Right to Work
and Rural India

Right to Work and Rural India

Working of the Mahatma Gandhi National Rural Employment Guarantee Scheme (MGNREGS)

Edited by
Ashok K. Pankaj

SAGE www.sagepublications.com
Los Angeles • London • New Delhi • Singapore • Washington DC

First published in 2012 by

SAGE Publications India Pvt Ltd
B1/I-1 Mohan Cooperative Industrial Area
Mathura Road, New Delhi 110 044, India
www.sagepub.in

SAGE Publications Inc
2455 Teller Road
Thousand Oaks, California 91320, USA

SAGE Publications Ltd
1 Oliver's Yard, 55 City Road
London EC1Y 1SP, United Kingdom

SAGE Publications Asia-Pacific Pte Ltd
33 Pekin Street
#02-01 Far East Square
Singapore 048763

Published by Vivek Mehra for SAGE Publications India Pvt Ltd, typeset in 10/13 Minion Pro by Diligent Typesetter, Delhi and printed at Saurabh Printers Pvt. Ltd.

Library of Congress Cataloging-in-Publication Data

Right to work and rural India: working of the Mahatma Gandhi National Rural Employment Guarantee Scheme (MGNREGS)/edited by Ashok K. Pankaj.
p. cm.
Includes bibliographical references and index.
1. India. National Rural Employment Guarantee Act, 2005. 2. Manpower policy, Rural—India. 3. Guaranteed annual income—India. 4. Job security—India. 5. Right to labor—India. 6. Rural poor—Employment—India. I. Pankaj, Ashok, K. 1970–
HD5710.85.I4R54 331.01'1—dc23 2012 2012024064

ISBN: 978-81-321-0899-3 (HB)

The SAGE Team: Sharel Simon, Shreya Lall, and Anju Saxena

To Millions of MGNREGS Workers

Contents

List of Tables

Appendix Tables

List of Figures

List of Abbreviations

ADS	Area Development Society
AEN	Assistant Engineer
AP	Andhra Pradesh
APDAI	AP Drought Adaptation Initiative
APL	Above Poverty Level
APNA	Andhra Pradesh NGO Alliance
APNREGS	Andhra Pradesh National Rural Employment Guarantee Scheme
APOs	Assistant Project Directors
BAG	Backward Area Grant
BDO	Block Development Officer
BJP	Bhartiya Janata Party
BN	Bharat Nirman
BNPP	Bank-Netherlands Partnership Program
BPL	Below Poverty Line
BPO	Block Program Officer
BRGF	Backward Regions Grant Fund
BRLP	Bihar Rural Livelihoods Promotion Society
CAG	Comptroller and Auditor General of India
CAPART	Council for Advancement of People's Action and Rural Technology
CCT	Conditional Cash Transfer
CDS	Community Development Society
CEGC	Central Employment Guarantee Council
CF	Corpus Fund
CFT	Cubic Feet
CGE	Computable General Equilibrium
CITI	Confederation of Indian Textile Industries
CPI-M	Communist Party of India-Marxist
CPLRs	Common Property Land Resources
CPR	Common Property Resources
CRIDA	Central Research Institute for Dry-land Agriculture
CSO	Civil Society Organisation
DDG	Deputy Director General
DG	Director General
DPC	District Programme Coordinator
DPP	District Perspective Plan

DRDA	District Rural Development Agency
EAS	Employment Assurance Scheme
EGA	Employment Guarantee Assistant
EGC	Employment Guarantee Council
EGP	Employment Guarantee Programme
EGS	Employment Guarantee Scheme
EGS-LDP	EGS Land Development Project
EPWP	Extended Public Works Programme
FGD	Focus Group Discussion
ForWaRD	Forum for Watershed Research and Policy Dialogue
GAD	Gender and Development
GDI	Gender-related Development Index
GDP	Gross Domestic Product
GEM	Gender Empowerment Measure
GP	Gram Panchayat
GSDP	Gross State Domestic Product
GVS	Gram Vikas Sankul
HDI	Human Development Index
HH	Household
HP	Himachal Pradesh
HPP	Horticulture and Plantation Project
IAY	Indira Awas Yojana
ICDS	Integrated Child Development Scheme
ICESCR	International Covenant on Economic, Social and Cultural Rights
ICRISAT	International Crop Research Institute for the Semi-arid Tropics
ICT	Information and Communication Technology
IFP	Irrigation Facilities Project
IFPRI	International Food Policy Research Institute
IIA	Indian Industry Association
IKP	Indira Kranti Patham
ILO	International Labour Organization
IRDP	Integrated Rural Development Programme
IT	Information Technology
ITDA	Integrated Tribal Development Agency
JEN	Junior Engineer
JFM	Joint Forest Management
JGSY	Jawahar Gram Samridhi Yojana
JRY	Jawahar Rozgar Yojana
MEC	Marginal Efficiency of Capital
MEGS	Maharashtra Employment Guarantee Scheme
MGNREGA	Mahatma Gandhi National Rural Employment Guarantee Act
MGNREGS	Mahatma Gandhi National Rural Employment Guarantee Scheme

MIS	Management Information System
MKSS	Mazdoor Kisaan Shakti Sangathan
MoRD	Ministry of Rural Development
MP	Madhya Pradesh
MPC	Marginal Propensity of Consumption
MPDOs	Mandal Parishad Development Officer
MTA	Mid Term Appraisal
NAC	National Advisory Council
NAM	National Authority for MGNREGA
NCEUS	National Commission for Enterprises in the Unorganised Sectors
NDA	National Democratic Alliance
NFFWP	National Food for Work Programme
NFHS	National Family Health Survey
NGO	Non-governmental Organisation
NIRD	National Institute of Rural Development
NREP	National Rural Employment Programme
NRM	Natural Resource Management
NSSO	National Sample Survey Organization
OBCs	Other Backward Classes
PACS	Poorest Area Civil Society
PCI	Per Capita Income
PIM	Participatory Irrigation Management
PO	Programme Officer
Pop	Population
PPP	Purchasing Power Parity
PRIs	Panchayat Raj Institutions
REGS	Rural Employment Guarantee Scheme
RFID	Radio Frequency Identification Technology
RH	Rural Household
RKVY	Raashtriya Krishi Vikas Yojana
RLEGP	Rural Landless Employment Guarantee Programme
RLH	Rural Labour Households
RW	Rural Work
SAM	Social Accounting Matrix
SAP	Sustainable Agriculture Project
SCs	Scheduled Castes
SEGC	State Employment Guarantee Council
SERP	Society for Elimination of Rural Poverty
SEZ	Special Economic Zone
SGRY	Sampoorna Grameen Rozgar Yojana
SHGs	Self-help Groups
SME	Small and Medium Enterprises

SNA	System of National Accounts
SOR	Schedule of Rates
SRIJAN	Self-reliant Initiatives through Joint Action
SSS	Shram Shakti Sangham
ST	Scheduled Tribes
TCS	Tata Consultancy Services
TDP	Telugu Desam Party
TSI	Total Score of Implementation
UP	Uttar Pradesh
UPA	United Progressive Alliance
UT	Union Territory
VLS	Village-level Study
VMKS	Vagad Mazdoor Kisan Sangathan
VOs	Village Organisations
WDF	Watershed Development Fund
WDPs	Watershed Development Projects
WSAs	Wage Seekers Associations

Preface

> [T]he economic constitution of India … should be such that no one under it should suffer from want of food and clothing … everybody should be able to get sufficient work to enable him to make the two ends meet (Gandhi, 1947: 70).

These words of Gandhi encapsulate the core objective of the National Rural Employment Guarantee Act (NREGA), 2005, that has been rightly renamed as the Mahatma Gandhi National Rural Employment Guarantee Act (MGNREGA; *Gazette of India* [2009]). Gandhi was the first to articulate right to work as a basic policy goal of independent India, and was the leading theorist of social and economic reconstruction of the self-sufficient village republics. Right to work and dignity of labour, decentralised planning and development, and village autonomy and local governance were essential components of his plan.

However, Gandhi's vision of idyllic self-sufficient village republics did not find favour with the makers of modern India. Ambedkar, the chairman of the draft committee of the Indian Constitution, abhorred Indian villages for their deeply entrenched and regressive social structures and practices. Nehru, the architect of the economic policy of Independent India, was unable to romanticize Indian villages, and was averse to the archaic idea of self-sufficient village republics. He revered big industries (steel plants), multipurpose big dams and mega power projects as the temples of modern India. The village republic was not among his favourite projects.

Under the Directive Principles of State Policy (Part IV of the Indian Constitution), provisions were made for right to work, local self-government and other principles and policies of Gandhi, but were emasculated by making them non-justiciable, and enforceable only as per the convenience of the State (Article 37). The economic policy of post-Independence India was completely out of sync with the goals of Gandhi. The ideological battle inside the Congress over the course of economic policy ended with the death of Sardar Patel and culminated in the articulation of the Second Industrial Policy, followed by the Second Five Year Plan that preferred a heavy industry and high investment-led economic growth model. Small and cottage industries and self-sufficient autonomous village republics were left abandoned.

Remnants of the Gandhian plan have, however, formed part of the various rural development and poverty alleviation programmes; an impressive number of them have been experimented with since the early 1970s. The 73rd and 74th Constitutional Amendment Acts, 1993 were a decisive step in realising decentralised and participatory development through institutions of local self-government, an important component of the Gandhian plan. Twelve years later, another milestone came in the form of the MGNREGA with a view to ensuring that 'no one in rural India should suffer from want of food and clothing and everybody should be able to get sufficient work to enable him to make the two ends meet'.

By devolving powers, functions and functionaries to the panchayati raj institutions, this also complements the objectives of the 73rd Amendment Act.

The problem of development in India is not simply lack of savings and investment and its translation into growth rate (Harrod–Domar model). Except for initial years, that is, upto the 1960s, the savings rate has been reasonably good. The problem of development in India is more of redistribution and investment in the appropriate sectors. The issue of distribution has acquired prominence in the reform phase as the high growth rate in GDP, instead of improving, resulted in deterioration of personal, sectoral and regional distribution.

There are sound theoretical reasons and empirical evidences to question sustainability of the growth process characterised by a disjunction between growth and employment and income and distribution. Its social and political consequences are far more serious. In the reform phase, India has witnessed a series of social and political discontents (Dalit and backward-class movements, communal conflicts, Naxal movement, farmer agitations), which are not completely disconnected with the growth process. The MGNREGA is a (political) realisation of the consequences of inegalitarian growth process of the reform phase. At least the timing and the context of this Act suggest so.

The issue of distribution has been ignored for years under the influence of various growth-centric Western development models, which were not designed for highly inegalitarian and unequal societies such as of India. The MGNREGA is an attempt to address, although partially, the issue of distribution that has become more pressing in the reform phase of high growth and increasing inequality.

Working of the Mahatma Gandhi National Rural Employment Guarantee Scheme (MGNREGS), however, suggests gigantic gap between its goals and achievements. Apart from lacunae and deficits in implementation, the intra- and inter-state variations in implementation are other serious shortcomings. The protagonists are collecting evidences to prove that the MGNREGS has worked successfully, or even if it has not worked so far, will do so. Its critics are equally active in amassing data on malpractices in implementation, leakages and corruption, and raising questions about the outcomes of the investment. Implementation of the MGNREGS has not disappointed either. There are evidences to prove its working as well as its failure.

This book, without getting engaged in the debate on merits and demerits of this massive programme of rural employment generation and assets creation, attempts to understand the working of the MGNREGS on the ground and documents evidences of implementation and impacts across better and poor implemented, agriculturally developed and backward states of India. The essays in this volume will be helpful for both the protagonists and critics of MGNREGA/MGNREGS to firm up their respective positions.

In preparation of this book, I have received support and cooperation from a number of individuals. Without listing them, I express my sincere thanks to all of them. When the idea of this book was formulated, the list of contributors was rather big and impressive. I wish to thank to all of them, who were unable to contribute, and who finally contributed in this volume. The keen interest of SAGE, in particular of Sugata Ghosh, encouraged me to complete this project, which was once abandoned. The SAGE team maintained the same interest in the production of the book. Muchkund Dubey has been a constant source of encouragement in this venture. D.N. Reddy, apart from contributing a chapter, has been always helpful in formulation of the design of the chapters and eager to discuss this book. Sandip Sarkar and Rukmini Tankha took the pain to go through the rather long 'Introduction'. I express my sincere gratitude to all of them. I would also like to thank *Economic and Political Weekly* for giving permission to use the article 'Empowerment Effects of the NREGS on Women Workers: A Study of Four States'. Last but not the least, my sincere gratitude to my family and friends, whose support is invaluable.

Delhi
October 2011

Ashok K. Pankaj

References

Gandhi, M. K. (1947) *India of My Dreams*. Ahmedabad: Navjivan Publishing House, p. 70.
Gazette of India (2009) Extraordinary Part II, Section I, No. 53, New Delhi, Thursday, 31 December.

SECTION I

Introduction

1

Guaranteeing Right to Work in Rural India

Context, Issues and Policies

Ashok K. Pankaj

I

Why MGNREGA?

The Mahatma Gandhi National Rural Employment Guarantee Act 2005 (MGNREGA)[1] is a bold experiment in providing a minimum livelihood security to rural households through public works–based employment programme. The act-based employment guarantee scheme, the primary objective of which is to ensure the transfer of a minimum income to rural households through self-seeking wage employment, is a departure from the erstwhile employment and public works programmes, which were designed to create community infrastructure first, and then, simultaneously generate income and employment to local residents. The demand-based entitlement to 100 days of employment at minimum wages and a corresponding legal obligation on the agencies of the state to provide so within a stipulated period of time is a major departure. The compensatory provisions like unemployment allowance, compensation for the delay in wage payment and a punitive provision for the government officials in case of their failure to provide employment within 15 days of the demand complete the cycle of entitlement. More importantly, the act exalts the position of the citizens from the receivers of state's dole to a legally entitled shareholder in the development pie, irrespective of the size of the pie.

The act (MGNREGA) has laudable objectives, and the operational part, that is, Mahatma Gandhi National Rural Employment Guarantee Scheme (MGNREGS) contains innovative and unique features. Nonetheless, questions are raised about the timing and purpose of the legislation, design and structure of the programme, desirability of the state-sponsored employment programme in the phase of liberalisation and the likely impacts of such a massive wage employment and public works programme. Critics of the programme are also sceptical about its success.

What is the necessity of a state-guaranteed employment programme in the phase of liberalisation, and how it suits with the goal of a free market economy that India has gradually moved towards since 1991? What will be the micro- and macro-level economic impacts of such a massive programme of rural income and employment generation and assets creation? Will it be able to mitigate household-level rural poverty which, in spite of various and varying estimations,[2] continues to be at unacceptable level? What will be its impacts on rural and agrarian economy, labour market conditions, rural–urban economic linkages and overall multiplier effects? What will be its other consequences for India's internal and external economy? Will the wage income transferred under the MGNREGS help India in sustaining domestic-demand–driven high growth rate in gross domestic product (GDP) that she has achieved since the 1990s? Will this guaranteed employment programme be able to address income, sectoral and regional inequalities that have increased in the reform phase? Will it be sufficient to address the issue of distribution that has become more uneven in this phase?

Then, there are questions about the objectives as well: What is the nature of this programme, which is loaded with multiple objectives? Is it a programme of social security, or of employment generation and assets creation with larger macroeconomic effects? If it is a programme of social security, then why is it linked to employment generation and assets creation, and how these two objectives have been reconciled in the programme?

Finally, there are issues about its sociopolitical significance: What does this MGNREGA mean to the people of this country whose constitution enshrines right to work (livelihood) as a goal of socio-economic development, but that has been denied by the successive governments for nearly 56 years—ironically for about 40 years under the regime of avowed socialism and welfare state? What will be the social and political impacts of the right to work–based largest public works programme in the largest democracy of the world? And last, given the numerous difficulties in implementation of such a massive programme, will this programme be able to meet key objectives of the act?

These questions have been (and are being) frequently asked since the commencement of this programme. Numerous plausible explanations and (hypothetical) answers have also been provided, although firm trends about its impacts are yet to be established. There are divisions of opinion about the way the programme should have been designed and structured. There are divergent views on the thrust of the objectives as well. To some it is primarily an income-transfer programme, but to others it is both an income-transfer and assets-creation programme. The former evaluates its working from the viewpoints of workers and the latter from the viewpoints of investment and community assets. There are divergent views on its working and success as well. There are some who have already written the elegy of the programme. But there are some who are determined to make it an agent of rural transformation. The working of the programme has not disappointed either: if there are some success stories to celebrate, there are plenty of implementation bottlenecks to doom its failure.

This book is an attempt to answer some of these questions based on the theoretical positions and empirical evidences. The next part of this chapter explains the contexts—economic, political and constitutional—of the act. Part III describes in brief the changing thrust of India's anti-poverty programme and, then, her experiments with various employment programmes. It also explains MGNREGS as a new approach to employment programme and describes its main objectives and features to understand its distinct character and nature. Part IV describes in brief Keynes' position on public works programme as a macroeconomic policy to achieve full employment equilibrium and the working of the multiplier and accelerator effects in the economy. Part V analyses poverty-alleviation role of employment guarantee scheme and compares it with that of the cash-transfer programme to understand why the former has been and should be chosen over the latter in India. Part VI examines the working of the MGNREGS and evaluates its performance with respect to its major objectives. Finally, a brief summary of the chapters gives an overview of the working of this programme.

II

Contexts

Economic Reforms and Growth without Distribution

While India's GDP grew at a faster rate in the post-reform period, the disjunction between growth and employment and income and distribution has accentuated income, sectoral and regional inequalities. Between 1993–94 and 2004–05, GDP per capita increased at a higher rate, but income inequality both within the rural and urban and between rural and urban areas has also increased. The high growth rate in GDP has been obtained largely through higher growth rate in the secondary and tertiary sectors, but the pace of job creation has been incommensurate with the growth rate, resulting in further overcrowding of the primary sector. States and regions with greater ability to attract private and foreign investments have grown faster,[3] leading to increased regional disparity. At the same time, the space for the Centre's role in balanced regional development has decreased under the new (economic) policy regime.

Income inequality has increased since 1983–84. However, the situation has worsened since 1993–94 (Datt and Ravallion, 2002a & b, 2009; Deaton and Drèze, 2002; Bhaduri, 2008, Desai et al., 2010; Sarkar and Mehta, 2010; Vakulabharanam, 2010). Between 1983–84 and 1993–94, income inequalities declined within the rural and urban areas, but overall inequality increased because of the widening rural–urban income gap. The Gini index of income inequality (income as a proxy of average per capita monthly expenditure) was 0.33 of overall, 0.31 of rural and 0.36 of urban in 1983–84. It marginally increased to 0.34 in case of overall, but declined to 0.29 in case of rural and 0.35 in case of urban in 1993–94. In contrast to that, Gini index of income inequality increased from 0.34, 0.29 and 0.35 in 1993–94 to 0.37, 0.32, and 0.38, respectively of overall, rural and urban in 2004–05 (Sarkar and Mehta, 2010). It seems that the situation has not improved between 2004–05 and 2009–10, although it has not worsened either (Ahluwalia, 2011).

Rising personal inequality has also manifested through increasing wage inequalities, which have shown overall increase in the post-reform period. In the pre-reform period, say, between 1983–84 and 1993–94, wage inequality of all workers, except urban regular, declined. In the post-reform period, that is, between 1993–94 and 2004–05, it increased in case of all workers—rural regular and casual, and urban regular and casual. Further, wage differentials increased significantly across educational and earning groups; wages of high-earning groups and educated and skilled workers in contrast to those of unskilled and less-educated workers rose sharply in this period (Sarkar and Mehta, 2010). Increasing intra- and inter-class income differential is another dimension of rising personal inequality in the post-reform period (Vakulabharanam, 2010).

The sectoral inequality has widened in the post-reform period; the secondary and tertiary sectors have grown at a much faster rate than the primary sector. While agriculture GDP grew at an average rate of 2.8 per cent and 2.6 per cent between 1993–99 and 1999–2004, respectively, the non-agriculture GDP grew at the average rate of 8.11 and 7.22 per cent, respectively, in the same period. Growth differential between the agriculture and non-agriculture sectors has widened further since 2003–04 (Kundu, 2010). More important, the share of agriculture in GDP has declined sharply in the post-reform period, although the share of labour force engaged in agriculture has not declined in that ratio. The sectoral inequality has also increased in terms of income and wage inequalities across agriculture and non-agriculture sectors.

Inter-state and intra-state regional disparities have widened in the reform phase. The standard deviation of per capita state GDP has increased from 0.30 in the 1980s to 0.40 in the 1990s (Kanbur, 2010). Southern and western states grew at a faster rate in the 1990s and maintained the high growth rate in the 2000s, although states of Hindi heartland have also achieved higher growth rate in the 2000s (Ahluwalia, 2011). Another dimension of the increasing spatial disparities is widening intra-state inequalities that have increased considerably in some fast-growing states, namely, Gujarat, Haryana, Karnataka, Andhra Pradesh, West Bengal, Kerala, Maharashtra and Tamil Nadu (Ahluwalia, 2011: 92; Vakulabharanam, 2010: 71).

Poverty and Unemployment

The post-reform trends in poverty reduction are worrisome. First, the absolute number of the poor declined only marginally in the reform phase. In 1983, 324.34 million persons were poor and 315.48 million remained so in 2004–05—a decline of merely 9.07 million over a decade. Even otherwise, in 2004–05, 27 per cent of the total population were living below the official poverty line (as per Lakdawala Committee Methodology), which is contested for underestimation. Second, while high growth rate in GDP has resulted in steeper decline in poverty, there are indications that the post-reform growth process 'has become less pro-poor in the sense of the headcount index becoming less responsive to growth in per-capita consumption' (Datt and Ravallion, 2009: 57). The preliminary findings of the 66th round of the National Sample Survey Organization (NSSO) consumption expenditure survey shows that the pace of poverty decline has slowed down further between 2004–05 and 2009–10 (Ahluwalia, 2011: 89). Third, poverty inequality across states and even within states has increased significantly (Himanshu, 2007; Dev and Ravi, 2007). The income and wealth inequality across states and socio-economic groups has also increased between 1992 and 2002. (Jayadev, Motiram and Vakulabharanam, 2007).

The employment scenario in the post-reform period suggests deterioration of the situation. First, between 1983–84 and 2004–05, even though the rate of overall unemployment has not increased, yet the rate of unemployment in the youth and educated persons has increased. Second, there has been a decline in the percentage of population employed in the organised and formal sectors. Between 1983–84 and 2004–05, organised sector employment decreased from 14.8 per cent to 9.7 per cent and formal employment declined from 10.2 per cent to 6.6 per cent (Ghosh, 2010). Moreover, there has been a massive increase in self-employment, which is largely an increase in casualisation of employment. Third, there has been a steady decline in employment elasticity in aggregate, and more so in agriculture and manufacturing sectors (Bhaduri, 2008; Nayyar, 2006; Dasgupta and Singh, 2005; Papola, 2005).

The stagnation in employment generation in agriculture and inability of the industry and service sectors to absorb the labour force in the ratio of the growth rate indicates disjunction between growth and employment in the liberalisation phase. The slow growth of agricultural employment is not primarily due to high labour-productivity growth in agriculture. On the other hand, the non-agricultural sectors have registered high growth in output and labour productivity, but with an aggregate employment elasticity of around 0.30, which is insufficient to absorb surplus labour force from agriculture (Bhaduri, 2008: 4). The consequence is an increasingly overcrowded, low-productivity agricultural sector with little impacts on the livelihood conditions of the population dependent on it.

Agriculture and Rural Economy in Distress

The condition of the agriculture sector that still provides livelihood to the majority of the population and absorbs about 56.5 per cent of the total workforce[4] has worsened in the reform phase. While the growth rate in agriculture declined from 3.08 per cent in the 1980s to 2.57 per cent in the reform period (1992–93 to 2004–05), the sectoral contribution of agriculture in GDP decreased, but without any (significant) decline in the number of workforce absorbed in and population dependent on agriculture. This implies a relative decline in labour productivity in agriculture compared to other sectors. Moreover, disguised unemployment in the agriculture has increased as there is a decline in productivity in spite of increasing absorption of labour force.

The inability of the industrial and service sectors to absorb workforce in the same ratio as increase in the rate of growth in these two sectors has resulted in increasing dependence of the rising population on the agriculture sector. A major consequence of this has been the decline in the average size of operational holdings from 2.63 hectares in 1960–61 to 2.20 in 1970–71; 1.67 in 1981–82; 1.34 in 1991–92 and 1.06 in 2003. This has lowered agriculture productivity, profitability of the operational holdings and surplus of the farmers.

Increasing indebtedness and rising suicide rates among farmers show that agriculture is in distress. As per the Report of the Expert Group (Government of India, 2009a) on agricultural indebtedness in 2007, based on NSSO Situation Assessment Survey of Farmers, 2003, 48.6 per cent of farmers in India were indebted. The percentage of indebted farmers varied across states, but was high in Andhra Pradesh (82 per cent), Tamil Nadu (74.5 per cent), Punjab (65.4 per cent), Kerala (64.4 per cent), Karnataka (61.6 per cent), Maharashtra (54.8 per cent) and Haryana (53.1 per cent). It was relatively low in the poor states of Bihar (33 per cent), Uttar Pradesh (UP) (40.3 per cent) and Orissa (47.8 per cent). The average (of all India) amount of indebtedness was ₹12,585, but varied across states. It was high in the Punjab (₹4,1576), Andhra Pradesh (₹23,965), Kerala (₹33,907) and in some other states.[5] The incidence of suicides has increased among the farmers in Andhra Pradesh, Maharashtra, Punjab with high incidence of indebtedness.

Rural India retains the largest proportion of population (70 per cent) as well as of labour force. Of 467 million estimated labour force in 2004–05, 348 million (71.4 per cent) lived in the rural areas and the majority of them (56.5 per cent of the total workers) earned their livelihood from agriculture. This also shows a low level of diversification of occupation in the rural areas.

The declining agriculture productivity and surplus of the farmers, increasing disguised and open unemployment and low occupational diversification in the rural economy has triggered large-scale intra- and inter-state migration from rural to urban areas. However, distress migrants from the rural areas, unable to get any regular employment, become casual labour in the urban areas. Their low earnings and high living costs leave them either no better or only marginally better off, but with a (high) social cost as well.

Moderating Social and Political Consequences of Reforms

Social and political consequences of the reform-phase growth process are much more serious. Declining employment opportunities for educated rural and urban youth (unemployment rate is higher in youth and educated persons), and shrinking sources of livelihood in rural areas have increased despair and despondency among the youth and others. Social and political extremism is one of the manifestations of growing discontent among the people.

Since the commencement of the reform process, India has witnessed a series of social and political discontent movements. Hindu–Muslim riots, backward-class mobilisation for job reservation and upper-caste reaction against other backward classes (OBCs) mobilisation leading to intense social conflicts in the early 1990s, Dalit and backward-class assertions, farmer's agitations, people's movement against land acquisition (for industrialisation in Singur and Nandigram in West Bengal, urban estate in Greater Noida, nuclear power plant in Maharashtra and against special economic zones [SEZs] and Naxalism that has spread like wildfire (about 220–30 districts out of 615 are affected and about 90–100 are worst affected) are manifestations of increasing discontents in the society. All of them may not be the direct consequences of the reform process, yet some of them are obviously related to the reform process.

The larger political consequence is volatile and unstable politics. Since 1991, there has not been a single case of one-party government completing the tenure on its own majority at the Centre. The Narasimha Rao–led Congress government (1991–96) that started liberalisation process survived the full term only by engineering defections in opposition camps during the vote of no confidence. The other governments have been coalitions of political conveniences. Anti-incumbency and midterm elections became more frequent than earlier. Re-election of governments at the centre and in states became uncommon in the reform phase, although the tendency has declined recently. To beat the anti-incumbency factors, political parties devised a strategy to replace the existing members of legislature with new faces during the parliamentary and assembly elections.

People have openly shown their discontent with the rejection of 'India Shining' and its votary—National Democratic Alliance (NDA) government, led by the Bhartiya Janata Party (BJP)—at the Centre in the 2004 parliamentary elections, and voting out of the icons of blatant reforms, like, Chandra Babu Naidu of Telugu Desam Party (TDP) in Andhra Pradesh and S. M. Krishna of Congress in Karnataka assembly elections. The rural voters cutting across castes and classes revealed their anti-reform posture, for the first time in a more articulate manner. The National Election Study (Suri, 2004) confirms that those who voted against the BJP-led NDA were also opposed to economic reforms. Similarly, it is learnt that the surprising defeats of Chandra Babu Naidu in Andhra Pradesh and S.M. Krishna in Karnataka were masterminded by the rural voters. Further, it has been found that the poor, lower castes, and a large part of farmers and peasantry held a negative perception about the reforms, whereas the urban, middle and professional classes, and business and trading people generally favoured it (Suri, 2004).

In order to regain the lost political base among the poor, lower castes and rural voters, the Congress that started liberalisation in 1991 and, then, remained out of power between 1996 and March 2004 at the Centre—the longest ever since Independence—was desperately trying to get back its pro-poor image. Realising the electoral importance of rural constituencies that still dominate the Indian Parliament, and to dispel their negative perceptions about economic reforms, the party promised in its election manifesto the intention to bring suitable schemes and policies for the development of rural areas and the rural and poor people.[6] The commitment towards an employment guarantee scheme was formalised with the coalition partners through common minimum programme. It is learnt that the MGNREGS and other pro-poor programmes, launched by the Congress during United Progressive Alliance-I (UPA-I), helped it in increasing its seats and vote percentage, although it was still short of majority in 2009 parliamentary elections. The Congress managed to form the UPA-II government with the reshuffling of coalition partners, and has been making more such attempts Right to Education Act and Food Security Act to wean away the poor and rural voters. But, masses are still unsure about its pro-poor commitment, primarily because of its inability to turn the growth process from GDP-centric to people-centric.

Redeeming Constitutional Promises

Right to work and livelihood are constitutional promises to citizens of India. There is an explicit provision for that under Articles 39 (a) and 41 of the Directive Principles of State Policy contained in Part IV of the Indian Constitution. Article 39 (a) reads: 'The State shall, in particular, direct its policy towards securing that—the citizens, men and women equally, have the right to an adequate means to livelihood', and Article 41 directs: 'The State shall within the limits of its economic capacity and development, make effective provision for securing the right to work to public assistance in cases of unemployment ... and in other cases of undeserving want' (The Constitution of India, 2007: 21–22).

The provision for right to work and livelihood can also be inferred from Article 21 (right to life and liberty) under Fundamental Rights. While interpreting Article 21 of the Indian Constitution, the Supreme Court of India in *Olega Tellis versus Bombay Municipal Corporation* held that the word 'life' in Article 21 includes 'right to livelihood', as nobody can live without the means of livelihood (1986). The Preamble to the Constitution of India, which sets the goal of Indian Republic, is a collective promise '... to constitute India into a sovereign socialist democratic republic and to secure to all its citizens: justice, social, economic and political ...'. The promise of the Preamble is also a promise to right to livelihood to every citizen of this country.

The successive governments have shown little interest in enforcing various socio-economic rights including the 'right to livelihood' and 'right to work' contained in Part IV of the Constitution. One reason for this is the nature of Directive Principles of State Policy itself. Unlike Fundamental Rights under Part III of the Constitution, various socio-economic rights under the Directive Principles have been rendered non-justiciable by Article 37 that provides: 'The provisions contained in this part shall not be enforceable by any court, but the principles therein laid down are nevertheless fundamental in the governance of the country and it shall be the duty of the State to apply these principles in making laws' (The Constitution of India, 2007: 21). Constraint of resource mobilisation due to low level of economic development and, hence, low resource base to enforce these provisions could be another plausible explanation for keeping these rights in abeyance. But the inability of political parties and their governments to prioritise development policies and goals in consonance with the Directive Principles and the failure of the civil society to bring these issues to the forefront of their social and political mobilisation is perhaps a more realistic explanation for keeping Articles 39(a) and 41 (right to work and livelihood) dormant for 55 years.

Interestingly, increased resource base and greater collection of revenues in the liberalisation phase has enhanced financial position of the governments to redeem some of these dormant constitutional promises. The Supreme Court of India has also taken a proactive position[7] (in some cases, radical step like asking the Union Government to distribute food grain free to the poor instead of allowing it to rot in the open) and has given a new meaning to some of these non-justiciable rights. It has also broadened the meaning of right to life under Article 21 of the Constitution.

Thus, the rising income, sectoral and regional inequalities in the reform phase, nearly jobless growth of the 1990s, stagnation or even decline in the growth of agricultural productivity, distressed farmers committing suicides in various parts of the country and increasing distress migration from the rural to urban areas were the larger socio-economic contexts of the MGNREGA, and the realisation of unsustainability of economic reforms which resulted in high but exclusive and skewed growth trajectories was the political context of the MGNREGA. Its legal–constitutional root lies in Part III and Part IV of the Indian Constitution that deal with justiciable and non-justiciable rights, respectively. Increased revenues of the government in the post-reform phase, judicial assertion for enforcement and realisation of some basic rights of the citizens, and rising civil society also helped in translating a constitutional promise into a legal entitlement through the MGNREGA.

III

India's Experiment with Employment Programme

The thrust of India's anti-poverty programme has been changing. The land- and assets-based approach of the 1970s gave way to income- and employment-based programmes in the 1980s. Long-term investment in human capital through better education, health and nutrition facilities acquired equal importance in the 1990s. And more recently, that is, in the 2000s, entitlement-based approach with guaranteed transfer of income and services has entered into development discourse and is practised with three important developments, namely, MGNREGA 2005, Right of Children to Free and Compulsory Education Act 2009 and the proposed Right to Food Act. The MGNREGA provides for guaranteed income; the proposed Right to Food Act provides for foodgrain and the Right of Children to Free and Compulsory Education Act 2009 provides for free education of children upto 14 years of age.

The land-based approach has failed mostly (exception Operation Barga of CPI-M Government in West Bengal) because of various difficulties associated with the procurement of surplus land and its distribution among the poor population. The dynamics of land, caste and local power structure was not favourable to land distribution. The static nature of the approach was another limitation, as the availability of land is given. It can cater to the needs of only a limited number of households and cannot be increased in case of increased requirement. The assets-based programme, say, Integrated Rural Development Programme (IRDP), failed because of various reasons, but mainly due to massive leakages and corruption. It also suffered from design defects. For example, under the IRDP, providing milch cattle to the poor household without ensuring that the household has a minimum amount of land and resources to rear the animal did not prove helpful.

Public works–based employment programme has been found more efficacious; India has experimented with a series of them since 1980. Some of the important programmes were: National Rural Employment Programme (NREP) 1980–89; Rural Landless Employment Guarantee Programme (RLEGP) 1983–89; Jawahar Rozgar Yojana (JRY) 1989–99; Employment Assurance Scheme (EAS) 1993–99; Jawahar Gram Samridhi Yojana (JGSY) 1999–2002; Sampoorna Grameen Rozgar Yojana (SGRY) since September 2001 and National Food for Work Programme (NFFWP) since 14 November 2004. SGRY and NFFWP were merged with the MGNREGS in 2006. These were Centre-sponsored programmes wherein the central government shared major part of the financial burden and left the implementation in the hands of the state governments. Varying degrees of success and failures have been attributed to these programmes. Nevertheless, some common problems observed in their successful implementation were:

1. Schemes formulated and implemented by the bureaucracy in a centralised manner without community participation;
2. Supply-driven scheme, that is, employment provided based on the supply;
3. Poor mechanism of social accounting, monitoring and in the absence of transparency and accountability, plenty of complaints of wastages of resources, leakages and corruption;
4. Inadequate employment generation, and employment generation not linked to providing minimum livelihood security;
5. Income, minimum wages, and workers' amenities not part of entitlement;
6. Low participation of women; and
7. Employment opportunities inflexible to workers' demand.

An important departure was the Maharashtra Employment Guarantee Scheme (MEGS) that was started as a drought-relief measure in 1972–73 and converted into a legally guaranteed programme in 1975. It stood out for its entitlement-based approach and distinct design. Unlike the other employment programmes of the past, the MEGS adopted entitlement- and demand-based approach wherein a minimum income through a minimum number of employment days became a legal entitlement, guaranteed through an act of the state legislature. In spite of mixed results (Dattar, 1990; Mahendra Dev, 2005; Krishnaraj et al., 2004), the MEGS has been lauded for its entitlement-based approach. The MGNREGS draws heavily on the objective, design and structure of the MEGS.

MGNREGA: Objectives, Design and Features[8]

The MGNREGA was passed by the parliament in its monsoon session of 2005, within one year of the formation of the Congress-led UPA-I government at the Centre. The act received the assent of the President on 5 September 2005 and was notified in the Gazette of India on 7 September 2005. The MGNREGS that originates from the act came into force in 200 selected (backward) districts of the country on 2 February 2006[9] and its coverage has been extended in phases to 130 more districts since 1 April 2007 and to the rest of the districts since 1 April 2008.[10] At present, the employment guarantee scheme is in implementation in 615 districts, covering the entire rural population of the country.

Objectives: The primary objective of this act is to provide minimum livelihood security to rural households. The act states the purpose as:

> To provide for the enhancement of livelihood security of the households in rural areas of the country by providing at least one hundred days of guaranteed wage employment in every financial year to every household whose adult members volunteer to do unskilled manual work ....' (*Gazette of India*, 2006)

The other objectives of the act include reduction in distress migration from the rural to urban areas and from one part to another part of the rural areas; creation of durable assets in rural areas; invigorating civic and community life, strengthening of decentralised and participatory development process through panchayat raj institutions (PRIs) as they have been entrusted to formulate, implement and monitor the scheme; empowerment of rural women through increased earning opportunity and participation in community development process; overall development of the rural economy; promotion of inclusive growth and development and to create multiplier effects on the economy.

Features: To achieve these objectives, the MGNREGS contains new provisions, which were not part of the erstwhile employment generation and public works programmes.

1. While the other employment programmes owe their origins to executive orders, MGNREGS originates from an act of Parliament that gives it legal–constitutional superiority over its predecessors.
2. It is irreversible and can be terminated only by another act of Parliament.
3. It aims more at guaranteeing minimum livelihood security than removing rural poverty or other development objectives.
4. Its overall thrust is entitlement and, hence, the provisions like minimum wages, worksite facilities, and mandatory participation of female workers (one third of the total).
5. It is the first major experiment in at least partially decentralised planning; monitoring and implementation through PRIs across states.

Other features that give MGNREGS a distinct character are as follows:

1. Hundred days of wage employment at prescribed minimum wages (not less than ₹60 and has been raised to ₹100) to all rural households with a provision to give priority to women workers in the ratio of one third of the total workers;
2. self-selection and demand-based employment;
3. unemployment allowances in case of the inability of the implementing agency to provide job on demand;
4. providing fund is a legal obligation and not restricted to budgetary allocations;
5. 60 per cent of the project cost to be spent on the wages of unskilled workers and 40 per cent on the wages of skilled and semi-skilled workers and materials;
6. Centre funding 100 per cent of the wage cost and 75 per cent of the material and wage cost of skilled and semi-skilled workers;

7. non-lapsable corpus of fund, unlike other budgetary allocations;
8. emphasis on the works of water conservation and harvesting;
9. institutions of local self-governance (PRIs) are the principal agencies for planning, implementation and monitoring of the works;
10. social auditing to enforce transparency and accountability;
11. workers' entitlement to four facilities at worksite: (*a*) drinking water, (*b*) shelter, (*c*) first aid and (*d*) crèche for children of female workers, who are below six years of age;
12. no contractors and, as far as possible, no use of machines;
13. three-tier grievance-redressal mechanisms and provision of ombudsman.

The objectives of the act and features of the programme suggest that as a policy instrument, it broadly fits into many shoes. It can be termed as a social security measure, an employment-generation programme, a conditional cash transfer (CCT), a rural development programme and a macroeconomic policy as well. But in spite of its multiple objectives that also create confusion about its exact nature, it enshrines the principle that a minimum livelihood security is a non-negotiable democratic development right of the citizens, whatever may be the course of development. The concept of right to development as a basic democratic right is gradually becoming part of popular imagination, which will have significant implications for the future.

IV

Keynes, Public Works and Multiplier-accelerator Effects

The origin of public works programme as a macroeconomic policy lies in the theories of business cycle and employment/unemployment. Business cycle is a phenomenon associated with the free market laissez-faire economy where the boom and recession follow in a cyclical manner, and are considered a natural part of the capitalist production system. A situation of full employment is arrived during the boom, and further investment without corresponding increase in demand triggers recessionary situation, which leads to massive unemployment and subsequent fall in the economy. However, there is a limit to this fall, as even in recession a minimum demand for goods and services remains in the economy.

Classical economists prescribe a monetary-policy-based interventionist measure to fight recession and restore the economy to its full-employment situation. Rate of interest holds key to the classical economists' prescription for fighting recession. It is held that the reduced rate of interest will make capital cheaper that will induce investment in the economy. The increased investment will generate further employment and income, and will increase the effective demand via additional income in the economy.

Keynes disagrees with the classical economists' position, and holds that the marginal efficiency of capital (MEC) is key to the explanation of trade cycle. He interprets MEC in broader terms, and includes the factor of expectation of the rising demand that generates confidence in entrepreneurs. He prescribes that public works programme will increase the MEC via increased effective demand in the economy that, in turn, depends on higher marginal propensity of consumption (MPC).

The classical theory of full employment is based on wage rate and marginal productivity of labour. It is assumed that a worker is willing to employ himself or herself, so long as his or her wage is equal to the marginal utility of his labour. And the producer is willing to employ at a wage rate which is equal to the marginal productivity of labour. Based on the proposition of marginal utility and wage rate, classical economists argue that a situation of full employment equilibrium is achieved in an economy by the intersection of demand and supply curves at a level where wage rate is equal to the marginal productivity of labour. The wage rate plays a critical role, as an increase in the wage rate may enhance supply of the labour and decrease in it may decrease its supply. Thus, a full employment equilibrium position (full employment) is achieved based on the interplay of demand and supply forces.

The Great Depression of 1929 and its devastating effects on the capitalist economies throughout the world demonstrated the weakness of the classical theory of full employment equilibrium and inability of the monetary policy to correct the situation (fall). Without much fall in the monetary wages, the real wages toppled. Unemployment increased sharply and there was hardly any demand for labour even at the reduced (monetary) wages. The full employment assumptions of the classical economists broke down and the monetary-policy-based prescription to correct the situation was not showing any results. Recession-hit industries were trenching workers and, in the absence of demand for their products, were closing industries. They were reluctant to invest further even if they had the option of getting cheap labour and credit.

The classical economists consider full employment as a normal condition and explain only two types of unemployment: (*a*) frictional, and (*b*) voluntary. Keynes explains the existence of a third type of unemployment that he calls 'involuntary unemployment'; classical economists did not admit its existence. He defines 'involuntary unemployment' as:

> Men are involuntarily unemployed if, in the event of a small rise in the price of wage goods relatively to the money wage, both the aggregate supply of labour willing to work for the current money-wage and the aggregate demand for it at that wage would be greater than the existing volume of employment. (Keynes, 1951: 15)

In a simpler manner, there are people who are willing to work on the existing wage rate, but there is no demand for this additional labour in the economy. Keynes suggests that public works programme can satisfy this additional demand for job and can restore the full employment equilibrium.

Keynes, however, adds that full employment equilibrium is not a stable condition, but less than full employment is a more normal and stable condition. And aberrations from the normal condition, that is, less than full employment can be corrected through public investment in public works programme. Since private investment will not be forthcoming in the recession, a condition of low expectation of return, Keynes explains it as low MEC, and, hence, public investment is the only choice. Thus to Keynes, public investment in public works programme is a remedial measure to fight recession and remove involuntary unemployment. However, the desirable effects of public works programme can be achieved only if the economy has the capacity to meet the additional demand for goods and services without increasing prices (inflation). Also, multiplier effects work only if the additional demand does not lead to inflation, or the demand is met through import in the economy.

Keynes and MGNREGS

MGNREGS in India has been adopted in the context which is different from the recessionary condition and Keynesian presumption. The Indian economy is growing fast, but the high growth rate in GDP is in disjunction with the employment growth rate. Also, per capita GDP has increased, but in the absence of distribution, inequality has also increased. The increased inequality has implications for sustainability of the high growth rate. If income accumulates only in the hands of the rich people whose MPC is less than that of the poor people, the effect of increased income on effective demand via MPC is also less. The multiplier effects of increased income will be greater in an equal than in an unequal society.

Similarly, unemployment problem in India is of a different type. Even though open unemployment was only about 3.5 per cent in 2004–05, underemployment is massive. A large number of people are seemingly employed, but they earn very little—this is known as the phenomenon of working poor. In 2004–05, 39 per cent of the working population were from below poverty line (BPL) families. The National Commission for Enterprises in the Unorganised Sectors (NCEUS) estimates that 79 per cent of India's working population were poor in 2004–05. Thus, unlike the post-recession situation, the problem of unemployment in India is of a different type. It is a problem of creating productive employment at a rate commensurate with the growth rate in working population, or rather higher than that.

In the above context, the public works–based employment programme under MGNREGS has been adopted more as a distribution measure than as an anti-recession course-corrective mechanism. However, the multiplier effects in the economy would be greater, as this programme creates wage employment and mostly for the poor people whose MPC is greater. The role of public works–based decentralised guaranteed employment programme in obtaining full employment equilibrium for the Indian economy has been explained by Bhaduri as an alternative model of development (Bhaduri, 2005). He argues that there is a huge unutilised capacity in wage goods industries, and income transfer to the poor households under the employment guarantee programme will not only lead to the full utilisation of the existing capacity but its multiplier effects would be significant.

Multiplier-accelerator and MGNREGS

Multiplier explains the net effect of change in investment on overall employment, and accelerator explains change in demand for capital goods derived from change in demand for consumption goods. Keynes explains multiplier as a definite ratio between income and investment and between total employment and employment directly employed on investment. He defines it as: 'For in given circumstances, a definite ratio, to be called multiplier, can be established between income and investment and, subject to certain simplifications, between the total employment and the employment directly employed on investment (also called primary employment).' He further describes it as a part of his full employment theory, as 'it establishes a precise relationship, given the propensity to consume, between aggregate employment and income and investment' (Keynes, 1951: 113).

Although multiplier explains the net total effects of change in investment on income and employment, yet Keynes distinguishes between investment and employment multipliers. He defines the investment multiplier as: 'when there is an increment of aggregate investment, income will increase by an amount which is k times the increment of investment' (Keynes, 1937: 115). Here k denotes multiplier.

Similarly, he defines employment multiplier as the ratio of the total employment which is associated with a given increment of primary employment in the investment industries.

The MPC is fundamental to the working of multiplier. Higher the MPC, the greater is the multiplier effect and lower the MPC, the lesser is the multiplier effect. Since the MPC of the rich population is less than that of the poor, the multiplier effect of increased income is greater in the poor than in the rich society. Moreover, it is greater in an equal than in an unequal society where additional income goes to the rich with less MPC.

While the MPC determines the value of multiplier, the multiplier effects of public works operate under certain assumptions. An important assumption relates to no change in other investment. In other words, the public works should not offset other investment. This, in turn, is related to the method of financing. If financing policy results in offsetting other investments, multiplier effects are likely to be less on the economy. For the extra money which flows in the market because of the new income and consumption, it might increase inflation and might result in increased rate of interest. But if there is an increase in the rate of interest, it will reduce MEC and that will work as a disincentive to the private entrepreneurs. Another important assumption relates to the nature of consumption goods and ability of the economy to produce it locally. If the increased demand for the wage goods is met through imports, the multiplier effects will not work effectively. In a sense, the domestic economy must have the capacity to produce the wage goods locally without pushing inflation.

While multiplier explains the net effects of change in investment on income and employment, accelerator explains the net effects of change in consumption outlay on total investment. When there is an increased demand for consumption goods—here wage goods, a result of public investment—there is an increase in the demand for capital goods to produce the additionally demanded consumer goods. But like in the case of multiplier, the MPC plays a critical role in accelerator effects. If the MPC is zero, say the entire new income is saved, there is no demand for consumption goods and, hence, no corresponding demand for capital goods to produce additional consumption goods. In other words, to produce additional consumption goods, additional capital goods are required. However, if there is unused additional capacity in the economy and the increased demand can be met without additional investment in capital goods, then there would not be accelerator effects. But if there is unutilised capacity in terms of labour and raw material, but still there is a demand for machine and technology, the additional investment will be required. But like in the case of multiplier, accelerator depends on the MPC and existing unutilised capacity in the economy to produce the additional consumption goods.

The MGNREGS is primarily an income-transfer programme that transfers income to the poor population in the ratio of 60 per cent of the total cost as wages, and since the MPC of the poor population is greater, multiplier is likely to be greater. There are some studies that capture consumption expenditure of MGNREGS workers and show that most of the workers are using the major part of their wage income from MGNREGS to meeting their daily consumption necessities (Pankaj, 2008a; Pankaj and Tankha, 2009). This shows that the MPC of MGNREGS workers is not only higher, but they are spending major part of the earning on wage goods, which increases demand for the wage goods and there remains unutilised capacity in the economy. Thus, it is unlikely that the higher MPC of the MGNREGS workers will push inflation, as the increased demand for wage goods can be easily met through unutilised capacity in the economy.

It has been observed that most of the MGNREGS workers are spending their MGNREGS earnings for daily consumption necessities and on items like food, clothes, tea, sugar, medicines, household items, small agricultural appliances, etc. The Indian economy has unutilised capacity in terms of raw materials and labour to produce most of these consumption goods. The additional demand for these items can be met without resorting to import. However, demand for some goods may need additional capital investment. The increased demand for consumption goods might trigger demand for capital goods. Private entrepreneurs will mobilise their resources to produce additional demand. In this way, the MGNREGS might induce the combined forces of multiplier and accelerator in the Indian economy. It is not surprising that the Indian economy was the least affected by the recent global recession. For example, in 2008, the year of global recession, India maintained 6.8 per cent growth rate in GDP. In the successive years too, India's GDP grew at the rate of 8 per cent and 8.6 per cent in 2009–10 and 2010–11, respectively.

V

Employment Programme and Poverty Reduction

The public works-based employment guarantee programme helps in poverty reduction largely through two effects: (*a*) income benefits to the individual beneficiary, and (*b*) benefits of rural infrastructure and community assets. Gaiha (1997: 301–14) has explained individual-level benefits in terms of (*a*) transfer and (*b*) stabilisation effects. By transfer effects, he means a net transfer of income including benefits of community assets. By stabilisation effects, he means that the beneficiary household can depend on the additional income to cope with the difficulties during lean season, distress, calamities and difficult conditions. It works as a cushion against adversity and stops fall of the families from the existing position.

The transfer of income helps in poverty reduction if it results in saving that can be used for the purchase of productive assets, converting unproductive into productive assets, increasing productivity of the existing assets like land and agriculture, and other investment that generates regular income. Saving and investment in productive investment, however, depends on two conditions: first is the adequacy of the amount transferred, and the second is the existing income and assets base of the households that allow savings out of additional income. The additional income through employment programme is generally low and marginal propensity of the poor households to consume is generally high. Thus, the net effects in terms of saving and, hence, investment in productive assets is rather low in the above conditions. Nonetheless, some of these households have been found to be utilising the additional income for productive investment (purposes) like buying seeds, small appliances, cattle, etc.

On the other hand, the stabilisation effects of such a programme are more robust. First, a large number of these households remain sagged in poverty due to adverse fall like lack of income during the lean season, sudden loss of income and increase in expenditure due to illness, etc. Most of these poor households meet the adverse situations through borrowing money and mortgaging/selling of assets and property. This not only robs them of their surplus, but makes them often fall into a debt trap. The additional and assured income through employment guarantee programme cushions these families against adverse fall. This adverse fall is so frequent in the life of these poor households that they are unable to move out of this. The regular guaranteed income over a reasonable period might help these poor families in moving out of this situation.

The poverty-reducing effects of community assets are indirect, although the benefits of community assets are reaped both by the beneficiary and the non-beneficiary, poor and the non-poor households alike. It has been observed that increased rural connectivity and higher agricultural productivity have greater poverty-reducing effects (Nayyar, 2002: 10–11). Since the majority of the community assets created under employment programme, at least in the case of MGNREGS, are related to water conservation, harvesting and rural connectivity, its poverty-reducing effects are (supposedly) greater.

However, the poverty-reducing effects of the employment scheme are linked to the design of the programme. The important design issues relate to: (*a*) targeting and coverage, (*b*) adequacy of the amount transferred and its certainty, (*c*) length (period) of income transfer and (*d*) types and quality of assets created. First, if the employment programme is not well targeted, its impact on poverty would be negligible/nil. The employment programme is generally better in targeting, as it is based on the principle that only the most needy person will come forward to work and earn. The rights-based universal and guaranteed programme has another advantage of self-targeting. It also rules out the possibility of exclusion of the deserving households even though some better-off households may also become beneficiary. Second, the amount of income should be adequate enough to generate some effects; it should be certain and regular and the programme should have a reasonably long period of life. The short-duration programme has been found more useful for stabilisation than for poverty-reducing purposes. Third, the types and quality of assets created also matter, as inappropriate assets and those of poor quality would not be very helpful.

Employment Guarantee versus Cash Transfer

Cash transfer and, in particular, the CCT as a means of income transfer to the poor households has emerged as an alternative to the employment programme. At present, about 28 countries are running the cash-transfer programme. The protagonists of the cash transfer argue that if income transfer is the instrument of poverty reduction, then cash transfer is a better and more efficient instrument, as it is less demanding in terms of implementation and administrative cost. The CCT has added advantage of addressing transmission of intergenerational poverty by investment in health and education of the children of the poor families.

Like in the case of guaranteed employment programme, the cash transfer too helps in poverty reduction largely through income and multiplier effects, although to some, multiplier effects of employment guarantee programme are greater than that of cash transfer (Narayana, Parikh and Srinivasan, 1988). But while the CCT has another advantage of removing transmission of intergenerational poverty by linking income transfer with the conditionality of education and health of children, the employment guarantee scheme has another advantage of creating productive assets that trigger many local level effects. But even under employment guarantee scheme, there is no bar to put such conditionalties on the beneficiaries. But even without explicit conditionality of educating children and giving health care, most of the poor families have been found investing in health and education of their children, if additional income permits such expenditure. A large number of MGNREGS workers in India have been found using additional income from the MGNREGS to meet education- and health-related expenditure. This has been more so in case of women workers (Pankaj and Tankha, 2010).

VI

Working of the MGNREGS and Critical Issues

Income, Employment Generation and Multiplier

Employment generation is the instrument and income transfer is the objective of the programme. Nonetheless, instrument and objective are interrelated, as income transfer depends on employment generation, but both create their own discrete effects. The guaranteed employment days are to ensure transfer of a minimum income and effects of the additional income, say, multiplier works depending on: (*a*) coverage, that is, the number of households provided with additional income; (*b*) adequacy, that is, the amount of additional income transferred and (*c*) consistency in the transfer over the years. Even the labour market effects depend to a great extent on these two factors.

The coverage of the scheme is massive; the entire rural population that constitutes 72 per cent of the total population of India (as per the census 2001) is (notionally) covered. In a state like Bihar, this goes upto 90 per cent of the total population. But even in terms of actual beneficiaries, the number is huge. For example, Figure 1.1 shows that out of the total rural households (137,747,384 as per 2001 Census), 39.8 per cent (54.83 million) were provided employment in 2010–11. This figure has increased from 15.26 per cent in 2006–07 to 24.62 per cent in 2007–08, 32.75 per cent in 2008–09 and 38.14 per cent in 2009–10.[11] The number of people (at least one person per household) provided employment is more than the total population of a large number of African, Asian and Latin American countries. None of India's past employment programme provided employment at such a large scale, and no democratic country has ever implemented a universal right-to-work programme. Of course, it is universal at the rural household level.

Figure 1.1: Households Provided Employment as Percentage of Total Rural Households

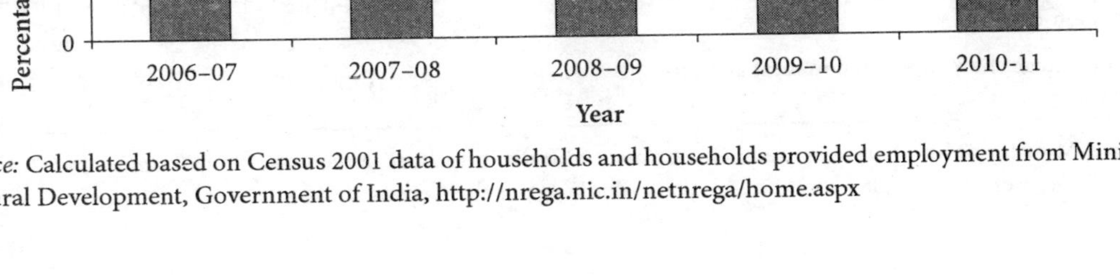

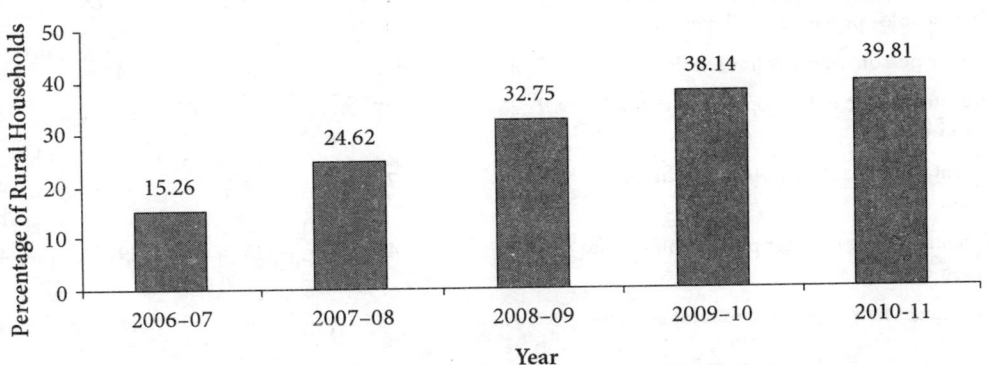

Source: Calculated based on Census 2001 data of households and households provided employment from Ministry of Rural Development, Government of India, http://nrega.nic.in/netnrega/home.aspx

Although average person-days of employment provided per household fall short of the minimum guarantee of 100 days, yet this figure has reached an all-India average of 54 person-days per household in 2009–10.[12] In the same year, Himachal Pradesh (HP) (57.30), Karnataka (56.62), Madhya Pradesh (MP) (55.66) and Tamil Nadu (54.67) were able to provide employment days greater than the national average; and a few—Rajasthan (68.97), Andhra Pradesh (65.67), UP (64.91) and some smaller states of the north-east like Tripura (79.56), Sikkim (79.92), Mizoram (94.57) and Nagaland (87.40) generated about 60–70 days on an average per household (Table A1.3).

A significant number of households have also completed 100 days of employment. For example, in 2009–10, 7.8 million households (13.47 per cent of the households provided employment) also completed 100 days. The ratio of households which completed 100 days has increased from 10.2 per cent in 2006–07 to 13.47 in 2009–10. It is likely that with the streamlining of the implementation, this figure will reach a higher level. Field observations suggest that most of the households joining the employment guarantee scheme would like to work for 100 days.

Table 1.1 shows that about 10 billion person-days of employment has been generated in the five years up to 2010–11. It was 0.9 billion person-days in 2006–07, 1.4 in 2007–08, 2.2 in 2008–09, 2.8 billion in 2009–10 and 2.56 billion in 2010–11. This has been generated with an expenditure of 88.2 billion rupees in 2006–07, 158.5 billion in 2007–08, 272.5 billion in 2008–09, 379 billion rupees in 2009–10 and 392 billion in 2010–11.

More than 50 per cent of the total employment days have been earned by the scheduled castes (SC) and scheduled tribes (ST) households who are mostly poor (See Table A1.4. and Table A1.5 for state-wise

Table 1.1: Snapshot of Employment Generation at All-India Level (2006–07 to 2010–11)

Employment Generated and Provided	*2006–07*	*2007–08*	*2008–09*	*2009–10*	*2010–11*
1. No. of households provided employment in million	21.01	33.9	45.11	52.58	54.83
2. No. of households provided employment as per cent of total rural households	15.26	24.62	32.75	38.14	39.81
3. Household completing 100 days as per cent of households provided employment	10.2	–	14.45	13.47	10.20
4. Average person-days per households	43	42	48	54	47
5. Percentage share of SC population in total person-days	25	27	29	30	31
6. Percentage share of ST population in total person-days	36	29	25	21	21
7. Percentage share of other population in total person-days	38	43	45	49	49
8. Percentage share of women in total person-days	41	43	48	48	48

Source: Ministry of Rural Development, Government of India, http://nrega.nic.in/netnrega/home.aspx
Note: There were 137,747,384 rural households in India as per the Census 2001.

detail). The incidence of poverty is highest among the SC and ST, and they constitute the largest proportion of India's total poor population. Women's share in total person-days has exceeded their share in the erstwhile employment programmes like the SGRY, and has also exceeded the minimum reserved participation of 33 per cent in all the five years of implementation since 2006–07. Women's share in total person-days has reached 48 per cent of the total person-days in 2008–09 and remained at the same level in 2009–10 and 2010–11 (see Table A1.7 for state-wise detail). This constituted the highest ever share of women in any public works-based employment programme in India.

The federal government has allocated a budget of 113 billion rupees in 2006–07, 120 in 2007–08, 300 in 2008–09, 391 in 2009–10 and 401 billion rupees in 2010–11. This budget constituted 0.27 per cent of GDP in 2006–07, 0.25 in 2007–08, 0.56 in 2008–09, 0.67 in 2009–10 and 0.64 in 2010–11. This budget does not include the share (25 per cent of the material and wage cost of skilled workers) of different state governments. About two thirds of the total expenditure has been incurred on wages. As a whole, up to 2010–11, 85,985 crores of rupees have been spent on wages, which is a huge income transfer to the poor people with high marginal propensity to consume.

The huge transfer of income to the people with high MPC has positive implications for the working of the multiplier. It has been observed that most of these poor use their additional income from MGNREGS on consumption goods like food, clothes, sugar, tea, edible oil, shoes, utensils, medicines, cheap cosmetics, transport, etc. (Pankaj, 2008a; Pankaj and Tankha, 2009). The additional demand for these goods will generate further employment and income in the economy. Production of some of these goods might require capital investment as well and this will trigger accelerator effects in the economy.

Poverty-reducing Effects

Wage income from MGNREGS constitutes significant part of the annual income of these households. It is about 20–30 per cent of the annual income of the poor households at the existing level of poverty line. A study of four states, namely, Rajasthan, HP, Bihar and Jharkhand shows that it constitutes about 19 per cent of the total annual income of the MGNREGS workers' households (Pankaj and Tankha, 2009). This figure varies across states and individual households depending on the number of person-days realised by the household and the availability of other sources of income.

It has been observed that apart from using additional income from MGNREGS on consumption, these workers are using this additional income also for health and education, repaying of debt, and buying little household items. The low income and the pressure of necessity do not permit sufficient savings and investment in assets like land, but some households were found purchasing fixed deposit instruments of bank from where they were collecting their MGNREGS wages (Pankaj and Tankha, 2009: 63). Investment in health and education of children is likely to reduce transmission of intergenerational poverty—one of the major advantages of CCT programme.

The incidence of indebtedness is huge in rural areas. As per the NSSO Situation Assessment Survey of Farmers, 2003, 48.6 per cent of the agricultural households were indebted. The average amount of debt was ₹12,585, which is almost equal to the annual minimum income guaranteed under the MGNREGS. The percentage of indebted households and the amount of debt varied across states and size of the holding. The MGNREGS supports the economically vulnerable households during the lean season. A large number of these poor households used to take loan at a very high rate from non-institutional sources just to buy food and other necessary goods. Now, they are able to earn under the scheme even during the lean season. In fact, the large part of employment generation under the MGNREGS is only during the lean season.

After the revision of MGNREGS wages in January 2011, the MGNREGS guarantees a transfer of about 12,000 rupees per household per annum (assuming the payment of minimum wage and 100 days of employment). Thus, the guaranteed annual income under the MGNREGS is only marginally less than the average amount of indebtedness of these households. A study of MGNREGS workers of Bihar shows that while in 2006, 38 per cent of these households were indebted, only 31.37 per cent of them remained so in 2008. The ratio of indebted households declined by about seven percentage points in two years (Pankaj, 2008a: 130). Other studies also suggest that the incidence of borrowing for meeting daily necessities by these poor households has come down because of getting employment in the lean season.

Distress and seasonal migration constitutes major proportion of rural-to-urban migration in India. However, because of the high cost of living in urban areas and lack of regular employment for these workers, migration does not help these poor families beyond meeting immediate daily necessities. There is a social cost of migration as well; most of these workers were found unhappy with their migrant conditions.

The MGNREGS has resulted in reduced distress and seasonal migration from the rural areas. A study of Bihar, the state with high incidence of rural migration, suggests that migration of MGNREGS workers households declined by about 12 percentage points in between 2006 and 2008 (Pankaj, 2008a: 132). Similar trends have been found in other states. Moreover, workers were found more satisfied while working in their own villages. Even the savings of the MGNREGS workers were greater, because of no cost involved in getting job at home under the MGNREGS. And if the work is provided beyond five kilometres of the radius of the home, there is a provision of addition of 10 per cent of the wage in the total wage.

Community Assets and Local Economy

About 15 million public works have been undertaken up to 2010–11. Most of the works pertain to water conservation and harvesting, rural connectivity and land development. A large number of works also relate to small and minor irrigation and land development. The land-development works include those of the land of small and marginal farmers who constitute about 80 per cent of India's farmers. The effects of community assets are geographically widespread, as these assets are being constructed in almost every village of the country. The variety of works undertaken shows the types of assets created. Figure 1.2 shows the types of work undertaken in between 2008–09 and 2010–11 (only since 2008–09, all the districts have been covered).

The community-level impacts of the above works are yet to be registered in a big way. Nonetheless, there are some indications of the working of multiplier effects on the village economy. Hirway et al. (2010) has used social accounting matrix (SAM) to study multiplier effects of the MGNREGA in Nana Kotda village of Gujarat and finds that its employment, income and output multiplier effects are noticeable.

The huge number of works undertaken in the rural areas have enhanced rural infrastructure. Up to 2010–11, about 15 million works have been undertaken, spread over six lakh villages. It means that in each village, on an average 25 works have been undertaken so far. A major impact of such works, in particular of water conservation, irrigation and flood control, is on agricultural economy. The amount

Figure 1.2: Types of Works Undertaken between 2008–09 and 2010–11

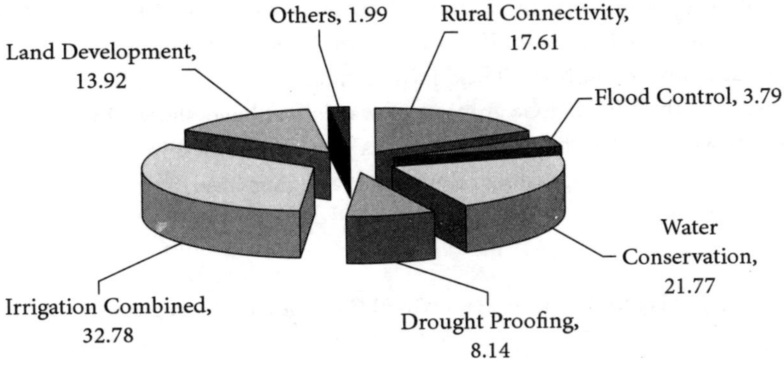

Source: http://nrega.nic.in/netnrega/home.aspx

of cultivable land has increased and agricultural productivity has also increased. The land-development works undertaken on the farm of small and marginal farmers and poor SC and ST households would significantly increase the agricultural productivity. These farmers are unable to invest in the land development, and MGNREGS is helping them in bringing their uncultivable land under cultivation. For example, a large number of wells are being constructed on the land of the small and marginal farmers. It is learnt that each well can irrigate upto two acres of land. And most of these small and marginal farmers, who were unable to cultivate those lands, will benefit hugely from this project.

It has been found in several places that increased rural connectivity triggers many effects. Rural connectivity increases two-way linkages—the sale of the product and buying of inputs—with the market. It reduces transportation cost on agricultural inputs like fertilisers, diesel and agricultural appliances, and gives better price of agricultural products by direct selling in the market.

Nevertheless, there are concerns about the quality of assets being created, its durability and sectional control over the benefits. There is a bit of difficulty in creating quality assets, as the act prescribes 60:40 wage and material ratio. Also the earth-related work, although more labour intensive, is yet not very durable because of less material component. There are some complaints about the improper selection of work and benefits of the assets derived by the more resourceful persons. There are also some complaints about leakages and corruption in works.

Wage Rate and Labour Market

There are significant labour market implications of 52 million households getting work for an average of 54 days in a year (2009–10) under the MGNREGS. High participation of women and enforcement of the provisions of equal and minimum wages are other important influences. The labour market effects of these forces work, however, mostly through employment generation and wage rate.

A large number of people are working under the MGNREGS and getting wage which is higher than the wage rate of casual workers in the agriculture and non-agriculture sectors of the rural economy. In

2004–05, the all-India average daily wage of a casual rural worker was 55.03 rupees for male and 34.94 rupees for female. As against this, the average daily wage of an MGNREGS worker was 65 rupees in 2006–07, which increased to 75 in 2007–08, 84 in 2008–09, 86 in 2009–10 and 99 in 2010–11. The minimum wages under the MGNREGS have increased very substantially within five years. The state-wise increase in the MGNREGS minimum wages has been shown in Figure 1.3. In fact, the average minimum wage under the MGNREGS has almost doubled in the last five years, which is unprecedented. This is bound to push rural wages at a higher level, and there are indications that it has increased significantly.

Figure 1.3: State-wise MGNREGS Wages in 2006 and 2011

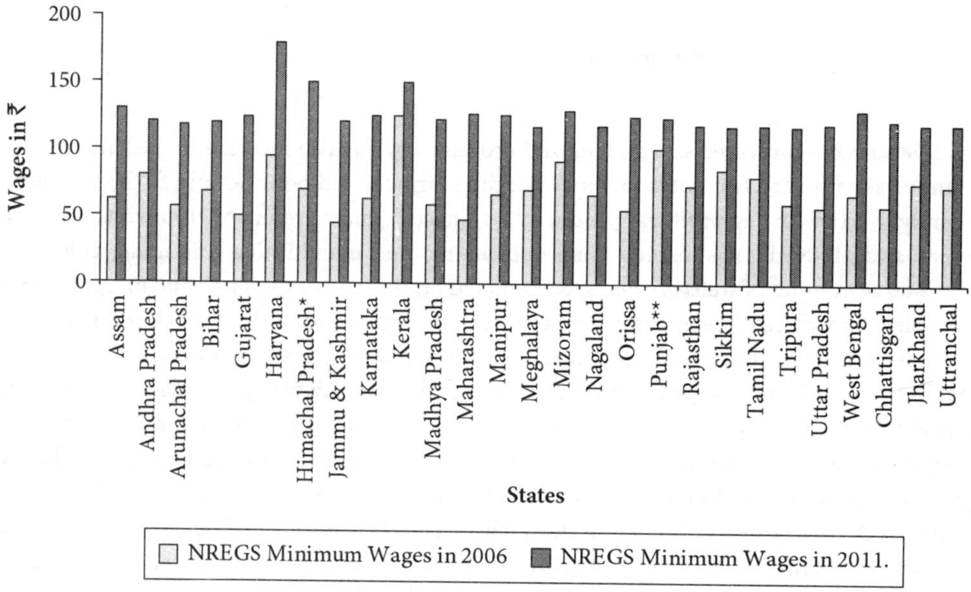

Source: http://nrega.nic.in/netnrega/home.aspx
Notes: * 120 for non-scheduled areas.
** 130 for Amritsar district.

The higher wage rate under the MGNREGS will create supply-side pressure on the local wages that remain suppressed because of monopsonic and oligopolistic control over the local labour market, apart from other factors. The enhanced income security increases bargaining power of the poor households, as they are assured of a minimum income, and can afford to bargain competitive wage rate. Also, because of the higher wage rate under the MGNREGS, some of the rural workers might withdraw from the low-paid job and will compensate for the loss of income through high-paid job under MGNREGS. High participation of women will create its own supply-side pressure, as they would withdraw from the low-paid job and refuse to accept non-discriminatory wages.

However, this pressure on the wages of the local economy would not work uniformly and with equal degree in all the districts and states, as there are differential conditions in terms of agriculture, landholding pattern, unemployment and agriculture wage rate in different places. It is anticipated that the wage rate in the farm sector would increase in those areas where there is a shortage of labourers, and still the wage rate is depressed. On the other hand, its effects, at least in the short run, will be limited where there is abundant supply of labour and a large number of them migrate to other states in search of wage employment. For example, in flood-prone districts of north Bihar, drought-prone districts of southern Rajasthan, tribal-dominated north-eastern districts of Gujarat, famine-affected districts of Orissa and in many other places, the agricultural wage rate is depressed because of the abundant supply of labour. A large number of them migrate in search of wage employment because of the lack of employment opportunities in agriculture and non-agricultural sectors there.

The pressure on the wage rate will create many positive effects. It is argued that it will break the low income equilibrium of the rural economy and push it on higher income equilibrium, as it happened in the industrialised developed economies. The other positive effects of increased wage rate relate to the change in agricultural practices, cropping pattern and productivity. The increased wage cost would influence farmers to change the cropping pattern, agriculture practices and enhance productivity. In states where agriculture is still predominantly driven by man and animal power (eastern and central India) and the level of mechanisation is low, enhanced wage cost would create cost-related pressure for the mechanisation, improvement in agriculture practices and techniques. The low level of mechanisation continues to be sustained by easy availability of cheap labour, apart from other factors. But once the wage rate increases substantially as an impact of the MGNREGS, scale of profit would decline due to increase in input cost for labour. This would create positive effects in terms of crop substitution, encouragement to mechanisation and changes in agricultural practices/methods.

However, the substantial increase in wage rate might trigger some negative effects as well. The enhanced wage rate will make many tiny and small manufacturing units (in the rural economy first) uncompetitive, and over a period of time, these industries will shut down. This will lead to a loss of employment and income in the non-agriculture sectors. The multiplier effects will be negated. If the process continues, it might also trigger reverse multiplier. Since the number of employment days has been capped at 100 days per family in a year, the chances of the working of the reverse multiplier are minimum.

The practice of discriminatory wages in case of casual workers is found both in rural and urban areas. In 2004–05, the all-India average daily wage of a casual rural worker was 55.03 rupees for male and 34.94 rupees for female, a difference of about 20 rupees (Karan and Selvaraj, 2008: 43). In other words, the average daily wage of a female casual worker was only 63 per cent of that of a male worker. The difference was much higher in some states. There was a difference of 69.11 rupees in Kerala, the highest among all the states. In contrast to that, the MGNREGS provides equal wages for male and female workers, and field reports suggest that male and female workers are getting equal wages under the MGNREGS.

Realisation of equal wages for male and female workers under MGNREGS has significant implications for the rural labour market.[13] If women are able to earn higher wages under the MGNREGS, there is a likelihood that in most cases, they would not be willing/available to work for less than what they are getting under the MGNREGS. The reduction in the supply of women labour force, because of their joining of MGNREGS, would create supply-side pressure on labour market that would push the wage floor. It has been observed that many tea gardens in Kangra were finding it difficult to hire workers on the basis of their pre-MGNREGS wages (Pankaj and Tankha, 2009). They had to increase the wages, and this revision had to be done frequently, as with the revision in the MGNREGS wages. Some of these tea gardens were on the verge of closure, as they were finding it difficult to operate at profit with increased wage cost.

Participatory Development Process

Social audit, transparency and accountability: Social impacts of MGNREGS are noteworthy. It is the first policy instrument that has practically strengthened participatory decentralised development process uniformally across states, which continued to be missing in most of the states even after the 73rd Constitutional Amendment Act. There are reports that the MGNREGS works are being selected through the *gram sabha* (village assembly); the gram sabha meeting has become more frequent and people's participation including participation of women has increased in these meetings. The PRIs (institutions of local self-governance) are not only selecting the work, but also executing it.

Transparency, accountability and monitoring of public works programme have acquired a new dimension, as it no longer remains a distant mysteriously secret process of the bureaucracy. Although, transparency and accountability provisions are not working well, yet a beginning has been made, and the process is being strengthened. For the first time, workers are able to sign muster rolls, which are also found at worksites in some places. But all these documents are under the domain of the GP, and any adult member of the GP can ask for these documents to see and verify it.

Social audit of the work is still missing in most of the cases. Nonetheless, some civil society organisations (CSOs) have played effective role in mobilisation of the people to activate social audit process. Mazdoor Kisan Sangram Samiti in Rajasthan has played critical role in this area. In Andhra Pradesh, the state government has tried to institutionalise the social audit process, even it is state-driven. In other states too, social audit is heard of taking place, but only on and off. Some socially aware citizens are using the Right to Information Act to seek information and bring anomalies and leakages in the public domain that generates pressure on the implementing agencies to adhere to the provisions of the act.

Entitlements and Empowerment

Demand-based job creation, unemployment allowance and worksite facilities are largely missing. Nonetheless, it is happening and being talked of. While under the Maharashtra Employment Guarantee Scheme, not a single case of the payment of unemployment allowance happened over 30 years of the implementation of the programme, under the MGNREGS, it has been paid in MP, Chhattisgarh and other states also. Wage compensation for delayed wage payment is unheard of even in the organised sector. But in the Khunti district of Jharkhand, mobilisation of workers by civil society actors resulted in payment of compensation for delayed wage payment. These incidents are still rare. Nevertheless, they are happening.

The MGNREGS has empowered the poor workers in many other ways as well. About nine crore bank and post office accounts have been opened in the name of these workers. Most of them have got access to these financial institutions for the first time in their life. The linkages with the financial institutions trigger several other benefits. A saving habit is developing, and getting loan from these institutions has become easy for these poor. For the government, it will be helpful in delivery of other social-assistance programmes involving cash transfer. Further, guaranteed employment can liberate the poor families from the clutches of the local employers (landlords).

The MGNREGS has positive impacts on rural women workers (Khera and Nayyar, 2009). Women's empowerment is another significant social impact of the programme. A study of women workers in four north Indian states shows individual and community-level empowerment effects of the MGNREGS on women workers (Pankaj and Tankha, 2010). At individual level, there are three significant effects, which are: (*a*) income–consumption effects, (*b*) intrahousehold (increased decision-making role of women) effects and (*c*) broadening of choice and capability. At the community level, the high participation of women under the MGNREGS, apart from bringing male–female wage parity, would correct the skewed labour market conditions. Women's participation in gram sabha and their joining public works in large numbers will have several other effects. The introduction of female mate system has been found favourable to change gender relations: for male workers, it is an entirely new experience to work under a female mate.

Gaps and Deficits

There are difficulties and challenges in the realisation of the main objectives of the MGNREGS. The programme is yet to become demand-driven and civil society–oriented. In most of the states, employment is being provided based on the availability of the work, and the local bureaucracy is controlling the implementation process to a great extent. The realisation of low number of person-days and other entitlements are happening because of the low level of quality awareness among the poor households and low, rather lack of, civil society mobilisation.

There is a huge variation in implementation and, hence, in impacts across the states. Residents of a few states are able to realise more number of person-days and other entitlements than the residents of other states. If the realisation of person-days remains low in the Punjab, Haryana and Kerala, there is not much concern. But the low realisation of person-days in states like Bihar, Jharkhand, MP, Chhattisgarh, Orissa and West Bengal, with high incidence of poverty and migration of rural population, is a matter of concern. The objective of bridging regional disparities based on demand-based approach will be defeated primarily because of this. Of course, state like Rajasthan has taken full advantage of the scheme, and has been able to corner about 30–40 per cent of the total MGNREGS budget of the federal government. Other states with high incidence of poverty and low level of development can learn lessons from Rajasthan.

The PRIs are weak in most of the states. They suffer from poor institutionalisation, low delivery capacity and weak resource base, apart from others. On the other hand, the implementation of the scheme under the MGNREGS is dependent on the capability and efficiency of these institutions in realising entitlements. These institutions are getting strengthened through the programme, but the process is exogenous, and it will not be able to address the structural weaknesses of these institutions.

There are defects of design as well. MGNREGS is overcentralised in design, although implementation process has been decentralised to a considerable extent. Its implementation design is neutral to differential delivery capacities of PRIs and bureaucracy, and mobilisation of the civil society in different states. It clubs too many objectives and, sometimes, there is an inherent tension between these objectives. For example, its main objective to provide minimum livelihood security through 100 days of guaranteed wage employment in public works, preferably *kacha* one, appears to be incompatible with its another important objective of creating durable assets. *Kacha* work is generally considered employment intensive, provided it is done manually. However, it is non-durable in nature. The problem gets aggravated as the MGNREGA guidelines prescribe distribution of cost on the wages of unskilled workers and material including the wages of skilled workers in the ratio of 60:40.

Last, it leaves the entire urban population outside its purview. And probably it will be difficult to launch such a programme in urban areas unless there is a massive change in the design and structure. Public works in urban areas are generally less labour intensive. Even in rural areas, the programme cannot be run for years and years. In areas with well-developed rural infrastructure, there is already a problem of getting public land for creating community assets. In irrigated areas, there is limited scope for taking work on the land of individual farmers. But then it is also expected that the multiplier effects will gradually reduce demand for such employment in the long run.

In spite of difficulties, there is a hope for the success of the programme. The hope arises from the following developments:

1. Right to work has entered into the imagination of the common man.
2. Unprecedented political consensus backs the programme.
3. Civil society is rising for the realisation of their entitlements.
4. Local institutions have started responding to the demand.

VII

Chapters

Section II contains three chapters that explain public works–based employment programme as a full-employment strategy, and explore its role in poverty reduction. Indira Hirway describes various strategies of reaching full employment, and suggests that public works–based guaranteed employment programme can be a component of full employment strategy for a country like India. She explains MGNREGS as a part of labour-intensive growth strategy, and argues that there are three sectors that can be critical to growth and employment generation. These three are: (*a*) regeneration of natural resources to stabilise and promote growth of agriculture and allied activities, where the bulk of the workforce and the poor are located; (*b*) construction of socio-economic infrastructure that can promote growth of big, small and unorganised sector units and (*c*) reduction in unpaid work of the poor and women (working poor) to release them to take up for productive employment in the market economy. Based on the assessment of the design and implementation of MGNREGS in India, she suggests that inclusion of skill training, maintenance of the public assets and services as permissible work under the MGNREGS would be helpful in this respect.

Gerry Rodgers has explored the linkages between right to work and poverty reduction, and argues that right to work can address employment-related poverty that is one of the important causes of poverty in the country. He first explains the ethical and other dimensions of right to work and its evolution and integration with development discourse as part of entitlement approach, and then, he examines the linkages between right to work and poverty reduction by posing the following questions: (*a*) How far is poverty the consequence of deficits in work, such as a shortfall of employment or inadequate conditions of work, and—correspondingly—to what extent is employment creation a primary instrument for poverty reduction, either through income it generates or through the empowerment of those employed? (*b*) Given the relationship between employment and poverty, how the right to work might lead directly or indirectly to an increase in employment, improvement in the quality of work and an increase in income? He argues that for the majority of the poor, employment deficit is an important reason for poverty, although there are equally important factors like low productivity, wages and income in the existing employment, and shortfall in social security measures. He, however, concludes that while employment creation is an essential element of poverty-reduction strategies, a range of mutually reinforcing policies is required to raise the pace of employment creation, improve the quality and productivity of work and strengthen the economic and political capabilities of the poor to demand and take advantage of economic opportunities.

Eduardo Zepeda and Diana Alarcón have reviewed the poverty-reducing effects of employment guarantee scheme and cash-transfer programme, and argue that both help poor families mainly through the transfer of additional income. Most of the poor households use large part of this additional income for consumption purposes that triggers multiplier effects in the economy, and multiplier effects, in turn, increase productive employment opportunities in the economy. The poor also gain by this growth process, that is, increased productive employment opportunities. But while employment guarantee scheme has another advantage of creating community assets that trigger many other effects in the local economy, the CCT helps in reducing transmission of intergenerational poverty by better human capital development. Based on the review of the modelling exercises of the two programmes, they arrive at a conclusion that as a whole, the employment guarantee scheme has greater poverty-reducing effects than CCT. However, the former (employment guarantee scheme) is more demanding in terms of design and implementation and, therefore, the outcome is also dependent to a great extent on these two factors. Further, the quality of the community assets is another factor that needs attention under the employment guarantee scheme.

The four papers in Section 3 are empirical that bring field-based state-specific experiences of implementation and impact. All the four papers of this section are survey based and examine working of the MGNREGS in agriculturally backward and developed states, north and south Indian states and better and poor performer states. *Demand and Delivery Gap: Strengthening Grass-roots Institutions in Bihar and Jharkhand* by Ashok K. Pankaj examines the working of the MGNREGS in Bihar and Jharkhand, the two most backward states of India. The paper argues that the high incidence of rural poverty, low occupational diversification in rural areas, heavy seasonal and distress migration from the rural areas in search of wage employment and poor infrastructure in rural areas of these two states make them ideal candidates for the employment guarantee scheme. But while the socio-economic conditions of the rural population suggest huge demand for (wage) employment in both the states (which is not reflected in the official statistics of the number of households that demanded employment), the implementation of the scheme suggests wide gap between actual demand and delivery. On the one hand, because of the low level of literacy, lack of procedural and substantial awareness, absence of social mobilisation for the realisation of entitlement and very weak presence of CSOs, the local population in both the states have limited capacity to articulate their demand effectively. On the other hand, the grass-roots institutions are weak enough to translate demand into delivery. Lack of vibrant CSOs that could play the mobilisation role is an important gap in these two states. Like the previous and the erstwhile (government-sponsored) employment-generation programme, the MGNREGS remains largely supply driven in both the states.

Nonetheless, there are indications that the scheme has been able to create some impact on the livelihood conditions of beneficiary households including reduction in their indebtedness and distress seasonal migration in both the states. Because of the low level of implementation and procedural weaknesses, community-level impacts are not very visible. Finally, this paper suggests some measures for strengthening of the grass-roots institutions and emphasises that the MGNREGS provides a unique opportunity to both the states to transform the livelihood conditions of the rural population by strengthening of implementation. Based on the number of BPL families, it is estimated that Bihar could have got upto 10,000 crores of rupees from the Centre, which was more than the annual plan of the state say, in 2006–07 and 2007–08. Similar is the case with Jharkhand.

Rajasthan has been one of the leading performers in terms of the implementation of the MGNREGS. The overall employment generation has been high; households have been able to realise greater number of employment days and, hence, income and relatively more number of households have completed hundred days of employment. The state has taken out the major share (30–40 per cent) of total MGNREGS budget of the Centre. It has also shown the way in terms of high participation by women and active mobilisation of CSOs.

Surjit Singh, Varsha Joshi and K. N. Joshi evaluate the working of the MGNREGS in five districts of Rajasthan and examine in detail implementation issues like availability of work within 15 days of demand; work made available within 5 km of the radius of the village; payment of wages and within 15 days of the completion of the work; payment of unemployment allowance in case of failure to provide work within 15 days of demand; role of the gram sabha; gender discrimination in allocating work and wage payment and scope for unionisation of the workers. They also assess impacts on benefited households, their migration, women's participation and its larger social impacts. The impact of social audit on the quality of the work, quality of the assets created, the level of awareness about and enforcement of entitlements has been further examined.

This paper shows that notwithstanding implementation difficulties related to work measurement and wage payment, types and quality of assets created, low efficiency and capacity of local-level bureaucracy and leakages as well, the scheme has generated some tangible impacts on the rural population. An interesting finding of Rajasthan experience is playing of local power dynamics; people from upper-caste households have also joined to benefit from the scheme, but most of them actually do not work and take to themselves the role of supervisors, even when there is an official mate present.

Andhra Pradesh is another state that has been in the limelight for state-driven implementation of the MGNREGS. The success story of Andhra Pradesh has been woven around the massive use of modern technology and its guided penetration at the village level. The use of existing organisation like Indira Kranti Patham (IKP), a self-help group of women has been another attractive feature of Andhra Pradesh.

The paper by S. Galab and E. Revathi in this section examines the role of state-enabled institutions in facilitating implementation of the MGNREGS in the state. This paper deals with the role of IKP, a woman self-help group, social audit and wage seekers associations (WSAs) in enhanced performance of MGNREGS in the state. Based on a case study of Ananthapura district, it argues that these organisations have played crucial role in mobilisation of the workers and facilitating demand-based employment generation in the state. This paper also uses findings of a primary survey to show the preliminary impacts of the programme.

The MGNREGS has not been designed for agriculturally developed states like the Punjab and Haryana. Nonetheless, there is a demand for wage employment among the landless SC population of the state; the customary (law) practices deny landownership to SCs in the state. The decline in agricultural productivity and profits of the farmers and decreasing non-farm-sector employment opportunities have increased the demand for productive employment in other segments of society as well. However, low wage rate under MGNREGS, poor administrative preparedness and limited space for taking public works in large numbers in rural areas of the state have been major constraints.

The case of Punjab is a bit tricky, as the MGNREGS has both positive and negative implications for the agriculture economy of the state that depends heavily on the migrant labourers during the peak agriculture season. The MGNREGS may create further shortage because of the likelihood of withdrawal of some local workers and their joining the MGNREGS, and reduction in the number of migrant workers because of their getting MGNREGS employment at their home, the origin of migration. This has implications for pushing wage rate further, and hence, decline in profits of the farmers. Amidst declining profits, farmers will be tempted to divert agriculture land for non-agriculture purposes.

The paper by R. S. Ghuman and Parvinder Kaur examines the implications of MGNREGS for the developed but declining agricultural economy of the Punjab. It is argued that amidst declining agriculture productivity, employment generation under MGNREGS is expected to attract unemployed and underemployed unskilled labour in rural Punjab. The case study of Hoshiarpur district, however, suggests that the ground realities are different. The study also highlights that there is a need to review the scope and coverage of activities under MGNREGS with a region-/state-specific approach.

Section four examines MGNREGS as an agent of rural transformation. Apart from household-level effects that have been explained in the previous section, there are larger social and economic effects of the programme. The four papers in this section deal with three important aspects of impacts. Amita Shah has analysed the various aspects of the creation of community assets and outlined the challenges of creating productive community assets under the MGNREGS. T. Haque explores the impact of MGNREGS on agrarian economy with respect to increased irrigation, production and productivity, and cropping pattern. D. N. Reddy analyses how MGNREGS has created opportunities for Indian agriculture and yet there are new challenges arising out of MGNREGS. Ashok K. Pankaj and Rukmini Tankha have examined the empowerment effects of MGNREGS on rural women for whom there is unprecedented opportunity to earn independently. The individual- and community-level women's empowerment effects have been explained through a case study of four north Indian states.

Amita Shah explains the scope and challenges of assets creation under the MGNREGS and argues that enhancing wage income through creation of productive assets, especially in the farm economy, is a hallmark of the employment-generation programmes in India and elsewhere. It could be postulated that increased wages and capital formation within rural economies may unleash significant amount of effective demand and productive capacities, which, in turn, may redress poverty and also boost up overall growth in the country. The strategy may do marvel in an economy such as India, where agriculture sector continues to play crucial role in sustaining the momentum of overall economic growth besides reducing poverty. It concludes that while the right to work under MGNREGS could enhance and help realise the full potential of productive capacities in rural economies, it is essential that the work under it is planned, synchronised and placed in the context of planned economic growth so as to be able to impact local economy within short or medium time frame.

T. Haque explores the linkages between MGNREGS and agriculture and argues that the MGNREGS has been able to generate positive effects on agriculture mainly through irrigation, water-harvesting and land-development works undertaken in huge numbers. The main effects have been found on the cropping pattern, crop productivity and cost of production. This paper also raises some issues arising because of the rise in cost of production mainly because of increase in the wages, a clear effect of MGNREGS. The paper draws on primary and secondary sources to support the arguments.

D. Narshimha Reddy argues that the two dimensions of MGNREGS—ensuring employment of 100 days at minimum wages and creating assets that would improve the resource base of rural areas—are likely to have different implications for agriculture of especially marginal and small farmers. The paper examines the implications of the MGNREGS for agricultural labour market; impacts of creation and augmentation of rural water and land resources; the resulting changes in irrigation, area cultivated and agricultural productivity and impacts of the above on the farming community, especially those belonging to the SCs, STs, and other individual land-development beneficiaries and small and marginal farmers. At the same time, he outlines some of the challenges arising out of seasonal fluctuations in labour supply and demand, migration, agricultural wages and cost of cultivation, and implications of these changes to the small-farm economy, especially in dry-land regions. The paper examines the above implications also with a case study of Andhra Pradesh.

Among the important social consequences of the MGNREGS is high participation of women as workers and its effects on their individual and social life. The paper by Ashok K. Pankaj and Rukmini Tankha, based on a field survey, examines individual- and community-level empowerment effects of the MGNREGS on rural women in the states of Bihar, Jharkhand, Rajasthan and HP. It argues that a woman worker has benefited from the scheme primarily because of the paid-employment opportunity, and benefits have been realised through: (*a*) income–consumption effects, (*b*) intrahousehold effects (decision-making role) and (*c*) enhancement of choice and capability. Women as a community have also gained to some extent in terms of: (*a*) realisation of equal wages under MGNREGS with its long-term implications for correcting gender skewness and gender-discriminatory wages prevalent in the rural labour market of India; (*b*) recognition of the need for engendering of public works programme and (*c*) increased participation in the gram sabha that might change the male-dominant character of decision making at the grass-roots democratic institutions. The paper finally pleads that despite difficulties and hurdles for women, prospects lie, inter alia, in their collective mobilisation, more so in laggard states, for: (*a*) greater process participation, (*b*) realisation of sufficient number of person-days and wages paid through the individual account of women workers, (*c*) enforcement of provisions like crèche and (*d*) engendering of the nature of work, including types of assets created with a view to derive lateral benefits from the work and assets.

The two papers in the prospects section address two most important but overlapping issues of implementation. Paper by Katharina Raabe et al. addresses the issue of governance and outlines challenges based on insight from Bihar using Process-Influence-Mapping.[14] It is argued here that there are two types of governance challenges that make the large-scale implementation of social safety nets in rural areas, such as those implemented under MGNREGA, inherently difficult: (*a*) the challenge to avoid elite capture and to actually reach the poor and the disadvantaged and (*b*) the challenge to manage the funds allocated to the programme effectively and to avoid leakages and corruption. This paper presents the results from a case study in which Process-Influence-Mapping was applied in two districts in Bihar to analyse the implementation of MGNREGA.

Pramathesh Ambasta examines the scope of transforming rural governance through effective community participation under the ambience of PRIs. He argues that local-community-based development approach can be instrumental in promoting inclusive growth agenda and MGNREGS is a suitable policy instrument for this. However, the PRIs are handicapped due to ineffective devolution of funds, functions and functionaries in spite of the constitutional mandate. In this context, he examines the experiences of the MGNREGA to see how its outcomes have fallen short of its potential due to inadequate support structures at the grass roots. He also outlines a comprehensive reform agenda and gives special focus on the use of information and communication technology (ICT) for the above purpose. Finally, he argues that the reforms in governance and use of ICT will serve limited purpose in the absence of community mobilisation and in particular empowerment of the rural poor.

Notes

1. The National Rural Employment Guarantee Act, 2005, was renamed as the Mahatma Gandhi National Rural Employment Guarantee Act 2005 by an amendment in the act, passed by Parliament in 2009, and assented to by the President of India on 31 December 2009. See *The Gazette of India* (2009). Accordingly, Mahatma Gandhi is prefixed before the name of the scheme that is now called 'Mahatma Gandhi National Rural Employment Guarantee Scheme'.
2. The Planning Commission of India estimates rural poverty at 28.3 per cent of the total population in 2004–05. The Tendulkar Committee, appointed by the Planning Commission itself to address the issue of poverty measurement, estimates it at 41.8 per cent. The Saxena Committee, established by the Ministry of Rural Development, Government of India, to examine the issue of identification of BPL families, estimates it at 50 per cent. The National Commission for Enterprises in the Unorganised Sectors estimates it at 77 per cent.
3. Growth rate of some laggard states such as Bihar, Jharkhand, Orissa, etc., has also picked up recently.
4. Workforce calculated on the basis of usual principal and subsidiary status for the year 2004–05 (NSSO 61st round).
5. NSSO Situation Assessment Survey of Farmers, 2003. Table adopted from the Report of the Expert Group on Agricultural Indebtedness, July 2007.
6. The formation of the UPA (Congress, various Communist and other parties) made a formal commitment on these issues through the Common Minimum Program that talked of an employment guarantee scheme to ensure livelihood security to the rural people through the enactment of a legislation.

7. For example, in the famous Keshavnanda Bharati v. State of Kerala, the Supreme Court held that the object of Directive Principles is to embody the concept of a welfare state (1973, 4 SCC: 28). Similarly, in Jacob v. Kerala Water Authority (1999, 1 SCC: 28), the Supreme Court remarked that the judiciary should so interpret an Act as to advance Article 41, that is, right to work. In yet another case, Air India Statutory Corporation v. United Labour Union (AIR, 1997 SC: 645), it was observed that the Directive Principles contained provisions relating to 'Right to Development' that stands elevated as human right as it was made by the UN Convention on 'Right to Development'.
8. For details, see, Pankaj (2008). I have drawn on context and features in parts from my article, 'Guaranteeing Right to Work'.
9. On 2 February 2006, Prime Minister Manmohan Singh formally launched implementation of MGNREGA at Bandlapalle Gram Panchayat (GP), Narpala Mandal, Ananthapura District of Andhra Pradesh. Most of the states also chose to launch it on the same date.
10. The act mandates that all the districts are required to be covered within five years of its notification, that is, by 7 September 2010. However, the UPA-I government extended it to the rest of the districts from 1 April 2008, preponing it by two years.
11. The increase in 2007–08 and 2008–09 is also because of the increase in the coverage of the districts. In 2006–07, only 200 districts were covered and in 2007–08, 330 districts were covered. But the figure shown relates to all-India rural population.
12. Although, the minimum guarantee of 100 days are demand based and, hence, average person-days of less than 100 days should not be understood as non-fulfillment of the entitlement.
13. Ratna Sudarshan has examined rural labour-market conditions in Palakkad district of Kerala and found that differential wages existed for men and women in non-formal agriculture and non-agriculture sectors. A women worker in Palakkad district earned about ₹70 upwards per day while a male worker earned about ₹150 upwards per day. In contrast to this, the MGNREGS provided equal wages for both male and female workers (₹125). See Sudarshan (2008).
14. Process-Influence-Mapping is a participatory mapping technique, which is based on the Net-Map tool and combines elements of various tools that have been developed to analyse stakeholder interaction and political processes. The Process-Influence-Mapping is a new research method that throws light on these questions.

References

Ahluwalia, M. S. (2011) Prospects and policy challenges in the twelfth plan. *Economic and Political Weekly* XLVI, No. 21: 88–105.

Bagchee, A. (2005) Political and administrative realities of Employment Guarantee Scheme. *Economic and Political Weekly* 40, No. 2: 4531–37.

Bhaduri, A. (2005) *Development with dignity: A case for full employment.* Delhi: National Book Trust.

——— (2008) *Growth and employment in the era of globalization: Some lessons from the Indian experiences*, ILO Asia-Pacific Working Paper Series.

Dasgupta, S. and A. Singh (2005) Will Services be the new engine of economic growth in India, Working Paper 310, Centre for Business Research, University of Cambridge, UK.

Datt, G. and M. Ravallion (1994) Income gains for the poor from public works employment, evidence from two Indian villages. Living Standards Measurement Study Working Paper 100, March.

——— (2002a) Has India's post-reform economic growth left the poor behind. *The Journal of Economic Perspectives* 16, No. 3: 89–108.

——— (2002b) Why has economic growth been more pro-poor in some states of India than others? *Journal of Development Economics* 68, No. 2: 381–400.

——— (2009) Shining for the poor too? *Economic and Political Weekly* 45, No. 7: 55–60.

Dattar, C. (1990) Maharashtra Employment Guarantee Scheme. Mumbai: Tata Institute of Social Sciences.
Deaton, A. and J. Drèze (2002) Poverty and inequality in India: A reexamination. *Economic and Political Weekly* 37, No. 36: 3729–48.
Desai Sonalde B., Amaresh Dubey, Brij Lal Joshi, Mitali Sen, Abusaleh Shariff and Reeve Vanneman (2010) *Human development in India: Challenges for a society in Transition*. Delhi: Oxford University Press.
Dev, S. M. and C. Ravi (2007) Poverty and inequality: All India and states, 1983–2005. *Economic and Political Weekly* 42, No. 6.
Gaiha, Raghav (1997) Do rural public works influence agricultural wages? The case of the employment guarantee scheme in India. *Oxford Development Studies* 25, No. 3: 301–14.
Gazette of India, No. 231, 6 March 2007.
——— Extraordinary Part- II, Section- I, No. 53, New Delhi, Thursday, 31 December 2009.
Ghosh, Ajit K. (2010) India's employment challenges. Paper presented during an international consultation on Human Development in India: Emerging Issues and Policy Perspectives, organised by the Institute for Human Development, ICSSR and World Bank on 5–6 February at New Delhi.
Government of India (2009a) *Report of the Expert Group to Advise the Ministry of Rural Development on the Methodology for Conducting the Below Poverty Line (BPL) Census for 11th Five Year Plan (August 2009)*, Ministry of Rural Development, Krishi Bhavan, New Delhi.
——— (2009b) *Report of the Expert Group to Review the Methodology for Estimation of Poverty (November 2009)*, Planning Commission, New Delhi.
Himanshu (2007) Recent trends in poverty and inequality: Some preliminary results. *Economic and Political Weekly* 42, No. 6: 497–508.
Hirway, Indira, M. R. Saluja and Bhupesh Yadav (2010) *Employment guarantee programme and pro-poor growth: The study of a village in Gujarat*. Delhi: Academic Foundation.
Jayadev, Motiram and Vamsi Vakulabharanam (2007) Patterns of wealth disparities in India during the liberalisation era. *Economic and Political Weekly* 42, No. 39: 3853–63.
Kanbur, Ravi (2010) Regional disparities and Indian development, *India in the world: Growth stability and equity*, National Council of Applied Economic Research, Delhi.
Karan, Anup K. and Sakthivel Selvaraj (2008) *Trends in wages and earnings in India: Increasing wage differentials in a segmented labour market*, ILO Asia-Pacific Working Paper Series. New Delhi: ILO subregional office for South Asia.
Keynes, John Maynard (1951) *The general theory of employment interest and money*. London: Macmillan and Co. Ltd.
Khera, Reetika and Nandini Nayak (2009) Women workers and perceptions of the National Rural Employment Guarantee Act. *Economic and Political Weekly* 44, No. 43: 49–57.
Krishnaraj, Maithreyi, Divya Pandey and Aruna Kanchi (2004) Does EGS require restructuring for poverty alleviation and gender equality? II—Gender concerns and issues for restructuring. *Economic and Political Weekly* 39, No. 17: 1741–17.
Kundu, Amitabh (2010) Rural urban economic disparities in India: Database and trends, *India in the world: Growth stability and equity*, Delhi: NCAER.
Mahendra Dev, S. (1995) Alleviating poverty: Maharashtra Employment Guarantee Scheme. *Economic and Political Weekly* 40, No. 14: 1410–13.
Ministry of Law and Justice (2007) *The Constitution of India*. Delhi: Ministry of Law and Justice, Government of India.
Ministry of Rural Development, http://nrega.nic.in/netnrega/home.aspx
National Rural Employment Guarantee Act (2005) No. 42 of 2005 published in *Gazette of India, Extraordinary Part-II, Section-I, No. 48*. New Delhi, Wednesday, 7 September.
Nayyar, Rohini (2002) The contribution of public works and other labour-based infrastructure to poverty alleviation: The Indian experiences, issues in employment and poverty. Discussion Paper 3, ILO, Geneva.
Nayyar, D. (2006) India's unfinished journey: Transforming growth into development. *Modern Asian Studies* (UK: University of Cambridge) 40, No. 3: 797–832.
Narayana, N. S. S., Kirit Parikh and T. N. Srinivasan (1988) Rural works programmes in India: Costs and benefits. *Journal of Development Economics* 29: 131–56.
National Rural Employment Guarantee Act (2005), *Operational Guidelines 2008* (3rd edition), Ministry of Rural Development, Department of Rural Development, Government of India, New Delhi. http://nrega.nic.in/Nrega_guidelinesEng.pdf
——— Review by Prime Minster on 20th June 2007, NREGA.nic.in.
Olega Tellis and Others v. Bombay Municipal Corporation and Others. All India Reporter 1986, SC 180.
Pankaj, Ashok K. (2008a) *Processes, institutions and mechanisms of implementation of NREGA: Impact Assessment of Bihar and Jharkhand*. Delhi: Institute for Human Development.

Pankaj, Ashok K. (2008b) The National Rural Employment Guarantee Act: Guaranteeing the right to livelihood. In *India: Social Development Report*. Delhi: Oxford University Press.

Pankaj, Ashok K. and Rukmini Tankha (2009) *Women's empowerment through guaranteed employment*. Delhi: Institute for Human Development.

——— (2010) Empowerment effects of the NREGS on women workers: A study in four states. *Economic and Political Weekly* 44, No. 30, (24 July): 45–55.

Papola, T. S. (2005) Emerging structure of the Indian economy. Presidential address to the Indian Economic Association (mimeo).

Patel, S. (2006) Empowerment, co-option and domination: Politics of Maharashtra's employment guarantee scheme. *Economic and Political Weekly* 41, No. 50: 5126–32.

Ravallion, M., G. Datt and S. Chaudhuri (1991) Reaching the rural poor through public employment: Arguments, evidence, and lessons from South Asia. *World Bank Research Observer* 6, (July): 153–76.

Report on Conditions of Work and Promotion of Livelihoods in the Unorganised Sector (2007) National Commission For Enterprises in the Unorganised Sector, Government of India.

Sarkar, Sandip and Balwant Singh Mehta (2010) Income inequality in India: Pre- and Post-reform periods. *Economic and Political Weekly* 44, No. 37: 44–55.

Savale, S. (2006) Is local really better? Comparing EGS and locally-managed rural works programmes in Nasik district. *Economic and Political Weekly* 41, No. 50: 5133–39.

Sudarshan, Ratna (2008) Impact of NREGA on rural labour market in Kerala: Preliminary findings on women's work. Presentation made at international conference *NREGS in India: Impacts and implementation experiences* (16–17 September), New Delhi, India.

Suri, K. C. 2004. Democracy, economic reforms and election results in India. *Economic and Political Weekly* 39, No. 51: 5404–11.

Vaidyanathan, A. (2005) Employment guarantee and decentralisation. *Economic and Political Weekly* 40 No. 16: 1582–87.

Vakulabharanam, Vamsi (2010) Does class matter, class structure and worsening inequality in India. *Economic and Political Weekly* 44, No. 29: 67–76.

Appendix A1

Table A1.1: State-wise Number of Households Provided Employment

States	*2006–07*	*2007–08*	*2008–09*	*2009–10*	*2010–11*
Andhra Pradesh	2,161,395	4,803,892	5,699,557	6,158,493	6,200,423
Arunachal Pradesh	16,926	4,490	80,714	68,157	26,712
Assam	792,270	1,402,888	1,877,393	2,137,270	1,797,864
Bihar	1,688,899	3,859,630	3,822,484	4,127,330	4,684,724
Gujarat	226,269	290,691	850,691	1,596,402	1,093,302
Haryana	50,765	70,869	162,932	156,406	235,281
Himachal Pradesh	63,514	271,099	445,713	497,336	444,247
Jammu and Kashmir	121,328	138,303	199,166	336,036	470,993
Karnataka	545,185	549,994	896,212	3,535,281	2,224,468
Kerala	99,107	185,392	692,015	955,976	1,175,816
Madhya Pradesh	2,866,349	4,346,916	5,207,665	4,714,591	4,385,376
Maharashtra	384,944	474,695	906,297	591,547	441,920

(Table A1.1 contd.)

(Table A1.1 contd.)

Punjab	31,648	49,690	149,902	271,934	278,021
Rajasthan	1,175,172	2,170,460	6,373,093	6,522,264	5,859,667
Sikkim	4,107	19,664	52,006	54,156	56,401
Tamil Nadu	683,481	1,234,818	3,345,648	4,373,257	4,969,140
Tripura	74,335	423,724	549,022	576,487	557,055
Uttar Pradesh	2,573,245	4,096,408	4,336,466	5,483,434	6,431,213
West Bengal	3,083,757	3,843,335	3,025,854	3,479,915	4,998,239
Chhattisgarh	1,256,737	2,284,963	2,270,415	2,025,845	2,485,581
Jharkhand	1,394,108	1,679,868	1,576,348	1,702,599	1,987,360
Uttarakhand	134,312	189,263	298,741	522,304	542,391
Manipur	18,568	112,549	381,109	418,564	433,845
Meghalaya	96,627	106,042	224,263	300,482	346,149
Mizoram	50,998	88,940	172,775	180,140	170,894
Nagaland	27,884	110,052	296,689	325,242	350,815
Orissa	1,394,169	1,100,497	1,199,006	1,398,300	2,004,815
Puducherry	–	–	12,264	40,377	33,522
Andaman and Nicobar	–	–	5,975	20,337	16,278
Lakshadweep	–	–	3,024	5,192	4,507
Chandigarh	–	–	00	00	00
Dadra & Nagar Haveli	–	–	1,919	3,741	2,290
Daman & Diu	–	–	00	00	00
Goa	–	–	00	6,604	13,897
Grand Total	**21,016,099**	**33,909,132**	**45,115,358**	**52,585,999**	**54,723,206**

Source: http://nrega.nic.in/netnrega/home.aspx

Table A1.2: State-wise Total Employment Generation (Person-days in lakh)

States	*2006–07*	*2007–08*	*2008–09*	*2009–10*	*2010–11*
Andhra Pradesh	678.77	2010.28	2735.45	4044.3	3351.61
Arunachal Pradesh	4.53	2.79	34.98	16.98	10.32
Assam	572.92	487.61	751.07	732.97	470.08
Bihar	596.87	855.1	991.75	1136.91	1597.59
Gujarat	100.48	90.06	213.07	585.1	491.84

(Table A1.2 contd.)

(Table A1.2 contd.)

States	*2006–07*	*2007–08*	*2008–09*	*2009–10*	*2010–11*
Haryana	24.12	35.76	69.11	59.03	84.2
Himachal Pradesh	29.9	97.53	205.28	284.94	219.46
Jammu and Kashmir	32.3	33.4	78.8	128.71	198.01
Karnataka	222.01	197.78	287.64	2003.49	1097.84
Kerala	20.48	60.75	153.75	339.72	480.34
Madhya Pradesh	1971.77	2753.02	2946.97	2624.03	2204.86
Maharashtra	159.28	184.86	419.85	274.33	195.1
Punjab	15.57	19.15	40.27	77.15	75.08
Rajasthan	998.87	1678.38	4829.55	4498.09	3026.21
Sikkim	2.42	8.6	26.34	43.28	48.14
Tamil Nadu	182.79	645.23	1203.59	2390.75	2685.93
Tripura	50.13	181.05	351.12	460.23	374.51
Uttar Pradesh	822.91	1363.06	2272.21	3559.26	3348.97
West Bengal	440.08	968.8	786.61	1551.67	1553.08
Chhattisgarh	700.21	1316.1	1243.18	1041.57	1110.35
Jharkhand	520.47	747.56	749.97	842.47	830.9
Uttarakhand	40.6	80.34	104.33	182.39	230.21
Manipur	18.57	48.32	285.62	306.17	267.86
Meghalaya	24.22	41.33	86.31	148.48	196.81
Mizoram	7.85	31.53	125.82	170.35	166
Nagaland	13.08	24.33	202.7	284.27	334.34
Orissa	799.34	405.23	432.58	554.08	976.56
Puducherry	–	–	1.64	9.07	8.82
Andaman and Nicobar	–	–	1.00	5.82	3.29
Lakshadweep	–	–	1.82	1.41	1.34
Chandigarh	–	–	00	00	00
Dadra & Nagar Haveli	–	–	0.48	0.7	0.47
Daman & Diu	–	–	00	00	00
Goa	–	–	00	1.85	3.7
Grand Total	**9,050.54**	**14,367.95**	**21,632.86**	**28,359.59**	**25,643.8**

Source: http://nrega.nic.in/netnrega/home.aspx

Table A1.3: State-wise Average Person-days per Household

States	*2006–07*	*2007–08*	*2008–09*	*2009–10*	*2010–11*
Andhra Pradesh	31.40	41.85	47.99	65.67	54.05
Arunachal Pradesh	26.76	62.14	43.34	24.91	38.63
Assam	72.31	34.76	40.01	34.29	26.15
Bihar	35.34	22.15	25.95	27.55	34.10
Gujarat	44.41	30.98	25.05	36.65	44.99
Haryana	47.51	50.46	42.42	37.74	35.79
Himachal Pradesh	47.08	35.98	46.06	57.29	49.40
Jammu and Kashmir	26.62	24.15	39.56	38.30	42.04
Karnataka	40.72	35.96	32.10	56.67	49.35
Kerala	20.66	32.77	22.22	35.54	40.85
Madhya Pradesh	68.79	63.33	56.59	55.66	50.28
Maharashtra	41.38	38.94	46.33	46.38	44.15
Punjab	49.20	38.54	26.86	28.37	27.01
Rajasthan	85.00	77.33	75.78	68.97	51.64
Sikkim	58.92	43.73	50.65	79.92	85.35
Tamil Nadu	26.74	52.25	35.97	54.67	54.05
Tripura	67.44	42.73	63.95	79.83	67.23
Uttar Pradesh	31.98	33.27	52.40	64.91	52.07
West Bengal	14.27	25.21	26.00	44.59	31.07
Chhattisgarh	55.72	57.60	54.76	51.41	44.67
Jharkhand	37.33	44.50	47.58	49.48	41.81
Uttarakhand	30.23	42.45	34.92	34.92	42.44
Manipur	100.01	42.93	74.94	73.15	61.74
Meghalaya	25.07	38.98	38.49	49.41	56.86
Mizoram	15.39	35.45	72.82	94.57	97.14
Nagaland	46.91	22.11	68.32	87.40	95.30
Orissa	57.33	36.82	36.08	39.63	48.71
Puducherry	–	–	13.37	22.46	26.31
Andaman and Nicobar	–	–	16.74	28.62	20.21
Lakshadweep	–	–	60.19	27.16	29.73
Chandigarh	–	–	–	–	–
Dadra & Nagar Haveli	–	–	25.01	18.71	20.52
Daman & Diu	–	–	–	–	–
Goa	–	–	–	28.01	26.62
Grand Total	**43.06**	**42.37**	**47.95**	**53.93**	**46.86**

Source: http://nrega.nic.in/netnrega/home.aspx

Table A1.4: State-wise Share of SCs in Total Person-days (in per cent)

States	*2006–07*	*2007–08*	*2008–09*	*2009–10*	*2010–11*
Andhra Pradesh	29.82	27.72	26.14	24.68	24.32
Arunachal Pradesh	0.00	0.00	1.68	0.00	0.00
Assam	8.65	7.60	10.41	12.15	11.02
Bihar	47.08	45.66	50.07	45.3	45.38
Gujarat	7.04	5.92	12.67	14.87	14.54
Haryana	60.03	53.80	53.03	53.59	48.93
Himachal Pradesh	30.40	32.31	33.51	33.36	32.58
Jammu and Kashmir	5.42	9.85	8.46	8.39	7.26
Karnataka	33.05	30.23	27.77	16.7	16.16
Kerala	20.12	16.87	19.47	16.77	16.22
Madhya Pradesh	15.87	17.87	17.82	18.48	19.43
Maharashtra	16.19	18.44	16.51	25.61	22.36
Punjab	69.36	76.29	74.22	78.92	78.26
Rajasthan	15.97	19.24	28.79	26.53	25.5
Sikkim	0.83	7.09	5.71	9.66	12.04
Tamil Nadu	56.06	57.36	60.27	59.07	57.71
Tripura	15.92	20.83	23.45	18.03	17.95
Uttar Pradesh	56.85	53.75	53.56	56.41	53.96
West Bengal	36.08	36.28	37.45	36.86	36.91
Chhattisgarh	12.01	14.91	16.41	15.32	14.57
Jharkhand	23.48	20.74	18.1	16.04	13.44
Uttarakhand	26.70	27.30	27.15	26.04	26.37
Manipur	0.00	0.27	1.65	27.53	1.95
Meghalaya	0.29	0.46	0.45	0.52	0.38
Mizoram	0.00	0.00	–	0.01	–
Nagaland	0.00	0.00	–	–	–
Orissa	23.65	24.33	20.24	19.16	18.13
Puducherry	–	–	49.5	46.15	34.6
Andaman and Nicobar	–	–	–	–	–
Lakshadweep	–	–	–	–	–
Chandigarh	–	–	–	–	–
Dadra & Nagar Haveli	–	–	–	–	–
Daman & Diu	–	–	–	–	–
Goa	–	–	–	5.2	4.09
Grand Total	**25.36**	**27.43**	**29.29**	**30.48**	**30.7**

Source: http://nrega.nic.in/netnrega/home.aspx

Table A1.5: State-wise Share of ST in Total Person-days (in per cent)

States	*2006–07*	*2007–08*	*2008–09*	*2009–10*	*2010–11*
Andhra Pradesh	13.01	12.79	12.95	14.71	16.02
Arunachal Pradesh	100.00	66.31	81.06	97.75	98.42
Assam	46.26	39.12	34.45	31.02	27.31
Bihar	3.21	2.46	2.65	2.16	2.14
Gujarat	64.26	65.92	50.56	39.46	41.18
Haryana	0.00	0.00	0	0.01	0
Himachal Pradesh	22.41	11.03	7.79	8.7	8.19
Jammu and Kashmir	23.22	24.34	27.43	26.13	23.86
Karnataka	20.35	19.18	13.87	8.57	9.36
Kerala	12.40	16.89	9.26	5.33	3.1
Madhya Pradesh	48.64	48.76	46.81	45.34	43.31
Maharashtra	40.88	38.49	44.17	33.16	24.15
Punjab	0.00	0.00	0	0	0.02
Rajasthan	64.36	46.39	23.24	22.5	23.28
Sikkim	98.35	42.56	44.14	42.53	39.89
Tamil Nadu	2.37	2.63	1.74	2.5	2.19
Tripura	62.18	41.95	45.19	40.98	43.45
Uttar Pradesh	3.11	1.85	1.96	1.48	2.1
West Bengal	18.61	13.80	14.81	14.38	13.41
Chhattisgarh	45.55	41.39	41.32	38.2	36.51
Jharkhand	40.29	41.65	39.97	42.99	42.08
Uttarakhand	1.40	4.34	5.15	4.04	4.24
Manipur	100.00	99.42	72.91	42.85	75.74
Meghalaya	83.15	88.07	94.72	94.09	94.43
Mizoram	100.00	100.00	99.95	99.86	99.84
Nagaland	100.00	100.00	100	100	100
Orissa	49.27	39.65	35.81	36.26	35.55
Puducherry	–	–	0.00	0.00	0.05
Andaman and Nicobar	–	–	9.85	6.86	0.00
Lakshadweep	–	–	99.56	99.87	100
Chandigarh	–	–	0.00	0.00	0.00
Dadra & Nagar Haveli	–	–	100	100	100
Daman & Diu	–	–	0.00	0.00	0.00
Goa	–	–	0.00	26.89	24.26
Grand Total	**36.45**	**29.2707**	**25.43**	**20.71**	**20.76**

Source: http://nrega.nic.in/netnrega/home.aspx

Table A1.6: State-wise Share of Others in Total Person-days (in per cent)

States	*2006–07*	*2007–08*	*2008–09*	*2009–10*	*2010–11*
Andhra Pradesh	57.17	59.49	60.91	60.62	59.66
Arunachal Pradesh	0.00	33.69	17.27	2.24	1.55
Assam	45.08	53.28	55.14	56.83	61.67
Bihar	49.72	51.88	47.28	52.53	52.49
Gujarat	28.70	28.16	36.77	45.67	44.28
Haryana	39.97	46.20	46.97	46.40	51.07
Himachal Pradesh	47.19	56.66	58.70	57.94	59.23
Jammu and Kashmir	71.36	65.81	64.11	65.48	68.88
Karnataka	46.60	50.59	58.35	74.72	74.49
Kerala	67.48	66.22	71.27	77.90	80.68
Madhya Pradesh	35.49	33.37	35.37	36.17	37.26
Maharashtra	42.92	43.07	39.33	41.23	53.49
Punjab	30.64	23.71	25.78	21.08	21.72
Rajasthan	19.67	34.37	47.97	50.97	51.22
Sikkim	1.24	50.35	50.15	47.80	48.07
Tamil Nadu	41.56	40.01	37.99	38.43	40.10
Tripura	21.90	37.22	31.35	40.99	38.61
Uttar Pradesh	40.04	44.40	44.48	42.11	43.94
West Bengal	45.31	49.92	47.74	48.76	49.67
Chhattisgarh	42.44	43.69	42.28	46.48	48.92
Jharkhand	36.23	37.61	41.93	40.97	44.47
Uttarakhand	71.90	68.36	67.70	69.92	69.39
Manipur	0.00	0.29	25.44	29.62	22.32
Meghalaya	16.56	11.47	4.83	5.39	5.19
Mizoram	0.00	0.00	0.05	0.13	0.16
Nagaland	0.00	0.00	0.00	0.00	0.00
Orissa	27.07	36.02	43.95	44.58	46.32
Puducherry	–	–	50.61	53.80	65.31
Andaman and Nicobar	–	–	90.00	93.13	100.00
Lakshadweep	–	–	0.55	0.00	0.00
Chandigarh	–	–	0.00	0.00	–
Dadra & Nagar Haveli	–	–	0.00	0.00	0.00
Daman & Diu	–	–	0.00	0.00	–
Goa	–	–	0.00	68.11	71.62
Grand Total	**38.19**	**43.29**	**45.28**	**48.80**	**48.54**

Source: http://nrega.nic.in/netnrega/home.aspx

Table A1.7: State-wise Share of Women in Total Person-days (in per cent)

States	*2006–07*	*2007–08*	*2008–09*	*2009–10*	*2010–11*
Andhra Pradesh	54.79	57.75	58.15	58.1	57.05
Arunachal Pradesh	30.02	29.75	26.12	17.24	40.27
Assam	31.67	30.85	27.16	27.7	26.53
Bihar	17.38	26.62	30.02	30.04	28.46
Gujarat	50.20	46.55	42.82	47.55	44.23
Haryana	30.60	34.42	30.64	34.81	35.62
Himachal Pradesh	12.24	30.10	39.02	46.09	48.25
Jammu and Kashmir	4.46	1.08	5.76	6.67	7.73
Karnataka	50.56	50.27	50.42	36.79	46.01
Kerala	65.63	71.39	85.01	88.19	90.39
Madhya Pradesh	43.24	41.67	43.28	44.23	44.42
Maharashtra	37.07	39.99	46.22	39.65	45.88
Punjab	37.76	16.29	24.62	26.28	33.73
Rajasthan	67.14	69.00	67.11	66.89	68.34
Sikkim	24.79	36.74	37.66	51.23	46.68
Tamil Nadu	81.11	82.01	79.67	82.91	82.59
Tripura	75.00	44.51	51.01	41.09	38.55
Uttar Pradesh	16.55	14.53	18.11	21.67	21.42
West Bengal	18.28	16.99	26.53	33.42	33.69
Chhattisgarh	39.32	42.05	47.43	49.21	48.63
Jharkhand	39.48	27.17	28.51	34.25	33.47
Uttarakhand	30.47	42.77	36.86	40.28	40.3
Manipur	50.89	32.80	45.92	47.97	49.66
Meghalaya	194.05	30.87	41.35	47.2	44.59
Mizoram	33.38	33.62	36.59	34.99	33.93
Nagaland	29.97	29.35	36.71	43.53	35.02
Orissa	35.60	36.39	37.58	36.25	39.4
Puducherry	–	–	67.02	63.49	79.79
Andaman and Nicobar	–	–	39.53	44.88	49.75
Lakshadweep	–	–	40.68	37.67	34.33
Chandigarh	–	–	–	–	–
Dadra & Nagar Haveli	–	–	79.13	86.15	86.93
Daman & Diu	–	–	–	–	–
Goa	–	–	–	62.3	68.42
Grand Total	**40.65**	**42.52**	**47.88**	**48.1**	**47.94**

Source: http://nrega.nic.in/netnrega/home.aspx

Table A1.8: State-wise MGNREGS Minimum Wages in 2006 and 2011

States	*MGNREGS Minimum Wages in 2006*	*MGNREGS Minimum Wages in 2011*
Assam	62	130
Andhra Pradesh	80	121
Arunachal Pradesh	57	118
Bihar	68	120
Gujarat	50	124
Haryana	95	179
Himachal Pradesh	70	150*
Jammu & Kashmir	45	121
Karnataka	63	125
Kerala	125	150
Madhya Pradesh	59	122
Maharashtra	47	127
Manipur	66	126
Meghalaya	70	117
Mizoram	91	129
Nagaland	66	118
Orissa	55	125
Punjab	101	124**
Rajasthan	73	119
Sikkim	85	118
Tamil Nadu	80	119
Tripura	60	118
Uttar Pradesh	58	120
West Bengal	67	130
Chhattisgarh	59	122
Jharkhand	76	120
Uttaranchal	73	120

Source: http://nrega.nic.in/netnrega/home.aspx
Note: * 120 for non-scheduled areas.
** 130 for Amritsar district.

SECTION II

MGNREGS

Alleviating Poverty through Employment Generation

2

MGNREGS

A Component of Full-employment Strategy for India

Indira Hirway

I

This chapter argues that the Mahatma Gandhi National Rural Employment Guarantee Scheme Programme (MGNREGS) designed under the Mahatma Gandhi National Rural Employment Guarantee Act (MGNREGA) needs to be treated as a component of a full-employment strategy for India. This is because the programme has the potential to lead the economy towards labour-intensive growth and full employment. After making this argument, the paper examines the design of the MGNREGS in this context and studies its performance during its first two years.

It is now recognised that ensuring 'decent' employment to all those who are willing and ready to work is an important goal for any economy. It is accepted that benefits of employment are microeconomic as well as macroeconomic, and there is an important mutually reinforcing relationship between economic and social benefits of employment. At the individual level, employment increases financial security and promotes higher living standards; improves physical and mental health; raises self-esteem and self-confidence; and enables a person to become a responsible citizen. At the macro level, full employment ensures financial and macroeconomic stability (Fullwiller, 2006); promotes social and political stability by reducing social tensions, crime and conflicts; and enhances economic and social multiplier effects (Forstater, 2006). As Amartya Sen has put it,

> there is plenty of evidence that unemployment has many far reaching effects other than loss of income, that includes psychological harm, loss of work motivation, skill and self confidence; increase in ailment and morbidity (and even mortality); disruption is family relations and social life; hardening of social exclusion and accentuation of racial tensions and gender asymmetries. (Sen, 2000)

The goal of ensuring employment to all is very much in line with the Article 23 of the UN Declaration of Human Rights that states, 'every one has a right to work, to free choice of employment, to just and favourable conditions of work and to protection against unemployment' (UN, 1948). The ILO Convention

122 also declares, 'with a view to stimulating economic growth and development, raising levels of living, meeting manpower requirements and overcoming unemployment and underemployment, each Member shall declare and pursue, as a major goal, an active policy designed to promote full, productive and freely chosen employment'. This right is also incorporated in the Indian Constitution as right to life. Legal guarantee of work, thus, is a part of global commitment to full employment by nations.

Apart from having the intrinsic value of guarantee of work, an employment guarantee programme (EGP) answers the present employment crisis in India.

II

MGNREGA: Answer to Employment Crisis in India

The Employment Challenge in India

India has achieved a high rate of economic growth in the recent decades. The economy came out of the Hindu growth-rate syndrome in the 1980s, and registered an average annual growth rate of 5.8 per cent during 1981–2005. In the recent years, the growth rate has shown continuous acceleration, from an annual average of 5.5 per cent during the Ninth Plan (1997/98–2001/02) to 7.7 per cent during the Tenth Plan (2002/03–2006/07), with 8.7 per cent growth rate in the last four years of the plan. With this kind of growth, India is one of the fastest growing countries in the world, and with per capita GDP of US $ 1,033, it is now regarded as a middle-income developing country (Planning Commission, 2008).

The structure of the Indian economy, however, has not shown a balanced growth. While agriculture registered 2.0 per cent and 1.7 per cent growth during the Ninth and Tenth Plans, respectively, the service sector showed 8.1 per cent and 9.0 per cent, and the manufacturing sector showed 4.6 and 8.3 per cent growth in the Ninth and Tenth Plans, respectively. In other words, the agricultural sector, where the majority of workers (56.67 per cent) as well as majority of the poor is located, has shown a very low rate of growth (Figure 2.1). The impact of the overall high growth has not been very positive on poverty reduction either. One does not observe any acceleration, along with the acceleration of the GDP, in poverty reduction. The incidence of poverty declined from 36.00 per cent in 1993/94 to 27.5 per cent in 2004/05, implying a very small rate of decline per year during the period. The elasticity of poverty reduction with respect to per capita GDP growth has also declined from 1.13 per cent during 1993/94–1999/00 to 0.69 per cent during 1999/00–2004/05. In the case of some marginalised groups like the ST, the reduction in poverty has been almost zero. The absolute number of the poor declined from 320 millions in 1993/94 to 302 millions in 2004/05. In short, the glorious performance of economic growth is not really reflected in poverty reduction.

Two major challenges on the employment front are the slow growth of employment accompanied with the declining employment elasticity and the rapid deterioration in the quality of employment. The long-term annual rate of growth of employment has declined from 2.1 per cent during 1983–1993/94 to 1.84 per cent during 1993/94–2004/05. Though one observes a marked improvement in the recent years (1999/2000–2004/05), during which period the employment increased by an annual rate of 2.46 per cent, this increase cannot be considered as a positive development, first because a large part of this new employment is in self-employment, which is emerging as a residual sector for all those who cannot

Figure 2.1: NRM and Sustainable Agriculture

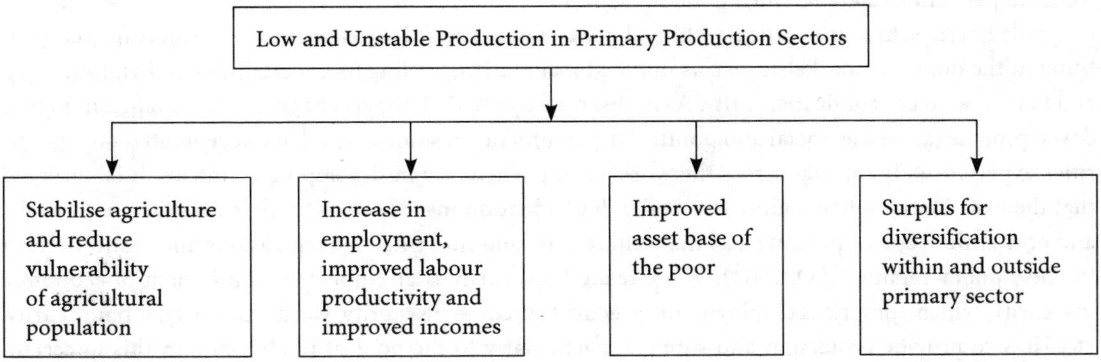

Source: Author.

get any work in the labour market; second, a significant part of this increase is of subsidiary employment, that is, part-time, marginal employment and third, because almost entire increase (60 millions) is of informal employment—either in the informal sector or in informal jobs in the formal sector. The official data indicates that there has been a *decline* in the employment in the organised sector by 0.31 per cent per year during 1993/94–2004/05 (Planning Commission, 2008). As G. S. Bhalla observes, the increase in the rate of growth of employment in the recent years cannot be interpreted as India's faster move towards industrial revolution and diversification of its employment to higher productivity non-agricultural sectors (G. S. Bhalla, 2007).

The changes in the structure of employment have not been very positive: the share of agriculture in the national GDP has declined to less than one-fifth of the GDP, while its share in the total employment still remains high, at 56.67 per cent, and it declined at a very low rate, from 65.42 per cent in 1993 to 61.03 per cent in 1993/94 and to 56.67 per cent in 2004/05. Conversely, the share of industry in total GDP increased by 10 percentage points, while its share in employment increased by only 1.00 per cent (from 11.24 per cent in 1983 to 12.20 per cent in 2004/05). This indicates the wide as well as the widening gap between the labour productivities in agriculture and manufacturing sectors. As the official data shows, the annual rate of increase in the per worker productivity in agriculture during 1993/94–2004/05 has been 1.80 per cent, as against 3.48 per cent in manufacturing and 4.51 per cent in the tertiary sector. It is not surprising, therefore, that the poverty in India is concentrated largely in rural areas and particularly among agricultural/rural labour and small/marginal farmers, as observed by Sheila Bhalla (2007). The agricultural sector, which houses more than 55 per cent of the work force, suffers from low labour productivity, low labour-productivity growth and a high level of unemployment/underemployment.

A related problem is the low and fast-declining employment elasticity of economic growth in all the major sectors in the economy. The overall employment elasticity in the Indian economy was 0.40 during the period 1983–1993/94. It declined to 0.32 during 1993/94–2004/05. The sectoral elasticities also show a decline during this period. Another worrisome feature of the employment scene in India is the rising incidence of unemployment. The overall rate of unemployment has increased from 6.1 per cent in

1993/94 to 8.3 per cent in 2004/05. The unemployment rate of agricultural labour households has risen from 9.5 per cent to 2004/05 during the same period (Mitra, 2008).

Trade liberalisation under the neo-liberal policies has exposed the economy to the increased competition in the domestic market as well as in the global market, leading to uncertainties and vulnerability, and to increased economic insecurity. As is observed by the ILO, the recent economic and technological developments (as well as social and political developments in some cases) have accentuated the insecurities experienced by people across the world, and particularly in developing countries. It is observed that the neo-liberal policy regime is actually dependent on insecurity, as there is no state-based social and economic security, portrayed as the welfare state and no protective regulations and institutions in the new policy regime (ILO, 2004). Work-related insecurity is an important component of economic insecurity, which comprises employment insecurity, income insecurity, work insecurity, job insecurity, etc. How to provide protection and support, particularly to the poor at the bottom, in this uncertain environment is one more challenge to the policymakers. And last, feminisation of employment along with rapid deterioration in the quality of employment of women is another major development on the employment front in India. One also observes rising gender gaps in the major labour-market outcomes in the recent years.

In short, the major areas of concern in the field of employment in India are the low and declining rate of growth of productive employment; the rising incidence of unemployment; the rapid deterioration in the quality of employment; the rising employment insecurity and work insecurity as well as increasing gender gaps in the labour-market outcomes. How to reverse these trends is a major policy question at present.

T. S. Papola has quantified the size of the employment that needs to be generated in the economy on the basis of the (*a*) unemployment rates and (*b*) underemployment rates of the workforce. This is estimated at 76.8 million in 2007. Adding the working poor, who are too vulnerable in their present jobs and who need new employment, the total employment required to be generated during the 11th Plan has been estimated at 92.3 million by him (Papola, 2008).[1] The present growth path, if continued, is not likely to create this size of employment with its low and declining employment elasticity. It has been estimated that with the employment elasticity of 0.25 (which seems to be realistic), the Indian economy will have to grow at 11.00 per cent, just to absorb the new labour force and the openly unemployed (at 2.7 per cent growth of employment). This growth will not offer employment to the vulnerable working poor. Considering the fact that this growth is neither feasible nor adequate, one has to look for alternatives.

Alternative Approaches

One approach could be to mainstream employment in developing strategy and policies by treating it as the primary objective of development and making other dimensions, namely, growth rate, technology, balance of payments, etc., dependent upon it. For this approach to be applied, the amount of employment required to be generated has to be assessed as also the employment likely to be generated by any given rate and structure of growth. Such an approach has not been found feasible and has, therefore, never been attempted (Papola, 2008). This is because (*a*) the growth required to generate the needed employment during a given period of time may be much higher than the available resources, (*b*) the structure of output resulting from purely employment-oriented growth may not correspond to the pattern of demand and (*c*) in an economy with low level of income and high incidence of poverty, it may prove self-defeating, as it may not ensure a reasonable level of income from work.

Since rapid technical progress, arising from borrowing technologies from the countries which are at the frontier of technological development, is largely responsible for the declining employment elasticity (and for the high rate of growth), it can be argued that restricting technical progress to ensure low employment elasticity of economic growth, that is, reverting backward from the neo-liberal policies, could be another approach to promote employment growth. Such an approach implies restrictions on foreign trade (going back to protectionism) and on the market forces, and increasing the role of the state in the economy. However, this is not feasible, as it is not feasible to put the clock back! Also, it does not automatically lead the economy towards full employment.

Promotion of labour-intensive sectors is yet another approach recommended by many experts. This approach ensures that economic growth tends to be labour intensive, along with rising labour productivity. This in turn ensures that the levels of incomes of the workforce improves, raising the aggregate demand in the economy. In other words, this approach generates employment for the unemployed on the one hand, and raises the aggregate demand to push the economy upwards on the other hand. The Government of India has adopted this strategy in India, and was is to be implemented with fresh efforts in the Eleventh Five Year Plan (Planning Commission, 2008). According to the Plan, this has to be achieved (*a*) by encouraging the corporate sector to move into more labour-intensive sectors and (*b*) by facilitating expansion of employment and output of the unorganised enterprises that operate in the labour-intensive sectors.

It has been estimated by T. S. Papola that 9.3 per cent growth at the overall employment elasticity of 0.44 during the Eleventh Plan should enable the employment to grow at 4.09 per cent and it will be able to generate adequate employment in the economy during the Eleventh Plan. The primary, secondary and tertiary sectors will have to grow at 4.00, 11.00 and 10.00 annual rates, respectively, with 0.45, 0.68 and 0.58 employment elasticities, respectively. The Twelfth Plan has also set a target of 9–9.5 per cent growth rate in the economy. Shifting the employment elasticities in the different sectors to the required levels, however, appears to be a tall order! How can we reach this rate and pattern of economic growth? In other words, promotion of labour-intensive sectors is a sound strategy, but achieving this is a big challenge. Will providing incentives to the corporate sector to move into more labour-intensive sectors work well? And what kind of enabling environment is required to facilitate expansion of employment and output of the unorganised enterprises that operate in the labour-intensive sectors?

Two Critical Questions

There are two critical questions that need to be answered at this stage: First, what will happen to the poor till this massive employment is generated? How will they survive till then? And second, what kinds of interventions/inputs are needed to promote labour-intensive sectors? Is it possible to use the present surplus labour through an employment guarantee programme to create an enabling environment for the labour-intensive sectors? It is argued that a well-designed employment guarantee programme, preferably with the legal component of guarantee to work, can reply both these questions positively. It is also argued that the MGNREGS designed under the MGNREGA has the potential of replying to both the questions positively.

The effective promotion of labour-intensive sectors in India, that is, agriculture and allied sectors like animal husbandry and dairying, forestry, fishery; industries such as food processing, textile and garments, leather and leather goods and other similar industries; and basic social services, etc., requires three major inputs: (*a*) strong natural resource management (NRM) on a massive scale, for raising productivity and acquiring stability in agriculture and allied activities; producing raw materials for several labour-intensive industries like textiles and garments, (*b*) basic infrastructural facilities to promote tiny, small and medium enterprises and (*c*) drinking water, sanitation and infrastructure for health and education to improve labour productivity. A well-designed employment guarantee scheme can contribute significantly here. To put it differently, the role of an EGP has to be much more than guaranteeing work to the poor because guarantee of employment by itself does not change the basic process of employment generation in the economy. An employment guarantee can be treated as an end in itself only under the assumption that the development process under the neo-liberal policy regime will generate adequate employment opportunities in the medium term to absorb the surplus manpower, including additions to the labour force. However, looking at the experiences in the recent past, this assumption does not seem to be realistic. If the employment guarantee scheme (EGS) is designed without any long-term perspective, it is likely to end up as a permanent burden on the national exchequer as it will always be needed for the growing size of the bypassed and marginalised labour force.

Evidences from Other Countries

Several developing countries and developed countries have used an EGP or massive wage-employment programmes to ensure minimum incomes at the bottom, to raise aggregate demand in the economy and to lead the economy towards full employment. Such programmes have been used to ameliorate the after-effects of financial crisis (for example, Jefes programme in Argentina, Padat Karya in Indonesia, Master Plan for Tackling Unemployment in South Korea); to ensure food security and to promote employment in the mainstream economy (Rural Maintenance Programme and Food for Work Programmes in Bangladesh, Ethiopia and in many other countries); to address structural poverty and to promote employment-intensive growth through construction of labour-based infrastructure (Expanded Public Works Programme in South Africa, Ghana, Zimbabwe and many other African countries) and to stabilise economy during the downward trend of business cycles and ensure full employment in developed countries (the Netherlands, Sweden and the USA). Though there have been several shortcomings in many of these programmes, what is worth noting is that they all guarantee/provide employment in crisis so as to move towards full employment in the medium/long term. In other words, the strategy of guaranteeing work to address the immediate needs and to ensure a minimum income to the households affected by economic crisis, starvation or poverty, on the one hand, and to make use of the labour to move towards full employment, on the other hand, is gradually emerging as a strategy at the global level.

III

Strengthening Links between EGS and Full-employment Path

MGNREGS and Employment-intensive Sectors

As seen above, the three important, rather critical inputs that can help the growth of labour-intensive sectors in the Indian economy are (*a*) regeneration of natural resources to stabilise and promote growth of agriculture and allied activities, where the bulk of the workforce and the poor are located, (*b*) construction of socio-economic infrastructure that can promote growth of big, small and unorganised sector units and (*c*) reduction in unpaid work of the poor and women (working poor) to release them to take up for productive employment in the market economy. Though there are policies and programmes to promote all the three inputs, MGNREGS does have a role here. It can contribute in utilising the present surplus labour to create an enabling environment for the labour-intensive sectors in the economy (Tinbergen, 1994).[2]

It needs to be underlined at the outset that the present size of the MGNREGS is not small. In the year 2007/08, the amount spent on MGNREGS was ₹16,000 crores, which was 15–18 per cent of the total money spent on the central schemes in India. This generated 1,440 million person-days for 33.9 million households! With the expanded coverage from 330 districts in 2007–08 to 615 districts in 2008–09 and the expected rise in demand for work with the growing awareness of people about the scheme and improved preparedness of the institutions to implement the scheme, the total amount to be spent on NREGS may go up significantly. In short, the size of the scheme is big enough to make an impact on the employment scene in the country. MGNREGS needs to be integrated systematically with the process of expansion of employment opportunities in the economy.

In all the three sectors, namely, NRM, infrastructural development and unpaid work, one finds that (*a*) ongoing programmes suffer from some gaps, that is, some components are left out, (*b*) frequently they are implemented in a scattered and ad hoc manner and in isolated locations, without any comprehensive framework, (*c*) in some cases their size is much smaller than required, largely due to the shortage of funds and (*d*) frequently they fail to address the local-level needs and tap local-level potential. It is argued that it is feasible to use NREGS to address these shortages systematically.

Regeneration of Environmental Resources for Strengthening Sectors

Where Poor are Located

One major reason why the regeneration of NRM has been included in the list of the permitted works under MGNREGS is perhaps the fact that the management of natural resources, on which the livelihoods of majority of rural population including the poor depends, is not addressed sufficiently by the ongoing programmes. The majority of the poor, the marginalised and unemployed/underemployed are located in agriculture and allied activities, which suffer form low productivity and uncertainty arising from fluctuating production and incomes, thanks to the uncertainty of the rainfall and less irrigation facilities.

We describe below the NRM activities which can be undertaken/strengthened through the MGNREGS:

- Land and water management in a systematic and scientific manner through watershed development programmes has been accepted as a major strategy for NRM in the country. However, the work done under this flagship programme is much less than what is required in the country, thanks to the limited funds available (Joy, Gujja, Paranjape et al., 2008). There is therefore an urgent need to give a big push to this programme through MGNREGS along with the guarantee of work. Madhya Pradesh is a good example of the use of MGNREGS funds for watershed development and watershed plus development.[3]
- Forestation is another area where funds are a constraint. This refers particularly to forestation on degraded forests in the periphery of villages and on common lands which can be regenerated through watershed development and plantation. Plantation on wastelands and forestation on non-forest areas under social forestry are also important. The last is important for mangroves also, most of which are badly neglected as well as badly needed for ecological, economic as well as protection reasons (Hirway and Goswami, 2007).[4] These gaps in forestation are closely connected with people's livelihood and well-being.
- Diversification of agriculture and primary sector is a much talked about subject, but not much is done for promoting livelihood in some important sectors, like inland fisheries, which have a good scope in many parts of the country. Inland fisheries can be promoted by digging ponds and constructing other water harvesting structures in suitable regions. This can promote livelihood and food security at the local level. Similarly, medicinal plantation, horticulture, jetropha plantation etc are the programmes where a lot can be done for promoting livelihood.
- Animal husbandry and dairying is another area, which needs small scale interventions in the form of grassland development, roads, etc. at the local village and block levels.
- One finds several small gaps in the area of irrigation, including minor irrigation at the village, block and district levels. Construction of small check dams and *bandharas*, de-silting of check dams, digging small farm ponds, deepening tanks, ponds and rivulets etc can be identified and undertaken at the local level. In addition, manufacturing of green manure, compost etc. also can be taken up under the MGNREGS.

In short, there is a good scope for (*a*) expanding some of the present interventions, (*b*) filling in the gaps and (*c*) undertaking small NRM activities to promote local livelihood in crop farming, animal husbandry, dairying, horticulture, fishery, etc.

The long experience of NRM in India, however, shows that ad hoc selection of NRM works at a local level can distort and harm natural systems, sometimes irreparably, can create conflicts between villages or between regions and can become non-sustainable. It is necessary, therefore, to see that natural resources are planned systematically. NRM needs to be viewed in the context of a larger scene. For example, water-conservation and water-harvesting structures at the village level need to be planned with reference to concerned macro watersheds and the relevant river basin. Water-harvesting structures like check dams planned at the village level in isolation may corner water at the cost of neighboring villages. Also, an isolated structure here and another there is not likely to help systematic watershed development. Similarly, drought proofing has to be promoted under a sound regional strategy. Isolated forestation or water structures will not lead to drought proofing. Ad hoc works recommended by people at the village panchayat level will not be of much use. The lessons learnt from the long experience of NRM have been incorporated under the Bopal Declaration, which presents 'non-negotiable principles of development and management of natural resources in sustainable manner' (Development Support Centre, 2005).[5] These principles underscore the importance of systematic planning on the one hand and emphasise the role of community participation on the other hand. It will be necessary to dovetail MGNREGS with ongoing NRM programmes.

The MGNREGS interventions, thus, will contribute towards stabilisation of agriculture, encourage multiple cropping and enhance its productivity, improve assets base of small and marginal farmers and promote diversification within the primary sector. The MGNREGS, thus, will create an enabling environment for the growth of the sectors which are predominated by the poor including the working poor, the unemployed and the underemployed.

Construction of Socio-economic Infrastructure for Improved Quality of Life and for Promoting Labour-intensive Sectors

Absence of adequate socio-economic infrastructure is one of the major causes of low level of development of developing economies. Provision of basic infrastructure can provide improved quality of life to people including the poor and improved employment opportunities (Figure 2.2). There are several flagship programmes of the central government in this area. Bharat Nirman,[6] Pradhan Mantri Gram Sadak Yojana,[7] National Rural Health Mission,[8] Sarva Shiksha Abhiyan,[9] Total Sanitation Campaign,[10] Indira Awas Yojana,[11] etc. In spite of these programmes, there are several infrastructure facilities, which are left out and there are several gaps in the present programmes at the district and below district levels. The MGNREGS can fill in these gaps and also supplement these programmes.

Figure 2.2: Impact of Creation of Socio-economic Infrastructure

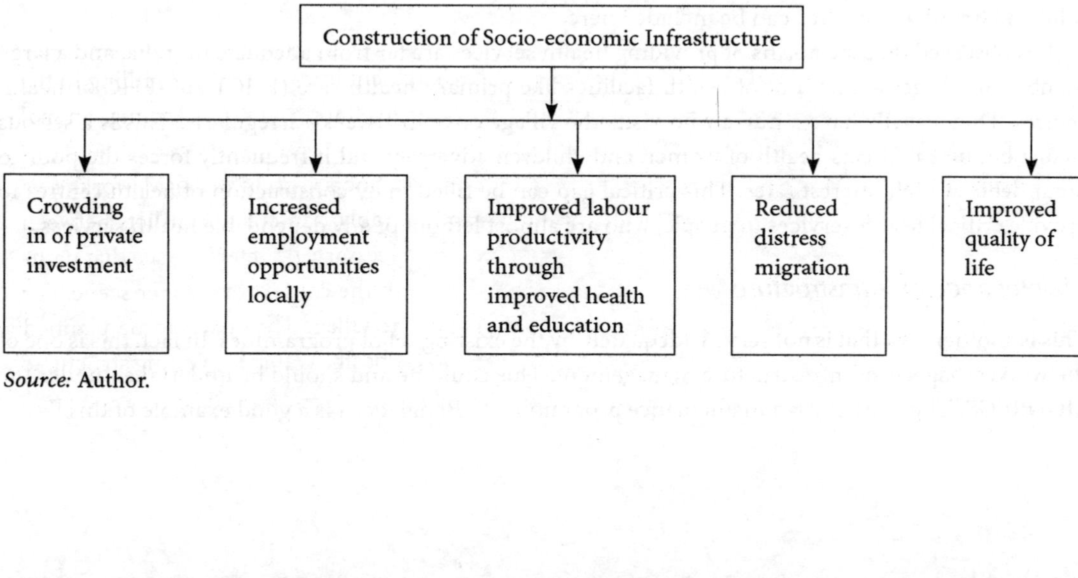

Source: Author.

Basic socio-economic infrastructure required at the village level will include (*a*) all-weather approach road including feeder roads, link roads to improve connectivity; (*b*) facility for potable drinking water, largely through water harvesting, and construction of pipelines for ensuring water supply at the door step; (*c*) drainage, sanitation and arrangements for disposal of solid and liquid waste; (*d*) paving of internal roads; (*e*) housing for the poor; (*f*) construction of buildings for basic educational and health services and (*g*) other infrastructure like community centres, etc. It is observed that all these facilities are not made available to all villages because (*a*) the norms of some of the flagship programmes do not cover smaller villages, (*b*) infrastructure like internal paving of roads, drainage, waste disposal, etc., are not covered in relevant programmes and (*c*) community facilities pertaining to the poor are not covered adequately. Some of the major facilities which can be undertaken under MGNREGS are as follows:

Connectivity

All-weather approach roads to smaller villages; paving of internal roads particularly in the settlements of the poor, SC, ST, OBC communities; collecting storm water/rain water through suitable structures to prevent isolation of smaller villages and settlements of the poor in the rainy season, etc., can be undertaken under the MGNREGS.

Drinking Water Supply

In spite of the central schemes, potable water supply to all is still a distant dream for many small and big villages in India. Considering the fact that local water harvesting is the most feasible solution in most parts of the country, the provision of drinking water could be one of the major infrastructural facilities that can be undertaken under the MGNREGS. The present drinking water schemes can be up scaled through MGNREGS. Arrangements for disposal of used water, which is usually neglected in the government programmes, can also be undertaken under the MGNREGS.[12]

Health Infrastructure

Sanitation and public hygiene is another area that can be covered comprehensively through the MGNREGS. Construction of drainage, creating infrastructure for public sanitation and disposal of solid and liquid wastes, etc., can be included here.

It is observed that the norms of providing health services are far from adequate in India, and a large number of villages are left out of health facilities like primary health care (PHC), sub-PHC or health centres. They usually have a nurse who visits the village once in a week—irregularly. This is a serious lacuna because it affects health of women and children adversely and it frequently forces the poor to incur debts at high interest rates. This critical gap can be filled in by construction of health centres to provide critical health services to people, who are almost left out of any dependable health services.

Maintenance of Infrastructure

This is another area that is not served adequately by the existing set of programmes. In fact, this is one of the weakest aspects of infrastructure management. This could be and should be undertaken under the MGNREGS. The famous road maintenance programme of Bangladesh is a good example of this.[13]

Other Infrastructure

MGNREGS can also contribute in filling in gaps in educational infrastructure (school rooms, drinking water facility for schools, mid-day meal kitchens, pre-school rooms, etc.) for which no adequate funds are made available to most villages. Certain economic infrastructure, such as godowns, marketing yards, etc., which are critical for development and for which funds are in short supply, can also be taken up under the MGNREGS.

Once again, there is a need to plan these systematically. Ad hoc selection of works, based on the 'needs' of local people can be both inefficient as well as expensive. All infrastructure facilities cannot be located anywhere and everywhere. For example, each village cannot have a secondary school, or a hospital or a marketing yard. The location of a service/infrastructure depends as the threshold population, on the one hand, and the distance that people are willing to travel, on the other hand.[14] According to the service-centre approach, primary service centre at the lowest level is expected to provide all the basic physical infrastructure and social services, which are important for ensuring a minimum quality of life, for reducing their vulnerability (by providing health facility and educational facility) and for ensuring their access to developmental opportunities by improving their capabilities. The secondary service centres will have a higher level of facilities and the tertiary centres will have a still higher level of facilities.

The first major impact of construction of basic socio-economic infrastructure facilities will be crowding in of private investments in these villages, as better opportunities will be available for starting local enterprises. This will increase employment opportunities locally. And since the new employment will increase purchasing power of the masses, it will have (output, income and employment) multiplier impacts on the local/regional economy. Again, improved health and educational facilities will enhance labour productivity, which will, in turn, give a push to economic growth. Another impact could be in terms of reduced distress migration of the poor. And finally, improved social infrastructure will improve quality of life of people in multiple ways (Rania and Fontana, 2008). By providing basic facilities in SC, ST localities, one can bring about changes in the quality of life of the poor, which in turn can bring about considerable increase in their productivity.

Addressing Unpaid Work of Women for Promoting Women's Work in the Labour Market

A paradox observed in developing countries is the simultaneous existence of sizable unemployment/underemployment, on the one hand, and sizable unpaid work, on the other hand. If a part of unpaid work is brought into the public domain through constructing suitable infrastructure, unpaid workers can be released for productive work in the labour market. Since these unpaid workers are the poor and women (poor as well as non-poor), construction of this public infrastructure will help poverty reduction and contribute towards gender equality by improving opportunities for productive employment for women.

Unpaid work is unpaid SNA work (that is, work included in UN System of National Accounts) and unpaid non-SNA work (that is, work not covered under national income accounts, domestic services and care, and community services). The former includes subsistence work like collection of basic necessities (fuel wood, water, wood for repairs and construction of shelter, vegetables, fish, etc.) and collection of raw materials for family enterprises (fodder for animals, bamboo for crafts and artisan work, etc). The Indian time-use study has shown that women spend between 10–25 per cent of their productive time on these activities (Hirway, 2008), which are drudgery and which (*a*) result in time stress of women, (*b*) provide them less time for productive work in the labour market and (*c*) deny them equal opportunities to develop capabilities. Unfortunately, not much attention has been paid by policymakers to unpaid work in a systematic manner, and some ad hoc interventions are far from adequate.

Though there are programmes for rural water supply and rural energy (plantations on common lands/waste lands, etc.), the fact remains that 80 per cent of the rural households use fuel wood and it is not feasible to reduce this significantly in near future. There is an urgent need to provide fuel wood (with fuel-efficient stoves) and drinking water as seen above, at the doorstep to ensure that women do not have to spend long hours to collect it. The MGNREGS can help by fuel plantation, fodder development, water harvesting structures, etc.

Domestic services and care including child care also take away up to 30 per cent of women's time. India has now some excellent schemes for child care, such as Integrated Child Development Scheme (ICDS), Midday Meal Scheme, etc. What is lacking, however, is universal child care, which requires one ICDS centre for every 40 children; universal day care for working mothers, and universal health services for pregnant women and young mothers. These could be partly subsidised. There is no provision for such infrastructure under the present programmes. The MGNREGS can create this infrastructure.

This unequal distribution of domestic work creates several problems for women: since this work is invisible in statistics[15] and unpaid in nature, women's work is not recognised and women are assigned inferior status (subordinate) at home, leading to patriarchal values in the household. This inferior status at home is reflected in their inferior status in the labour market, because (*a*) women enter the labour market with the burden of domestic responsibilities that deprives them of level playing field in the labour market, (*b*) women experience less opportunities for human capital formation due to the patriarchal values at home as well as limited time and energy to access opportunities for skills in the labour market, (*c*) women are less mobile in their job due to domestic responsibilities and (*d*) women tend to be subordinate to men and tend to become meek and docile as workers. As a consequence of all this, women enjoy lower status in the labour market in terms of their participation, employment status, the incidence of unemployment, wage rates, diversification and opportunities for upward mobility. Though women's lower status in the labour market has been attributed by scholars to their lower human capital, discrimination against women, segmentation of labour market for women and to low access to information of women, at the root of these explanations is the higher burden of unpaid work on women and the consequences thereof.

Appendix 2.1 at the end of the chapter presents how different infrastructure facilities, which can be undertaken under the MGNREGS, can reduce the burden of unpaid work on women. Such works can release women for productive work in the labour market; can reduce time stress of women to enable them to access leisure and educational/skill-related opportunities, which in turn can improve women's labour productivity and can raise their participation in the market activities, which can improve their status at home (Figure 2.3). In short, reduction in unpaid work can promote gender equality in the labour market, as women will be in a better position to access opportunities in the market. And last, all

Figure 2.3: Employment Programme and Impact on Women

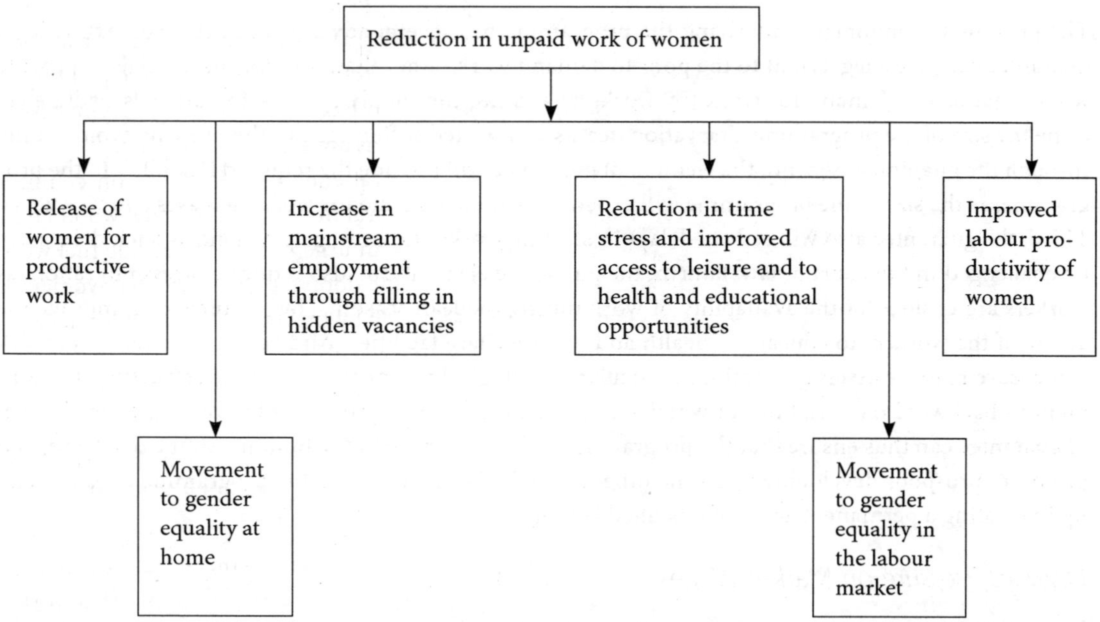

Source: Author.

these developments will increase mainstream employment opportunities in the labour market, as the 'hidden vacancies' of unpaid work, so far filled in by women, will appear openly in the labour market (Antonopoulos and Fontana, 2006). That is, larger employment opportunities will be created in the labour market in the basic services like child care services, managing local water supply, organising sanitation services, etc.

To sum up, MGNREGS has good scope for promoting the three inputs, namely, NRM, socio-economic infrastructure and reduction in unpaid work, which can be instrumental in promoting labour-intensive sectors in the economy. The guarantee component of MGNREGS can have some special advantages here (in addition to the advantages of the rights-based approach). To start with, the demand for work (by workers) and not the supply of work (by officials) will determine the size of the scheme. This will provide flexibility to the size of the scheme, which implies that when needed, the size of the scheme can be expanded. Again, the guarantee of work can ensure massive assets generation, particularly ecological regeneration and infrastructure development in backward regions, both of which can promote economic growth of the regions.

Other Links between MGNREGS and Labour-intensive Development Process

There are several other possible links between NREGS and labour-intensive development process in developing countries.

The Guarantee Component

The guarantee component underlying the programme has several advantages in this context: A legal guarantee can give a legal right to the poor to demand work rather than wait for the officials to provide work. That is, the demand for work (by workers) and not the supply of work (by officials) will determine the size of the programme. Starvation deaths and related sufferings can therefore be avoided only through the guarantee. Second, the element of guarantee will provide the required flexibility to the programme, as the size of the programme will expand when the demand for work increases and vice versa. Third, the guarantee also will reduce delays in starting works and in wage payment, as such delays can be challenged in the court of law. Fourth, the guarantee element can also reduce distress migration, as workers are ensured of the availability of work during the lean season. This, in turn, can improve the access of the workers to education, health and other welfare facilities. And last, the guarantee of work can ensure massive assets generation, particularly, ecological regeneration and infrastructure development in backward regions, both of which can promote economic growth of the regions. The element of guarantee can thus ensure that the programme reaches the poor at the bottom, on the one hand, and promotes pro-poor development, on the other hand. It also ensures that the programme does not end up in creating a permanent army of unskilled labour.

Upward Pressure on Market Wages

Fixing the wage rate under an EGP has been a controversial point in most developing countries. On the one hand, there is an argument made that the wage rate should be lower than the market wage rate to assure self-targeting, while on the other hand, it is argued that paying a legal minimum wage rate (which is usually higher than the market wage rate) will ensure minimum incomes to the poor. The latter will also put an upward pressure on the market wage rate. In the countries, where there is a minimum wages act, payment of the minimum wages will be not only legally correct, but it will also help in the enforcement of the act. However, there is no conclusive evidence on this so far on whether payment of legal minimum wages will put a pressure on the market wage. Consequently, instead of taking a stand on this issue, we only observe that payment of higher than the market wage rate on an EGS may result in reduction in exploitation of labour, which is observed to be there in some parts of the country.

Impact on Labour Market

An MGNREGS can have several other positive impacts on the labour market in terms of employment and quality of employment.

1. By paying legal minimum wages, EGS can help in the effective enforcement of the minimum wages act.
2. Since the wage rates in EGS like MGNREGS are equal for all, throughout the year, the programme will reduce/remove wage-rate inequalities across seasons as well as across different socio-economic groups including gender.
3. The EGS can improve the quality of employment, as the government programme can ensure a minimum package of entitlements of workers, namely, social security, working conditions and facilities and amenities at worksites.

4. Large number of workers working together for a long time can lead to formation of labour unions. That is, the EGS can encourage workers to develop their collective strength and bargaining power in the labour market. This can improve the bargaining strength of workers outside the NREGP also.

Women's Empowerment and Gender Equality

Another link will be between women's empowerment and reduced inequalities, with the development process. This link will be outside the impact on unpaid work. Women will be empowered under the EGS in multiple ways (Autonpoulos and Fontana, 2008):

1. In almost all countries, the participation of women has been very high in the EGS works, and in most cases, women's participation has been higher than that of men. This participation is likely to improve women's status at home.
2. Working outside home is likely to improve women's exposure to the outside world. This exposure, along with cash in hands, is likely to improve their clothes, as well as their confidence and self-esteem (Dandekar, 1983).
3. The overall employability of women is likely to improve after they get work experience on the EGS.
4. Large-scale participation of women in the EGS can encourage them to form unions. This collective strength, in the long run, can improve women's bargaining power in the labour market.
5. As seen earlier, reduction in unpaid work is likely to improve their employment and labour-market status, along with enhancement in the employment opportunities in the economy.

In short, the EGS can promote integration of women in the labour market.

Directing Economic Growth towards Domestic Markets

The linkages between the employment guarantee and the macro-development path are likely to expand domestic employment and domestic markets, raising aggregate demand in the economy. Expansion of agriculture and allied activities will generate large-scale demand for wage goods, and this will give a push to labour-intensive agriculture as well as labour-intensive industries. Second, infrastructure development including basic services will once again expand local markets by attracting private investment. The EGS can thus trigger a process that will enrich the domestic economy and domestic markets.

EGS is only a Component of Full-employment Strategy

In the end it needs to be underlined that though a well-designed EGS can contribute significantly towards the movement of developing economies, it has to be supplemented by supplementary efforts. In order that the EGS is able to establish meaningful linkages with the growth process, for example, it is necessary that productive use of the assets generated under the EGS is ensured. This can be organised mainly through supplementary policies and programmes. One famous example here is the development of horticulture that happened in Maharashtra when the land and water development works under the

Maharashtra Employment Guarantee Scheme were supported by the supply of the required inputs and technology along with loans for horticulture.

In the final analysis, a well-designed EGS can take on the challenges posed by the changing employment scene in the country. It cannot only address the immediate problem of ensuring employment and wages to the poor at the bottom, but it can also promote full employment and pro-poor economic growth. The planning under the EGS, therefore, requires a long-term perspective and systematic approach to create and strengthen meaningful linkages between NREGP and the macroeconomic growth process.

The EGS, however, needs to be supplemented by supportive interventions so that productive use of the assets generated under the programme is ensured. It is a critical component of a full-employment strategy. If planned and implemented well, it can modify the development path by acting as a thin edge of the wedge.

IV

Assessment of MGNREGS

Can the MGNREGS, the way it is designed and implemented at present, perform the role described above? Or is there any need to modify the design and to improve its implementation? We discuss below these questions briefly.

Implications for Modifying the MGNREGS Design

The above discussion has important implications for reorienting and to an extent redesigning of the MGNREGS. Some of the required characteristics are already there, but need to be made explicit, while some others are absent and need to be incorporated in the design.

Long-term Perspective

The MGNREGS will have to be viewed in terms of its medium- and long-term impact on the economy, and its design will have to facilitate this long-term role. It will have to be planned at the different levels, keeping in mind its role in the development process. Such a plan can be indicative at the macro and concrete at the lower levels.

Strong Planning Component

Designing long-term perspective plan, organising horizontal coordination and ensuring convergence of EGP with ongoing programmes and processes will have to be an essential element of the programme. Also, it will be necessary to use multi-level planning when necessary, for example, in infrastructure planning and in NRM.

Decentralised Planning and Implementation

Decentralisation will help in (*a*) ensuring local participation, (*b*) incorporating local needs for assets, (*c*) bringing transparency and accountability and (*d*) in systematic monitoring.

Labour-based Infrastructural Development

ILO has initiated a very useful programme on labour-based infrastructural development in many African countries (Miller, 2006; ILO, 2006). The Extended Public Works Programme (EPWP) of South Africa is a good success story in this context. The rationale of this programme is to maximise employment in the construction of infrastructure like roads, buildings, bridges, airport, etc. The programme uses light equipments in the place of heavy machines whenever feasible. This reduces cost of construction of infrastructure, on the one hand, and expands employment avenues, on the other hand. This approach emphasises that the quality of infrastructure is up to the mark, that is, the quality of infrastructure is not compromised to generate employment.

The issue of the ratio of labour cost and material cost is important here. However, this can be worked out by selecting the right kind of infrastructure and the labour-intensive component of infrastructure for the MGNREGS. Convergence of infrastructure-development programmes like Bharat Nirman and PM's rural road programme (Pradhan Mantri Gram Sadak Yojana) with the MGNREGS will be very important here.

Skill Training

Skill training will have to be an important component of NREGP. Many countries have included skill training in their respective programmes, for example, EPWP in South Africa, Jefes in Argentina, labour-based infrastructure programmes in many African countries, etc. It needs to be noted that construction of quality infrastructure, systematic management of natural resources, etc., requires skilled labour. Again, unskilled workers will not be able to get mainstream jobs which are likely to be created through the MGNREGS works. Skill acquisition will help in improving productivity as well as employability of workers. We, therefore, believe that skill training, even on-the-job training will have to be an essential part of the MGNREGS.

Maintenance of Public Assets

Several countries have designed EGS or wage-employment programmes for maintenance of public assets like roads (for example, rural-maintenance programme in Bangladesh, Padata Karya in Indonesia and infrastructure-based programmes in Africa). Considering the facts that (*a*) lack of proper maintenance of roads and other infrastructure is a common problem in many developing countries, (*b*) this results in serious losses in the economy and (*c*) regular maintenance can generate regular wage employment, it is very desirable that maintenance of roads and other infrastructure is incorporated in the design of EGS.

Inclusion of Services

This brings us to the question of including services or regular jobs under the MGNREGS. Several countries have included services, such as child care, care of the old and the sick (particularly HIV-AIDS patients), cooking for community, and other social services as a part of employment guarantee. Argentina (Jefes), Indonesia (Padat Karya), South Africa (EPWP) are some of the examples of this. This type of employment is given for a limited period of three to four months or so. The rationale behind the inclusion of services is that (*a*) the persons performing these services are trained on the job so that their employability improves, (*b*) these services, which are very important, are provided to the community on rotation basis but continuously and (*c*) in the long run, these services can be converted into permanent services available to communities. Though these services are desirable, the government does not have resources to make them permanent and government-funded services.

Except for the last three points (that is, skill training, maintenance of assets and inclusion of basic services), the rest of the characteristics are already there in the present design. The programme needs to be reoriented towards these points. The last three, however new, deserve serious consideration of policymakers.

Brief Assessment of Performance of MGNREGS

The overall performance of MGNREGS has not been poor at the all-India level (Table 2.1). In the first year (2006–07), 905 million person-days were generated in the selected most backward 200 districts in the country. This was much more than the 856 million person-days of total employment generated under the two major national programmes, namely, SGRY and NFFWP, which covered all the

Table 2.1: Performance of MGNREGS during 2006–07 to 2010–11

Item	*2006–07*	*2007–08*	*2008–09*	*2009–10*	*2010–11*
No. of districts	200	331	615	615	615
HH provided work (in millions)	21.02	33.91	45.11	52.58	54.83
MGNREGS income per household	1,920.0	2,972.4	3,899.0	4,400.7	3,979.9
Person-days (in millions)	905.06	1,436.8	2,163.35	2,830.35	2,003.4
Person-days per household	**43.05**	**42.37**	**47.96**	**53.54**	**47.00**
Women days (in millions)	367.90	610.91	1,035.72	1,377.84	953.00
Percentage of women days	40.65	42.52	47.88	48.68	47.57
SC days (in millions)	229.50	394.23	633.59	863.85	439.40
Percentage of SC days	25.36	27.44	29.29	30.52	31.00
ST days (in millions)	329.88	420.56	550.16	586.97	348.50
Percentage of ST days	36.45	29.27	25.43	20.74	21.00
Funds allotted (in millions)	120,736	192,788	363,005	496,437	519,258
Funds used (in millions)	88,233.6	159,998	272,501	379,483	392,622
Percentage of funds used	73.08	81.98	75.07	76.44	75.61
Works: Total (in lakhs)	8.42	17.92	39.89	46.03	54.76
Ongoing	4.49	9.69	27.75	23.70	30.79
Completed	3.97	8.24	12.14	20.95	23.78

Source: http://nrega.nic.in/netnrega/home.aspx

districts in the country. The employment generated under the MGNREGS increased to 1,436 million person-days in 2007–08 (330 districts) and to 2,160 million person-days in 2008–09 (615 districts) in the country. It increased to 2,830.35 million days in 2009–10 and to 2,003.4 million days in 2010–11. It is worth noting that the number of households participating in the MGNREGS increased to 54.83 million in 2010–11.

The total funds spent on the programme has continuously increased, from ₹88,236 million in 2006–07 to ₹192,788 million in 2007–08 to ₹379,483 million in 2009–10 to ₹392,622 million in 2010–11. Again, the total number of works taken up under the MGNREGS increased from 8.42 lakhs in the first year to 39.89 lakhs in 2008–09 and to 54.76 lakhs in 2010–11. It is also worth noting that a large number of the works have been for water conservation, connectivity (rural roads) and the remaining for land development (Hirway, 2004).

Another positive aspect about the performance of the MGNREGS has been the high and increasing share of women in the total person-days generated under the programme. This share which was 41 per cent in the first year increased to 43 per cent in the second year, to 47.96 per cent in the third year to 48 per cent in 2010–11. The consistently high participation of women in the programme indicates that women find this programme continuously attractive perhaps because it is available locally, it is a government programme and it is without contractors. This participation by women is likely to have several positive impacts on women in terms of improvement in their employability, their exposure to outside world and their human capabilities (Ambasta, Shanker and Shah, 2008).

The participation of the scheduled castes in the programme has continuously increased in the initial years and remained high throughout. The share of the STs has marginally declined mainly because the programme has entered into non-ST areas gradually (Aakella and Kidambi, 2007; Bhaduri, 2007).

In all, about 66 lakhs works have been completed in the five years of the MGNREGS. In the year 2010–11, 30.79 lakh works were ongoing in addition to the completed works.

An important aspect of the performance of the MGNREGS is that there is a slight decline in certain variables of performance in the last year, that is 2010–11. A careful view of the statistics show that this decline is not observed in all the states. At least 50 per cent states are doing better than the earlier year in their performance in the MGNREGS. For the other 50 per cent states, some of the likely reasons for the decline in some of the performance indicators could be (*a*) delayed payment of the MGNREGS wages that encourages households to move away from the MGNREGS, (*b*) non-fulfilments of most of the entitlements including guarantee of work is also pushing households away from the MGNREGS, (*c*) scattered and intermittent nature of the MGNREGS work encourages workers to depend on their earlier coping strategies like out-migration, long-term work with local farmers (though at lower wages), etc., and (*d*) unwillingness of local leaders—Sarpanch, Talati, big farmers, etc., to raise the level of the MGNREGS employment beyond a minimum level. In a very few cases, it is also possible that MGNREGS works have increased the mainstream employment as a result of which the demand for work under the MGNREGS has declined. It is clear that there is a need to investigate this development carefully.

Along with the achievements it is important to note some disappointments which primarily refer to the low level of performance, on the one hand, and low level of empowerment of the poor, on the other hand. A large number of small and big studies have been carried out by scholars, officials and CSOs. Some of the weaknesses noted by these studies (Acharya, 2004; Das and Pradhan, 2007; Devasia and Khaleej, 2007; Jacob and Varghese, 2006; Krishnamurthy, 2006) are:

1. The guarantee component is almost absent in the implementation of the programme. The data which shows a very narrow gap between the number of households demanding work and getting work does not reflect the reality. Field-level studies show that there is hardly any system of recording the date of demanding work.
2. Except for a few households in a few pockets, households do not receive any unemployment allowance.
3. The planning for works has been largely top down and ad hoc. Even when a shelf of projects exists, it is not a result of any systematic planning. The MGNREGS is not really integrated with the development process of the economy.
4. Transparency and social accountability in the scheme is very poor. Social audits have been, at best, perfunctory and, at worst, non-existent (Aakella and Kidambi, 2007; Ambasta, Shankar and Shah, 2008).

A careful view of the performance of MGNREGS at the district level, however, presents interesting results. Our district-level analysis shows that there are some districts which have performed very well in terms of some basic indicators like (*a*) per cent of SC and ST households in the district participating in the scheme, (*b*) per cent of women participating, (*c*) daily wage rate, (*d*) average number of days of work per household, (*e*) per cent of households completing 100 days, (*f*) per cent of disabled beneficiaries and (*g*) per cent of allotted funds spent. Our analysis shows that there are at least 25–30 districts from the 200 districts of the first year, which have performed well and also improved their performance over the years. These districts are spread over several states such as Rajasthan, MP, Assam, Andhra Pradesh, Chhattisgarh, etc. In these districts the average number of days of employment per the MGNREGS household is above 80 days; more than 50 to 90 per cent of the households have completed 100 days; the average daily wage rate has been ₹80.00 and above; women's share in the total employment has been more than 60 per cent, a large percentage of the district SC and ST households have participated in MGNREGS works; and a large number of works have been undertaken under the programme.

These are the districts that give hope for the future as they show that implementing MGNREGS successfully is feasible. While concluding this paper we would like to recommend that a careful study of these districts will have some important lessons for improving the working of this programme.

Appendix A2

Table A2.1: Unpaid Work and its Implications for Public EGSs

Type of Activity	*Description of Activities*	*Implications for EGSs: Works/Assets*	*Impact*
1. Non-market economic activities: acquiring/ collecting basic necessities	1. Fetching water	1. Construction of water harvesting structures	Public provisioning of necessities
		2. Deepening tank/improving traditional structures	
		3. Organising distribution of water supply and laying pipelines	
	2. Fetching fuel wood from common lands	1. Regeneration of common lands and plantation: social forestry	1. Access to low cost healthy energy
		2. Regeneration of forest lands	2. Promotion to income-generating activities
		3. Constructing smokeless stoves/improved stoves	3. Improved environmental resources
		4. Constructing biogas plants running on cow dung, bio mass	
		4. Plantation of biofuel trees	
	3. Walking long distance for relieving activities	1. Construction of latrines	1. Improved health facilities
		2. Construction of drainages	
2. Non-market economic activities: collection of raw material for income-generating activities	1. Collection of fodder from common lands	1. Regeneration of common lands for fodder crops or fodder farms	1. Improved income/ productive employment
	2. Collection of wood/ bamboo, etc., for crafts/manufacturing goods	1. Regeneration of common lands: social forestry	1. Improved incomes/ productive employment
		2. Regeneration of forest lands	2. Improved environmental resources
		3. Wasteland (public) development	

(Table A2.1 contd.)

(Table A2.1 contd.)

Type of Activity	*Description of Activities*	*Implications for EGSs: Works/Assets*	*Impact*
3. Unpaid domestic work: care-related activities	1. Child care	1. Constructing child care centres	1. Improved child health
		2. Constructing child development centres for children below five years of age	2. More time for women to rest or to work in productive employment
		3. Constructing school rooms & school facilities	3. Improved education: more enrolment and less drop out
		4. Construction of mid-day meal kitchens	
	2. Care of the sick, old and disabled in the household	1. Constructing health centres/ dispensaries	1. Improved health facilities
		2. Improving/repairing expanding existing health facilities	
		3. Constructing facilities for public sanitation and hygiene	
5. Unpaid domestic work: household repair in non-durable shelter	1. Repair and maintenance of house: floor, walls and ceiling	1. Construction of durable housing for the poor	1. Improved homes of people
			2. More time available for rest/work
6. Unpaid work: Travelling	1. Travelling for different reasons on foot	1. Construction of roads: approach roads, feeder roads, paving of internal roads	1. Less drudgery of walking
			2. More time for rest/work

Notes

1. Papola has estimated this required employment based on the following calculation:

1.	Unemployment 2007	21.6 million
2.	Addition to labour force (2007–12)	44.7 million
3.	Working poor that need employment	26.0 million
	Total	92.3 million

2. Jan Tinbergen has observed that rural public works promote strategic use of surplus labour to move towards full employment in developing countries (Hirway and Terhal, 1994).
3. Government of MP has taken a successful initiative to integrate MGNREGS with the watershed development projects successfully.
4. The recent tsunami experience has shown that mangroves are critical for the safety of the coastal population. The study on Valuation of Coastal Resources by Indira Hirway and S. Goswami has shown that a major problem in regeneration of mangroves on the Indian coast is shortage of funds. The shortage is felt by the forest department as well as by local villages under local programmes (Hirway and Goswami, 2007).
5. This declaration is called 'Bopal Declaration' named after Bopal village that is a village in the outskirts of Ahmedabad where the meeting of non-governmental organisations (NGOs) working for NRM made this declaration. There are eight principles which are: (*a*) community-based organisations of primary stakeholders at the centre of planning, budgeting, implementation and management of natural resources, (*b*) management of natural resources for achieving social, economic and economic equity, (*c*) decentralisation in the planning and management of natural resources, (*d*) appointing a facilitating agency (NGO) with professional and multiple skills for motivating and organising people, (*e*) participatory evaluation and monitoring—concurrent, midcourse and outcome based, through independent expert agency, (*f*) allocation of resources for training and software inputs, (*g*) ensuring use of the works completed and (*h*) organisational restructuring for implementing these principles.
6. Bharat Nirman is a time-bound plan for rural infrastructure of the Government of India in partnership with state governments and PRIs (2005–09).
7. Pradhan Mantri Gram Sadak Yojana or Prime Minister's Rural Roads Programme is to provide connectivity to unconnected habitats as a part of rural poverty reduction strategy. In the first phase, villages with population of 1,000 and above (500 in the case of hilly, tribal and desert areas) will be covered. The scheme is a part of Bharat Nirman (2005–09).
8. The National Rural Health Mission (2005–12) has been launched to carry out necessary architectural corrections in the basic health-delivery system. It covers nutrition, sanitation, hygiene and safe drinking water.
9. Sarva Shiksha Abhiyan aims at achieving universalisation of elementary education in a time-bound manner, it seeks to open new schools when necessary and strengthen infrastructure of the existing schools.
10. Total sanitation programme is a national scheme that aims at extending sanitation facilities in rural areas gradually.
11. Indira Awas Yojana is a rural housing programme for the rural poor. The objective of the programme is to help construction of dwelling units by members of SC/ST, freed bonded labour and other BPL households by providing them grant-in-aid.
12. The present rural drinking water schemes have not been able to cover all the villages so far. They are not likely to cover all the villages even after the Eleventh Plan!
13. A study by Menhnaz Rabbani (2006) has shown that this programme has, in spite of its limitations, given positive results (Rabbani, 2006).
14. For a detailed discussion, refer to Indira Hirway (2006).
15. Time-use surveys are not common in most developing countries. India conducted its first (national) time use survey in 1998–99 in six major states in India.

References

Aakella, K. V and S. Kidambi (2007) Challenging corruption with social audit. *Economic and Political Weekly*, (3 February).
Acharya, Shankar (2004) Guaranteeing a job or Fiscal Crisis? *BS*, (30 November).

Ambasta P. P. S., Vijay Shankar and Mihir Shah (2008) Two years of NREGA: The road ahead. *Economic and Political Weekly*, (23 February).

Antonopoulos, Rania and Marzia Fontana (2008) Gender awareness and time use Data: Why it matters for macro economic policies. In towards mainstreaming time use surveys in national statistical system in India. New Delhi: Ministry of Women and Child Development, UNDP and World Bank.

——— (2006), Hidden Vacancies? From Unpaid Work to Gender-Aware Public Job Creation: Toward a Path of Gender Equality and Pro-Poor Development, Paper Prepared for Levy Economics Institute Conference on Public Employment Guarantee, 13–14 October.

Bhaduri, Amit (2007) Alternatives in industrialization. *Economic and Political Weekly*, (5 May).

Bhalla, G. S. (2007) Globalization and employment trends in India. Presidential Address, Indian Society of Labour Economics, CESS, Hyderabad.

Bhalla, Sheila (2007) Inclusive growth? Focus on employment. Paper presented at a seminar on 'Making growth inclusive with special reference to employment generation, 28–29 June 2007, in Delhi.

Dandekar, Kumudini (1983) *EGS of Maharashtra an employment opportunity for women*. Pune, India: Gokhale Institute of Economics and Politics.

Das Vidhya and Pramod Pradhan (2007) Illusion of change. *Economic and Political Weekly*, (11 August).

Development Support Center (2005) *Bopal declarations non-negotiable principles of development and management of national resource in sustainable manner*. Bopal, Ahmedabad: DSC.

Forstater, Mathew (2001) Full employment policies must consider effective demand and structural and economic change. Working Paper No 14, The Centre For Full Employment and Price Stability, University of Missouri, Kansas City, USA.

Fullwiler, Scott T. (2006) Macro-economic stabilization through an employer at last resort. Working paper No. 44, Center for Full Employment and Price Stability, University of Missouri Kansas City, USA.

Ghosh, Jayati and C. P. Chandrasekhar (2007) Recent employment trends in India and China: An unfortunate convergence? Paper presented at seminar on 'Making growth inclusive with special reference to employment generation', 28–29 June, Delhi.

Government of India (2005) The National Rural Employment Guarantee Act 2005. New Delhi: Ministry of Law and Justice.

——— (2006) *Report of Technical Committee on Watershed Programme in India: From Hariyali to Neeranchal*. New Delhi: Department of Land Resources, Ministry of Rural Development.

Hindu (2007) State govt considers providing creche in Villupuram district work sites in Tamil Nadu. The Hindu, 5 August.

Hiraman, Bharat (2007) In Bilapur they have started dreaming again! Financial Express, 24 May.

Hirway, Indira (2004) Providing employment guarantee in India: Some critical issues. *Economic and Political Weekly*, India, (November).

——— (2006) Employment Guarantee for Promoting Pro-Poor Development Issues and Concerns with Reference to MGNREGA in India. Paper prepared for Conference on Employment Guarantee Policies: Theory and Practice, 13–14 October, Levy Institute, New York.

——— (2008) Plan for long term. *Indian Express*, 2 February.

Hirway, Indira and P. Terhal (1994) *Towards employment guarantee in India: Indian and international experiences in rural public works programme*. New Delhi: Sage Publication.

Hirway, Indira and Subhrangsu Goswami (2007) *Valuation of coastal resources: The case of mangroves in Gujarat*. New Delhi: Academic Foundation.

ILO (2004a) A fair globalization creating opportunities for all. International Labor Organisation, February.

——— (2004b) Economic Security for a better world, ILO Socio-Economic Security Programme, International Labour Organisation, Geneva, Switzerland.

Jacob, Arun and Varghese Richard (2006) 'Reasonable beginning in Palakkad, Kerala' NREGA Implementation -1. *Economic Political Weekly*. 2 December.

Joy, K. J., Biksham Gujja, Suhas Paranjape, Vinod Goud and Shruti Vispute (eds) (2008) *Water conflicts in India: A million revolts in the making*. London, New York, New Delhi: Routledge.

Khan, Etmad (2007) Poverty guaranteed. *Tehelka*. 7 September.

Krishnamurthy, J. (2006) Employment guarantee and crisis response. *Economic and Political Weekly*. 4 March.

Miller, Steven (2006) *Employment intensive strategies: Linking sustainable infrastructural development and social transfers*. Geneva: ILO.

Mitra, Arup (2008) The Indian labour market an overview. International Labour Organisation Working Paper Series.

MoRD (Ministry of Rural Development) (2008) *National Rural Employment Guarantee Act (NREGA) 2005 operational guidelines 2008*, 3rd Edition. India: Ministry of Rural Development, Government of India.

Papola, T. S. (2008) Employment challenges and strategies in India. Discussion Paper, International Labour Organisation, New Delhi.

Rabbani, Mehnaz (2006) *Employment of poverty reduction in Bangladesh: A review of the rural maintenance program, research and evaluation dvision*. Bangladesh: BRAC.

Sen, Amartya (2000) The ends and means of sustainability. Keynote Address at Inter-Academy Panel on International Issues, Tokyo, May.

Tinbergen, Jan (1994) Foreword to *Towards employment guarantee in India*, by Indira Hirway and P. Terhal. New Delhi: Sage Publications.

United Nation (1948) Universal declaration of human rights. United Nations, New York: General Assembly of the United Nations.

3

Interpreting the Right to Work
What Relevance for Poverty Reduction?

Gerry Rodgers

Introduction

The Universal Declaration of Human Rights states, 'Everyone has the right to work, to free choice of employment, to just and favourable conditions of work and to protection against unemployment' (Article 23(1)). At first sight, this is not a controversial statement. Most societies are built around the ability of their people to earn a decent living through access to employment.

And yet the negotiations around this phrase in the Universal Declaration were difficult, for behind this statement were hidden two different conceptions of society. In one, the right to work was absolute, and the State was therefore obliged to provide employment for all—but to this obligation of the State, there corresponded a duty to work on the part of citizens. In the other, the right to work was expressed in terms of the freedom to choose of the individual, but within a wider market economy that provided no guarantees that the choices would be realised in practice. As Eleanor Roosevelt put it in a speech in 1948,

> The Soviet Union insists that this [the right to work] is a basic right which it alone can guarantee because it alone provides full employment by the government. But the right to work in the Soviet Union means the assignment of workers to whatever task is given to them by the government ... We in the United States have come to realise [the right to work] means freedom to choose one's job, to work or not to work as one desires. (Glendon, 2001: 138)

This fundamental difference in interpretation has greatly influenced the role that the right to work has played in national social and economic policies. Indeed, for much of the period from 1948 to 1990, the realisation of the right to work through the achievement of full employment in socialist economies was presented by the Soviet bloc as proof of the superiority of their economic system, while Western industrialised countries focused on freedoms in work—freedom of association and collective bargaining, freedom from forced labour and from discrimination—rather than on the right to work as such.

And in most developing countries, the right to work was subordinated to broader development goals. The ILO's main employment convention, No. 122, 1964, merely has a preambular reference to the Universal Declaration's enunciation of the right to work, and expresses the goal as 'full, productive and freely chosen employment', not as a right, but as the result of an active policy that should aim at ensuring that 'there is work for all who are available for and seeking work'.

The right to work is therefore complex politically; but it is also complex substantively. First, it is both an end in itself, and a means to other ends. Work may and should have intrinsic value for those that perform it, but it is also the means by which other rights—to an adequate standard of living, to a dignified existence—are realised for the majority of people.

Second, the right to work does not stand on its own, but involves other rights—notably, in the words of the Universal Declaration of Human Rights, 'just and favourable conditions of work ... [and] remuneration', 'rest and leisure, including reasonable limitation of working hours', 'social protection', 'the right to form and join trade unions ....'

Third, work itself is not necessarily desired. There is a compulsion to work because people need the product of their labour in order to live, but much work is experienced as unpleasant drudgery. For many people, work has negative value rather than positive, and the right to leisure is surely as important as the right to work.

A right to work is thus a paradox, because work is, for most people, an unavoidable part of life. In some circumstances, the right not to work is as valid as the right to work (for example, maternity, retirement), and the conditions under which work is performed are as important as the work itself. It is not surprising that writings on work since the early days of capitalist development have been ambiguous about the meaning and content of this right (see, for instance, the review in Standing [2002: 247–55]).

The idea of the right to work was nevertheless incorporated into the International Covenant on Economic, Social and Cultural Rights (ICESCR), adopted in 1966 and now ratified by the great majority of the world's countries. It therefore has become an important element of the international human rights agenda.

In developing countries, rights language was not widely used as a way of expressing economic, social and cultural goals in the period following the wave of decolonisation from the 1940s to the 1960s. The right to work was no exception; indeed, there was a greater stress on the duty to work than the right to work, as certain countries perceived an obligation on the part of their citizens to work for the common good. Mainstream development policy aimed to overcome constraints on social and economic progress by building up social and physical infrastructure, capital and institutions. Rights were regarded as abstract concepts in the absence of the social and economic means to realise them. And this was particularly true of the right to work, which clearly depended on economic factors. In any case, in most countries most people were working; indeed, many of them were working far too much—the basic problem was the low productivity of their work. There was no point in expressing a right to work without the means for its realisation, and without, at the same time, dealing with the productivity of work; it was rather to be expressed as a development goal, to which a number of different policies could contribute.

Since the 1970s, however, rights-based language has become more widespread in development discourse—in part, as a reaction to the extreme economic policies that dominated the international economy in the 1980s and 1990s. As Amartya Sen put it, '... the *rhetoric* of human rights is much more widely accepted today—indeed much more frequently invoked—than it has ever been in the past' (Sen, 1999). The use of the word rhetoric implies a certain scepticism; but the possible contribution to development strategy of the notion of the right to work merits further consideration.

The Content of a Right to Work

Amartya Sen has investigated the relationships between rights and economic goals and outcomes in a series of writings. In his book *Development as Freedom*, Sen examines the validity of a rights-based approach to development in some depth (Sen, 1999: 227 ff). He considers and rejects three possible critiques of rights-based arguments:

- The argument that rights are not innate, but must derive from some authority or legislation (legitimacy). Sen rejects this argument on the grounds that rights should be seen as ethical claims, and distinguished from legislated entitlements.
- The argument that rights exist only where there is a corresponding duty on the part of some agent to ensure their realisation (coherence). On this, Sen considers that rights can exist (in the sense of unfulfilled claims) even if no one has the responsibility to realise them.
- The argument that rights are not universal but vary from one society to another (cultural). This Sen denies, arguing that basic freedoms and their formulations in terms of rights are indeed universal.

But despite Sen's rebuttals, all three of these critiques pose problems for the right to work. The first critique draws attention to the lack of a precise definition of the right to work outside a particular legislative environment. The second highlights the problem of agency and responsibility, to which we return below—a right to work in the absence of an agent to provide this work is not very compelling. And the third abstracts from cultural and social differences that are important for those concerned. Work plays different roles in different societies.

In order to overcome these objections, first it is necessary to consider the meaning of the word 'work'. In its broadest sense, it encompasses all socially valued activities, from wage employment to child care, from gainful self-employment to domestic chores. And work can be done under an enormous variety of social statuses and relationships, ranging from a formal employment contract to an individual drive for self-realisation. This makes the right to work a very amorphous and all-embracing concept.

An alternative is to consider the right to work as referring essentially to gainful employment. Definitions vary, but employment is generally interpreted as referring to economic activity, embracing both waged work and own account work, not including unpaid work in the domestic and voluntary spheres. Interpreting the right to work as a right to employment makes the notion more practical and meaningful, and probably closer to popular understanding. A right to work could then be understood as a right to waged employment, or to the resources and market opportunities required for self-employment.

The second point, perhaps more important still, is that an unqualified right to work makes little sense. A right to work is not meaningful if it refers to work in unhealthy or exploitative conditions, for less than subsistence wages, at ages that are inconsistent with education or retirement, on precarious or insecure terms. There must be some measure of the acceptability of work. The Universal Declaration recognises this and sets conditions on work, as noted above. The ICESCR specifies in article 6 fair wages and equal remuneration for work of equal value, safe and healthy working conditions, equal opportunity for promotion to an appropriate higher level, rest and the limitation of working hours.

But this raises difficult issues. How can one possibly set conditions that are universally valid? Wages and working conditions vary with productivity; indeed, the fundamental logic of economic development is precisely to improve standards of work and life through rising productivity. And so with economic development comes the possibility of higher wages, shorter hours, better working conditions and less drudgery. It follows that the substantive content of the right to work cannot be uniform across economic differences.

The conventional way to bypass this issue is to consider that all societies should set minimum standards for wages and conditions of work, but that the level of these standards will differ according to the resources and possibilities of the societies concerned. Then the right to work (or employment) is a right to work or employment that meets those minimum standards. This, though, runs the risk of circular reasoning—if the content of the right is determined by the possibilities, then the notion of a right adds little of value. We are better off with the notion of employment as a development goal.

Another route is offered by the ILO's decent work agenda. Instead of the right to work, we may consider the right to decent work. Decent work, as formulated by the ILO, brings together basic rights and freedoms at work, access to employment, social protection and social dialogue between representatives of workers and employers (ILO, 1999). This goes beyond minimum standards to incorporate aspirations for security and safe working conditions, dignity at work, representation and negotiation, equality of treatment. As a statement of the goal, it is appealing, and perhaps more appealing than the alternatives above. A right to decent work could then be seen as a central focus of development policy, valid in itself while, at the same time, contributing to many other development goals.

But while the rhetoric may be appealing, this formulation does not avoid the conceptual problems raised above. The concrete specification of the goal of decent work depends on the level of development, so that the 'right to decent work' in Western Europe will look quite different from the same right in India. There may be common underlying principles, but the acceptable levels of safety, income or leisure, to take three examples, depend on economic and social context. The main advantage of going down this route is that in principle it offers a coherent and constant overall framework, from which may be derived the substantive content of the right in any particular circumstance.

Beyond these issues of the quality of work, there are other complicating factors too. An important one concerns skill and occupation. Work is not homogenous, and most people seek work in which they are able to apply their skills and capabilities. Should this too be considered a right? More generally, as a part of the right to work, we may wish to consider other aspirations that should be realised through work, such as creativity, self-fulfilment and social inclusion. But the risk then is to make the concept unworkable in practice.

So the right to work faces severe conceptual problems, if one attempts to give it real content. To capture the diversity of goals and of situations requires a framework that is so broad as to be unusable. The notion of a right to decent work is promising, but does not solve all the problems by any means, and one of the difficulties faced in applying the decent work agenda lies precisely in the difficulty of giving it unambiguous and concrete content. A more limited right to employment might be more viable. But one can equally argue that work and employment are better considered as broad development goals, rather than as rights.

Another approach, which is perhaps less satisfying, but more practical, is to consider the right to work in a purely instrumental sense. As noted above, most people work because they are remunerated, not because of the value to them of undertaking the work itself; indeed, much work is drudgery. The relevant right is then the right to the product of labour, that is, to the incomes and entitlements that it generates; and to that right corresponds an obligation to work. The right to work is then a pseudo-right, in reality the reflection of a particular stage of social and economic development in which all who can do so contribute their labour, and in return are entitled to a share of the product of their work. It is a means, a mechanism, an investment that delivers a return, both for the individual and for the collectivity.

Expressed in this way, it nevertheless raises a series of further questions. If the right to work is a proxy for the right to an income, what should be the relationship between income and work? Should income be determined by the productivity of work, should it rather reflect some social goal (a living wage, an adequate income), should it be determined in the market, should there be a minimum? Then there are fundamental questions about the pattern of inequality in returns to work, between sexes, ages, social groups; and about the fact that some people are inclined or able to work more than others. In practice, the right to income from work cannot be divorced from more general consideration of how income should be divided and distributed. But despite these complexities, a focus on income offers one direct link between the right to work and the reduction of poverty, a question to which we now turn.

The Right to Work and the Reduction of Poverty

The standard criterion for identifying poverty is low income or consumption. As noted above, the right to work can be considered as a proxy for a right to income, and this gives us a first aspect of the relationship between the right to work and the reduction of poverty. But a wider set of issues is also involved. If we follow Sen's capability approach, and consider work and employment as freedoms that enhance peoples' ability to undertake valued activities, then employment may play additional roles in overcoming disadvantage.

We need to separate two aspects. The first is the connection between work and employment, on the one hand, and poverty, on the other. How far is poverty the consequence of deficits in work, such as a shortfall of employment or inadequate conditions of work, and—correspondingly—to what extent is employment creation a primary instrument for reducing poverty, either through the income it generates, or through the empowerment of those employed?

The second is, given the relationship between employment and poverty, how the formulation and promotion of a right to work might lead directly or indirectly to an increase in employment, improvements in the quality of work or an increase in income from employment.

Work, Employment and Poverty

It is a banal and frequent observation that the poor cannot afford to be unemployed. However, there are a number of situations where lack of employment is an important factor in poverty:

- In many occupations, notably but not exclusively in agriculture, there are large seasonal variations in demand for labour, or otherwise precarious or unstable employment relationships.

- In some occupations, low productivity may take the form of long periods available for work but with little to do, as occurs with many casual workers and petty shopkeepers.
- Particular groups (defined by sex, race, sexual preference, social stigma or other factors) face discrimination in the labour market, which excludes them from some or all types of work.
- Short-term crises, whether economic, war or natural disasters, often lead to dramatic employment shortfalls.
- Among the poor, a substantial group of people seek work but cannot obtain it because of poor health, disability or physical condition, inability to move to available jobs, lack of skills and competences and other factors.

At different times and in different places, employment policy has been designed to respond to some or all of these situations as part of an effort to reduce poverty. Public works programmes have long been the response to employment shortfalls due to short-term economic downturns, droughts and other disasters. In their classic and influential study of poverty in India, Dandekar and Rath (1971) argued that while the poorest 10 per cent of the population needed to be supported through income transfers and other social policies, the central policy instrument for eliminating poverty among the majority of the poor should be a programme of employment creation through public works programmes. The same basic idea has continued to underlie policy formulation in India, notably giving rise to the Maharashtra Employment Guarantee scheme and its successor, the MGNREGS. The employment guarantee offered in these programmes consists mainly of employment in public works programmes of one sort or another.

A rather different argument can be built on a Keynesian foundation. Bhaduri argues that there is considerable economic slack, even in a developing country such as India, which shows up as disguised rather than open unemployment—as in low-productivity self-employment. This means that action to increase aggregate demand, especially if focused on employment-intensive activities, will generate growth and employment in a virtuous circle (Bhaduri, 2005). Again, it is the creation of employment that is the key to reducing poverty.

The primary goal of these programmes is income generation. But some programmes, especially those which provide an employment guarantee, aim to do more: to empower poor individuals and groups by giving them the right to make demands—in this case, the demand for work—that must be satisfied. It is an explicit aim of the MGNREGS to be a first step towards a right to work, 'as an aspect of the fundamental right to live with dignity' (Drèze and Khera, 2011).

On the question of discrimination, various forms of affirmative action to increase the access of deprived groups to jobs are widely practised, although there is little evidence that they increase the overall volume of employment, rather than redistributing the employment that already exists.

These policy approaches, and others like them, are certainly effective up to a point. There is little doubt that programmes and policies that create employment can have a substantial impact on poverty. Even when the employment deficit as such is not large, a tighter labour market can help to raise wages and draw in additional workers. While the effectiveness of MGNREGS varies from state to state in India, few people now doubt that it has made a substantial contribution to the reduction of poverty in recent years (Government of India, 2009; Khera and Nayak, 2009).

Some provisos are necessary, however. First, direct employment creation, notably through public works programmes, clearly helps to mop up seasonal unemployment, and to compensate for loss of employment due to crisis or economic fluctuations. But such programmes often miss large segments of the population, in many places including the poorest.

Second, most poor people are not unemployed. Many of the poor, notably women, already work far too much; employment-creation programmes merely increase the pressure on them to work more. In reality, for the majority of the poor, the main employment problem is one of overwork at low productivity, whether in self-employment or wage work. The issue is then not creating employment but rather raising productivity, notably in peasant agriculture or small informal enterprises, so as to raise incomes.

Third, the quality of the jobs that are created is often poor. Much of it consists of hard unskilled labour, in poor working conditions, with little development of skills. As a means of redistributing income, it is rather inefficient, and its main advantage is self-selection—only those who are really in need will accept to undertake the type of work concerned. Such policies fail to take into account the fundamental questions about the quality of work discussed above.

The Impact on Employment of the Right to Work

The second question is how far policies to promote the right to work can in practice lead to more and better employment. At least three issues need to be resolved. The first is the responsibility for ensuring that the right is realised. The second is the productivity of the work that is done. And the third is dealing with the diversity of needs.

On the first issue, in practice, where attempts have been made to introduce the right to work, the ultimate responsibility has fallen on the State—either because the State itself becomes the sole employer, or because it has to put in place a frame of regulation that ensures that private employers provide the necessary employment. In rights-based employment schemes such as the employment guarantee scheme (MGNREGS) in India discussed above, it is again the State that is the funder of last resort. This is a paradox in economies where employment is essentially generated in the private sector. But imposing employment targets, goals or conditions on private enterprises, whether through persuasion or through legislation, has rarely been very successful. High levels of private-sector employment can certainly be achieved with the right incentives, sufficient economic growth and a high level of demand. But it is again the State that has to design and implement policies which cause enterprises to respond in such a way that the right to employment is realised.

The second question, the productivity of the work that is done, is a fundamental one. A right to work that ignores the relationship between employment and production is not sustainable. This was one of the fundamental difficulties of the implementation of the right to work in the European socialist economies—the growing numbers of unproductive workers in state enterprises was a major contributor to the ultimate economic failure of the system. A right to work that is merely a camouflage for redistribution may be viable in the short term; indeed, this is the logic underlying many employment-creating public works programmes. But in the long run, a right to work is about the effective organisation of the production system, and has to be connected to a wider strategy of investment, of skill development, of enterprise creation and of economic growth, which can create opportunities for productive work to which the poor have access.

That is also the precondition for the creation of decent work. Where the right to work is interpreted as an employment guarantee in public works, the question of the quality of work receives little attention. Yet, as we have seen above, if there is no consideration of the quality of work, the right to work may turn out to be drudgery in exchange for a dole. There has to be a broader vision in which work and employment play a more positive role in people's lives. But the economic preconditions remain the same. Decent work has to be productive if it is to be viable. The key to a right to decent work, therefore, lies in finding ways to ensure that improvements in work contribute at the same time to economic goals, in terms of output and productivity. If so, implementing a right to decent work can be an important contribution to a strategy for employment creation. Unfortunately this does not appear to be typically the case. In practice, most economies, both industrialised and developing, are dualistic in their employment structures, with only a minority of high-productivity, decent jobs. Unless ways are found to address the challenge of improving work and employment in the informal segment of the economy, the right to decent work will remain in the sphere of good intentions.

And the third question, diversity, raises complex questions to which there are no easy answers, for needs and demands for work vary greatly. If the goal is limited to poverty reduction, however, the participatory approach adopted by the MGNREGS, which gives people the right to demand employment at the local level, in other words making right a claimable right, and giving different groups the chance to make different demands, has shown promising results. The evidence from the initial years of implementation of the programme suggests that it has been successful in increasing the employment levels of women and of SCs and STs, and so empowering different groups among the poorest. See, for example, Khera and Nayak (2009) and Pankaj and Tankha (2009).

Some Implications

The concept of the right to work, as specified in the Universal Declaration and the ICESCR, is appealing. But as soon as one digs deeper into the content of this right, many complicating factors emerge, in terms of the type of work to which this right refers, its desirability or otherwise, how it is remunerated, how it is connected with the broader system of production and distribution and how the right can be realised.

One of the difficulties of the notion of the right to work, as specified in these international instruments, is in fact its breadth. It encompasses a wide range of key features of the world of work, all intrinsically desirable—but not necessarily all compatible or easy to achieve simultaneously. A more limited notion, such as access to gainful employment, may be a more practical way forward.

The basic point, from an economic perspective, is that work has a dual role: as a source of identity, income and other rewards for the individual; and a factor of production, from the point of view of the enterprise or the economy. The rights discourse is of course built on the former role; but in an economic analysis, it cannot be separated from the latter.

Ultimately, the value of the idea of the right to work depends on the existence of mechanisms for it to be realised, and many of these lie in the economic domain—notably a state commitment to economic policies that deliver high levels of demand for labour. The notion of a right to work may add political pressure on governments to put such policies in place, and may, if it is legislated, give people the power to demand that the authorities provide employment. But the need for economic policies to satisfy this demand remains. At the same time, an economic approach alone is too limited. Realising the right to work is also a question of empowerment and social institutions, legal frameworks and political action. Integrating these different elements calls for a more sophisticated cross-disciplinary approach; as we have seen, Sen's frame of analysis in terms of freedoms and capabilities offers one possible route forward.

As for the linkage with poverty, for the majority of the poor, while employment deficits are important, poverty is also the result of low productivity, wages and incomes in existing employment, along with shortfalls in social protection. So while employment creation is an essential element of poverty-reduction strategies, it is only one element among others.

The notion of the right to work can play a useful supporting role in strategy to reduce poverty, but is unlikely to form its core. A range of mutually reinforcing policies is required to raise the pace of employment creation, improve the quality and productivity of work and strengthen the economic and political capabilities of the poor to demand and take advantage of economic opportunity.

Acknowledgements

This is a revised version of a chapter in the volume entitled *Poverty and human rights: Economic perspectives*, edited by Bård Anders Andreassen, Stephen P. Marks and Arjun K. Sengupta, UNESCO (forthcoming). I am grateful to Stephen Marks, Claire La Hovary, Janine Rodgers and Lee Swepston for their comments on that chapter.

References

Bhaduri, Amit (2005) *Development with dignity: A case for full employment*. New Delhi: National Book Trust.

Dandekar, V. M. and N. Rath (1971) *Poverty in India*. Pune: Indian School of Political Economy.

Drèze, Jean and Reetika Khera (2011) Presentation on the National Rural Employment Guarantee Act (PowerPoint presentation). http://www.righttofoodindia.org/rtowork/ega_keydocs.html (accessed 12 May 2012).

Glendon, Mary Ann (2001) *A world made new: Eleanor Roosevelt and the Universal Declaration of Human Rights*. New York: Random House.

Government of India, National Commission for Enterprises in the Unorganised Sector (2009) *The challenge of employment in India, Volume I—Main Report*, chap. 9. New Delhi.

ILO (1999) *Report of the Director General: Decent Work*, 87th Session of the International Labour Conference, Geneva, June. http://www.ilo.org/public/english/standards/relm/ilc/ilc87/rep-i.htm.

Khera, Reetika and Nandini Nayak (2009) Women workers and perceptions of the National Rural Employment Guarantee Act. *Economic & Political Weekly* xliv, No. 43: 50.

Pankaj, Ashok and Rukmini Tankha (2009) *Women's empowerment through guaranteed employment: A case study of NREGA implementation in Bihar, Jharkhand, Rajasthan, and Himachal Pradesh*. New Delhi: Institute for Human Development.

Sen, Amartya (1999) *Development as freedom*. Oxford University Press.

Standing, Guy (2002) *Beyond the new paternalism*. London: Verso.

4

Which Way to Reduce Poverty

Cash Transfers or Employment Guarantee Scheme?

Eduardo Zepeda and Diana Alarcón

I

Introduction

Like public works programmes, cash transfers to the poor have a long history. Britain was perhaps the first country to enact laws, known as the Poor Laws[1] to assist women, children, elder and handicapped through cash transfers, and to provide work and work-based payments to the able-bodied in the sixteenth century. The laws made a distinction between those who were able to work and those who were not able to work. The former were employed in public works and the latter were provided with a cash transfer. The distinction between those who are able to work and those who are not able to work still forms part of poverty-alleviation strategies and, in a sense, laid the foundations of cash transfers and employment-based social assistance programmes.

Similarly, public works programmes have formed an important part of public policy for centuries, but they became institutionalised and grounded in economic theories in the early decades of the twentieth century. China's public works programmes of the 1920s, India's several famine-relief-based public works programmes in the colonial period and the US New Deal of the the1930s were landmark developments in this regard. The New Deal was an immediate test of the Keynesian theory that pleaded for deficit-finance-based public works programmes to fight recession in the economy. The 1980s and 1990s witnessed a renewed interest in public works programmes, and an even more remarkable interest in cash transfer programmes, particularly in Latin America.

In the last 20 years, the number of countries adopting cash-transfer programmes has increased significantly. According to Fieszben and Schady (2009), the number of countries with such programmes expanded from 3 in 1997 to 28 in 2008.[2] These are not traditional welfare programmes but a transfer of income to poor households that requires the fulfilment of certain actions from beneficiaries, deemed positive to the individuals and the society as a whole. Beneficiary households are typically requested to send kids to school and ensure that families receive basic health care, including vaccinations, nutrition education and pregnancy care. *Bolsa Familia* in Brazil and *Oportunidades* in Mexico are the best known examples from Latin America. Beyond the introduction of conditions to enact the transfer, these programmes feature a number of innovations, including careful targeting of beneficiaries and comprehensive systems of monitoring and evaluation of results. Because of a corresponding obligation on the beneficiaries, these programmes have been labelled as a new generation of cash-transfer programmes.

This chapter first examines the salient features of the public works and programmes. It then briefly discusses cash transfer programmes. The chapter next compares works programmes and cash transfer programmes in relation to their poverty impact, their economy-wide impacts, and issues of implementation. The fourth section offers concluding remarks.

II

Public Works and Employment Programmes

There are a number of studies that have examined public works programmes from various perspectives. Drèze and Sen (1989) have examined India's public works programme in the context of famines; Mukherjee (1997) has examined public works programmes in Africa, India and Latin America Africa and Subbarao et al. (1997) have examined public works programme as a safety net in Asia, Latin America and the Middle East. More recent reviews of public works programmes include Devereux and Solomon (2006), Lal et al. (2010), McCord (2009) and Nino et al. (2009).

Most of these studies draw the conclusion that well-designed public works programmes are a powerful tool to transfer income to the poor and can contribute significantly towards poverty reduction in the long run. Devereux and Solomon (2006) argue that although public works programmes were generally adopted for their self-targeting capabilities, it is increasingly recognised that the assets created by these programmes may have long-term benefits to individuals and communities at large. The authors also argue that public works programmes may provide workers with skills that can help them to escape poverty and they contribute to build institutions—for planning, managing and monitoring—that improve the capacity of individuals and communities to improve their development outlook. India's public works programme created by Mahatma Gandhi National Rural Employment Guarantee Scheme (MGNREGS) calls, for example, for strong local capacities.

Public works programmes can be suitably classified into short- and long-term programmes based on their objectives. Short-term public works programme's aim is temporary relief measure to deal with crisis situation arising from a sudden fall in family income due to natural calamities or economic crises. These are short-lived and relatively small programmes, but there are a number of countries that have adopted this programme. In fact, short-term public works programme constitute the majority of such interventions in recent years. The long-term public works programmes are designed to attend long-term economic objectives like reducing poverty, regenerating the local economy through asset creations and long-term structural stability in the economy. These programmes tend to be large and long-lasting, rich in experience and lessons, but there are few of them. The two types of programmes—short and long term—share important characteristics, but they are also different in important ways.

Short-term Public Works Programme: Crisis Interventions

Most of the public works programmes of recent years form part of short-term crisis interventions (McCord, 2009). McCord (2009) has examined a list of 125 programmes and found that about half of them were conceived as one-time interventions. Of the total, 3 out of 4 programmes lasted less than 6 years, 15 had a lifetime of 6 or more years and only 3 were open ended. Their average lifespan was three years.[3] Similarly, Nino et al. (2009) have reviewed a number of programmes and found that 11 out of 27 were a one-time intervention (shock). Since most programmes are designed to deal with temporary shocks, they tend to be small, limiting their reach to the regions affected by the shocks or to those mostly affected by economic downturns. According to Nino et al. (2009), programmes in the sub-Saharan African and South Asia regions typically cover no more than 10 per cent of the economically active population, while other regions cover no more than 2 per cent of the economically active population.

The above studies suggest that effective implementation of a well-designed short-term programme is essential to reach its objectives. There are two basic components of design: one, the programme should be able to meet the crisis situation. It should be able to respond to people's request for work, coming into operations at the right moment and lasting for as long as it is required. Jobs created by the programmes need to be easily accessible to the people, and the size of the programme needs to be large enough to offer appropriate coverage to the population in need. Two, the wage rate should be structured in a manner that will provide suitable income transfer to the target population and should not disturb the financial and other equilibrium of the economy. Apart from the above, the wage rate has implications for its ability to reach the poor, its capacity to exclude better-off households, ability to increase household income and its overall labour-market impact.

Self-selection is an important feature of the employment programmes. It reduces the administrative costs of the programme and reduces the selection errors incurred by other methods used in the selection of beneficiaries. The wage rate also plays an important role in this self-selection process. An extremely low wage rate might not attract the deserving households while too high a wage rate might make these jobs attractive to much better-off households. There are also leakages-related risks of high wage rates. As a course-correcting mechanism, it has been suggested that self-selection should be complemented with geographical and ethnical targeting to increase the participation of the poor and deprived population groups.

The definition of the wage rate also matters for the efficiency of the programme to increase poor's income. The list of beneficiaries of a programme might include people who worked in unpaid activities, were unemployed or economically inactive before the programme and people who left other paid jobs to join the programme. The addition of household income in these cases will be different in these cases. While those who had no paid job prior to the programme will add the total wage received to the income of the household, those who left a paid job to join the programme will only add the difference between the programme wage and the wage in the previously held job. In the latter case, the programme will add to household income only the difference between the programme's wage and the foregone income of these workers. Foregone income lowers the efficiency of the programme to improve household income. One should expect that the higher the wage paid by the programme, the more attractive it will be and the higher the foregone income becomes.

The definition of the wage rate also has implications for the array of businesses effectively or potentially active in the region. The obvious implication is that a high wage rate tends to drive competitive activities out of the market. Under the short-run crisis response programme, it should not be a major concern, and the short-term lifespan of temporary programmes reduces further the danger of serious disruption of market activities. Nevertheless, the risk is there. The higher the wage rate, the larger the risk of disrupting local market activities. At the same time, not all market activities are socially worth to keep. To insist, the rule should not be to set the lowest possible wage rate as to minimise the risk of disturbing markets. Broad economic and social factors should be considered when deciding the wage rate of employment programmes.

Public Works Programme: Long-term Objectives

In contrast to the short-term public works programmes, the long-term programmes with objectives like addressing high unemployment, structural underemployment and poverty are not in huge numbers. McCord and Slater (2009) have found that out of the 161 employment programmes reviewed by them, only seven were of long-term objectives; they have called these programmes as employer of the last resort. Such programmes include New Deal employment programmes, Egypt's employment guarantee programme to university graduates, Ethiopia's Productive Safety Net Program, South Africa's Community Work Programme and the employment guarantee programmes of India.[4] These programmes were not only of long-term duration, but also of wide coverage. For example, Ethiopia's Productive Safety Net Program caters to seven million people, while the NREGP of India provided employment to more than 50 million households in 2009/10; in both cases, the number of beneficiaries represents well above 10 per cent of the economically active population.

A good design and effective implementation constituted the core of the success of these programmes.[5] A good poverty-reduction work programme needs first to be efficient in transferring income; the wage rate plays a crucial role in this. Also, targeting matters. However, the aim of removing structural unemployment and poverty reduction demands more complex design and implementation processes. There are four issues that need attention in this respect: (*a*) the quality of assets, (*b*) the size of the programme, (*c*) its flexibility to respond to the demand for this kind of jobs and (*d*) the definition of the wage rate.

First, these programmes should be designed in a manner that leads to the creation of appropriate and quality assets. While the quality of assets may not be a prime concern for a temporary programme, the capacity of medium- and long-term work programmes to reduce poverty depends very much on the quality of the assets created and its collateral distribution effects. Assets should positively add to local productive capacities and, to the extent possible, their benefits should accrue to the poor.

Second, the size of such programmes is likely to be large, as to cover a large proportion of the poor in the whole country or a particular region. While temporary work programmes can be confined to the area of crisis; the long-term objectives demand adequate coverage of the entire poor population in a country or a region.

Third, given the relatively large size and long-term objective, these programmes should be able to respond to changing needs. If the ability of temporary work programmes to assist the poor during the crisis depends on being able to come in time and last long enough to cover the period of distress, the ability of a work programme to reduce poverty depends on its sustainability over a significant length of time and its ability to adjust to changes in beneficiaries' demand for work. To be sure, the need for public works jobs is likely to be lower during times of rapid growth than during times of slow or regressive growth, and the programme needs to be able to adjust and respond appropriately. Large and long-lasting work programmes need to have the flexibility to make jobs available to workers in need.[6] At the same time, these programmes should avoid interfering with labour markets. Such flexibility and sensitivity call for detailed and complex information systems and require an elaborated and large decision-making structure, which demands good planning and execution on the part of policymakers and its implementation agencies.

Fourth, the definition of the wage rate in these programmes is critical. The large size and long time horizon of these programmes increase the relevance of adopting appropriate mechanisms to set an appropriate wage rate. The wage rate has implications for generating adequate income for the household; cost of the programme; capacity to target the right population groups; definition of the size of foregone income and overall impact on labour markets. By making available a potentially significant number of jobs outside the market, at a programme-determined wage rate, the impacts on the local economy could be significant.

The large, long-lasting employment programmes impose strong demands on the managerial capacities of the institutions in charge of the design and implementation. A decentralised, demand-driven programme can be better suited to take up the challenges. Employment guarantee schemes (EGS) are designed to respond to the demand for jobs where and when it arises. Rather than centrally deciding where and when jobs will be created, the programme develops technical and organisational capacities to appropriately respond to the demand for jobs. These are also complex tasks, but of a different kind. The international experience with EGSes reduces to a few programmes, but rich in lessons. The largest and most interesting in terms of its design and impact are the India's Maharashtra Employment Guarantee Scheme and the more recent MGNREGA. Job creation in an EGS can be thought as the result of the interaction of at least five factors, namely, the need for work of potential beneficiaries; the set of rules and specifications governing the programme; the technical and organisational capacities to implement the programme; the social and economic conditions of localities and the interplay between the programme and market forces in the local economy.[7] In this context, the decision on the wage rate becomes particularly important.

The definition of the wage rate in an EGS seeking to reduce poverty is crucial to the functioning of local markets. If the EGS is credible, that is, if the EGS is believed to be capable of responding to workers' demand for work over a reasonably long period of time, the EGS will effectively set a new wage floor and most likely, will force wages to increase. This is so because most urban and rural labour markets in developing countries are highly imperfect and dominated by few employers, that is, with monopsony or oligopsony structures where the market wage rate tends to be below its theoretical competitive level (Manning, 2005; Oya, 2010). In this context, it is thus important that the EGS wage rate be set above the monopsony or oligopsony market wage. A higher wage market not only makes jobs attractive to the poor, especially when the poor have to perform important unpaid tasks to ensure livelihoods, but it might also help to reduce labour-market imperfections and accelerate development. Low wages in local economies are part of the sluggish dynamism that characterises them and the slow pace of development.

Thus, contrary to the conventional thinking, the EGS-induced increase in wages may have the positive effect of bringing local labour market closer to competitive conditions, thereby increasing employment and efficiency (Basu, Chau and Kanbur, 2008). More efficient labour markets and the injection of additional cash to the local economy can trigger dynamic pro-development effects in otherwise stagnant economies.

The contribution of EGS to poverty reduction also depends on broader definition of wages. In the context of scant local development, the participation of poor people in the work programmes is usually not cost free. In some urban markets in developing countries, it is customary, for example, to set a transport allowance as an explicit part of the wage. The wage rate of an effective EGS should include the cost of access. If worksites are far from the residence of the intended beneficiaries, the cost of accessing those jobs may outweigh the benefit that the wage programmes intend to bring. Similarly, if other costs to access the jobs are not properly accounted for, the demand for EGS jobs may be small. In addition to transportation, other important costs that should be accounted for are the necessary facilities in the worksite, such as drinking water, shady areas or child care—especially important to facilitate the participation of women in the programme. The development consequences of inadequately setting wages or improper accounting for access costs to the programme's jobs may be significant to the point of rendering the programme inadequate to respond to the needs of the poor.

III

Conditional Cash-transfer Programmes

A number of studies have addressed the issues involved in CCT programmes.[8] While income transfers to the poor, especially in the form of non-contributory pensions to the old, have a long history in both developed and developing countries, large-scale CCT programmes were introduced in Latin America in the 1990s as part of poverty-alleviation policies, actions to increase education and, in some cases, as part of longer-term strategies seeking a sustained reduction in poverty. By imposing a condition to the transfer of income, CCT programmes linked the income transfer to the larger aim of human-capital development through increased education and improved health of the poor families. It was argued that the fulfilment of such conditions and the money transferred would contribute to break the intergenerational transmission of poverty. The programme was not just *giving money away*, it was transferring money in exchange for an action or the fulfilment of a condition on the part of the beneficiary. Generally, thus, poor families will receive an income transfer conditional to keep children at school and have regular health check-ups.

As in the case of public works, CCT programmes can make a significant contribution to poverty reduction, at least in the short term, if they are sufficiently large to cover most, if not all, of the poor and if the amount of the transfer is sufficiently large to bring family income above the poverty line. A good part of the popularity and interest on CCT programmes owes to the successful experiences of Brazil and Mexico and much of their success owes to their size. In mid-2009, there were 11.6 million beneficiary families covered by *Bolsa Familia* in Brazil; this was around 50 million people, which represents around 26 per cent of the population. In 2010 there were 5.8 million families receiving income grants from *Oportunidades*, which represents about one quarter of the population. However, the conditions that allow these two countries to have massive programmes to cover virtually all families in extreme poverty might not be available to other countries. The budget for *Oportunidades* and that of *Bolsa Familia* represent less than one per cent of GDP. A good design, good organisational capacities and good implementation have contributed to their success and their affordability. But the affordability is also explained by the fact that these two are medium-income countries with high inequality, which means that a small amount of money, relative to average income in the country, can be transferred to a large number of families and still make a significant addition to the income of the poor. Poorer countries with higher incidence of poverty, and less inequality, may find it difficult to sustain massive income-transfer programmes. Not surprisingly, CCT programmes in other countries are small with a relatively weak impact on poverty reduction and, in most cases, they largely depend on resources from donor countries and international agencies, which, according to McCord, are adopting the practice of restricting transfers to the poorest 10 per cent of the population.

The monthly income these programmes transfer to the poor is small; between US$31 and 91 per family in Brazil in 2009 and around US$38.00 average in Mexico. But such a small transfer does help poor families, and the poorer the family, the most welcome the transfer is. But the transfer by itself is not likely to permanently take them out of poverty.

There are two ways through which CCT helps these poor families in moving out of poverty. First, the transfer of income to the poor has multiplier effects, which might lead to a significant increase in employment and in the income of a larger group of local producers and service providers (many of whom would be poor themselves). Second, the income transfer along with educational and health improvement would help in arresting intergenerational transmission of poverty. More education and better health improve, in turn, the income-earning opportunities of poor young people when they join the labour market.

The very transfer of income from the rich to the poor triggers changes that in principle can increase the incomes of the poor. For one thing, poor people tend to spend a larger proportion of their incomes on goods that are more likely to be produced by the poor themselves—as in the informal sector. In the case of poor rural localities, one can easily expect that the increases in income the programme brings can benefit local activities and increase the income of residents engaged in these activities; income transfer to the poor can have multiplier effects in the local economy. Through a comprehensive review of the literature, Hanlon et al. (2010) identified various mechanisms through which the very income transfer to the poor has a positive impact on the local economy: (*a*) liquidity-constrained households are able to increase investment in microenterprises and agricultural production; (*b*) decreasing precautionary savings which liberates resources for investment; (*c*) since migration requires some initial capital, there are reports indicating an increase of migration among families receiving income from Mexico's *Oportunidades.* Despite the noticeable impact that the inflow of cash of these programmes can have in poor local economies, studies have not found sizeable general equilibrium impacts, on either local or national economies, as wages and prices have reportedly changed little as a result of CCTs (Fieszben and Schady, 2009). Nevertheless, a study of Mexico's *Oportunidades* programme found that incomes of non-beneficiary households have also increased due to the presence of the programme (Angelucci and Giorgio, 2009).

The idea that CCTs could, by themselves, break the intergenerational transmission of poverty is fading from the debate. Once praised as a development silver bullet, it is now widely accepted that CCTs might be an important part of social policies, but not the main way out of poverty.[9] Nevertheless, it is useful to revisit one of the important arguments that were proposed in favour of incorporating the fulfilment of specific behavioural conditions in order to receive the transfer of income. The argument started with the assumption that the poor underinvest in human capital; thus, creating incentives to correct for such underinvestment would allow the next generation of a poor family to escape poverty through better job opportunities. The story of social mobility through education is well known to the poor, but growth needs to be broad based to create job opportunities to a growing number of young workers. Without a major improvement in the quality and relevance of education, deeper credit markets to respond to the needs of small-scale producers and better market access to rural producers, small cash transfers to improve school attendance may not be enough to break the intergenerational transmission of poverty.

CCTs have been successful in increasing human capital. Among the poor, school attendance has risen and education achievements are now higher, nutrition has improved and the use of health services has gone up. In some cases, the simple increase in income explains the improvement in human capital; in others, the conditions associated to the income transfer have made the difference.[10] But the question remains: is a little more human capital enough to break the intergenerational transmission of poverty? Consider the case of Mexico. After 13 years of operation, few would agree that the children that benefited from *Oportunidades* that are now joining or about to join the labour force will escape poverty in the next few years as a result of their increased endowment of human capital. Despite better human capital, Levy (2009) argues that the children of today's beneficiaries of the programme *Oportunidades* will be likely to remain in low-productivity, informal jobs and unable to escape poverty.[11] Few would agree that a massive CCT in a poorer country will suffice to eradicate poverty in the time span of a generation.

IV

The Way Forward: Cash Transfers or Employment Guarantee?

The extensive experience with public works and cash transfers demonstrates their effectiveness to redistribute income to the poor;[12] but the choice between these two programmes is not easy. The choice of the programme—cash transfer or employment guarantee—depends on factors like the specific conditions of the target population, the underlying objectives of the programme and the institutional capacity of government to design and deliver them. Nevertheless, there are advantages of EGS and similarly certain advantages of cash transfer. While both types of programmes have proved their effectiveness in reducing poverty in the short term, we have examined the general advantages and disadvantages of these two programmes from the viewpoints of poverty reduction in the long term.

There are two aspects in which EGS will have an effect on poverty reduction that are absent in CCT programmes. First, the EGS directly improves the employment skills of beneficiaries, which can be relevant for their lifelong work careers. Second, public works create assets that may increase the productivity of activities populated by the poor. Furthermore, EGS have stronger multiplier effects compared to cash transfers. While a monetary unit transferred to households has the same multiplier effect regardless of its origin (as a wage, a scholarship or a cash transfer), the assets built by the EGS increase output in the construction sector, which further increases the demand for labour from poor households.[13]

There are three advantages of CCTs over EGS. First, while the added income of both programmes equally contributes to improve education and health through the income effect, by conditioning the transfer, CCTs may induce a larger investment among families that underinvest on their children's education.[14] Second, the total cost of a transfer of one monetary unit to households is lower in the case of CCTs because there are no additional investments involved (as in the case of public works programmes). Third, the required administrative capacities are also lower in CCTs when compared to EGS. Management of CCTs requires verification of the income of potential beneficiaries and the fulfilment of conditions, that is, school attendance and clinical check-ups. EGS, on the other hand, require the management of construction processes for the building of productive assets.

But to properly balance out the advantages and disadvantages of work programmes and cash transfers, one needs to look beyond the direct and immediate impacts. Some studies have found small negative effects on the supply of labour of households that receive CCTs. The effect of work programmes on labour markets, as has been discussed here, is more nuanced. If the wage rate paid by the programme is adequately high, particularly in the case of guarantee schemes, the programme contributes to the development of labour markets. If the wage rate is unduly high, however, the work programme may crowd out competitive businesses which will diminish the positive impact on the welfare of the poor. A full comparison of work programmes and cash transfers needs to take into account immediate impacts and second-round economic effects, including the benefits derived from the assets built by public works.

EGS and CCT in a Modelling Setting

To illustrate the interplay of these factors, we looked at two modelling exercises. The first uses a national SAM and a CGE model to simulate the impact of a national public works programme similar to the one proposed in India's 1985 Five Year Plan (Narayana, Parikh and Srinivasan [NPS], 1988). The main conclusion of this study is that if well designed and executed, a large public works programme could significantly reduce poverty and do so at a moderate cost. They also compared the public works programme with a uniform rural transfer of income and concluded in favour of the public works programme. The second exercise reviewed involves a SAM multiplier analysis of the Maharashtra Employment Guarantee Scheme in a poor village (Imai, 2007). The study concludes that the EGS in Maharashtra is the appropriate policy to transfer income and reduce poverty only if assets are adequately built and maintained.

NPS ran a dynamic CGE model to assess the impact of a rural public works programme (Rural Works [RW]) on growth, welfare and the income of the poor. The simulated programme provides 200 person-days per year to every household in the bottom 40 per cent of the income distribution in rural areas. The programme is assumed to operate only in the lean season and it is assumed to have no impact on agriculture wages. The paper presents a number of simulations that shed light on the various aspects of work programmes: their impact in reducing poverty, the importance of creating productive assets, the consequences of the choice of financing and the effect of leakages to the non-poor. The simulations are framed as transfers of food (wheat) in exchange for work, but the modelling perfectly applicable to a cash-for-work programme.

The implementation of the work programme results in poverty reductions that are proportionally larger to the poorer the household is: the calorie intake of the poorest 20 and 40 per cent households increase by 70 and 40 per cent, respectively.[15] If the investment of the work programme is assumed to be as productive as the average investment in the economy, which implies that the creation of standard-quality assets, then running the work programme decreases the average growth rate of GDP (1980–2000) by 0.25 per cent points.[16] However, if the programme creates assets with a productivity that is lower than that of the average investment in the economy, the implementation of the programme reduces the growth rate of GDP by 0.47 per cent points and 0.73 per cent points in the case of zero productivity. These results highlight the importance of ensuring that works are efficiently carried out.[17]

The paper discusses the effect of leakages in the programme. For that effect, the authors run a simulation assuming that half of the benefits leak to the upper 60 per cent of the rural population. The leak has two effects.[18] The first obvious consequence is that leakages weaken the capacity of the programme to reduce poverty. The second not so obvious result is that the leaking of the transfer to the upper part of the rural distribution gives resources to population groups that save and pay taxes, which gives a boost to the economy. The simulation assuming no leakages results in a reduction of 0.25 per cent points in the average growth rate; if the simulation assumes leakages, the growth rate falls by 0.20 per cent points. The model suggests that targeting comes with a cost, but the cost is small. It is thus desirable to increase the targeting efficacy of work programmes.

The result of comparing the RW programme with a uniform transfer of food critically depends on the productivity of the assets produced by the work programme. The simulation assumes a similar budget for both programmes, which in principle would produce a similar impact on GDP. By construction, the works programme is bound to have a better distributive impact than the uniform transfer: the rural poor are much better off in the work programme simulation. The results show that assuming average productivity, the cost of both programmes is quite similar: 0.25 per cent points of the growth rate in the case of the work programme and 0.23 per cent points in the case of the uniform transfer. Moreover, the social welfare associated with the work programme is clearly superior to that of the uniform transfer. The simulations thus show that a work programme that is realistically well designed and implemented—that is, creates assets at average productivity—can reduce poverty at a moderate cost to GDP, and compares favourably with a uniform transfer programme.

Imai (2007) analyses the direct and indirect effects of the EGS in the village of Kanzara in Maharashtra.[19] The paper deals with four major issues. First, it distinguishes between direct and indirect (multiplier) effects of the EGS. Second, it analyses the issue of foregone income.[20] Third, it compares the effects of transferring a given amount of income to households through an EGS and through a uniform transfer. Fourth, it looks at the impact of the assets created by the EGS. Imai concludes that once EGS forgone income and multiplier effects are taken into account, a uniform transfer is a more effective policy to reduce poverty than public works. However, if the EGS creates productive assets and maintains them adequately, the EGS can reduce poverty more effectively than a uniform transfer.[21]

Since the data for the Kanzara village already includes the contribution of the EGS to household income, its impact on the economy is simulated by actually subtracting EGS wage payments. Through this exercise, the model estimates that the EGS is increasing household income by 2.6 per cent and that the landless unsalaried and small farmers and low-income households are among the groups benefiting the most. The estimation of EGS indirect effects suggests that multiplier effects are significant, as the EGS induces an increase in output of 1.3 per cent.

The analysis of foregone income looks at two variants of the EGS wage injection: the first one considers that the EGS wage payments are all an addition to households income, that is, it assumes that people taking EGS were all unemployed or inactive, so forgone income is zero; the second variant assumes that some EGS beneficiaries shifted jobs, which means that their forgone income is positive and should be subtracted from the EGS income flow to households. One difficult issue to quantify is how big is foregone income? To get around this, the model uses an early estimate of average forgone income based on a conditional time allocation model (Datt and Ravallion, 1994; and Ravallion and Datt, 1995). If the EGS is run under the assumption that some beneficiaries left their jobs to join the EGS, that is, allowing for forgone income, then EGS brings to households an additional 1.6 per cent. If the simulation assumes zero forgone income, implementing the EGS increases household income by 2.6 per cent.

The comparison between the EGS and a uniform universal transfer is constructed in such a way that both programmes transfer the same total amount of income to households. This facilitates the analysis of the impact of the transfer.[22] To the extent that the low-income households predominate among the EGS beneficiaries, the EGS has better distribution effects than a uniform transfer to all households or all individuals. But the introduction of foregone income into the analysis changes the picture, for it reduces the net income accruing to precisely those low-income households that participate in the EGS. Imai's simulations show poor households receiving a lower net income from the EGS than what they get from a uniform transfer. His simulations also show that multiplier effects are stronger in the case of a uniform transfer than in the EGS with forgone income.

The issue of the quality of the assets created is handled by assuming that works introduce irrigation in agriculture, which brings the productivity of dry land at par with the productivity of wetlands. The total cost of the EGS in this scenario is composed of wages (two-thirds of the cost) and investment (one-third of the cost). Accounting for the effect of the assets created by the EGS gives a further boost of 0.5 per cent to household income and about 0.4 per cent to village output. Yet, these increases are slightly smaller than the ones delivered by a uniform transfer. The balance is so far in favour of the uniform transfer. However, Imai notes that the benefits of the uniform transfer only last for as long as transfer stays in place while the introduction of irrigation might last for many years, provided it is properly maintained. This last consideration makes the long-term balance comparing an EGS and a uniform transfer to lean in favour of the EGS.

Both the general equilibrium and multiplier analysis comparing cash transfers and public works programmes tend to favour public works programmes, assuming these programmes are well defined and properly implemented. Critical to the good results of a work programme is its ability to self-select the poor population and the capacity to generate productive assets. The modelling exercises reviewed here both lean in favour of work programmes, but only if the investments in these programmes are as productive as the average investment in the economy, in one case, or are able to transform a dry land into an irrigated land.

Neither of the two models fully takes into account the dynamics that an EGS might trigger in local labour markets. One model simply assumes that the work programme has no effect on labour markets, while the other limits the analysis to foregone income assuming wages remain the same. Further research and experimentation is needed to inform policies on the effect of EGS on local wages and the overall effects of increasing the participation of unpaid labour and other household members at working age into the labour force. Among other things, allowing for these transformational changes will reduce the size of foregone income and hence lean the balance in favor of EGS and away from transfers in the short and long term.[23] These are areas, among others, in which more knowledge and experimentation is required.

Implementing Employment Guarantee and Cash Transfers

Good design and efficient implementation are crucial for both EGS and CCTs. But EGS are more demanding. EGS require stronger capacities, have bigger costs than cash transfers and make more decisions on sensitive issues. The definition of the wage rate is a case in point due to the potential negative consequences on labour markets. In addition to this, the integration of a portfolio of projects ready to be drawn from the shelves is equally critical for the success of any guarantee programme. If institutional capacities are not strong, EGS and work programmes can be difficult to implement and their cost would increase. Many public works have proved to be expensive undertakings. According to Nino et al. (2009), work programmes have transferred income to households at a cost of six dollars per dollar transferred. The experience of MGNREGA is encouraging, however. It says that it is possible to massively increase the scale of a guarantee programme and keep its costs in check. According to official MGNREGA data, the programme is transferring income at a cost lower than one dollar per dollar transferred, with most of the cost accounted by construction materials. Adding up all costs, the total programme expenses do not add up to one per cent of GDP.

The implementation of MGNREGA was started in 2006. That year it provided close to one billion person-days of work to 21 million household. By 2009/10, the number of person-days of work tripled to almost 3 billion, while the number of households covered doubled to about 50 million.[24] This is an impressive record. Yet, the programme faces daunting challenges. There are doubts about the quality of the assets it creates. With a strong mandate not to exceed a 60 per cent to 40 per cent labour to other costs ratio and the explicit prohibition of recurring to contractors, to ensure high employment intensity, the durability and adequacy of assets might not be the optimum. Independent evaluations, including mandated social audits, frequently point to deficiencies in the creation of assets. Yet, Drèze and Khera (2008), after acknowledging problems with the quality of assets, suggest that the return on MGNREGA investments may not be inferior to the return on many other investments elsewhere in the economy. Moreover, they argue that it is not necessary to change MGNREGA rules for asset creation and that the quality of assets can greatly be enhanced with affordable, well-directed research and development. Research aiming to improve the productivity of the poor's activities can in turn feed back into the overall development process.

There are questions about the ability of the programme to effectively guarantee employment. The act guarantees a minimum of 100 days per household. As impressive as the expansion of the programme is, MGNREGA is providing an average of 50 days of work per year to households. In some states, average number of work days is very low. Households do not need more work, or are there constrains limiting the provision of jobs? Evaluations suggest that the potential demand for MGNREGA jobs is large and that many people fail to obtain a job because they ignore that they have the right to demand one. This might be the case because local authorities do not make jobs available and because poor people often fall trapped in discrimination or corruption. It is very likely that the programme has not yet reached the needed capacity to effectively guarantee employment and communities have not acquired the necessary empowerment to enforce their rights.

The work facilities—such as the provision of drinking water in worksites, shades for rest periods and crèches where needed—are not always there. Their absence is particularly notorious in the case of crèches, which is a critical deficiency for a programme where females provide half of the workers. Providing work facilities is important because among other things, it reduces the cost of taking the MGNREGA job and makes the programme wage more attractive.

To improve the effectiveness of MGNREGA, it seems like there is need to strengthen administrative, managerial and technical capacities to effectively guarantee employment and efficiently build productive assets. Institutions for community participation, democratic decision making, transparency and anti-corruption need to be created and reinforced. Significant resources, efforts and energies will have to be funneled to their achievement if MGNREGA is to effectively contribute to longer-term poverty reduction and local development.

If the benefits of an EGS were short-term poverty alleviation, one could perhaps look for an alternative lower-cost programme such as a CCT. For the long-term poverty alleviation, a programme such as the MGNREGA is required. The larger cost such a programme entails and the strong administrative and institutional requirements it imposes are worth undertaking. The argument we are trying to make here is that beyond balancing costs and benefits, the costs an EGS such as MGNREGA have are not dead costs, they should be considered instead as part of the critical investments that countries need to do to induce the creation of well-functioning markets for broad-based development.

Well-functioning markets need individuals that can claim their rights and have the necessary capacities to manage production processes and responsibly take part in the decisions concerning community investments. Markets need institutions that foster community engagement, transparency and accountability. Markets need institutions with low tolerance to corruption and rent seeking. The capacities and institutions that an EGS needs for proper operation are also capacities and institutions that markets need to operate efficiently. In most countries, business- and market-development initiatives have not been very effective in reaching rural communities and the poor. Market development has had a tendency to concentrate in large business with little trickle-down effects to rural communities and the markets of the poor. Programmes such as EGS, which build institutions and capacities for development, have the potential to induce greater dynamism to the local markets that are relevant to the poor.

Would countries engaging in the implementation of an EGS be stuck with the programme for many, many years to come? The fortune of an effective EGS is that it endogenously becomes redundant whenever it succeeds in eliminating poverty. When rural or urban dwellers find it advantageous to leave a modest but dignified standard of living for better opportunities and prospects, there is an automatic exit from the programme. When rural or urban residents opt out of the guarantee scheme to work in farms or in factories because wages are better and labour conditions are acceptable, they exit the programme. These two events occur when markets are flourishing and societies are progressing.

Conclusion

The chapter discussed the advantages and limitations of CCT programmes and rural employment-guarantee schemes to achieve sustained reductions in poverty. The chapter looked at some of the conditions that can contribute to the good operation of an EGS to suggest that the good functioning of EGS critically depends on three factors. First, on the level at which wages are set, to avoid distortions in labour markets and large forgone-income deduction to the benefits of the programme. Second, the degree in which benefits of the public works programme leak to the non-poor population. Third, the productivity of the assets public works programmes create.

Drawing from several studies, the chapter attempted a comparison of the two programmes and found that CCTs pose less demands on capacities and institutions and operate with lower administrative costs when compared to EGS. On the other hand, CCTs have more limitations than EGS to achieve longer-term poverty reduction. Indirect and multiplier effects have been an important issue in the discussion of the ability of these programmes to reduce long-term poverty. To shed some light on the issue, the chapter reviewed two modelling exercises that estimate direct and indirect effects of public works programmes and compare them with a uniform transfer programme. The review of these studies suggests that work programmes are an effective policy to reduce poverty and that they can do so at relative small cost of GDP. The comparison with a cash-transfer programme gives nuanced results, but the overall balance leans in favour of work programmes. The positive note on work programmes and its favourable comparison with a uniform transfer depend on the not unreasonable assumption that the programme can build assets with a productivity that is similar to that of other investments in the economy.

The chapter finally addresses the issues of implementation and the high pressure that EGS exerts on national capacities and institutions. Such demands have hitherto suggested that the idea of running a continuous and sufficiently large EGS is unrealistic. The chapter argues that the successful unfolding of India's MGNREGA programme shows that it is feasible to implement an effective EGS to achieve sustainable poverty reduction. That does not mean that MGNREGA has established the factual possibility. The chapter suggests that along the evidence coming from independent evaluations of MGNREGA, the programme still needs to effectively guarantee employment and improve significantly the quality of the assets it creates. Effectively guaranteeing employment and significantly improving the quality of assets might be a costly endeavour. However, the chapter argues that investing to achieve these two goals amounts to investing in long-term development, for the conditions necessary to effectively run an EGS are the same as those needed to build properly functioning markets.

Acknowledgements

We thank the excellent research assistance of Chandan Sapkota. We also thank the comments and suggestions of Ashok K. Pankaj and the participants in a panel in the Ten Years of Chronic Poverty Conference. The views expressed in this chapter do not represent the views of the organisations where the authors work.

Notes

1. The Poor Laws were developed in the medieval period and codified between 1587 and 1598 as a legislation to provide assistance to the poor, and were the first of their kind to provide state assistance to the poor people.
2. The report mainly covers programmes and studies sponsored by the World Bank.
3. The study is based on 167 programmes but data on the length of operation was available for only 125 programmes.
4. On Egypt's employment programme, see Assad (1997).
5. In their review of 37 work programmes spanning over 20 years, Nino et al. (2009) highlight the potential of these programmes to contribute to the reduction of poverty in low-income countries.
6. In the context of developed market economies, these schemes recognise the limitations of market economies to continuously achieve full employment and assign to the government the role of employer of last resort. The New Deal policies of the US designed to confront unemployment rates above 20 per cent are a classical example of government intervention aiming in the direction of guaranteeing employment. In a more articulated way, the post-war Swedish centralised and restrained wage-bargaining process coupled with active labour policies managed to achieve full employment and price stability over a number of years (Kaboub, 2007).
7. Breaking down the monopsony or oligopsony power that permeates the rural and urban labour markets of developing countries, and opening up the possibility of unleashing market process previously trapped by low-wage, low-demand structures (found that policy designs that favor poverty reduction might be more efficient).
8. See, for example, Fieszben and Schady (2009), Sojo (2009).
9. See, for example, the Fieszben and Schady (2009).
10. The literature is vast. See, for example, Fieszben and Schady (2009), McCord (2009) and McCord and Slater (2009), Hailu and Soares (2008), McCord (2009), Lal et al. (2010). See also Bastagli (2009).
11. See Berry's paper to this conference for a discussion of Levy's (2009) assessment of *Oportunidades*.
12. See Hanlon et al. (2010) for a comprehensive review of cash-transfer programmes and their various social and economic impacts.
13. We might also include the already mentioned flexibility of EGS to provide support during shocks in contrast with the relative rigidity of CCTs to cope with shocks. On this last point, see, for example, Soares (2009).
14. Yet, a behavioral conditionality can easily be added to a public works programme, as in the case of the *Jefes* programme in Argentina, see Galaso and Ravallion (2003). On the other, it can also be argued that CCTs should limit themselves to the case in which a behavioral change can actually take place. See de Janvri and Sadoulette (2004).
15. Since the programme does not model changes in employment, the increase in the amount of food, the wage paid, has the simple expected effect of reinforcing, almost lineally, the reduction of poverty.
16. Here we only present the simulations assuming the programme is financed at the expense of investments in other programmes. However, the simulations of the RW include two alternative sources of funds. One assumes the budget of the programme comes entirely from cutting investments in other programmes. A second alternative is to finance the programme by increasing taxes. If the programme is financed through taxes, the average growth rate increases by 0.22 per cent points. If the programme is run at the expense of investments in other programmes, the implementation of rural works reduces the average rate of GDP growth by –0.25 per cent points.
17. Three possibilities are considered regarding investments in rural works: (*a*) no investment failure, that is, RW is as efficient as other investments in the rest of the economy; (*b*) RW fails completely to bring any benefit; (*c*) RW investment is half as efficient as other investments in the economy.
18. The simulation assumes that 50 per cent of the transfers 'leak' to the upper 60 per cent of the distribution.

19. The analysis uses the Kanzara (1984) village SAM that integrates data from the International Crop research Institute for the Semi-arid Tropics (ICRISAT) Village-level Studies (VLS) and data collected by Subramanian (1988). Building on Subramanian and Sadoulet (1990) and Subramanian (1996).
20. The inputted forgone income is based on the estimates of Datt and Ravallion (1994) and Ravallion and Datt (1995).
21. The EGS capacity to reduce poverty can be enhanced by supplementing its self-targeting mechanism with other targeting instruments.
22. This means Imai makes the harmless but unrealistic assumption that the non-wage costs of the EGS are equal to the non-transfer costs of the uniform transfer programme.
23. In an ex ante partial equilibrium analysis of MGNREGA, Murguia and Ravallion (2005) estimate that foregone income might represent about 25 per cent of the wage bill. However, their modelling of workers' participation in MGNREGA grossly underestimates the proportion of jobs that females have actually filled in, suggesting that their estimates of forgone income might be too high, as women tend to work in unpaid activities.
24. Figures are from MGNREGA official website. For a discussion of MGNREGA, see Sharma (2010).

References

Angelucci, M. and G. de Giorgi (2009) Indirect effects of an aid program: How do cash transfers affect ineligibles' consumption? *American Economic Review* 99, No. 1: 486–508.

Assad, Ragui (1997) The effects of public sector hiring and compensation policies on the Egyptian labor market. *World Bank Economic Review* 11:1: 85–118.

Bastagli, Francesca (2009) From social safety net to social policy? The role of conditional cash transfers in welfare state development in Latin America. International Policy Centre for Inclusive Growth Working Paper No. 60.

Basu, Arnab, Nancy H. Chau, Ravi Kanbur (2008) A theory of employment guarantees: Contestability, credibility and distributional concerns. IZA Discussion Papers No. 3002, April.

Datt, Gaurav and Martin Ravallion (1994) Transfer benefits from public works employment: Evidence from rural India. *The Economic Journal* 104: 1346–69.

Devereux, S. and C. Solomon (2006) Employment creation programmes: The international evidence. Issues in employment and poverty. Discussion Paper No. 24, International Labour Office, Geneva.

de Janvri, Alain and Elisabeth Sadoulet (2004) *Conditional cash transfer programs: Are they really magic bullets?* Berkeley: Department of Agricultural and Resource Economics, University of California.

Drèze, Jean and Amartya Sen (1989) *Hunger and public action. Wider studies in development economics.* Oxford: Clarendon Press.

Drèze, Jean and Reethika Khera (2008) The battle for employment guarantee. *Frontline* 26, No. 1.

Fieszbein, A. and N. Schady (2009) *Conditional cash transfers. Reducing present and future poverty.* The World Bank.

Galaso, Emmanuela and Martin Ravallion (2003) Social protection in a crisis: Argentina's plan Jefes y Jefas. Working Paper 3165, World Bank.

Hailu, Degol and Fabio Soares (2008) Cash transfers—Lessons from Africa and Latin America. *Poverty in Focus* No. 15, International Policy Centre for Inclusive Growth.

Hanlon, Joseph, Armando Barrientos and David Hulme (2010) Just give money to the poor. The Development Revolution from the Global South. Kumarian Press.

Imai, Katsushi (2007) Targeting versus universalims: An evaluation of indirect effects of the employment guarantee scheme in India. *Journal of Policy Modeling* 29, No. 1: 99–113.

Kaboub, Fadhel (2007) Employment guarantee programs: A survey of theory and policy experiences. Working Paper 498, The Levy Institute of Brad College.

Lal, Radhika, Steve Miller, Maikel Lieuw-Kie-Song and Daniel Kostzer (2010) Public works and employment programmes: Towards a long-term development approach. Working paper No. 66, International Policy Centre for Inclusive Growth.

Levy, Santiago (2009) *Good intentions, bad outcomes: Social policy, informality, and economic growth in Mexico.* Washington, D.C.: The Brookings Institution.

Manning, Alan (2005) *Monopsony in motion: Imperfect competition in labor markets.* Princeton: Princeton University Press.

McCord, Anna (2009) Cash transfers: Affordability and sustainability. Project Briefing No. 30, Overseas Development Institute.

McCord, Anna and Rachel Slater (2009). *Overview of public works programmes in sub-Saharan Africa.* London: Overseas Development Institute.

Mukherjee, Anindita (1997) Public works programmes: Some issues. *The Indian Journal of Labour Economics* 40, No. 2: 289–306.

Murguia, Rinku and Martin Ravallion (2005) Is a guarantee living wage a good anti-poverty policy? Working paper No. 3640, World Bank.

Narayana N. S. S., Kirit Parikh and T. N. Srinivasan (1988) Rural works programmes in India: Costs and benefits. *Journal of Development Economics* 29: 131–56.

Nino, Carlo del, Kalanidhi Subbarao and Annamaria Milazzo (2009) How to make public works work: A review of the experiences. Social Protection Discussion Paper No. 905, World Bank.

Oya, Carlos (2010) Rural inequality, wage employment and labour market formation in Africa: Historical and micro-level evidence. Integration Policy Department Working Paper 97, International Labour Organisation.

Ravallion, M. and G. Datt (1995) Is targeting through a work requirement efficient? Some evidence for rural India. In *Public spending and the poor theory and evidence*, ed. Dominique Van De Walle and Kimberley Nead, 413–14, chap. 15. Washington, D.C.: The World Bank.

Sharma, Amita (2010) Rights-based legal guarantee as development policy: The Mahatma Gandhi National Rural Employment Guarantee Act. NREGA-UNDP Discussion Paper No. 2.

Soares, F. (2009) Do CCTs minimize the impact of the current economic crisis? One Pager No. 96, International Policy Centre for Inclusive Growth.

Sojo, A. ed. (2009) *El financiamiento de la proteccion social en paises pobres y desguales.* CEPAL.

Subbarao, K., A. Bonnerjee, K. Ezemerari, J. Braithwaite, C. Graham, S. Carvalho and A. Thompson (1997) *Safety net programs and poverty reduction: Lessons from cross-country experience. Directions of development.* The World Bank.

Subramanian, S. (1988) *Production and distribution in a dry-land village economy*, Ph.D. Dissertation, University of California, Berkeley.

——— (1996) Production and distribution in a dry-land village economy. In *Villages economies: The design, estimation, and use of village wide economic models*, ed. J. Edward Taylor and I. Adelman, 59–100, chap. 4. New York: Cambridge University Press.

Subramanian, S. and E. Sadoulet (1990) The transmission of production fluctuations and technical change in a village economy: A social accounting matrix approach, *Economic Development and Cultural Change* 39, No. 1: 131–76.

SECTION III

Working of the MGNREGS

Regional Variations in Implementation and Impact

5

Demand and Delivery Gap

A Case for Strengthening Grass-roots Institutions in Bihar and Jharkhand

Ashok K. Pankaj

I

Introduction

Socio-economic conditions of rural Bihar and Jharkhand are ideal for meeting objectives of the MGNREGS. Both the states are primarily agrarian and rural. In 2001, 90 per cent of the total population of Bihar and 78 per cent of Jharkhand were residing in rural areas, and 82.4 per cent of rural workers in Bihar and 77.8 per cent in Jharkhand were dependent on agriculture. A very high proportion of the rural poulation in both the states are poor: 41.4 per cent of the total and 42.1 per cent of the rural population in Bihar and 40.3 per cent of the total and 46.3 per cent of the rural population in Jharkhand were living below the poverty line in 2004–05 (Government of India, 2009).[1]

Poverty is higher in the SC, ST and (lower) OBC, the traditionally marginalised social groups. In 2004–05, 57.2 per cent of the rural SC, 64 per cent of ST and 37 per cent of OBC against only 26.6 per cent of other (general) caste population in Bihar were living below the poverty line. Similarly, in Jharkhand, 54.1 per cent of the rural SC, 57.5 per cent of ST, 40 per cent of OBC and 36.9 per cent of other (general) castes were living below the poverty line in the same year. Poverty differential across caste groups was higher in the rural area of Bihar than in Jharkhand (61st round of NSSO).

Agriculture is the main source of livelihood of the rural population in both the states. In 2001, out of the total rural workers in Bihar, 82.4 per cent were engaged in agriculture: 31.4 per cent were cultivators and 51 per cent were agricultural labourers. In Jharkhand, 77.8 per cent of the rural workers were engaged in agriculture: 45 per cent were cultivators and 32.8 per cent were agricultural labourers. The proportion of cultivators was relatively higher in Jharkhand, whereas the proportion of agricultural labourers was relatively higher in Bihar (Primary Census Abstract, 2001).

A high proportion of rural workers are casual wage-earners, but even self-employed workers earn a significant part of their income through wages. In 2004–05, in Bihar, 60.2 per cent of rural workers were self-employed in agriculture (small and marginal farmers) and non-agriculture (petty traders), and 37 per cent were casual labourers. Only 2.7 per cent were in regular employment (61st round of NSSO 2004–05). Similarly, in Jharkhand, 71 per cent of rural workers were self-employed in agriculture (marginal and small farmers) and non-agriculture (petty traders), and 24.80 per cent were casual labourers. Only 4.20 per cent were in regular employment. Even among the self-employed in agriculture, there was dependence on the multiple sources of income. For example, in Bihar, a farmer household earned on an average 46.7 per cent of the total income from cultivation, 14.6 per cent from animal husbandry and 27.5 per cent from wages. In Jharkhand, a farmer household earned on an average 41 per cent of the total income from cultivation and 45 per cent from wages.

While the majority of the rural population in both the states is dependent on agriculture and allied sectors, the share of agriculture in the gross state domestic product (GSDP) is quite low. In 2008–09, agriculture and allied sectors (primary sector) contributed 26 per cent of the GSDP of Bihar and 20 per cent of Jharkhand. This means that the average per capita income of an agricultural worker is quite low and much lower than that of a secondary and tertiary sector worker. Moreover, while there has been a marginal decline in the percentage of population engaged in agriculture, the share of agriculture in the GSDP has fallen sharply over the years, thereby indicating declining productivity of agricultural workers.

The fundamentals of agriculture are quite weak in both the states: agriculture is low in intensity, yield and productivity. The average size of holding in Bihar is very low. About 84 per cent of the farmers have less than one hectare of operational holding. In 2006–07, the net sown area and total cropped area as percentage of total geographical area was 60.16 and 81.97, respectively, but the area sown with more than one crop was only 21.81 per cent. The average yield per hectare of rice and wheat, the two major crops of the state, is almost half of that of the agriculturally developed states (IHD, 2009a; Government of Bihar, 2010).

In Jharkhand, the overall cultivable land as percentage of total geographical area is 52.20 per cent. But, net sown area as percentage of total geographical area is 22.11 per cent and the area sown with more than one crop is 14.92 per cent of the net sown area and merely 3.3 per cent of the total geographical area. The average size of the holding in the state is 1.58 hectares, which is higher than the average size of holding in Bihar. However, like Bihar, 80 per cent of the land holding is less than two hectares. Agriculture is mainly rain-fed, as only 8.9 per cent of the net sown area is irrigated. The productivity, that is, yield per hectare is also low (IHD, 2009b).

While the socio-economic conditions of the rural population suggest that there is a huge demand for (wage) employment in both the states (which is not reflected in the official statistics of the number of households demanding employment under the MGNREGS),[2] the implementation of the scheme suggests a wide gap between the actual demand and delivery. Because of the low level of literacy, lack of awareness (procedural and substantial), absence of social mobilisation and weak presence of civil-society organisations, people are unable to articulate their demand effectively (Bhatia and Drèze, 2006; Drèze, 2008; Louis, 2006; Pankaj, 2008a; Reddy et al., 2011). On the other hand, grass-roots institutions are weak enough to create sufficient jobs to meet the demand. Like the previous and the erstwhile (government-sponsored) employment generation programmes, the MGNREGS remains largely supply driven, and this remains a fundamental challenge of implementation in both the states.

Nevertheless, there are indications that the scheme has been able to create some impacts on the livelihood conditions of the MGNREGS workers' households. The impacts are primarily due to the additional earning opportunity and availability of job in the lean season. There are also reports of reduction in the indebtedness of and distress and seasonal migration from these households. As against the household-level impacts, the larger social and economic community-level impacts are yet to be registered in a significant manner, although huge potentialities remain to be exploited there. Both the states have low levels of rural infrastructure and community assets; the multiplier effects of the creation of community assets could be significant.

The next part of this chapter gives an overview of the implementation of the MGNREGS with respect to demand and delivery gap in these two states. This has been explained in terms of overall coverage—number of households provided employment, average person-days per household and the number of households completing 100 days of employment, etc. Part three explains the reasons for the low level of implementation, and analyses it in the context of structural weaknesses of the local institutions. In spite of the low level of implementation, there are clear indications of household- and community-level impacts of the scheme in both the states. Because of the very low income base of these households, even small additional earning makes a difference to their livelihood conditions. These individual- and community-level impacts have been explained in chapter four. The final part argues that the MGNREGS provides a big opportunity for both the states to transform the rural livelihood conditions and local economy. However, the weak local institutions (PRIs) must be strengthened to tap this. Bihar has a very progressive Panchayat Raj Act 2006, and Jharkhand has recently elected PRIs for the first time after the 73rd Constitutional Amendment Act.[3] Proactive state can also fill the critical gap till the local institutions become stronger.

II

A large number of districts—23 out of 38 districts in Bihar[4] and 20 out of 23 districts in Jharkhand—were covered in the first phase of MGNREGS implementation, that is, 2 February 2006. With the extension of the coverage to all the remaining districts in the two states on 1 April 2007, 90 per cent of the total population of Bihar and 78 per cent of Jharkhand have now the protection of 100 days of guaranteed employment. The coverage of the total population is one of the highest in these two states. But notwithstanding high coverage and high level of demand for employment, the overall implementation including employment generation remains very low in both the states.

Demand for Employment under MGNREGS

There is a huge demand for MGNREGS employment in both the states. A 2008 study of six districts of Bihar and three districts of Jharkhand shows the level of demand (Pankaj 2008a). About 95 per cent of the rural households in Bihar were aware of the employment-guarantee scheme and out of that, 76.32 per cent were interested in seeking MGNREGS wage employment. The demand was a little higher in Jharkhand where 96.2 per cent of the rural households were aware of the scheme and out of that, 90 per cent were also interested in getting employment under the MGNREGS. The intensity of demand was higher among the landless and marginal landholder SC, ST and OBC households (Table 5.1). The demand was low from the upper castes, although some of them were also poor.

The demand was in inverse correlation with the size of the landholding in both the states: it declined with the increase in the size of the holding. But while in Bihar, the demand was concentrated among the landless and nearly landless households, and declined substantially among the households owning more than 2.5 acres of land, in Jharkhand, it was more widespread across land categories (see Table 5.1). Because of the very low irrigation facilities (about nine per cent of the cultivable area) and hilly terrain, the intensity of demand was higher even among the small and medium farmers in Jharkhand.

Table 5.1: Percentage of Households Interested in Seeking Wage Employment under the MGNREGS in Bihar and Jharkhand in 2008

	Bihar		*Jharkhand*	
Social Categories	*Total Aware HHs (in %)*	*Interested as Percentage of Aware HHs*	*Total Aware HHs (in %)*	*Interested as Percentage of Aware HHs*
Caste				
Upper Caste	86.52	54.83	98.71	64.05
OBC-I*	94.31	72.15	89.41	83.55
OBC-II**	92.94	65.16	98.88	83.83
SC	97.94	93.41	95.24	98.13
ST	100	100	96.9	93.73
Others	100	92.31	100	100
Land				
Landless	97.24	87.67	97.51	93.71
>0.5 acres	92.53	76.75	96.82	92.15
0.5 to 1 acres	91.37	56.03	94.44	91.02
1 to 2.5 acres	89.30	39.70	97.08	89.7
2.5 to 5 acres	86.67	12.82	91.37	74.8
5 to 10 acres	85.94	14.55	96.55	57.14
Above 10 acres	63.16	16.67	100.00	00.00
Total	**94.49**	**76.32**	**96.2**	**90.02**

Source: Table adapted from Pankaj (2008a: 73, 79, 80).
Notes: * OBC-I means lower OBCs, generally service castes.
** OBC-II means upper OBCs that include yadav, koeris, kumris, etc.

Because of high level of poverty and lack of employment opportunities, the demand was uniformly high across the districts. Another factor for high level of demand under the MGNREGS was the prevalence of low wage rate in both the agriculture and non-agriculture sectors (the wage rate is depressed also because of high supply of labour and low demand for it) and relatively high wage rate under the

MGNREGS. This, to some extent, explains uniformly high demand across developed, less developed and backward districts of these two states. If the demand was high in Kishanganj, Supaul and Gaya, the backward districts of Bihar, it was equally high in Rohtas, a developed district of the state (Pankaj, 2008a: 72). It was the same situation in Jharkhand (Pankaj, 2008a: 78).

Households Provided Employment

Households Provided Employment as Percentage of Interested Households

While there is a high demand for employment under the MGNREGS, the level of job creation remained low in both the states. For example, in a study of 18 villages of Bihar, 72.1 per cent of the rural households were interested in seeking wage employment under the MGNREGS, but only 25.2 per cent were provided employment in the year 2007–08 (Pankaj, 2008a: 71). The coverage was relatively better in Jharkhand. In a survey of 12 villages, 89.6 per cent of the rural households were interested in getting wage employment, but only 52.5 per cent were provided employment (Pankaj, 2008a: 79). The incompleteness of the various stages of the process of getting job under the MGNREGS has been shown through Figure 5.1 in Bihar and Figure 5.2 in Jharkhand.

Figure 5.1: Status of Job Card Registration and Distribution and Job provided as Percentage of Total Rural Households in Bihar

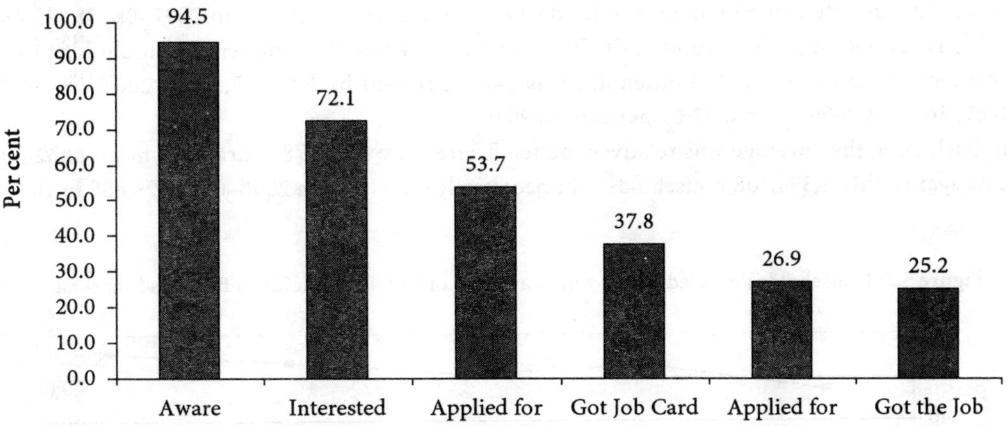

Source: Pankaj (2008a: 71).

Employment Provided as Ratio of BPL Households

In both the states, the number of households provided employment as the ratio of BPL households has been low in all the five years of implementation since 2006 (see Figure 5.3). For example, as per the 2007 BPL survey, there were 11,340,990 rural BPL households in Bihar. On the other hand, the number

Figure 5.2: Status of Job Card Registration and Distribution and Job Provided as Percentage of Total Rural Households in Jharkhand

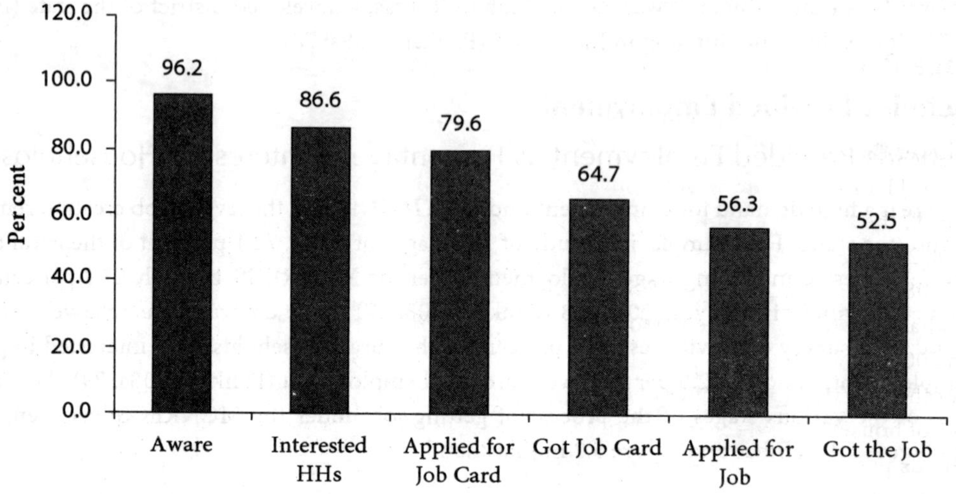

Source: Pankaj (2008a: 79)

of households provided employment was 1,6 88,899 in 2006–07, 38, 59,630 in 2007–08, 38, 22,484 in 2008–09, 41, 27,330 in 2009–10, and 1,550,708 in 2010–11. Thus, the number of households provided employment as the ratio of BPL households was 14.89 per cent in 2006–07, 34 in 2007–08, 33.70 in 2008–09, 36.39 in 2009–10 and 13.67 per cent in 2010–11.

In Jharkhand, the coverage was relatively better. There were 2,554,780 rural BPL households in the state. As against this, 1,394,108 households (not necessarily only BPL) in 2006–07, 1,679,868 in 2007–08,

Figure 5.3: Households Provided Employment as Ratio of BPL Households in Bihar and Jharkhand

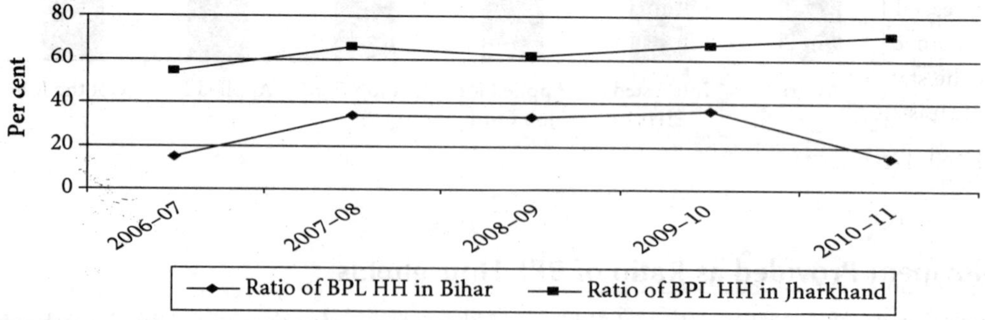

Source: MGNREGA data from the website of the Ministry of Rural Development, Government of India and the number of BPL households from the respective Rural Development Department of the Government of Bihar and Jharkhand.

1,576,348 in 2008–09 and 1,702,599, 2009–10 and 1,751,434 were provided employment. As ratio of BPL households, it was 54.5 per cent in 2006–07, 65.8 in 2007–08, 61.7 in 2008–09, 66.6 in 2009–10 and 68.55 in 2010–11.

Average Person-days and Households Completed 100 Days

Apart from the low coverage of households, average person-days of employment provided was also low. It was lower than the national average in all the five years of implementation, that is, between 2006–07 and 2010–11 in Bihar, and in four out of five years in between 2006 and 2011 in Jharkhand. At all-India level, the average person-days of employment generation was 43, 42, 48, 54 and 47 in 2006–07, 2007–08, 2008–09, 2009–10 and 2010–11, respectively. In Bihar, it was only 16 days in 2006–07, 23 days in 2007–08, 26 days in 2008–09, 27.55 days in 2009–10 and 35 days in 2010–11. It was relatively better in Jharkhand with the average person-days of 37 in 2006–07, 46 in 2007–08, 47.58 in 2008–09, 49.58 days in 2009–10 and 42.80 in 2010–11.

In both the states, the number of households which completed 100 days remained low. In Bihar, the number of households which completed 100 days of employment constituted only 1.37 per cent of the households provided employment in 2007–08, 2.68 per cent in 2008–09, 4.76 in per cent in 2009–10 and 5.02 per cent in 2010–11. In Jharkhand, it was 3 per cent in 2007–08, 6.05 per cent in 2008–09, 7.82 per cent in 2009–10 and 6.98 per cent in 2010–11. In Bihar, the performance of most of the districts remained poor in this respect; in Jharkhand, it was relatively better in a few districts. But while only a little number of households completed 100 days of employment, a large number of these households were interested in working for more than even 100 days, the official limit (Pankaj, 2008a). In other words, the problem seems to be more on the supply side.

Share of SCs, STs and Women in Total Person-days in Bihar

Table 5.2 gives an overview of employment generated in Bihar between 2006–07 and 2010–11. While the share of SCs was higher, the share of STs and women was lower. The share of SC was higher than the national average in all the five years. On the other hand, the share of women was lower than the national average in all the five years, although it has shown an increasing trend over the years. For example, it has increased from 17.38 per cent in 2006–07 to 26.62 per cent in 2007–08, 30.02 per cent in 2008–09 and remained at 30 in 2009–10. It has marginally declined to 28.56 per cent in 2010–11. This is much below the state average of some better performing states like Rajasthan, Tamil Nadu, Andhra Pradesh and HP. It is also less than the stipulated 33 per cent share of women workers. The low share of ST was because of their very low population (about one per cent of the total) in the state after the separation of Jharkhand.

The relatively high share of SCs in Bihar is because of high intensity of demand for manual wage employment among the SC households, as most of them are landless or nearly landless, and are dependent on casual labour in agriculture and non-agriculture. The high share of 'others' is due to the inclusion of OBCs in 'others'. The socio-economic conditions of lower OBCs in Bihar are only marginally better than those of the SCs. Like the SCs, they are also mostly wage-earners and are economically vulnerable.

Table 5.2: Employment Generation under MGNREGS in Bihar (2006–07 to 2010–11)

Some Indicators of Employment Provided	*2006–07*	*2007–08*	*2008–09*	*2009–10*	*2010–11*
Total number of HHs provided employment	1,688,899	3,859,630	3,822,484	4,127,330	1,550,708
HHs provided employment as percentage of rural HHs (19,874,783)	8.50	19.42	19.23	20.77	7.80
HHs provided employment as percentage of rural BPL HHs (11,340,990)	14.89	34.03	33.71	36.39	13.67
HHs completed 100 days as percentage of HHs provided employment	0.0	1.37	2.68	4.76	5.02
Average person-days per HH	16	23	26	27.55	35.16
Percentage share of SC in total person-days	47.08	45.66	43.86	45.3	26.37
Percentage share of ST in total person-days	3.21	2.46	4.58	2.16	1.69
Percentage share of women in total person-days	17.38	26.62	30.02	30.04	28.56

Source: MGNREGA-related data downloaded from the Ministry of Rural Development, Government of India website nrega.nic.in, and BPL population figure from Department of Rural Development, Government of Bihar.

Share of SCs, STs and Women in Jharkhand

In Jharkhand, the STs, followed by SCs, are the major beneficiaries of the job guarantee scheme (see Table 5.3). The share of ST was higher than the national average in all the five years. The high share

Table 5.3: Employment Generation under MGNREGS in Jharkhand (2006–07 to 2010–11)

Some Indicators of Employment Provided	*2006–07*	*2007–08*	*2008–09*	*2009–10*	*2010–11*
Total number of HHs provided employment	1,394,109	1,679,868	1,576,348	1,702,599	1,807,665
HHs provided employment as Percentage of rural HHs (3,736,524)	37.31	44.96	42.19	45.57	48.38
HHs provided employment as Percentage of rural BPL HHs (2,554,780)	54.57	65.75	61.70	66.64	70.76
HHs completed 100 days as percentage of HHs provided employment	0.36	3.0	6.05	7.82	6.98
Average person-days per HH	37	46	47.58	49.58	42.8
Percentage share of SC in total person-days	23.48	20.74	19.03	16.04	12.14
Percentage share of ST in total person-days	40.29	41.65	40.51	42.99	43.16
Percentage share of women in total person-days	39.48	27.17	28.51	34.25	32.14

Source: MGNREGA-related data downloaded from the Ministry of Rural Development, Government of India website Nrega.nic.in, and BPL population figure from the Department of Rural Development, Government of Jharkhand.

of the STs was also because of their high share in the total population of the state and high demand for wage employment among the ST population.

The low participation of women in Jharkhand is against the trend in other states with high SC, ST population. It has been found that participation of women has been high in the districts and states with high concentration of tribal population. Jharkhand defies this general trend as participation of women has been less than the national average in all the five years. For example, the share of women in total person-days was 39.47 per cent in 2006–07, 27 per cent in 2007–08, 28.51 per cent in 2008–09, 34.25 in 2009–10 and 32.14 in 2010–11.

The low participation of women in Bihar and Jharkhand has social and economic contexts, which can be defined in terms of low level of human and gender development, social and cultural restrictions and low mobilisation of women (Pankaj and Tankha, 2009). But apart from the above sociocultural reasons, the low level of employment generation was also a factor. Because of limited number of employment days provided, it was being worked mostly by male members. In states with high participation of women, the average person-days is also higher than the national average.

Unemployment Allowance[5]

Based on the level of demand and actual realisation of person-days of employment, one can argue that there should have been huge number of cases of the payment of unemployment allowance in both the states. However, like in other states, the payment of unemployment allowance was rare in both the states.[6] The non-payment of unemployment allowance is due to two factors. One is lack of procedural awareness on the part of jobseekers, and another is reluctance on the part of officials to pay unemployment allowance, even if there are such cases. Further, in the absence of the issuing of receipt of the application for job, the jobseekers have no documentary proof to claim unemployment allowance. The reluctance on the part of officials is primarily due to the punitive provision of the act. The payment of unemployment allowance has to be followed by a suitable explanation as to why the official failed to provide job on demand, and instead paid unemployment allowance. Also, the state government has to bear the cost of unemployment allowance, while the cost of wages is borne by the Centre. Risk-averse bureaucracy (officials) considers it as a negative remark on their performance and, therefore, tries to avoid it. Some of the applicants are also unscrupulous, as some households with a reasonably good economic and social status have managed to obtain job cards in an attempt to use them for claiming unemployment allowance and other possible benefits in future. This has made the implementing agencies wary of giving unemployment allowances even in genuine cases.[7]

Payment of Minimum Wages

The payment of minimum wages was closer to the prescribed minimum and higher than the prevailing rural wages in both the states. A survey of 23 worksites across six districts in Bihar (see Table 5.4) and 14 worksites across three districts in Jharkhand (see Table 5.5) shows that the actual wage payment was closer to, but less than, the prescribed minimum wages in most of the cases. For example, in Bihar, the average actual wage payment was 68 rupees against the MGNREGS minimum wage of 82 rupees in 2008. Similarly, in Jharkhand, the actual average wage payment was 78 rupees against the MGNREGS minimum wage of 86.40 rupees.

Table 5.4: Payment of Minimum Wages to MGNREGS Workers in Bihar in November–December, 2008

	Actual Average Wage Payment at (23) Surveyed Worksites in 2008					*Minimum Wage Under MGNREGS in 2008**
Districts	*(1)*	*(2)*	*(3)*	*(4)*	*(5)*	
Gaya	68	50	50	–	–	82
Kishanganj	60	81	60	–	–	82
Nalanda	81	60	60	–	–	82
Rohtas	68	60	60	75	81	82
Samastipur	75	60	81	71	–	82
Supaul	81	81	81	81	77	82
State average	–	–	**68**	–	–	**82**

Source: Adapted from Pankaj (2008a).
Note: *It has increased to ₹89 in 2009, ₹114 in 2010 and ₹120 in 2011.

Table 5.5: Payment of Minimum Wages to MGNREGS Workers in Jharkhand in November–December, 2008

	Actual Average Wage Payment at (14) Surveyed Worksites in 2008					*Minimum Wage under MGNREGS in 2008**
Districts	*(1)*	*(2)*	*(3)*	*(4)*	*(5)*	
East Singhbhum	77	77	81	77	81	86.40
Pakur	81	81	81	65	–	86.40
Palamu	100	86	77	76	86	86.40
State average	–	–	**78**	–	–	**86.40**

Source: Adapted from Pankaj (2008a).
Note: *It has increased to ₹92 in 2009, ₹111 in 2010 and ₹120 in 2011.

The trend was found uniformly across the districts in both the states. Out of the three worksites surveyed in Gaya district of Bihar, the actual wage payment was 68 rupees in one case and 50 rupees in the other two cases. In Kishanganj, it was 81 rupees in one case, which was only one rupee less than the prescribed minimum and 60 rupees in other two cases. The wage payment was most satisfactory in Supaul; in four out of five worksites surveyed, the actual wage payment was 81 rupees, only one rupee less than the prescribed minimum. In East Singhbhum, Pakur and Palamu districts of Jharkhand, the actual wage payment was only a little less than the prescribed minimum in most of the cases surveyed.

Wage payment under MGNREGS was better than in many states, but not because of greater enforcement of the minimum wage provisions. On the contrary, it was happening because of weak enforcement of the provisions apart from other reasons. First, in most of the cases, the payment was still based on daily wage system and the procedure of measurement and payment as per the schedule of rate (SOR) was not followed strictly. Out of the 23 worksites surveyed in Bihar, piece-rate-based wage payment was followed only in 10 cases and the time rate was followed in the rest of the 13 cases. In Jharkhand, on the other hand, the piece rate was followed in 50 per cent of the cases and the time rate in the rest 50 per cent. Second, the intensity of the working class (Ultra-Left) movement has some impacts on wage payment. Some of the officials in the Naxal-affected areas reported that they were made to pay minimum wages, even though workers had not earned it as per the SOR. With the introduction of the account payment, the situation has improved further. Third, the revision of the SOR[8] in 2008 in both the states was also helpful. The revised SOR of Bihar was also a progressive measure in terms of prescribing different tasks for male and female workers for the same wage rate.

This, however, does not mean that there were no leakages of the wages. For example, when the actual wages paid to the workers were cross-checked with the muster rolls and job cards, the entries were different. In almost all the cases examined, the job cards and muster rolls mentioned the payment of prescribed minimum wages. In some cases, the workers were working without job cards and their names were not found in the muster rolls. Muster rolls and job cards were generally not available at the worksites. When asked for them, some of these workers could produce the job cards while others could not. Muster rolls were found to be incomplete in most of the cases.

Timely Payment of Wages

The act prescribes that wages shall be paid on weekly basis, but not later than 15 days from the date of completion of the work. Table 5.6 shows the periodicity of wage payment in both the states. In Bihar, about two-thirds of the beneficiary households were paid weekly, and one-fifth daily. About 7 per cent

Table 5.6: Frequency of Wage Payment in Bihar and Jharkhand in November–December, 2008 (percentage of households)

Districts	*Daily*	*Weekly*	*Fortnightly*	*Monthly*	*After a Month*	*Yet to be Paid*	*Others*
			1. Bihar				
Gaya	11.54	75.00	13.46	00	00	00	00
Kishanganj	8.47	91.53	00	00	00	00	00
Nalanda	27.27	58.18	3.64	1.82	00	7.27	1.82
Rohtas	11.86	81.36	6.78	00	00	00	00
Samastipur	22.03	59.32	6.78	11.86	00	00	00
Supaul	38.00	44.00	14.00	2.00	00	00	2.00
Total	**19.46**	**68.86**	**7.19**	**2.69**	**00**	**1.2**	**0.6**
			2. Jharkhand				
East Singhbhum	6.90	35.63	20.69	29.89	5.75	00	1.15
Pakur	7.50	87.50	1.25	1.25	00	00	2.50
Palamu	29.63	45.68	19.75	3.70	1.23	00	00
Total	**14.52**	**55.65**	**14.11**	**12.1**	**2.42**	**00**	**1.21**

Source: Adapted from Pankaj (2008a).

of these households were paid fortnightly and 3 per cent were paid even monthly. In Jharkhand, 56 per cent of the beneficiary households were paid weekly, 15 per cent daily, 14 per cent fortnightly, 12 per cent monthly and 2.5 per cent after more than a month. Because of the practice of daily wage and cash payment in a large number of cases, the wage payment as per the prescribed provision was better in both the states.

It has been learnt that with the introduction of account payment of the wage, it has got further delayed in both the states. One of the main reasons for this is the low administrative abilities of the local institutions to process the wage payment that has become more challenging after the introduction of the account payment. The delay in wage payment has been found in most other states except for Andhra Pradesh that has made use of modern technology for facilitating timely payment of wages. The Andhra model is worth emulating for other states as well.

There are some other difficulties as well. One is that the implementing agents at the grass-roots level are not very receptive to the idea of payment through the bank or post office accounts.[9] Two, there is a practical difficulty due to the poor density of post office and bank accounts in rural areas. For example, in one block of Pakur district of Jharkhand, there was only one bank available. Similarly, the situation was no better in case of the post office. This creates a genuine problem in this regard. In some of the cases, the workers have to walk for 15 km to receive their wages as a bank or a post office was not available in the vicinity. Sometimes, even after reaching the post office or bank, they were returned, as money had not been transferred in their accounts. Delayed wage payment remains a major difficulty and payment through account has increased the delay, as officials are not able to complete the process of wage transfer in the account on time.

Although there is a punitive provision for the delayed wage payment, like many other provisions, it remains un-enforced. However, in Khunti district of Jharkhand, after mobilisation of the workers by civil-society actors, the administration was made to pay compensation at the rate of ₹3,000 per worker. In Latehar and Dhanbad districts of Jharkhand also, workers were given compensation for the delayed wage payment. Seventy-six workers in Manika block of Latehar district and 40 workers in Topchanchi block of Dhanbad district were paid compensation at the rate of ₹3,000 per worker. This was more of a symbolic victory of workers, as delayed payment continues to be there.

Worksite Facilities

There is a provision of four worksite facilities, which are parts of workers' entitlements. However, these facilities remained mostly missing from most of the worksites. Out of the 23 worksites surveyed in Bihar, drinking water facility was available in 12 cases, first aid in 10 cases and the facilities for shelter and crèches each in only one case. In Jharkhand, out of the 14 worksites surveyed, drinking water was available in seven, first aid in eight, shelter in five and crèche in only one case.

It appears that the implementing agencies/agents have not taken the issue of providing worksite facilities seriously, as providing these facilities does not require much effort. The implementing agencies/agents were not sensitive to the issue of providing facilities for the workers at the worksites. Workers were neither fully aware of these rights, nor were they willing (capable) to raise these issues. The provision of worksite facilities remain mostly on paper in other states as well.

III

Explaining Low Level of Implementation

The MGNREGS is a big test of the capacity of local institutions (PRIs) and bureaucracy as well. Both the states have weak local institutions. Bihar has a very progressive legislation, that is, Bihar Panchayat Raj Act 2006. But this Act was not followed by adequate devolution of power, functions, functionaries and funds to these institutions. There are organic weaknesses as well: the gram sabha has not emerged as a vibrant collective decision-making body. While the PRIs are weak, the lack of adequate staff, training and capacity building, infrastructure and, above all, 15 years of negligence have emasculated the local bureaucracy. The Nitish Kumar–led JD-U-BJP government in the state has taken some initiatives in improving the efficiency of local bureaucracy. But it would take years of systematic efforts and investment to improve so.

Jharkhand was implementing the scheme with the help of bureaucracy, as formal PRIs were not constituted in the state till 2010. As a result of that, the implementation was bureaucracy-centric and largely centralised. The state has elected the formal PRIs in 2010. But it will take some years of systematic devolution of power, functions and finances to these bodies to emerge as vibrant and effective grassroots delivery institutions. Until then, bureaucracy will continue to dominate the scene. In addition to that, the state has been quagmired in political instability, unstable governments and corruption since its formation as a separate state in 2000.

Apart from the generic problem of weak local institutions, there are MGNREGS-specific issues and problems. The level of awareness among citizens is critical to the realisation of entitlement in a demand-based approach. There was a high level of general awareness among the people about the MGNREGS—a government programme that provides 100 days of employment. However, most of these people were unaware of other provisions like how and where to apply, unemployment allowance, work within five kilometres of the radius of the residence, worksite- and wage-related provisions, etc.

Lack of Quality Awareness

In Bihar, 91.34 per cent of the respondents were aware of the fact that the MGNREGS is a government programme to provide 100 days of employment. But 22.89 per cent were aware of minimum wages, 10.72 per cent about crèches and other facilities, 35.88 per cent about distance provision, 2.47 per cent about the planning process and 27.42 per cent about the role of the GP (Figure 5.4). In Jharkhand, 93.45 per cent of the respondents were aware of the fact that the MGNREGS is a government programme to provide 100 days of employment, but only 33.90 per cent knew about minimum wages, 7.98 per cent about worksite facilities, 35.04 per cent about distance provision, 7.98 per cent about the role of the GP and 2.85 per cent about some other provisions of the scheme (Figure 5.5).

Inactive Gram Sabha

In both the states, the selection of the work was being done generally outside the gram sabha. It was much more problematic in Jharkhand than in Bihar. While in Bihar, the work was usually being selected

Figure 5.4: Level of Quality Awareness in Bihar in 2008

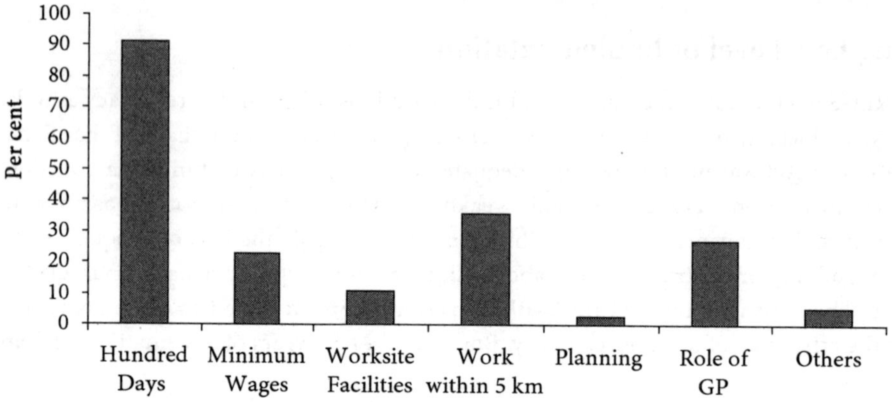

Source: Pankaj (2008a).

Figure 5.5: Level of Quality Awareness in Jharkhand in 2008

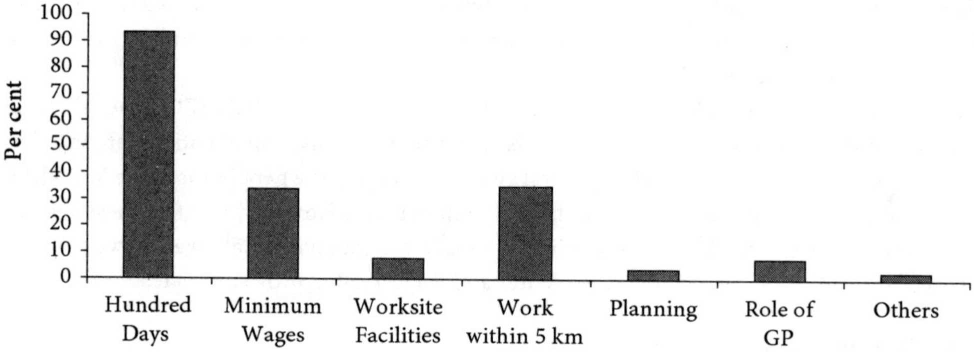

Source: Pankaj (2008a).

and approved without the meeting of the gram sabha, in the latter (Jharkhand), the bureaucracy was playing the main role in the selection and implementation of the work. The selection of the work was being imposed from the above: sometimes it was selected by the Block Development Officer (BDO), sometimes by the District Programme Coordinator (DPC) and sometimes even by the state Rural Development Department.

In Bihar, the GP head (*Mukhia*) in consultation with the MGNREGS programme officer (PO) and a few of his supporters generally selected the work and sent for administrative and technical approval as a work formally selected by the gram sabha. Some of the PRI representatives also have a tendency to accord benefits to the people who are supposedly their voters. For instance, while selecting rural connectivity, they give preference first to the area where their voters reside. This affects the utility of the work, as it is not selected based on overall community interests.

In Jharkhand, the selection of the work was more centralised. In the absence of formal PRIs, the gram sabha was not playing any meaningful role. The more important issue is that of the selection of implementing agencies and agents, which is again much more problematic in Jharkhand than in Bihar. In the absence of formal PRIs in Jharkhand, the line departments were implementing 50 per cent of the works supposed to be done by the Panchayat Samiti and Zila Parishad. The rest 50 per cent of the works, which were to be implemented by the GP, were being given to the individuals who were reportedly chosen by the gram sabha. However, the implementing agents were generally chosen by the BDOs who were functioning as POs in connivance with some important villagers. Even the gram sabha meeting was called; it was merely a ritual.

Social audit has been found of significant impact in improving delivery of the MGNREGS (Galab and Revathi, 2012). In the absence of a vibrant gram sabha, working of vigilance and social monitoring remained ineffective in both the states. The mandatory social audit is almost absent in both the states. Some initiatives by some agents of civil society in certain pockets of the states are quite inadequate to substitute for institutionalised social audit, an important provision to enforce transparency and accountability. Both the states were also found lacking in terms of assets management. There was hardly any plan for the maintenance and use of the assets by the community.

Low Capacity of Local Bureaucracy

In Bihar, the acute shortage of staff at the level of BDOs, POs, panchayat secretary and junior engineers hampered the implementation process in the initial years. To meet the shortage of staff and technical personnel, the state government initiated a process of recruitment in the year 2007 and completed it by 2008. However, the newly recruited staff needed training, orientation and proper facilities to work on. The government organised some training and capacity-building programme for the newly elected PRI representatives and newly appointed officials like the POs, but this was quite inadequate and not very fruitful. There is structural problem as well. The state has limited institutional capacity to impart training to such a large number of functionaries. The Bihar State Institute of Rural Development was not able to provide training at such a large scale and panchayat raj training institutes in the state were practically defunct.

The shortage of staff hampered the implementation process in Jharkhand as well. For instance, one panchayat secretary was in charge of two GPs; one junior engineer had the responsibility of all the public works under one block. Jharkhand also initiated the process of recruitment, but the process remained slow and tardy. In addition, uniform pattern of recruitment was not followed across the state. The newly created state has established a number of new districts and blocks, which were still in the process of being firmly established as an administrative unit.

Bihar also lost the initial years of implementation. Like most other states, the scheme was implemented without much preparation in the commencement year, that is, 2006. In addition, the state announced panchayat elections in 2006 that were staggered into 10 phases, spread over two months. The election process commenced in February 2006, and was completed only in July 2006. The process began in terms of determination of reservation and accordingly determination of reserved constituencies because of the new legislation that had introduced a new formula of vertical reservation of 50 per cent of the seats for women and 20 per cent of seats for the lower OBC. Newly elected representatives, most of them were first-timers, took some time to settle down and understand the process. In the process, the first half of 2006 was lost. This includes the lean season (summer of 2006) when the demand for employment is high among the casual agricultural workers and taking (public works) is easy. Most of the earth-related and other works become feasible only after the harvesting of Rabi crops. Again, during the summer of 2007, the entire local-level administrative machinery and PRI representatives were preoccupied in the preparation of rectified BPL list in the state.

Lack of Vibrant Civil-society Organisations

The civil society organisations are weak in both the states. Unlike in Rajasthan where these organisations were instrumental in mobilisation of the people and playing very active role since the commencement of the programme, there has been hardly such efforts by civil-society organisations in these two states. On the one hand, there were little efforts on the part of civil-society organisations, and on the other, the state government did not play a proactive role, unlike in Andhra Pradesh. Of late, the Nitish Kumar–led JD-U-BJP combined government has started talking of the MGNREGS. Some civil society organisations have also started taking up the issue of MGNREGS implementation. Nonetheless, initial years are lost.

IV

Impact Assessment

Implementation and impacts are interrelated under MGNREGS. The low implementation leads to the low level of impacts and vice versa. In both the states, the impacts of the scheme have been found at a low level because of the low level of job creation, income transfer to the poor and creation of private and community assets. Nevertheless, there are some noticeable impacts at the household level and also at the community level.

The household-level impact is essentially an impact of additional income. However, this impact of additional income depends to a great extent on the economic conditions of the households. The impact is more in case of the household with low income level and less in case of the household with more income level. Because of the low income level and low economic conditions of the MGNREGS workers' households in Bihar and Jharkhand, the income effects of MGNREGS earning is sharply noticeable, and so are the income-related effects like reduction in distress seasonal migration and indebtedness. But well-targeting of the household is the first major condition of this.

Well-targeting through Self-targeting

The household-level impacts depend on targeting of the appropriate sections of the population. Although it is a universal programme, yet if the poor households remain outside the reach of the programme, the impacts will be limited. Poor targeting of beneficiaries has been one of the major difficulties with most of the government programmes. The self-targeting and universal approach under MGNREGS is supposed to address this problem in a better manner. Table 5.7 shows the level of appropriateness of self-targeting under the programme.

Table 5.7: Caste-, Land- and Occupation-wise Beneficiary Households (in per cent)

Categories	*Bihar*	*Jharkhand*
Caste		
Upper caste	5.76	4.29
OBC-I	15.13	7.43
OBC-II	21.45	11.83
SC	53.39	27.85
ST	3.99	48.17
Others	0.28	0.42
Land		
Landless	80.41	29.95
>0.5 acres	13.65	28.38
0.5 to 1 acres	3.16	20.63
1 to 2.5 acres	2.04	13.72
2.5 to 5 acres	0.37	6.18
5 to 10 acres	0.37	1.15
Above 10 acres	0.00	0.00
Occupation		
Self-employed in agriculture	5.01	21.88
Casual labourers in agriculture	77.99	40.21
Casual labourers in non-agriculture	15.60	34.45
Self-employed in small business	1.02	2.20
Self-employed in large business/salaried	0.09	0.73
Others	0.28	0.52
Total	**100.00**	**100.00**

Source: Pankaj (2008a: 121).

Social and economic profile of MGNREGS workers' households in Bihar suggests that the most vulnerable segments of population have benefited the most from the scheme (Pankaj, 2008a). For instance, SC and OBC (ST constitutes only one per cent of the state population after separation of Jharkhand) constituted about 90 per cent of the MGNREGS workers' households. In terms of land category, more than 94 per cent of the households were either landless or nearly landless (those owning >0.5 acres). Similarly, casual labourers in agriculture and non-agriculture households constituted about 95 per cent of the beneficiaries. What emerges from this is that more than 90 per cent of the beneficiaries in Bihar belonged to SC and OBC, who are invariably landless or nearly landless, and most of them are casual labourers in agriculture and non-agriculture.

Similarly, in Jharkhand, most of the MGNREGS workers' households belonged to the most marginalised and vulnerable sections. However, the beneficiary groups in Jharkhand were more diverse than they were in Bihar. Although as in Bihar, in Jharkhand too, ST, SC and OBC constituted about 95 per cent of the beneficiaries, yet in terms of the land category, more than 90 per cent of the beneficiaries belonged to the landless households or households owning up to 2.5 acres of land. Also, the number of beneficiary households decreased consistently with the increase in the size of the landholding. Another interesting departure from Bihar is that while in Bihar, the number of beneficiaries from the self-employed in agriculture was insignificant, this category constituted more than one-fifth of the beneficiaries in Jharkhand. Thus, in both Bihar and Jharkhand, the most disadvantaged economic and social groups have benefited the most from this scheme.

Income Generation

The average annual income of a beneficiary household was quite low in both Bihar and Jharkhand. While the average annual income of a beneficiary household was ₹19,707 in Bihar, it was ₹23,414 in Jharkhand. Most of the beneficiaries earned a major part of their income from their labour in agriculture and non-agriculture in Bihar, and through labour in non-agriculture or through own agriculture in Jharkhand (Pankaj, 2008a; Reddy et al., 2010).

Because of the low income base of these households, the earning from MGNREGS, in spite of low amount, contributed significantly to the annual income of these households. It contributed about 8 per cent of the total income of a beneficiary household in Bihar and 2.41 per cent of the total annual income of a beneficiary household in Jharkhand.

The contribution of the MGNREGA income to the total income of the beneficiary households varied across caste and land categories. It contributed more to the income of the households of SC, OBC-I landless and marginal landholders. The relatively high contribution of MGNREGS income to the total annual income of the SC, OBC-I category and the landless and nearly landless households is primarily because of: (*a*) low annual income base of these households and (*b*) relatively higher number of days worked by these households.

While the earning from the MGNREGS contributed maximum to the income of the SC and landless households in Bihar, it contributed so to the income of ST and marginal landholders in Jharkhand (see Table 5.8). This is also because the average number of person-days of the ST and marginal landholders was greater than that of the other categories. A comparison between Bihar, a relatively low-income state, and Jharkhand, which has higher income levels than that of Bihar, shows that the share of MGNREGS income to the total annual income of a worker household was higher in the former.

Expenditure out of MGNREGS Earnings

Even though the earnings from MGNREGA are not very substantial, yet the manner in which the beneficiary uses this amount is important in understanding the role of the MGNREGA in meeting critical necessities of these households. Most of the MGNREGS workers' households were found spending the largest proportion of their income on items of basic necessities. In both Bihar and Jharkhand, MGNREGS workers' households spent a substantial part of their earnings on food and daily consumption items first

Table 5.8: Share of MGNREGS Earning in the Total Annual Income of a Beneficiary Household

	MGNREGA Income as Percentage of the Total Annual Income of the Households	
Categories	*Bihar*	*Jharkhand*
Caste		
Upper caste	3.29	0.27
OBC-I	5.14	1.55
OBC-II	4.22	2.36
SC	11.74	0.97
ST	2.74	3.91
Land		
Landless	8.90	0.89
Marginal	7.81	3.18
Small	2.31	2.02
Medium	–	1.39
Total	**8.37**	**2.41**

Source: Adapted from Pankaj (2008a: 125–26).

and after that, on health care, social ceremonies and education of the children. Debt repayment also formed a component of the expenditure met from the MGNREGA earnings.

MGNREGS workers in Bihar used substantial part of their wages on food and other daily consumption items followed by expenditure on medical care and social ceremonies (see Figure 5.6). Expenditure on household durables like utensils, cots, quilts, etc., and on the education of the children formed

Figure 5.6: Percentage Share of Items of Expenditure out of MGNREGS Income of a Worker in Bihar (2007–08)

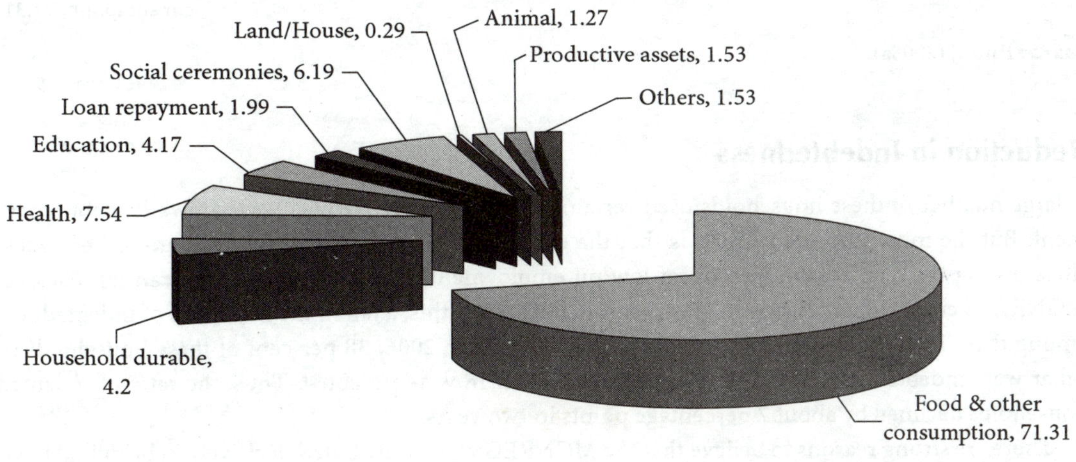

Source: Pankaj (2008a).

another important component of the expenditure met out of the MGNREGA earnings. An important trend is variation in items of expenditure across land categories. Although the landless, marginal and small landholders among the beneficiaries spent a substantial share on food and other daily consumption items, yet the marginal and small landholders spent relatively more on health and social ceremonies than what their landless counterparts did.

A similar trend was found in Jharkhand. Most of these workers spent substantial proportion on food and other daily consumption items followed by expenditure on health care, social ceremonies and purchase of durable assets (see Figure 5.7). A little variation across caste and land categories was found in Jharkhand as well. OBC-I beneficiaries spent relatively more on household durables and OBC-II on social ceremonies. Similarly, small landholders spent relatively more on health care and marginal landholders on health care and social ceremonies.

Figure 5.7: Percentage Share of Items of Expenditure out of MGNREGS Income of a Worker in Jharkhand (2007–08)

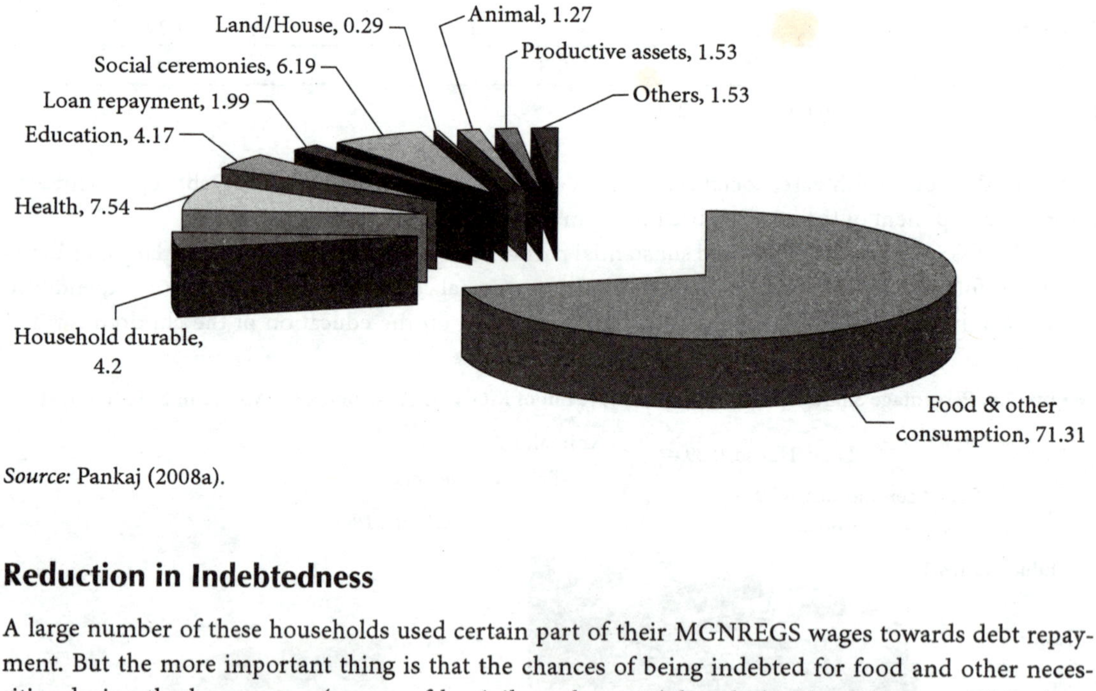

Source: Pankaj (2008a).

Reduction in Indebtedness

A large number of these households used certain part of their MGNREGS wages towards debt repayment. But the more important thing is that the chances of being indebted for food and other necessities during the lean season (season of low/nil employment) has declined, as they can fall back on MGNREGS employment during the lean season. Because of this, a fall in the incidence of indebtedness among these households was noticed. For instance, while in 2006, 38 per cent of these households in Bihar were indebted, in 2008, only 31.37 per cent of them were indebted. Thus, the ratio of indebted households declined by about 7 percentage points in two years.

There are strong reasons to believe that the MGNREGS has contributed decisively in bringing down this indebtedness. Most of these households take loans for a short period and for meeting expenditures on food, medicine, clothes, social ceremonies, etc. Moreover, the average amount of money they borrow is not very high. Further, most of them borrow money during the lean season. MGNREGS, by providing income and employment during the lean season, cushions these households against borrowing. Second, the trend in expenditure out of MGNREGA income suggests that most of these households are spending on items like food and other items of daily consumption, medicine and health care and on social ceremonies, for which they normally borrow money.

The most important aspect, however, is the potential of the scheme to rid these households of their entire debt burden. For example, the average amount of debt of an MGNREGS worker household was 2,771 rupees in Bihar and 1,241 rupees in Jharkhand. Assuming that an MGNREGS worker spends entire wages on debt repayment and works for a minimum of 20–30 days and gets payment of minimum wages (presently 114 in Bihar and 111 in Jharkhand), the entire debt can be retired in just one year.

Impact on Migration

Two factors drive migration: first is prospects for better income and employment opportunity, and the second is distress conditions at home. However, migration of the landless, unskilled and casual wage-earners is generally caused by distressed conditions at home. The migration from rural Bihar and Jharkhand appears to be the case of a distress seasonal migration wherein one member from the household migrates to earn for the entire family during the lean season.

Post MGNREGS, there is a reduction in migration from these households. For instance, in Bihar, about 35 per cent of the MGNREGS workers' households reported migration in 2006. This figure came down to 23 per cent in 2008, a decline of about 12 percentage points in two years, which is significant. Reduction in immigration across caste and land categories has been shown in Table 5.9.

This decline could have been much more substantial, but for the low person-days of employment generation and difficulties related to the payment of minimum wages. People continued to migrate, as they were not able to get upto 100 days of employment and there was uncertainty of getting it under MGNREGS. In some villages of Gaya district of Bihar, the migrant families had stopped going outside

Table 5.9: Reduction in Migration from MGNREGS Workers' Households in Bihar (between 2006 and 2008)

	2006	*2008*
Caste		
OBC-I	55.56	31.43
OBC-II	45.83	17.65
SC	25.37	19.15
ST	30.00	n.a.
Land Category		
Landless	32.74	19.23
Marginal	40.82	33.33
Small	33.33	33.33
Total	**34.73**	**22.55**

Source: Pankaj (2008a).

after getting wage employment under the MGNREGS in 2006. In expectation of getting employment, they stayed at home in 2007, but did not get any. Because of this uncertainty, they preferred to migrate in 2008 than to wait and not get employment here.

The minimum wage under the MGNREGS is another factor. The minimum wage and even the actual wage under MGNREGS are competitive with the average wage of a migrant worker at destination. Moreover, the saving of an MGNREGS worker is greater than that of a migrant worker, as migrant worker has to spend part of wages on living, transportation and other costs. On the other hand, the MGNREGS workers have the advantage of working from home.

Migration has a social cost as well. The migrant workers feel alienated at the place of destination. There are cases of different types of exploitation of migrant workers as well. More recently, local residents in states like Maharashtra and Assam have raised their protest against the migrant workers of Bihar and Jharkhand, and sometimes these protests have taken violent turns. Violence against the migrant workers puts their lives at risk. Discussions with the migrant workers revealed that except for a lucky few, most of them have had some unpleasant experiences as migrants.

Impact at the Macro Level

While individual household-level impacts are largely results of income transfer, the community-level (macro) effects are results of a number of factors including procedural aspects and creation of community assets. The community-level impacts include impact of the community assets (rural infrastructure), changes in the local wages and their impact on the labour market and local (agrarian) economy. Invigorating the PRIs, strengthening of the decentralised development process and increased transparency and accountability in public works programme are some other larger social impacts of the scheme, generated through the procedure of the implementation.

Community Assets

The community-level impacts are not very sharp. Nonetheless, there are some important trends and developments. The most obvious impact is the number of community assets created in both the states. Apart from the number, the nature of the works undertaken in these two states is also important. In spite of local biasness in the selection of the work, the types of works undertaken suggest that they fill some critical gaps in rural infrastructure. For example, works of water conservation and harvesting, irrigation and rural connectivity constitute the largest number of works undertaken in both the states with low irrigated areas and low density of roads. There is a huge amount of uncultivated but cultivable land lying in both the states. Land development under the MGNREGS will increase the overall cultivated land. The scope for land development is greater in Jharkhand than in Bihar.

The nature of the works undertaken in various districts of these two states suggests that the MGNREGA works can contribute significantly to the creation of the much-needed rural infrastructure in both the states. For example, most of the districts of north Bihar face the problem of rural connectivity as frequent floods wash away the roads. Most of the districts of north Bihar have given preference to works of rural connectivity. On the other hand, the districts south of the Ganges including those in Jharkhand, which were earlier parts of Bihar, have given preference to works of water conservation and harvesting, as a large part of these districts remain un-irrigated, and face the problem of water shortage.

A number of works constructed under the MGNREGS show that these assets have proved to be of immense use. Although concrete evidence in terms of the contribution of these assets is not available at this stage, yet what is learnt through observation is that the schemes of water conservation and harvesting and rural connectivity are proving to be very useful in both the states. Some of the un-irrigated areas became irrigated now. For instance, some check dams were constructed on the low edge of the hill in Littipara block of Pakur district. This has helped in the recharging of water in the downhill area. People were able to grow crop at the foothill that was uncultivated earlier.

The types of works undertaken fill critical infrastructure gap. Nonetheless, there are problems related to the location of the work, maintenance and upkeep of the assets created and lateral use of these assets. For example, in the Littipara block of Pakur district (Jharkhand), a very grand project was conceived and designed. The idea was to construct a check dam at the gulley point of the hillock and to arrest the water there for two purposes—one was to use it for recharging of the ground water at downhill, and another was to revive the dead distributory canal down the hillock. More interestingly, the idea was to use free boulders and stones available on the hillock to arrest the water at the gulley. However, the first rain of the season washed the check dam, as it was built without using appropriate materials. In such a case, none of the purposes was served, as it neither led to recharging of the groundwater, nor did it revive the old distributory canal.

In Palamu district of Jharkhand, a big pond was constructed at a cost of about 800,000 rupees on the farmland of a villager, who had 40 acres of land. But the location of the pond was not ideal for irrigation. It was learnt that the owner of the pond would use it for fishing purposes. This raises the issue of subsidising the better-off families through the MGNREGS.

The quality of the assets was generally found to be poor, though not necessarily because of the low cost or material–labour component. In most of the cases, sufficient technical supervision was lacking, and workers were left to execute the works on their own. The problem of technical supervision was more acute wherein construction was left entirely on the beneficiary like in case of *jalkund* (a pond of 15 × 15 metre) without providing any technical support.

Labour Market and Local Economy

There would be significant impacts on labour market and local and agrarian economy in both the states. For instance, in Bihar, the MGNREGS wage has increased from 68 rupees in 2006 to 120 rupees in 2011. Similar is the increase in Jharkhand. Such a sharp increase in MGNREGS wage will create upward pressure on the local wages, which continues to be depressed due to excess supply of labour in the economy. This will have some positive effects as well. One, the rural economy will reach to a high level of income equilibrium that continues to be trapped at a low-level equilibrium. Two, the high wage cost would generate pressure for mechanisation of agriculture that is mainly driven by man and animal power in both the states. The high wage cost would also affect cropping pattern, agricultural practices and, more important, diversification of agriculture also.

Another impact could be found in terms of equalisation of wages of male and female workers, which is a major challenge of rural labour market. Although under the MGNREGS, male and female workers were getting equal wages in both the states, yet it would not translate easily in other works of the rural areas. In states with high participation of women, the trend in terms of equalisation of wages of male and female workers has been noticed. However, low participation of women in both the states and problem of plenty would remain as a hurdle for equalisation of wages of male and female workers in both the states.

Decentralised Development

Strengthening of the participatory development process at the grass-roots level is a major contribution of MGNREGS. Apart from the provisions like selection of the work through gram sabha, social audit, vigilance committee, there are material aspects of strengthening of the local institutions (PRIs) in these two states. For example, most of the GPs in Bihar and Jharkhand have no office space and no building of their own. There is a provision of the construction of Rajiv Gandhi Samudayik Bhavan under the MGNREGS. All the GPs in Bihar and Jharkhand can take advantage of the provision and construct GP bhavan. This will help in institutionalising offices of GPs in both the states. Once the office infrastructure is created, it will be easy for the people to meet their GP head and Panchayat secretaries who remain elusive, as people do not have any fixed place to meet them.

Before MGNREGS, the GPs in these two states had hardly any fund, except for small transfer under the recommendations of the 12th Finance Commission. In the absence of its own revenue and limited fund under the 12th Finance Commission, GPs were unable to make its own plan and were reduced to an adjunct public works department. The MGNREGS gives free money to the GPs and allows them to plan the works as per the requirement. Also, the flow of fund under the MGNREGS is linked to the planning and execution of the work by the GPs.

The process of selecting work through the gram sabha meeting, social monitoring and social auditing are still weak. Nonetheless, there are indications that gram sabha meetings have started taking place, people's participation including that of women has increased and questions are being raised and discussed in the gram sabha meeting (Pankaj and Tankha, 2009; Reddy et al., 2010). In some places, social audit, with the help of civil-society organisations, has also started taking place. The vigilance committee remains mostly inactive, but aware citizens were found taking help of the right to information act to bring leakages in public domain. All these developments hold significant potentialities to transform the character of grass-roots participatory development.

Social Empowerment

Some other community-level impacts remain weak primarily because of low level of implementation. An important issue is women's participation that remains low in both the states. There are studies that suggest that high participation of women and their independent earning under MGNREGS have significant liberating/empowerment effects on the rural women (Khera and Nayak, 2009; Pankaj and Tankha, 2010). These effects have been realised at both the individual and community levels, although the former has been stronger than the latter.

The availability of 100 days of guaranteed employment can also loosen the traditional feudal–worker relations that still operate in some pockets of these two states. The poor SC, ST landless households have got the opportunities to liberate them from the traditional relations which were reinforced by their economic dependence.

V

Conclusion

It appears that even after five years of the MGNREGS, its implementation has not really taken off in both the states. The overall implementation remains at a low level and because of this, impacts too remain at a low level. Both the states have performed poorly in terms of overall coverage of the total rural and BPL population, average person-days of employment, number of households completing 100 days and creation of useful community assets. There are process-related weaknesses as well. The participatory process like the selection of the work through the gram sabha, social auditing and local-level vigilance remain weak. The low participation of women has not been able to trigger empowerment and other labour-market effects to the desirable extent.

Nevertheless, there are evidences that show that the scheme holds tremendous potentialities to transform the livelihood conditions in the rural areas. First, in spite of universal character, it has reached the most needy households. The majority of beneficiaries are from the lowest socio-economic segments. The income–consumption effects of the additional income are noteworthy and so are its effects on reduction in indebtedness and migration. The filling of some critical infrastructure gap and selection of the work as per the local needs would be helpful in meeting critical infrastructure gap. Generation of additional irrigation capacity, increased rural connectivity and land-development works would trigger many other economic effects with long-term impacts on the local rural economy.

Among the major weaknesses of the programme is gap in the demand and supply sides, as the scheme remains supply-driven against the objectives of the act. The low realisation of person-days has limited the scope of greater income–consumption and household-level effects. The non-adherence to the participatory process of the selection of the work, its social monitoring and supervision have resulted in weak decentralisation effects.

There are demand-and-supply-side problems. The low level of literacy, lack of qualitative awareness and weak mobilisation by civil-society organisations are constraints on demand articulation. This demand-side gap has been filled by active civil-society organisations in Rajasthan and by a proactive state in Andhra Pradesh. On the supply side, low delivery capacity of local institutions—of both PRIs and local bureaucracy—remains a fundamental problem.

The road ahead lies in the strengthening of the local institutions—both PRIs and bureaucracy. The effects of progressive Bihar Panchyat Raj Act 2006 have not been realised to the possible extent because of little follow-up in terms of devolution of power, functions, functionaries and finances (Pankaj, 2008b). Jharkhand was implementing the scheme without the formal PRIs. With the formation of the PRIs in the state in 2010, a major institutional gap has been filled. However, systematic efforts towards strengthening of these institutions would be required to make them viable local bodies of decentralised development.

The efficiencies of local bureaucracy were hampered because of the shortage of staff, infrastructure and low investment in their training and capacity building. With the completion of the recruitment of

PO, Rozgar Sevak and other staff for the MGNREGS, the minimum manpower is now available. But the administrative efficiencies have to be improved at other levels as well. Bihar has taken some bold initiatives in toning up of the administration. However, these efforts have not been able to generate much impact at the lower-level bureaucracy. Jharkhand has been in continual political trouble since its formation as a new state in 2000. Political instability and corruption take a toll on the efficiencies of bureaucracy.

Acknowledgement

This chapter draws on the author's study, 'Processes, Institutions, and Mechanisms of Implementation of MGNREGA: Impact Assessment of Bihar and Jharkhand', sponsored by the Ministry of Rural Development, Government of India and UNDP.

Notes

1. As per the Tendulkar Committee Report that used a different methodology, 55.70 per cent of rural and 54.40 per cent of total population in Bihar and 51.60 of rural and 45.30 per cent of total population in Jharkhand were living below the poverty line in 2004–05. See *Report of the Expert Group to Review the Methodology for Estimation of Poverty* (Governemnt of India, 2009).
2. The official figure shows that almost cent per cent of the households which demanded employment were provided with the same in both the states. This is, however, misleading. In both the states, there is a serious procedural lacuna, as the households demanding employment are not provided with a receipt of an acknowledgement. The problem is acute because of the high level of illiteracy and inability of these people to submit written applications. The lack of awareness about the procedure to be followed for applying for the job is another issue. In states like Rajasthan, vigilant and active civil-society organisations have played a critical role in mobilisation of the jobseekers and facilitated application processes, but this was not the case in Bihar and Jharkhand.
3. The formation of PRIs in Jharkhand got embroiled in litigation on the issue of reservation for the tribal population. However, elections were held in 2010 to constitute formal PRIs in the state.
4. The Government of Bihar extended the coverage of the MGNREGS to all the remaining 15 districts of the state through its own resources on 2 February 2006. This gave Bihar the unique distinction of covering cent per cent of the total rural population of the state in the very first phase of implementation.
5. The act provides for the payment of unemployment allowance in case of the inability of the implementing agencies to provide jobs within 15 days of the applicant household demanding so. There is also a punitive provision that the implementing officials will be responsible for the payment of unemployment allowance, except under certain circumstances. Moreover, the unemployment allowance will be paid by the state government and not by the Centre.
6. However, in 2010, about 800 workers in Araria district of Bihar were paid unemployment allowance after a long-drawn struggle.
7. In Nalanda district, there was a flood due to heavy rainfall in the rainy season of 2007. All the *Kacha* works were suspended and a large part of the district remained waterlogged for a considerable period and hence, it was difficult for the implementing agencies to provide job on demand. Taking advantage of the difficulties, many people, who had never came for job, started demanding it and realising the inability of the officials to provide so, started claiming unemployment allowance. It is also to be noted that in the Noorsarai block of the district, unprecedented crowd had come to the BDO office to get the job card; although later on,

construction of a pond just a little away from the block office was left incomplete, as people were not reporting for job.

8. The revised SOR in Bihar is a progressive provision. It prescribes different tasks for male and female workers under the MGNREGA. It will certainly help women workers in earning minimum wages. The SOR, as it was in December 2008, is shown below.

Soil Category	*Male (CFT)**	*Female (CFT)*	*Wages*
Soft	80	68	89
Semi-hard	77	63	89
Hard	73	60	89

* CFT = cubic feet

The Government of Jharkhand has revised the wage rate based on the time and motion study conducted by the Birla Institute of Technology, Mesra (Ranchi). See the notification Department of Rural Development, Government of Jharkhand, Ref. No: 4-548-NREGA/2008 No. 6873122-10–08. The wage rate is given below.

Soil Category	*Task (CFT*)*	*Wages*
Soft	73	90
Hard	54	90
Very hard	44	90

* CFT with prescribed lead and lifting.

9. An interesting thing about the payment through bank and post office accounts is that implementing agents are not comfortable with the payment through bank and post office accounts. A number of officials told in a complaining manner that payment through accounts creates difficulties for the workers. However, not a single worker told that he or she has difficulty in getting the payment. In fact, in Pakur district, some workers were found walking 15 to 20 km to get their wages from the post office and bank. The non-availability of bank and post office at a suitable distance and their inflexible working hours definitely create hardship for the workers. Nevertheless, they are happy with the system.

References

Bhatia, Bela and Jean Drèze (2006) Employment guarantee in Jharkhand: Ground realities. *Economic and Political Weekly* 41, No. 29: 3198–202.

Drèze, Jean (2008) Ship without rudder? *Hindu*, 19 July.

Galab, S. and Revathi, E. (2012) MGNREGS in Andhra Pradesh: Examining the role of state-enabled institutions. In *Right to Work and rural india: Working of the Mahatma Gandhi National Rural Employment Guarantee Scheme (MGNREGS)*, ed. Ashok K. Pankaj. New Delhi: SAGE.

Government of Bihar (2010) *Towards Accelerated Agricultural Development in Bihar*. Report of the Steering Group on the Vision of Agriculture Development in Bihar, Department of Agriculture, Government of Bihar.

Government of India (2006) *Level and Pattern of Consumer Expenditure, 2004 -2005, NSS 61st Round (July 2004–June 2005)*. NSS Report No. 508(61/1.0)/1), National Sample Survey Organisation, Ministry of Statistics and Programme Implementation, New Delhi.

——— (2009) *Report of the Expert Group to Review the Methodology for Estimation of Poverty*, November 2009, Planning Commission, New Delhi.

IHD (2009a) *Food security atlas of rural Bihar*. Delhi: IHD and World Food Programme and Institute for Human Development.

——— (2009b) *Food security atlas of rural Jharkhand*. Delhi: IHD and World Food Programme and Institute for Human Development.

Khera, Reetika and Nandini Nayak (2009) Women Workers and Perceptions of the National Rural Employment Guarantee Act. *Economic and Political Weekly* 44, No. 43: 49–57.

Louis, Prakash (2006) Birth pangs in Bihar. *Economic and Political Weekly* 41, No. 48: 4946–47.

Pankaj, Ashok K. (2008a) *Processes, institutions and mechanisms of implementation of NREGA: Impact assessment of Bihar and Jharkhand*. Delhi: Institute for Human Development.

——— (2008b) Meeting social deficits through legislation: Bihar Panchayat Raj Act 2006. *Journal of Social Sciences* 10, No. 2: 273–84.

Pankaj, Ashok K. and Rukmini Tankha (2009) *Women's Empowerment through Guaranteed Employment*. Delhi: Institute for Human Development.

——— (2010) Empowerment effects of the NREGS on women workers: A study in four states. *Economic and Political Weekly* 44, No. 30, (24 July): 45–55.

Primary Census Abstract (2001) Office of the Registrar General, Government of India.

Reddy, D. N., C. Upendranadh, R. Tankha and A. N. Sharma (2011) *Institutions and Innovations in the Implementation Process of the Mahatma Gandhi National Rural Employment Guarantee Scheme in India*. CSP Research Report 09. Brighton: IDS.

6

Working of the Employment Guarantee Scheme in Rajasthan

Some Grass-roots Experiences

Surjit Singh, Varsha Joshi and K. N. Joshi

I

Introduction

India has experimented with land-, assets-, income- and employment-based anti-poverty measures with various levels of success and failures since the early 1970s. The sheer unavailability of huge surplus land for distribution and increasing population pressure make land-based strategy unviable (Singh and Sagar, 2004). Even if we manage to distribute a minimum size of holding to all the landless poor, the small holding does not generate sufficient income for the household to ensure minimum income security. The assets- and welfare-oriented anti-poverty programmes have generally been marred by the targeting inefficiency, leakages and corruption. Public works–based income- and employment-generation programme has proved more effective. The role of public works–based employment-generation programme has been well accepted (Gaiha, 1997; Lipton, 1998; Nayyar, 2002). The MGNREGS is a new approach to the erstwhile employment programme; instead of targeting at removing poverty, it aims at providing minimum income security that might lead to poverty reduction.

The socio-economic conditions of rural population in Rajasthan make it an ideal state for such programme. Rajasthan has been running public works-based drought-relief programme frequently for years in various districts (southern Rajasthan) of the state. Because of the extreme economic vulnerability of rural population, there is a massive demand for wage employment in the state, at least in the drought-prone southern parts. Low irrigated area, largely seasonal and rain-fed agriculture and lack of employment opportunities in non-farm sectors compel rural population to migrate in large numbers in search of livelihood.

The Rajasthan Context

Rajasthan has been in attention for the implementation of the MGNREGS from the very beginning. The state has led from the front in the formation of the act, and even before the act was formulated, civil society organisations in southern Rajasthan had been running right-to-work movement for years. Their active involvement in the policy formulation of the MGNREGS and, subsequently, their efforts in the mobilisation of the civil society for the realisation of the right to work made Rajasthan a leading state in implementation of the act. Apart from realising about 30–40 per cent of the total MGNREGS budget of the Centre, the state has been outstanding in ensuring high participation of women. This is more interesting, as the state forms part of the larger cultural belt of Hindi heartland, characterised by low human development, social conservatism and slow pace of modernisation.

In the above context, this chapter examines the implementation of the scheme, and also attempts to assess its impact on the rural society and economy of Rajasthan. For this purpose, this chapter addresses the issues of implementation and impacts. The important issues addressed in this chapter include availability of work within 15 days of demand; work made available within five km of the village; payment of wages (minimum wage of ₹73 in 2008 and increased to ₹100 in 2009) within 15 days of the completion of the work; payment of unemployment allowance in case of failure to provide work within 15 days of demand; role of the gram sabha; gender discrimination in allocating work and wage payment and scope for unionisation of the workers. In terms of impact, this chapter analyses the impact of the scheme on individual beneficiaries, migration, women's participation and its larger social impacts; social audit and its impact on the quality of the work, quality of the assets created, the level of awareness about the entitlements. Apart from that, this chapter also examines implementation of transparency and accountability mechanisms, availability of worksite facilities and other provisions of the act and guidelines.

This chapter is based on the study of five districts, namely, Dungarpur, Jhalawar, Banswara, Jalore and Karauli (Joshi, Singh and Joshi, 2008); all the five districts are first-phase districts. A total of 3,293 households selected from 660 works (five workers on an average per work) were interviewed in November–December 2008. The types of work included all the then permissible eight category works.

The next section provides a brief description of implementation status in all the five districts. Section three explains impacts of the scheme and section four describes the administrative set-up that has been implementing the scheme in the state. And in the final section, some conclusions have been drawn.

II

Implementation Status and Issues

In 2007–08, the study period, about 8.40 lakh households demanded work and 8.45 lakh households were provided employment in the selected five districts (see Table 6.1). The number of households provided employment exceeded because some households were asked by the implementing agencies to join the work, although this is against the norms and guidelines. A total of 581.25 lakh person-days of employment were generated, and Banswara, Jhalawar and Dungarpur led in employment generation. The share of women was the highest in Jalore (80.12 per cent) and the lowest in (59.28 per cent) in Jhalawar. The share of ST in total person-days was the highest in Banswara and the share of the SCs was the highest in Jalore (see Table 6.2).

Table 6.1: District-wise Job Creation in Jhalawar, Banswara, Dungarpur, Jalore and Karauli Districts of Rajasthan under MGNREGS in 2007–08

Districts	*Employment Demanded (HH, lakh)*	*Employment Provided (HH, lakh)*	*Person-days (lakh)*
Jhalawar	1.36308	1.40708	80.99
Banswara	2.15294	2.15294	115.24
Dungarpur	2.09270	2.09270	181.55
Jalore	1.23055	1.23003	81.23
Karauli	1.56511	1.56511	122.24
Total	**8.40438**	**8.44786**	**581.25**

Source: www.nrega.nic.in

Table 6.2: District-wise Social Category-wise Employment Provided in Rajasthan in 2007–08

	SCs		*STs*		*Women*		*Others*	
Districts	*Average Person-days*	*% Share*	*Average Person-days*	*% Share*	*Average Person-days*	*% Share*	*Average Person-days*	*% Share*
Jhalawar	25.45	31.42	13.46	16.61	48.02	59.28	42.09	51.97
Banswara	5.40	4.69	101.62	88.19	78.97	68.53	8.22	7.13
Dungarpur	11.52	6.35	145.56	80.18	133.79	73.69	4.47	13.48
Jalore	30.98	38.14	11.77	14.49	65.08	80.12	38.48	47.37
Karauli	37.75	30.88	37.09	30.34	78.17	63.95	47.40	38.78

Source: www.nrega.nic.in

The Issues Related to Job Card

Who Owns the Job Card

The job card distribution seems to be largely non-discriminatory across caste and religious groups. In all the five districts surveyed, most of the households, irrespective of BPL or above poverty level (APL) categories, were having a job card, although initially the 2002 BPL list was made the basis for job card distribution. In some villages, 2002 voters' list was also used for this purpose. This, however, left those households who were neither listed in the BPL list nor in the voter list, but needed employment.

People generally approached the sarpanch (head of the gram panchayat), mate and *sachiv* for the job card. Some of the respondents mentioned that they had paid money to get a job card, although most had paid ₹2 to ₹60 for the photographs that are pasted on the job card.[1] In village Karji of Bagidora panchayat samiti in Banswara, all job cardholders paid ₹25 for getting the job cards. The panchayat samiti, in turn, gave them a receipt in the name of *Shiksha Upkar* (education sub-tax).[2]

The job card was generally distributed household wise. However, there were cases of individuals also having separate job cards. This was more often the case with those who were locally powerful and influential. In a few cases, the names of women were not mentioned in the job card. At least three such cases were found. In Banswara and Dungarpur districts, the names of women were generally included in the job card. In Punjpur GP of Dungarpur, widows were also having a job card. The job cards are made for the family and they carry the name of the head of the household. However, there were examples where sons within a joint family had separate cards. This was amongst the 'influential families of the village'. Officials and sarpanch found the official definition of household—people residing together and having common kitchen—difficult in operationalising for household-based job card and other provisions. This is also unfavourable to widows and joint families. It was also found that quite a few households (5.41 per cent) of the sample possessed more than one job card. The proportion of such households was about 8 per cent in Dungarpur, Karauli and Jhalawar districts.

Social Categories

In Masana village of Dungarpur district, 136 families (Ramgarh, 94 and Masana, 42) had not applied for the work and 400 families had not got job cards. They were mostly upper-caste households—Jains, Brahmins and Rajputs.[3] Interestingly, some Brahmin families (in Ramgarh) had got job cards, though they never applied for work. They found the manual work under the MGNREGS derogatory of their social status. Still they had applied for the job card, as it might serve some other purposes like getting a ration card in the future. In Todabhim and Nadauti, panchayat samitis of Karauli district, it is largely the Jatavs followed by the Meenas and Gujjars who predominantly owned job cards. In Banswara district, mostly ST and in Dungarpur, both the SC and non-SC were job cardholders.

The sample workers belonged to different caste categories: SCs (13.48 per cent), STs (62.1 per cent), OBCs (32.5 per cent) and upper caste (5.44 per cent) (Table 6.3). Distribution across districts shows the highest proportion of beneficiaries from the SCs in Karauli, STs in Banswara, Jalore and Dungarpur and OBCs in Jhalawar. It appears that self-targeting, seen as a unique selling proposition of the MGNREGA, is actually working.

Table 6.3: Socio-religious Category-wise Distribution of MGNREGS Workers Households in Rajasthan (number and percentage)

Social Categories	*Karauli*	*Banswara*	*Dungarpur*	*Jhalawar*	*Jalore*	*Total (%)*	*Total No.*
Caste							
SC	34.93	3.60	7.82	27.25	13.75	13.48	444
ST	27.15	93.87	63.56	23.69	48.75	62.10	2,045
General	8.78	0.09	6.93	10.90	5.00	5.44	179
OBC	29.14	2.43	21.69	38.16	32.50	18.98	625
Religion							
Hindu	97.01	99.73	100		98.74	98.75	99.24
Muslim	2.99	0.27	–	1.26	–	1.25	0.76
Total	100	100	100	100		100	100

Source: Survey.

In districts like Dungarpur and Jalore, Jain, Rajput, Rajpurohit and Brahmin families have also started seeking wage employment under the MGNREGS. Traditionally they did not work as a manual worker on other's call. Even now, the number is small, but a beginning has been made under the MGNREGS work. However, participation of women from these households is still very low. From Jain households, only men are participating. In some villages, upper caste women from Brahmin and Rajput families were found working under the MGNREGS. According to the villagers, they do not maintain any caste discrimination amongst themselves. This was specifically among the women who mentioned that 'we drink water from the same place and maintain friendly relations with all women irrespective of the caste'. In the sample districts, the majority of cardholders were Hindus followed by Muslims. The proportion of Muslims was the highest at three per cent in Karauli. It is largely dependent on composition of the village population.

Age, Sex and Marital Profile of Workers

In Karauli district, the minimum age of a worker was 22 years and the maximum was 70 years; although the majority of workers came from the age group of 21–50 (Table 6.4). A good number of workers of 60 years and above were also found working. The proportion was high in Dungarpur, Jalore and Jhalawar, compared to other districts. The proportion of workers from below 20 years was negligible, only 0.88 per cent.

Table 6.4: Age Profile of MGNREGS Workers in Rajasthan

Age in yrs.	*Karauli*	*Banswara*	*Dungarpur*	*Jhalawar*	*Jalore*	*Total (%)*	*Total No.*
<20	0.40	1.53	0.44	1.05		0.88	29
21–30	28.74	23.15	21.78	19.92	17.50	22.93	755
31–40	37.33	36.85	30.67	31.66	32.50	33.95	1,118
41–50	21.16	22.52	23.38	26.83	26.25	23.32	768
51–60	7.78	10.36	11.91	14.26	13.75	11.14	367
60 plus	4.59	5.59	11.82	6.29	10.00	7.77	256
Total	**100**	**100**	**100**	**100**	**100**	**100**	**3,293**

Source: Survey.

Job cards are generally in the name of (male) head of the family, but women in large numbers have joined as workers. The proportion of women with job cards in their own name varied between 6.4 per cent in Dungarpur and 15 per cent in Jhalawar (Table 6.5).[4]

Table 6.6 shows that about 95 per cent of the job cardholders were married; about 2 per cent were unmarried and about 3 per cent were widows and widowers. The percentage of widow job cardholders was the highest (8.75 per cent) in Jalore and the lowest in Karauli (widows have got job cards in Todabhim and Naduati blocks). However, widowers have obtained cards in all but Karauli district; though the proportion is very small.

Table 6.5: Male–Female Distribution of MGNREGS Workers in Rajasthan (in per cent)

Sex	*Karauli*	*Banswara*	*Dungarpur*	*Jhalawar*	*Jalore*	*Total*	*No.*
Male	86.23	90.18	93.60	93.08	85.00	91.04	2,998
Female	13.77	9.82	6.40	6.92	15.00	8.96	295
Total	**100**	**100**	**100**	**100**	**100**	**100**	**3,293**

Source: Survey.

Table 6.6: Marital Status of MGNREGS Workers in Rajasthan (in per cent)

Status	*Karauli*	*Banswara*	*Dungarpur*	*Jhalawar*	*Jalore*	*Total*
Married	97.60	93.51	95.29	94.55	90.00	94.81
Unmarried	2.20	4.23	0.62	1.26	–	2.16
Widow	0.20	1.62	2.67	3.56	8.75	2.22
Widower	–	0.45	1.33	0.21	1.25	0.67
Others	–	0.18	0.09	0.42		0.15
Total No.	100	100	100	100	100	100

Source: Survey.

Economic Conditions of these Households

The average monthly income of a job cardholder was ₹1,117 in Karauli, ₹1,069 in Banswara, ₹1,337 in Dungarpur, ₹1,206 in Jhalawar and ₹1,496 in Jalore (Table 6.7). The personal income of the job cardholder constituted around 60 per cent or more of the total monthly income of a household across districts. The highest contribution was in Jhalawar (67.86 per cent). It is also noticed that the monthly

Table 6.7: Monthly Family Income of an MGNREGS Worker in Rajasthan (in ₹)

District	*Personal Income*	*Family Income*	*Income of the Respondent as Percentage of Family Income*
Karauli	1,117	1,882	59.32
Banswara	1,069	1,657	64.48
Dungarpur	1,337	2,199	60.83
Jhalawar	1,206	1,778	67.86
Jalore	1,496	2,233	67.02
Total	**1,198**	**1,908**	**62.80**

Source: Survey.

personal income of the workers varied widely across and within the districts too. For instance, in the two panchayat samitis, it ranged from ₹200 to ₹7,000 per month.

Most of these households earned mostly through agriculture and wages that varied across districts (Table 6.8). For instance, 71.25 per cent replied in Jalore that agriculture is the source of income, while 66.27 per cent replied in Karauli that wage labour is the major source of income. There are job cardholder households with income accruing from service, petty business and combination of sources. MGNREGS is now contributing to this income. The results show that agricultural labour and other labour relied on MGNREGS programme to supplement their incomes.

Table 6.8: Sources of Family Income of an MGNREGS Worker in Rajasthan (in percentage)

Source	*Karauli*	*Banswara*	*Dungarpur*	*Jhalawar*	*Jalore*	*Total*	*Total No.*
No response	0.80	0.36	–	–	–	0.24	8
Agriculture	26.15	65.50	54.58	43.19	71.25	52.69	1,735
Labour	66.27	33.78	42.67	55.97	25.00	44.76	1,474
Service	0.20	0.18	0.89		3.75	0.49	16
Business	0.60		0.71	0.21	–	0.36	12
Others	5.99	0.18	1.16	0.63	–	1.46	48
Total	**100**	**100**	**100**	**100**	**100**	**100**	**3,293**

Source: Survey.

Awareness about the MGNREGS

Most of the people were aware of the Rozgar Guarantee. In Banswara and Dungarpur, it is popular by the name of EGS. Jalore being the second-phase district, there was low level of awareness at the time of survey there. What is the source of information about MGNREGA? Ward panch was the major source of information about the programme in all the districts except for Jhalawar where mate was the main source. The role of the Panchayat secretary was only marginal. However, the role of TV and newspapers was important in Banswara, Jhalawar and Dungarpur.

Most of the people were aware of only 100 days of employment provision (Table 6.9).[5] The knowledge about minimum wage varied across districts with 35 per cent job cardholders reporting that they knew about minimum wages in Jalore, but only 2.4 per cent in Karauli knew that. Except for Dungarpur and Jalore, in all other districts, people were hardly aware of the four worksites facilities of crèche, shed, water and first aid. In Dungarpur, 63.73 per cent had knowledge about these facilities, but only 0.20 per cent in Karauli was aware of this. It is again in Dungarpur and Jalore that people were well versed with work availability within 5 km of distance. On the issue of planning of projects and law, very few job cardholders had any knowledge; although around 8 per cent in Dungarpur and Jalore were aware of that. On the role of the GP, the awareness was very little, although the GP is the nodal implementing agency.

Table 6.9: Awareness about MGNREGA in Rajasthan (in per cent)

Items	*Karauli*	*Banswara*	*Dungarpur*	*Jhalawar*	*Jalore*	*Total %*	*No.*
Aware of MGNREGA	99.80	97.93	100	98.53	100	99.06	3,262
Per family 100 days' employment	98.80	94.23	97.60	93.08	100	96.05	3,163
Minimum wage	2.40	11.17	29.78	25.37	35.00	18.83	620
Crèche, Shed, Water, First aid	0.20	3.69	63.73	14.47	52.50	26.42	870
Availability of work within 5 km	11.58	7.39	42.58	15.30	46.25	22.14	729
Planning process	2.20	1.80	7.82	1.47	7.50	4.01	132
Role of GP	–	0.18	2.49	0.21	1.25	0.97	32

Source: Survey.

Number of Days Worked

On an average, the sample households worked for 82.68 person-days in a year (Table 6.10). However, the average person-days of a respondent worker was only 36.52 days. That means that more than one member from a family was working in MGNREGS. This is also because of the high share of women. The average person-days worked by the job cardholder varied between 29.91 days in Banswara and 46.54 days in Dungarpur. The family workdays ranged between 71.08 days in Jhalawar and 88.58 days in Dungarpur.[6] Men's person-days was only 31.16 days compared to 51.52 days of women. On an average men had worked for a minimum of 21.11 days in Jalore and a maximum of 34.04 days in Jhalawar, while women had worked for 37.04 days on an average in Jhalawar and 65.49 days in Jalore.[7]

In some districts, a few households had worked for more than even 100 days. Out of the total sample, 11.38 per cent in Dungarpur,[8] 8.6 per cent in Jhalawar, 4.41 per cent in Banswara, 2.59 per cent in Karauli and 2.5 per cent in Jalore had worked for more than 100 days.[9] The above results however do not match with the quoted official figures (Mehrotra, 2008) for Rajasthan.[10] This means that official figures and field results are at variance.

Table 6.10: Average Employment Days Earned by a Household in Rajasthan in 2007–08

Districts	*Self*	*Family*	*Men*	*Women*
Karauli	32.11	75.30	29.29	46.00
Banswara	29.91	84.72	32.82	51.90
Dungarpur	46.54	88.58	29.85	58.74
Jhalawar	31.51	71.08	34.04	37.04
Jalore	44.22	86.60	21.11	65.49
Total	**36.52**	**82.68**	**31.16**	**51.52**

Source: Survey.

The scrutiny of job cards in Sabalpura GP in 2006–07 showed that 25 per cent of the job cards had entry of more than 100 days of work and paid wages of ₹45 to ₹50. In the year 2007–08, in the same GP, none of the job cards had entry of 100 day of work and the average workdays were 40 to 60 days and wages about ₹40 to ₹50. In all these job cards, the name, date and muster roll number and even days of work were not mentioned accurately. In Dungarpur, a case came up where an educated couple of Bhil tribe showed their job card where there was a wrong entry of 60 days. *Sachiv* had kept the job card with him and after few days of continuous request, the card was returned. When they saw the wrong entry, they complained to the *sachiv*. He offered the couple ₹100 and pressurised them not to talk to anybody about the incident.

Unemployment Allowance

The act enjoins upon the concerned officials to pay unemployment allowance to those holding valid job cards if they were unable to provide work to the applicants. This provision had hardly been implemented even when work was not granted. One reason for this is low level of awareness about the provision of unemployment allowance. Moreover, it is found that filling of Form 6 (job application form) is a mere formality, which is done only after entry into the muster roll, that is, after joining the work.[11] Only 19 of the 3,293 job cardholders knew about unemployment allowance and 12 were from one district—Banswara. But even out of that, only 13 were aware that it can be claimed after lapse of 15 days of seeking work.

Only 47.65 per cent of the respondents admitted receiving of receipt of job application form. The proportion varied across districts: Karauli (19.56 per cent), Banswara (22.34 per cent), Dungarpur (85.33 per cent), Jhalawar (43.4 per cent) and Jalore (70 per cent). The practice adopted by mates is that entries are made in muster roll on the day employment is provided. Thus, normal process of application-based job providing was not followed. Mate plays a role of not registering the person on the day he or she applies for work. There were a few cases of a household being refused work on application (0.82 per cent), and such cases were in the highest number in Jhalawar (1.47 per cent) followed by Karauli (1 per cent), Banswara (0.72 per cent) and Dungarpur (0.62 per cent). In spite of that and the provision of unemployment allowance, none of them was paid any unemployment allowance. The onus of payment of this allowance rests with the state government and there is a punitive provision that makes the officials to adopt all kinds of means to avoid paying unemployment allowance.[12] In Jhalawar district, especially in Thanwad GP, it was found that only influential persons' names were recorded in the muster rolls. When families who actually needed work approached the mate, they were given a standard answer: 'you had already been given sufficient number' (*mazdoor purey hogaiey*), irrespective of the number of days worked by the families.

Work, Wages and Worksites

How People Get Work

There has been a mixed response to how the villagers get work (Table 6.11). In most cases, it came out that the *sachiv*, sarpanch and the mate usually inform them about work. However, it is the mate whom most of the workers contact for work first and then only sarpanch and secretary. The role of ward panch

Table 6.11: Awareness about the Employment Days and Wage Rate in Rajasthan (per cent of respondents)

Awareness about Days of Work	*Karauli*	*Banswara*	*Dungarpur*	*Jhalawar*	*Jalore*	*Total*	*Total No.*
Aware of 100 days employment	99.40	96.40	100	98.32	100	98.45	3,242
Did you apply for employment	95.81	95.59	99.38	95.60	100	97.02	3,195
Persons contacted you for employment							
No response	–	–	0.71	0.21	–	0.27	9
Sarpanch	21.16	23.15	23.73	25.79	30.00	23.60	777
Mate	60.68	59.73	66.93	62.26	56.25	62.62	2,062
Secretary	16.17	11.26	7.38	9.64	11.25	10.45	344
Ward panch	2.00	5.86	1.24	2.10	2.50	3.07	101
Aware of the wage rate	89.42	55.41	28.62	83.86	60.00	55.66	1,833

Source: Survey.

is only marginal. In cases of farm pond work on private land, it is largely the family members of the concerned household who are enrolled in the muster roll and are provided employment. In Dungarpur, it was found that the ward panches and sarpanches were conscious of the fact that which *phala* (a part of a village) had completed 100 days and accordingly provide work to different *phalas* in rotation. They make sure that the nearest *phala* gets the first priority and then the next one in distance.

Out of the total respondents, 54.63 per cent had knowledge of the prescribed minimum wage, which was ₹73 per day in 2008 and was increased to 100 rupees in 2009. The knowledge about the prescribed minimum wage rate was the highest in Karauli (89.42 per cent) and the lowest in Dungarpur (28.62 per cent). Some of these workers were also aware that the minimum wages can keep changing.

It was also found that in some cases, households did not join the work after being provided. Such cases were reported from all the districts surveyed. Some people did not join the work as there was pressure of own agriculture work. This happened generally with households having some amount of land. Higher demand for work in agriculture and higher wages elsewhere were other reasons. Some did not go to work because other important domestic works required attention. Illness was also a reason. However, this was not a situation where the household had applied for the work. Rather, the implementing agencies called the job cardholders for work and then they refused to join (see Table 6.12).

Wages

The operational guidelines provide that the wages should be paid on a weekly basis and, in any case, not later than a fortnight of the date on which the work was done (Section 3[3]). The average wage earned was in the range of ₹40–60 per day, against the then minimum wage of ₹73. In places where the mate was supervising the work properly, the wage was found in the range of ₹70–73 per day, nearer to

Table 6.12: District-wise Three Main Reasons for Refusal to Join MGNREGS Work

Districts	*Reason 1*	*Reason 2*	*Reason 3*	*No. of Respondents*
Karauli	Agriculture	Illness	Necessary work	6
Banswara	Necessary work	Illness	Agriculture	16
Dungarpur	Illness	Agriculture	Necessary work	157
Jhalawar	Agriculture	Necessary work	Illness	17
Jalore	Necessary work	Agriculture	Illness	20
Total	Illness	Necessary work	Agriculture	216

Source: Survey.

the prescribed minimum wage. Villagers, specifically in Karauli and Dungarpur, were unsatisfied with the wages that they had received. In Banswara, Dungarpur and Karauli, the average wage rate ranged between ₹45 and ₹60. In Karauli district, the wages received for the work done under farm pond construction ranged between ₹45 and ₹46, whereas in case of gravel road construction, the actual wage varied between ₹45 and ₹60. In Banswara and Dungarpur, the actual wages paid varied between ₹50 and ₹60.

The practice of allocating work to a group of five workers and group measurement had resulted in the realisation of higher and near-to-the-minimum wages. The format of daily record is quite useful according to the mates. According to the *gram sevak* of Sajjangarh panchayat samiti, 'earlier wage rates were ranging from ₹40 to ₹55 per day due to incorrect measurement'. The amount of the wages is decided by the junior engineer (JEN) who measures the work and task. However, the main problem lies in delay in measurement. It is reported that measurement is not done on daily basis and is done as per the convenience of the JEN who has to do this task at a number of worksites. It is usually once in 10 days or after a fortnight. This delay in measurement delays payment of wages. However, the act provides for weekly or fortnightly payments, but practically this was not happening. In Ramgarh GP of Dungarpur district, the wage payment through bank/post office account has been in practice since 1 April 2007. Now all payments are made through banks or post offices. Wage payment through bank/post office account has certainly minimised the leakages in the wage payment, although the distance of the bank and delay in payment continue to be issues.

The wages of the mate, drinking water supplier (who are usually women), skilled labour (*karigars*) and the person who handles the crèche are charged from the material cost. These days are not included in the 100 days. This makes the work of mate enviable and there is a local pressure for allocating such work.

Types of Work Undertaken

In the five districts surveyed, the largest number of works undertaken in 2006–07 and 2007–08 related to water harvesting. However, the district specificities and local demand have also governed the types of the works selected. For instance, in Banswara, works of road connectivity, and in Karauli and Dungarpur, works of renovation of traditional waterbodies were taken in the largest number. In

Banswara and Dungarpur, work providing irrigation facilities to the land owned by private individuals was not taken at all in the sampled villages, whereas in Jhalawar and Banswara, land development on the plot of individuals was the major activity. In Banswara, micro-irrigation works were also undertaken in large numbers.

In some places, works officially undertaken were not found on the ground. In Jhalawar's Pacholo village of Bakani panchayat samiti, two public wells were deepened and for each one, ₹50,000 were allotted. The three villagers showed their job cards, which mentioned that they had worked on the project of deepening of well site. But these villagers themselves clarified that they had not worked on such a site at all. It was reported that a muster roll was opened and wages of two days were also paid. But later on, machine was used to complete the work.

Facilities at Worksite

MGNREGA provides for facilities for safe drinking water, shade for children, place of rest and a first-aid box at the worksite (Section 27, Schedule II of the MGNREGA). Section 28 of Schedule II provides for crèche facility at the worksite for five or more children, below six years of age, accompanying working women. The worksite facilities were mostly missing. Crèche was not found to be available in a large number of worksites. Women with young children were being discouraged to participate in the scheme due to unavailability of crèche facilities at the worksite. Because of the lack of facilities at worksites, children accompanying their mothers were left unattended in the heat. As a consequence, women were hesitant to bring their children to the sites. This also discouraged participation of women with young children. In contrast to almost missing crèche facilities, drinking water was made available at all the worksites visited. In Banswara and Dungarpur districts, first-aid kits were also available with some panchayats. On the non-availability of tent for shade and cradle for crèche, some sarpanches and *sachivs* mentioned the problem of storage and carriage as a major factor for not providing this. In some panchayats, tents and cradles had been supplied just before the survey.

Use of Machinery at Worksites and Contractors

The act bans completely the use of contractors and machine as far as possible. This makes a decisive break with the contractor-based public works programme, considered to be a key factor of corruption. However, the use of machinery and appointment of contractors were noticed in some places. For instance, in Andhiakhera village in Karauli, for gravel road construction, tractor was used and the job was given on contract. The labour employed on the contract was of that of the tractor owner. Labourers registered in the muster rolls were given the job of spreading and levelling of stones on the road. In some places in Karauli district, machines did 40 per cent of the work on the farm pond. The workers and the sarpanches of Dungarpur and Banswara felt that as the area is hilly and rocky, the JCB (earth-mover) machines should be allowed since it is difficult to cut stones, and is very time consuming. Similar difficulties were pointed out in case of hard black soil in Karauli district. The use of machine was found mostly in Banswara district (18.3 per cent of the worksites) followed by Jhalawar (7.5 per cent), Karauli (4.6 per cent), Jalore (1.3 per cent) and Dungarpur (0.9 per cent). (This figure is based on the report of 273 job cardholders.)

Local Political Dynamics and Selection of Work

Local political dynamics have been found to be operating in the selection of work and also while allocating job to people. In Jhalawar, while calling people for the job, the sarpanch preferred his people—those who had voted for him—against those who had opposed him during the election. In Karauli, the local dynamics were found operating between the Gujjars and Meenas. The Gujjars were reluctant to work under a Meena mate. It was also found that the work was undertaken in the locality of the voters of sarpanch first and then in other places.[13]

Sustainability of Work Completed

The quality of the works was good where the sarpanch, village committee and the JEN were careful and watchful. Nonetheless, a number of works whose utilities were not sure, were also undertaken. At one place, the villagers complained that although the work is shown on paper as completed, it does not exist in reality, which was found true. Careless selection of work was found to be of no use. One such example is in village Upar Gaon, G.P. Kheda Kachwasa in Dungarpur district where forestation work took place in 2007. Ratanjot saplings were planted in order to increase the income from forest produce. Though the villagers said that they were satisfied with the work, the reality is that the plantation had wilted/died out by 2008. In village Sulai, G.P. Kheda Kachwasa, the work done was of anicut renovation (2006–07). The wall was made and the anicut's depth was increased. Due to improper construction material, inadequate use of cement and improper length of the wall, it (wall) had already fallen and the water was flowing in the fields; the purpose of arresting soil erosion was defeated. In Karji village, GP Bagidora, the villagers felt that though the site and work selection was right, the construction work was not up to the mark. The anicut did not have required depth and, therefore, there was leakage. Though quite a few of these anicuts and check dams were in a bad condition, yet a number of them, especially in Banswara and Dungarpur, were serving the purpose well. In fact, due to proper construction of the structures, water was able to reach the tail end of plots (*Kyari*). In Bichiwada panchayat samiti of Dungarpur, sarpanch himself intervened in the construction of the structure and made sure that it was according to the required measurements and the material used was also in the right proportion. This resulted in good quality of the assets. The lack of technical and administrative manpower was also found affecting work quality.

III

Impact

Increased Purchasing Power

All respondents mentioned that the wages earned through the MGNREGS have increased their purchasing capacity. A number of them were spending it on food and other consumption items. However, with spiraling inflation of food items, this increase was getting neutralised. Studies have shown that low nutrition leads to low productivity, which leads to low wages which leads to low nutrition—this completes the vicious circle (Jha, Bhattacharya and Gaiha, 2010). In Rajasthan, only 0.5 per cent of the households are adequately nourished in all nine nutrients. It has the highest deprivation of all nutrients (29 per cent households), though top 12 per cent of households in calorie consumption crossed the minimum norm (Jha, Bhattacharya and Gaiha, 2010). Thus, nutritional deprivation is acute in Rajasthan and it is expected that MGNREGS might contribute to its improvement.

Decreased Petty Loans

As for most of the families in the districts, outmigration was a survival strategy. Since they were not able to send money regularly to the families back home, very often women had to survive on borrowing for their daily household expenditures. But most of these families mentioned that now they do not need to borrow for petty consumption items because of the fact that they themselves have started working. In Jhalawar, a woman mentioned that before the MGNREGA, she was dependent on borrowed money for visiting her parents. But now as she earns herself, she need not borrow.

Migration

The youth and adults, who used to migrate earlier, were found staying in their villages. In cases where women were not migrating with their husbands because of household responsibilities, these women were getting job at their doorsteps. It was found that in all the surveyed districts, outmigration had been a major survival strategy. After MGNREGA's intervention, the migration in these districts had certainly decreased but not stopped completely. On being questioned about the impact of the MGNREGA, the respondent's first answer was that it had decreased migration as '*ghar baithey rozgar mil jata haey*'. In Jhalawar, most of the villagers used to migrate with families to neighbouring states like MP for work. After the MGNREGS, women were staying back as they got employment near the home.

Better Connectivity

With construction of village roads, whether *pucca* or gravel, the connectivity has certainly increased. The villagers of Banswara and Dungarpur especially mentioned that the approach road had facilitated access to the health services and town. It has made their conditions better. Linkages between the villages have also improved.

Improvement in Agricultural Production

In Banswara and Dungarpur, due to improvement and construction of water harvesting structures, agriculture production has risen. The waterlogging problem has largely been solved in these districts because of the fact that drains were repaired here. This has led to reduction in crop failure and destruction. In these areas where the land size is extremely small, villagers are now able to grow crops in the tail end plots of water spread areas. In Jhalawar, there used to be just one crop before 2006 because of drying of wells. But now, after creation of water harvesting structures under the MGNREGA in most villages visited, there has been an increase in the groundwater level up to 10–15 per cent. Some families have started growing wheat.

Improvement in the Environment Conditions

Due to water conservation, the vegetation cover has increased in the surrounding areas. Availability of drinking water for cattle has increased up to a minimum of four to five months, and this is also the result of favourable rains. Land erosion has decreased to a large extent, especially in Banswara and Dungarpur. This in turn has helped control siltation in waterbodies. Due to large number of construction of waterbodies, general groundwater of the area has increased to a large extent.

IV

Administration of the Programme

As per the operational guidelines, state governments are required to appoint a full-time PO at block level and an employment guarantee assistant (EGA) at GP level. State governments are also to constitute panels of accredited engineers at block and district levels, and appoint technical resource groups at the district and state levels to assist in planning, design monitoring, evaluation quality audit and trainings.

In Rajasthan, POs were appointed on deputation from various departments. The PO is placed in the same office as of the BDO. But at some places, BDOs have been given additional charge of PO. The POs are usually Rajasthan Administrative Service (RAS) officers (state administrative service officers), whereas the BDO is junior in hierarchy to an RAS officer. Nevertheless, the BDO commands greater obedience at the block level. The PO faces problems in getting the work done from the *sachiv* (secretary) as both BDO and PO are placed at the same level in the same office, and since the *sachiv* has to work more frequently with the BDO, he invariably gives preference to BDO over the PO. Similarly, the JENs who are in charge of 10–15 GPs are on deputation from departments like irrigation, Public Works Department (PWD), soil conservation, etc. In case where there is no JEN, an Assistant Engineer (AEN) is made in-charge. Interestingly, for the villagers it is the JEN, *sachiv* (secretary) and the sarpanch who are important functionaries of the programme. Due to low number of JENs and their wide geographical areas to be covered, they are not in a position to supervise the work at regular intervals. In fact, a suggestion came up from the *sachivs* and the sarpanches that the JENs should not supervise more than five GPs so that they are able to perform the assigned tasks of measurement regularly and timely. It would help in timely payment of wages, which is not a practice at present across the districts. There is an issue of travel allowance to *rozgar sahayak* and the *sachiv*.[14] JENs and *sachivs* were allegedly sometimes abused by workers over measurement issues and, hence, were asking for insurance cover. Some sarpanches and *sachivs* demanded technical assistant specially trained in water harvesting technology, as they found JENs were inadequate in knowledge.

Capacity Building of the Officers

Officers involved in the scheme were given two to three days of training, which was not very fruitful. Despite that, only 20 per cent of the officers have gone through the act carefully. As regards the copy of the act, it is available at the *sachiv* level, but the sarpanches largely do not possess a copy of the act and most of them have not gone through it. The trainings by the government and the NGOs did make them aware of the important provisions of the act. There is certainly a need for intensive training of the officials so that they are adequately aware of all the provisions of the scheme. The training needs to be a continuous process rather than just a one-time affair. They also need to be frequently updated of the information.[15]

Procedure of Complaints

Largely complaints have been lodged about the discrepancies in the payment of wages and the names in muster rolls. The procedure followed in all the districts is that initially a complaint is lodged with the *sachiv* and the sarpanch, who forward it to the PO. The PO either sets up a committee or requests the JEN to look into the matter. According to the *sachivs*, 'Usually the matter is solved at the village level itself after discussion with the concerned persons.' Only in one case in Banswara, a stay order of the court was obtained for the work, as according to the complainant, the selection of the site of anicut was wrong. He had a fear that it might affect his field. But this was also solved out of court and the case was withdrawn.

Role of Panchayat Functionaries

As per Section 16(1) of the MGNREGA, the planning of the works/projects to be implemented in the GP area should be undertaken by the GP. The plan proposals are then sent to the block and district level for final approval. It was found that in case of works that took place in 2006, top-down approach was adopted for planning. The projects were first formulated and then brought to the gram sabha for namesake approval. However, from 2007 onwards, gram sabha formulated the annual plans and prioritised the projects in many instances. In Karauli and Dungarpur districts, the sarpanches have played a major role. But in Banswara, it is the *sachiv* who played the important role. After finalisation of the project, the sarpanch and the *sachiv* appoint the mate who starts the work. Across the districts, it was observed that the gram sabha meetings were not held in the true spirit, as participation was minimal. Thus, the gram sabha formalities are completed largely on paper.[16]

Audit (Social Audits)

Government auditing has been taking place regularly twice in a year. But social audit, except for some done with the help of Mazdoor Kisan Shakti Sangathan (MKSS) in Karauli, was a rare phenomenon. The social audits appear to be mere formalities. The locally known people are appointed for social auditing who consider it as a mere formality. Even though vigilance committees have been set up, most of them have been inactive. The officials were expressing their reservations about the help to be taken by the NGOs. Sarpanches, however, felt that the NGOs are needed to create awareness about the scheme to facilitate planning of the projects, and to inspect the works. NGOs from outside Rajasthan were found visiting the districts.[17]

Task Management

According to the workers, the group and task measurement systems were not working appropriately. It was pointed out that if a particular person of a group does not perform the task, wage of other workers gets affected. Even the sarpanches, especially in Dungarpur, mentioned that people in the villages knew that they would get at least 50 rupees per day if they were registered in a muster roll for work. Very often they did not work which created problems for other workers. The discussions brought that the number of such people was increasing across villages. In Jalore block, the villagers themselves had come out with alternative for persons who do not perform work properly in a group. Such individuals were given work separately. The villagers feel that this system works efficiently as it ensures wage payment according to the task performed.

In Karauli district, women complained that they did not like to work on farm pond construction sites as they get less wages there. This is due to the fact that these constructions are on individual farms. The owner of farm provides a list of family members and relatives on the muster roll and these people do not perform any work. In Nangal sherpur village of Todabhim Panchayat in Karauli, it was found that non-job cardholders were also given work on such sites.

The person-days and the number of workers required are identified and the sarpanch, *sachiv* and JEN prepare the list. After that the sarpanch and *sachiv* appoint a mate. Once the mate is appointed, the muster roll is transferred to the mate. According to the villagers, the problem starts at the transfer of the muster roll. The final authority is the mate who signs on the muster roll and then the payments are made.

Role of Mates

Most of the mates were male only. However, in districts like Jalore, Banswara and Jhalawar, women mates were also found, but not too many. Mates are involved with daily supervision of the work and maintenance of the muster rolls. Although, it is mainly the mate who supervises the work at the construction site, however in few cases (Dungarpur and Jalore), sarpanches were also found supervising works. In some cases, it was observed that it is the mate who approaches the villagers for work. The quality of the work was found dependent on the efficiency and commitment of the mate. This also reduces complaints about low wages, measurement, etc. In Jalore panchayat samiti's Bandawadi village, a woman mate was 8th pass and was very popular. Women workers mentioned that they were getting maximum wage for the work done. She regularly supervises the work and maintains the muster roll properly. But in some cases, mates were also found tampering with the muster rolls.

V

Conclusion

The people of Rajasthan have perceived the MGNREGA as a very important programme for rural India and more so for Rajasthan that often faces the problem of drought, food insecurity, low irrigation and hence, of agriculture and low income and employment opportunities causing large-scale migration. People have benefited directly through increased income and security of income and indirectly through enhanced rural infrastructure. Women have got avenues to earn independently, and this has improved their decision-making power at the household level.

The implementation of the scheme does not vary much across districts and within a district. Nonetheless, there are problems in implementation. They are related to measurement, wage payment, planning of projects, involvement of people, mobilisation of community and training and capacity building of officials and representatives. The scale of implementation is bound to stress the capacity and efficiency of the local bureaucracy. The state is still not fully equipped with trained and adequate manpower to handle the MGNREGA. Much also needs to be done on how to construct sustainable assets and to provide sustainable employment to the rural population. Strict monitoring of each and every provision of the act and implementation needs to be done. SORs require a relook too which is based more on the contractor system. The notion of age and gender difference in productivity needs to be brought into the current SORs.[18] The scheme has to go beyond drought proofing and water harvesting. It should be used in the crisis situation too (see Krishnamurty, 2006).

There are also issues of local power dynamics. The powerful people and community are trying to maximise their benefits, which might affect the poor people and might defeat the objectives of the act.

The capacity of panchayat also needs to be properly assessed. There are no shelves of projects and it is compounded by large number of incomplete works. The major challenge at the local level for the panchayats would be to have sustainable projects on the shelf. The past experience of employment guarantee scheme in Maharashtra has shown us that it does not take long for drying up of projects. This will be the situation very soon because local communities have myopic vision on type of projects that the communities can have. We have also seen that civil society organisations also do not have a long-term vision on the type of development projects, which can provide long-term sustainable employment and livelihood to the poor in our villages. There is also a need for clustering villages for creation of sustainable assets, which are useful for the local communities.

There is also a case for strengthening of the wage payment and unemployment allowance provision. Increasing of the number of minimum of 100 guaranteed days to 150–200 days can be considered, as there is a demand for this. It seems that lots need to be done, so that the MGNREGA becomes an instrument of removing stark poverty from the rural India. There is no doubt that the MGNREGA has tremendous potentialities to achieve it and to transform rural India.

Notes

1. There are various types of discrepancies in job cards. The majority of job cardholders were contacted largely by the sarpanch, followed by the secretary. The role of the mate is very small. However, a number of people reportedly had given money to get a job card and 3.1 per cent in Banswara reported so. What is the amount paid? It varies between ₹5 and ₹100, which is quite significant if considered as a wage component—one can say a high transaction cost. This has occurred largely in Banswara district (28 of the 45 reporting so). It is also surprising that many paid for photograph too (14.64 per cent). Majority, who reportedly paid, had paid between ₹20 and ₹40. It is mainly in Jhalawar that people paid for photograph; 349 of 458 persons (73.2 per cent).

2. Those villagers who had not got their photographs taken in the camp organised by the panchayat had to pay for the photographs. The payment ranged from ₹20 to ₹50 per job card.
3. Three families from the Jain community have a job card and the males of these families have worked under the scheme.
4. The programme envisages that one-third of the beneficiaries shall be women who have registered for and requested for work.
5. In focus group discussion at large in the villages, the villagers are found to be aware about the fact that this scheme provides 100 days' employment.
6. Official figure of employment provided (number of person-days per household) stood at 85.4 in 2006–07 and a reduced number of 75 in 2007–08 (Mehrotra, 2008).
7. The number of days of work per households was far away from 100 days, but it was still higher than the 26 person-days per household of work in 2005–06 in SGRY (Mehrotra, 2008).
8. In Dungarpur, in many cases it was found that number of days exceeded 125 days.
9. Job card entries revealed that women have worked for more number of days than male members of the family. In fact, nearly 80 per cent have been women workers.
10. It is reported that in Rajasthan in 2006–07 percentage of households completing 100 days of employment is 54.4 and a reduced proportion of 42 per cent in 2007–08 (Mehrotra, 2008). Comptroller and Auditor General of India (CAG) (2007) pointed out that a bare 3.2 per cent of registered households in 200 poorest districts managed to get guaranteed 100 days' employment in a year. Our results are contrary to it though.
11. The formalities of Form 6 are completed at the worksite itself. Except for Dungarpur, it was observed that the Form 6 is filled once they have been registered for work in the muster roll.
12. It was observed that in large number of cases, wage payments were not written for the year 2007 and the number of days of work was also not entered properly. The spaces are left blank. Similarly, in Karauli, it is found that the job cards did not have the entry for the request for work, nor the payment entries were done properly.
13. In the 2010 panchayat elections in Rajasthan, there was hardly any village that did not have five to eight candidates for sarpanch's post.
14. The JENs were initially paid ₹7,000 and recently the remuneration has been increased by ₹500 to cover their travel expenses.
15. For example, in Dungarpur, a *Sachiv* said it is 70 per cent from the central government and 30 per cent from the state government. Another said that it is in 80:20 ratio. This is found across the districts. In Karauli, a *Sachiv* mentioned that the funds come from the District Rural Development Agency (DRDA).
16. There is not only shortage of staff, but also technical skills are lacking.
17. PRIA is one organisation that has been actively working with the sarpanches. Similarly, in Karauli, State Vikas Sansthan has been active in some of the panchayat samitis.
18. Though, this is a difficult proposition at the state level.

References

Gaiha, Raghav (1997) Do rural public works influence agricultural wages? The case of the employment guarantee scheme in India. *Oxford Development Studies*.

Jha, Raghbendra, S. Bhattacharya and Raghav Gaiha (2010) NREG, PDS & Nutritional deprivation. *Economics Times*, (11 May).

Joshi, Varsha, Surjit Singh and K. N. Joshi (2008) *Evaluation of NREGA in Rajasthan*. Report prepared for UNDP, New Delhi.

Krishnamurty, J. (2006) Employment guarantee and crisis response. *Economic and Political Weekly* 41, No. 9, (4 March): 789–93.

Lipton, Michael (1998) *Successes in anti-poverty*. Geneva: ILO.

Mehrotra, Santosh (2008) NREG two years on: Where do we go from here? *Economic and Political Weekly* 40, No. 7, (2 August): 27–36.

National Rural Employment Guarantee Act, 2005, No. 42 of 2005, published in *Gazette of India*, Extraordinary Part- II, Section- I, No. 48, Wednesday, 7 September 2005, New Delhi.

Nayyar, Rohini (2002) Issues in employment and poverty. Discussion Paper 3, Recovery and Reconstruction Department, International Labour Office, Geneva.

Singh, Surjit and V. Sagar (2004) *Agriculture credit in India, A millennium study of Indian Farmer*. New Delhi: Academic Foundation and Ministry of Agriculture, Govt. of India.

7

MGNREGS in Andhra Pradesh
Examining the Role of State-enabled Institutions

Shaik Galab and E. Revathi

I

Introduction

The MGNREGS was implemented in only 13 out of 22 districts in February 2006 in the first phase of MGNREGS in Andhra Pradesh. It was extended to another six districts in April 2007 and to the rest three on 1 April 2008. Thus, 1,098 mandals (blocks) across the state in all the 22 districts (excluding Hyderabad) are now covered. With the extension of the coverage to entire rural districts, 72.7 per cent of the total state population is covered by the employment guarantee scheme.

The MGNREGS held tremendous potential for employment generation and income security to the vast number of rural poor households in the state which has high concentration of poor population in the rural areas; low cropping intensity; low level of irrigation in the large part of the state—particularly in Telangana and Raylaseema regions—and the low level of rural infrastructure. On the one hand, there is a huge demand for wage employment under the MGNREGS in the state, and on the other hand, the state has also responded actively and geared all its resources to create employment under the MGNREGS. This has made the state of Andhra Pradesh one of the leading states in implementation of the MGNREGS.

The state has been able to spend about ₹15,178 crore on the MGNREGS in between February 2006 and May 2011 (20 May 2011) that constitutes more than one-tenth of the total MGNREGS budget of the Government of India. A total of 125.83 crore person-days of employment have been generated and a total of 91.33 lakh households have got employment on an average of 54.66 days per household per annum. About 32 lakh households have already completed 100 days of employment so far and this number constitutes about one-third of the total households provided employment. About 15 lakh public works have already been undertaken under the MGNREGS in the state. The state has also been a leading state in terms of employment generated and shared by women. The percentage share of women in total employment generated has been higher than the national average in all the five years (2006–11) of implementation. High demand for wage employment under the MGNREGS and ability of the local institutions to generate employment in response to the demand has made Andhra Pradesh one of the leading states in implementation of the MGNREGS.

In Rajasthan, the MGNREGS implementation has been largely driven by the civil society organisations that have played crucial role in the mobilisation of the people and have been in the forefront of right-to-work movement, while in Andhra Pradesh, the proactive state has played greater role in pushing the implementation to greater heights. The state has facilitated the implementation through the use of modern technology in synergising with the local institutions that were already there to take up the responsibilities. This also shows that the synergisation of the efforts of state and local institutions and use of technology can dramatically change the nature of service delivery at the grass-roots level.

The ability of the people to access information on their rights and entitlements provided in the MGNREGA, and the ability to negotiate with the local bureaucracy and Panchayati Raj Institutions (PRI) representatives, given the exclusive administrative arrangements made at various levels of administration, are important determinants of effective realisation of entitlements under the MGNREGS. On the other hand, the low ability of the people to realise their entitlements on their own is a major hindrance to the rights-based development approach. To fill this critical gap, both the government as well as the non-government organisations (NGOs) in the state, have taken initiatives in this direction. Fortunately, Andhra Pradesh has already built a number of local institutions which are capable to play that role.

The state is endowed with an effective network of women Self-help Groups (SHGs: IKP) in the villages and their federations at the village level (village organisations), mandal level (mandal samakhyas) and district level (zilla samakhyas) under the IKP. It has been found that the IKP has enhanced the ability of women to access information and the ability to negotiate with the government, market and civil society that have enhanced their abilities to fight poverty as well (Galab and Prudhvikar Reddy, 2010).

The government has also put in place the administrative structures at all levels to conduct social audit of the MGNREGS. The conduct of social audit has increased the level of awareness among the workers regarding their rights and entitlements and also contributed to their increased abilities to negotiate with the bureaucracy and elected PRI representatives in implementing the programme efficiently (Aakella and Kidami, 2007a and 2007b; Gopal, 2009; Pokharel, Aiyar and Samji, 2008; Raju, 2009).

Similarly, the NGOs have promoted Wage Seeker's Associations (WSOs) in the villages and their federations at the mandal level to improve the abilities of these workers to access information regarding their rights and entitlements and the abilities to negotiate with the concerned bureaucracy and elected PRI representatives. There is also evidence that the WSAs have increased the abilities of the wage seekers to realise their rights and entitlements (People's Monitoring Committee, 2009).

The present chapter has explained the implementation context of the MGNREGS in Andhra Pradesh with respect to five factors: the overall implementation by the state, state-promoted and state-enabled institutions; community; households and individuals. First, the programme has to be implemented by the state as per the guidelines of the MGNREGA. The state-promoted and state-enabled institutions played an important role in terms of implementation at the grass-roots level. The Andhra Pradesh government has promoted institutions like IKP (SHG), social audit and state-enabled institutions like WSAs. The members of households who are members of SHGs and/or WSAs and/or social audit acquire ability to access information about their rights and entitlements and ability to negotiate with the implementing agency and to realise their entitlements and rights. Third, the community or village contexts of implementation have been explained in terms of variables like the percentage of irrigated area in the village, drought proneness of the region, per capita income, percentage of SC and ST population and percentage of female population. These village contexts determine the level of demand for and supply of employment under the MGNREGS in the state. The first two characteristics, namely, percentage of irrigated area and drought proneness of the villages reflect the demand situation for wage seekers in the villages; whereas, the latter two reflect the supply situation of wage seekers in the villages. Fourth, the socio-economic conditions like poverty, caste affiliations, occupation, number of workers per household and gender of the head of the households are some of the characteristics of the households that determine the demand for employment under the MGNREGS. Last, individual factors like age, literacy, disability and skill required for working under the MGNREGS have been found important determinants of demand for wage employment under the programme in the state (Figure 7.1).

Part II gives an overview of the implementation and impacts of the MGNREGS in the state. This section explains implementation and impacts based on both the primary and secondary data. Section III of the chapter analyses the role of local institutions, especially SHGs, WSAs and social audit in improving implementation in the state. This section explains implementation and impacts based on both the primary and secondary data. This also analyses the role of IKP (SHG), WSAs and social audit through a regression analysis. The final section argues that the investment in these local institutions was a useful exercise and would go a long way in improving service delivery at the grass-roots level. The Andhra Pradesh model of MGNREGS also suggests that synergisation of the efforts of the state and civil society are equally important for strengthening of grass-roots service delivery, and this will have better effects on the livelihood conditions of the poor households in the rural areas.

II

An Overview of Implementation and Impact in Andhra Pradesh

Level of Implementation of MGNREGS in Andhra Pradesh

The implementation of the MGNREGS in Andhra Pradesh has been improving over time. The utilisation of funds and employment provided stand as a testimony to this. The utilisation of funds increased from 60 per cent in 2006–07 to 98 per cent in 2009–10. The employment days provided per household went up from 37 to 46 and the percentage of households provided with 100 days of employment has gone up from 3 per cent to 12 per cent during 2009–10 and to 15.5 per cent during 2010–11 (Table 7A.1). The position of Andhra Pradesh among all the states has improved from 20 in 2006–07 to 2 in 2009–10 in this regard. The performance of the scheme varied widely across the districts (Table 7A.2). Districts located in dry-land regions of the state like the Telangana and Rayalaseema have higher participation rates compared to the coastal Andhra region (Galab et al., 2010). The improvement in the implementation of this scheme ensured more benefits to the poorest of the poor (Galab et al., 2010). The composition of the works undertaken reveal that the lion's share of works undertaken—around 70 per cent—are related to common property resources (like water) for strengthening dry-land agriculture. At the same time, development works on lands (private property resources) of the SC and ST constitute

Figure 7.1: Conceptual Framework for Understanding Determinants of Different Dimensions of Employment under MGNREGS

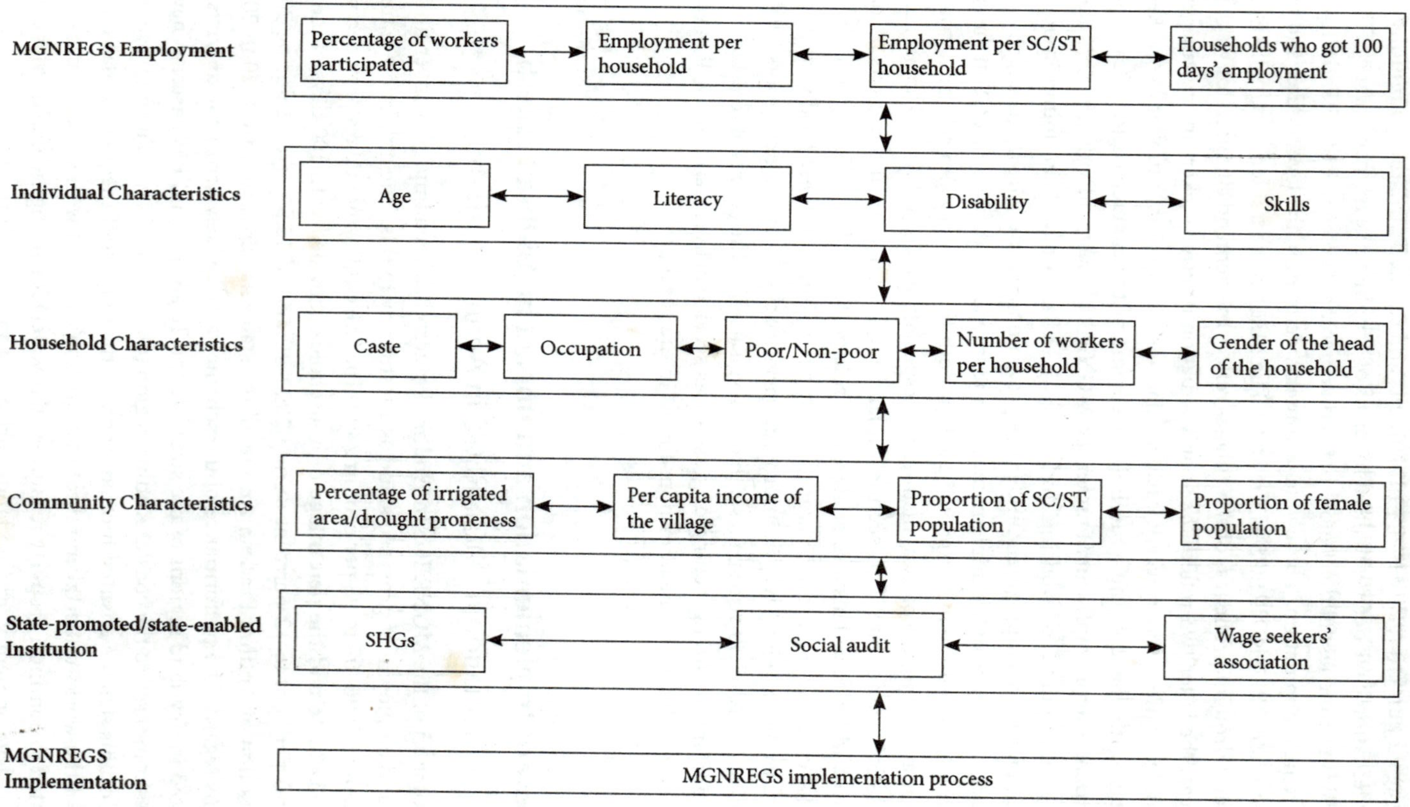

around one-fifth of the works (MGNREGS, Mid Term Appraisal [MTA] XI Plan, Andhra Pradesh). However, it is argued that the larger share of the centrally decided programmes reduces the voice of the wage seekers in the exercise of evolving the shelf of works in the gram sabha (Kumar et al., 2008).

Impact Assessment

Households have experienced positive impact in terms of employment, incomes and consumption due to the MGNREGS. The employment gain due to MGNREGS is highest for both casual labour and the self-employed in agriculture among the occupation groups. While casual labour in agriculture has substituted MGNREGS work with non-MGNREGS work, the self-employed in agriculture (farmers) have complemented it with farm work. Employment gain has been the largest for marginal farmer, followed by medium farmer. Under usual conditions, the number of wage days falls as landholding rises, but it is the converse in case of MGNREGS work indicating landholding households (marginal, medium, large and small in that order) made use of MGNREGS more than agriculture labour (Galab et al., 2010). Employment gain is high in the case of women. They have substituted self-employment for MGNREGS work. Moreover, unemployment days are more for females, indicating high demand for work (Galab et al., 2010).

The agriculture labour among the occupational groups, landed groups over landless groups among the landholding groups and poverty groups compared to non-poor groups have experienced higher participation rates across the districts. The per household employment gain for the state according to a study of four districts shows that it was around 20 days (Galab et al., 2009). The MGNREGS has also widened the choice of work for the participant households. Besides, wages earned from the MGNREGS work were helpful to the participant families in meeting the household needs. Male–female wage disparities have reduced for MGNREGS work in comparison with market wage disparities.

Wage rates have increased in agriculture as well as non-agriculture for men and women. The percentage rise in wages is more for agriculture compared to non-agriculture and more in the case of women compared to men. The labour market has undergone changes due to MGNREGS works due to tightening of labour market as wage workers are substituting non-MGNREGS work with MGNREGS work, indicated by rise in the market wage. However, wage rise takes place only when MGNREGS work is seen as an alternative or competing type of employment to regular wage work available. In other words, if MGNREGS works like a complementary employment, then wage rise may not be effected, but when it plays a substituting role that will lead to wage rise. Land-use pattern, crops cultivated, cropping intensity and irrigation intensity may be some demand-side factors and number of agricultural labour households, number of SC households and the size of categories of farmers mostly determine the supply factors in the labour markets. Besides, both inward and outward migration also affect the labour market in the village. MGNREGS works done in kharif season led to higher increase in wage rates than works during rabi and kharif.

The MGNREGS has also affected local labour-employment conditions. The system of annual farm servants has been on the wane. Within the casual labour system, advance payments have increased to enable labour tying because of the alternative employment from the MGNREGS. The change in the casual labour system (advance payments) indicates the increased bargaining power of the agricultural labour because of the MGNREGS. Land lease market has become vibrant with MGNREGS in two districts in Karimnagar and Ananthapura (Galab et al., 2009; Table 7A.3).

III

Contribution of IKP, Social Audit and Workers' Associations

This section explains the contribution of the state-enabled institutions, namely, IKP, social audit and workers association in improving delivery of the MGNREGS in the state. This study adopts 'Before and After approach' to assess the contribution of social audit, although it gives an overestimate of the contribution of these institutions. For this purpose, financial years 2007–08 and 2009–10 are considered to represent the 'Before' and 'After' situations. This is because the entire study area considered had been exposed to social audit in the year 2008–09. It is also important to note that there has been improvement in the implementation of the MGNREGS over time in the state of Andhra Pradesh, and this is another factor that gives overestimation of the contribution of social audit. The selection of the year 2009–10 to represent the 'After' situation is the immediate succeeding year after the study area was exposed to these institutions. Thus, the estimates of the contribution of these institutions presented in this chapter may provide the upper limit.

The assessment of the WSAs has been done adopting 'Double Difference Method'. The study area considered had been exposed to WSAs in the year 2008–09. Further, the WSAs are present in 5 out of 14 villages of Parigi mandal, the study area. This gives us the opportunity to classify the villages into the villages with WSAs and villages without WSAs. Thus, we have 'With' and 'Without' situations of WSAs. This chapter considers financial years 2007–08 and 2009–10 to represent the 'Before' and 'After' situations of WSAs.

A different approach has been adopted to assess the contribution of SHGs of IKP under district contexts. As the SHGs are omnipresent in the state of Andhra Pradesh, the variations in the intensity of the presence of these institutions, measured through number of SHGs per 1,000 female population, across the districts has been analysed to assess the contribution of SHGs of IKP.

The study area selected for assessing the contribution of social audit and WSAs is Parigi mandal (the administrative unit below district level) of Ananthapura district of Andhra Pradesh. Ananthapura district has been selected because of being the first phase district and because of the presence of WSAs promoted by an NGO in some of the villages. The entire Parigi mandal has been exposed to social audit. This gives an opportunity to assess the interaction effect of social audit, and WSAs. Further, a total of 14 villages have been selected from the mandal and about 6,560 households have been analysed for the study. Thus, we have taken household as a unit of analysis to assess the contribution of social audit and WSAs.

The data has been obtained from Department of Rural Development, Government of Andhra Pradesh, and the village and town directory, Census 2001. Unit-level data has been explored for the selected villages in Parigi mandal from the state Management Information System (MIS) data (nrega.ap.gov.in, 2010).The data on social audit is collected from the Parigi mandal in Ananthapura district of Andhra Pradesh. Unit-level data from the Andhra Pradesh National Rural Employment

Guarantee Scheme (APNREGS) website has been utilised for the selected villages for the dependent variables, namely, average days of employment obtained per household under the MGNREGS, average days of employment per SC and ST household under the MGNREGS and percentage of households which achieved 100 days of employment. Data on some of the independent variables like percentage of irrigated area from groundwater sources, percentage of female population, percentage of SC and ST population, total income of village and total population (to derive PCI [Per Capita Income]) has been collected for the selected villages from the village and town directory, Census 2001, Ananthapura district. The interrelationships among the selected variables have been established through regression analysis. All these models contain continuous dependent variable and dichotomous independent variables. It gives an opportunity to assess the interaction among the independent variables.

The Contribution of IKP

The IKP is the flagship programme of the Government of Andhra Pradesh with the main objective to enable all the rural poor families in 22 rural districts of the state to improve their livelihoods and quality of life. The formation of SHGs and their federations at the village, mandal and district levels meant for generating micro-processes to influence the institutions and policies for improving the livelihoods of the poor is central to the IKP. This project aims at enhancing the assets, capabilities and ability of the poor to deal with shocks and risks. The role of women in public spaces is equally important for interacting with the state, civil society and the market to establish the agency of women, which would then improve the functioning of these institutions for addressing the barriers to poverty alleviation. As the Village panchayats are still dominated by the village oligarchies, the participation of women in collective actions in regard to problems encountered like quality of drinking water, irrigation facilities, access to education, sanitation conditions, access to approach roads and quality of internal roads, which are undertaken by the Village Organisations (VOs) and Mandal Samakhyas (MSs) has increased due to their participation in the IKP. The data relating to this indicates that the women did address the functioning of all the formal institutions considered for the analysis. It is evident that women's participation has had a positive impact on the functioning of institutions dealing with drinking water, electricity, irrigation, education, sanitation, roads and poverty alleviation (Galab and Prudhvikar Reddy, 2009). Percentage of households which participated in MGNREGS from among the job card households, percentage of workers who participated from among the workers registered, number of days of employment per household (on average) and number of households who got 100 days of employment for *IKP households* have been invariably higher than those obtained by *all households* for all the years starting from 2006–07 to 2009–10. This is true across all the social groups—caste and gender groups (Table 7.1).

The relationship between these indicators and the IKP has been examined across the districts. The IKP has been characterised in terms of two parameters, namely, number of SHGs per 1,000 females in a district and corpus funds per SHG (rupees in crores) in a district. The correlation coefficients estimated between these parameters of SHGs and the above performance parameters of the MGNREGS unfold that the number of SHGs per 1,000 female population is positively related with the overall performance

Table 7.1: Employment Dimensions under MGNREGS for All Households and IKP Households (2006–07 to 2009–10)

		Year of Implementation							
Sl.		*2006–07*		*2007–08*		*2008–09*		*2009–10*	
No.	*Description of Parameters*	*All*	*IKP**	*All*	*IKP*	*All*	*IKP*	*All*	*IKP*
1.	**Percentage of households participating in MGNREGS to the total HHs having job cards**								
	Total HHs	18.23	36.98	39.31	68.34	47.85	86.73	44.00	85.45
	SC	21.05	38.63	42.29	69.35	50.12	87.43	45.52	86.11
	ST	21.00	39.44	41.10	68.74	51.07	83.65	48.35	83.45
	OBC	18.14	68.77	40.22	68.77	49.12	87.42	46.10	86.21
	OC	12.38	31.88	31.02	61.32	38.66	86.05	32.81	82.81
2.	**Percentage of workers participating to the workers registered**								
	SC	8.04	23.90	17.48	48.98	22.64	67.39	22.16	68.40
	ST	3.67	10.09	8.22	20.93	11.48	27.90	12.21	28.12
	Male	12.81	28.85	29.08	58.39	39.34	81.72	39.21	82.58
	Female	14.22	30.28	34.04	66.57	45.96	93.80	46.87	95.56
3.	**Average employment days per HH**	30.15	34.08	42.68	59.02	39.86	59.01	49.42	80.51
4.	**No. of HHs completing 100 days of employment**	3.09	4.13	8.76	17.60	8.43	16.89	11.72	17.14

Source: Compiled on the basis of data from http://nrega.ap.gov.in, documents from Society for Elimination of Rural Poverty (SERP).
Note: * denotes the percentage of IKP HHs in the total HHs with job cards.

(overall rank) of the programme across the districts, while the corpus fund per SHG is negatively related with the overall performance(overall rank); contrary to the corpus fund per SHG, the number of SHGs per 1,000 female population have positive relationship with the average days of employment per household as well as percentage of households which completed 100 days of employment and that both the parameters of SHG have positive relationship with the drought proneness (Table 7.2). Thus, each of these two parameters of SHGs has kept varied relationship with the different parameters of performance, and each of these two parameters of SHGs have a positive relationship with the drought proneness of the districts, indicating the greater role of SHGs in the context of drought. These leads have become the hypotheses to be tested in the multiple regression analysis conducted. The details on the multiple regression analysis are in order.

Table 7.2. Zero-order Correlation Matrix SHG and Corpus Fund (CF)/SHG and Performance Parameters in the State

Variables	*Score for Working HHs*	*Average Days per HH Score*	*Timely Payment Score*	*Score for SC and ST (population)*	*Score for Completion of Works*	*Score for HHs Completing 100 Days*	*Overall Rank*	*Percentage of Average Drought-affected Mandals to Total*
SHG/ 1000W	.50 (0.05)	.52 (0.05)	–.46 (0.05)	.41	–.38	.52 (0.05)	.42 (0.05)	0.16
CF/SHG	–.35 (0.10)	–.61 (0.01)	.38 (0.07)	–.47 (0.05)	.23	–.61 (0.01)	–.61 (0.01)	–0.40

Source: Computed from unit-level data for the selected villages from APMGNREGS website.

Regression Analysis

The regression results presented in Table 7.3 for *all households* indicate that the households in the districts with higher number of SHGs, compared to the households in the districts with lower number of SHGs, have obtained an additional 10 days of employment per household (Model 1), on average. Similarly, the SCs and STs in the districts with higher number of SHGs have gained an additional employment of 11 days and 8 days per household (Model 1), on average, respectively. The households residing in the districts with higher drought proneness (percentage of mandals declared as affected by drought, on average, during the last 16 years in each district indicates drought proneness) have got an additional employment of 14 days per households (Model 1). With respect to two parameters—namely, households getting 100 days of employment and early payment of wages—the number of SHGs and intensity of drought proneness have made little difference. Further, the households in the districts with higher corpus fund per SHGs have not obtained any additional employment, compared to those in the districts with lower corpus fund per SHG. This is true in case of SC households and ST households too. Moreover, either in regard to households getting 100 days of employment or early payment of wages, the households in the districts with higher corpus fund have not derived any advantage over those in the districts with low corpus fund per SHG. Drought proneness has contributed to the increase in households obtaining 100 days of employment by five percentage points. However, drought proneness of the districts has had no effect on the early payment of wages.

The Contribution of Social Audit

There are also provisions for the mechanisms in MGNREGA to ensure guaranteed employment to the people. Provision for the regular conduct of social audit for assessing planning, implementation and impact of the MGNREGS in gram sabhas is evidence to this. Social audit has contributed by increasing the awareness levels of the workers in regard to the MGNREGS and the entitlements and rights provided in the programme such as guaranteed employment for one hundred days, ban on the use of machines and contractors, minimum wages, demand for work, payment of wages within 15 days, unemployment allowance, payment slips and worksite facilities. It has also contributed to identifying anomalies in the

Table 7.3: Determinants of Employment of All Households under MGNREGS at District Level—Regression Results

Dependent/Independent Variables	*No. of SHGs per 1,000 Women*	*Percentage of Drought-affected Mandals*	*Percentage of Marginal Holdings*	*Corpus Funds per SHG*	*Constant*	*Adj. R Square*
EMPMGNREGS						
Model 1	9.91*	13.58*	–2.48		31.72	.27
Model 2		9.97*	–3.8	–1.8	39.0	.16
Model 3	10.06*	13.75*	–2.73	.58	31.27	.26
EMPSCMGNREGS						
Model 1	10.824*	15.81*	–.767		30.65	.36
Model 2		11.60*	–2.3	–3.3	39.47	.23
Model 3	10.61*	15.59*	–.81	–.79	31.283	.35
EMPSTMGNREGS						
Model 1	7.41*	11.37*	–.67		36.67	.16
Model 2		9.08*	–1.6	.75	40.85	.08
Model 3	8.13*	12.13*	–.47	2.67	34.57	.15
PHHEMGNREGS						
Model 1	3.07	4.70*	–1.0		6.3	.17
Model 2		3.73	–1.4	–.03	8.3	.066
Model 3	3.273	4.96*	–.96	.73	5.8	.09
WPWTDMGNREGS						
Model 1	–3.7	13.3	8.6		35.45	–.006
Model 2		14.8	9.2	1.4	32.4	–.01
Model 3	–7.84	7.55	7.63	–2.53	39.93	–.08

Source: District-level data from APMGNREGS website.
Notes: Number of observations is 44.
EMPMGNREGS = employment per HH obtained through MGNREGS.
PHHEMGNREGS = percentage of HH obtained 100 days of employment under MGNREGS.
EMPSCMGNREGS = employment per HH obtained by SC HH under MGNREGS.
EMPSTMGNREGS = employment per HH obtained by ST HH under MGNREGS.
WPWTDMGNREGS = percentage of workers for whom payments were initiated within three days.
Level of significance: * denotes <1, ** denotes 1–5, *** denotes 5–10.
The independent variables are considered as dichotomous; district having higher value than the state average as one and otherwise as zero.

implementation process like fudging of muster rolls, financial irregularities, poor maintenance of related records, deviations in wage payments to the labourers, fabrication of muster rolls and non-existence of works shown as having been completed. The amounts siphoned off have been recovered before and during the social audit process. This has led to improvements in the implementation of the programme (Aakella and Sowmya, 2007a and 2007b; Gopal, 2009; Pokharel, Aiyar and Samji, 2008; Raju, 2009).

A comparison of the different parameters of employment before (2007–08) and after (2009–10) social audit in the villages of Paragi mandal indicates that the employment per household, percentage of households that obtained 100 days of employment, employment per household for SC and participation of worker from among the eligible workers have increased considerably after the social audit over the situation before social audit. Thus, it is evident that the social audit has contributed to improvements in all the dimensions of employment considered for the analysis (Table 7.4).

Table 7.4: Different Parameters of Employment from MGNREGS in the Villages before and after Social Audit

Sl. No.	*Dependent Variable*	*Before Social Audit*	*After Social Audit*
1.	Average number of days worked	34	66
2.	Average of total wage (₹)	2,890.78	6,887.10
3.	Percentage of MGNREGS participants out of total eligible workers	48.85	66.14
4.	HH completed 100 days of employment	53	1065
5.	Average number of days worked by SC	36	76

Source: Unit-level data for the selected villages from APMGNREGS website.

Regression Analysis

The related results are presented in Table 7.5. The households had gained an additional employment of 30 days per household from the villages when they were exposed to social audit compared to the situation when they were not exposed to social audit (column 2, row 1). But, the SC and ST households had gained an additional employment of 38 days per household in the villages due to social audit (column 3, row 1). Thus, social audit has enabled the SC and ST households in demanding more employment. In other words, social audit has enhanced the negotiating skills of SC and ST households to bargain with the implementing agency. Social audit is found to be more effective in enabling the households in obtaining more employment in the villages which have higher irrigated area (the source of irrigation is groundwater and subject to instability due to frequent droughts) for crop cultivation and larger proportion of female population, compared to those in the villages that have lower irrigated area and lower proportion of female population. Further, it is also found to be more effective in the villages with lower per capita income and lower proportion of SC and ST population in raising the employment per household. This also indicates that the authorities had not been able to meet the increased demand due to social audit for employment from the SC and ST households in the villages which have larger proportion of SC and ST population. Thus, the social audit had enabled the households in the villages which have higher irrigated area, higher proportion of SC and ST population, higher proportion of female population and higher per capita income to get additional employment. Further, the household's probability of obtaining 100 days of employment had increased by 0.20.

Table 7.5: Contribution of Social Audit to Employment from MGNREGS: Regression Results

		Dependent Variables		
Sl. No.	*Independent Variable*	*EMPNREGS*	*SC and ST EMPNREGS*	*Households Completed 100 Days of Employment*
	1	2	3	4
1.	Social audit (dummy)	29.75***	37.74***	0.196***
2.	Percentage of irrigated area (dummy)	2.41**	6.84***	0.039***
3.	Percentage of SC and ST population (dummy)	-2.36**	-2.469	-0.01
4.	Percentage of female population (dummy)	5.94***	8.97***	0.071***
5.	Per capita income (dummy)	-35.37***	-21.53***	-0.047***
Constant		38.93	37.31	-0.0036
Adj. R-Square		0.106	0.117	0.1
Number of Observations		6,560	2,046	6,560

Source: Unit-level data for the selected villages from APMGNREGS website.
Notes: EMPNREGS = Employment per HH obtained through MGNREGS.
Level of significance based on t values: * denotes <1%, ** denotes 5%, *** denotes 5—10%.
The independent variables are considered as dichotomous; district having higher value than the state average as one and otherwise as zero.

The Contribution of WSAs

Even though the MGNREGA spells out clearly the rights and entitlements of wage seekers, individual wage seekers from socially marginalised communities, particularly SC and ST, are not in a position to access their rights and entitlements due to their dependence on the local land-owning dominant castes for work, loans, foodgrains when in distress, and for other needs. The implementation of MGNREGS as per the act in letter and spirit could change the relations between dominant caste landlords and SC/ST labour, and this may ultimately result in an increase in the bargaining capacity of the SC and ST with the land-owning upper castes. The latter may not like to lose their control over the socially marginalised communities. Hence, they may see to it that the programme is not implemented effectively through their nexus with the political leaders and bureaucracy at various levels. Hence, there is a need for organising wage seekers to access their rights and entitlements of MGNREGS through their negotiations with the implementing agency controlled by the land-owning elites and bureaucracy. The government of Andhra Pradesh, through G.O.M.s No. 339 dated 7 November 2009, has encouraged wage seekers to organise potential labour into groups that can be registered with mandal parishad development officer (MPDOs)/assistant project directors (APOs) at the mandal level for demanding and claiming all their rights and entitlements under the MGNREGS and effectively participate in the social audit process and be a part of social audit forums. WSAs in Andhra Pradesh focus on the following issues relating to the planning and implementation of the MGNREGS: job cards, preparation and updating of list of wage-seekers, identification of shelf of works, interaction with MGNREGS officials, allotment of work, facilities at worksites, work measurements and muster roll verification, payslips issue, wage payments, peer leaders identification from WSAs, members enrolment in WSAs, WSA formation at the village level, awareness camps to WSAs, WSAs federation at the mandal and district levels, WSAs meetings at the village and mandal levels, participation in mandal-level review meetings on MGNREGS and facilitating the participation of WSAs in social audit (People's Monitoring Committee, 2009). The data in this regard indicates that WSAs have contributed to an increase of 16 percentage points of participation of workers from among the eligible workers. They have also led to the increase of 32 days of employment per household and an increase of 26 days of employment per households in case of SC and ST households. Further, they have increased the percentage of households who got 100 days of employment (Table 7.6).

Table 7.6: Different Parameters of Employment from MGNREGS in the Villages before WSAs and after WSAs

Sl. No.	*Parameters of Employment*	*Before WSAs (2007–08)*	*After WSAs (2009–10)*	*Increase/ Decrease*
1.	Percentage of workers participating in MGNREGS from total eligible workers	53.24	69.39	16.15
2.	Average number of days worked per household	31	63	32
3.	Average number of days worked per HH by SC and ST HHs	30	56	26
4.	HHs completed 100 days of employment	6	281	275

Source: Unit-level data for selected villages from APMGNREGS website.

Regression Analysis

The results are presented in Table 7.7. The households in the villages have obtained a low level of employment by 26 days per household due to the presence of WSAs (column 2, row 1). Further, the households belonging to SCs and STs in these villages got a low-level employment by 60 days (column 3, row 1). The WSAs are found to be more effective in the villages that have large proportion of irrigated area and larger proportion of female population. On the other hand, they are found to be less effective in the villages that have higher proportion of SC and ST households. This indicates that the demand for employment from SC and ST households has not been met by the implementing authorities in the village where large proportion of SC and ST households live. This has become more severe in the context of WSAs enhancing the participation of wage seekers into the programme. In other words, the increased demand for employment due to more participation of wage seekers in the villages after the WSA took roots, especially in the villages where large proportion of SC and ST households live, has not been met by the authorities and this has resulted in the lower employment days for the households on average. This had further reduced the household's probability of obtaining 100 days of employment.

Table 7.7: Contribution of WSAs to Employment from MGNREGS: Regression Results

Sl. No.	*Independent Variable*	*Dependent Variables*		
		EMPNREGS	*SC and ST EMPNREGS*	*HH Completed 100 Days of Employment*
	1	2	3	4
1.	WSA (dummy)	−26.1***	−59.66***	−0.137***
2.	Percentage of irrigated area (dummy)	3.045***	8.05***	0.044***
3.	Percentage of SC and ST population (dummy)	−16.68***	−36.33***	−0.085***
4.	Percentage of female population (dummy)	18.31***	29.16***	0.13***
5.	Per capita income (dummy)	−29.17***	−55.61***	−0.132***
6.	Constant	66.54	91.09	0.182
7.	Adj. R-Square	0.051	0.114	0.042
8.	Number of observations	6,560	2,046	6,560

Source: Unit-level data for the selected villages from APMGNREGS website and village and town directory, Population Census 2001, Ananthapura District.
Notes: EMPNREGS = Employment per HH obtained through MGNREGS.
Level of significance based on t values: * denotes <1%, ** denotes 5%, *** denotes 10%.
The independent variables are considered as dichotomous; district having higher value than the state average as one and otherwise as zero.

Synergy between WSA and Social Audit: Regression Analysis

The contribution of WSAs and social audit to the different dimensions of employment has been assessed in the foregoing analysis. The village which has WSAs and is exposed to social audit gives the opportunity to examine the following two issues:

1. How far do WSAs and social audit together contribute to the additional gains in different dimensions of employment for the households in villages?
2. What are the village contexts in which WSAs and social audit are together effective in ensuring gains in different dimensions of employment for the households in villages?

The results are presented in Table 7.8. The years 2007–08 and 2009–10 are considered to capture the employment situation before social audit/WSAs and the employment situation after social audit/WSAs, respectively. The villages which were exposed to both WSAs and social audit are considered .The employment situation in these villages before (2007–08) after (2009–10) experiencing both WSAs and social audit helps to examine the issues raised above. The estimated results of the above equation unfold that the employment for the households on an average per household in the villages had declined after exposure to WSAs compared to the situation of non-exposure to WSAs by these villages; the employment demanded by the households was shared among the increased participant households due to the exposure to WSAs and, as a result, the employment per households in these villages had declined after

Table 7.8: Contribution of Social Audit and WSAs to Employment under MGNREGS: Regression Results

		Dependent Variables		
Sl. No.	*Independent Variable*	*EMPNREGS*	*SC and ST EMPNREGS*	*HHs Completed 100 Days of Employment*
1.	Social audit (dummy)	31.106***	40.572***	0.203***
2.	Percentage of irrigated Area (dummy)	–1.972*	3.26	0.012
3.	Percentage of SC and ST population (dummy)	–19.706***	–38.82***	–0.105***
4.	Percentage of female population (dummy)	19.264***	30.147***	0.136***
5.	Per capita income (dummy)	–29.183***	–55.028***	–0.132***
6.	WSA (dummy)	–29.612***	–64.286***	–0.16***
7.	Constant	51.75	69.58	0.080
8.	Adj. R-Square	0.131	0.205	0.119
9.	Number of Observations	6,560	2,046	6,560

Notes: EMPNREGS = Employment per HH obtained through NREGS.
Level of significance based on t values: * denotes <1%, ** denotes 5%, *** denotes 10%.
The independent variables are considered as dichotomous; district having higher value than the state average as one and otherwise as zero.

exposure to WSAs; the social audit, on the other hand, had contributed to increase in the employment per household, despite the increased participation of the workers in the villages; the households in the villages exposed to both these institutions had a gain of one additional day of employment. It is also evident from the results that the combination of these two institutions is found to be more effective in the villages where the proportion of female population is high. The combination is also found to be effective in the villages that have low proportion of SC and ST population and low per capita income. This is also true with regard to gain in employment and also the village contexts in which the combination of these institutions are found to be effective in case of SC and ST households. It is also further evident that the probability of households getting 100 days of employment has increased due to the combined effect of WSAs and social audit. This is more so in the village contexts where the proportion of female population is high and percentage of irrigated area is high, and also the village contexts where the proportion of SC and ST population is low and per capita income is low.

Conclusion

SHGs and social audit have enabled the households in general to obtain additional employment. Moreover, they have increased the probability of getting 100 days of employment by the households. The SHGs were found to be more effective in enabling the households in getting more employment in highly drought-prone situations. This indicates that MGNREGS has provided social protection in the vulnerable situation. Social audit is found to be more effective in enabling the households in obtaining more employment in the villages which have highly unstable irrigated area (groundwater source in drought situation) and larger proportion of female population. Further, it is also found to be more effective in the villages with lower per capita income and lower proportion of SC and ST population in raising the employment per household. But this institution has not enabled SC and ST households in obtaining additional employment in the villages which have larger proportion of SC and ST population.

WSAs have not contributed in obtaining additional employment in general and also to the SC and ST households. They are found to be effective in the villages which have high unstable irrigation source and large proportion of female population with low per capita income. But WSAs are found to be ineffective in villages with larger proportion of SC and ST population. The social audit and the WSA together have also not enabled the SC and ST households to gain additional employment in a similar situation. This indicates that the authorities had not been able to meet the increased demand or there is large unmet demand due to social audit/WSAs/combination of social audit and WSAs for employment from the SC and ST households in the villages with larger proportion of SC and ST population. As a result of this, the households had shared the employment provided and this, in turn, reduced the employment per household. This process had ultimately led to reduction in the probability of households getting 100 days of employment in the villages with larger proportion of SC and ST population. All these indicate that implementing agency has not geared up itself to meet the increased demand for employment from SC and ST sections due to the presence of state-led and state-enabled institutions. The increased demand from these sections is due to two factors: one, entry of new wage seekers and two, the enhanced demand from the existing wage-seekers. When the poorest of the poor sections largely consisting of SC and ST population have geared up to demand larger employment due to state-enabled institutions, the implementing authority is not able to cater to the increased demand. This is much against the very spirit of guaranteed employment.

References

Aakella, K. and S. Kidami (2007a) Challenging corruption with social audits. *Economic and Political Weekly* No. 5 (3 February): 345–47.

——— (2007b) Social audits in Andhra Pradesh: A process in evolution. *Economic and Political Weekly* No. 47 (24 November); 18–19.

Galab, S. and P. Prudhvikar Reddy (2009) *End-term Appraisal of Andhra Pradesh Rural Poverty Reduction Project*. Unpublished project report, CESS, Hyderabad.

——— (2010) *Impact Assessment of Andhra Pradesh Rural Poverty Reduction Project*, Centre for Economic and Social Studies (CESS), Hyderabad.

Galab, S., E. Revathi, P. Prudhvikar Reddy and C. Ravi (2010) Mahatma Gandhi National Rural Employment Guarantee Programme in Andhra Pradesh: An assessment. LBS *Journal of Management and Research* VIII, (January–June No. 1): 14–34.

Galab, S., P. Prudhvikar Reddy, E. Revathi and C. Ravi (2009) *Report on Management of National Rural Employment Guarantee Scheme, Issues and Challenges: The Case of Andhra Pradesh*. Submitted to the Lal Bahadur Shastri Institute of Management, New Delhi.

Gopal, K. S. (2009) NREGA social audit: Myths and reality. *Economic and Political Weekly* No. 3 (17 January): 70–71.

Government of Andhra Pradesh, Department of Rural Development. http://nrega.ap.gov.in.

MGNREGS (2011) *Report on the Mid Term Appraisal of the 11th Plan of Andhra Pradesh*. Sponsored by Planning Commission, GoI, Vol II CESS, Hyderabad.

People's Monitoring Committee (2009) *Empowering wage seeker's federations: To access NEGS in AP.* PMC: Hyderabad.

Pokharel, Atul, Y. Aiyar and S. Samji (2008) Understanding social audits: Learning's from the AP experience. www.rd.ap.gov.in/SAudit/drasft_Social Audit_Feb08.pps (accessed 12 November 2009).

Raju, K. (2009) Social audit immersion clinic. Presentation made at World Bank, Washington D.C. on 23rd March.

Ravi Kumar, C. H., D. Rakesh Kumar and S. Seethalakshmi (2008) National Rural Employment Guarantee Act in Andhra Pradesh: Claims and questions in operationalisation (2007–08). www.nregaconsortium.in/resources.html (accessed 12 November 2009).

Appendix 7A

Table 7A.1: Employment Days per Household, Percentage of Households Who Obtained 100 Days of Employment and Wage Rate (₹) for All and IKP Households under MGNREGS during 2009–10

	Average Days of Employment Provided Per HH						*Percentage of HH Completed 100 Days of Employment*		*Average Wage Rate*	
	All	*IKP*	*All*	*IKP*	*All*	*IKP*	*All*	*IKP*	*All*	*IKP*
Districts	*Total HH*		*SC*		*ST*				*HH*	
Adilabad	46.7	83.4	44.8	68	46.2	60.9	12.2	17.4	90.8	83.4
Ananthapura	50.6	87.9	48.7	85.5	53.7	83.8	14	17.1	97.7	87.9
Chittoor	66.1	76.1	60.8	94.7	53.2	75.7	23.1	25.1	86.8	76.1
East Godavari	41.7	78.8	30.4	104.2	65.3	133.9	12.4	17.5	85.5	78.8
Guntur	17.2	88.7	15.7	30.4	24.8	38.6	1.4	9.5	96.6	88.7
Kadapa	65.7	77.6	62.3	93.1	54.8	65.7	23.2	23.4	84.8	77.6
Karimnagar	44.6	85.8	39.4	83.5	52.7	88.8	11.2	18.1	91.1	85.8
Khammam	52.4	82.8	44.6	62.1	59.9	68.5	16.1	25.2	84.3	82.8
Krishna	22.3	78.7	22.4	72.8	27.3	69.9	2.4	0.8	83.7	78.7
Kurnool	63.1	89.2	63.3	77.6	58.7	57.6	21.5	26	88.7	89.2
Mahabubnagar	49.6	87	48.6	68	47.1	72.2	13.1	30.1	91	87
Medak	50.8	92	53.8	75.2	45.7	76.2	13.7	16.4	96.9	92
Nalgonda	42.6	79.3	41.7	71.6	46.1	105.1	9.3	10.4	86.1	79.3
Nizamabad	52.9	91.3	47.5	86.6	58.7	110.2	15.7	14.7	94.5	91.3
Prakasam	53.5	80.8	46.9	94.5	48.9	23.5	16.4	6.7	86.6	80.8
Ranga Reddy	62.4	92.7	64.7	93.8	73.6	98.3	20.7	21.3	102.8	92.7
S.P.S Nellore	44.8	71.8	39.7	81	38	65.4	12.5	13	85	71.8
Srikakulam	53.2	72.6	51.8	89.9	54.5	83.1	15.3	10.3	87.3	72.6
Visakhapatnam	44.8	79.9	42.1	93.7	29.9	70.6	12.9	8.5	89.7	79.9
Vizianagaram	63.8	76.3	64.4	90.1	50.9	84.7	19.6	32.9	84	76.3
Warangal	41.7	83.1	38.4	56.9	45.9	44.8	8.4	9.6	86.1	83.1
West Godavari	32.9	73.3	34.9	82.2	50.9	94.1	8	3.5	77.1	73.3
Total	**49.4**	**82.4**	**45.5**	**80.8**	**49.4**	**74.3**	**14.1**	**17.1**	**88.8**	**82.4**

Table 7A.2: Performance of MGNREGS across the Districts in Andhra Pradesh during the Year 2010–11 (as on 16 November 2010)

		Parameters for Measuring Performance of MGNREGS									
Sl. No.	*Districts*	*Score for Working HHs*	*Average Days per HH Score*	*Timely Payment Score*	*Score for SC and ST (Population)*	*Score for Completion of Works*	*Score for HHs Completing 100 Days*	*Overall Rank*	*No. of SHG/ 1000 Women*	*Corpus Funds/ SHG (₹ Lakhs)*	*Percentage of Average Drought-affected Mandals to Total*
1.	Adilabad	59.15	76.71	71.63	76.35	86.83	56.02	5	25.70	0.21	36
2.	Ananthapura	50.73	81.28	84.08	41.78	67.18	57.73	11	39.62	0.15	49
3.	Chittoor	32.3	79.08	90.49	37.25	50.13	48.29	17	19.66	0.67	49
4.	East Godavari	60.99	43.01	88.83	50.41	100	20.3	16	14.00	1.04	22
5.	Guntur	30.54	36.27	88.53	16.8	90.93	15.89	22	11.46	1.52	25
6.	Kadapa	46.34	82.36	84.92	46.89	71.49	65.02	9	31.11	0.57	50
7.	Karimnagar	66.8	49.18	74.53	46.15	95.6	19.4	18	26.90	0.42	36
8.	Khammam	65.8	58.47	83.68	55.22	70.23	33.95	13	41.36	0.45	25
9.	Krishna	41.86	32.96	89.4	23.67	81.16	10.74	21	12.18	0.82	23
10.	Kurnool	61.41	75.49	80.81	48.61	85.52	54.25	7	25.32	0.47	43
11.	Mahabubnagar	60.58	71.55	73.37	47.55	93.05	51.97	10	18.57	0.40	47
12.	Medak	62.96	76.09	76.75	61.35	82.32	56.56	6	22.88	0.57	39
13.	Nalgonda	79.63	60.26	70.43	58.96	70.23	36.99	12	23.13	0.56	41
14.	Nizamabad	74.14	100	73.05	100	78.93	100	1	37.91	0.15	34
15.	Prakasam	64.07	65.94	63.7	53.15	64.7	47.69	15	30.75	0.17	49
16.	Ranga Reddy	53.99	74.61	75.95	55.48	94.53	56.76	8	23.17	0.32	36
17.	S.P.S Nellore	44.4	54.02	88.12	27.19	81.01	29.57	19	23.29	0.32	49
18.	Srikakulam	93.74	80.76	85.77	87.56	92.08	64.65	2	37.81	0.32	32

19.	Visakhapatnam	80.83	61.57	100	72.4	59.32	36.42	4	21.98	0.35	28
20.	Vizianagaram	100	80.43	71.44	66.98	46.3	62.54	3	47.22	0.14	33
21.	Warangal	88.73	57.77	59.01	55.91	70.78	31.24	14	37.48	0.67	35
22.	West Godavari	51.45	47.61	80.31	40.45	76.05	30.33	20	26.84	0.84	21

Source: http/ nrega.ap.gov.in.

Notes: Overall rank is calculated based on the following weightages.

20 per cent weightage on working HHs, 25 per cent weightage on average person-days per HH,
20 per cent weightage on timely payments, 15 per cent weightage on average days by SC and ST,
10 per cent weightage on works completion, 10 per cent weightage on HHs completing 100 days (considered from September in every Financial year).

Table 7A.3: Performance of MGNREGS and Other Indicators in the Villages of Parigi Mandal of Ananthapura District

Sl. No.	Villages	*EMPNREGS*		*SC and ST EMPNREGS*		*HH Completed 100 days of Employment*		*Total Score of Implementation (TSI)*		*WSA 1=Y 0=N*	*Social Audit 0=Before SA, 1=After SA (Social Audit Year= 2008–09)*		*Pecent-age of Female Popula-tion*	*Percent-age of SC and ST Popula-tion*	*Percent-age of Irrigated Area*	*Percentage of area Irrigated under Ground-water*	*PCI*
		2007	2009	2007	2009	2007	2009	2007	2009	2009	2007	2009	2001	2001	2008	2008	2008
1.	Beechiganipalle	30	93	36	126	4	154	5	1	0	0	1	49.6	30.0	12.0	100.0	0.03
2.	Honampally	25	71	28	79	3	97	9	7	0	0	1	NA	NA	NA	NA	NA
3.	Kodigenahalli	19	35	8	10	0	17	14	12	0	0	1	46.2	13.7	29.6	75.4	0.53
4.	Moda	41	54	40	56	6	56	6	10	0	0	1	48.5	32.5	24.9	100.0	0.10
5.	P. Narasapuram	30	43	34	36	0	21	8	11	1	0	1	48.2	18.7	16.0	100.0	0.06
6.	Parigi	39	46	34	42	8	54	1	6	0	0	1	48.9	21.8	22.7	94.3	0.51
7.	Pydeti	27	61	21	63	1	59	11	14	0	0	1	48.4	16.1	31.7	100.0	0.07
8.	S. Rangarajpally	28	62	27	65	4	66	2	2	1	0	1	NA	NA	NA	NA	NA
9.	Sasanakota	28	62	20	14	1	0	7	5	1	0	1	50.5	32.7	31.1	100.0	0.07
10.	Seegipalle	34	17	24	80	0	83	12	13	1	0	1	51.1	14.8	12.0	100.0	0.08
11.	Sirekolam	21	89	44	150	7	155	4	9	0	0	1	48.7	20.4	40.4	100.0	0.04
12.	Utakur	46	71	49	82	14	130	3	4	0	0	1	48.6	24.1	48.0	100.0	0.05
13.	Vittapalle	0	55	0	61	0	35	13	8	1	0	1	49.6	21.0	30.7	100.0	0.05
14.	Yerragunta	38	102	33	109	5	142	10	3	1	0	1	49.0	18.0	32.4	100.0	0.05

Source: Compiled on the basis of data from http://nrega.ap.gov.in; social audit reports; Village Directory, 2001, Census Ananthapura district.

8

Employment Guarantee Scheme in Punjab

A Case Study of Hoshiarpur District

Ranjit Singh Ghuman and Parvinder Kaur Dua

I

Introduction

This chapter examines working of the guaranteed employment scheme in the state of the Punjab that has been the bedrock of green revolution, and is one of the most prosperous states of India. However, with the deceleration in agriculture since the last two decades, various facets of agrarian distress have surfaced. Amidst declining agricultural productivity and increasing input cost, debt-ridden farmers are committing suicides in large numbers. Unemployment in general and rural unemployment in particular has increased. Inability of the agricultural sector to productively absorb rural labour force further and incommensurate growth in the non-farm sector employment have resulted in increased number of unemployed population.

The Punjab has been a net importer of agricultural labourer. However, the heavy mechanisation in the course of green revolution has reduced the demand for agricultural labourer only for non-mechanised parts of farming like transplanting paddy, grass weeding, etc. Thus, the scarcity of labourer is only seasonal in character. Moreover, mechanisation has also reduced the overall number of employment days in agriculture, although it has increased in the non-farm sectors.

This chapter examines the demand for government-sponsored wage employment in the rural areas of Punjab, and probes the level and intensity of such demand, across various segments of population. It also examines the impact of the scheme on the agrarian economy in general and local wages, rural labour market and agriculture productivity in particular.

The next part gives an overview of the agrarian and rural economy and employment–unemployment situation in the rural Punjab. The overall implementation of the employment guarantee scheme in Punjab has been discussed in Part III. In Part IV, the implementation conditions and performance of the scheme have been examined in detail through a case study of Hoshiarpur district, the only first-phase district of the Punjab. Last, some general conclusions about the relevance and utility of the scheme and its likely impact on the rural and agrarian economy of the state have been summed up.

II

An Overview of Agrarian and Employment Scenario in Punjab

The decline in the agriculture productivity, income and employment generation and the overall agrarian economy of the Punjab since the last two decades have been explained in a number of studies (Bhalla, 1987 and 1989; Bhalla and Singh, 2009; Ghuman, 2001; Gill, 2002; Johl, 2002). This decline has been partly explained as adverse effects of excess use of chemical fertilisers and pesticides, heavy exploitation of groundwater, heavy mechanisation (mainly in the form of under utilisation of capacity) and increasing input cost and declining productivity in agriculture (Chadha, 1986; Chopra, 2002; Gill and Ghuman, 2001; Raikhy, 1999; Ray, 2002; Singh, 2007). As such the rural Punjab in general and agrarian economy in particular is passing through a critical phase which has resulted in a serious crisis (Ghuman, 2005, 2008a; Gill, 2005; Shergill, 1998, 2010; Singh et al., 2007a, 2007b).

Agriculture sector in the Punjab has been experiencing a deceleration for about the last two decades in terms of stagnating yield and rising cost. The annual trend growth rate of per hectare net return, over operational costs in wheat and paddy combined (two major crops), at constant prices, was –2.18 per cent per annum during the decade of 1990s. In the case of cotton, it was –14.24 per cent (Ghuman, 2001). The ever rising cost of cultivation and declining net return has resulted in heavy indebtedness of farmers. According to the NSSO (2005) estimates, the average amount of outstanding loan on each farm household is the highest (₹41,576) in the Punjab amongst all the major states in India. About 52 per cent of this debt is from non-institutional sources. Moreover, next to Andhra Pradesh and Tamil Nadu, the debt incidence of farmers is the third highest in Punjab. About 65 per cent farm households in Punjab are under debt.

A recent study (Singh et al., 2007b) highlights that about 89 per cent farmers are under debt and per household debt was ₹56,442. According to this study, 48 per cent of the debt was from non-institutional sources. According to Shergill (2010), the total farm debt in Punjab was ₹303,941 million in 2008. His earlier study (1998) estimated the farm debt at ₹57,009 million. The burden of debt per operated acre in Punjab increased from ₹5,721 in 1997 to ₹28,942 in 2008. At constant prices (1997–98 prices), the total farm debt in Punjab in 2008 was ₹138,293 million (2.43 times higher than that in 1997). The debt per operated acre (at 1997–98 prices) increased from ₹5,721 in 1997 to ₹13,169 in 2008, an increase of 2.3 times. Significantly, 54.17 per cent of this farm debt was from non-institutional (commission agents and money lenders) sources. Nearly 17 per cent farmers in Punjab are in debt trap (Shergill, 2010). It is significant to note that the debt burden on the households in which farmers committed suicides was to the tune of ₹270,419 (Singh, G., 2008).

The ever-shrinking net income, led to an increasing economic distress which, in turn, resulted in farmers' suicides in the Punjab. It is estimated that more than 10, 000 farmers in the Punjab might have committed suicide during, approximately, the last 15 years.[1] The incidence of suicide is not only confined to farmers, but is found in agricultural labourers also (Singh, G., 2008). It is estimated that about

3,000–4,000 labourers have committed suicide during the same period. A recent study (PAU, 2009) has revealed that 1,757 farmers and 1,133 agricultural labourers committed suicides in only two districts of Punjab—Sangrur and Bathinda—during 2000–08. The study further shows that about 73 per cent of farmers and 59 per cent of labourers had committed suicide because of indebtedness.

Unemployment in general and rural unemployment in particular has increased in recent years. One of its reasons is shrinking employment opportunities in agriculture in particular and rural economy in general. Out of the total workers in the Punjab nearly 70 per cent are engaged in rural sector. Further, out of the total rural workers, 31.5 per cent are cultivators, 22.0 per cent are agricultural labourers, 3.1 per cent are engaged in household industry and 43.4 per cent are other workers. The proportion of agricultural workers (cultivators + labourers) in all the workers in the state has declined from 55.2 per cent in 1991 to 39.4 per cent in 2001 (Government of India, 2002b). This clearly shows the declining employment opportunities in the agricultural sector.

The agricultural sector and rural economy, unable to absorb rural labour force further, have been pushing out the surplus workers for about the last two decades in the Punjab. However, incommensurate growth of employment generation in non-agricultural sectors has increased the incidence of unemployment in rural population (Ghuman, 2005). It has been estimated, based on the cost of cultivation data, that 1.29 million (1.01 million cultivators and 0.28 million labourers) agricultural workers have been rendered surplus in agriculture and livestock. Total person-days employment in crop-rearing sector alone declined from 480 million person-days in 1983–84 to 430 million person-days in 1996–97, according to estimates generated from cost of cultivation data (Gill, 2002).

The labour-absorption capacity of agriculture in the Punjab has been experiencing a negative trend growth rate (Bhalla, 1987). The fact of the matter is that growth rate of employment in agriculture was just 0.02 per cent during 1993–94 and 1999–2000 in India. The employment elasticity in agriculture during the same period was just 0.01 (Government of India, 2002c).

As per the Punjab Government estimates (Government of Punjab, 1998), 1.04 million persons (0.58 million educated and 0.46 million uneducated) in the 18–35 years age group were unemployed in the rural Punjab in 1998. In view of very low growth rate of employment, this might have gone above two million by now.[2] The employment growth rate in Punjab during the Ninth and Tenth Five Year Plans was far below the growth rate of labour force. The Kaldor-Kuznets (Kaldor, 1967; Kuznets, 1965) long-term dynamics of growth of an agrarian economy have been partially reflected in the case of Punjab agriculture. The share of agriculture in state's net income declined substantially from 47 per cent in 1960–61 to about 22 per cent in 2005–06, at 1993–94 prices (Ghuman, 2008b). Contrary to it, the share of workforce in agriculture declined from 55.89 per cent in 1961 to 55.26 per cent in 1991. Perhaps slow structural change in occupation has been one of the most serious limitations of Punjab's development model.

It is significant to note that the proportion of agricultural workers in total rural workers in Punjab declined from 73.5 per cent in 1991 to 53.5 per cent in 2001 (Government of India, 2002b). This means 46.5 per cent of rural workers are in the non-agricultural sector. However, the empirical studies do not support such a high percentage of rural workers in non-agricultural sector in the state. According to one of those studies (Ghuman, 2005) about 16 per cent of the rural workers in the state are in non-agricultural sectors. In fact, the agricultural sector has started pushing the labour out and non-agricultural sectors are not absorbing those pushed-out workers.

The share of casual labour in total hired labour agriculture in Punjab increased from 29 to 71 per cent in 1970s to 68 to 84 per cent in 1990s (Gill and Ghuman, 2001). Due to shrinking employment opportunities in agriculture, these casual labourers are able to find work for a lesser number of days in agriculture in a year. Little more than 16 per cent casual labourers could find work only for 8 to 10 days in a month. Another 79 per cent could get work for 10 to 20 days in a month. On an average, the agricultural labourers in Punjab got ₹73 per day during 2006–07, whereas non-agricultural labourers earned ₹95 per day. As regards rural workers, working partially in agriculture and partially in non-agricultural sectors, the average wage earnings were ₹77 per day during 2006–07 (Ghuman et al., 2007). Taking five persons as the average size of the household, it comes out to be nearly 15 rupees per capita. Significantly, at the all-India level, 77 per cent population is living on only up to ₹20 a day (Sengupta et al., 2008).

In fact, the agricultural labourers are also committing suicides in Punjab, mainly due to their poor economic conditions and outstanding loan (AFDR, 2000; Iyer, 2000). The average amount of outstanding loan of the deceased agricultural labourers was ₹57,121 per household in 2007 (Singh, G., 2008).

It is significant to note that there has been a large-scale migration of labour into Punjab ever since the success of green revolution since 1970s. A sizeable proportion of that in-migration was into agriculture sector. The in-migration of labour in rural Punjab was 0.41 million in 1981, which increased to 0.67 million in 1991 (Government of India, 1981, 1991). In 2006–07, the estimated in-migration of labour in rural Punjab was 0.82 million (Ghuman et al., 2007). This was a unique phenomenon as on the one side, Punjab agriculture was pushing labourers out of agriculture and, on the other hand, there was a continuous in-migration of labourers in the state. In fact, most of the employment in the agriculture sector has become seasonal due to heavy mechanisation and shrinking of busy season days in agriculture. As such, 0.70 million migrant labourers (out of 0.82 million labourers) were seasonal and were employed on casual basis.

III

Employment Scenario under MGNREGS across the Districts in Punjab

The MGNREGS became operative in only one district (Hoshiarpur) of the state on 2 February 2006 (Phase I). It was extended to Amritsar, Jalandhar and Nawanshahr districts on 1 April 2007 (Phase II) and to the rest 16 districts on 1 April 2008 (Phase III). The scheme provides a minimum annual income through 100 days of guaranteed employment to all the rural households who (have limited income and employment opportunities) are willing to work on the prescribed minimum wages.

The MGNREGA became operative in all the districts of the state with effect from the financial year 2008–09. As such, the district-wise employment scenario under the MGNREGS has been examined for only three years, that is, 2008–09, 2009–10 and 2010–11. In 2008–09, in all the 20 districts of Punjab, 524,928 households were issued job cards and, out of them, 72.98 per cent were SC households (Table 8.1). But in district like Moga, 96.30 per cent of the job cardholders were SC households. Out of the total job cardholder households, 28.56 per cent were also given employment. Again, out of the total employment provided (4,017 thousand person-days), the share of SCs was 74.17 per cent. The SCs constituted 28.85 per cent of the total and 33.04 per cent of the rural population in Punjab (Government

Table 8.1: Employment Status under MGNREGS across the Districts in Punjab during 2008–09

	Cumulative no. of HHs Issued Job Cards			*HHs Provided Employment*		*Employment Generated (Thousand Person-days)*		
Districts	*Total*	*SC*	*SC (%)*	*Total*	*SC (%)*	*Total*	*SC (%)*	*Women (%)*
(1)	*(2)*	*(3)*	*(4)*	*(5)*	*(6)*	*(7)*	*(8)*	*(9)*
Hoshiarpur	**45,135**	**27,590**	**61.13**	**35,512**	**78.68**	**1,206**	**59.45**	**26.04**
Amritsar	36,163	32,751	90.56	14,913	41.24	617	89.95	0.49
Jalandhar	16,566	14,086	85.03	4,234	25.56	108	97.22	36.11
Nawanshahr	16,373	12,176	74.37	4,154	25.37	146	86.99	52.74
Barnala	17,385	12,385	71.24	1,268	7.29	090	96.67	48.89
Bathinda	23,532	22,208	94.37	17,036	72.40	340	99.41	1.76
Faridkot	11,899	8,946	75.18	5,319	44.70	37	86.49	10.81
Fategarh Sahib	15,830	12,568	79.39	1,955	12.35	85	80.00	29.41
Firozpur	72,543	49,392	68.09	9,943	13.71	50	86.00	100.00
Gurdaspur	51,378	28,445	55.36	7,036	13.69	193	60.10	0.00
Kapurthala	9,237	7,813	84.58	2,566	27.78	38	68.42	23.68
Ludhiana	11,450	9,786	85.47	996	8.70	183	82.51	4.35
Mansa	25,134	21,403	85.16	7,241	28.81	95	91.58	22.11
Moga	18,137	17,466	96.30	1,703	9.39	52	86.54	1.92
Muktsar	25,038	23,488	93.81	11,259	44.97	174	95.40	100.00
Patiala	22,748	15,572	68.45	4,398	19.33	147	80.95	29.25
Rupnagar	14,233	7,915	55.61	1,046	7.35	29	55.17	17.24
Sangrur	43,082	22,600	52.46	11,652	27.46	265	28.68	19.62
SAS Nagar	12,101	6,333	52.33	5,763	47.62	124	59.68	94.35
Tarn Taran	36,964	29,832	80.71	1,908	5.16	48	81.25	0.00
Total	**524,928**	**383,115**	**72.98**	**149,902**	**28.56**	**4027**	**74.17**	**24.61**

Source: www.nrega.ntc.in, accessed 13 May 2010.

Notes: 1. Hoshiarpur was covered under the first phase of the MGNREGS and the three districts—Amritsar, Jalandhar and Nawanshahr—were covered under the second phase. The remaining 16 districts were covered in the third phase.

2. The number of job cardholder households that demanded employment under the MGNREGS and the number of households that were provided employment is exactly the same, as per the official record.

3. 10 lakh = 1 million.

4. Nawanshahr is now SAB Nagar.

of Punjab, 2008). Across the districts, the proportion of SCs in rural population varied between 26.15 per cent (Gurdaspur) and 45.78 per cent (Jalandhar). Women's share in total person-days of employment under the scheme was only one-fourth of the total (24.61 per cent). Thus, the demand for the government-sponsored guaranteed wage employment in the rural Punjab is largely confined to the SCs and women.

It is significant to note that Punjab has the highest proportion of SCs population amongst the major states in India. During the British period, all the non-tillers were not allowed to own/purchase agricultural land. Hence, the SCs in Punjab have historically been non-owners of land. Of late, however, they have been having some operational holdings and their share in the total operational holdings and in total operated area is only 4.67 per cent and 2.14 per cent, respectively. The average size of their operational holdings is 1.77 hectares (Government of India, 2003).

The overall level of demand for the government-sponsored wage employment in the state is low, which further varied across districts. The number of job cardholder households was only 9237 in Kapurthala, but 72,543 in Firozpur. The share of SC households varied between 52.33 per cent in SAS Nagar and 96.30 per cent in Moga. Similarly, the number of households that were provided with employment varied between 996 in Ludhiana and 35,512 in Hoshiarpur. The proportion of such households in the total number of job cardholder households varied between 5.16 per cent in Tarn Taran and 78.68 per cent in Hoshiarpur (Table 8.1).

The number of households provided employment as a ratio to the job cardholders is low in most of the districts. Out of the total 20 districts, the proportion of households with employment to the job cardholder households was only up to 25 per cent in 11 districts. In another seven districts, this proportion was between 25 per cent and 50 per cent. Only in two districts, the proportion of such households was above 50 per cent, but below 80 per cent (Table 8.1).

The amount of employment generation during 2008–09 varied between 37,000 person-days (Faridkot) and 12.06 lakh person-days (Hoshiarpur). The share of SC in the total person-days is quite sizeable and varied between 28.68 per cent in Sangrur and 99.41 per cent in Bathinda. In 14 districts, more than 80 per cent of the person-days of employment were availed by the SC households. The proportion was between 50 per cent and 80 per cent in another five districts. Only in one district, this was 28.68 per cent. It is to be noted that the share of SCs in the total job cardholder households was also very high in all the districts of the state (Table 8.1).

The proportion of women in the person-days employment was, however, not very high, except in some of the districts (Table 8.1). Their share was less than 50 per cent in 17 of the 20 districts. In two districts, the share of women was nil. This means that women in Punjab are either not participating in the work or are not encouraged to undertaking work under the MGNREGS.

The average person-days of employment per households varied between 5 days (Firozpur) and 43 days (Fatehgarh Sahib) across the districts of Punjab during 2008–09 (Table 8.2). The districts of Ludhiana and Barnala, with 184 days and 71 days, respectively, were an exception. In the case of Ludhiana, the number of households that demanded work was very small. Almost similar was the case in Barnala district.

The number of households completing 100 days of employment is quite low and almost negligible in most of the districts. In 10 out of 20 districts, not a single household completed 100 days of employment (Table 8.2).

Table 8.2: Generation of Employment under MGNREGS across the Districts and Employment Gap in Punjab during 2008–09

	Employment Generated (Person-days)		*HHs Employed for 100 Days*		*Required Employment (Thousand Person-days) to Provide 100 Days' Employment*		*Employment days' gap (in thousand)*	
Districts	*Total (in thousand)*	*Average per HH*	*No.*	*%*	*For HHs Demanding Work*	*For HHs with Job Cards*	*For HHs Demanding Work*	*For HHs with Job Cards*
(1)	*(2)*	*(3)*	*(4)*	*(5)*	*(6)*	*(7)*	*(8)*	*(9)*
Hoshiarpur	**1,206**	**33.96**	**3,534**	**9.96**	**3,551**	**4,514**	**2,345**	**3,308**
Amritsar	617	41.37	78	0.52	1,491	3,616	874	2,999
Jalandhar	108	25.51	00	0.00	423	1,657	315	1,519
Nawanshahr	146	35.15	172	4.14	415	1,637	269	1,491
Barnala	90	70.78	01	0.08	127	1,738	37	1,648
Bathinda	340	19.96	00	0.00	1,704	2,353	1,364	2,013
Faridkot	37	6.96	00	0.00	532	1,190	495	1,153
Fategarh Sahib	85	43.48	33	1.69	195	1,583	110	1,498
Firozpur	50	5.03	00	0.00	994	7,254	944	7,204
Gurdaspur	193	27.43	00	0.00	704	5,138	511	4,948
Kapurthala	38	14.81	00	0.00	257	924	219	886
Ludhiana	183	183.73	23	2.31	99	1,145	84	962
Mansa	95	13.12	18	0.25	724	2,513	629	2,418
Moga	52	30.53	00	0.00	170	1,814	118	1,762
Muktsar	174	15.45	12	0.11	1,126	2,504	952	233
Patiala	147	33.42	98	2.23	440	2,275	293	2,128
Rupnagar	29	27.72	01	0.09	105	1,423	76	1,394
Sangrur	265	22.74	00	0.00	1,165	4,308	900	4,043
SAS Nagar	124	21.15	00	0.00	576	1,210	452	1,086
Tarn Taran	48	25.16	00	0.00	191	3,696	143	3,648
Total	**4,027**	**26.86**	**3970**	**2.65**	**14,990**	**52,493**	**10,963**	**48,466**

Source: www.nrega.ntc.in, accessed 13 May 2010.

Notes: Column 6 has been computed by multiplying column 5 of table 1 by 100 and then dividing by hundred thousand; column 7 has been computed by multiplying column 2 of table 1 by 100 and then dividing by hundred thousand.

In another two districts, only one household completed 100 days of employment. However, in Hoshiarpur, about 10 per cent of the households could complete 100 days of employment. In five districts, the proportion of such households was less than one per cent. In another four districts, the proportion of such households varied between 1.69 per cent and 4.14 per cent.

Based on the presumption that all those households that are demanding employment would work for 100 days, the state should have generated 14.99 million person-days of employment in 2008–09. As against this, only 4.02 million person-days of employment were generated, thereby leaving a gap of 10.97 million person-days in 2008–09. The required extent of employment, across the districts, varied between 99 thousand person-days (Ludhiana) and 3.55 million person-days (Hoshiarpur). The employment gap across the districts ranged from 76 thousand person-days (Rupnagar) to 2.34 million person-days (Hoshiarpur). If all the job cardholder households were to be provided with 100 days' employment during 2008–09, the required employment generation would have been 52.49 million person-days. Accordingly, the employment gap would have been 48.47 million person-days (Table 8.2) in Punjab. The employment gap across the districts varied between 0.87 million person-days (Kapurthala) and 7.20 million person-days (Firozpur).

There is an overall increase in the employment demanded and provided in 2009–10 (Table 8.3). The number of job cardholder households increased from 524,928 in 2008–09 to 709,186 in 2009–10. Out of them, 77.61 per cent were the SCs. An increase of 184,258 (35.10 per cent) job card households in one year indicates the increasing level of demand for the scheme in the state.

The total number of households that were provided with employment increased to 270,713 in 2009–10 from 149,902 in 2008–09. The percentage of such households to the total job card households increased from 28.56 per cent in 2008–09 to 38.17 per cent in 2009–10. Across the districts, this percentage varied mainly between 6.34 per cent (Moga) to 43.94 per cent (Jalandhar) in majority of the districts. In three districts, this proportion was around 67 per cent, with Sangrur (93.21 per cent) as an exception.

The employment generation during 2009–10 (Table 8.3) was 7.66 million person-days. Out of this, 79.90 per cent were availed by the SCs and 26.35 per cent by women. Across the districts, the proportion of SCs varied from 52.03 per cent in Gurdaspur to 97.90 per cent in Bathinda. The proportion of women, across the districts was between 2.44 per cent in Moga and 73.38 per cent in Sangrur. The number of woman workers was nil in Faridkot district.

The average days of employment per household were 28.30 days in 2009–10. Across the various districts, it varied between 8.79 days (Sangrur) and 57.21 days (Mansa). District Rupnagar, with 70.35 days of average employment, was an exception (Table 8.4).

In terms of 100 days of employment, only 7,657 households (2.83 per cent) with employment completed 100 days in 2009–10 (Table 8.4). In two districts, no household got employment for 100 days. In another seven districts, the proportion of households that got employment for 100 days was less than one per cent. In 11 districts, this proportion varied between 1.38 per cent and 10.60 per cent of the households. Presuming that all those households that were provided employment would like to work for 100 days, the state was required to generate 27.07 million person-days as against 7.66 million person-days generated in 2009–10. This required an additional employment generation of

Table 8.3: Employment Status under MGNREGS across the Districts in Punjab during 2009–10

	Cumulative No. of HHs Issued Job Cards			*No. of HHs Provided Employment*		*Employment Generated (Thousand Person-days)*		
Districts	*Total*	*SC*	*SC (%)*	*Total*	*SC (%)*	*Total*	*SC (%)*	*Women (%)*
(1)	*(2)*	*(3)*	*(4)*	*(5)*	*(6)*	*(7)*	*(8)*	*(9)*
Hoshiarpur	**66,025**	**39,242**	**59.43**	**44,581**	**67.52**	**1,286**	**62.36**	**25.19**
Amritsar	55,126	47,224	85.67	37,425	67.89	1,524	85.70	3.08
Jalandhar	29,612	27,437	92.66	13,012	43.94	405	94.07	53.09
Nawanshahr	20,026	14,969	74.75	7,835	39.12	293	77.13	54.27
Barnala	19,552	14,449	73.90	7,100	36.31	98	89.80	50.00
Bathinda	36,425	34,506	94.73	14,942	41.02	763	97.90	12.32
Faridkot	14,731	11,784	79.99	4,647	31.55	109	80.73	0.00
Fategarh Sahib	22,208	17,615	79.93	3,133	14.11	75	86.67	50.67
Firozpur	81,953	65,789	80.28	18,564	22.76	313	79.87	22.68
Gurdaspur	57,049	30,162	52.87	23,602	41.37	542	52.03	4.43
Kapurthala	15,690	14,038	89.47	3,270	20.84	8	82.50	18.75
Ludhiana	40,390	32,032	79.31	7,188	17.80	219	82.65	32.42
Mansa	40,425	36,382	90.00	6,135	15.18	351	80.06	33.33
Moga	26,665	23,119	86.74	1,690	06.34	41	92.68	2.44
Muktsar	40,996	38,156	93.07	27,594	67.31	604	92.22	59.27
Patiala	29,606	20,554	69.43	9,378	31.68	333	76.88	50.45
Rupnagar	16,964	92,13	54.31	3,090	18.27	218	60.55	17.89
Sangrur	33,942	25,688	75.68	31,638	93.21	278	71.58	73.38
SAS Nagar	17,509	12,691	72.48	3,094	17.67	57	82.46	24.56
Tarn Taran	44,292	35,317	79.74	2,786	31.04	73	86.30	15.07
Total	**709,186**	**550,367**	**77.61**	**270,713**	**38.17**	**7,662**	**79.90**	**26.35**

Source: www.nrega.nic.in, accessed on 13 May 2010.

19.41 million person-days. The requirement for additional employment generation would have gone up to 63.26 million person-days in order to provide 100 days' employment to all the existing job cardholder households.

Thus, the level of implementation across districts reflects wide variations in the demand for employment under the MGNREGS and employment provided. However, the level of demand has to be understood in the context of employment available in the agriculture and non-agriculture sectors. It is

Table 8.4: Generation of Employment across the Districts under MGNREGS and Employment Gap in Punjab during 2009–10

	Employment Generated (Person-days)		*HHs employed for 100 days*		*Required Employment (in thousand) to Provide 100 Days'*		*Employment Gap (Thousand Person-days)*	
Districts	*Total (in thousands)*	*Average per HH*	*No.*	*%*	*For HHs Demanding Work*	*For HHs with Job Cards*	*For HHs Demanding Work*	*For HHs with Job Cards*
(1)	*(2)*	*(3)*	*(4)*	*(5)*	*(6)*	*(7)*	*(8)*	*(9)*
Hoshiarpur	**1,286**	**28.85**	**614**	**1.38**	**4,458**	**6,603**	**3,172**	**5,317**
Amritsar	1,524	40.72	3,966	10.60	3,743	5,513	2,219	3,989
Jalandhar	405	31.13	359	2.76	1,301	2,961	896	2,556
Nawanshahr	293	37.40	502	6.41	784	2,003	491	1,710
Barnala	98	13.80	11	0.15	710	1,955	612	1,857
Bathinda	763	51.06	787	5.27	1,494	3,643	731	2,880
Faridkot	109	23.46	34	0.73	465	1,473	356	1,364
Fategarh Sahib	75	23.94	52	1.66	313	2,221	238	2,146
Firozpur	313	16.86	00	0.00	1,856	8,195	1,543	7,882
Gurdaspur	542	22.96	75	0.32	2,360	5,705	1,818	5,163
Kapurthala	80	24.46	19	0.58	327	1,569	247	1,489
Ludhiana	219	30.47	244	3.39	719	4,039	500	3,820
Mansa	351	57.21	130	2.12	614	4,041	263	3,690
Moga	41	24.26	03	0.18	169	2,667	128	2,626
Muktsar	604	21.88	418	1.51	2,759	4,100	2,155	3,496
Patiala	333	35.51	141	1.50	938	2,961	605	2,628
Rupnagar	218	70.35	234	7.55	310	1,696	92	1,448
Sangrur	278	8.79	65	0.21	3,164	3,394	2,886	3,116
SAS Nagar	57	18.42	00	0.00	309	1,751	252	1,694
Tarn Taran	73	26.20	03	0.11	279	4,429	206	4,356
Total	**7,662**	**28.30**	**7,657**	**2.83**	**27,071**	**70,914**	**19,409**	**63,257**

Source: www.nrega.nic.in, accessed on 13 May 2010.
Note: Column 6 has been computed by multiplying column 5 of table 3 by 100 and then dividing by hundred thousand; column 7 has been computed by multiplying column 2 of table 3 by 100 and then dividing by hundred thousand.

significant to note that 63.43 per cent of labourers in Punjab get employment in agriculture between 96 days and 120 days in a year (Ghuman et al., 2007:40). For them, there is a demand for employment under the scheme. However, 79 per cent of the labourers get employment between 120 days and 240 days in year, both in agriculture and non-agricultural activities (Ghuman et al., 2007: 41). This, inter alia, may be one of the reasons for a low demand for employment under the MGNREGS.

The cumulative number of households with job cards in Punjab increased from 709,000 in 2009–10 to 808,000 in 2010–11 (Table 8.5). Across the districts, it varied between 13,046 (Kapurthala) and 70,049 (Hoshiarpur). The SC job cardholders accounted for a little more than 76 per cent. Across the

Table 8.5: Employment Status under MGNREGS across the Districts in Punjab during 2010–11

	Commutative No. of HHs Issued Job Cards			*No. of HHs Provided Employment*		*Employment Generated (Thousand Person-days)*		
Districts	*Total*	*SC*	*SC (%)*	*Total*	*SC (%)*	*Total*	*SC (%)*	*Women (%)*
(1)	*(2)*	*(3)*	*(4)*	*(5)*	*(6)*	*(7)*	*(8)*	*(9)*
Hoshiarpur	**70,049**	**40,604**	**57.97**	**30,553**	**43.62**	**970**	**56.80**	**39.69**
Amritsar	62,896	54,299	86.33	28,565	45.42	814	86.12	12.04
Jalandhar	33,005	30,561	92.60	11,251	34.09	354	93.50	57.91
Nawanshahr	21,058	14,009	66.53	42,88	20.36	131	70.99	54.96
Barnala	22,392	18,254	81.52	78,01	34.84	224	91.07	62.50
Bathinda	40,200	35,567	88.48	17,971	44.70	394	89.34	51.27
Faridkot	19,076	16,842	88.29	5,910	30.98	136	91.91	51.47
Fategarh Sahib	24,793	19,905	80.28	4,920	19.84	173	86.13	63.01
Firozpur	98,039	78,153	79.72	28,562	29.13	579	81.00	23.14
Gurdaspur	60,139	24,824	41.28	14,844	24.68	456	38.16	07.68
Kapurthala	13,046	10,715	82.13	3,560	27.29	96	77.08	42.71
Ludhiana	53,209	42,749	80.34	16,849	31.66	475	85.05	48.84
Mansa	34,585	28,034	81.11	8,342	24.12	216	84.72	31.94
Moga	33,874	29,657	87.55	10,602	31.30	257	90.66	38.52
Muktsar	48,483	44,491	91.77	22,112	45.61	539	93.51	56.77
Patiala	35,725	24,512	68.61	10,758	30.11	287	70.38	49.13
Rupnagar	21,496	11,791	54.85	4,787	22.27	214	47.66	34.58
Sangrur	43,639	35,141	80.53	16,493	37.79	346	83.53	50.87
SAS Nagar	17,361	11,043	63.61	3,517	20.26	130	63.85	31.54
Tarn Taran	54,570	43,078	78.94	16,319	29.90	306	83.33	15.36
Total	**807,631**	**614,229**	**76.19**	**268,004**	**33.18**	**7098**	**77.18**	**37.71**

Source: www.nrega.nic.in, accessed on 3 May 2011.

districts, it varied between 41.28 per cent (Gurdaspur) and 92.60 per cent (Jalandhar). It is significant to note that the proportion of SC population in rural population in Jalandhar is the highest (45.38 per cent) among all the districts of Punjab. On the other hand, the proportion of SC population in the rural population of Gurdaspur district is on the lower side (26.15 per cent) among all the districts of Punjab. These SC rural households are largely the landless and invariably the resource poor households.

Table 8.5 also reveals that the proportion of households, that got employment under the MGNREGS in the total job cardholder households was only 33.18 per cent. Across the districts, it varied between 45.42 per cent (Amritsar) and 19.84 per cent (Fatehgarh Sahib) during 2010–11. It is significant to note that in half the districts, the proportion of households with employment in the total job cardholder households was less than 30 per cent. In one-fourth of the districts, this proportion was between 30 per cent and 40 per cent.

During 2010–11, 7.1 million person-days employment was generated in Punjab. Across the districts, the extent of employment generation varied between 96 thousand person-days (Kapurthala) and 970 thousand person-days (Hoshiarpur). Out of this employment, about 77 per cent person-days were availed by the SC job cardholder households. Across the districts, it varied between 38 per cent (Gurdaspur) and 93.5 per cent (Jalandhar). The proportion of women workers, who availed employment, was 37.71 per cent across the job card households in the state during 2010–11 (Table 8.5). Across the districts, it varied between 76.8 per cent (Gurdaspur) and 63 per cent (Fatehgarh Sahib). Clearly, the SCs and women got a higher share in the total employment generated under the MGNREGS during 2010–11.

The total employment generation under the MGNREGS in Punjab during 2010–11, on an average, gave 26.49 days employment to the households that demanded job (Table 8.6). It is far less than the target of 100 days' employment. Across the districts under the MGNREGS, per household mean days employment varied between 18.75 days (Tarn Taran) and 44.68 days (Rupnagar).

Only 1.89 per cent households, that were given employment, got employment for 100 days during 2010–11 (Table 8.6). The remaining 98.11 per cent households got employment for lesser number of days. Across the districts, the proportion of households, with 100 days' employment, varied between 0.15 per cent (Tarn Taran) and 3.49 per cent (Amritsar) during 2010–11. Clearly, 100 days' employment has been a distant dream in Punjab.

In order to provide 100 days' employment to all those households that demanded job, we needed to generate 26.8 million person-days of employment during 2010–11 in Punjab (Table 8.6). Compared to it, only 7.1 million person-days of employment could be generated. The table also reveals a huge variation across the districts. If all the households with job cards demand 100 days' employment, then the required employment generation in 2010–11 would have been 80.8 million person-days. Clearly, there is huge employment gap between the actual and required employment generation.

At the state level, the gap comes out to be 19.7 million person-days if 100 days' employment was to be given to all those households that demanded work (Table 8.6). Across the districts, it varied between 222 thousand person-days (SAS Nagar) and 2.28 million person-days (Firozpur). This gap could further increase to 73.7 million person-days for the whole of the state if all the job cardholder households demanded 100 days' employment during 2010–11. Across the districts, this gap ranged between 1.2 million person-days (Kapurthala) and 9.2 million person-days (Firozpur).

Table 8.6: Generation of Employment across the Districts under MGNREGS and Employment Gap in Punjab during 2010–11

	Employment Generated (Person-days)		*HHs Employed for 100 Days*		*Required Employment (Thousand Person-days) to Provide 100 Days' Employment*		*Employment Gap (in Thousand Person-days)*	
Districts	*Total (in thousand)*	*Average per HH*	*No.*	*%*	*For HHs Demanding Work (in thousand)*	*For HHs with Job Cards*	*For HHs Demanding Work*	*For HHs with Job Cards*
(1)	*(2)*	*(3)*	*(4)*	*(5)*	*(6)*	*(7)*	*(8)*	*(9)*
Hoshiarpur	**970**	**3,175**	**1,036**	**3.39**	**3,053**	**7,005**	**2,083**	**6,065**
Amritsar	814	2,849	997	3.49	2,857	6,290	2,043	5,476
Jalandhar	354	3,147	333	2.96	1,125	3,301	771	2,947
Nawanshahr	131	3,054	108	2.52	429	2,106	298	1,975
Barnala	224	2,872	101	1.29	780	2,239	556	2,015
Bathinda	394	2,193	194	1.08	1,797	4,020	1,403	3,626
Faridkot	136	2,301	88	1.49	591	1,908	455	1,772
Fategarh Sahib	173	3,516	247	3.29	492	2,479	319	2,306
Firozpur	579	2,027	200	0.70	2,856	9,804	2,277	9,225
Gurdaspur	456	3,073	141	0.95	1,484	6,014	1,028	5,558
Kapurthala	96	2,697	79	2.22	356	1,305	260	1,209
Ludhiana	475	2,819	372	2.21	1,685	5,321	1,210	4,846
Mansa	216	2,590	114	1.37	834	3,459	618	3,243
Moga	257	2,425	48	0.45	1,060	3,387	803	3,130
Muktsar	539	2,438	268	1.21	2,211	4,848	1,672	4,309
Patiala	287	2,667	229	2.13	1,076	3,573	789	3,286
Rupnagar	214	4,468	267	5.58	479	2,150	265	1,936
Sangrur	346	2,098	127	0.77	1,649	4,364	1,303	4,018
SAS Nagar	130	3,693	90	2.56	352	1,736	222	1,606
Tarn Taran	306	1,875	25	0.15	1,632	5,457	1,326	5,151
Total	**7,098**	**2,649**	**5,064**	**1.89**	**26,800**	**80,763**	**19,707**	**73,665**

Source: www.nrega.nic.in, accessed on 3 May 2011.
Note: Column 6 has been computed by multiplying column 5 of table 5 by 100 and the dividing by hundred thousand; column 7 has been computed by multiplying column 2 of table 5 by 100 and then dividing by hundred thousand.

But the number of households that demanded job and number of households that were given employment has been recorded as exactly the same in the official data, which has to be viewed with a note of caution. The job provided is not based on the demand placed through application. Contrarily, the head of the gram panchayat calls people for work as and when required. There was no other mechanism to inform the potential jobseekers about the availability of work. It is significant to note that under the MGNREGS, the public announcement about the availability of work is mandatory.

Also, the demand for the MGNREGS employment is confined mostly to the SC households that constituted 77.61 per cent of the job cardholders and accounted for 79.90 per cent of the employment days provided in 2009–10. During 2010–11, the share of SCs in job cardholders was 76.19 per cent and their share in employment was 77.18 per cent. The share of SCs in employment varied across districts. However, in most of the districts, the SCs constitute the largest proportion of the job cardholder households and got the largest share in the total person-days of employment generated under MGNREGS.

The low participation of women in most of the districts indicates that women are yet to come forward to avail employment opportunities under the scheme in large numbers. In most of the districts, the percentage share of women in total person-days is less than the national average and less than the stipulated minimum of 33 per cent. In districts like Amritsar and Gurdaspur (known as Majha region), the participation of women was very low in 2009–10.

This needs to be understood in the context that the female work participation rate has always been low in Punjab. The female work participation rate in the state in 2001 was 18.7 per cent (26th rank, among the states and Union Territories (UTs) in India, in the descending order). It was only 16.3 per cent in Amritsar and 12.7 per cent in Gurdaspur. Compared to it, the male work participation rate in the state has been above 53 per cent during 1961 to 2001. It is significant to note that the female work participation rate in the state was merely 2.3 per cent in 1981 and 4.4 per cent in 1991 (Government of India, 2002b: 54). In the districts of Amritsar and Gurdaspur, it was 2.7 per cent and 2.4 per cent, respectively in 1991.

The low women work participation rate in Punjab, particularly in the rural area, may be mainly attributed to social reasons. Women are normally not encouraged to go in for out-of-home work. Women in rural Punjab are largely engaged in unpaid household work.

It is significant to note that the average female work participation rate in India was 25.6 per cent in 2001, whereas in the rural India, the female work participation rate was 30.8 per cent (Government of India, 2008: 12).

The supply-side constraint is also visible. For, the number of households seeking job cards has increased from 524,928 in 2008–09 to 709,186 households in 2009–10, an increase of nearly 35 per cent. It further increased to 807,631 households during 2010–11. Moreover, the average person-days of employment provided was only 27 days in 2008–09, 28 days in 2009–10 and 26 days in 2010–11, which was a little less than the national average for the three years.

One fundamental reason for the low level of employment generation under the MGNREGS is the provision of employment generation through eight types of work which are practically applicable more in the case of dry areas. Because of the high percentage of irrigated area, in almost of all the districts, the scope of work of water conservation and harvesting has almost saturated. In view of this, Punjab would have to devise new ways and means to conserve and harvest water, particularly rain water. As a large part of the Punjab is plain (except Hoshiarpur district), the scope of taking land development work is also limited. Further, most of the villages are connected with all weather *pucca* roads that also limit the scope for road construction under the scheme.

It is significant to note that being a success story of green revolution, Punjab is beset with specific limitations in regard to the MGNREGS. The peak season work in agriculture is confined to a maximum of three months. The market wage rate (earnings by the labourers) is almost three times higher than the wage rate under the MGNREGS during these months. So, during the peak season, hardly any worker is available for work under the rural employment guarantee scheme. During the remaining period of the year, the work is mainly available in the urban and semi-urban areas in construction-related activities and in other seasonal activities. The market wage rate earnings in such activities are also higher (say, by 25 to 50 per cent) than the wage rate under the MGNREGS. In many seasonal activities, the earnings are almost double of the stipulated minimum wage rate.

The availability of work under the MGNREGS in other states (particularly in Bihar and UP, the main supplier of migrant labourers to Punjab) has further tightened the supply side. Recently, the Punjab government has launched an interest-free loan (ranging from ₹2,500 to ₹15,000) scheme for daily wage-earners (*Tribune*, 2010a). The scheme is mainly a strategy to attract migrant workers who are known as the backbone of the rural economy of Punjab. It is pertinent to note that the number of migrant laboures in Punjab in 2001 was 1.75 million, out of which 0.95 million were in urban area (Government of India, 2002a). According to a recent study (Ghuman et al., 2007), the estimated number of migrant labourers in Punjab in 2007 was 0.82 million. In view of the shortage of labour, mainly due to declining supply of migrant labour, the government of Punjab has offered heavy subsidy on paddy transplantation machines (*Tribune*, 2010b). The extent of subsidy is to the tune of ₹75,000 on each transplanting machine and, in addition, the farmers who will help the fellow farmers will be given an additional subsidy of ₹5,000 per acre.

In view of the above, Punjab would have to plan its employment generation under the MGNREGS during the non-peak season. Also, the minimum wage rate would have to be raised so as to make this scheme attractive to the workers. In addition to that, the scope and coverage of works under the scheme shall have to be widened, keeping in view the requirements of the developed states like Punjab.

IV

A Case Study of Hoshiarpur District

Hoshiarpur, the only first-phase district of the Punjab, is predominantly rural with 80.33 per cent population residing in the rural area. Further, 80 per cent of the male and 90 per cent of the female population lives in rural area (Table 8.7). The proportion of rural workers in total workers of this district is nearly 82 per cent, whereas the average of all districts of Punjab is approximately 70 per cent. The proportion of male rural workers in total male workers in Hoshiarpur district is nearly 80 per cent, whereas in Punjab, it is about 66 per cent. The corresponding proportion of females in Hoshiarpur district is approximately 89 per cent and, in Punjab, it is nearly 83 per cent.

About 79 per cent main workers[3] and 94 per cent marginal workers,[4] respectively, of Hoshiarpur district are rural workers. As regards males, 78 per cent are main workers and 92 per cent are marginal workers. In the case of female workers, 83 per cent are main workers and 96 per cent are marginal

Table 8.7: Percentage Share of Rural Population and Rural Workers in Punjab and Hoshiarpur District

	Persons		*Male*		*Female*	
	Punjab	*Hoshiarpur*	*Punjab*	*Hoshiarpur*	*Punjab*	*Hoshiarpur*
In total population	66.05	80.34	65.55	79.82	66.62	80.88
SC in rural population	33.04	36.40	32.97	36.59	33.12	36.20
Rural workers in total workers	69.82	81.94	65.96	79.71	82.60	88.97
Rural main workers in total main workers	67.70	78.99	64.72	78.05	77.96	83.51
Rural marginal workers in total marginal workers	86.75	94.35	80.97	91.99	90.79	96.43
Total rural workers in rural population	39.73	35.43	54.45	50.91	23.15	19.08
Rural main workers in total rural workers	82.30	77.92	65.79	63.71	16.51	14.21
Rural marginal workers in total rural workers	17.70	22.08	34.21	36.29	83.49	85.79
AWs in total workers	39.40	40.70	59.60	40.10	36.20	42.50
AWs in total rural workers	53.51	48.33	60.06	48.81	36.17	46.99
Rural cultivators in rural workers	31.51	28.42	27.30	22.61	4.21	5.81
Rural ALs in rural workers	22.00	19.91	16.30	13.41	5.70	6.50

Sources: 1. Government of India.
2. Government of Punjab, 2006.
Note: AWs and ALs stand for Agricultural Workers (cultivators + agricultural labourers) and Agricultural Labourers, respectively. A person who works on another person's land for wage in money or kind or share is regarded as an agricultural labourer.

workers. The share of rural marginal workers in the total rural workers in the district is also higher than the corresponding average of rural Punjab. Such a high proportion of marginal rural workers in the district is expected to avail the wage employment under the MGNREGS.

The proportion of marginal[5] (tiny operational holdings) and small farmers and agricultural labourers in the district is higher than the state average. The proportion of marginal operational holdings in district Hoshiarpur is more than double (26.72 per cent) than the average in Punjab (12.31 per cent). The proportion of small operational holdings in the district is 23.49 per cent, whereas in Punjab, their proportion is 17.35 per cent (Government of Punjab, 2006). The marginal and small farmers, alongwith rural agricultural labourers, particularly the marginal workers, are expected to be the potential beneficiaries of the MGNRGES in the district.

In spite of economic backwardness, the district has the highest literacy rate in the state. Its economic backwardness is mainly due to its topography. The Shivalik Hills, from the north-east and south-east alignment, run throughout the length of the district. The foothill plains and flood-prone plains of the river Beas constitute the remaining part of the district. The hill track known as *kandi* area, covers roughly one-half of the district. Such topography does not allow intensive agriculture as in the other parts of the state.

Socio-economic Status of Sampled Job Cardholders in Hoshiarpur District

The district has 10 development blocks consisting of 1,426 villages,[6] out of which 1,396 are inhabited. The number of gram panchayats is 1,317.[7] The number of panchayats varies from 82 to 168 across the blocks. The total number of households is 0.24 million in the district. The number of job card-holder households in the district was 42,225 by the end of March 2008, which is nearly 18 per cent of the total households. It increased to 45,135 by March 2009 and further to 66,025 by March 2010. In other words, the job cardholder households constitute 27 per cent of the total rural households in the district.

The proportion of BPL households to total households is 7.85 per cent in the district and, across the blocks, it varies from 5.21 per cent to 14.69 per cent. The proportion of BPL households to job card-holder households was 43.66 per cent in the district and, across the blocks, it varied from 20.70 per cent to 88.95 per cent.

Most of the blocks of the districts are ranked very poor in terms of development indicators. The most developed block (Tanda) has 31st rank in Punjab in the descending order. The second-highest developed block of the district ranks 62nd in the state and the least-developed block in the district ranks 109 in the state.

The case study of Hoshiarpur is based on a survey conducted in 10 randomly selected villages, choosing one village from each development block. Out of the each selected village, 10 job cardholder households (who were provided employment under the MGNREGS) were also selected randomly. Out of the 100 sampled job cardholder households, 93 per cent were BPL. Only seven per cent of the job cardholder households in the sample were APL households. Even these seven per cent households were only marginally above the poverty line. In 50 per cent of the sampled villages, there was not a single job cardholder from the APL category.

About two-thirds of the jobseekers were from the age group of 35–65 years and only 35 per cent were from the age group of 18–35 years. In 3 out of the 10 sampled villages, 90 to 100 per cent of the jobseek-ers were in the 35–65 age groups (Table 8.8). It shows that the MGNREGS is not the first preference for the relatively young workers.

About 75 per cent of the jobseekers (job cardholders) were SC households. Only 16 per cent of the job cardholders were from the general castes and another nine per cent were from the backward castes. However, in 4 out of the 10 sampled villages, 100 per cent job cardholders were SC households. In an-other two villages, 90 per cent were SC households and, in one village, 80 per cent were SC households. Of the total job cardholders in the district, 65.2 per cent were from the SC households; 21.3 per cent from the general castes and another 13.5 per cent were from the backward castes (District Programme Coordinator, 2007). Hoshiarpur being the highest literate district of the state, 71 per cent of the job cardholders were literate. The average family size of the sampled job cardholders was 5.2 persons per households.

Table 8.8: Caste, Poverty, Educational Status and Family Size of the Job Cardholders and Family Size of their Households

Name of the Village	*Job Cardholder HHs* — *Sex*		*Age (Years)*		*Caste*			*Poverty*		*Education Level*			*Family Size*
	M	*F*	*18—35*	*36—65*	*General Caste*	*SC*	*OBC*	*APL*	*BPL*	*Illiterate*	*≤8th*	*≤10th*	*(Persons)*
Hasipind	6	4	3	7	1	9	—	1	9	3	6	1	6.0
Beh Fatto	7	3	6	4	3	—	7	2	8	2	7	1	5.0
Fathuwal	7	3	3	7	4	6	—	1	9	2	8	—	5.0
Passi *Kandi*	6	4	1	9	—	10	—	—	10	4	5	1	5.2
Bassi Maruf Hussainpur	5	5	6	4	—	10	—	—	10	1	8+1*	—	5.3
Bhawanipur	3	7	—	10	6	3	1	2	8	5	4	1	6.7
Bassi Hasatkhan	7	3	4	6	—	10	—	—	10	3	5	2	3.4
Muggowal	3	7	5	5	0	10	0	0	10	2	5	3	5.1
Johal	9	1	6	4	1	9	0	0	10	3	6	1	5.3
Dagan	4	6	1	9	1	8	1	1	9	4	4	2	5.0
Total	57	43	35	65	16	75	09	07	93	29	58	13	5.2

Source: Field survey.

Notes: 1. In the villages at serial numbers 3, 6 and 7, there were 1, 2 and 3 job cardholders, respectively, whose ages were above 65 years.

2. * He was graduate.

Occupation of Job Cardholder Households and Age and Gender of Labourers under MGNREGS

As is evident from Table 8.9, about 77 per cent of the job cardholders were agricultural labourers, although 23 per cent of the job cardholders were also from cultivators, but the average size of operational holdings varied between 0.13 acres to half an acre,[8] which can not productively absorb all the adult members. In one village, the proportion of job cardholders from cultivator households was 80 per cent. Compared with the proportion of agricultural labourers (19.91 per cent) in the rural workers in the district, 77 per cent share of agricultural labourers show low labour-absorbing capacity of the agriculture sector.

Out of 100 sampled job cardholder households, 126 persons were actually provided employment between February 2006 and March 2008. Out of that, 63.5 per cent were male and 36.5 per cent were female. In the entire district, the ratio of male and female workers was 75.05: 24.95. Further, 41.3 per cent of the workers were in the age group of 18–35 years and 52.4 per cent were in the age group of 36–65 years. It is interesting to note that 6.4 per cent workers (all male) were above 65 years of age. In the absence of social and economic security, this old population found in the MGNREGS a source of livelihood, although hard and strenuous physical work is an obvious deterrent for them. Of the district total, 91.3 per cent workers were in the age group of 18 to 50 years and 7.5 per cent workers were in the age group of 51 to 65 years.

Table 8.9: Occupation of Job Cardholder Households and Sex and Age of Persons Employed and Employment Generated under MGNREGS in the Sampled Villages in Hoshiarpur District

			Age and Sex of Workers Who Were Actually Called for Work (years)						
	Occupation (in %)		*18–35 year*		*36–65 year*		*65+ (year)*	*Employment (Person-days)*	
Name of the Villages	C	AL	M	F	M	F	M	*2006–07*	*2007–08*
Hasipind	01	09	02	01	05	02	—	107	41
Beh Fatto	08*	02	05	05	03	02	—	668	108
Fathuwal	01	09	02	03	04	03	01	800	600
Passi *Kandi*	01	09	02	01	06	05	—	242	126
Bassi Maruf Hussainpur	02	08	02	03	03	02	—	570	395
Bhawanipur	03	07	01	01	05	05	03	266	42
Bassi Hasatkhan	03	07	05	01	03	—	03	680	62
Muggowal	02	08	02	04	03	02	—	945	15
Johal	01	09	06	—	03	—	01	131	122
Dagan	01	09	04	02	06	04	—	178	133
Total No.	23	77	31	21	41	25	08	4,587	1,644
Total (%)	(23.0)	(77.0)	(24.6)	(16.7)	(32.5)	(19.8)	(6.4)	(73.6)	(26.4)

Source: Field survey.
Notes: 1. The average (per person) employment days came out to be 49.45 in two years. The yearly average thus comes out to be 24.73 person-days.
2. C and AL stand for Cultivators and Agricultural Labourers, respectively.
3. No female worker above the age of 65 years reported for work.
4. * The ownership of land ranges from 0.13 acres to 0.5 acres.

Only 1.2 per cent workers were in the age group of 65 and above. The proportion of female workers in each age group was lower. The low participation of women must be, however, understood in the context of their low work-participation rate and their low proportion (6.50 per cent) in the rural agricultural workers. Amongst the entire 126 workers, 24.6 per cent male and 16.7 per cent female workers were in the age group of 18–35 years. The proportion of male in total workers in this age group was 59.6 per cent. In the age group of 36–65 years, 32.5 per cent were males and only 19.8 per cent were females. The proportion of males within this age group was 62.1 per cent. The ratio of female workers was found declining with the advancing of age. In fact, all the workers in the age group of 65 and above were males.

The overall employment generation was quite low in all the villages. It was only 4,587 person-days in 2006–07 and 1,644 person-days in 2007–08. On an average, every person was provided only 24.73 person-days in a year (Table 8.9). In terms of households, on an average, each household worked for 37 days in the district in 2006–07 (Mathur, 2008).

In terms of completing 100 days, only 17 per cent households completed 100 days in 2006–07 and not a single one in 2007–08 (Table 8.10). In 2006–07, 47 per cent households got employment only up

Table 8.10: Number of Workdays Completed by the Households under MGNREGS in the Sampled Villages in Hoshiarpur District during 2006–07 and 2007–08

Name of the Villages	*Workdays Completed: Number of HHs*													
	1–10		*11–20*		*21–30*		*31–40*		*41–50*		*51–60*	*71–80*	*91–99*	*100*
	2006–07	*2007–08*	*2006–07*	*2007–08*	*2006–07*	*2007–08*	*2006–07*	*2007–08*	*2006–07*	*2007–08*	*2006–07*	*2006–07*	*2006–07*	*2006–07*
Hasipind	08	09	02	—	—	—	—	—	—	—	—	—	—	
Beh Fatto	—	—	02	03	03	—	01	—	01	—	01	—	01	04
Fathuwal	—	—	—	—			—	—	—	—	10	10	—	
Passi *Kandi*	—	—	02	07	07	01	01	08	—	—	—	—	—	
Bassi Maruf Hussainpur	—	—	—	—	01	01	—	—	01	—	09	—	—	
Bhawanipur	—	—	02	03	07	—	—	—	01	—	—	—	—	
Bassi Hasatkhan	—	—	01	04	02		—	—	01	—	01	—	01	04
Muggowal	—	—	—	—		—	—	—	01	01	—	—	—	0[illegible]
Johal	02	02	04	08	03	—	—	—	—	—	—	—	—	
Dagan	—	—	—	02	01	—	—	—	—	—	—	—	—	
Total	10	11	13	27	24	02	02	08	05	01	21	10	02	1[illegible]

Source: Field survey.

Notes: 1. No HH got employment between 61–70 days during any of the year.
2. During 2007–08, no HH got employment between 51 and 60 days, 71 and 80 days, 91 and 99 days, and 100 days.
3. Total number of HHs/workers who got work during 2006–07 and 2007–08 was 104 and 49, respectively.

to 30 days, whereas this proportion was 40 per cent in 2007–08. In fact, during 2007–08, not a single household got employment beyond 50 days. It seems that the employment potential got exhausted during 2006–07, the first year of the implementation of the MGNREGS.

Panchayat head informed that inadequate flow of funds to the panchayat and limited scope for employment generation were the two main reasons for low job creation.[9] However, most of the job cardholders were willing to work and would have worked provided they were given employment. No sampled worker ever declined the work offer. Because of the inability to provide job, the panchayat heads were discriminatory in calling people for the job and demand-based job creation was nowhere on the scene. The capacity of different panchayats to create job also varied. A few panchayats were able to generate more work than others.

The demand-side problem was equally evident. The level of awareness about the MGNREGS and rights of workers was very low. Not even a single worker among the sampled job cardholders was aware about the statutory provision of unemployment allowance in the absence of non-availability of work within the stipulated period of 15 days. At the same time, no worker knew about the prevailing minimum wage rate in the district. The job cardholders also did not know that they were to apply for work. They simply knew that once they got the job card, they would be called for work by the panchayat head as and when required. At the same time, however, they denied any bribe for getting the job card or work.

The actual wage payment was less than the prescribed minimum wage under the MGNREGS in the state. The average wage payment was 92.50 rupees against the then prevailing minimum wage of 126 rupees. Moreover, the market wage rate during busy/peak seasons is more than double the wage rate under MGNREGS. This high wage difference makes the employment under this scheme less attractive.

V

Summing Up

Under the green revolution, the agrarian economy of Punjab had generated large-scale employment opportunities for local and migrant labourers during the 1970s and 1980s. Moreover, the vertical integration of agriculture and other sectors created productive employment in non-farm sectors in large numbers. Most of this employment was, however, in informal and unorganised sectors. The heavy mechanisation of agricultural operations reduced the demand for labour in the agriculture, but simultaneous employment generation in non-farm sectors allowed local labourers to shift to non-farm employment. On the other hand, the seasonal heavy demand for labourers for plantation and harvesting purposes, which were not mechanised, was easily met through the import of migrant labourers from Bihar and UP.

Agriculture, however, started decelerating in the 1990s. Cost of production increased, productivity declined, and the net income of the cultivators also decreased. As a result of that, employment generation in agriculture and non-agriculture sectors alike (both were vertically integrated) started declining. The employment elasticity of agriculture declined substantially. Agriculture was unable to absorb labour force in the ratio of the growth rate of labour force. A serious problem of income and employment has emerged in the rural economy of Punjab. An indicator of agrarian distress is the fact that both the farmers and agriculture labourers have been committing suicide in the rural Punjab in recent years.

The ideal target of the MGNREGS is the state with high incidence of rural BPL population, low-productivity of agriculture and lack of non-agricultural activities, low level of irrigation and high incidence of outmigration of rural population in search of wage employment. The Punjab with very low rural BPL population, highly intensive agriculture, vertical integration of agriculture and non-agriculture sectors, very high proportion of irrigated areas and net importer of agricultural labourers is not a suitable candidate for the scheme (at least in its present form) that provides wage employment to rural population at the prescribed minimum wages in the rural areas.

Nonetheless, there is a demand for guaranteed wage employment in the state and the demand is increasing, although unlike some other states, the demand varies sharply across the districts. Moreover, the demand for such employment is largely concentrated in the SC and BPL population. Marginal and small farmers were also found seeking wage employment. The small and marginal holdings are unable to productively absorb even the family labourers. Also the decline in productivity and income make these farmers to search for additional sources of income. Women, potential jobseekers, are yet to avail these opportunities in large number.

The record of job creation under the MGNREGS is rather poor in the state. The number of households provided employment as proportion of households with the job cards and even of the BPL households is quite low. The average person-days per household is almost half of the national average. The mean days of employment under the MGNREGS per households (who were provided work) in Punjab were around 27 days, 28 days and 26 days in a year during 2008–09, 2009–10 and 2010–11, respectively. The proportion of households that completed 100 days of employment (out of those with employment) during 2008–09, 2009–10 and 2010–11 was 2.65 per cent, 2.83 per cent and 1.89 per cent, respectively. Thus, there was hardly any improvement in the performance of MGNREGS during the three years under study. Besides, there is a huge gap between actual generation of employment and the potential demand for employment under the MGNREGS in Punjab.

The demand for employment among the job cardholders is genuine. There is not a single incidence of job cardholder who did not turn for work, provided he or she was called for work. It must be emphasised here that against the norms of the act to provide employment based on demand, employment is provided based on supply. The field survey testifies that there is a genuine demand among the job cardholders.

There is a fundamental constraint in providing employment under the types of work permitted under the MGNREGS in the state. There is saturation of irrigated area and little scope to undertake work of water conservation and harvesting. Most of the villages are connected with all-weather *pucca* roads. Even the scope for land development is limited. Except for Hoshiarpur district (Shivalik hills), other districts are in plains. There is, thus, a need to review the MGNREGS so as to make it compatible with the requirements and ground realities of the state of Punjab. Given the declining employment elasticity in agriculture, the development of rural non-farm sector is sine qua non for the diversification of rural economy of Punjab. At the same time, the MGNREGS should focus more and more on the assets building along with employment generation.

Nonetheless, the MGNREGS are affecting rural labour market in many ways. The impact is more because of its implementation in other states than in Punjab. There are anecdotal reports that suggest that there is a decline of in-migrant labourers in the state. This decline is because of their absorption in their own home states. This may increase the local wage rate, thereby further increasing input cost in the agriculture, already facing a serious problem of declining productivity and profit generation. Moreover, if the local workers get sufficient number of employment days under the scheme, this would push the local non-farm sector wages. The upward revision in the rural farm and non-farm sector wages would increase the overall cost in the rural economy. And there are many implications of this. Agriculture would decline further. There are also dangers of converting farm land into non-farm land, provided there are opportunities. Moreover, the net income of the rural households would further decline and there would be adverse multiplier effects of this.

Of course, the investment in the rural economy and creation of local assets would have its own positive effects. Moreover, the income added to the poor households would most likely be spent on consumption goods. This will increase the demand for these goods in the local economy, but probably push the price as well.

Nevertheless, the rural employment guarantee scheme has a potential to provide livelihood security to the poorest of the poor in rural areas, provided it is made commensurate with the local needs and ground realities of the state, and above all the scheme is properly implemented.

Notes

1. So far, there is no study on the estimation of the total number of farmers' suicides for the entire state of Punjab. However, some farmers' unions and certain NGOs tried to estimate the farmers' suicides in Punjab by preparing a list of such farmers. The Punjab Agriculture University (PAU), Ludhiana, has estimated that 2,890 (1,757 farmers and 1,133 farm labourers) farmers and farm labourers have committed suicides during 2000–08 in two districts—Sangrur and Bathinda. The Government of Punjab has now asked the three universities in the state to conduct a census survey about farmers and labourers' suicides in all the remaining districts of the state.
2. According to Census 2001 (Government of India), the total workers in Punjab were 91.42 lakhs (10 lakhs = 1 million). It indicates that nearly 21 per cent of workforce in Punjab is either unemployed/grossly underemployed/disguisedly unemployed.
3. A person who has worked for six months or more during the year preceding to the census year (Census year is a calendar year from 1 January to 31 December) is termed as Main Worker.
4. A person who has worked for less than 6 months (may be even for a day) during the year preceding to census year is termed as Marginal Worker.
5. In the census, a person is classified as cultivator if he or she is engaged in cultivation of land owned or held from government or held from private persons or institutions for payment of money, kinds or share. Cultivation also includes effective supervision or directions in cultivation. Tiny operational holding is generally the marginal holding (less than one hectare of land).
6. According to the Indian population census, the 'village' has been taken as the basic unit for the purpose of data tabulation. The definition of village used in the census is identical with that of 'Estate', under the Punjab Revenue Act. As per jurisdictional frame of 2001 census, there are 12,729 villages in the state of Punjab. Village is synonymous with rural area.

7. Panchayat (gram/village panchayat) is the lowest unit of local self-government in rural area. After the 73rd Constitutional Amendment, the panchayats got a constitutional status as units of self-government. The head of the gram panchayat in Punjab is called 'Sarpanch', while other members are called 'Panches'.
8. One hectare is approximately equal to 2.5 acres.
9. The panchayat heads of all the 10 sample villages were having educational attainment above 8th standard. Similarly 98 per cent panchayat members were having academic qualifications equal to or beyond 8th standard.

References

AFDR, Punjab (2000) Suicides in rural Punjab: A report. Association for Democratic Rights, AFDR, Patiala, Punjab.

Bhalla, G. S. and G. Singh (2009) Economic liberalisation and Indian agriculture: A state-wise analysis. *Economic and Political Weekly* 44, No. 52: 34–44.

Bhalla, Shiela (1987) Trends in employment in Indian agriculture, land and asset distribution. *Indian Journal of Agricultural Economics (IJAE)* 42, No. 4: 548–49.

——— (1989) Employment in Indian agriculture: Retrospect and prospect. *Social Scientist* 17, No. 5–6: 3–21.

Chadha, G. K. (1986) The off farm economic structure of agriculturally growing regions: A study of Indian Punjab. In *Off farm employment in development of rural Asia*, ed. R. T. Shand, vol. 2. Canberra, Australia: Canberra National Centre for Development Studies.

Chopra, Kanchan (2002) Sustaining agricultural growth in Punjab: Role of interventions in the water sector. In *Future of Agriculture in Punjab*, eds. S. S. Johl and S. K. Ray. Chandigarh: CRRID, 69–78.

District Programme Coordinator Hoshiarpur (2007) *Impact of MGNREGA in district Hoshiarpur, Punjab: From February 2006 to February 2007*, District Hoshiarpur, Punjab.

Ghuman, Ranjit Singh (2001) WTO and Indian agriculture: Crisis and challenges. *Man and Development* 23, No. 2: 82–83.

——— (2005) Rural non-farm employment scenario: Reflections from recent data in Punjab. *Economic and Political Weekly* 50, No. 41: 4473–80.

——— (2008a) Socio-economic crisis in rural Punjab. *Economic and Political Weekly* 53, No. 7: 12–15.

——— (2008b) Growth and structural changes in Punjab since 1960s: A politico-economic analysis. Paper presented at the workshop organized by Institute of South Asian Studies, NUS, Singapore, 18 September 2008.

Ghuman, Ranjit Singh, Inderjeet Singh and Lakhwinder Singh (2007) Status of local agricultural labour in Punjab, The Punjab State Farmers Commission, Government of Punjab, SAS Nagar, Mohali.

Gill, Sucha Singh (2002) Agriculture, crop technology and employment generation in Punjab. In *Future of agriculture in Punjab*, eds. S. S. Johl and S. K. Ray, 56–68. CRRID; Chandigarh.

——— (2005) Economics distress and farmers' suicides in Punjab. *Journal of Punjab Studies* 12, No. 2: 219–38.

Gill, Sucha Singh and Ranjit Singh Ghuman (2001) Changing agrarian relations in India: Some reflections from recent data. *Indian Journal of Labour Economics (IJLE)* 44, No. 4, 810–26.

Government of India (1981) *Census of India, 1981*. New Delhi.

——— (1991) *Census of India, 1991*. New Delhi.

——— (2002a) *Census of India*. 2001, New Delhi.

——— (2002b), *Census of India 2001*, Series 4, Punjab, paper—3 of 2001, Distribution of workers and non-workers, New Delhi.

——— (2003) *Agricultural census: 1995–96*, Ministry of Agriculture, New Delhi.

——— (2006) Statistical abstract of Punjab, Economic and Statistical Organization, Punjab.

——— (2008) *Census of India 2001: Workers and non-workers*. New Delhi, 12.

——— (2008) Statistical abstract of Punjab, Economic and Statistical Organization, Punjab, Chandigarh.

——— *Census of India, 2001*, Series 4, Punjab, Paper 1, 2 and 3.

Government of Punjab, Economic Advisor (1998) *Report on unemployed persons (age group 18–35 years) desirous of seeking employment in Punjab*, unpublished, Chandigarh.

Iyer, G. K. (2000) *Indebtedness, improvement and suicides in rural Punjab*. Delhi: Indian Publishers.

Johl, S. S. (2002) Problems and prospects of agricultural sector development in Punjab. In *Future of agriculture in Punjab*, eds. S. S. Johl and S. K. Ray, 5–10. Chandigarh: CRRID.

Kaldor, Nicholas (1967) *Strategic factor in economic development*. New York: Carnell University Press.

Kuznets, Simon (1965) *Economic growth and structure*. New Delhi: Oxford and IBH Publishing Company.

Mathur, Lalit (2008) Employment guarantee: Progress so far. *Economic and Political Weekly* 52: 17–20.

NSSO (2005) *Indebtness of Farmer Households*, Report No. 498, NSS 59th Round.

PAU, Ludhiana, Department of Economics (2009) Farmers and agricultural labourers suicides due to indebtedness in the Punjab state—A pilot project of Sangrur and Bathinda districts, The project was commissioned by the Government of Punjab, Punjab Agricultural University (PAU), Ludhiana.

Raikhy, P. S. (1999) Mechanisation and cost of cultivation in Punjab during eighties. In *Mechanisation of Punjab agriculture and its impact*, ed. T. S. Chahal, 35–42. Amritsar, Punjab: Indian Society of Agricultural Economics.

Ray, S. K. (2002) Prologue: Crisis in Punjab agriculture. In *Future of agriculture in Punjab*, eds. S. S. Johl and S. K. Ray. Chandigarh: Centre for Research in Rural Industrial Development (CRRID).

Sengupta, Arjun, K.P. Kannan and Ravi Shankar Srivastava (2008) India's common people: Who are they, how many are they and how do they live. *Economic and Political Weekly* 43, No. 11: 49–63.

Shergill, H. S. (1998) *Rural credit and indebtedness in Punjab*. Chandigarh: Institute for Development and Communication (Monograph Series-IV).

——— (2010) *Growth of farm debt in Punjab: 1997 to 2008*. Chandigarh: Institute for Development and Communication.

Singh, Gurpreet (2008) Farmers suicides in Punjab: A socio-economic analysis. M. Phil. Dissertation, Punjabi University, Patiala.

Singh, Karam (2007) Punjab: The dame of water table. The Punjab State Farmers Commission, Government of Punjab, S.A.S. Nagar, Punjab, India.

Singh, Karam, Sukhpal Singh and H. S. Kingra (2007a) Status of farmers who left farming in Punjab. The Punjab State Farmers Commission, Government of Punjab, S.A.S. Nagar, Punjab, India.

——— (2007b) Flow of funds to farmers and indebtedness in Punjab. The Punjab State Farmers Commission, Government of Punjab.

Tribune (2010a) NREGA fuels labour shortage in Punjab. *Tribune*, 21 April 2010, Chandigarh.

——— (2010b) Tackling farm labour woes: State offers subsidy on transplantation machines. *Tribune, 15 May 2010, Chandigarh.*

SECTION IV

MGNREGS and Agents of Rural Transformation

9

Assets Creation and Local Economy under MGNREGS

Scope and Challenges

Amita Shah

I

Context

Developmental Planning and Right to Work: Some Dilemmas

Enhancing wage income through creation of productive assets, especially in the farm economy, is a hallmark of the employment-generation programmes in India and elsewhere.[1] It could be postulated that increased wages and capital formation within rural economies may unleash significant amount of effective demand and productive capacities which, in turn, may redress poverty and also boost up overall growth in the country. The strategy may do marvel in an economy such as India, where agriculture sector continues to play crucial role in sustaining the momentum of overall economic growth, besides reducing poverty (Panda, 2003; Majumdar, 2006; Planning Commission, 2007; The World Bank, 2007).

Basic investment in land and water is an essential precondition for enhancing productivity of agriculture, besides generation and dissemination of technology across different agro-climatic conditions in the country. The proportion of investment in agriculture, with a single exception of irrigation infrastructure, however, has undergone significant decline owing to a number of reasons emanating mainly from the neo-liberal economic polices adopted since the 1990s (Bhaduri, 2005). Public investment in land and water resources and other economic infrastructure, ideally, could provide significant boost-up to the farm economies, particularly in regions with low endowment and limited agronomic potential. In fact, the growing importance of policy initiatives like watershed development projects (WDPs), Bharat Nirman (BN), backward area grant (BAG), etc., in the recent plans signifies recognition of the critical need for enhancing basic investment in natural resource management for promoting the farm economy. If adequately funded and appropriately implemented, these schemes may create and unleash the requisite productive capacities for boosting up agricultural growth, which is also broad based and poverty reducing.

The ideal scenario of a well-planned development of land and water resources, however, is far from being realised. Even if such developments were in place, coverage of such programmatic interventions may have fallen short of creating demand for the massive army of rural labour force in the country, waiting to be fully employed—both in terms of time as well as income—in productive sectors within the economy. Right to demand and seek work, therefore, could possibly work as an effective mechanism for bridging the gap between rural development and people's well-being, given the constraints posed by the neo-liberal economic policies on the one hand, and the programmatic failures on the other.

It may, however, be noted that the MGNREGS is envisaged as providing minimum livelihood security to rural households rather than reducing rural poverty or attaining other developmental objectives (Pankaj, 2008). Although the distinction is quite clear, it may not necessarily resolve the dilemmas that actually arise while operationalising various rural works, especially for creating productive assets within rural economies. Essentially, the operational dilemmas emanate because of the increasing presence of programmatic interventions dealing with land and water resources; keeping the distinction noted above, thus, is difficult. In any case, a conceptual clarity on the interface between the two sets of interventions, often dealing with the same set of natural resources within local economies, is important for attaining the two (not so separable objectives) of livelihood security and poverty reduction or rural development.

It is the contention of this chapter that whereas right to work under the MGNREGS could enhance and help realise the full potential of productive capacities in rural economies, it is essential that the work under the MGNREGS is planned, synchronised and placed in the context of planned economic growth so as to be able to impact local economies within short or medium time frame.

The chapter examines the potential impact of various assets created under the MGNREGS on local economies and discusses policy implications for ensuring realisation of the potential. The specific objectives are to (*a*) identify potential linkages of the assets and impact on rural economies; (*b*) discuss imperatives for convergence with developmental programme, especially watershed development and (*c*) draw policy implications. Given the fact that the implementation of the MGNREGS is still in the initial stage, and that realisation of impact of the assets created under the scheme may often take longer than two to three years, the analysis presented in the chapter is mainly exploratory and draws upon the vast and growing literature as well as secondary data.

The analysis is divided into six sections including this introduction. The next section briefly recapitulates the experiences on assets creation from various employment-generation schemes and highlights the major corrective measures introduced in the MGNREGS. Sections three and four present a broad mapping of the linkages, and assess various dimensions of the impact that the assets may generate in rural economy. This has been attempted in the light of the evidence from watershed projects as there is a fair amount of similarity in the nature of the assets created under these two initiatives. This is followed by assessing the scope for meeting the requirement of large sections of poor and vulnerable households and identifying implication for MGNREGS. The last section, section seven, summarises main conclusions.

II

Creation of Assets under Wage Employment Programmes: Experiences and Corrective Measures under MGNREGS

A number of studies have gone into examining the aspect of assets creation under the various wage employment schemes. The two most important observations emerging from the studies are (*a*) low employment intensity of the work while creating the assets and (*b*) low quality as well as durability, especially of the productive assets, which pertain mainly to land and water resources development (Papola, 2005; Hirway and Terhal, 1994; Government of India, 2006). Lack of planning and involvement of labour contractors and use of machinery were often found to be the most common factors leading to what appeared to be poor outcomes with respect to asset creation.

A major exception seems to be in the case of the Maharashtra Employment Guarantee Scheme where the works, with a central thrust on drought proofing, had focused mainly on creation of irrigation infrastructure. The land-owning class thus became direct beneficiaries, and hence the important stakeholders in the process of creation of such assets. Presence of social movements also helped keeping the contractors away. The outcome, therefore, turned out to be more effective (Patel, 2006).

The concerns about low quality and durability of the assets assume central importance in the context of not only wage employment schemes but also in the context of development programmes like watershed development, waste land development, small irrigation, etc. In fact, it is mainly these concerns combined with the objective of ensuring post-project management of the assets that have led to evolution of participatory approaches by setting up local institutions in the context of the various land and water resources development programmes.[2]

Unfortunately these participatory processes are yet to take roots within the local communities, owing to a number of factors—procedural, financial and socio-political. We do not intend to get into the debates on the limitations of participatory approaches as well as outcomes. However, what is important to note is that the issues of quality, durability and future maintenance continue to remain, by and large, un-addressed even in these programmes. For instance, a recent study of nearly 1,000 micro watershed projects, constituting 5 per cent of the completed projects in MP, Maharashtra and Karnataka revealed that a majority of the physical assets like water harvesting structures, contour trenches, village tanks, farm ponds and pasture land were not in 'good condition'. It was also noted that limited efforts were made to take care of repair/maintenance/post-project management of such assets.[3] While this may not be very surprising, given the limitations of the participatory processes adopted so far, the issue continues to pose the most critical challenge with respect to sustainability of such interventions and, hence, impact on rural economies.

Prima facie, there could be two sets of responses: first is to treat this as a hard reality and hence make provision for recurring investment for repair and maintenance year by year where the works under MGNREGS could serve as supplementary investment as noted above. The second approach could be to evolve mechanisms within the MGNREGS, whereby local institutions could be strengthened. Whereas it is not quite clear as to what kind of institutional arrangements would get evolved under the MGNREGS, an important provision under the MGNREGA is for involving NGOs for overseeing the implementation processes. This, in fact, opens up a substantial scope for strengthening the participatory processes and institutions thereof. The scope for such developments to take place, however, may be significantly enhanced if MGNREGS works are converged with developmental programmes like watershed development, which has already set the process of institution building in motion. In absence of this, the two processes may work at cross purposes—the point already made earlier.

Corrective Measures under MGNREGS

Table 9.1 presents a synoptic view of the problems faced with respect to assets creation and the corrective measures within MGNREGA for overcoming the limitations.

The above depiction highlights the fact that the MGNREGA has made adequate provisions for addressing the limitations with respect to creation of assets under the various wage employment programmes. These are some of the most needed improvements over the earlier schemes. However, two interrelated aspects need special attention in this context: (*a*) relatively greater emphasis on ensuring right choice of works with appropriate planning, and hence expecting better quality of assets rather than on mechanisms for future management and (*b*) the focus is more on implementation as against the outcomes. Of course, there is a valid justification for assuming that right kind of processes would lead to right kind of outcomes. This, however, may not necessarily hold good, especially in the initial phase of implementation of the scheme as highlighted by a number of studies (Mehrotra, 2008; Pankaj, 2008; Ambasta, Vijay Shankar and Mihir, 2008).

While it may take some time before these provisions actually get operationalised, it is imperative to note that convergence with the various developmental programmes may hold the key for realisation of the corrective mechanisms noted above. According to a recent study covering 17 districts under the MGNREGS, only three districts had treated the rural works, especially for water conservation, as developmental initiatives (Mahapatra et al., 2008: 55). The process of convergence, however, is yet to be

Table 9.1: Limitations and Corrective Measures for Assets Creation under MGNREGS

Sl. No.	*Major Limitations in Asset creation under Wage Employment Programmes*	*Corrective Mechanisms under MGNREGS*
1.	Predominance of road and other physical infrastructures	Focus on land and water resources development with prescribed priorities under schedule I.
2.	Lack of planning for creating productive assets focusing on land water resources	Multi-layer planning at village, block and districts; use of information technology in planning; provision of technical support team
3.	Involvement of contractors, use of machinery and neglect of direct labour employment	Ban on contractors; involvement of NGOs besides village panchayats in project implementation
4.	Absence of institutional mechanism for future management of assets	Provision for forming local institutions like SHGs, user groups; special emphasis on social auditing and generating awareness on capacity building
5.	Relative isolation from developmental programmes	Emphasis on convergence with other programmes

Source: Author.

fully worked out. In what follows, we have discussed some of the important challenges in attaining the convergence, with special reference to WDPs.

Convergence between WDPs and MGNREGS: Some Issues

As noted earlier, much of the assets created by various employment-generation programmes in the past have focused on development of land and water resources besides construction of roads and other physical infrastructure. Nevertheless, given the disjointed nature of the wage employment programmes (and other scattered efforts for conservation), a comprehensive approach for land and water resources development, under what has evolved as watershed development programmes, came to the centre stage of livelihood enhancement under different agro-climatic conditions in the country (Shah, 1998).

It is therefore essential that assets creation under employment-generation programmes is in tandem with the rapidly increasing scope and coverage of watershed development and other schemes for development of irrigation infrastructure in the lagging regions. It is here that the primary goals of employment generation and assets creation may need reconciliation. It is plausible that need for employment generation and priorities for land and water resources development may not necessarily coincide across time and space. This may hold good particularly in a situation where employment generation is driven by rights-based approach, as in the case of the MGNREGS where demand for employment may not be amenable to any perspective planning for the area/spatial unit, which is the primary unit for schemes like watershed or irrigation development.

On the other hand, the actual experience from area-based and planned interventions under programmes like watershed development also point out serious limitations arising out of a number of constraints—financial, administrative and institutional. The outcomes, therefore, are often suboptimal (Kerr, 2002). Absence of institutional mechanisms for maintenance and future management of the structures created under WDPs and mobilising supplementary investment for enhancing efficiency of these structures have remained the most important challenges despite adopting participatory processes for project implementation. Similar experiences have been noted under other schemes for land and water resources development. Given this scenario, creation of productive assets through the MGNREGS could work as complementary investment to those under the various developmental programmes.

Faced with the challenges of (*a*) mismatch between the needs and priorities of employment guarantee and developmental programmes and (*b*) suboptimal conditions with respect to implementation of the various developmental programmes, the MGNREGS has worked out some pragmatic solutions to attain complementarity or convergence between the two sets of policy initiatives. These have been manifested by the two important provisions made under the scheme. First, eight out of the nine activity types prescribed for undertaking rural works pertain to soil–water conservation or irrigation infrastructure.[4] And second, dovetailing the other developmental schemes, without substituting funds earmarked for MGNREGS, is strongly recommended. In the process, the MGNREGS could strengthen the implementation of developmental programmes such as watershed development and irrigation, without compromising the rights-based approach for employment generation.[5] Potentially MGNREGS may contribute not only in terms of providing additional financial resources to the existing programmes, but it could also help in promoting institutions for local governance—an important feature of the various developmental programmes (including watershed and irrigation) adopting participatory approaches.

This could be attained by promoting institutions for democratic governance such as gram sabha at the village level, setting up participatory processes through social auditing and establishing strong links with Right to Information, etc.

While these are some of the pragmatic solutions for attaining the convergence, they may not completely reconcile the problem of a mismatch between needs and priorities of employment generation and asset creation, at least in the initial phase.

One of the risks involved in converging the two sets of programmes is that the MGNREGS could be viewed not only as a source of supplementary investment during and after the project, but also as a means to ensure continuous flow of funds for repair/maintenance and/or replacement of the assets created under the developmental programmes like watershed and irrigation. This may have a serious dampening impact on the quality of the assets in the first place, and also on the institutional mechanisms for ensuring efficacy of the assets thereby mobilising additional (private) investment essential for sustaining the flow of surplus generation within the context of rural economies.

Of course, the MGNREGS does provide for certain checks for ensuring quality of work and social audit for monitoring the execution of rural works. It is, however, likely that the focus of these processes is mainly on the aspect of job creation as compared to quality of assets creation.[6] In this situation, the assurance that funds from the MGNREGS could be obtained for carrying out repair/maintenance of replacement of the assets created earlier, may result in certain unwarranted outcomes that may undermine quality, sustenance and future development of the assets created for land and water resources development. This essentially may result in putting the participatory processes for creating community's stakes in creation of assets as well as future management and development and, thereby, accountability, in the back gear. All these may jeopardise sustained flow of benefits from the assets created jointly under development projects and the MGNREGS. This essentially may imply reverting to the earlier scenarios of unplanned, scattered and haphazard approach to assets creation and development.

One could possibly argue that the actual experience from several of the developmental programmes, especially watershed development, is in any case far from creating good-quality assets, with strong institutional mechanisms for future management and sustainable impact on rural economies. And that all these happen without adequate and guaranteed employment. The issue, therefore, is to first correct the limitations/inadequacies in the existing projects which, in turn, may generate additional demand for labour—short term as well long term. Meanwhile, the MGNREGS may continue to supplement and, at times, work parallel to the process of asset creation in rural economies.

While this may be a valid argument, it is not clear as to the kind of impact MGNREGS may have on long-term sustainability of the assets created, and hence the impact on rural institutions and economies. Of course, one could argue that one should not bother much about the sustainability of the assets as long as MGNREGS could ensure continuous flow of funds for repairing or replacing them year by year. The question is whether the administrative wherewithal, including the institutions of local governance, is adequate to undertake rural works on a large scale with at least minimum assurance of quality control.

Given the inadequacies in the implementation of developmental programmes on the one hand and MGNREGS on the other, it is crucial that the convergence between them adds to the strength, rather than diffuse the effectiveness of the two sets of policy initiatives. There are, of course, possibilities of both these to happen since the promoters (the state) as well as recipients (the people) are same in the case of both the programmes. Consolidating the strengths would require much more detailed planning and implementation than what each of the two would call for. This is a huge challenge. In the absence of this, the impact of MGNREGS on asset creation and growth of local economies may remain lower than the full potential, notwithstanding the multiplier impact it may generate for growth at macro level.

Issues at Micro Level

Apart from criticality of convergence with the ongoing developmental programmes, the impact of asset creation and wages within the local economy may largely get governed by factors such as composition of assets, scale and technology, equity and coverage of beneficiaries and sustainability of benefits that may actually (rather than potentially) get generated through the MGNREGS.

Since a large proportion of the MGNREGS work is focused on land and water resources development, assets created through such activities are likely to have significant forward linkages within the local economies. Among these, the most important, at least in the short run, is increased access to irrigation. A number of studies have highlighted the pivotal role that irrigation plays in promoting growth in agriculture and poverty reduction (Bhattarai, Sakthivadivel and Hussain, 2002). Also, evidence from a number of WDPs suggest a fairly favourable benefit–cost ratio, where a large proportion of the benefits tend to emanate from additional availability of water. However, unlike irrigation, the impact of watershed development programmes on poverty reduction or livelihood security is not very clear.

Nevertheless, with the extent to which the MGNREGS supplements the programmatic investment in land and water resources development, the impacts of such investments are likely to be direct, immediate and substantial. The issues that need further attention are that of the scale at which such assets are created, the technology used, spread of benefits among different categories of households and, of course, the second-round impact of increased wage rates on demand for farm labour, etc. Besides these, there are issues of efficiency in the use of natural resources such as land and water and the environmental implications thereof.

Also there are issues of weather-induced uncertainties and fluctuations in the impact on local economies; investment in land and water resources development is expected to reduce such vulnerabilities. How far it is actually realised would depend on how systematic is the planning, what is the quality of work undertaken and how sustainable the assets are. These aspects bring us back to the issues of careful synthesis and convergence between programmatic interventions through schemes like watershed development and the MGNREGS.

The issues discussed above assume special significance in the context of the local economies, notwithstanding the significant multiplier impact to be generated at the macro level due to the increased wage income in the economy.

III

Forward Linkages and Local Economy: Experience and Issues

It has been argued that rural employment programmes may help enhancing asset base in rural economies and also improve efficacy of the various developmental initiatives by putting supplementary investment into these assets, besides generating wage income, a part of which may be channelised through additional demand in the local economies. Together, these may have significant multiplier impact in the overall economy. For instance, the initial estimates by Patnaik (2005) suggested that ₹1 spent on MGNREGS may generate ₹1.33 as wage bill in the economy. While these are macro-level projections based mainly on income multiplier, ascertaining the impact of productive assets within local economies is somewhat tricky.

This section presents a broad mapping of the linkages that the assets created under the MGNREGS may generate within the context of local economies. The mapping of linkages would include mainly the first- and second-round effects. Whereas the first-round effect may include aspects like increased wage income and the associated changes in demand for consumer goods as well as labour, wage rates and on-farm investment, etc., the second-round effects may encompass a wide range of outcomes in terms of production, food security, market development, equity and local governance.

Although the linkages are fairly well recognised, the actual realisation, however, could be fairly diverse and complex. It is difficult to gauge the nature and extent of such linkages, given the wide variations in the operating environment, including climatic variations across the states and regions. Besides these, the impact on local economies is likely to be significantly influenced by the macroeconomic policies, especially pertaining to agriculture sector with which most of the assets have direct linkages.

Another important aspect that needs special mention at this stage is the complementary/supplementary nature of investment in assets creation under the MGNREGS. As noted earlier, all the eight prescribed categories of work pertain to various measures for land and water resources development. Since most of these works are to be planned at the village level, and because there is a cap of 40 per cent for the material cost and a relatively limited time flexibility for executing the works, it may be difficult to plan out large-scale activities such as creation of medium-scale irrigation infrastructure; major treatments on drainage line, especially on a highly undulating terrain; structures for preventing flood; land shaping and fencing and mulching–manuring of private land, etc.

As a result, the kind of activities that are likely to be undertaken for development of land and water resources would be more of the nature of (*a*) creation of small irrigation/water harvesting structures; (*b*) plantation on degraded land and (*c*) repair and maintenance of the existing irrigation infrastructure, including preparation of field channels, drainage-line treatments and replantation, etc. It may be noted that the first two constitute the central thrust of watershed/small irrigation development programmes, whereas the last one pertains to the future management of the treatments already carried out through the first two activities.

The activities remain complementary/supplementary in nature in so far as they fill in the gaps in the coverage of the watershed/small irrigation development programmes on the one hand, and undertake the tasks of recurring maintenance for which there is no effective arrangement—individually or collectively—on the other.[7] This, at times, makes it difficult to assess the impact on local economy, in absence of information regarding (*a*) extent of initial investment in the structures and (*b*) nature of arrangement for future maintenance on a recurring basis.

Given these caveats, in what follows we have presented a typology of linkages of the major sets of assets likely to be created under the MGNREGS and assess the second-round effects of the assets created under the scheme.

Assets and the Linkages

The assets created through the MGNREGS consist mainly of two categories: (*a*) those related to physical infrastructures such as roads and other amenities and (*b*) the productive assets that directly help promoting productive capacities within the local economy. Whereas the former may have significant bearing on the effective functioning of the latter, it is relatively difficult to capture direct linkages of the physical infrastructure with the local economies. Besides, the physical infrastructure plays a pivotal role in improving quality of life by enhancing the access to basic services for health, education, commutation for work and, thereby, economic well-being. Figure 9.1 presents a broad mapping of the forward linkages, mediating factors and the requisite corrective measures for realising the potential impact of the productive assets generated under the MGNREGS, which is quite self-explanatory.

Figure 9.1: Productive Assets and Forward Linkage within Local Rural Economy

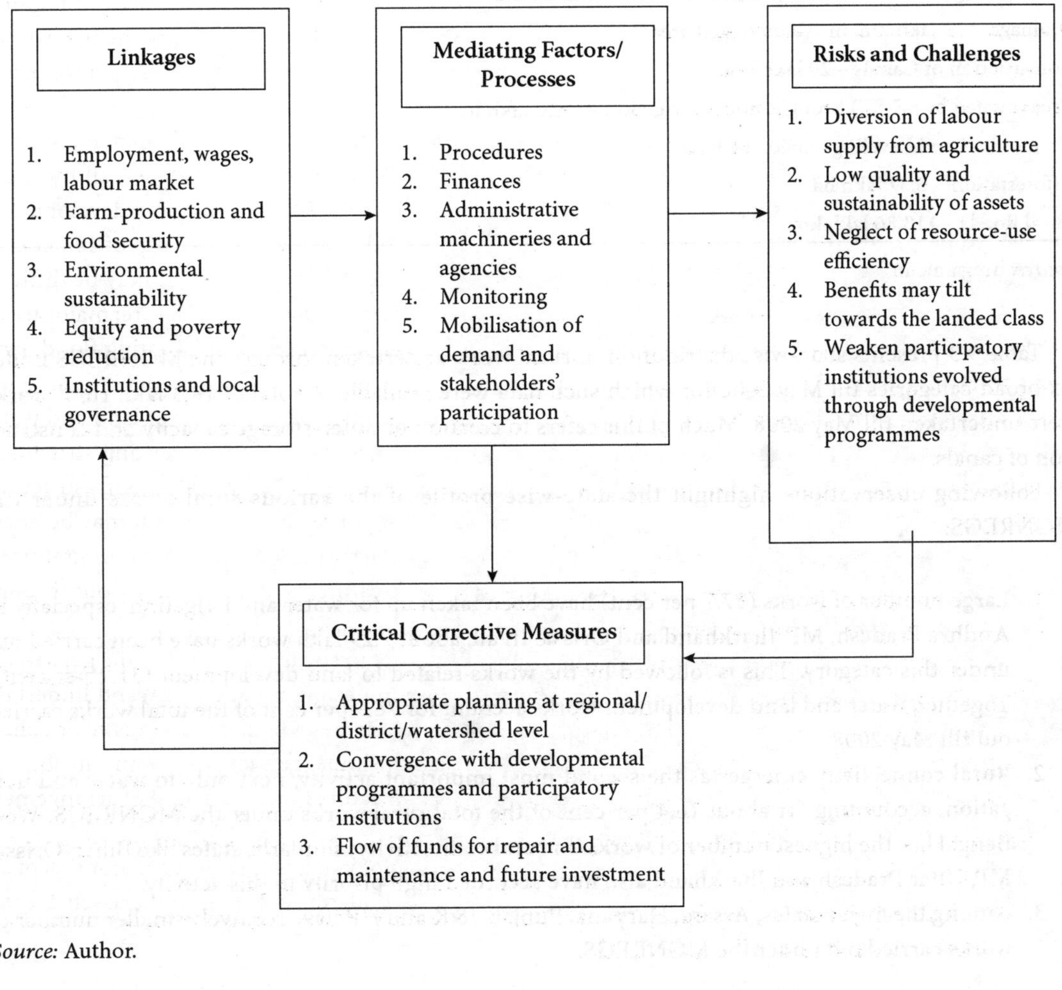
Linkages
1. Employment, wages, labour market
2. Farm-production and food security
3. Environmental sustainability
4. Equity and poverty reduction
5. Institutions and local governance
Mediating Factors/ Processes
1. Procedures
2. Finances
3. Administrative machineries and agencies
4. Monitoring
5. Mobilisation of demand and stakeholders' participation
Risks and Challenges
1. Diversion of labour supply from agriculture
2. Low quality and sustainability of assets
3. Neglect of resource-use efficiency
4. Benefits may tilt towards the landed class
5. Weaken participatory institutions evolved through developmental programmes
Critical Corrective Measures
1. Appropriate planning at regional/ district/watershed level
2. Convergence with developmental programmes and participatory institutions
3. Flow of funds for repair and maintenance and future investment

Source: Author.

Profile of Assets Created under MGNREGS: A State-level Profile

By the mid of 2010–11, a total of about 120.18 million households were provided job cards and nearly 55.8 million households had demanded employment under the MGNREGS during 2006–07; this works out to be approximately 40 per cent of the rural households in the country. The total number of employment generated was 255.53 person-days, which worked out to be 46 per household. Table 9.2 presents a snapshot of the main features of MGNREGS activities at the all-India level.

A large number of works (19.3 lakhs) carried under the scheme had brought in substantial benefits in terms of irrigation infrastructure and improved vegetative cover as shown in Table 9.2.

Table 9.2: Assets Created under MGNREGS: A Bird's Eye View (2010–11)

Types of Assets (Up to May 2010)
Water Storage (New Structures) Capacity – 3266 lakh cu. mt.
Drainage – 12 lakh km. in Water logged area
Construction of Canals – 20 lakh kms.
Area (owned by SC/ST) Brought under Irrigation – 8820 lakh ha.
Plantation, Land Leveling – 55.02 lakh ha.
Afforestation – 6.57 lakh ha.
Rural Roads – 113.86 lakh km.

Source: nrega.nic.in

Table 9.3 presents state-wise distribution of rural work undertaken through the MGNREGS under six broad categories till May 2008 for which such data were available. A total of 19.3 lakh rural works were undertaken till May 2008. Much of this refers to creation of water-storage capacity and construction of canals.

Following observations highlight the state-wise profile of the various rural works under the MGNREGS:

1. Large number of works (37.7 per cent) have been taken up for water and irrigation, especially in Andhra Pradesh, MP, Jharkhand and Orissa. In all, about 7.29 lakh works have been carried out under this category. This is followed by the works related to land development (31.2 per cent). Together, water and land development works account for 78.9 per cent of the total works carried out till May 2008.
2. Rural connectivity emerges as the second most important activity, next only to water and irrigation, accounting for about 16.4 per cent of the total rural works under the MGNREGS. West Bengal has the highest number of works on rural connectivity; similarly, states like Bihar, Orissa, MP, Uttar Pradesh and Jharkhand also have accorded high priority to this activity.
3. Among the major states, Assam, Haryana, Punjab, J&K and HP have relatively smaller number of works carried out under the MGNREGS.

Table 9.3: Distribution of the Rural Works (Completed) across Major States (till May 2008)

	Water and Irrigation	*Drought Proofing*	*Flood Control*	*Rural Connectivity*	*Land Development*	*Other Activity*	*All*
Andhra Pradesh	192,230	47,278	1,765	1,503	454,256	0	697,031
Arunachal Pradesh	29	182	3	52	0	131	397
Assam	2,377	791	1,694	7,773	2,181	875	15,691
Bihar	25,580	1,354	2,411	34,734	608	12,390	77,076
Gujarat	21,984	2,948	1,261	6,093	976	133	33,394
Haryana	1,729	200	115	2,323	705	62	5,134
Himachal Pradesh	6,390	437	3,718	13,884	3,158	1,852	29,439
Jammu & Kashmir	695	54	795	763	522	87	2,916
Karnataka	19,250	12,703	7,286	13,126	15,468	1,231	69,064
Kerala	10,013	2,112	19,358	1,974	16,023	30	49,510
Madhya Pradesh	153,388	23,117	2,103	36,718	29,827	438	245,590
Maharashtra	6,791	2,278	67	1,234	272	497	11,139
Manipur	368	171	5	129	228	0	901
Meghalaya	1,708	555	93	1,365	244	1	3,966
Mizoram	24	70	12	387	6	20	519
Nagaland	58	31	6	104	11	0	210
Orissa	41,660	3,801	677	40,088	1,925	5,218	93,369
Punjab	187	390	68	1,277	311	171	2,404
Rajasthan	36,721	1,457	415	9,055	4,430	1,298	53,377
Sikkim	69	1	150	39	2	0	261
Tamil Nadu	10,390	7	82	996	0	0	11,475
Tripura	9,098	3,745	639	12,908	10,497	33,168	70,056
Uttar Pradesh	25,493	10,505	5,358	39,006	16,221	9,929	106,512
West Bengal	52,640	14,056	9,128	48,668	14,501	2,124	141,117
Chhattisgarh	27,821	6,994	597	17,414	22,957	1,727	77,509
Jharkhand	75,954	2,282	208	24,843	9,144	11,502	123,933
Uttaranchal	7,114	1,557	3,131	1,402	754	414	14,372
Total	**729,761**	**139,076**	**61,145**	**317,858**	**605,227**	**83,298**	**1,936,362**
Percentage	**37.7**	**7.2**	**3.2**	**16.4**	**31.2**	**4.3**	**100**

Source: Ghosh, Satpathy and Mehta (2008).

Table 9.4 presents the estimates of expenditure per work under the major states. It is observed that the average expenditure per completed work ranges significantly from ₹40,000 in Karnataka and Orissa to ₹3.11 in Tamil Nadu and 2.94 lakhs in Assam. Kerala and Gujarat are the other two states with lower amount of expenditure, that is, ₹41000–42,000 per work. Four states, namely, Bihar,

Table 9.4: Expenditure on Completed Works under MGNREGS

States	*Total No. of Workers by May 2011*	*No. of Works Completed by May 2011*	*Proportion of Works Completed— (%)*	*Total Expenditure— ₹ lakhs*	*Expenditure on Completed Works— ₹ lakhs*	*Expenditure per Completed Work ₹ lakh*
Andhra Pradesh	1,286,311	864,989	67.24	543,938.6	365,744.31	0.42
Assam	31,134	10,650	34.21	916,11.16	31,340.18	2.94
Bihar	194,776	39,386	20.22	266,413	53,868.71	1.37
Chhattisgarh	156,226	89,287	57.15	163,397.8	93,381.84	1.05
Gujarat	85,049	45,158	53.1	78,822	41,854.48	0.93
Haryana	12,832	7,532	58.7	21,421.04	12,574.15	1.67
Jharkhand	211,379	42,812	20.25	128,375.6	25,996.06	0.61
Karnataka	637,731	61,037	9.57	256,693.3	24,565.55	0.40
Kerala	166,509	62,808	37.72	67,564.28	25,485.25	0.41
Madhya Pradesh	686,703	290,912	42.36	364,179.7	154,266.52	0.53
Maharashtra	49,368	18,707	37.89	35,767.08	13,552.15	0.72
Orissa	367,597	52,961	14.41	148,788.8	21,440.47	0.40
Punjab	14,867	6,265	42.14	16,576.84	6,985.48	1.12
Rajasthan	195,206	51,976	26.63	328,907.1	87,587.96	1.69
Tamil Nadu	73,073	28,003	38.32	227,340.7	87,116.96	3.11
Uttar Pradesh	752,067	448,148	59.59	562,825.9	335,387.95	0.75
Uttarakhand	42,206	29,749	70.48	380,19.87	26,796.40	0.90
West Bengal	246,013	142,974	58.12	253,246.1	147,186.63	1.03

Source: Data from nrega.nic.in

Haryana, Punjab, Rajasthan and West Bengal have spent between one to two lakhs per work. There is, however, no systematic inverse relationship between the number of completed works and average expenditure per work.

The information presented in Tables 9.3 and 9.4, thus, does not help in identifying the specific nature of work undertaken in different locations. This may make it difficult to ascertain the impact that such works may generate on rural economies. It may, however, be useful to consider some broad attributes of the major works under the MGNREGS in Table 9.5.

An important feature observed from Table 9.5 is that employment gain is mostly direct rather than indirect and recurring. This is mainly because of the high incidence of underemployment among those already working on agriculture and allied activities. There is, of course, a possibility of increasing the productivity of labour time put to farm activities. It may, however, be noted that development of public/common property resources may help in creating additional flow of employment over time.

Table 9.5: Salient Features of the Various Rural Works: Some General Observations

	Type of Assets				
Potential Linkages and Challenges	*Water and Irrigation (water storage capacity including irrigation for SC/ST HH; construction of canals)**	*Drought Proofing (drainage-line treatment; additional water storage)**	*Flood Control and Protection (drainage; construction of canals)**	*Land Development (land levelling; afforestation)**	*Rural Connectivity (rural roads)**
1. Employment and Labour Market	Increased area under cultivation; this may lead to intensification of on-farm employment	Direct employment on the worksite	Direct employment	Direct employment; additional employment after a lag of time after the growth of plantation and additional fodder	Direct employment; may generate more/better employment opportunities due to increased mobility
2. Farm Production and Food Security	Enhance productivity and help food security—directly/indirectly at HH as well as macro level	Indirect impact on productivity through increased soil-moisture profile	Significant impact on land productivity and reduced risk due to flooding	Increased availability of non-timber forest produce including fuel wood; and fodder	Not much
3. Environmental Sustainability	Limited emphasis on water-use efficiency; likely to shift towards water-intensive crops and further depletion of groundwater	Fairly substantial	Significant impact on reducing soil erosion/land degradation	Fairly significant	No positive impact
4. Equity and Poverty Reduction	Significant impact on reducing poverty/poverty gap; implications on intravillage equity is not clear	Could benefit those not having irrigation; also help in regeneration of Common Property Land Resources (CPLRs)	Not so clear	Substantial, since the poor depend more on the forest resources	May help the poor to explore better opportunities outside the village
5. Institutions and Local Governance	Not much	Need local institutions for repair and maintenance as much of the works are on Common Property Resources (CPRs)	Not clear	Need local institutions for collective action	No impact

(Table 9.5 contd.)

(Table 9.5 contd.)

Potential Linkages and Challenges	*Type of Assets*				
	*Water and Irrigation (water storage capacity including irrigation for SC/ST HH; construction of canals)**	*Drought Proofing (drainage-line treatment; additional water storage)**	*Flood Control and Protection (drainage; construction of canals)**	*Land Development (land levelling; afforestation)**	*Rural Connectivity (rural roads)**
6. Size, Certainty and Gestation Period of the Flow of Benefits	Reasonably good	Marginal and takes long time for realising the benefits	Fairly substantial and immediate	Significant benefits, but takes long time for plantation to grow; generally low survival rate	Indirect impacts are difficult to discern
7. Measures Needed for Sustaining the Benefits	Need to promote water-use efficiency	Comprehensive approach based on watershed development may help realising the full potential	Systematic planning based on watershed/basin as unit	Strengthening of local institutions for protection is a critical precondition for the success	Not clear

Source: Author's conceptualisation.
Note: * The specific activities indicated in parentheses are based on the general impression as such information is not available at aggregate level.

The profile of the impact in Table 9.5 may give a broad picture of the typology of impact that each of category of the rural works could generate. The above presentation, however, is subject to two limitations: (*a*) it assumes specific nature of activities, for which information is available, under each of the major categories of works; there is no information on the specific activities carried out under each category of works and (*b*) the depiction of the typology of impact is based on the understanding derived from the actual experiences from a number of projects pertaining to natural resources development across different parts in India;[8] generalisation may not be appropriate. In this sense the typology presented above may be treated only as indicative. Given this backdrop, the next section tries to assess the impact of some of the specific activities taken up under MGNREGS across different states in the country.

IV

Assets and the Impact: A Preliminary Assessment

At the outset, it may be mentioned that the attempt made in this section to assess the impact of the various assets created under the MGNREGS is somewhat premature and is based on the limited data availability on the specific nature of the assets. A national-level study was carried out by the National Institute of Rural Development (NIRD), which sought to conduct a census survey of all the assets created under the MGNREGA in a few villages across the major states; the results are yet to be put in the public domain. Meanwhile, a few studies have looked into the impacts of the assets created under the scheme, although most of these could only be viewed as initial evidence, in absence of further information on the quality as well as durability of such assets and the specific institutional arrangements thereof. Given this scenario, this section draws from the limited evidence obtained mainly from the initial impact assessment of the MGNREGA and subsequently draws upon the evidence from impact assessment of various projects, especially WDPs with which the MGNREGS seems to have the closest linkages.[9] Since watershed projects have fairly large coverage across states in the country, using the evidence from impact assessment of watershed projects may be reasonably justified. The analysis in this section draws upon three sets of evidences from WDPs: (*a*) meta-analysis covering a large number of states, (*b*) treatment-specific assessment and (*c*) status of the assets in the post-project period.

Assets Created and Impacts under MGNREGA: Some Evidence

A number of studies have been carried out assessing the impacts of the MGNREGA on wage employment and also on the usefulness of the assets created under the scheme.[10] A study by Drèze and Khera (2009) noted that about 87 per cent of the households covered by the survey reported that the assets created/repaired under the MGNREGA were useful.[11] This, of course, is generally true, at least in the initial phase, of most of the assets created through developmental schemes such as watershed and various rural development programmes. There are, however, two important issues that need to be addressed in medium or long-term contexts, as already flagged in the initial part of the chapter. These are: (*a*) whether the assets have direct implications for enhancing productivity and earnings in future; and (*b*) what are the institutional mechanisms to ensure that the flow of benefits also reach the poor and sustain in the future?

Besides these critical concerns, the issue of the right choice or composition of the assets remains relevant, notwithstanding the widespread perceived utility of the assets created under the MGNREGA. For instance, a study by Centre for Science and Environment (CSE, 2008) observed that notwithstanding the officially 'stated non-negotiable focus' on water and soil conservation, funds are used largely on roads and building. This was evident by the fact that only three states— Andhra Pradesh, MP and Jharkhand accounted for 96 per cent of water conservation works under MGNREGA (Drèze and Khera, 2009: 6). According to the study, 'irrational wage calculation formula has made productive assets creation less lucrative to local communities in terms of accessing minimum wage on time' (ibid; 6).

Concerns have also been raised with respect to the equity aspects of the access to the benefits from the assets created under the scheme (Shah and Mehta, 2008; Hirway, 2010). The earlier experience from Maharashtra Employment Guarantee Scheme suggested that the scheme, though useful to the poor, had low impact on poverty reduction and also that much of the benefits had gone to resource-rich farmers with access to irrigation. A similar scenario may arise in the case of MGNREGA, especially in absence of the corresponding institutional processes and mechanisms to ensure that the poor may also get a share in the benefits from the assets created under the scheme.[12]

It is in this context that the provisions for creating assets on private lands of the marginalised communities deserve special attention. Though debatable, the issue is fairly pertinent if the process of asset creation is seen as a mechanism to simultaneously address the issue of equity and poverty reduction among the rural communities. The recent evidence on the overall upward movement in the rural wages, a part of which could be attributed to the MGNREGS, may provide further fillip to the argument that the scheme should proactively help in creating productive assets on the poor's land; in absence of this, the poor may either gradually start abandoning the land and/or get into the practice of reverse tenancy—both may have adverse and certainly unintended socio-economic implications.

It is, therefore, important to look into the experience of how assets created under a similar intervention like watershed development in the past have performed in terms of sustainable and equitable flow of benefits in the post-project scenario. This aspect has been discussed subsequently in the light of the existing evidence in the Indian context.

Evidence from Meta-analysis of Watershed Projects

A recent study based on 636 watershed projects spread across different parts in India brings out useful findings on benefits from the project (Joshi et al., 2008). Drawing from a subset of 311 studies, the analysis indicates an average benefit–cost ratio of the order of 2.01:1, with a median value of 1.7:1 (see Table 9.6). This is fairly moderate, given the fact that it includes the entire project costs as well as benefits, which may also include wage income from the direct employment on the project sites. This is an important limitation of meta-analysis, which is difficult to address as the estimates have been generated through the existing studies, often using different methodologies.

Table 9.6: Summary of Benefits from the Sample Watershed

	Particulars	*Unit*	*No. of Studies*	*Mean*	*Mode*	*Median*
Efficiency	BC ratio	Ratio	311.00	2.01	1.70	1.70
	Internal Rate of Return (IRR)	Per cent	162.00	27.43	25.90	25.00
Equity	Employment	Person-days/ha/year	99.00	154.53	286.67	56.50
Sustainability	Increase in irrigated area	Per cent	93.00	51.55	34.00	63.43
	Increase in cropping intensity	Per cent	339.00	35.51	5.00	21.00
	Run-off reduced	Per cent	83.00	45.72	43.30	42.53
	Soil loss saved	Tons/ha/year	72	1.12	0.91	0.99

Source: Joshi et al. (2008).

On employment gains, the evidence from 99 studies indicates that the project activities generated an average of about 155 person-days of work per hectare per year for the project period of about five years. Assuming an average size of watershed area of 500 ha, this may generate total employment of about 77,000 person-days per year. At the rate of 100 days per household per year (as per the MGNREGS norm), this could provide employment to 77 households per micro watershed or village for five years. This may fall short of the actual requirement, especially in villages with significant proportion of households facing severe poverty. It may, however, be noted that the estimated employment gain is likely to be lower than the actual potential of a micro watershed project. This could be due to two reasons: (*a*) use of machinery to substitute labour and (*b*) incomplete treatments of watershed owing to several constraints including finance. We will get back to this issue in the next section.

Benefits from Specific Treatments—Evidence from Gujarat

The above evidence, based on the meta-analysis, provides estimates of benefits for the entire set of activities carried out under a micro watershed project. While these activities cover almost all the rural works covered under the five major categories listed in Table 9.5, it is important to get at least a broad idea of the impact from specific activities, as the MGNREGS, unlike WDPs, does not adopt a systematic/comprehensive approach to natural resource development to which most of the assets are linked.

Studies on WDPs, on the other hand, seldom look at the impact of each of the treatments separately. However, an attempt was made to gauge broad magnitude of benefits in a disaggregated manner such as this (Shah, 2005). The analysis, based on some micro-level evidence from Gujarat, provided estimates of the net returns from some of the major treatments such as water harvesting structures/small check dams, field bunding, land levelling, plantation and pasture development, drainage-line treatments, etc. Table 9.7 presents information on this aspect. It may, however, be noted that the estimates of costs and benefits pertain to the prices prevailing in the study region during 2000–01. At present, the estimates could be twice that of the original. These estimates are presented in the parentheses in column three of Table 9.7. The estimates are drawn from the projects from dry-land regions in Gujarat; the returns could be higher in the case of areas with moderate rainfall as indicated by the meta-analysis noted above, and also those with moderately sloppy topography where immediate gains from soil–water conservation are generally higher than those having a relatively plain terrain (Shah, 2004).

Table 9.7: Economic Returns form Major Treatments

Watershed Treatments	*Cost ₹/ha*	*Benefits ₹/ha (2000–01 prices)*	*Remarks*
Field bunding on private land	2,500–3,000 on land with moderate slope	15–20 % increase in yield during normal rainfall	In most cases, field bunds exist. They need to be strengthened and improved in terms of size and material. In absence of any other incentives like irrigation, Farm Yard Manure (FYM) or farm forestry, field bunds alone will not provide sufficient incentives even for proper maintenance. Hence, this treatment should become a part of a larger package of increasing land productivity.
Farm forestry/ plantation and private and public land	5,000–6,000	15,000–20,000 with about 60 % survival rate (30,000–40,000)	Need to be accompanied by provision for survival irrigation, good quality of planting material and fencing.
Regeneration of pastures on CPLRs	4,000–5,000	1,500–2,000 for fodder + fuel wood (3,000–4,000)	Need to treat a part of the gaucher through proper protection. The other part should be kept open for tree grazing. Provision of fodder pool in the first five years or regeneration measures might help protection. Similarly, deep ploughing, manuring and seedling might also help expediting the process of regeneration.

(Table 9.7 contd.)

(Table 9.7 contd.)

Watershed Treatments	*Cost ₹/ha*	*Benefits ₹/ha (2000–01 prices)*	*Remarks*
Irrigation from water harvesting structures like check dams on public land	20,000–100,000	7,500–10,000 through additional water for irrigation (15,000–20,000)	People have very high preference and hence willingness to pay. Scope for attaining better equity through provision of water rights to all HH and cross-subsidy.
Farm ponds on private land	10,000–15,000	2,000–3,000 during normal year (4,000–6,000)	Provide credit support to make basic investment in the structures. Subsidies farm forestry or plantation on performance (survival) basis.
Land levelling	4,000–7,000	5,000–7,000	High preference in the regions having moderate–high slopes and small holdings
Mulching, composting and other agronomic practices	NA	NA	Farmers do recognise the importance of such measures. But these need proper extension as well as organisational support, besides (wage) income support for putting family labour on such on-farm treatments.

Source: Adapted from Chart 2 in Shah (2005).

The information in Table 9.7 reveals that direct benefits from various treatments (in current prices at present) varies from ₹30, 000–40,000 per ha from farm forestry to ₹15,000–20,000 per ha from irrigation and water harvesting structures, to ₹3, 000–4,000 per ha from pasture development. It may, however, be noted that the estimated benefits could further increase provided (*a*) quality of the assets is good and (*b*) post-project maintenance is taken care of. In absence of these two, the flow of benefits may reduce over time. This phenomenon was widely observed during a recent exercise, mentioned earlier, of revisiting the physical structures/assets created under watershed projects covering a sample of nearly 1,000 micro watershed in three states,namely, MP, Maharashtra, Karnataka.[13] In what follows, we bring out certain important findings from MP, which incidentally has created large number of such assets under the MGNREGS, as already seen in Table 9.1.

Evidence from a Post-project Assessment in MP

The evidence from post-project scenarios in MP draws from a sample of 347 micro watersheds, constituting roughly five per cent of the completed WDPs in the state for which information was available (Shah, Joshi and Desai, 2008). As part of the exercise, physical verification of a sub-set of the major structures (assets) created under the WDPs was carried out. The structures included in this exercise covered those with average–good conditions as per the local community; these excluded those who, according to the village community, were severely damaged or were in the best condition at the time of the visit.

The information in Table 9.8a indicates that whereas nearly 50 per cent of the check dams using concrete material were already damaged, more than 60 per cent of the *kacha* check dams/water harvesting structure were damaged at the time of the study. Compared to this, a significantly large proportion of

Table 9.8a: Status of Selected Structures and Coverage of Beneficiaries

Type of Treatments	*Total Nos.*	*No. of Structures in Good Condition (%)*
Pucca check dams	885	465 (52.5)
Kacha check dams	1,048	401 (38.3)
Village tanks	733	645 (87.9)
Deepening of village tanks	135	100 (74.0)
Percolation tanks	283	255 (90.1)
Farm ponds (public)	362	276 (76.2)
Plantation (public)	122	39 (32.0)

Source: Adapted from Shah, Joshi and Desai (2008).
Note: Figure in parenthesis is in per cent.

village/percolation tanks were still in good conditions. This could partly be due to the fact that many of the village tanks or ponds are traditional structures, relatively larger in size, existing over a longer period of time and undergoing periodical repairs through drought-relief programmes as compared to the check dams created through the WDPs, which are generally smaller in size and not having institutional mechanisms for maintenance through local institutions. Compared to water harvesting structures, impact of the CPLRs is found to be fairly limited as more than 60 per cent of the plots under plantation had lower than even 30 per cent of survival rate. The above observations may reinstate the widely acknowledged phenomenon of limited and selective coverage of benefits arising out the various treatments/assets created under the WDPs as shown in Table 9.8b.

Table 9.8b: Summary of the Physical Verification—Status, Arrangements for Future Management and Beneficiaries

Type of Treatment (Total no. of villages covered under the treatment)	*No. of Structures*	*Structures in Good Condition (%)**	*% of Villages with Arrangements for Future Management*	*Average No. of Direct Beneficiaries (No beneficiaries)***
Pucca check dams (217)	189	52.6	47.1	7 (25)***
Kacha check dams (78)	42	38.3	45.2	3 (11)
Village tanks (209)	166	88.0	54.2	5 (40)
Percolation tanks (74)	33	90.0	48.5	6 (5)
Farm ponds on public land (41)	21	76.2	80.9	2.5 (5)
Plantation on public land (253)	122	32.0$ (survival rate > 30 %)	82.8	NA

Source: Shah, Joshi and Desai (2008).
Notes: * Based on Table19a in Shah, Joshi and Desai (2008).
** Based on the median value.
*** No. of structures not reporting any benefits.
$ Survival rate >30%.

The phenomenon of limited coverage of beneficiaries is particularly true in the case of check dams where the direct benefits in terms of additional irrigation is obtained by about 7–10 beneficiaries at the most. Since these structures often do not have any specific arrangements for repair and maintenance (as it is generally assumed that the user group would take care of them), it is often observed that the initial benefits may get reduced over time.

In this context, the evidence from Table 9.9 is quite revealing. It is observed that the association between the proportions of the sample WDPs reporting 'high' level of overall benefits increased significantly from about 12 per cent in the pre-1994 period and 21 per cent during 1995–97 to 45 per cent in the post 2001–02. It may be noted that less than one-fourth of the WDPs had reported 'high' overall benefits from the projects as compared to about 29 per cent reporting low and another 47 per cent reporting medium levels of benefits from watershed projects.

Table 9.9: Overall Benefits of Watershed Development Programme by Year of Starting

Level of Benefit	*Before 1994*	*1995–97*	*1998–2000*	*2001–02*	*All*
Low (%)	37.5	30.5	27.7	19.3	28.7
Medium (%)	50.0	48.7	45.8	35.5	47.4
High (%)	12.5	20.8	26.5	45.2	23.9
All (%)	100.0	100.0	100.0	100.0	100.0
Total No.	16	187	83	41	327

Note: Excludes 10 out of 13 villages for which year of starting is not clear, and the six villages for which information on overall benefits is not available.

Overall, the evidence presented in this section, though selective, highlights certain critical features of the impact of WDP treatments on rural economies. These could be summarised as follows: (*a*) employment gain is confined mainly to on-site work; (*b*) whereas overall benefit–cost ratio for watershed projects is fairly moderate, the major economic benefits emanate from various water harvesting structures which, in turn, may have limited coverage of beneficiaries; (*c*) physical structures, especially small check dams, created under the WDPs tend to get damaged in absence of institutional mechanisms for maintenance and (*d*) overall benefits from the WDPs appear to be low or medium and that the benefits tend to decline over time. This may imply that much of the impact on productivity, employment and capital formation, by and large, may remain confined to direct/first-round effects. Sustaining the impact may, however, necessitate institution building and strengthening of the local governance.

There are three important implications for the MGNREGS. These are need for: (*a*) exploring the scope for expanding the extent of employment generation; (*b*) ensuring good quality and maintenance of the assets and (*c*) widening the net of beneficiary households so as to complement the coverage of direct beneficiaries from WDPs; greater focus on development of resources under common property regimes may assume the importance in this context. We may address some of these issues in the next section.

V

Reaching Out to the Poor: Exploring the Full Potential in the Context of WDPs

A number of studies in the recent past have tried to address the issue of the extent of households requiring and actually demanding obtaining employment under MGNREGS (Box 9.1). The analyses indicate a fairly large range from 33–40 per cent of the total of about 5,000 million person-days of unemployment (Papola, 2005), to about 40–43 per cent of the rural households (Patanaik, 2005), to 80 per cent of the rural labour households (RLH) (Ambasta et al., 2008) to a larger estimate of person-days to be generated (including those requiring less than 100 days of work) (See Table 9.10).

Table 9.10: Projected and Actual Demand for Employment under MGNREGS: Some Scenarios

Scenarios by	*Main Features*	*No. of Rural HH (out of the total of 200 million)*	*Remarks*
1. Papola (2005)	Based on the estimated quantum of unemployment and the actual turnout during MEGS	Seeking employment for 2,000 million person-days/ year, particularly by the uneducated in rural areas	This may be gross under estimation in the light of the fact that (a) it ignores the extent of underemployment and (b) assumes no improvement in the actual implementation of MGNREGS over MEGS, notwithstanding the significantly higher wage rates under MGNREGS as compared to the actual.
2. Patanaik (2005)	Based mainly on the estimates of RLH, that is, approximately 60 million HHs	60 million rural HHs (6,000 million person-days/year)	These may require employment for all the 100 days
3. Considering marginally non-poor and the extent of underemployment to meet the requisite expenditure level	Poor and those marginally above (25 % higher expenditure than poverty line—that is, ₹21,375 per hh) the poverty line (about 40–43 % of rural HHs as per NSSO 43rd round) Estimating the total no. of paid work to attain the income of ₹21,375 per HH. This amounts to about 428 person-days of paid employment/hh, that is, 214 days per worker (assuming two workers/hh) @ of ₹50 per day.	Assuming that two full-time workers may get paid employment for say a total of about 320 days per HH, these HH may still need an addition of 100 days of work per year. This would imply significantly larger number (than 6,000 million) of employment days to be generated through MGNREGS.	These HH may be spread over the entire segment having expenditure up to ₹21,375 per HH per year. Those much below the poverty line, however, may require much more than 100 days of employment to reach the above level of expenditure.

(Table 9.10 contd.)

(Table 9.10 contd.)

Scenarios by	*Main Features*	*No. of Rural HH (out of the total of 200 million)*	*Remarks*
4. Actual Scenario	2.1 million HHs in 2006–07 (Mehrotra, 2008)	About 3.9 million HHs in the districts covered under phase I & II. 36 % of the rural HHs in these districts (Ghosh et.al., 2008).	The achievement in the first two years thus, tend to confirm the conservative estimate provided by Papola (2005).
A Significant gap still exists between the estimated no. of 60 million and the actual 2.1 million hhs demanding work. Also the intensity of employment is 43 days as against 100 days per hhs per year.			

The estimates presented above clearly suggest the need to expand the coverage of MGNREGS in terms of both HH (Table 9.11) and no. of days of employment per household (as seen in Table 9.2). According to Ambasta, et al. (2008), about 50–60 million HHs may need such employment. Against

Table 9.11. MGNREGS: Participation Rate of Households

States	*No. of Rural HHs covered under MGNREGS (Phase 1 and 2 Districts) (in lakhs)*	*Employment Demanded by HHs (in lakhs)*	*Percentage of Households Participated*
Andhra Pradesh	105.92	48.04	45.36
Assam	19.88	14.48	72.86
Bihar	124.07	38.63	31.13
Chhattisgarh	29.43	22.97	78.05
Gujarat	19.88	2.91	14.62
Haryana	5.07	0.71	13.99
Jharkhand	37.37	16.80	44.96
Karnataka	29.39	8.64	29.39
Kerala	10.50	2.59	24.69
Madhya Pradesh	53.26	43.47	81.62
Maharashtra	53.50	4.75	8.87
Orissa	51.98	11.35	21.83
Punjab	8.18	0.50	6.07
Rajasthan	24.64	21.73	88.19
Tamil Nadu	31.35	12.35	39.38
Uttar Pradesh	120.95	41.04	33.93
Uttarakhand	5.05	1.89	37.45
West Bengal	108.69	39.20	36.07

Source: nrega.nic.in

this, the actual coverage of households appears to be in the range of 10–12 per cent. What is a more realistic assessment of the number of households actually requiring (hence, demanding) the work? And, how to go about attaining that?

We discuss this issue in the light of the scope within WDPs which, as of now, does not emphasise much of on-farm treatments, somewhat similar to the MGNREGS.

Box 9.1. Employment Guarantee through MGNREGS–WDP Combined: Some Projections

The assessment of the scope for rural works under MGNREGS has been attempted by considering a village with about 500 ha of land under a micro watershed and 250 households inhabiting this. The need for additional employment is estimated on the basis of following assumptions (against the national average of 300 household per village).[14]

Demand for Work: 100 out of 250 households (that is, 40 per cent) of the households would require additional employment for 100 days on an average. This works out to be 10,000 person-days of additional work required in the village per year.

Wage Bill: Assuming a relatively low wage rate of ₹50 per day, the wage bill would amount to ₹7.5 lakh per year.

Provision for Wage Bill under WDPs (with a Total budget of ₹30 lakh): Of the total budget, 82.5 per cent is to be spent for various treatments, of which 60 per cent should go towards wage bill. This works out to be about ₹15 lakh for five years. This at the rate of ₹50 per day as wages could generate 30,000 person-days of employment over five years, that is 6,000 person-days per year.

The Gap: 9,000 person-days per year, which at the rate of ₹50 per day may require ₹4.5 lakh per year or 22.5 lakhs for five years. The total wage bill, thus, may go up to ₹37.5 lakhs per watershed village over a period of five years.

Revised Budget for WDPs: It is, however, contemplated that the budget for WDPs may be revised upward to make it double, that is, ₹60 lakhs per micro watershed. Simultaneously, the time frame is also increased from five to seven years. Accordingly, the wage bill may go up to ₹30 lakhs for seven years. It is envisaged that this kind of upward revision would help taking care of both the rise in costs (including wage cost) and completion of the required treatments, which was not possible due to financial constraints.

The revised budget with a wage bill of ₹30 lakhs may generate employment of 60,000 person-days over seven years, that is, about 8,500 person-days per year. However, factoring in for the higher wage rate of say, ₹70 per day, employment generation would be of the order of about 42,000–43,000 person-days over seven years, that is, roughly 6,000 person-days per year. This may still leave a gap of 9,000 person-days of employment over the project period of seven instead of five years.

Assuming that the MGNREGS could help in mobilising the additional fund required for generating the flow of 15,000 person-days of employment over a period of at least seven years, the issue that remains to be addressed is what kind of work could be undertaken for generating the additional employment beyond what has been envisaged in the watershed project. Also, it is important to address the issue pertaining to increase in the demand for work, at least among the very poor sections of the society, given the situation of severe underemployment. If the demand for work is more than 100 days among the 40 per cent of households that demand the work, then the gap would be more than 1,500 person-days per year.

We try to discuss some of these issues in the light of the unfinished agenda of watershed development and beyond that.

First of all, the present approach to watershed development leaves out a number of measures that need more intensive treatments. These include both public or common resources, and private land. The emphasis on public resources refers mainly to wasteland and/or pasture development which, in turn, has significant bearing on the development of livestock, thereby sustained increase in employment throughout the year and over time. At present, watershed treatment suffers from two major limitations—poor quality of material and low/no protection. These issues need to be addressed by mobilising additional fund for taking up the labour works under the MGNREGS; funds from the WDPs could then be utilised for improving the quality of material/protection.

On private land, the need is to undertake labour-intensive measures for mending the bunds/trenches, preparing mulch and manure and biomass generation. A model focusing on biomass-based approach to increasing productivity of land suggests that about 200 person-days of work may be required to regenerate cultivable land facing degradation and, hence, low vegetative cover. It is postulated that a poor household having one acre of land could be brought to the level of self-sufficiency (rather than self-provisioning) through biomass regeneration (Datye, 1997). Such models need to be promoted by supporting labour inputs on the farm of the poor. At present, the MGNREGS permits on-farm work related to irrigation on the land of SC/ST. The provision needs to be extended to all households willing to adopt more sustainable technologies for productivity enhancement such as this. At present, the very poor households are not able to take out time and/or other resources as they often are too busy making the two ends meet by undertaking scattered, multiple and low-productive tasks at the cost of long-term investment in their land and allied activities like livestock.

Second, a number of water harvesting structures need supplementary investment for making field channels, direct recharging of wells and taking up labour-intensive rather than water-intensive crops. Watershed projects may provide special incentives for cultivation of such crops; the funds required for this could be created by dovetailing the WDPs with MGNREGS. It may, however, be noted that funds from MGNREGS should not be used indiscriminately for recurring repair and maintenance as it may send negative signals for the users/communities to take care of the assets created under the WDPs/MGNREGS.

Last, there is a substantial need for promoting value addition through agro-processing and allied activities, given the initial investment in land and water resources. It is in this context that convergence between WDPs and MGNREGS may help in fulfilling the incomplete agenda of watershed-based development which, in turn, may pave way for sustained increase in income and employment. Absence of this may lead to perpetual dependence on wage income earned through employment guarantee schemes. This may work counterproductive if the central thrust of the rural works/asset creation moves away from creating additional production capacities in the rural areas as indicated by Bhaduri (2005: 269). Increased connectivity may play an important role in facilitating expansion of productive capacities and employment opportunities rather than being seen as stand-alone infrastructure, per se, to benefit the rural communities.

Towards Convergence between MGNREGA and WDP: Recent Developments

An important mechanism for fostering the developmental objectives alongside the employment guarantee is to explore convergence with several other developmental programmes that already carry out similar works. This may not only strengthen the ongoing processes of developmental initiatives, but may also help in avoiding undue overlaps and duplication of efforts. More important, a carefully carved out mechanism for convergence may help dovetailing the participatory processes as well as institutions at local levels, evolved during implementation of the various developmental schemes, with those being set up for the implementation of the MGNREGA.

Driven by this objective, the Government of India had set up a task force for working out the norms and procedures for convergence of a number of developmental schemes with MGNREGA. One of the most important areas of convergence has been with watershed development, for which a special expert group has been set up.[15] The expert group is in the process of working out the modalities for convergence where enhancing the quality as well as sustainability of soil and water conservation works assumes a central place. The basic arguments for seeking the convergence are threefold: (*a*) improved resource planning and management; (*b*) avoiding overlap of financial resources and (*c*) ensuring better maintenance of the assets in the post-project phase through institutional linkages.

It is in this context that the works in the next phase of MGNREGA, especially those having direct link with farm productivity, need to be planned, prioritised and implemented.

VI

Concluding Remarks

The foregoing analysis tried to explore the likely impact of the assets created under the MGNREGS at this initial stage. In doing so, the chapter discusses the issue of dilemmas of linking the MGNREGS with various developmental initiatives, especially those focusing on livelihood enhancement through management of natural resources. Given the fact that over 70 per cent of the rural works under the scheme pertain to development of land and water/irrigation facilities, the assessment could be attempted in the light of the experiences from developmental programmes like watershed development, having the closest resemblance to the scheme.

The discussion in the initial part of the chapter highlighted the specific corrective measures undertaken in the design of the MGNREGS, which potentially may help overcome some of the widely prevalent limitations of assets creation under the earlier employment generation programmes, especially, the Maharashtra Employment Guarantee Scheme. The analysis, however, points out that whereas these are some of the most needed improvements over the earlier schemes, two interrelated aspects need special attention in this context: (*a*) relatively greater emphasis on ensuring right choice of works with appropriate planning, and hence, expecting better quality of assets rather than on mechanisms for future management and (*b*) the focus is more on implementation as against the outcomes. This may, of course, be justified by asserting that the right kind of processes would lead to right kind of outcomes.

It is further noted that much of the assets created under the MGNREGS are likely to be supplementary/complementary in nature. This may open up both an opportunity for convergence and also the risk of diluting the processes of development already being set through the various natural resources-based initiatives.

Supplementary nature of the assets may create additional difficulties in assessing the actual impact, besides the data limitations pertaining to the specific nature of the assets created under the MGNREGS.

The assessment, ideally, should take into consideration the multifunctional nature of the impact that the assets, related mainly to natural resources, are expected to generate, especially if initiated through a developmental mode. The various facets of the impact may thus include not only income and employment, but also larger developmental objectives such as environmental sustainability, intra-village equity and building up of institutional capacities through democratic decentralisation.

Given these broad contours, the analysis brought to the fore some of the important evidences from the experiences of watershed projects in different parts of the country. The evidence highlighted certain critical features such as (*a*) employment gain is confined mainly to direct on-site work; (*b*) whereas overall benefit–cost ratio for watershed projects is fairly moderate (around 1.7), the major economic benefits emanate from various water harvesting structures which, in turn, may have limited coverage of beneficiaries; (*c*) physical structures, especially small check dams, created under the WDPs tend to get damaged in absence of institutional mechanisms for maintenance and (*d*) overall benefits from the WDPs appear to be low or medium and that the benefits tend to decline over time. This may imply that much of the impact on productivity, employment and capital formation, by and large, may remain confined to direct/first-round effects. Sustaining the impact may, however, necessitate institution building and strengthening of the local governance.

There are three important implications for the MGNREGS. These are need for: (*a*) exploring the scope for expanding the extent of employment generation; (*b*) ensuring good quality and maintenance of the assets (*c*) widening the net of beneficiary households so as to complement the coverage of direct beneficiaries from the WDPs.

Widening the coverage of the MGNREGS work may involve intensification of several of watershed treatments (both on private and common property resources), which often remain incomplete, and also going beyond that. Investment of additional labour inputs on the farms of the poor may hold significant promises in terms of enhancing productive capacities of the marginal land, often subject to severe degradation, held by the poor. There are technological options for promoting a more regenerative agriculture, which is often more labour intensive. It is essential that corresponding changes are made in the macroeconomic policies to support such production systems. Similarly, efforts should be made to create basic infrastructure for strengthening forward linkages for the increased on-farm production resulting form the assets.

The central thrust, therefore, should be to facilitate convergence among the various processes of assets creation aiming at enhancement of productive capacities in the stagnant and eroding base of the rural economies. Absence of this may lead to perpetual dependence on wage income earned through the employment guarantee scheme. This may be counterproductive for the larger goals of development for which the MGNREGS, if properly synchronised, holds a great potential by setting up new pathways.

Given the difficulties in overcoming the limitations of various developmental programmes on the one hand, and MGNREGS on the other, it is crucial that the convergence between the two add to the strength, rather than diffuse the effectiveness thereof. There are, of course, possibilities of both these to happen since the promoters (the state) as well as recipients (the people) of both these initiatives are the same. Consolidating the strengths, however, would require much more detailed planning and careful implementation than what each of the two, separately, may call for. In the absence of this, the impact of MGNREGS on assets creation and growth of local economies may remain far lower than the full potential, notwithstanding the substantial multiplier impact it may generate for overall growth at the macro level.

Notes

1. The idea of the state providing employment guarantee as 'employer of the last resort' has been prevalent in economic literature since the seventeenth century. The concept has gained currency in serious policy-making, especially in the industrialised economies in the developed countries (Kuboub, 2007). In India, the concept has undergone progressive evolution from relief to employment guarantee and right to work and livelihood.
2. Apart from improving efficiency in resources management, the participatory approaches adopted in various schemes aim at strengthening democratic decentralisation. These schemes include: Integrated WDP, Waste Land Development, Participatory Irrigation Management (PIM) and Joint Forest Management (JFM).
3. The exercise is undertaken in three states, namely, MP, Maharashtra and Karnataka under the collaborative initiative, namely, Forum for Watershed Research and Policy Dialogue (ForWaRD). For details, see www.forward.org.in.
4. These are: (*a*) water conservation and water harvesting; (*b*) drought proofing including afforestation; (*c*) irrigation canals; (*d*) provision of irrigation on the land of SCs/STs; (*e*) renovation of traditional water bodies; (*f*) land levelling; (*g*) flood control works; (*h*) road connectivity and (*i*) any other works notified by the central government in consultation with the state governments.
5. It may, however, be noted that as per the recent circular, the labour component of WDPs is to be obtained from the MGNREGS; this essentially would mean shrinkage in the actual allocation of funds for such programmes as WDPs.
6. For instance, the emphasis even in the discussion on the MGNREGA till now has focused mainly on planning, job creation, transparency in record keeping, etc. The issue of what kind of assets, with what kind of technical specificity and, above all, with what kind of arrangement for repair and maintenance is yet to figure as an important element in the monitoring system.
7. As part of the budgetary allocation for the WDPs funded by the Ministry of Rural Development, each micro watershed should create Watershed Development Fund (WDF) of the order of about ₹2 lakhs, which ideally could take care of the future needs of investment, including repair and maintenance. Unfortunately, the fund has remained unutilised for the want of procedural clarity; as a result, a huge amount of about ₹300–400 crores seems to have been locked up in the bank accounts of the watershed committee.
8. These projects refer to watershed development, wasteland development, joint forest management, minor irrigation, drought proofing, etc.
9. The linkage or convergence with the MGNREGS has been envisaged as part of the operational guidelines of watershed projects suggesting that major part of the labour work should be undertaken by dovetailing funds from the MGNREGS.
10. A study, carried out in six states looking at the implementation and initial perceptions of the beneficiary as well as non-beneficiary households, reported positive responses about the nature of the assets created (For details, see Chhabra, Raina and Sharma, 2009). A similar observation was also noted by a study in Rajasthan (Joshi et al., 2008).
11. The study was based on a survey conducted in six states covering 100 worksites and 1,000 randomly selected workers.

12. Similar concerns about the equity issue have been raised in the present context of watershed development in the country (For details, see Shah, Samuel and Joy, 2011).
13. See note 11.
14. The lower number of average household per village is worked out by considering 750 million rural population with an average size of five persons per household, spread over 0.6 million villages.
15. The expert group has been set up by the Ministry of Rural Development, Government of India, during August 2010 to look into the implementation of the MGNREGA on a watershed platform. The author has an opportunity to serve as a member of the expert group.

References

Ambasta, P., P. S. Vijay Shankar and S. Mihir (2008) Two years of NREGA: The road ahead. *Economic and Political Weekly* 43, No. 8: 41–50.

Bhaduri, A. (2005) Guarantee employment and right to information. *Economic and Political Weekly* 41, No. 3: 267–69.

Bhattarai, M., R. Sakthivadivel and I. Hussain (2002) Irrigation impact on income inequality and poverty alleviation: Policy issues and options for improved management of irrigation system, International Water Management Institute, Colombo, Sri Lanka.

Chhabra, S., R. L. Raina and G. L. Sharma (2009) *A report on management of National Rural Employment Guarantee Scheme: Issues and challenges*. Delhi, Lal Bahadur Shastri Institute of Management.

CSE (2008) NREGA: Opportunities and challenges, Natural Resource Management and Livelihood Unit, Centre for Science and Environment, New Delhi.

Datye, K. R. (1997) Banking on biomass, Centre for Environment Education, Environment and Development series, Ahmedabad.

Drèze, J. and R. Khera (2009) The battle for employment guarantee. *Frontline*, 16 January. http://www.hinduonnet.com/fline/f12601/stories/20090116260100400.htm

Ghosh, Saurabh, Trishna Satpathy and Asha Kapur Mehta (2008) National Rural Employment Guarantee Scheme, Alternative Economic Survey. New Delhi: Daanish Books.

Government of India (2006) *National Employment Guarantee Act*, Administration Reforms Commission, New Delhi.

Hirway, I. and P. Terhal (1994) *Towards employment guarantee in India: Indian and international experience in rural works programmes*. New Delhi: Sage Publications.

——— (2010) NREG after four years: Building on experiences to move ahead. *Indian Journal Labour Economics* 53, No.1: 113–36.

Joshi, P. K., A. K. Jha, S. P. Wani, T. K. Sreedevi and F. A. Shaheen (2008) Impact of watershed programme and conditions of success: A Meta Analysis-Approach (draft paper), prepared for the Comprehensive Assessment of Watershed Projects in India, ICRISAT, Patancheru.

Kerr, J. (2002) Watershed Development, Environmental Services, and Poverty Alleviation in India. *World Development* 30, No. 8: 387–1400.

Kuboub, F. (2007) Employment guarantee programmes: A survey of theories and policy experiences. Working Paper No. 498, The Levy Economic Institute, New York.

Mahapatra, R., Neha Sapuja, Sandip Das and Supriya Singh (2008) The National Employment Guarantee Act (NREGA): Opportunities and challenges, Centre for Science and Environment, New Delhi.

Majumdar, N. A. (2006) *Centrality of Agriculture to India's Economic Development, Economic Developments in India*, Vol. 98, 51–61. New Delhi: Academic Foundation.

Mehrotra, S. (2008) NREG two years on: Where do we go from here? *Economic and Political Weekly* 43, No. 31: 27–35.

Panda, M. (2003) *Role of agriculture in the poverty reduction process in India*, (unpublished), Indira Gandhi Institute of Development Research, Mumbai.

Pankaj, Ashok K. (2008) The National Rural Employment Guarantee Act: Guaranteeing the right to livelihood. *India: Social Development Report*. Delhi: Oxford University Press.

Papola, T. S. (2005) A universal programme is feasible. *Economic and Political Weekly* 41, No. 5: 594–99.

Patnaik, P. (2005) On the need for providing employment guarantee. *Economic and Political Weekly* 41, No. 2: 203–07.

Planning Commission (2007) Salient Recommendations: Working Group on Natural Resource Management for XI Plan, Sub Group—IV, 2006, Ministry of Agriculture, Government of India, New Delhi.

Shah, A. (1998) Watershed development programmes in India: Emerging issues for environment development perspective. *Economic and Political Weekly* 32, No. 26.

———. (2004) Benchmark survey for impact assessment of participatory watershed development projects in India, (mimeo), Gujarat Institute of Development Research, Ahmedabad.

———. (2005) Economic rationale, subsidy and cost sharing in watershed projects. *Economic and Political Weekly* 40, No. 26: 2663–72.

Shah, A. and A. K. Mehta (2008) Experiences of the Maharashtra Employment Guarantee Scheme: Are there lessons for NREGs? *Indian Journal Labour Economics* 51, No. 2: 197–212.

Shah, A., A. Samuel and K. J. Joy (2011, forthcoming) Equity in watershed development: Imperatives for property rights, resource allocation and institutions. In Integrated watershed management and improved livelihoods: Upgrading rainfed agriculture, ed. S. P. Wani, Johan, Rockstrom and K. L. Sarawat. USA: CRC Press/Balkema, Taylor and Francis Group.

Shah, A., H. Joshi and J. Desai (2008) Revisiting watershed development in Madhya Pradesh: Evidence from a large survey, (unpublished), Gujarat Institute of Development Research, Ahmedabad.

World Bank (2007), *Agriculture for Development*. World Development Report-2008, Washington DC.

10

MGNREGS and its Effects on Agriculture
Exploring Linkages

T. Haque

I

Introduction

Agriculture in India has been in stagnation after reaching a new height in the 1970s and 1980s. While the growth rate in GDP has accelerated since the 1980s, the growth rate in agriculture has decelerated. The agriculture sector has grown only at one-third of the rate of growth in the secondary and tertiary sectors combined in the last two decades (Balakrishnan, Golait and Kumar, 2008). Consequently, while the share of secondary and tertiary sectors in GDP has increased; it has declined in the case of agriculture and allied sectors. Besides, the incommensurate growth in job creation in the secondary and tertiary sectors has left agriculture burdened with surplus labour. While the share of agriculture in GDP has come down to merely 14.2 per cent in 2010–11, agriculture continues to be the main source of livelihood for about 60 per cent of the total population (Economic Survey 2010–11).

The stagnancy in agriculture has been a result of a number of factors, including deterioration in soil, technology fatigue, decline in farm profitability, resource constraints of small farmers, decline in public investment in real terms, etc. Even though there has been an increase in investment in irrigation, the increase in the irrigated areas is not in proportion to the increase in the investment. Moreover, 60 per cent of the net sown area is still rain-fed.

Amidst above conditions, the MGNREGS that aims[1] at creation of community assets in rural areas with a focus on works of water conservation, irrigation and land development, holds significant development implications for the agriculture sector. The inclusion of land development works on the land of small and marginal farmers[2] who constitute more than 80 per cent of the total landholdings, can uplift the sagging agriculture sector. Those potentialities can be realised through increased acreage of lands under cultivation, increased production and productivities. The implementation of MGNREGS has shown some positive trends in the above direction.

This chapter is an attempt to analyse the nature and extent of the effects of MGNREGS on agriculture including irrigation, water management, cropping pattern, crop productivity and costs of production due to MGNREGS-propelled rise in agricultural wages and labour shortage, if any. The study is based on both the secondary and primary data. State-wise trends in types of assets created have been shown based on the secondary data. Then it uses primary data on types of assets created, its impact on the local and agriculture economy and livelihood conditions of the people.

The primary data have been collected from 23 selected districts in the states of Andhra Pradesh, Bihar, Chhattisgarh, Rajasthan, Jharkhand, Karnataka, MP, Maharashtra, Orissa, Gujarat, Tamil Nadu, UP and West Bengal. The districts were selected purposively from among the 200 backward districts chosen for the implementation of MGNREGS in the first phase with effect from 2006–07, keeping in view the level of agricultural development in these districts, SC/ST population and MGNREGS implementation. Further, two representative blocks from each district were selected in consultation with the district officials. From each block, 60 households in a particular village or cluster of villages were interviewed with the help of a structured schedule. However, in seven districts, namely, Dhamtari, Bastar, Malkangiri, Dhenkanal, Khunti, Gumla and Adilabad, only 20 households per cluster of villages were selected for the sake of convenience in data collection, as these are areas worst affected with the Naxal movement. Thus, the overall sample size was 2,200 households. Besides, the perceptions of beneficiaries in a focused group and officials and panchayat functionaries through interview methods were obtained.

The next part of this chapter analyses the impacts of MGNREGS on agriculture. This section is based on both the primary and the secondary data. The secondary data pertains mainly to the types of assets created that could be useful for the agriculture sector. The primary data shows how and to what extent these assets have been useful for the agriculture sector. Part three underlines some of the negative implications particularly because of the upward push to the wage sector and its consequences for the increasing input cost of agriculture and hence, surplus generation. Finally, some general conclusions are drawn based on the analysis and observation of the previous sections.

II

MGNREGS and its Effects on Agriculture

The main objective of the MGNREGS is to enhance the livelihood security of poor households in rural areas of the country by providing at least 100 days of guaranteed wage employment in a given financial year. Another important objective is to create durable community assets with MGNREGS works, which would enhance agricultural productivity along with increase in the demand for labour. While the effects of the assets creation on agriculture are direct and obvious, the effects of additional employment generation and income creation are indirect.

Assets Creation and Agriculture

The focus of MGNREGS in order of priority is on (*a*) water conservation and water harvesting, (*b*) drought proofing, including afforestation and tree plantation, (*c*) irrigation, including micro and minor irrigation works, (*d*) provision of horticulture plantation and land-development facilities owned by households belonging to the SC or ST or BPL families or beneficiaries of land reforms, Indira Awas Yojana (IAY) or that of the small farmers or marginal farmers, as defined in the Agricultural Debt Waiver and Debt Relief Scheme, 2008, (*e*) renovation of traditional water bodies, including desilting of tanks, (*f*) land development, (*g*) flood control and protection works, including drainage in waterlogged areas and rural connectivity to provide all-weather access and (*h*) any other work which may be notified by the Central government in consultation with the state governments. All of these works, except the last one, are of direct significance to agriculture.

Up to 2010–11, about 15 million public works have been undertaken. Most of them are works of water conservation, harvesting, irrigation, land development and rural connectivity. In between 2008–09 and 2010–11, about 12.4 million works have been undertaken; the largest number are irrigation works including irrigation on the land of SC/ST, BPL families and IAY beneficiary households who are unable to invest on irrigation even if they have land. Its effects will be maximum in the rain-fed areas where economic vulnerabilities of the small and marginal farmers and agricultural labourers are high.

Out of the total works undertaken in between 2008–09 and 2010–11, 32.78 per cent are works of irrigation; 21.77 per cent of water conservation; 13.92 per cent of land development; 3.79 per cent of flood control; 17.61 per cent of rural connectivity; 8.14 per cent of drought proofing and 1.99 per cent of others. Most of these works are of direct significance to agriculture. Even the works of rural connectivity have importance for the agriculture sector. These assets have been helpful in improving structural conditions of agriculture in a number of ways.

Land development, water conservation, water harvesting, drought proofing, flood control, etc., would help reduce soil erosion as well as loss of organic matter, thereby improving crop yields per unit of land in a sustainable manner. One of the main reasons for decline in agriculture productivity over the last years is deterioration in the quality of soil and negligible investment in its improvement. However, the increase in private investment in recent years has limited ability to address the problem of soil conservation and erosion, as it is caused by flood and uncontrolled flow of water. The works of flood control, water conservation and drought proofing that have been taken in large numbers in some states would be helpful in improving soil conditions. In eastern India, flood remains a perennial problem. It inundates the large part of fertile land, and carries away good-quality soil.

The distribution of works undertaken across states suggests that some of the states facing serious problem of soil erosion because of the regular flood have taken works of flood control in large numbers. For example, out of the total works undertaken in between 2008–09 and 2010–11, 13.56 per cent in Arunachal Pradesh, 10.92 per cent in Assam, 12.36 in Himachal Pradesh, 22.91 per cent in Jammu and Kashmir, 11.86 per cent in Sikkim, 23.87 per cent in Uttarakhand, 25.14 per cent in Manipur and 31.69 per cent in Kerala are flood control works. The working group of sub-committee of National Development Council on Agriculture and Allied and Related Issues has identified soil erosion as a major constraint on increasing agricultural production and productivity in these states.

Second, irrigation, including both micro and minor irrigation works and renovation of traditional water bodies, including desiltation of tanks and construction of farm ponds are intended to improve irrigation capacity. This would be much helpful, as the overall increase in irrigated areas has been only marginal in recent years despite increased allocation and expenditure on public irrigation. Also, renovation of traditional water bodies would increase their utility, as some of these bodies were not being used at its optimum level because of the lack of maintenance of these bodies. More important, only 40 per cent of the total net sown area is irrigated. Depletion of water table because of the overexploitation of groundwater is another serious problem in some states.

Under the MGNREGS, works of water conservation and irrigation have been given top priority. Out of the total works undertaken in between 2008–09 and 2010–11 (Table 10.1), about 22 per cent of

Table 10.1: State-wise Types of MGNREGS Works Undertaken in between 2008–09 and 2010–11

States	*Rural Connectivity*	*Flood Control*	*Water Conservation*	*Drought Proofing*	*Irrigation**	*Land Development*	*Others***	*Total No.*
	%	%	%	%	%	%	%	
Andhra Pradesh	5.30	0.56	35.67	3.69	36.07	18.69	0.02	2,982,084
Arunachal Pradesh	35.27	13.56	8.02	10.29	19.24	9.17	4.44	5,625
Assam	53.04	10.92	6.84	8.82	9.15	10.87	0.35	70,626
Bihar	35.94	5.71	10.98	26.21	17.07	3.87	0.23	466,923
Gujarat	6.42	3.28	60.60	7.91	13.47	3.16	5.16	428,468
Haryana	35.75	3.66	21.52	4.46	19.81	11.78	3.03	26,909
Himachal Pradesh	41.41	12.36	14.30	2.02	21.09	7.58	1.24	170,282
Jammu and Kashmir	33.82	22.91	9.50	1.56	21.32	10.76	0.13	98,602
Karnataka	10.53	7.01	16.38	14.21	28.67	18.47	4.73	1,058,775
Kerala	3.77	31.69	11.15	3.21	29.27	20.29	0.63	350,697
Madhya Pradesh	11.20	0.73	12.08	15.20	42.35	18.35	0.08	1,767,901
Maharashtra	9.86	1.57	51.98	17.24	14.66	4.19	0.50	99,207
Punjab	28.94	2.97	3.00	12.16	38.78	10.48	3.69	32,000
Rajasthan	23.15	1.11	14.63	4.12	51.40	4.20	1.40	638,558
Sikkim	25.06	11.86	13.51	26.39	10.75	12.41	0.02	5,647
Tamil Nadu	23.88	0.73	11.50	0.00	63.83	0.06	0.00	162,385
Tripura	21.40	1.78	19.23	6.63	18.47	21.41	11.08	313,180
Uttar Pradesh	32.65	4.54	11.73	4.97	27.24	13.65	5.21	1,606,609
West Bengal	30.17	5.99	18.19	14.65	22.70	8.22	0.09	529,576
Chhattisgarh	22.42	0.68	7.57	4.92	43.29	21.05	0.07	349,961
Jharkhand	18.82	0.31	32.14	2.37	35.11	10.26	0.99	548,913
Uttarakhand	5.97	23.87	36.02	10.99	17.55	5.27	0.34	99,358
Manipur	28.53	25.14	9.96	13.22	10.36	9.76	3.03	35,166

(Table 10.1 contd.)

(Table 10.1 contd.)

States	*Rural Connectivity*	*Flood Control*	*Water Conservation*	*Drought Proofing*	*Irrigation**	*Land Development*	*Others***	*Total No.*
	%	%	%	%	%	%	%	
Meghalaya	48.50	4.09	18.09	9.46	10.54	5.66	3.66	31,231
Mizoram	65.74	2.56	5.46	8.44	0.98	13.85	2.98	10,038
Nagaland	24.06	6.50	25.70	8.42	11.64	22.95	0.74	25,383
Orissa	32.59	0.47	18.72	4.72	36.56	1.80	5.15	568,539
Puducherry	0.00	0.00	0.00	1.16	98.84	0.00	0.00	1,898
Andaman and Nicobar	17.24	20.29	33.90	0.86	10.95	13.71	3.05	1,050
Lakshadweep	0.35	0.11	26.70	41.35	2.86	28.60	0.03	3,741
Chandigarh	0.0	0.0	0.0	0.0	0.0	0.0	0.0	0.0
Dadra & Nagar Haveli	83.16	14.74	2.11	0.00	0.00	0.00	0.00	95
Daman & Diu	0.0	0.0	0.0	0.0	0.0	0.0	0.0	0.0
Goa	28.54	28.54	3.09	0.00	12.44	27.07	0.33	1,230
Grand Total	**17.61**	**3.79**	**21.77**	**8.14**	**32.78**	**13.92**	**1.99**	**12,490,657**

Source: Ministry of Rural Development, Government of India. http://nrega.nic.in/netnrega/home.aspx

Notes: *Irrigation includes micro-irrigation and irrigation on the land of SC/ST, BPL, IAY and land beneficiary households.

** Includes Bharat Nirman Rajiv Gandhi Samudayi Vikas Kendra (a type of panchayat bhavan).

the total works are of water conservation and 33 per cent are of irrigation. Altogether 55 per cent of the total works undertaken between 2008–09 and 2010–11 address the issue of irrigation. States like MP, Punjab, Rajasthan, Tamil Nadu, Chhattisgarh, Jharkhand and Orissa have given the highest priority to irrigation works.

The improvement in irrigation capacity, apart from bringing new area under cultivation, will also improve crop yields due to availability of more water, and will result in multi-cropping as well. It can also promote other activities like fish culture. An integrated rice-and-fish-farming system in water-logged areas, especially when supported by appropriate technology and infrastructure, has the potential of raising farm productivity and income quite significantly.

Field observation and interactions with the villagers suggest that in most of the villages where such types of works have been undertaken, people have reported recharging of the groundwater. It was borne out from the discussion with gram panchayat heads in most of the surveyed villages that renovation of ponds/canals using MGNREGS resources helped improve irrigated area and cropping patterns positively. The changes in irrigated areas and cropping pattern in the surveyed villages are shown in Table 10.2.

Table 10.2: Changes in Average Area under Various Crops in the Selected Villages before and after MGNREGS (area in hectare)

		In 2006		*In 2009–10*	
States/Districts	*Crops*	*Total Area Sown*	*Irrigated Area*	*Total Area Sown*	*Irrigated Area*
Andhra Pradesh					
Cuddapah	Sunflower	90.00	67.50	83.50	81.00
Khammam	Paddy (Bhadai)	933.00	319.00	1140.00	386.00
Chhattisgarh					
Raigarh	Paddy (Aghni)	13.60	22.00	30.29	30.28
	Paddy (Bhadai)	441.10	56.00	441.10	91.00
	Pulses	1.30		4.50	3.00
Karnataka					
Chitradurga	Chilly	10.00	10.00	25.00	25.00
	Maize	24.00	24.00	36.00	36.00
	Onion	24.00	24.00	36.00	36.00
	Paddy (Bhadai)	20.00	20.00	30.00	30.00
	Tomato	1.00	1.00	3.00	3.00
Madhya Pradesh					
Balaghat	Paddy (Garma)	100.00	100.00	165.00	165.00

(Table 10.2 contd.)

(Table 10.2 contd.)

		In 2006		*In 2009–10*	
States/Districts	*Crops*	*Total Area Sown*	*Irrigated Area*	*Total Area Sown*	*Irrigated Area*
Orissa					
Kalahandi	Paddy (Bhadai)	760.00	315.00	722.50	345.00
	Vegetables	125.00	75.00	152.50	127.50
Tamil Nadu					
Dindigul	Banana	85.00	85.00	150.00	150.00
	Cowpea	2916.00	835.00	3290.00	1182.00
	Paddy (somba)	6450.00	6450.00	6642.00	6642.00
West Bengal					
Paschimi Medinipur	Lady finger	3.00	3.00	8.00	8.00
	Patal/Parmal	6.00	6.00	18.00	18.00
	Rapeseed and mustard	120.40	26.30	146.00	60.20
	Sesamum	210.00	10.20	280.00	80.40

Source: Survey based on the response of the gram panchayat heads.

The districts where such impact could be observed prominently include Cuddapah, Khammam, Raigarh, Dang, Chitradurga, Balaghat, Gondia, Banswara, Sonbhadra, West Medinipore and Bankura. In the districts of Khammam, Raigarh, Chitradurga, Balaghat, Kalahandi, Banswara, Dindigul, Lalitpur and Sonbhadra, gram panchayat functionaries reported that there was a change in the cropping pattern in favour of crops such as fruits and vegetables, cotton and paddy, which yielded more returns. Anyway, increase in irrigated area and change in cropping patterns are expected to help increase agricultural productivity and income.

Other studies have also pointed out similar improvements. In Pakur district of Jharkhand, check dam on the hill has resulted in recharging of the ground water in the plain down the hill. It was found that wells which were lying dry before the construction of check dam, were filled with water and the farmer on whose land this well was located, was able to grow paddy in his farm. Before that, he was unable to grow anything on that land and did not have money to invest further for construction of a deeper well (Pankaj, 2008).

The overall expenditure on the MGNREGS works has been significant (Table 10.3). This is all the more important, as there has been real-term decline in agricultural investment over the last two decades. The MGNREGS has not only arrested the decline in capital investment in agriculture sector, but effects of investment are likely to be more inclusive.

A significant amount of expenditure on assets created under the MGNREGS goes to the types of works like water conservation, irrigation and flood control which will be egalitarian in their effects. Moreover, the inclusion of irrigation and land-development works on the land of SC/ST, BPL and IAY

Table 10.3: State-wise Cumulative Expenditure on Types of Works Undertaken in Financial Year 2008–09 to 2010–11 (₹ in lakhs)

States and Union Territories	*Flood Control*	*Rural Connectivity*	*Water Conservation and Water Harvesting*	*Renovation of Traditional Waterbodies*	*Drought Proofing*	*Irrigation Canals*	*Irrigation Facilities to SC/ST/IAY/LRB*	*Land Development*	*Other Works*	*Rajiv Gandhi Seva Kendra*	*Total*
Andaman and Nicobar	26.90	47.86	87.62	4.43	8.71	12.84	0.00	71.34	0.01	0.32	260.01
Andhra Pradesh	15,939.00	106,962.53	63,028.49	96,697.30	18,798.23	21,362.31	17,015.76	96,659.06	1,099.27	0.00	437,561.96
Arunachal Pradesh	56.64	106.56	3.55	0.00	0.64	34.77	0.89	33.33	4.47	0.00	240.85
Assam	19,496.48	89,685.11	7,557.17	2,562.72	5,353.01	5,299.24	248.90	13,000.10	5,749.25	581.70	149,533.69
Bihar	10,254.44	163,773.94	22,573.39	13,219.86	29,046.26	22,550.51	437.56	12,288.55	5,818.91	385.36	280,348.78
Chhattisgarh	9,124.41	137,160.39	62,890.75	49,443.78	14,988.03	22,741.95	15,162.28	15,258.78	1,714.44	111.56	328,596.38
Goa	339.64	337.55	19.04	72.96	0.00	9.45	2.35	353.91	0.39	0.00	1,135.29
Gujarat	15,868.27	35,482.87	45,136.38	6,840.35	8,900.16	1,249.04	13,731.02	4,062.90	4,621.07	1,375.40	137,267.45
Haryana	1,276.28	14,596.39	8,523.20	2,504.77	1,522.59	3,012.28	37.68	5,057.52	861.22	2,494.74	39,886.67
Himachal Pradesh	16,576.82	48,833.50	14,875.87	3,377.02	1,026.93	12,146.52	1,538.20	9,784.18	2,798.09	3.25	110,960.37
Jammu and Kashmir	2,421.84	4,710.24	986.58	288.07	62.98	1,034.35	55.30	1,887.00	298.58	0.00	11,744.95
Karnataka	2,523.86	133,780.90	145,170.37	21,126.89	10,063.74	3,524.98	11,209.45	15,345.82	12,635.92	4,550.69	359,932.63
Kerala	72,834.20	84,202.14	87,003.70	35,651.42	42,966.24	46,937.10	25,452.03	60,764.39	24,724.47	2,988.86	483,524.56
Gujarat	30,169.79	5,076.72	15,961.29	17,141.66	3,929.82	10,865.82	5,506.47	35,210.10	901.81	0.30	124,763.78
Lakshadweep	10.48	0.00	15.14	12.78	24.31	0.00	0.00	22.00	5.93	0.00	90.65
Madhya Pradesh	6,335.63	271,956.38	297,141.16	27,160.09	45,535.76	7,575.27	85,274.45	30,265.58	12,521.23	0.00	783,765.52
Maharashtra	643.42	21,082.85	33,117.36	17,225.68	4,805.78	542.77	1,247.28	5,618.17	828.26	32.81	85,144.39

(Table 10.3 contd.)

(Table 10.3 contd.)

States and Union Territories	*Flood Control*	*Rural Connectivity*	*Water Conservation and Water Harvesting*	*Renovation of Traditional Water-bodies*	*Drought Proofing*	*Irrigation Canals*	*Irrigation Facilities to SC/ST/ IAY/LRB*	*Land Development*	*Other Works*	*Rajiv Gandhi Seva Kendra*	*Total*
Manipur	387.41	1,044.87	232.82	190.08	188.35	336.18	0.00	382.74	6.31	0.00	2,768.77
Meghalaya	1,724.93	17,941.29	4,934.90	786.15	1,569.99	798.51	4.58	1,764.36	560.97	802.34	30,888.02
Mizoram	853.59	21,122.37	521.42	12.64	1,356.93	152.28	12.87	3,132.52	236.46	936.77	28,337.86
Nagaland	1,940.63	55,826.45	3,692.66	177.96	1,972.03	4,235.67	79.65	3,971.44	4,628.20	0.00	76,524.69
Orissa	1,711.03	152,135.77	29,641.37	50,572.00	7,480.85	5,639.45	10,910.42	3,398.48	8,823.64	33,394.00	303,707.02
Puducherry	0.00	0.00	0.00	1,066.35	2.44	2.14	0.00	0.00	0.00	0.00	1,070.92
Punjab	946.73	9,172.53	570.08	10,422.25	1,111.13	1,007.85	3.73	2,567.80	851.47	988.55	27,642.12
Rajasthan	13,872.62	356,893.52	203,274.70	103,363.79	32,870.68	39,793.91	38,914.76	42,532.87	25,134.89	23,123.68	879,775.42
Sikkim	1,320.38	2,326.13	264.50	34.84	1,611.82	1,082.73	1.42	1,451.68	60.57	8.14	8,162.22
Tamil Nadu	2,544.04	75,805.85	75,087.72	172,293.97	84.97	46,127.24	376.62	267.63	0.00	0.00	372,588.06
Tripura	2,437.55	61,709.02	25,048.81	4,523.81	9,569.53	12,288.24	1,644.55	24,508.90	23,041.64	786.91	165,558.95
Uttar Pradesh	55,414.45	459,705.37	253,867.56	52,566.71	37,314.07	41,319.93	17,120.83	62,340.51	65,468.60	649.89	1045,767.93
Uttarakhand	15,652.10	1,882.55	10,748.99	2,321.01	3,432.72	6,151.73	215.88	4,796.08	597.23	41.22	45,839.49
West Bengal	28,996.76	178,009.25	89,122.05	51,385.51	14,963.94	20,143.53	6013.39	24,716.91	4,264.95	255.44	417,871.72
All India	**331,700.31**	**2,511,370.72**	**1,501,098.63**	**743,046.83**	**300,562.63**	**337,978.59**	**252,218.30**	**481,514.66**	**208,258.25**	**73,511.93**	**6,741,260.86**

Source: Ministry of Rural Development, Government of India, http://nrega.nic.in/
Note: UTs: Union Territories.

beneficiaries has given them a hope to bring their land under cultivation. Because of the limited resource base of these households, they are not able to invest in development of land or providing irrigation on their lands.

In between 2008–09 and 2010–11, out of the total MGNREGS expenditure in the country, agriculture-related activities such as water conservation and water harvesting, renovation of traditional waterbodies, drought proofing, irrigation and land development accounted for as much as 53.6 per cent. Rural connectivity which also influences diversified agricultural development shared about 37.2 per cent of the total work expenditure (Figure 10.1).

Figure 10.1: Percentage Share of MGNREGS Expenditure on Types of Works between 2008–09 and 2010–11

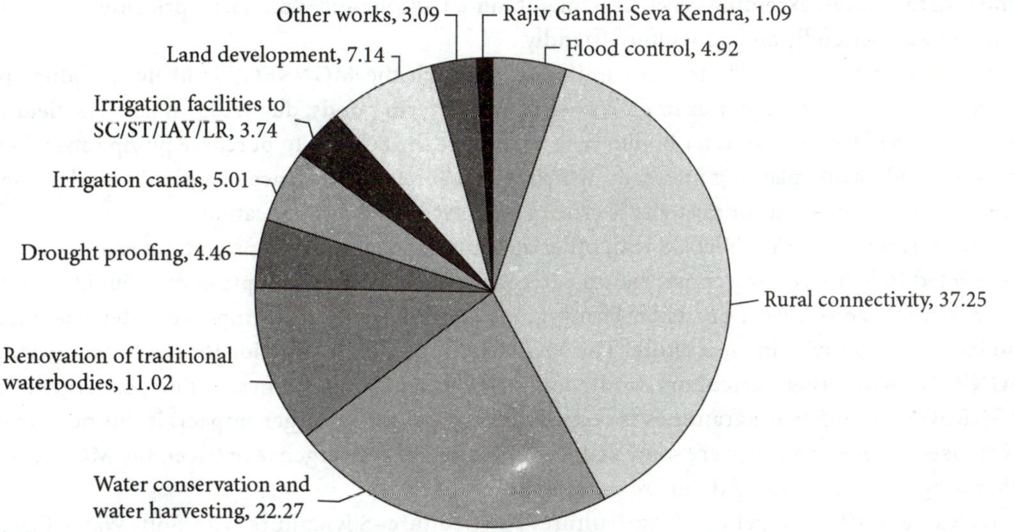

Source: Ministry of Rural Development, Government of India.

The state-wise trend in expenditure shows that in Jharkhand (40.3 per cent), MP (37.9 per cent), Maharashtra (38.9 per cent), Gujarat (32.9 per cent), Rajasthan (23.1 per cent), UP (24.3 per cent), Uttarakhand (23.4 per cent) and Andaman & Nicobar (87.6 per cent), water conservation and water harvesting accounted for relatively higher percentage of the total MGNREGS expenditure. Irrigation shared as much as 11.9 per cent in MP, 10.0 per cent in Maharashtra, 4.6 per cent in Chhattisgarh and 4.4 per cent in Rajasthan. In other states it remained around or below the national average. Renovation of traditional waterbodies accounted for about 99.6 per cent of the total MGNREGS expenditure in Puducherry followed by Tamil Nadu (46.2 per cent), Punjab (37.7 per cent), Andhra Pradesh (22.1 per cent), Orissa (16.6 per cent), Chhattisgarh (15.0 per cent), Arunachal Pradesh (14.1 per cent), Kerala (13.7 per cent), West Bengal (12.3 per cent) and Rajasthan (11.7 per cent), respectively. In all other states, its share in the total MGNREGS expenditure was below the national average.

Drought proofing was given importance in Bihar (10.4 per cent), Sikkim (19.7 per cent) and Lakshadweep (26.8 per cent). Land development accounted for as much as 31.2 per cent of the total expenditure in Goa, followed by Bihar (28.2 per cent), Andaman & Nicobar island (27.4 per cent), Lakshadweep (24.3 per cent), Andhra Pradesh (22.1 per cent), Sikkim (17.8 per cent), Jammu & Kashmir (16.1 per cent), Tripura (14.8 per cent), Manipur (13.8 per cent), Haryana (12.7 per cent), Karnataka (12.6 per cent), Mizoram (11.0 per cent) and Uttarakhand (10.5 per cent), respectively. Rural connectivity was given priority in almost all the states, excepting Uttarakhand (4.1 per cent), Kerala (4.1 per cent), Puducherry (0.0 per cent) and Lakshadweep (0.0 per cent).

In the course of our field survey also, it was observed that of the total work, irrigation accounted for nearly 41 per cent to 54 per cent in Gujarat and Rajasthan. Check dam shared about 19 per cent of the work in Cuddapah and 34 per cent in Bankura (Table 10.4). Renovation of pond was given priority in almost all the places, excepting Gaya, East Singhbhum, Lalitpur and Gondia. So priorities of investment seem to be eco-friendly and agriculture friendly.

This huge public expenditure on rural assets through the MGNREGS is likely to induce private investment in agriculture. For example, construction of farm ponds, dug wells on farmers' field as well as renovation of traditional water bodies may encourage the farmers to purchase pump sets, adopt drip irrigation and quality planting materials, which would accelerate the pace of agricultural development. Also, investment in rural connectivity is crucial for agricultural diversification.

The convergence of MGNREGS with other agricultural development programmes in rain-fed areas is expected to help promote conservation agriculture including the adoption of drought- and flood-tolerant seeds, zero tillage, precision farming, etc., which would help improve water-use efficiency and factor productivity in agriculture. The MGNREGA guidelines provide for the convergence of the MGNREGS with other agricultural and rural development programmes. While convergence of the MGNREGS and other programmes is considered critical for its larger impact, it did not happen in most cases. However, there were some successful models of convergence between the MGNREGS and other programmes; some of them are as follows:

(i) Model for Convergence of Agriculture–Horticulture–Silviculture with Soil–Water Conservation and Intercropping in Chhattisgarh—Badi, Marhan–Tikra (upland), Mal and Gabhar (lowlands) are five farming situations in Bastar district based on topography. Uplands were severely eroded due to slope and high rainfall. However, conservation of upland (soil and water) and water harvesting in lowland had tremendous potential for sustainable and profitable agriculture. In view of this, an integrated farming system model (integrating agriculture, horticulture and fishery) was developed through the MGNREGS in Tahakapal village (block Tokapal) in association with Dryland Research Project run by College of Agriculture, Jagdalpur. This involved soil and water conservation and planting of fruit trees as well as planting of multipurpose trees on farm boundary for vegetative fencing, fodder, fuel and green manuring, intercropping of maize, cowpea and vegetables.

By adoption of this model, 80 per cent of the soil could be saved with 100 per cent water conservation. The soil loss was 8t/ha from untreated area. This helped in converting wasteland into rain-fed farmhouse. The MGNREGS helped farmers in earning additional income of ₹65,000 from 1.5 acre land which was otherwise left fallow. Also, due to farm ponds, rice yield increased from 15 q/ha to 24 1/ha in lower side of ponds.

Table 10.4: Percentage Share of Cumulative Expenditure on Types of Works Undertaken in Financial Year 2008–09 to 2010–11

States	*Andhra Pradesh*		*Bihar*	*Chhattisgarh*	*Gujarat*	*Jharkhand*	*Karnataka*	*Madhya Pradesh*	*Maharashtra*	*Orissa*	*Rajasthan*	*Tamil Nadu*	*Uttar Pradesh*		*West Bengal*	
Districts	*Cuddapa*	*Khammam*	*Gaya*	*Raigarh*	*Dang*	*East Singhbhum*	*Chitradurga*	*Balaghat*	*Gondia*	*Kalahandi*	*Banswara*	*Dindigul*	*Lalitpur*	*Sonbhadra*	*Bankura*	*West Midinipur*
Types of work																
Road construction and repairing	13.21	9.39	48.20	35.06	37.41	39.06	32.76	54.93	98.59	52.10	0.00	26.14	22.94	45.16	44.12	33.20
Drain cleaning	3.77	11.84	48.92	0.00	0.00	37.50	23.71	8.45	0.00	0.00	0.00	1.14	28.82	7.53	0.00	0.41
Earth digging	0.94	3.67	0.00	0.00	0.00	20.31	0.00	0.00	0.00	0.00	0.00	0.00	14.12	2.15	0.00	0.00
Renovation of pond	4.72	13.88	0.00	53.25	21.77	0.00	7.76	5.63	1.41	38.66	45.83	30.68	0.00	25.81	19.23	40.57
Plantation	6.13	5.31	1.44	11.69	0.00	0.00	0.00	0.00	0.00	0.00	0.00	0.00	18.24	0.00	0.00	17.21
Check dam	0.00	8.16	0.00	0.00	0.00	0.00	18.53	1.41	0.00	0.00	0.00	1.14	2.35	1.08	34.25	0.00
Boulder removal	0.00	6.53	0.00	0.00	0.00	0.00	0.00	0.00	0.00	0.00	0.00	0.00	0.00	0.00	0.00	0.00
Irrigation work	2.36	3.27	1.44	0.00	40.82	0.00	0.00	0.00	0.00	0.00	54.17	14.77	5.29	0.00	0.00	0.41
Soil conservation	0.00	0.00	0.00	0.00	0.00	0.00	0.00	12.68	0.00	0.00	0.00	4.55	2.94	16.13	0.00	0.00
Land development	45.28	13.47	0.00	0.00	0.00	0.00	0.00	11.27	0.00	8.40	0.00	0.00	0.00	0.00	0.00	0.00
Other works	23.58	24.49	0.00	0.00	0.00	3.13	17.24	5.63	0.00	0.84	0.00	21.59	5.29	2.15	2.40	8.20

Source: Survey.

(ii) Convergence of MGNREGS (domestic ponds) with the BRGF, RKVY and Livestock Rearing in Chhattisgarh—A large tank was constructed under the MGNREGS which was used for fish production with support from Fisheries Department, thereby improving food and nutritional security of the beneficiaries. Besides, road-side plantation was undertaken in Machkot road under the technical guidance of the forest department. In addition, to encourage vegetable production, tube well and extension of electricity line was provided under the Backward Regions Grant Fund (BRGF). The farmers started growing onion, tomato, chilli and other seasonal vegetables along with rabi crops in these areas. Also funds were provided to Forest Department for training and production promotion of Lac. The training was imparted by the faculties of Central Lac Research Institute, Ranchi. The production of Lac started in January 2009. Moreover, about 15 unemployed youth from this village were sent to Mumbai for seeking training in masonry and other works. The training was given by Larsen & Toubro, Mumbai. In addition, horticulture department provided 250 pipes and sprinklers to 10 farmers with 70 per cent subsidy under micro-irrigation system. Due to this, the wastage of water stopped and water was made available to the distant land, which resulted in vegetable production. To promote use of bio fertilisers, the ready-made vermicompost kit was also made available to 25 farmers of village Machkot. The banana crop was introduced first time in the village by supplying good quality of plant by the horticulture department free of cost. Furthermore, the farmers of village Machkot were being enriched by receiving the backyard poultry unit (50 chicks in each unit) along with growing feed by linking them with the animal husbandry department. The routine health check-up, technical support and vaccination was being offered by the animal husbandry department, which resulted in better income. To upgrade the local goats, the 03 Jamunapari bucks were positioned in village which resulted in speedy increase in cross-bred progeny. Thus, even a few successful models indicate that the issue of convergence between various ongoing schemes of the government should be taken seriously for greater overall impact on productivity and income growth in rural areas.

Additional income generated through the MGNREGS works for agricultural workers and marginal and small farmers is likely to create increased demand for both food and non-food products which should help increase diversified agricultural growth. Figure 10.2 shows various sources of income of the MGNREGS beneficiary households. As can be seen from Figure 10.2, wage incomes through the MGNREGS work constituted as much as 44.25 per cent of total household income in Adilabad (AP), 43.18 per cent in Khammam (AP), 36.52 per cent in Sonbhadra (UP), 28.28 per cent in Dang (Gujarat), 24.85 per cent in Cuddapah (AP), 23.7 per cent in Lalitpur (UP), 21.23 per cent in Gaya (Bihar), 18.5 per cent in East Singhbhum (Jharkhand), 15.13 per cent in Chitradurga (Karnataka), 14.61 per cent in West Midnipur (West Bengal) and 10.89 per cent in Banswara (Rajasthan). In the remaining districts, it was in the range of 1 to 7 per cent.

In several places, the share of MGNREGS income was higher than that of traditional agricultural and non-agricultural wage incomes considered individually. These districts include Khammam (AP), Lalitpur (UP) and Sonbhadra (UP).

The beneficiary households were asked how they used the money earned through the MGNREGS during the past four years. It has been found that the expenditure pattern varied from region to region. In Gaya, Dang, Chitradurga, Gumla, Gondia, Lalitpur and Sonbhadra districts, about 60 to 98 per cent

Figure 10.2: Income from MGNREGS as Percentage of Total Annual Income of the Household

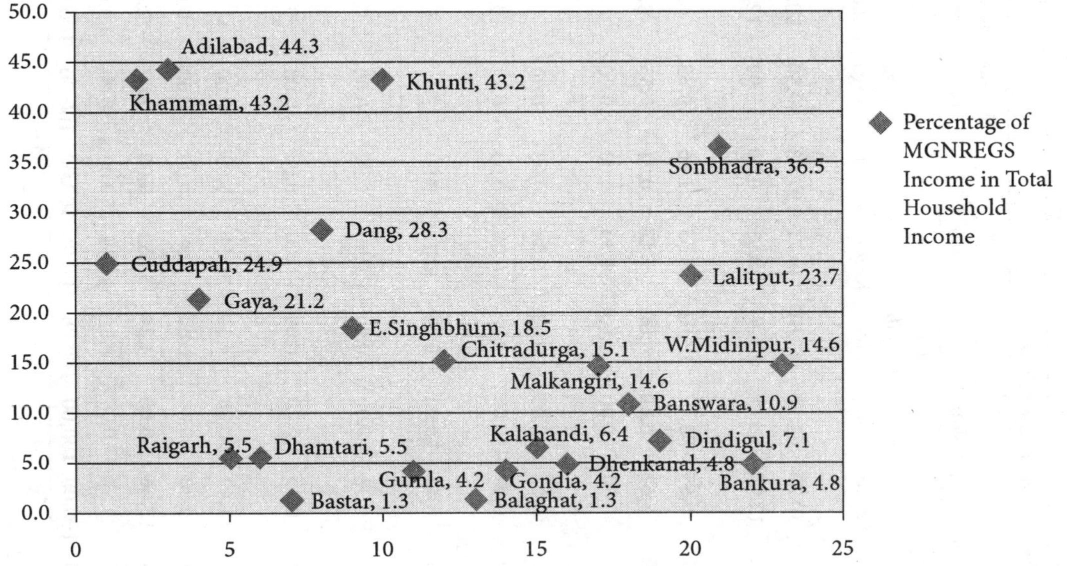

Source: Survey.

money earned was reported to have been used for foodgrains and other consumable items. This speaks quite a lot in the sense that the beneficiary households in these places would not have met even their day-to-day consumption need without having access to MGNREGS employment and income. In Kalahandi, Dhenkanal, Bankura, West Midinipur, Balaghat, East Singhbhum, Dhamtari, Bastar and Khunti, such consumption expenditure was in the medium range, that is, 40 to 57 per cent, while in Adilabad, Cuddapah, Khammam, Banswara and Raigarh, it was in the range of 11 to 28 per cent.

A significant portion of the money earned through the MGNREGS was used on education and health care in almost all the selected districts, except Gondia (Maharashtra), where 97.6 per cent expenditure was on foodgrains and other consumable items. The districts where expenditure on education and health care was quite significant include Sonbhadra (24.6 per cent), East Singhbhum (23.4 per cent), Lalitpur (19.7 per cent) Chitradurga (18.9 per cent) and Dindigul (17.7 per cent). On the other hand, in Gaya, Banswara and Dang districts, only a little proportion of MGNREGS income was spent to meet education and health expenditures. Investment on education and health would contribute towards increasing productivity of labour. In Khammam district of Andhra Pradesh and West Midinipur district of West Bengal, the beneficiary households also spent about 9.1 per cent and 1.7 per cent of their MGNREGS income, respectively, for the purchase of agricultural implements. In Khammam, Adilabad and Khunti districts, some beneficiaries also purchased agricultural land using MGNREGA income. In Adilabad, Cuddapah, Khammam, Raigarh and Dindigul, about 6 to 22 per cent of the MGNREGS income was used for debt repayment (Table 10.5).

Table 10.5: Utilisation Pattern of MGNREGS Income of Beneficiary Workers in 2010

	Percentage Share in Total Expenditure												
States	*Andhra Pradesh*			*Bihar*	*Chhattisgarh*			*Gujarat*	*Jharkhand*			*Karnataka*	*Madhya Pradesh*
Item of Expenditure / *Districts*	*Cuddapah*	*Khammam*	*Adilabad*	*Gaya*	*Raigarh*	*Dhamtari*	*Bastar*	*Dang*	*East Singhbhum*	*Khunti*	*Gumla*	*Chitradurga*	*Balaghat*
Food grains and other consumable items	**25.73**	**11.28**	**13.37**	**80.70**	**19.71**	**56.81**	**50.35**	**61.75**	**47.81**	**49.71**	**97.63**	**60.50**	**50.35**
Education and health	**11.68**	**13.19**	**11.54**	**6.08**	**8.55**	**23.40**	**12.05**	**4.08**	**23.40**	**8.55**	**0.00**	**18.94**	**12.05**
Festivals, social ceremonies, marriages	**19.27**	**9.17**	**10.07**	**5.91**	**18.55**	**17.02**	**6.65**	**34.17**	**17.02**	**18.55**	**1.66**	**10.35**	**6.65**
HH durables	**6.66**	**20.55**	**20.55**	**2.87**	**9.47**	**0.00**	**8.63**	**0.00**	**0.00**	**9.47**	**0.71**	**7.55**	**8.63**
Purchase of land	0.00	5.12	6.50	0.00	1.39	0.00	0.00	0.00	0.00	1.39	0.00	0.00	0.00
Redeeming of mortgaged land	0.00	0.00	0.00	0.00	0.00	0.00	0.00	0.00	0.00	0.00	0.00	0.00	0.00
Leased in land	0.00	1.73	1.73	0.00	0.00	0.00	0.00	0.00	0.00	0.00	0.00	0.02	0.00
Agricultural instrument	0.00	9.14	9.54	0.00	0.72	0.00	0.47	0.00	0.00	0.72	0.00	2.65	0.47
Non-agricultural instruments	0.00	0.00	0.00	0.26	0.00	0.00	0.00	0.00	0.00	0.00	0.00	0.00	0.00
Cattle (Cow, ox, goat, etc.)	1.80	0.63	0.63	0.46	0.00	0.00	0.70	0.00	0.00	0.00	0.00	0.00	0.70
Construction/maintenance of house, etc.	9.90	10.87	9.41	3.18	30.51	4.26	11.49	0.00	4.26	30.51	0.00	0.00	11.49
Others	0.00	0.68	0.68	0.00	0.00	0.00	0.00	0.00	0.00	0.00	0.00	0.00	0.00
Land/Assets	**11.71**	**28.16**	**28.49**	**3.89**	**32.62**	**4.26**	**12.66**	**0.00**	**4.26**	**32.62**	**0.00**	**2.67**	**12.66**
Others	24.95	17.65	13.30	0.55	11.11	8.51	9.67	0.00	8.51	11.11	0.00	0.00	9.67
Total	**100.00**	**100.00**	**100.00**	**100.00**	**100.00**	**100.00**	**100.00**	**100.00**	**100.00**	**100.00**	**100.00**	**100.00**	**100.00**

	Percentage Share in Total Expenditure									
States	*Maharashtra*	*Orissa*			*Rajasthan*	*Tamil Nadu*	*Uttar Pradesh*		*West Bengal*	
Item of Expenditure / *Districts*	*Gondia*	*Kalahandi*	*Dhenkanal*	*Malkangiri*	*Banswara*	*Dindigul*	*Lalitpur*	*Sonbhadra*	*Bankura*	*West Medinipur*
Food grains and other consumable items	**97.63**	**47.08**	**57.02**	**48.65**	**27.78**	**46.83**	**72.42**	**71.30**	**57.02**	**48.65**
Education and health	**0.00**	**10.36**	**11.13**	**11.85**	**6.35**	**17.70**	**19.68**	**24.63**	**11.13**	**11.85**
Festivals, social ceremonies, marriages	**1.66**	**14.42**	**7.41**	**11.32**	**65.87**	**4.38**	**4.62**	**3.48**	**7.41**	**11.32**
HH durables	**0.71**	**13.71**	**5.04**	**8.26**	**0.00**	**2.29**	**2.99**	**0.59**	**5.04**	**8.26**
Purchase of land	0.00	0.00	0.00	0.00	0.00	0.00	0.00	0.00	0.00	0.00
Redeeming of mortgaged land	0.00	0.00	0.00	0.44	0.00	0.00	0.00	0.00	0.00	0.44
Leased in land	0.00	0.00	0.00	0.00	0.00	0.00	0.00	0.00	0.00	0.00
Agricultural instrument	0.00	0.59	0.64	1.66	0.00	0.00	0.00	0.00	0.64	1.66
Non-agricultural instruments	0.00	0.00	0.00	0.11	0.00	0.00	0.00	0.00	0.00	0.11
Cattle (Cows/ox/goat/etc.)	0.00	1.91	0.03	2.95	0.00	0.80	0.00	0.00	0.03	2.95
Land/Assets	**0.00**	**13.40**	**3.08**	**12.81**	**0.00**	**2.90**	**0.29**	**0.00**	**3.08**	**12.81**
Others	0.00	1.02	16.32	7.11	0.00	25.89	0.00	0.00	16.32	7.11
Total	**100.00**	**100.00**	**100.00**	**100.00**	**100.00**	**100.00**	**100.00**	**100.00**	**100.00**	**100.00**

Source: Survey.

A major significance of this expenditure is increased demand for agricultural products—both foodgrains and non-food items. Because of the demand-side pressure on foodgrains, there would be an upward rise in the prices. It is expected to work as an incentive for the farmers who have been gradually losing interest in foodgrain products because of the low returns in comparison to commercial crops, say, cotton. Moreover, the diversification of consumption baskets of the poor people and increased expenditure on milk, fruits and vegetable will promote diversification in the agriculture sector.

MGNREGS Wages and Agriculture

The MGNREGS has resulted in substantial increase in the market wage rates of agricultural and non-agricultural labourers.[3] This was for both male and female labourers. The increase in the agricultural wages was found more sharply in Cuddapah, Khammam, Dindigul, Raigarh, Gaya, Chitradurga, Kalahandi, Lalitpur, Sonbhadra, West Midinipur and Bankura, in both the peak and lean seasons, for male and female workers. In fact, the district of Dindigul witnessed an increase in the agricultural wage rate by about 192 per cent for male workers and 207 per cent for female workers in the lean season and 97 per cent for male workers and 62 per cent for female workers in the peak season. Similarly, in Cuddapah and Khammam districts of Andhra Pradesh, the rise in agricultural wages was to the tunes of 50 to 85 per cent for male and 62 to 65 per cent for female workers in the lean season and 80 to 100 per cent for male workers and 42 to 75 per cent for female workers in the peak season (Table 10.6). In these southern districts, the non-agricultural wages of both male and female workers also increased substantially. It is often complained that many small farmers, being unable to meet the exorbitant labour cost are leaving farming and making a beeline to village officials seeking work under the MGNREGS (Rangarajan, 2009).

Most of the farmers, interacted with during the study, confirmed that the implementation of the MGNREGS had affected agriculture. First, it has increased the market wage rates of agricultural labourers which resulted in increase in the cost of production of various crops and, second, labour availability in the peak agricultural season became scarce, affecting agricultural operations adversely. At the same time, it is also true that in the rain-fed areas, improvement in water availability through MGNREGS work by way of renovation of ponds/canals and watershed development, land development, etc., has helped improve agricultural productivity in some places. Also the landless and semi-landless poor people, who benefited from employment under the MGNREGS, are now able to spend more on farm products that would create additional demand for various agricultural products, resulting in rise in the farm prices of agricultural commodities. Also, the additional cost of production due to a rise in agricultural wage rates gets compensated for the farmers by way of proportionate increase in the minimum support prices, which should impact the market prices of commodities, thereby benefiting the farming community in general. Regarding scarcity of agricultural labour during the peak agricultural seasons in some places, particularly Punjab, Haryana, coastal Andhra Pradesh and Tamil Nadu, due to competition from MGNREGS work, there would be a readjustment process in which farmers would now either do the farm work themselves or adopt more mechanisation. In fact, a practice has developed to suspend MGNREGS works during peak agriculture season so that it does not compete with agriculture work for getting workers.

Table 10.6: Percentage Change in Peak and Lean Season Rural Wages after MGNREGS between 2006–07 and 2009–10

		Increments in Agriculture Wage Rate due to MGNREGS				*Increments in Non-agriculture Wage Rate due to MGNREGS*	
State	*District*	*Peak Season (Male)*	*Peak Season (Female)*	*Lean Season (Male)*	*Lean Season (Female)*	*Male*	*Female*
Andhra Pradesh	Cuddapah	100	75	85	62.5	135	52.5
	Khammam	80	42.5	80	65	55	70
	Adilabad	88	45	82	70	72	80
Bihar	Gaya	46	46	46	46	50	50
Chhattisgarh	Raigarh	55	55	50	50	55	40
	Dhamtari	60	58	45	52	50	48
	Bastar	65	60	42	55	48	45
Gujarat	Dang	40	40	30	30	22.5	10
Jharkhand	Purvi Singhbhum	9.5	9.5	9.5	9.5	9.5	9.5
	Khunti	10	16	7	19	9	15
	Gumla	7	15	7	18	10	5
Karnataka	Chitradurga	50	30	40	20	65	55
Madhya Pradesh	Balaghat	27.5	20	25	25	55	55
Maharashtra	Gondia	35	20	20	15	40	15
Orissa	Kalahandi	80	80	60	60	40	40
	Dhenkanal	80	83	57	49	57	35
	Malkangiri	80	85	50	43	57	29.5
Rajasthan	Banswara	26	26	12.5	12.5	26	26
Tamil Nadu	Dindigul	97.5	62.5	192.5	207.5	125	75
Uttar Pradesh	Lalitpur	41	41	41	41	41	41
	Sonbhadra	31.5	31.5	31.5	31.5	31.5	31.5
West Bengal	Paschim Medinipur	36	36	36	36	55	40
	Bankura	40	40	40	40	35	40

Source: Survey.

III

Concluding Observations and Suggestions

An important objective of the MGNREGS is to create productive and durable assets of irrigation, drought proofing, water conservation and water harvesting, horticulture plantations and connectivity for generating sustainable livelihood in rural areas. In practice, this objective has been pursued in most places as revealed from the priorities of MGNREGS works and expenditure. However, there has been hardly any planned effort to ensure productive utilisation of whatever assets have been created. This is partly because of the lack of adequate coordination and convergence with other programmes and works, although some efforts are in progress in this direction. The Ministry of Rural Development has already issued guidelines for convergence between the MGNREGS and other development works to facilitate better planning and investments in rural areas. Apart from that, the absence of adequate socio-economic infrastructure such as roads, electricity, education, training, etc., the potentials of assets created under MGNREGS remains either unused or underutilised. Therefore, there should be greater efforts to ensure not only increased convergence between the MGNREGS, on the one hand, and agriculture, water conservation, irrigation canals and horticulture works, on the other be efforts, but also to promote education, training and skills of the rural people along with development of all-weather roads, markets, power connectivity, etc., so that the assets created under MGNREGS could be more productively utilised for sustainable rural development.

In quite a few places covered by the field study, it was observed that farmers have improved their irrigated area and changed the cropping patterns for realising higher productivity and incomes in areas treated through MGNREGS works. But in most cases, productivity-enhancing efforts are missing. Therefore, proper utilisation of assets created under the MGNREGS should receive an early attention by all those concerned at the state and local levels, through proper interdepartmental co-ordination and interprogramme/interactivity convergence.

This study clearly brings out that the wage rates of agricultural labourers have substantially increased in recent years, under the impact of MGNREGS. Also, there is scarcity of labour in the peak seasons in some places. These two factors are reportedly affecting agricultural productivity adversely in some developed pockets of the country. While the additional cost of production due to rise in agricultural wage rates can be compensated by way of a proportionate increase in the minimum support prices which also impact the market prices of agricultural commodities positively, thereby benefitting the farmers in general, the issue of seasonal labour shortage in agriculturally developed pockets would be taken care of through a process of readjustment in which farmers would now either do the farm work themselves or adopt more mechanisation. Moreover, the activities undertaken under the MGNREGS, such as water conservation and water harvesting, drought proofing, irrigation, renovation of traditional waterbodies, flood control and drainage improvement in waterlogged areas, horticulture plantation, land development and rural connectivity, are likely to improve significantly farm productivity and incomes, especially of small and marginal farmers, SC and ST households in the rain-fed areas where water scarcity, land degradation and monocropping system do not allow them to move to better economic conditions.

Acknowledgements

The chapter is based largely on the findings of a research study conducted by Council for Social Development, sponsored by Ministry of Rural Development, Government of India and UNDP, Delhi. The author acknowledges the research assistance provided by Kaustav Banerjee, Partha Saha and Gitesh Sinha as well as several other field investigators.

Notes

1. The primary objective of the MGNREGS is to provide minimum livelihood security through 100 days of assured employment on minimum wages to any rural household whose adult members volunteer to do unskilled manual works.
2. The inclusion of land development of small and marginal farmers is a later addition to the types of works undertaken under the MGNREGS.
3. Also confirmed by the NSSO 66th Round. See 'Key indicators of employment and unemployment in India 2009–10', NSSO 66th Round.

References

Balakrishnan P., Ramesh Golait and Pankaj Kumar (2008) *Agriculture growth in India since 1991*, Development Research Group Study No. 27, Department of Economic Analysis and Policy, Reserve Bank of India, Mumbai.

Economic Survey 2010–11, Ministry of Finance, Government of India.

Pankaj, Ashok K. (2008) *Processes, institutions and mechanisms of implementation of NREGA: Impact assessment of Bihar and Jharkhand*. Delhi: Institute for Human Development.

11

MGNREGS and Indian Agriculture
Opportunities and Challenges

D. Narshimha Reddy

I

Introduction

The Expectations

The MGNREGS is acclaimed as the world's largest public works programme. Based on its vast potential for creation of work and productive works, very high expectations are raised in terms of creation of employment that would protect the poor from hunger and poverty, reduction of rural–urban distress migration, changing power relations in rural areas, empowering PRIs and augmentation of rural water and land resources (Drèze, 2004) that would not only improve agricultural productivity but will have accelerator and multiplier effect on rural resource regeneration and rural livelihoods (Shah, 2009).

Of these multiplicity of expectations, one of the major areas of concern as much as an aspiration relates to the impact of MGNREGS on agriculture. The influence of MGNREGS on agriculture, including farming as much as farmers, may be analysed, in terms of three broad dimensions, namely, (*a*) agricultural labour market, (*b*) assets created with a bearing on agriculture and (*c*) works on the private lands of the poor peasantry; community, especially marginal-small farmers, in terms of changes in their asset position, costs and returns and overall household income including wage income. Given the magnitude of the scheme and the diversity of the agrarian conditions in the country, it is not surprising that although almost five years have passed since the launching, there are not many systematic and comprehensive studies on the impact of MGNREGS on agriculture. But there have been sporadic reports, mostly in the popular media, on the effect—often the adverse effect—of MGNREGA on agricultural labour supply, wages and costs of cultivation. There are also a few field-based studies. The evidence is in bits and pieces from different parts of the country with diverse agro-climatic conditions. Until a series of more systematic studies are made on the impact of MGNREGS on agriculture in different regions with different agro-climatic conditions, one way of answering the questions relating to agriculture is to pool the existing evidence for a nuanced reflection. And this chapter is an attempt in that direction.

Objectives of this Chapter

The main objectives of this chapter are to examine the available evidence on the impact of MGNREGS on (*a*) agriculture in terms of agricultural labour market; (*b*) the creation and augmentation of rural water and land resources, the resulting changes in irrigation, area cultivated and agricultural productivity and (*c*) the farming community, especially those belonging to SC, ST and other marginal and small farmers. It may be helpful, to begin with, to spell out each of these aspects in all their ramifications (see Figure 11.1) and to analyse them to the extent the available evidence permits.

Figure 11.1: Expected Linkages between MGNREGS and Agriculture

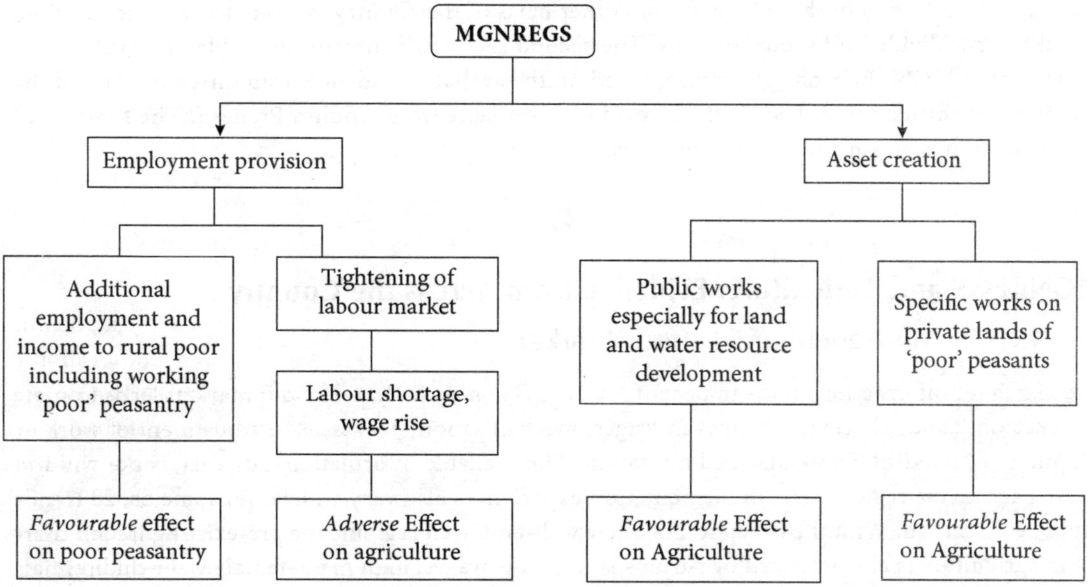

Source: Author.

First, the influence of the MGNREGS on labour market would cover a range of issues that include labour supply and demand in agriculture, especially in the peak season, agricultural wages in general and male–female differentials, responses to labour shortage in agriculture in terms of mechanisation, adjustment in working day including dual mode that combines two activities in one day, evolving a calendar of MGNREGS work to adjust to peak-season demand for agricultural labour and shifts in agricultural wage system from daily wage to piece rate or contract work. Second, the influence of MGNREGS on the rural water and land assets would be in terms of creation of new water-harvesting works, improvement in the existing works like bunding and desilting, soil conservation and plantation on the common lands. Third, the influence of MGNREGS works in the form of irrigation and land development, and horticulture on the private lands of certain category of farming community, especially SC and ST and marginal and small farmers.

The Approach

The study is based entirely on secondary sources except a brief case study of a village. But, as yet, there are no large-scale studies or surveys like the NSS on MGNREGS to provide systematic secondary sources of data. As a result, this chapter, by and large, depends on the scattered published and unpublished studies and reports, including some press reports relevant for the purpose. The methodologies of these studies or reports vary vastly from a few systematic surveys focused on an aspect of MGNREGS to opinion surveys or mere impressionistic observations. A great deal of caution is needed in teasing out any reliable interpretations. Often, the chapter adopts the method of a descriptive review, except for Andhra Pradesh for which a few systematic studies, with data on some aspects of MGNREGS and agriculture linkages, are available. And hence a separate section on Andhra Pradesh, while the rest of the evidence from other parts of the country is treated as another section. The chapter is divided into four sections. The second section documents available observations on the impact of MGNREGS on agriculture, based on the available evidence from different parts of the country. The third section deals with the evidence available from Andhra Pradesh. The fourth and the last section is on concluding observations.

II

MGNREGS and Agriculture: Evidence from Across the Country

MGNREGS and Agricultural Labour Market

The search for information on the impact of MGNREGS on agricultural labour markets leads to some evidence on labour shortage, changes in wages, mechanisation, peak-season adjustment of work or adoption of MGNREGS calendar and migration. The available information, however, is sketchy and uneven across the regions. The implementation experiences also vary widely. Yet some broad trends could be discerned. With the exception of a few well-endowed regions, the pre-existing labour market in agriculture is characterised by surplus labour, low wages, high male–female wage differentials and non-implementation of statutory minimum wages. The introduction of the MGNREGS, with minimum and equal wages for male and female workers, did bring about not only an increase in the overall agricultural wages but also reduction in the male–female wage differentials. For instance, wage increases were reported in a number of states right from Punjab and Haryana to Gujarat to West Bengal (Banerjee and Saha, 2010). Even in tea gardens of Silchar, wage hikes are attributed to the MGNREGS impact. That higher wages in the MGNREGS will divert workers from agriculture and create shortages of labour in agriculture is a theoretically valid proposition, but the extent to which it will happen is an empirical question (Papola, 2005). This question assumes importance especially in the context where still substantial underemployment prevails in rural areas (Shah, 2007)). The earlier Maharashtra experience with the employment guarantee scheme did put upward pressure on agricultural wages, but there was no clear evidence of shortage of labour (Acharya, 1990; Datt, 1994). In agriculturally well-endowed regions, the level of agricultural wages was higher even before the launching of MGNREGS, and peak-season labour demand was met by seasonal migration of labour from labour-surplus regions. The impact of MGNREGS on wages in such areas was not much, except in pockets where the migrant labour flow declined.

There have been a number of reports on labour shortage not only in agriculture but also in non-agricultural activities that depend on rural casual labour. There are reports from many states like Andhra Pradesh, Punjab, Haryana, UP and Tamil Nadu that after the introduction of MGNREGA, there has been shortage of labour during harvesting of crops like wheat and rice (*Financial Express*, 2008). Labour shortage is also reported during peak paddy sowing season in Punjab (*Tribune*, 2010b), and apple harvesting season in HP (http://greenworldinvestor.com/2010/07/17). There are reports as to how with the shortage of labour, the bargaining power of migrant labour in Punjab had increased to the extent of not only raising wages but also improving working conditions. One report reads:

> Besides the TV, cooler, freshly cooked food and accommodation, the labourers are now welcome to live in the houses of farm-owners and not in some dilapidated tubewell room out in the farm. Wages have gone up three-fold. Farmers say seasonal wages have increased from a mere ₹700 to ₹2,000-₹2,500 per acre, in just about two years. (*Times of India*, 2010)

While farmers of these regions tend to blame implementation of the MGNREGS in labour-surplus states like Bihar, UP and Jharkhand, the Commissioner of Agriculture of Punjab has a different explanation:

> Earlier, the labour force used to come to Punjab sometime by March-end, at the beginning of the harvesting season, and would stay put till paddy sowing was complete by July-end. This assured them ample work for nearly four months. But increased mechanisation of farm operations, especially in wheat production, has reduced the duration of employability for them and predictability of the workforce has shown a dwindling trend since the past six years or so. (*Sanhati*, 2008)

Agricultural Mechanisation

There are also reports that labour shortage is sought to be met by mechanisation. Farmers in the Gangetic belt of UP are reported to have resorted to mechanised harvesting of the wheat crop in many villages (*Pioneer*, 2010). The use of combined harvesters for paddy harvesting in Puducherry is also attributed to labour shortage resulting from the implementation of the MGNREGS (*Hindu*, 2010). Mechanisation of sugarcane harvesting in Maharashtra and provision of heavy subsidies to harvesting machines beginning with this year are also shown as a consequence of MGNREGS (*Business Standard*, 2011). In Andhra Pradesh, Tamil Nadu and Karnataka, mechanisation of paddy transplantation is promoted by providing subsidies on the machines (*Hindu*, 2011). Even in West Bengal there was resort to mechanisation to beat rising labour costs (Babu et al., 2011). An interesting report on the significant rise in the tractor market in India in recent years cites shortage of agricultural labour as one of the explanations (http://www.researchandmarkets.co/research/d5e163/indian_tractor-ind). There is a danger that these reports could be read as if the MGNREGS is responsible for mechanisation of Indian agriculture. It is a fact that introduction of combined harvesters, sugarcane harvesting machines and paddy transplanters have long preceded the MGNREGS. Some of these mechanisation processes themselves, as observed by the Commissioner of Agriculture of Punjab cited above, disturbed the stable stream of labour supply. However, there is no gainsaying that tightening of agricultural labour market along with the state policy of subsidising has been hastening agricultural mechanisation, especially in agriculturally better endowed regions.

Adoption of MGNREGS Work Calendar

One of the consistent and more sensible responses across the country is to manage peak-season agricultural labour demand by suspending MGNREGS work during peak farming seasons of sowing, transplanting and harvesting. Such measure would not only help farmers to avoid labour shortage but would also help workers to get more days of employment by way of peak-season agricultural employment as well as lean-season MGNREGS work. There are instances of a number of states where the panchayats were allowed, by mutual consent between farmers and agricultural workers, to work with a calendar that avoids MGNREGS work in peak season and ensures it in the lean season (*Asian Age*, 18 July 2011; *Financial Express*, 11 August 2008). Such a calendar is desired even in the context of tea gardens in West Bengal, as one executive observed: 'The Government would do well, and it would be a win-win situation for all, if they keep MGNREGS work between November and March when we do not need the workers. That way, even workers can make more money' (Bhagat, 2010). The recent initiatives by the Union Ministry of Agriculture and the Planning Commission appear to be towards making such an MGNREGS calendar as an official part of implementation (*Pioneer*, 2011).

Migration

The MGNREGS, by ensuring work for 100 days at assured minimum wage at the place of residence, is expected to have substantial impact on distress migration. Although there are no studies yet estimating the extent of decline in distress migration as a result of the MGNREGS, there are a number of studies which gathered the impression of participants on the impact of MGNREGS on migration. The responses vary from state to state and between districts within a state. The available responses from these surveys from Uttarakhand (Singh and Nauriyal, 2009), Orissa (Nayak, n.d.), Andhra Pradesh and Karnataka (Kamath, 2008), Tamil Nadu (Indian Institute of Technology, Madras [IITM], 2009) and Sikkim and Meghalaya (Panda, 2009) show, by and large, there has been decline in distress migration.

A study of select villages of Dhenkanal (Orissa), Bastar (Chhattisgarh), Khunti and Gumla (Jharkhand) districts shows that earlier due to lack of employment opportunities within the villages, there was outmigration to agriculturally more advanced states like Punjab and Haryana (Banerjee and Saha, 2010). The marginal and small farmers depended mostly on wage labour, with very little earnings from the low yields in agriculture. The commencement of MGNREGA works has not only ensured employment in their native places, but has also afforded them an opportunity to save for investment in their farming that has resulted in higher yields. As a result, although migration has not stopped entirely from these regions, the incidence of seasonal outmigration has come down.

A study with a specific focus on the impact of MGNREGS on ST in Kandhamal and Koraput districts of Orissa shows that distress migration declined by 72.5 per cent among males, and by 45.5 per cent among females. And also, the average duration of migration declined from 69 days to 23 days per worker (Rao et al., 2010). But a study of Purulia and Jalpaiguri in West Bengal shows marginal impact of the MGNREGS on distress migration, and the average number of days of migration declined by about 10 per cent (Babu et al., 2011). A study of five districts in Bihar finds that there was not much of incidence of migration in Siwan and Begusarai. And in Madhubani, with an incidence of as high as 50 per cent migration, only 11 per cent felt that there was any impact of the MGNREGS (Rao and Dheeraja, 2010).

There are interesting instances of return migration of marginal and small farmers of Barmer district of Rajasthan, who migrated to neighbouring Gujarat, Punjab and Haryana as wage-labour due to water scarcity and depletion of groundwater (Paliwal, 2011). In Barmer district, 47,779 *tankas* (small well-like structures made of concrete, cement and sand) and other water works were constructed under the MGNREGS to collect rain water which improved groundwater table that enabled crop cultivation. The improved water supply has brought the farmers back to agriculture.

Of course, migration is not a linear phenomenon, nor are its outcomes binary—like good or bad. The impact would depend on the nature and context of migration. One study shows that improved irrigation facilities, soil conservation, increase in area cultivated and crop diversification resulting in more employment reduced migration by 60 per cent in Sidhi district of Madhya Pradesh (CSE, 2008). Reports from Dungarpur, Udaipur and Rajsamand districts show that rural men continue to migrate to factory work in Mumbai, Udaipur and Gujarat (Joshi, Singh and Joshi, 2008). In all these cases, the wages in these activities are higher than that of the MGNREGS, and the duration of employment is also for longer periods. These can hardly be called distress migration. From these households, while men migrate for high-wage and relatively long-duration non-agricultural work, women and elderly remain in the village to take to MGNREGS work which certainly is an addition to overall household income. But to call this as a 'failure to curb distress migration' is misleading.[1]

That MGNREGS impacts distress migration is evident in the reports from non-farm activities like textiles, jute mills and large number of small and medium enterprises (SMEs). The textile industry is dependent on migrant workers especially from Uttar Pradesh, Bihar and Orissa. Since schemes like the MGNREGS provide livelihood to workers nearer home, it discourages labour migration from catchment areas to production centres. But this cannot be read as the cause for labour shortage but adds to the difficulties in mobilising 'additional workforce' needed in this sector. The growth projections of textile industry suggest that the workforce needs would increase from the current level of about 35 million to 47 million by 2015. Most of the workers earning about ₹7,000 a month are migratory in nature. They move from the agricultural sector to cities after the sowing season for half of the year, and get back to village when the harvest season starts. The MGNREGS is seen as discouraging labour migration from rural to urban areas (Rawat, 2011). But there is no evidence that migration for work that ensures higher wages and longer duration was discouraged by the MGNREGS. The Secretary General of Confederation of Indian Textile Industry (CITI) observes that the problem in the textile industry is not losing workers, but the industry is not getting additional workers, especially skilled workers. 'The challenge will be to find enough workers and to train them. Though the training needs are neither complicated nor time consuming, the magnitude of the requirements would make it a herculean task' (Nair, 2011). Within the textile industry, it is claimed that jute mills in West Bengal pay the maximum daily wages with a fresher getting ₹227 per day and a skilled worker ₹404. These wages are two to four times the MGNREGS wages. But yet, it is claimed that shortage of labour in jute mills is due to MGNREGS which discourages workers to migrate (*Fibre 2 Fashion*, 2011). Similarly, the Indian Industries Association (IIA), Ghaziabad Chapter, also considers MGNREGS as the cause for labour shortage in small and medium industries (*SME Times*, 28 April 2011). But there is evidence from field studies, as we shall see, that migration for high-wage employment, especially male members of the household has not declined due to MGNREGS.

MGNREGS Works and Agriculture

Since the thrust of MGNREGS works is on land and water conservation, the expected impact is substantial augmentation of agricultural production and productivity. The MGNREGS works on soil conservation and land development; renovation and construction of minor irrigation structures like tanks, ponds, percolation tanks and farm ponds for harvesting and augmenting storage of rain water; and undertaking of plantation and horticulture crops are likely to contribute to increase in area cultivated, irrigated area, improved quality of soil and result in improved agricultural productivity. However, given the diversity of agrarian conditions and the limited technical capacity of implementing agencies like PRIs, the quality and usefulness of these works are often called into question (NCCSO, 2009). The second problem is the evaluation of the contribution of these works to improved productivity, since direct measurement of such contribution, particularly at micro level to the exclusion of the effects on the contiguous basin or even watershed, is fraught with problems. At the same time, one may have to steer clear of the extremes, in the name of 'scientific assessment', that are being witnessed in the evaluation of the MGNREGS. For instance, a team of scientists assessing the contribution of MGNREGS works in Chitradurga district of Karnataka bring in allegedly heavy but inappropriate conceptual load like 'environmental services', and agricultural and irrigation 'vulnerability index' and 'carbon sequestration' (Tiwari et al., 2011). With their methodology of rapid scientific appraisal and their dependence on oral sources of data on water-storage level, it would have been much more sensible to narrate whether the design and location of the works were proper, whether there was any storage and percolation augmentation as reflected in water table, along with the information on area cultivated and irrigated. Instead, assuming an extreme scientific posture in the measurement of the impact on the basis of flimsy methodological approach and thin database, would, naturally invite severe criticism (Kumar et al., 2011). But strangely the critique itself lands in the other extreme of science by insisting that the authors should have quantified the total economic benefits (in terms of the positive and negative externalities) against the investments made for the MGNREGA (Kumar et al., 2011). The critique overlooks the fact that MGNREGS is a social protection programme where the investment is not based on the expected financial returns but benefits of employment, and the physical assets created. Benefit–cost analysis may not be a relevant method of impact assessment in this context.

This chapter, as pointed out earlier, confines to the available reports, and treats these as broadly indicative of the impact of MGNREGA works on quality of land, area cultivated, irrigation facilities, cropping pattern and overall agricultural production and productivity. A fairly large study by the Centre for Science and Environment (Mahapatra et al., 2008) covering 12 districts across nine states flags the development potential of the MGNREGA. The study sets out with the background of Maharashtra EGS in Ahmadnagar, a district with 400–500 mm rainfall. Over the years, the district experienced large amounts of investment on farm ponds, contour trenching, compartment bunding, building of over 1,000 check dams and about 70,000 water harvesting structures. Of the district's total area of 1.7 million hectares, roughly 11 per cent was brought under soil conservation works. In many cases, land which was barren was revived under own cultivation. Agriculture is booming and labour is short. Area under crops increased, and crops diversified. Marked increase was recorded in the water table by five metres between 2003–07. The case of the village Hiware Bazar receives special attention. The village experienced reverse migration. In 14 years, average household income increased 16 times, and out of 216 households, 54 are millionaires. And, now there is no demand for EGS work, since most of them are busy with own agricultural work. The study contrasts this experience with Bundelkhand region where such a potential for MGNREGS water harvesting and conservation exists, but it is yet to get the due priority. In contrast, the MGNREGS in Ranga Reddy district in Andhra Pradesh, where water conservation accounts for 67 per cent of MGNREGS works, and in Tsunami-affected Nagapattanam in Tamil Nadu, where 1,172 out of 1,406 works are relating to tanks, ponds and channels with a view to increase the water-holding capacity and to bring back normalcy into agricultural work, has had a lasting impact. Another study (CSE, 2008) focuses on two districts, Naupada in Orissa and Sidhi in Madhya Pradesh. In Naupada, 15 per cent respondents reported change in crop mix, and about 15 per cent reported increased water availability. There was also an increase of 18 per cent in area sown due to MGNREGS works. In Sidhi, 55 per cent of respondents reported increase in the area cultivated, and about 79 per cent reported increase in water availability. Another study of four districts across four states shows wide variation in the degree of utility of the works executed under the MGNREGS. In Ananthapura (Andhra Pradesh), out of a sample of 16 percolation tanks and farm ponds, 13 were in use. In Yewatmal (Maharashtra), out of 24 percolation tanks and farm ponds, only 14 were in use (Kareemulla et al., 2010).

There are reports on the revival of water bodies and canals under the MGNREGS. In Hanhat, panchayat of Lohardaga district of Jharkhand, farmers hardly had any crop for three years, but when renovation of a six-kilometre long canal was done under the MGNREGS, a large number of farmers in three villages could raise crops. In the barren district of Barmer in Rajasthan, the MGNREGS has brought about substantial improvement in water resources (Paliwal, 2011). As pointed out earlier, 47,779 *tankas* have been constructed under the MGNREGS. During the months when it does not rain, government water tankers fill them. Also, a dilapidated *poshal nari* (man-made pond) built 40 years ago was refurbished under the MGNREGS. This 33-hectare pond with about 10-metre depth built in the middle of sand dunes in Nagarda village was drying up. Its base was thickened with more layers of black soil which prevents seepage. The revival of this pond serves around 10,000 people and their livestock in 14 villages. Beginning with 2011, the Rajasthan government is augmenting allocation up to 40 per cent of the total MGNREGS funds for water harvesting, restoration of traditional waterbodies and desilting of waterbodies like ponds and lakes. In Assam, there are an estimated 3,000 natural waterbodies spread over one lakh hectares, and the government proposes to clear them of water hyacinth under MGNREGS (*Times of India*, 7 July 2011).

There are a number of reports on proactive promotion of diverse varieties of horticulture crops under the MGNREGS across the country. Since the MGNREGS envisages investment in promoting horticulture in private lands of the SC, ST and small–marginal farmers, and since in the earlier EGS in Maharashtra horticulture had a lasting impact, many governments have taken up this programme. The UP government plans to extend banana plantation in one lakh acres that would benefit 1.5 lakh farmers (*Indian Express*, 1 March 2011). In Assam, plantation of citrus trees on the plots of IAY houses and in the unutilised lands (through SHGs) is promoted under the MGNREGS (*Telegraph*, 2 July 2011). In Bongaigaon district of Assam, 1,000 of SC, ST and BPL families are targeted for involvement in cocoa cultivation under the MGNREGS (*Times of India*, 3 August 2011). A range of horticultural crops are taken up under the MGNREGS and in Gadag district, the choice of horticulture is 'sapota' trees (Ghanashyam, 2008).

MGNREGS and Farming Community

Besides providing employment and creation of public assets that would improve agro-ecological conditions in the countryside, the MGNREGS also provides for investment on private lands of SC, ST, BPL families and beneficiaries of IAY and land reforms, if the individual landowner is a job cardholder and also works under the scheme at least for 20 days in a year. It aims at provision of irrigation facility, horticulture plantation and land-development facilities on these individual landholdings. This is expected to benefit a large number of rural households since a very high proportion of even agricultural labour households in India actually own lands. The proportion of agricultural labour households owning land is as high as '50 per cent in Rajasthan and Madhya Pradesh, 60 in Orissa and Uttar Pradesh and over 70 in Chhattisgarh and Jharkhand. And if we focus on Adivasis, the proportion shoots up to as high as 76–87 per cent in Chhattisgarh, Jharkhand and Rajasthan' (Shah, 2009). The act was amended in 2008, and the scope of eligible categories of workers on whose land MGNREGS works can be taken up has been expanded to include small and marginal farmers.[2]

Small and marginal farmers account for about 80 per cent of all landholdings, and operate about 40 per cent of all cultivated land, which means that of the 142 million hectares of land under cultivation in the country, about 57 million hectares are under small and marginal farmers. If at least half of small and marginal farmers participate in the job scheme, then about 28 million hectares of private lands of the poor peasantry are likely to come under the MGNREGS. Most of these small and marginal farmers rely heavily on wage employment, often due to lack of capacity to invest and improve their own lands. The MGNREGS works on these lands, which have been starving for investment, is likely to improve productivity and enable small and marginal farmers gradually to move towards full-time farming. The available evidence does show that substantial proportion of participants in the MGNREGS do have land (Jha, Gaiha and Shankar, 2008). A study in a few Rajasthan villages showed that 46 per cent of participants in the job scheme were from those self-employed in agriculture. In Rajasthan, it transpires that the proportion of participation of those with some land is much higher than those without land. In fact, the share of those with land participating in the MGNREGS is much higher than the share of the landed in the population of the villages studied (Gaiha, Shankar and Jha, 2010). However, the available information also suggests that there is variation in the participation of the landed with the variation in agro-climatic conditions. For instance, a study of five districts with different agro-economic conditions in Tamil Nadu shows that in the highly irrigated deltaic region of Thanjavur district, 93 per cent of participants in MGNREGS are landless, whereas in drought-prone Cuddalore district, 35 per cent have land (IITM, 2009). And in Thanjavur no one with 2 acres or more participates in the scheme, whereas in Cuddalore, farmers with 4 to 10 acres also participate. Agro-climatic differences are also reflected in the beneficial effects that the MGNREGS could have on farming community. A study of Hoshiarpur (Punjab), Sirsa (Haryana) and Sirmur (HP) shows that in the semi-arid Sirsa district, 62 per cent of panchayats reported increase in agricultural productivity and, in the hilly Sirmur, three-fourth of the respondents felt the same way. But in agriculturally saturated Hoshiarpur, 87 per cent reported that the MGNREGS did not have any impact on irrigation and agriculture (CRRID, 2009).

Though detailed studies on the impact of MGNREGS works on individual lands of the poor peasantry are yet to come, the evidence trickling down from different parts of the country suggests that there has been positive effect on agricultural productivity and conditions of small–marginal farmers (Hirway, Saluja and Yadav, 2008; IAMR, 2008; Johnson, 2009; NCAER-PIF, 2009). A study of 12 blocks across three states, namely, Jharkhand, Chhattisgarh and Orissa (Banerjee and Saha, 2010) brings out the positive impact of the MGNREGA on the incomes of small–marginal farmers and on the investment and productivity of crops grown in most of the study regions. One study village did not have any irrigation facilities, and paddy cultivation was entirely dependent on rainfall. Before the advent of the MGNREGA, the marginal and small farmers had meagre income from crop cultivation and depended primarily on labouring out in various agricultural and non-agricultural activities. They could hardly save anything to invest in agriculture and, as a result, got very low yields.

> With the implementation of the NREGA, farmers (marginal and small farmers in particular) have additional income to invest in agriculture. In other words, in addition to consumption expenditure, a portion of the income earned through NREGA was invested in agriculture. Expenditure in agriculture was primarily in the form of purchase of chemical fertilisers and high yielding varieties of seeds. This has resulted in an increase in crop yield in the study regions. The increase in paddy yield is in the range of 50–55 per cent in the study regions of Chhattisgarh, and 90–100 per cent in the study regions of Jharkhand (Banerjee and Saha, 2010).

The authors observe that the increase in crop yield has reduced the livelihood vulnerability of the small and marginal farmers and that their livelihood security can be further improved if extension services and complementary inputs like irrigation are provided in these regions.

III

MGNREGS and Agriculture: Evidence from Andhra Pradesh

MGNREGS and Rural Labour Market in AP

One of the major impacts of MGNREGS in rural Andhra Pradesh, as in many other parts of the country, is on the labour market. Based on the reports of focus group discussions (FGDs), spread over a fairly large number of villages (77), Table 11.1 presents some broad indicators of the change in the rural labour market as a result of the MGNREGS. These indicators have to be interpreted in all their nuances to the extent the FGDs could capture them.

Table 11.1: Impact of MGNREGS on Rural Labour Market in Select Villages in Andhra Pradesh 2008–09

(Number of Villages)

Indicators	*Increased*	*Decreased*	*No Change*	*No Clear Response*	*All Villages*
1. Agricultural wages	70	Nil	2	5	77
2. Peak season shortage of agricultural labour	62	Nil	6	9	77
3. Male–female agricultural wage differential	Nil	71	Nil	6	77
4. Migration (a+b)	Nil	51	20	6	77
a) Villages with migration before MGNREGS	Nil	51	4	Nil	55
b) Villages with no migration before MGNREGS	Nil	Nil	12	Nil	12

Note: The evidence is based on reports of FGDs of 77 villages (panchayats) spread over eight districts (Chittoor, Nalgonda, Medak, Ranga Reddy, Adilabad, Karimnagar and Kurnool). These FGD reports are part of the two projects: Galab et al. (2008) and Reddy (2011).

Agricultural Wages

At the time of the fieldwork during 2008–09, the MGNREGS minimum wage for both male and female workers was ₹80. In some of the villages in the state, the male agricultural wage was equal or marginally more than the MGNREGS wage but the female agricultural wage level was much lower in almost all the villages. The introduction of MGNREGS increased the demand for labour in rural areas and resulted in increase in agricultural wages as well. The rise in female agricultural wages, which were at much lower level, was much steeper than the rate of increase in male wages. As a result, the difference between male–female agricultural wages declined substantially in almost all villages (71) for which information is available.

Shortage of Labour and Changes in Working Day

Even before MGNREGS, in peak agricultural season, labour shortage was experienced in many villages. Of course, there were a few dry-land villages where it was shortage of work, than shortage of labour, that continued to be a problem. But after the MGNREGS, 62 out of 68 villages reported increase in labour shortage. However, out of 77 villages, only two villages reported that there was any decline in area under cultivation due to rise in wages or shortage of labour in the peak season. In Kuppanagar village, there has actually been increase in the area cultivated in the last two years, due to MGNREGS investment in fallow and rain-fed lands of the SCs. A number of strategies are being adopted to meet the changing labour market situation, which in turn are also leading to many changes in the nature of rural, and especially agricultural, labour markets. Six villages reported labour being brought from outside the village by paying transport charges in addition to wages. In three villages, wages were paid in advance to ensure labour supply in the peak season for agriculture. There has been growing tendency towards piece rate or contracting out of agricultural work than employing labour on daily wages.

Agricultural workers reported better bargaining power, better treatment at the farm, visible change in the form of respect and less of pressure at the place of work. Besides rise in wages, in most of the villages, workers have been able to negotiate reduced duration of agricultural working day. And the growing shift towards piece rate or contract work on agriculture facilitated the change in the working day. Parallely, there has been increasing tendency in the MGNREGS working day to begin early in the day—by seven in the morning—and terminate by one in the afternoon. There are instances where the workers take to agricultural work in the afternoon, often on their own farms, after attending the MGNREGS work in the forenoon. There is in emergence, in some villages, a dual mode of work in a given day with MGNREGS work in the forenoon and agricultural work in the afternoon—the latter mostly on own farms. Such adjustments appear to soften the shortages of agricultural labour. And the very working day is being redefined due to changes in the labour market brought about by the MGNREGS.

MGNREGS Calender

Though there are reports elsewhere about mechanisation of agriculture as a response to labour shortage, there is no such perceptible change towards mechanisation as a response to the MGNREGS in the villages of the eight districts discussed here. But there is a widespread demand by farmers for stopping MGNREGS work during the agricultural peak season. In fact, a number of gram panchayats have evolved, through mutual negotiation, work calendar that avoids MGNREGS work during the local agricultural peak season. Such adjustment is seen as a mutually beneficial measure that helps farmers to avoid labour shortage in the peak season, and workers to get MGNREGS work in the lean season and, thus, increases the overall days of employment in a year.

Migration

Of the 77 villages reported in Table 11.1, in 12 villages, there was no migration before or after the MGNREGS. Of the remaining, in four villages, there was not much change in the migration situation even after the job scheme and, in six other villages, there was no clarity in the information recorded. In the rest of the 55 villages, there were varying degrees of decline in migration. Most of the decline is in distress migration, but not in the emerging process of movement towards higher-paying, relatively high-productivity non-agricultural work, and often, rural-to-urban mobility. At least four villages reported complete stoppage of distress migration. Some villages in districts like Ranga Reddy reported decline in long-distance distress migration to Mumbai and Pune. This is similar to the decline in migration from drought-prone Mahabubnagar district which was well-documented elsewhere (Sainath, 2008). In many other villages, the participants in discussions observed that there would be further decline in distress migration if MGNREGS work is provided for longer periods at a time, and if wages are paid without much delay. Their arguments were well reasoned. They were conscious of the costs of migration, including raising informal loans at high interest rates to meet the expenses of mobility, high rents and fuel costs in destinations; the ordeal of having to live in sub-human conditions and the risk of their children missing a chance to go to school.

The non-distress type of migration from these villages, which is not affected much by the MGNREGS, is of three types. One is the migration of male members of the households for high-paying non-agricultural work for relatively longer durations. For instance, from the villages of Kurnool district, which borders Karnataka, male members of the households migrate to Bellary to work in construction, mining and other activities. The second type of non-distress migration that continues even after MGNREGS is rural-to-rural migration from dry-land areas to fertile areas for agricultural work. For instance, from mandals like Aspari in Kurnool district, entire household members migrate to Guntur district during June–August to work in the mirch (chilli) and tobacco fields where each migrating couple make as much as ₹500 per day. These families return during September–October to their own villages to work in agriculture, and some, even in the MGNREGS. The third type of continuing migration is—strictly speaking, not migration—daily commuting to neighbouring towns. For instance, in Kurnool district, members of some rural households commute to neighbouring towns like Allagadda to work in shops and other establishments where the wages are high. Interestingly, some work in the MGNREGS in their villages in the forenoon, and commute in the afternoon to nearby towns to work in odd jobs including vegetable and fruit vending.

Additional Worker and Additional Employment Effect

A question often raised is if there were to be substantial increase in employment under the MGNREGS, what would be the impact on agriculture? Would there be shortage of labour for agriculture? Or decline in the area cultivated due to shortage of labour? The experience of Kuppanagar village, which we shall discuss more later, suggests that although initially there were signs of shortage of labour, over the past three years, there have been interesting developments in the working hours and the working day. Gradually, there has been shift in the daily work schedule of MGNREGS works. It is increasingly now tending to be confined to forenoon. With it, there is also a tendency on the part of workers who are engaged in the forenoon to take up either agriculture wage labour or own farm work in the afternoon. As observed earlier, many workers earn MGNREGS wages in the forenoon, and also earn on agriculture in the second half of the day, thereby doubling their day into two working and earning days. This is hard work, but preferred by many workers since there is substantial increase in income. This is a clear additional employment effect. The other factor contributing to additional worker effect is the inducement of relatively higher wages for women in the MGNREGS compared to agriculture. Some women from certain social groups, who did not perform wage labour, are participating in MGNREGS work. It is because of it being 'government' work, not work for a contractor or a landowner, which carried a social stigma for certain social communities. Thus, the additional employment and worker effects together appear to keep labour supply to agriculture not greatly disturbed.

MGNREGS Minimum Wages

In the first phase of the MGNREGS, the minimum wage fixed was ₹80 per day. It was increased in Andhra Pradesh to ₹100 in 2009. Since the MGNREGS wage is calculated on the basis of work done at the schedule of rates, the minimum wage level is only indicative and the wage level could be higher or lower depending on the turnover of work. But in Kuppanagar, a village that is used as a case study, the average wage level obtained has always been higher than the minimum indicated. Even in the earlier years when the minimum wage was ₹80, Kuppanagar workers logged wages ranging from ₹93 to ₹126. The results of the household survey show the average rate of ₹103 in 2009–10. In Kuppanagar, as in other places in the state, work is allotted to a group calibrating the quantity equivalent to the schedule of rates that would fetch minimum wage to each member. Often, some members of the group do not turn up but yet the remaining ones complete the total allotted work, and this increases the average wage to a level higher than indicated minimum wage. Wherever, the workers are formed into Shram Shakti Sanghams (SSSs), as in Kuppanagar, there is better motivation to work as a team and complete the work allotted even if some members do not turn up. The result is the average wage which is higher than the minimum wage. The average wages are paid equally to men and women. The average MGNREGS wages logged by Kuppanagar workers are higher than local agricultural wages, especially for women. The impact of MGNREGS wages are felt in two ways. First, overall agricultural wages have increased. Male wages in agriculture increased from ₹80 before the MGNREGS to the present level of ₹100, and female agricultural wages increased from ₹50 to ₹80. The male–female wage gap has declined substantively. The hours of agricultural work also has declined and it is invariably half-a-day work at the wages mentioned above. The net impact on agriculture is higher wage costs.

The responses in the group discussion reveal an interesting pattern. Regardless of the social group, most of the MGNREGS workers are also small–marginal farmers and they too feel the impact of rising agricultural wages on their farms, but marginally, because of two reasons. First, their earnings, especially those of women, from the MGNREGS are substantial. Second, they have substantial gains by way of improved productivity of their land due to MGNREGS land-development works on their private lands. Therefore, the small–marginal farmers do not complain much about rising wages. The landless workers acknowledge rising agricultural wages. Their main complaint is about the steep rise in prices of essential commodities.

The response of relatively bigger farmers, normally non-participants in the MGNREGS, is about the rising agricultural wages. Interestingly, in many villages, they do not complain about the MGNREGS as such, since most of them benefited from rise in water table in their wells and borewells due to MGNREGS works, especially due to desilting of tanks and ponds, and construction of a number of percolation tanks. These relatively bigger farmers have been repeatedly making a plea that half of their agricultural work and wages could be shared under the MGNREGS. Paradoxically, they have developed a vested interest in the MGNREGS, hoping that their wage costs would be shared under the scheme. And the political forces appear to be nursing this hope!

MGNREGS Works and Agriculture in AP

The extent to which assets created under MGNREGS could benefit rural development, in general, and agriculture, in particular, depends on not merely the resources available but on the extent of the commitment of the state as reflected in guidelines on prioritising and planning, and the ability of the local governments in identifying the works that would help in the realisation of larger objectives of resource improvement according to the prioritised works and social groups. In Andhra Pradesh, in the initial years, except for prioritising minor irrigation tanks, there was no clear direction or guidelines on what type of works should be taken up on priority. And this is reflected in Table 11.2 which shows that either in terms of employment created or wages paid, in the first three years, there was certain lack of clear direction, except in the case of minor irrigation. In the first three years, the very vague and diffuse categories like 'water conservation and harvesting' and 'others' together accounted for 80 per cent (2006–07) to 63 per cent (2008–09) of the employment generated under MGNREGS in Andhra Pradesh. But by 2009–10, there has been clarity in prioritization, and the priorities are clearly in favour of works that would have direct benefit to farming and SC, ST and other small–marginal farming communities. The two categories of works, namely, 'provision of irrigation facilities', which specifically addresses the needs of the poor peasantry, and 'renovation of traditional water-bodies', which together would have favourable impact on agriculture, acquire top priority. These two types of works together accounted for 64 per cent of employment generated in the state in 2009–10 and 58 per cent in 2010–11.

Table 11.2: Employment and Wages Paid Under Different MGNREGS Works in Andhra Pradesh

Year	*Water Conser-vation and Harvesting*	*Drought Proofing*	*Provision of Irrigation Facilities*	*Renovation of Traditional Waterbodies/ Desilting*	*Flood Control*	*Rural Connectivity*	*Others*	*Total*
Category-wise Person-days (₹000)								
2006–07	28	6	—	8	—	—	24	(100)
	(42)	(8)	(—)	(12)	(—)	(—)	(38)	
2007–08	56,415	2,923	7,526	45,506	3,682	3,947	79,979	(100)
	(28)	(1)	(4)	(23)	(2)	(2)	(40)	
2008–09	69,624	1,414	20,516	51,047	1,277	8,093	75,401	(100)
	(31)	(1)	(9)	(22)	(1)	(4)	(32)	
2009–10	73,226	1,152	134,248	118,645	645	7,056	55,114	(100)
	(19)	(Negl.)	(34)	(30)	(Negl.)	(2)	(15)	
2010–11	59,115	2,991	1,042,238	92,406	1,768	18,222	60,583	(100)
	(17)	(1)	(31)	(27)	(1)	(5)	(18)	
Category-wise Wages Paid (₹ lakh)								
2006–07	23,193	5,298	—	5,671	—	—	19,699	(100)
	(43)	(10)	(—)	(10)	(—)	(—)	(37)	
2007–08	49,760	2,393	6,680	39,324	3,377	3,337	66,148	(100)
	(29)	(1)	(4)	(23)	(2)	(2)	(39)	
2008–09	62,747	1,249	18,022	42,230	1,166	7,209	62,866	(100)
	(32)	(1)	(9)	(22)	(1)	(4)	(31)	
2009–10	67,929	1,116	123,172	105,505	596	6,060	49,060	(100)
	(19)	(Negl.)	(35)	(30)	(Negl.)	(2)	(14)	
2010–11	58,749	3,141	100,088	90,289	1,749	18,060	57,875	(100)
	(18)	(1)	(30)	(27)	(1)	(5)	(18)	

Source: http://MGNREGA.ap.gov.in (accessed 25 July 2011).
Note: Figures in parentheses show percentage.

Renovation of Minor Irrigation Tanks

The Government of Andhra Pradesh saw a great opportunity in the MGNREGA in operationalising their own long-pending programme of restoration of minor irrigation tanks. Soon after the launching of the first phase of MGNREGA in June 2006 in 13 districts of Andhra Pradesh, restoration of minor irrigation works received special attention. In October 2006, one of the earliest meetings of the state EGS council, chaired by the Chief Minister, decided that at least one minor irrigation tank in each gram panchayat shall be taken up for comprehensive restoration in the 13 districts of the first phase of MGNREGS.[3] Instructions were issued for conducting awareness programme at the village level and to identify a tank in each village for restoration. The process of identification of the tanks, planning and preparation of the estimates and execution was to be carried on by the Department of Rural Development in coordination with the panchayat raj and irrigation and command area development departments.

The tank restoration under the MGNREGS acquired certain political flavour, and was designated as 'Indiramma Cheruvu' programme. The priority accorded to the programme by the state government was reflected in the interest evinced by the Chief Minister in extending the programme to the second-phase districts of the MGNREGS, and taking up work on the second tank in gram panchayats where the first one was completed in the first-phase districts.[4] There was convergence of funds from the irrigation department and the MGNREGS to comprehensively restore minor irrigation tanks with a command area of less than 100 acres, and by June 2008, 12,500 tanks were taken up for strengthening of bunds, closing of breaches, repairs to sluices, weirs, feeder and field channels to stabilise 10.50 lakh acres of ayacut.[5]

By the middle of 2011, Table 11.3 shows, 61,257 tanks, each with an ayacut of less than 100 acres were brought under the MGNREGS-linked tank-restoration programme, and an estimated 30 lakh acres of ayacut under these tanks were claimed to have been stabilised. The average size of the tanks restored is about 50 acres. Though the estimated expenditure was much higher, the actual expenditure incurred was about ₹2,431 crore, which works out to an average of ₹3.95 lakh per tank or ₹7,900 per acre of ayacut stabilised. Considering the fact that over the years, there had been neglect of tank maintenance resulting in unattended breaches, erosion of bunds and silting up of tank beds, feeder and field channels that drastically eroded area under tank irrigation, the tank restoration under the MGNREGS is likely to be a big boost not only to surface irrigation but also in augmenting groundwater resources due to improved percolation and rise in water table. To assess the irrigation efficiency of the minor irrigation tanks restored under the scheme, a detailed survey was initiated by the government.[6] The evaluation is

Table11.3: Repair and Restoration of Minor Irrigation Tanks* under MGNREGS in Andhra Pradesh (2011)

Physical and Financial Aspects	*Planned*	*Completed as on 25 July 2011*
Number of Tanks (No.)	62,085	61,527
Expenditure (₹ lakh)	527,364	243,076
Ayacut (Acres)	3,005,059	–

Source: http://MGNREGA.ap.gov.in (accessed 25 July 2011).
Note: *Under a programme entitled 'Indiramma Cheruvu'.

expected to provide information about the extent of ayacut irrigated by each tank before and after restoration, which may provide the extent of irrigation impact of the MGNREGS-linked tank restoration.

Watershed Development

Another area of great opportunity for natural resource development is seen in the convergence of MGNREGS and watershed development programme. To avoid duplication and optimum utilisation of resources, works to be taken up under MGNREGS and watershed development programme were separately demarcated. Works which involve materials and machines were earmarked exclusively for watershed funds, while all other works as per the watershed action plan could be taken up with MGNREGS funds. As a result, there are visible signs of improvements of water storage, percolation and improvement of groundwater table in many locations in the state.

Horticulture

The convergence between the MGNREGS and horticulture department is another area where there has been direct benefit to small and marginal farmers belonging to different socio-economic categories eligible for works under the MGNREGS. Since most of the work being taken up under MGNREGA in Andhra Pradesh pertains to development of the land of the specified type of farmers, horticulture on their lands is expected to generate sustainable incomes. All costs, including labour and material costs, for plantation and maintenance of the same for three years are to be met from MGNREGS funds while the implementation is done through the Department of Horticulture, which is also the agency for implementing works under National Horticultural Mission. Here again, priority is accorded to the 'poorest of the poor' farmers and detailed horticulture development plans are prepared for each district. For instance, the plan for 2010–11 envisaged covering an area of about 79,000 hectares at a cost of about ₹500 crore.[7] Table 11.4 provides basic information on the progress made in horticulture plantation under the MGNREGS in the state.

The state also took a number of other initiatives towards convergence of the MGNREGS with other agencies. One such is the Andhra Pradesh Drought Adaption Initiative (APDAI) with a focus on improving production system on farms with pilot projects integrated with the MGNREGS. A project for the development of common lands by way of rejuvenating degraded common lands was launched in two districts involving MGNREGS funds, and as many as 24 NGOs providing facilitating

Table 11.4: Horticulture Plantation under MGNREGS in Andhra Pradesh (since inception up to 25 July 2011)

Particulars	*Coverage*
Number of works	91,731
Number of farmers	140,255
Area in which work commenced (acres)	742,090
Estimated expenditure (₹ lakh)	185,434

Source: http://nrega.ap.gov.in (accessed 25 July 2011).

cost. A biomass-based watershed project for improving biomass in dry lands through 'multi-tier' tree species was launched in Mahabubnagar district under MGNREGS with the technical support of an NGO, BAIF. Similar agreements are reached between Integrated Tribal Development Agency (ITDA) and Coffee Board for coffee plantation and with Rubber Board for rubber plantation in East Godavari agency areas; and the cost is shared by MGNREGS, ITDA and the respective boards. A coordination committee is formed at the state level with representation to various institutions like ICRISAT, Central Research Institute for Dryland Agriculture (CRIDA), etc., to provide technical support to the MGNREGS. The impact of these initiatives are expected to be substantial on agriculture in the state, but the progress made is yet to be assessed.

MGNREGS and Farming Community in AP

One of the major justifications for public works, in contrast to cash transfer, as a social protection measure is that these works not only generate employment but also create assets which would benefit the community as a whole. The nature of MGNREGS works is such that there is a built-in bias in favour of agriculture due to emphasis on conservation and development of land and water resources. Of particular importance to agriculture is the MGNREGS provision of irrigation facility, horticulture plantation and land development on private lands of SC, ST and BPL households or beneficiaries of land reforms and IAY; and its later extension to small and marginal farmers, (hereafter referred to as 'EGS-eligible farming communities'). This provision has far-reaching significance, especially to SC farming community in Andhra Pradesh.

Like many other states, small–marginal farmers constitute 80 per cent of farmers in Andhra Pradesh. More importantly, about 12.5 per cent of the cultivated area in the state is assigned land; the land has been assigned to the poor, either out of ceiling surplus or government land. But much of the assigned land has been of very poor quality requiring substantial investment if it were to be brought under plough. But most of these assignees could not afford such investment. Often, the state assistance for improvement of these lands was inadequate.

A sample survey of 800 beneficiaries of land assignment under land reforms in two districts of Andhra Pradesh shows that at the time of assignment, only in 17 per cent of the cases, the land assigned was cultivable; in about 26 per cent of cases, it was all shrubs and bushes and in 66 per cent, it was barren and rocky (Rani and Rao, 2011). Considerable amount of investment had to be made to bring them under plough. Only in those cases where institutional support like that of Scheduled Tribes Development Corporation investments could be made for land development and provision of irrigation facilities, the land could be cultivated. And in most of the other cases, either the assigned land was kept fallow or used for growing some rain-fed crops or in some cases, even abandoned. The Government of Andhra Pradesh saw the opportunity afforded by the provision of MGNREGS works on the lands of the 'eligible farming communities' and initiated steps to prioritise these works in the shelf of works planned for implementation under the scheme.

Of the nine categories of works provided under the MGNREGA, the fourth, 'Provision of Irrigation Facility ...' alone refers to works on private lands of certain eligible farming communities. The Government of Andhra Pradesh specified the fourth category of works into four projects:[8] (*a*) EGS

Land Development Project (EGS-LDP) to treat fallow and low-productive lands of the eligible farmers, with priority to SC and ST farmers; (*b*) Horticulture and Plantation Project (H&P); (*c*) Irrigation Facilities Project (IFP); (*d*) Sustainable Agriculture Project (SAP), and spelt out the nature of works to be taken up and priority to be assigned in selecting the farmers for implementation. The participation of SHGs was enlisted in identifying lands of the poorest of the poor with special emphasis on the land of SC and ST households. The Andhra Pradesh government has developed an ambitious plan to develop 2.5 million acres of assigned land belonging to SC, ST, small and marginal farmers under the MGNREGS at a cost of around ₹7,000 crore. The new works strategy evolved by the middle of 2010 emphasised completion of these works on *saturation basis* as could be observed from the following part of the guidelines: "a Land Development in the lands of SC/STs and Small and Marginal Farmers shall be taken up on a saturation basis. The Land Development includes various water conservation and water harvesting structures".[9] Table 11.5 provides a larger picture of the efforts of the state in bringing to record a strategy of project and works planning with the highest priority accorded to the development of the lands of the eligible farming community. About 32 lakh MGNREGS works are planned for execution in the private lands. Even if each of the work is likely to improve farming in at least one acre of land, the impact on farming and poor peasantry would be substantial. The sustained priority assigned to the works on the private land of the poor peasantry is revealed by the fact that the 'fourth category' of works alone accounts for almost a third of the total MGNREGS expenditure in recent years (Table 11.2). The benefits to poor peasantry and agricultural production are likely to be substantial, but still remain to be systematically assessed.

Table 11.5: Social Group-wise Prioritised MGNREGS Works on Eligible Private Lands in Andhra Pradesh, as on 25 July 2011

(Number of Works)

Status	*SC*	*ST*	*SC + ST*	*Others*	*Total*
1. Number of works in shelf	383,579	360,926	977	557,734	1,303,216
2. Number of works in sanction/start-up	561,547	243,669	1,254	484,511	1,290,981
3. Number of works in progress	204,305	132,505	2,237	308,426	647,473

Source: http://nrega.ap.gov.in (25 July 2011).

The MGNREGS provision for works on the private lands of the eligible farming communities has the effect of augmenting incomes of these communities by reinforcing their wage income, and by enabling them to earn income from self-employment in their own improved land. The available evidence shows that substantial portion of wage work in rural areas has been performed by the poor farming households. The results of an intensive micro-study of three villages in Andhra Pradesh shows that 16 to 48 per cent of the total hired work is performed by mostly poor and lower-middle peasants (Ramachandran, Rawal and Swaminathan, 2010). Another study of three villages shows that of those participating in MGNREGS works, about 50 per cent have land and 20 per cent are those usually self-employed in agriculture (Jha et al., 2008). There is a substantial participation of small–marginal farmers in the MGNREGS work. A large survey of six districts in Andhra Pradesh shows that farmers' participation in MGNREGS works ranges from 41 per cent in Kadapa to over 70 per cent in drought-prone Mahabubnagar and Ananthapura (Table 11.6). The MGNREGS participation of even large farmers goes with areas dependent on dry and rain-fed agriculture. Improving the lands of the poor farmers may help them to move to own cultivation.

Table 11.6: Landholding Status of Households Working in MGNREGS in Select Districts of Andhra Pradesh (2007–08)

(%)

District	*Landless*	*Marginal*	*Small*	*Medium*	*Large*	*All*
1. Mahaboobnagar	20.6	43.7	26.2	9.5*	—	100
2. Kadapa	58.9	32.8	6.9	1.3*	—	100
3. Karimnagar	57.0	10.1	11.3	11.9	9.6	100
4. Ranga Reddy	52.4	17.1	11.0	12.0	7.5	100
5. Ananthapura	25.7	19.8	18.6	17.8	18.0	100
6. Vijayanagaram	38.7	25.6	17.8	12.6	5.3	100

Source: Galab et al. (2009 and 2010).
Note: * Includes both medium and large holders.

MGNREGS and Private Lands of the 'Poor'—A Case Study

Drawn from a larger study of the author (Reddy, 2011), the case of Kuppanagar village in Medak district of Andhra Pradesh is presented here with specific focus on MGNREGS works on the private lands of eligible farming communities. A sample survey was conducted in the village, and Table 11.7 gives the details of the caste and class distribution of the sample households. The Panchayat has been proactive in identifying MGNREGS works on the private lands of special-category social groups, especially those of

Table 11.7: Caste- and Class-based (Size of Landholding) Classification of Sample Households (Kuppanagar)

Caste	*Landless*	*Marginal*	*Small*	*Semi-medium*	*Medium*	*Large*	*All*
SC	9	6	14	13	8	Nil	50
OBC	2	3	4	5	5	—	19
Others	4	4	4	7	4	—	23*
All	15	13	22	25	17	0	92

Source: Reddy, 2011.
Note: *20 HHs of these 'others' belong to Muslim community which is also mainly dependent on agriculture. Upper castes under 'others' in the village constitute very meagre proportion.

Table 11.8: MGNREGS Development Works on Private Lands under Progress in Kuppanagar during 2010–11*

Type of Work	*Community-wise Beneficiaries*				*Total Expenditure (₹ lakh)*	*Average per HH (₹)*
	SC	*OBC*	*Others*	*All*		
(1)	(2)	(3)	(4)	(5)	(6)	(7)
1. Tank silt application	103	13	1	117	13.08	11,178
2. Deep ploughing in hard soil	100	16	7	123	2.21	1,800
3. Development of fallow/dry lands	103	—	—	103	61.12	59,337
4. Open wells	4	2	—	6	2.48	41,358

Source: Mandal Computer Centre, Jarasangam, Medak District, Andhra Pradesh.
Note: *These works are approved and being implemented by the panchayat for the years 2010–11 and 2011–12.

SC households. Table 11.8 shows the MGNREGS development works on private lands of SC and others. Given the fact that the SCs constitute almost one-fourth of the population of the village and that most of them have some land, though mostly dry and uncultivable, one of the lasting ways of improving their economic condition is to make their lands more productive. Since most of them lacked resources for investment, the MGNREGS works on private lands have come as a boon.

What remained as unproductive pieces of assigned land are turning into productive agricultural assets. Application of tank silt to fallow or barren land enriches the soil, makes the land productive and ensures good crop even under rain-fed conditions. In developing fallow lands, one of the important works undertaken in some of these dry-land areas is the removal of overgrown *prosafis juliflora.* Most of the assigned lands when left fallow due to lack of resources for development turn into wild growth of *prosafis* which once sets in, becomes very difficult to clear unless completely rooted out—a task which needs about ₹40,000 per acre, and is beyond the means of poor farmers. There is no wonder that removal of *prosafis* overgrowth is one of the much sought-after work by the poor farmers.

Table 11.9 shows the beneficiaries under the MGNREGS in private lands, and the SCs get top priority in these works. The preponderance of SC households benefiting from the MGNREGS in the village is because of two reasons. One, most of the SC and other poor households in the village were assigned land out of two large tracts which were largely barren. Second, there were clear guidelines from the State that priority should be accorded to the SC and ST lands in undertaking land development on private lands, and special efforts were made through the SHGs to list the lands of the SC households in large number of villages for inclusion on priority in the shelf of projects prepared by the panchayats.[10] The state government's ambitious initiative in this regard could be gauged from the following part of the follow-up guidelines circulated:

> ... prepare the land inventory of SC/ST lands in all the villages in the state and (to) identify all the possible works in these lands with the objective to achieve an annual income of ₹25,000 per acre. The first and second priorities of projects are given as land development projects in fallow and cultivable lands of SC/ST farmers. *After saturation of the land development works in SC/ST lands* then other projects shall be identified to meet the demand of the labour budget of the habitation (emphasis added).[11]

Table 11.9: Households Benefiting from MGNREGS Works on Private Lands in Kuppanagar

Community	*All HHs*	*Landless HHs*	*HHs with Land*	*MGNREGS Private Land Improvement Work**	*Extent of Land Covered (acres)*	
					Total	*Average per HH*
SC	50	9	41	38 (93%)	62	1.6
OBC	19	2	17	8 (47%)	14	1.8
Others	23	4	19	8 (47%)	14	1.8
All	92	15	77	54 (70%)	89	1.6

Source: Reddy, 2011.
Notes: *HHs with land benefiting from MGNREGS improvement of private lands.
Figures in parentheses are percentages to HHs with land.

Table 11.10 shows that beneficiaries include farmers working on marginal-to-medium–sized land-holdings. Semi-medium or medium in dry-land conditions does not indicate a better resource position. In Kuppanagar, many of the SC households are also semi-medium and medium size landholders, but much of the land is of low productivity, requiring substantial investment to make it productive. Most of these households respond that they have an opportunity through the MGNREGS to raise good crops in their land for the first time. Table 11.11 shows the type of MGNREGS works on the private lands of the sample households. Most of them obtained the benefit of tank silt application to their lands. In fact, the results of tank silt application, by way of increased crop yields, had a visible impact and has created a very high demand from the SC and other eligible households for this programme, and the panchayat responded by according high priority to the same.

One of the interesting external outcomes of the state government's proactive initiation of measures to identify the lands of the SC and ST and other poor farmers' households through a series of systematic guidelines was the increased participation of these households in the meetings of the panchayat. Earlier,

Table 11.10: Size and Class of Holdings and MGNREGS Works on Private Lands in Kuppanagar

Size of Holdings	*Number of HHs with Land*	*HHs under MGNREGS Private Land Works*	*Total Extent of Area Covered (acres)*	*Average per HH (acres)*
Marginal	13	7	6	0.9
Small	22	18	30	1.7
Semi-medium	25	16	32	2.0
Medium	17	13	21	1.6
Large	—	—	—	—
All	77	54	89	1.6

Source: Reddy (2011).

Table 11.11: Type of MGNREGS Works Completed on Private Lands of Sample Households

Type of Work	*Marginal*	*Small*	*Semi-Medium*	*Medium*	*All Total*
Tank silt application	7	16	15	10	48 (89%)
Levelling and bunding	—	1	1	2	4 (7%)
Horticulture	—	—	—	1	1 (2%)
Other works	—	1	—	—	1 (2%)
All works	7	18	16	13	54 (100%)

Source: Reddy (2011).

when there was no priority for works on private lands, the poor farmers hardly evinced any interest in the deliberations of the panchayat. With the guidelines from the state to identify the lands of the poor, and to prioritise MGNREGS works in their favour, the passive indifference to panchayat meetings turned into active involvement. This process towards more democratisation of decision making at the grass-roots level has also turned as people's mobilisation in favour of more of MGNREGS works.

IV

Concluding Observations

MGNREGS, Labour Market and Agriculture

One of the clear evidences on the impact of MGNREGS on agriculture relates to labour market. Agricultural wages have increased across the country, and the rate of increase in the female agricultural wage has been much higher than male wages, and male–female differentials in agricultural wages have declined substantially. The tightening labour market has offered better bargaining power to agricultural labourers, better treatment at the place of work and ability to negotiate the duration of the working day. But the terms of wages are increasingly tending towards piece-rate contracts. The peak-period labour shortages in agriculture, which are confined to certain regions, are resulting in a number of changes in working hours, working day and MGNREGS work calendar. The ongoing process of agricultural mechanisation is being hastened, but not widespread. A more sensible response to peak-season agriculture labour shortage is the negotiated MGNREGS calendar that avoids implementing works during agricultural peak season and provides developmental works during lean season. And such a time schedule is welcomed by farmers as well as workers across the country.

There is no evidence that there has been a marked decline in the area cultivated either due to rise in agricultural wages or shortage of labour. On the contrary, there are counteracting forces by way of additional worker effect by drawing certain social groups into the 'government employment' of MGNREGS wage work; and additional area effect by making some of the fallow lands of the poor more productive. But there is a clear evidence that rise in wages is one of the contributing factors, along with other rising input costs, to increasing cost of cultivation. The SC, ST and other small–marginal farmers, who are also participants in the MGNREGS, were not affected much, or in many cases gained substantially, and the better-off farmers could face the rising costs partly through mechanisation. But the worst affected are the small–marginal farmers who are neither participants in MGNREGS work nor beneficiaries of works on their private lands. This section of the small–marginal farming community may not be small, and face serious crisis. In this context, the Planning Commission's proposal to make the scheme more farmer friendly by extending the coverage to some of the agricultural operations,[12] if designed properly, may address the problems of excluded small–marginal farmers.

One of the salutary effects of MGNREGS on poor rural households is the drastic reduction in distress migration. But there is no reason to share the apprehension, as expressed by some (Farrington, Holmes and Stater, 2007), that the scheme may discourage them from moving to more economically dynamic areas'. Just as in favour of decline in distress migration, there is equally strong evidence to show that migration for higher wage work that lasts for relatively longer period in a year remains unaffected, and possibly would improve if skill formation and activities that would improve human resource development are also brought under the MGNREGS.

MGNREGS Works and Agriculture

Since most of the works under the scheme are for land and water resource development and conservation, theoretically these works are expected to have lasting impact on agriculture. However, given the magnitude of the scheme and the diversity of the agrarian conditions in rural India, the benefits to agriculture are likely to be linked to the appropriateness of the choice of works to different regions, the quality of design and the competence and commitment in their effective execution (NCCSO, 2009). The evidence mustered in this chapter does suggest that works like tank restoration, silt application to degraded land, percolation tanks, farm ponds, rooting out of *prosafis* growth and deep tilling do have visible positive impact on agricultural productivity. And there is no room for believing, as some feel (Sjoblom and Farrington, 2008), that these works are prone to being taken over by wealthier sections of society or that these are poorly implemented, leading people to think that the MGNREGS is no better than any other government schemes that had little impact on poverty. The field experience in Andhra Pradesh suggests that most of the works under implementation are much sought after by the people. There is vast scope for learning from mutual experience of success. There is no reason why strategising works on the private lands of the SC, ST and small–marginal farmers, which is an overwhelming success in Andhra Pradesh, could be a non-starter in Tamil Nadu or Punjab. It is unfair on the part of the National Advisory Council (NAC) to criticise that all MGNREGS works so far have been like 'relief' works rather than being productive works (NAC, 2011). But, that does not mean that works implemented in Andhra Pradesh are appropriate in all locations and are technically perfect. In spite of the efforts of the state government, most of the panchayats are technically ill equipped. The situation in other states may not be any the better. There is much justification in the criticism:

> A key constraint to building high quality assets is the lack of technical support to communities as input to planning MNREG works (eg. through resource mapping exercises) as well as the storage of technical staff in designing and supervising works. A large number of works, particularly those related to water conservation, remain incomplete, either due to lack of technical support to GPs or the onset of monsoons (World Bank, 2011).

At the same time, one has to realise that there do not exist adequate technical capabilities that could be simply allocated as they do with the financial resources, but have to be created to suit the diversity of needs. There is need for broad regional resource-specific typologies for planning land development, water harvesting and conservation works, and for adoption with suitable local-level modifications (Bassi and Kumar, 2010). Reference to these limitations is not meant to digress from the beneficial effects of MGNREGS on agriculture, but only to draw attention to efforts needed if the vast positive potential has to be realised substantially.

Notes

1. For a very detailed report on how male members of the household migrate to high-paying factory work, and how women and elderly take to the MGNREGS, see *Business Standard* (2011) MGNREGS fails to curb distress migration in parts of Rajasthan. *Business Standard*, 14 August.
2. Para 1 of Schedule I of the MGNREGA was amended on 18 June 2008 to include small and marginal farmers, as defined in the Agriculture Debt Waiver and Debt Relief Scheme, 2008, as eligible for the works on individual land.
3. G.O. Rt. No. 1720 of the Irrigation and Command Area Development (MI.IV) Department dated 30 December 2006.
4. At the State MGNREGS Council meeting on 28 September 2007, the Chief Minister suggested extending the tank restoration programme to phase II districts and taking up of the second tank in each village in the phase I districts. Steps were initiated to this effect by the Department of Rural Development (Circular dated 27 November 2007).
5. A statement 'Best Practices in NREGS-AP' issued by the Commissioner of Rural Development, Government of Andhra Pradesh, dated 11 June 2008.
6. The Commissioner of Rural Development, Government of Andhra Pradesh, initiated a detailed survey of the minor irrigation tanks restored under the MGNREGS (Circular No. 71/EGS dated 20 June 2010). The results are awaited.
7. The G.O.Ms.No. 51, PR&RD (RDII) Department, dated 1 February 2010, lays down clearly the area, costs and the share of funds from the MGNREGS and Department of Horticulture, Government of Andhra Pradesh.
8. There were detailed instructions in two tranches of circulars specifying projects under each category and type of works under each project (Circular No. 653/EGS/PM(T)/2008 dated 6 October 2008 and 1 November 2008).
9. This is part of the guidelines issued under the MGNREGS New Works Strategy by the Commissioner of Rural Development, Government of Andhra Pradesh (Circular No. 1192/EGS/PM(T)/2010 dated 6 September 2010).
10. D.O. Letter No. 770/IKP-EGS/2009 dated 31 October 2009 and Circular Memo No. 1187/EGS/PM(T/08 dated 4 November 2009, Commissioner of Rural Development, Government of Andhra Pradesh, Hyderabad.
11. Circular No. 1192/EGS/PM(T)/2010 dated 28 September 2010, Commissioner of Rural Development, Government of Andhra Pradesh, Hyderabad.
12. It is reported that the draft proposal by the Planning Commission submitted to the Ministry of Rural Development suggests rechristening the scheme as MGNREGS-II so as to cover agricultural activities like sowing, harvesting, soil and compost preparation, irrigation and allied activities like tending livestock. It is also proposed that to begin with, the farm activities will be allowed under the revised scheme only in 2,000 backward blocks, with a goal of putting back small–marginal farmers on their own farms. (Sindhu, 2011 and *Tehelka*, 20 August 2011).

References

Acharya, S. (1990) *Maharashtra Employment Guarantee Scheme: A study of labour market intervention*. New Delhi: ILO-ARTEP.

Babu, V. Suresh, B. Dhanyashree, Joseph Abraham and K. Hanumatha Rao (2010) Impact of MGNREGS on scheduled castes in West Bengal, NIRD, Hyderabad (Processed).

Banerjee, Kaustav and Partha Saha (2010) The NREGA, the Maoists and development woes of the Indian state. *Economic and Political Weekly* XLV, No. 28, (10 July).

Bassi, Nitin and M. Dinesh Kumar (2010) NREGA and rural water management in India: Improving the welfare effects, Occasional Paper No. 3-0910, Institute for Resource Analysis and Policy, Hyderabad.

Bhagat, Rasheeda (2010) A world of cultivated taste. *Hindu Business Line*, 26 February.

Business Standard (2011) MNREGS fails to curb distress migration in parts of Rajasthan. *Business Standard*, 14 August.

——— (2011) Sugar mills go high-tech to beat labour shortage. *Business Standard*, 14 August.

Centre for Science and Environment (CSE) (2008) An Assessment of the performance of the National Rural Employment Guarantee Programme in terms of its potential for creation of natural wealth in India's Villages, CSE, New Delhi, September.

CRRID (2009) Appraisal of impact assessment of NREGS in selected districts of Himachal Pradesh, Punjab and Haryana, India Centre for Research in Rural and Industrial Development (CRRID), Chandigarh.

Datt, Gaurav (1994) Poverty alleviation through rural public works: The experience of Maharashtra Employment Guarantee Scheme. *The Indian Journal of Labour Economics* 37, No. 4.

Drèze, Jean (2004) Employment as a social responsibility. *Hindu*, 22 November.

Farrington, J., R. Holmes and R. Stater (2007) Linking social protection and the productive sectors. Briefing Paper 28, Overseas Development Institute, London.

Fibre 2 Fashion (online) (2011) 14 August.

Financial Express (2008) Government nulls 'lean period' for rural job scheme in harvesting season. *Financial Express*, 11 August.

Gaiha, Raghav, Shylashri Shankar and Raghabendra Jha (2010) Targeting accuracy of the NREGS: evidence from Rajasthan, Andhra Pradesh and Maharashtra. ASARC Working Paper 2010/3, Australian South Asia Research Centre, The Australian National University, Canberra.

Galab, S., E. Revathi, P. Prudhvikar Reddy and C. Ravi (2010) Mahatma Gandhi National Rural Employment Guarantee Programme in Andhra Pradesh: An assessment. *LBS Journal of Management and Research* 8, No. 1, (January–June): 14–34.

Galab, S., P. Prudhvikar Reddy, E. Revathi and C. Ravi (2008) *Evaluation Report on the Impact of NREGS in Andhra Pradesh*, Centre for Economic and Social Studies, Hyderabad (Processed).

——— (2009) NREGS in Andhra Pradesh: Issues and challenges, Centre for Economic and Social Studies, Hyderabad (for Commission of Panchayat Raj, GoAP, Hyderabad).

Ghanashyam, Bharathi (2008) NREGA: Bringing hope to small farmers, *Splash*, October.

Hindu (2010) Labour shortage affects paddy harvest. *Hindu*, 23 September.

Hirway, Indira, M. R. Saluja and Bhupesh Yadav (2008) *The impact of public employment guarantee strategies on gender equality and pro-poor economic development*, Research Project No. 34, The Levy Economic Institute and UNDP, Annandale-on-Hudson, New York, January.

IAMR (2008) *All India report on evaluation of NREGA: A survey of twenty districts*. New Delhi: Institute for Applied Manpower Research.

Indian Institute of Technology, Madras (IITM) (2009) Evaluation of National Rural Employment Guarantee Act, Rural Technology and Business Incubator, IIT, Madras.

Jha R., et al. (2008) Reviewing NREGP. *Economic and Political Weekly* 43, No. 11: 44–48.

Jha, Raghabendra, Raghav Gaiha and Shylashri Shankar (2008) National Rural Employment Guarantee Programme in Andhra Pradesh: Some recent evidence. ASARC Working Paper 2008/04.

Johnson, Doug (2009) Can workforce serve as a substitute for weather insurance? The case of NREGA in Andhra Pradesh. Working Paper Series No. 32, Centre for Micro Finance, Institute for Financial Management and Research, Chennai.

Joshi, Varsha, Surjit Singh and K. N. Joshi (2008) Evaluation of NREGA in Rajasthan, Institute for Development Studies, Jaipur, September.

Kamath, R (2008) NREGA surveys in Anantapur, Adilabad, Raichur and Gulbarga (2007–08) (MoRD and UNDP Sponsored), Indian Institute of Management, Bangalore.

Kareemulla, K., Shailendra Kumar, K. S. Reddy, C. A. Rama Rao and B. Venkateswarlu (2010) Impact of NREGS on rural livelihoods and agricultural capital formation. *Indian Journal of Agricultural Economics* 65, No. 3: 524–39.

Kumar, Dinesh M., Nitin Bassi, M. V. K. Sivamohan and V. Niranjan (2011) Employment guarantee and its environmental impact: Are the claims valid? *Economic and Political Weekly* XLVI, No. 34: 69–71.

Mahapatra, Richard, Neha Sakhuja, Sandip Das and Supriya Singh (2008) The National Rural Employment Guarantee Act (NREGA): Opportunities and challenges, Centre for Science and Environment, New Delhi.

Nair, D. K., Confederation of Indian Textile Industry (CITI) (2011) *SME Times*, 28 April.

National Advisory Council (2011) Strengthening natural resource management components under Mahatma Gandhi NREGA: Recommendations by National Advisory Council (AAC), NAC, New Delhi.

Nayak, N. C. (n.d.) Appraisal processes and procedures of NREGS in Orissa: A study of Mayurbhanj and Balasore district, Indian Institute of Technology, Kharagpur.

NCAER-PIF (2009) Study on evaluating performance of National Rural Employment Guarantee Act, National Council for Applied Economic Research, New Delhi.

NCCSO (2009) *NREGA reforms building rural India: First Annual Report of the National Consortium of Civil Society Organisation (NCCSO) on NREGA—2008-09*, Jatashankar, Dewas, MP.

Paliwal, Ankur (2011) Water turns the tide. *Down to Earth*, 15 April.

Panda, B. (2009) Appraisal of NREGA in the states of Meghalaya and Sikkim, Rajiv Gandhi Institute of Management, Shillong.

Papola, T. S. (2005) A universal programme is feasible. *Economic and Political Weekly* 40, No. 7 (12 February): 594–99.

Pioneer (2010) NREGS Lures Labourers Away from Fields. *Pioneer*, 4 May.

——— (2011) Agriculture Ministry wants MNREGA labour glitch uprooted. *Pioneer*, 24 July.

Ramachandran, V. K., Vikas Rawal and Madhura Swaminathan (2010) *Socio-economic surveys of three villages in Andhra Pradesh: A study of agrarian relations*. New Delhi: Tulika Books.

Rani, Radhika Ch. and D. V. L. N. V. Prasada Rao (2011) Status of Land allotment to poor under land distribution programmes: An evaluation, Centre for Agrarian Studies and Disaster Management, NIRD, Hyderabad (Forthcoming).

Rao, K. Hanumantha and C. Dheeraja (2010) *Changing gender relations through MGNREGS: Bihar state report*, NIRD, Hyderabad (Processed).

Rao, K. Hanumantha, S. Subrahmanyam, C. S. Murthy and V. Suresh Babu (2010) Impact of MGNREGS on scheduled tribes in Orissa, NIRD, Hyderabad (Processed).

Rawat, D. S., ASSOCHAM (2011) *India Infoline News Service*, 26 June.

Reddy, D. Narasimha (2011) Functioning of National Rural Employment Guarantee Scheme (NREGS) in Andhra Pradesh. Paper presented at final workshop under CDS-ASSR project on Monitoring the implementation of social security for the working poor in india's informal economy, Center for Development Studies, Thiruvananthpuram, India.

Sainath, P. (2008) NREGA hits buses to Mumbai. *Hindu*, 31 May.

Sanhati (2008) Aspirations within misery: Labour shortage in agriculture. *Sanhati*, 5 August.

Shah, Mihir (2007) Employment guarantee, civil society and Indian democracy. *Economic and Political Weekly* 42, Nos. 45 and 46: 43–51.

——— (2009) Multiplier–accelerator synergy in NREGA. *Hindu*, 30 April.

Sindhu, Seema (2011) NREGA to go farm-friendly. *Pioneer*, 19 August.

Singh, S. P. and D. K. Nauriyal (2009) System and process review and impact assessment of NREGS in the state of Uttarakhand, Indian Institute of Technology, Roorkee.

Sjoblom, D. and J. Farrington (2008) The Indian National Rural Employment Guarantee Act: Will it reduce poverty and boost the economy? Project Briefing No. 7, Overseas Development Institute, London.

Slter, Rachel, Rebecca Holmes and John Farrington (2007) *Social protection and growth: The agriculture case*. London: Overseas Development Institute.

SME Times (2011) 7 May.

Tehelka (2011) 20 August.

Times of India (2010) Punjab farmers reap bitter NREGA harvest. *Times of India*, 13 June.

——— (2011)1 April.

——— (2011) 7 July.

Tiwari, Rakesh, H. I. Somashekhar, V. R. Ramakrishna Parama, Indu K. Murthy, M. S. Mohan Kumar, B. K. Mohan Kumar, Harshad Parate et al. (2011) MNREGA for environmental service enhancement and vulnerability reduction: Rapid appraisal in Chitradurga district, Karnataka. *Economic and Political Weekly* XLVI, No. 20, (14 May): 39–47.

World Bank (2011) Social Protection for a Changing India, Vol. II, Chap. 4 'Public Works and Promotional Programs'. Washington, D.C.: World Bank.

12

Empowerment Effects of the MGNREGS on Women Workers

Ashok K. Pankaj and Rukmini Tankha

I

Introduction

Women's empowerment was not among the original intentions of the Mahatma Gandhi National Rural Employment Guarantee Act (MGNREGA), and is not among its main objectives. However, provisions like priority for women in the ratio of one-third of total workers [Schedule II (6)], equal wages for men and women [Schedule II (34)] and crèches for the children of women workers [Schedule II (28)] were made in the act, with the view of ensuring that rural women benefit from the scheme in a certain manner. Provisions like work within the radius of five kilometres from the house, absence of supervisor and contractor, flexibility in terms of choosing period and months of employment were made, though not exclusively for women, but nevertheless, conducive for rural women.

The flip side of the scheme is the nature of the job—hard manual work and wages based on piece rate—which make it difficult for women to earn minimum wages. Field reports (Bhatty, 2008; Sainath, 2007; Zila Panchayat, Bastar) suggest exclusion of single, divorced and separated, and old women in some places. In addition, entitlement to 100 days of guaranteed employment is applicable at the household level. In a male-dominant patriarchal society, it is difficult to believe that women's decision to avail of employment under the MGNREGS would get precedence over the decision of male members.

Nevertheless, women have availed of the paid employment opportunity under the MGNREGS in large numbers. The MGNREGS, being public works programme, has attracted rural women in large numbers. Women workers had a share of 40.65 per cent (national average) of total MGNREGS person-days in 2006–07, 42.52 per cent in 2007–08 and 47.88 per cent in 2008–09, exceeding expectations and the stipulated 33 per cent share. Interestingly, this occurred largely spontaneously. Women's participation under the MGNREGS (share in person-days) also exceeded their participation in the erstwhile employment-generation programmes like the SGRY and the MEGS, except for a few years under MEGS. For example, in 2005–06, under the SGRY, the share of women in total person-days was only 25.7 per cent, although it was a bit higher in some states like Rajasthan (42.32 per cent), MP (36.35 per cent), Andhra Pradesh

(37.44) per cent and Chhattisgarh (35.01 per cent) (CSO, 2007: 65). Similarly, women, on an average, constituted 40 per cent of the MEGS workers between 1978–79 and 1986–87 (Acharya, 1990: 63).

Women's participation in the MGNREGS, however, varies across regions. The share of women in total person-days was relatively high (exceeding 50 per cent) in Kerala, Tamil Nadu, Andhra Pradesh, Karnataka, Rajasthan and Tripura in all the three years, that is, 2006–07, 2007–08 and 2008–09 (except in Tripura where it was less than 50 per cent in 2007–08). It exceeded the national average (namely, 47.88 per cent) in Andhra Pradesh, Gujarat, Kerala, Tamil Nadu, Karnataka, Rajasthan and Tripura in all the three years. On the other hand, the share of women in total person-days was less than the national average in Bihar, Chhattisgarh, Haryana, HP, Jharkhand, Maharashtra, Orissa, Punjab, UP, Uttarakhand (except in 2007–08), West Bengal and most of the north-eastern states. Further, there is a gap of about 80 percentage points between the states with the highest and lowest participation rates, that is, Kerala (85.01 per cent) and Jammu and Kashmir (5.76 per cent). Even if we consider Jammu and Kashmir as an outlier, there is still a gap of about 67 percentage points between Kerala and UP (18.11 per cent). Moreover, there are pronounced regional north–south variations. The four southern states, namely, Andhra Pradesh, Karnataka, Kerala and Tamil Nadu with relatively better human and gender development indices have ensured high participation of women in all the three years (as their share in total person-days), although average person-days is low in Kerala. Rajasthan with high women's participation is the exception among the north Indian states.

In contrast to the high participation of women in the programme as workers, their participation in the processes like work selection, social audit, mobilisation of civil society and share in the control and management of assets created is not encouraging. This being the case, still in some places, women's participation in the gram sabha has increased, and there is even an increase in the number of women who speak in the gram sabha. In MP, women form parts of vigilance committee, and it is reported that women are the most vocal among the members of the vigilance committee in some places (Khera and Nayak, 2009: 56). There are also some examples of women's groups playing an important role in the management of community assets, for example, Jatropha plantation in Chhattisgarh (Zila Panchayat, Bastar). Nonetheless, the disjunction between 'work participation' and 'process participation' remains, and that would reduce the larger potential community-level impacts of the scheme.

Even so, the emergence of women workers as independent bread-earners, with control over their earnings, has significant empowerment effects such as a greater decision-making role in the family, discretion to spend and control the use of their earnings and confidence to earn independent of male family members. Moreover, reports of their increased participation in the gram sabha are encouraging, and might change the male-dominant character of decision making at the level of grass-roots democratic institutions that continue to be male dominated even after the increased representation of women following the 73rd Constitutional Amendment Act.

This chapter examines empowerment effects of the MGNREGS on rural women at both the individual and community levels. At the individual level, this has been examined through: (*a*) income–consumption effects, (*b*) intrahousehold effects (decision-making role) and (*c*) enhancement of choice and capability. The community-level effects have been assessed in terms of realisation of equal wages, increased participation in community development process and overall impact on gender relations, if any.

It argues that a woman worker has benefited from the scheme primarily because of the paid employment opportunity, and benefits have been realised through: (*a*) income–consumption effects, (*b*) intrahousehold effects (decision-making role) and (*c*) enhancement of choice and capability. Women as a community have also gained to some extent in terms of: (*a*) realisation of equal wages under MGNREGS with its long-term implications for correcting gender skewness and gender discriminatory wages prevalent in the rural labour market of India; (*b*) recognition of the need for engendering of public works programme and (*c*) increased participation in the gram sabha that might change the male-dominant character of decision making at the grass-roots democratic institutions.

The chapter finally pleads that despite difficulties and hurdles for women, prospects lie, inter alia, in their collective mobilisation, more so in laggard states, for: (*a*) greater process participation; (*b*) realisation of sufficient number of person-days and wages paid through the individual account of women workers; (*c*) enforcement of provisions like crèche and (*d*) engendering of the nature of work, including types of assets with a view to derive lateral benefits from the work and assets.

The next section describes perspectives, definition and methodology used in this study. Section three explains state and local contexts of variations in women's participation under MGNREGS. A brief description of characteristics of women workers and their households has been provided in section four. Individual and community-level empowerment effects including difficulties faced by women workers have been analysed in section five. The last section underlines the importance of MGNREGS for rural women and draws some general conclusions for policy purposes.

II

Perspectives, Definitions and Methodology

This study is informed by the Gender and Development (GAD) perspective[1] that argues that it is the gender discriminatory power structure and relations that lead to, and perpetuate, gender lopsided development outcomes, which are the main causes of women's deprivations. The empowerment effects of the MGNREGS have the potentialities to address unequal gender relations in the long run; some of them have been explained in terms of household and community-level effects in this chapter.

Under the rubric of GAD, Molyneux (1985) divided women's needs into 'practical' and 'strategic'. Practical needs are those related to food, clothes, housing, etc., and strategic needs are those related to the long-term issues of developing the ability to change the position of subordination and discrimination. The MGNREGS aims to meet the practical needs of women workers in the short run and their strategic needs in the long run. Women are able to buy food, clothes, medicines, etc., from their MGNREGS earnings that addresses their short-term needs. Their reduced dependence for these basic needs on the male members also addresses the issue of subordination and subjugation in the long term.

Household Economics, Paid Employment and Women's Empowerment

Till recently, intrahousehold affairs were considered outside the domain of mainstream economics that deals mainly with market institutions. With the assertion of feminist economics and emergence of 'bargaining' (Becker, 1981; Folbre, 1986) and 'cooperative-conflict' (Sen, 1990, 1996) models, the notion of household being a non-market institution has been challenged. It is argued that the perception of the family as an undifferentiated unit where cooperation, harmony and altruism define relations between members, camouflages the real nature of household affairs (Folbre, 1986; Sen, 1990). It is also contended that the notion of human behaviour guided by self interest in the market and altruism in family/household relations, is inconsistent.

Male–female intrahousehold relations, then, are (also) defined by their differential 'bargaining power', in turn determined by their differential access to economic, political and social resources. Property ownership and access to paid employment opportunity outside the household, apart from other factors, increases the bargaining capacity of a woman by giving her a better 'fallback position' (Agarwal, 1994). Since, in India and elsewhere, male members have greater control over property and other economic resources including access to paid employment, they enjoy better bargaining position inside their households. Moser (1993) holds that women's ability to earn outside their households increases their own self-perception of their contribution to the household, and this has similar effects. The paid employment opportunity under the MGNREGS holds similar prospects for rural women in India, who have little control over economic resources, and face social and other disadvantages in accessing paid employment outside the home.

The concept of empowerment gained prominence with the feminist movement in the 1980s. There are various views and perceptions on empowerment (Luttrell and Quiroz with Scrutton and Bird (2009)). To some, it is a process and, to others, it is an outcome. Many consider it to be both a process and an outcome. The process approach emphasises on organisational capacity building that enhances the access of disadvantaged groups to the process of development, while the outcome approach emphasises on increased access to economic resources. To Kabeer, 'empowerment refers to the expansion in people's ability to make strategic life choices in a context where this ability was previously denied to them' (Kabeer, 2001a: 19). She elaborates three dimensions of empowerment (*a*) resources (conditions), (*b*) agency (process) and (*c*) achievement (outcomes). The present study takes a broader view of empowerment and defines it 'both as a process and as an outcome that alters the position of women both inside and outside their households, and with this altered position, women are able to realise better individual and social life'.

Methodology and Sample Population

This study is largely empirical, based on a primary survey conducted in the four selected states of north India. The survey was conducted using a two-stage purposive and random sample technique (Table 12.1). In the first stage, states, districts and blocks were selected purposively and in the second stage, worksites and women workers were selected randomly. Methods of structured and non-structured interview and focused group discussions were also used for the purpose.

Selection of the Sample

States: The selection of states from north India is based on two main considerations. First, the human and gender development indicators of these states, except those of HP, are poor than those of their southern counterparts. It is believed that the empowerment effects (of MGNREGS) could be observed more sharply in states where women face poor socio-economic conditions, and where their participation in social and community development processes has traditionally been weak. Second, because of these factors, the issue of women's empowerment is more pertinent in these states than in others.

Further, the selected states consist of two pairs: Rajasthan and HP are two states with better implementation and Bihar and Jharkhand are two states with poor implementation records. This selection provides us with a contrast of two better implemented and two poorly implemented states across north India.[2]

Table 12.1: HDI, GDI and GEM of Selected States (2006)

States		*2006*	
States Selected for Study	***HDI[#]***	***GDI[##]***	***GEM[###]***
Bihar	0.552	0.525	0.385
Jharkhand	0.611	0.595	0.350
Rajasthan	0.591	0.577	0.387
Himachal Pradesh	0.705	0.702	0.473
Southern States			
Andhra Pradesh	0.627	0.617	0.509
Karnataka	0.658	0.647	0.480
Kerala	0.775	0.757	0.496
Tamil Nadu	0.694	0.683	0.482
Best Performing State[$]	***0.801***	***0.781***	***0.509***
All India Average	**0.648**	**0.633**	**0.451**

Source: Ministry of Women and Child Development, Government of India, 2009: 9, 10, 13.
Notes: [#] Human development index.
[##] Gender-related development index.
[###] Gender empowerment measure.
[$] **HDI** (Chandigarh), **GDI** (Chandigarh), **GEM** (Andhra Pradesh).

Districts and Blocks: Based on the consideration like SC, ST population, the level of overall and female literacy rate, agrarian conditions (irrigated areas, etc.) and overall implementation of the scheme in the district, particularly the participation of women, person-days per household and the number of works undertaken, one district each was purposively selected from all the four states—Gaya (Bihar), Ranchi (Jharkhand), Dungarpur (Rajasthan) and Kangra (HP). In Gaya, Ranchi and Dungarpur, the scheme has been implemented since 2 February 2006 and in Kangra, since 1 April 2007. This selection gives us a background of at least three years of implementation. The selection of Kangra from HP, despite it being a Phase II district, was based on the high participation of women, which was low in Chamba and abysmally low in Sirmour, the only two districts of the first phase. The selection of Ranchi, despite the low participation of women, was guided by the consideration of high

Table 12.2: Demographic and other Features of Population; MGNREGS Person-days and Share of SCs, STs, Others and Women in Total Person-days (2008–09)

Demographic and Other Features percent*	*Gaya*	*Ranchi*	*Dungarpur*	*Kangra*
Rural population	86.3	64.89	92.7	94.61
SC population	29.64	5.17	4.15	20.88
ST population	0.08	41.82	65.14	0.12
Literacy rate overall	50.45	64.57	48.57	80.08
Literacy rate–rural males	63.27	76.56	66.04	87.54
Literacy rate—rural females	36.66	51.72	31.77	73.01
Rural female workforce participation rate	28.15	46.81	39.48	38.6
Sex ratio	948	972	1,031	1,032
Share of SC, STs, Others and Women in MGNREGS Person-days				
Average person-days per household	17.9	36.7	47.48	72.17
Percentage share of SCs	62.99	10.61	4.96	28.88
Percentage share of STs	0.00	58.22	79.29	7.02
Percentage share of others	37.01	31.17	15.74	64.1
Percentage share of women	34.98	14.4	75.53	53.09

Sources: * Calculated from Primary Census Abstract, Census of India, 2001.
** Calculated from the data of the Ministry of Rural Development, Government of India (accessed 15 September 2009 from http://nrega.nic.in/netnrega/home.aspx

ST population. It has been observed that districts with high SC and ST population generally show high participation of women. Ranchi defies this general trend, and that made it an interesting case to probe.

From each district, three blocks were purposively selected, based on considerations like participation of women, the level of MGNREGS implementation and the socio-economic conditions of the population. Another important consideration was the availability of women workers at the worksites during the fieldwork, so that they could be interviewed while working at the worksites.

Worksites and Women Workers: Active worksites (worksites with working workers) and women workers were randomly selected (Table 12.2). But in the case of Gaya district, active worksites with women workers were not found in the selected blocks during the survey; women workers were selected from the most recently active worksites. A total of 428 women workers: 103 from Dungarpur (Rajasthan), 110 from Gaya (Bihar), 106 from Kangra (HP) and 109 from Ranchi (Jharkhand) were interviewed using a semi-structured questionnaire. Because of the selection of women in groups, the number is uneven across districts. Out of 428 women, 11 per cent had completed 100 days and 41 per cent had completed more than 50 days, whereas the national average of women's person-days is less than 50 in all the three years.

The sample consists of Hindus (86.2 per cent), Muslims (4.2 per cent), Christians (2.3 per cent) and indigenous religious groups such as *Sarna*,[3] a tribe in Jharkhand (7.2 per cent). In terms of caste category, the distribution is as follows: SC, 30.4 per cent; ST, 34.6 per cent and OBC, 34.6 per cent[4] —OBC-I, 7.71 per cent and OBC-II, 26.87 per cent.

III

Explaining Women Workers' Participation under MGNREGS

There are various explanations for the high and low participation of women workers under the MGNREGS. Factors such as the nature of job not requiring special knowledge and skill (Krishnaraj, Pandey and Kanchi, 2004, in the context of MEGS); outmigration of male members (Bhatty, 2006; Mehrotra, 2008; Talukdar, 2008); employment opportunity available at the doorstep (Bhatty, 2006; Khera and Nayak, 2009); tradition of rural women working in others' fields (Narayanan, 2008); equal, non-discriminatory wages (Sudarshan, 2008; Khera and Nayak, 2009) and innovative experiments in implementation like female mate system in Rajasthan (Khera, 2008), synergisation of the MGNREGS with Kudumbshree[5] in Kerala (Vijayakumar and Thomas, 2008) and gender differential tasks for uniform (minimum) wages in Bihar[6] (Pankaj, 2008a) have encouraged women workers' participation.

Slow implementation and overall low level of job creation in states like UP, West Bengal and Bihar, household-based job cards and definition of household based on common kitchen, thereby causing exclusion of single, divorced and separated women,[7] have restricted women's participation in some cases. Local socio-cultural factors also play a role. Women are subjected to discrimination at the level of household registration and issuing of job cards, including complete denial to single woman households in states like UP (Raja, 2007). In most parts of the Hindi heartland, there is a notion among the upper-caste landed communities that allowing women to work outside their homes would amount to a loss of honour and dignity of the family. Khera and Nayak have found that apart from socio-cultural restrictions, presence of contractors on the worksites (not permitted legally), schedule of rates-based wages and delay in wage payment and lack of childcare facilities have restrictive effects on women's participation as workers under the MGNREGS (Khera and Nayak, 2009: 54–55).

Bihar, Jharkhand, Rajasthan and Himachal Pradesh

The four states present a varied picture. In Bihar and Jharkhand, the nature and capacity of local institutions and socio-cultural factors are the main reasons for low participation of women. First, the scheme has been implemented in the backdrop of the same administrative and institutional set-up, not considered very efficient and effective in public service delivery. Bihar has improved its delivery efficiency since 2004–05, but in a top-down manner. The basic character of grass-roots institutions—local bureaucracy and PRIs—has not changed much. On the other hand, Jharkhand is doing without formal PRIs; implementation by the bureaucracy in a centralised manner goes against the spirit of the MGNREGS. Secondly, the demand for MGNREGS job is confined mostly to the SCs and OBCs in Bihar[8] and SCs, STs and OBCs in Jharkhand. Most of these workers are landless (though participation is more widespread across land category in Jharkhand) and characterised by low literacy and other economic deprivations (Pankaj, 2008a: 19–59). Local institutions are effectively controlled by a combination of landed upper castes and upper-middle ascendant castes in Bihar (Pankaj and Singh, 2004). Following the 2006 panchayat elections in Bihar, the dominance of erstwhile elite in local institutions has, however, declined (Pankaj, 2008b). Similar problems exist in Jharkhand, where MGNREGS jobseekers are unable to translate entitlements into effective demand, owing to the incapacity of local institutions. The problem is not unique to these two states. Contrastingly, civil society, in especially the southern part of Rajasthan and a pro-active state in Andhra Pradesh, has overcome this problem. Third, participation of women from upper castes is negligible and from the OBCs, limited. Due to social restrictions, upper-caste women, even from poor families, have not come forward. Upper OBCs have some amount of land and the women prefer to work on their own fields. The lower OBCs, mostly service castes, have traditionally been dependent on *jajmani* services, and vestiges of this still remain.

Rajasthan presents a different socio-economic context. First, the intensity of demand for wage employment is high and socially widespread in the rural areas, as there is low intensity of agriculture since large parts of the state are rain-fed. Second, the history of drought relief through public works programme[9] has seen large numbers of people, men and women, coming out to work. Third, because of the low income and employment opportunity in the local areas, men and women from rural Rajasthan have been migrating to nearby cities and towns inside and outside state. For migrant populations, local employment is preferable, as migration has both social and economic costs. Fourth, there is a strong presence of civil society organisations in some parts of Rajasthan. In the context of MGNREGA, the MKSS, Vagad Mazdoor Kisan Sangathan (VMKS) and the Rozgaar Evam Suchana Adhikar Abhiyan have played a critical mobilising role. Fifth, especially the southern districts of Rajasthan such as Dungarpur are tribal-dominant districts, where working of women outside of their homes is not socially tabooed, and further, this coupled with economic hardship compels male and female members to work to earn their minimum livelihood.

In HP, women's work participation has increased over the years, although it continues to be low in first-phase districts—Sirmour and Chamba. High levels of human and gender development indices and better delivery capacity of grass-roots institutions are important factors. Social practices tabooing women's participation are not entrenched here. The high participation of women in Kangra, in turn, has a specific context. Unlike other places, most of the women workers in Kangra were from relatively better socio-economic conditions: 97 per cent belonged to OBC households; 69 per cent were literate, the highest among the four districts; and 92 per cent were landed (marginal). The main reason for participation in the scheme by women here is not desperation to earn for livelihood purposes. Situated in the valley and having a conducive climate, agriculture is intensive and productivity is high. Even a marginal farmer is able to meet minimum livelihood requirements. Male members were found to work in agriculture and, if necessary, supplement income through casual wage employment in non-agriculture sectors. Women were usually found to be confined to domestic chores or sometimes did need-based work in their own farms, but were not regular wage seekers.

Women of Kangra were seen to view MGNREGS as an opportunity to earn independently. The *sarkari kaam* (government-sponsored work), timely payment of minimum wages[10] and payment into the individual account of women workers were other attractions. The availability of paid employment opportunity at the doorsteps, not available earlier and 'sarkari kaam' (government-sponsored work) were factors that attracted women to join MGNREGS as workers in other states as well (Khera and Nayak, 2009: 51). The liberal attitude of implementing agencies in issuing job cards facilitated participation of a large number of widows and single women.

IV

A Brief Background of Women Workers and Their Households

Empowerment narratives explained in the next section pertain to women belonging to lower social and economic status (Table 12.3).[11] Two-thirds of them were illiterate and another one-fourth were only functionally literate. Most of them were married and were from nuclear families. Eighty per cent of them were in the fertility age group: 60.5 per cent in the age group of 30–45 years and another 19 per cent in the age group of 18–29 years. Another 15 per cent were in the age group of 46–59 years, and 5 per cent were also above 60 years.

The income and assets base of these households were poor. The average annual income of a woman worker's household was ₹29,149 in Dungarpur, ₹21,422 in Gaya, ₹41,329 in Kangra and ₹27,140 in Ranchi. Two-thirds of these households were from BPL families: 45.1 per cent general BPL and another 25.5 per cent *Antyodaya* cardholders. 78.5 per cent of them were living in *kacha* houses and another 16 per cent in semi-*pucca* houses.

One-third households were landless and 93 per cent of those having land were only marginal land holders. Casual work in non-agriculture was the primary occupation of 65 per cent of these households and casual work in agriculture of another 15 per cent. Only a small proportion of households had their primary occupation as self-employed in agriculture and non-agriculture.

Sample women respondents were found to have earned a minimum number of days in the reference year (2008–09). A woman worker had completed 77 days on an average in Dungarpur, 61 days in Kangra, 35 days in Ranchi and 26 days in Gaya district. However, the average share of a woman worker in total person-days earned by the household was 93 per cent in Kangra, 79 per cent in Dungarpur, 67 per cent in Ranchi and 61 per cent in Gaya.

Table 12.3: Women's Share in Total Person-days Worked by the Household (2008 April–2009 March)

Districts	*Average Person-days of Women*	*Average Person-days of Other Members*	*Women's Share in Total Person-days of HH*(%)*
Dungarpur	77	40	79.34
Gaya	26	23	61.17
Kangra	61	26	93.48
Ranchi	35	28	66.95
Total	**49**	**29**	**77.19**

Source: Survey.
Note: * Women's share in total person-days of household has been derived as women's person-days divided by total person-days multiplied by 100.

Wage earning was the main source of income of these households. Earnings from non-agriculture wages constituted the highest proportion of the total annual income of a woman worker's household in all the four districts. Income from agricultural wages constituted the second highest proportion in Gaya and was the third highest source of household contribution after MGNREGA in Ranchi. Remittances from migration were also a major source of household income in Dungarpur, after MGNREGA. Their other sources of income are shown in Table 12.4.

Table 12.4: Earnings from Various Sources and Share of MGNREGS Income (2008–09)

Various Sources of Earnings of a Woman Worker's Household	*(Share in Percentage)*				
	Dungarpur	*Gaya*	*Kangra*	*Ranchi*	*Total*
Agricultural wages	2.22	34.10	0.84	14.46	10.54
Non-agricultural wages	42.98	42.34	43.62	45.46	43.80
Sale of agricultural products (grains)	0.67	3.25	0.07	5.36	2.04
Dairy	0.70	0.61	0.62	2.25	1.02
Sale of fruits and vegetables	0.00	0.00	0.87	0.64	0.45
Old age/widow and other pension	0.24	0.10	6.64	2.03	2.84
Remittances received	21.37	2.42	4.86	1.15	7.47
Others	4.86	4.31	24.58	12.45	13.38
MGNREGA	26.95	12.86	17.90	16.19	18.46
Total	**100.00**	**100.00**	**100.00**	**100.00**	**100.00**

Source: Survey based on reply of the respondent on recall basis.
Note: Figures may be taken as approximates.

The contribution of MGNREGS wages in the total annual income of a woman worker household was 27 per cent in Dungarpur, 18 per cent in Kangra, 16 per cent in Ranchi and 13 per cent in Gaya. More important, it has become the third largest source of a woman worker's household income in Dungarpur, and the second largest in Gaya, Kangra and Ranchi districts. The relatively high share of MGNREGS in the total annual income of these households is due to their low-income base.

V

Empowerments Effects: Some Evidences

How has paid employment under the MGNREGS transformed the (bargaining) position of rural women within their households? And to what extent has participatory development process under the MGNREGS been able to create larger social effects on women's empowerment? The former has been analysed at the household level and with respect to three interrelated processes and outcomes, which are:

1. income–consumption effects;
2. intrahousehold effects (decision-making role) and
3. enhancement of choice and capability.

The latter has been explained at the larger community level and through:

1. process participation;
2. wage equality and its long-term impacts on rural labour market conditions and
3. changes in gender relations, if any, because of the above and other factors.

Household-level Effects

Women's contribution to household income and to the national economy remains largely unaccounted as they undertake a significant amount of unpaid work. To many, this remains a fundamental challenge of women's empowerment (Boserup, 1980; Folbre, 2009; Hirway and Saluja, 2009). A Time Use Survey, conducted by the Central Statistical Organisation across six states (CSO, 2007: 77), revealed that on an average, rural women spent about 22.53 hours of their weekly time on SNA activities and 33.95 hours on extended SNA activities.[12] This, in fact, reiterates that the average number of hours spent by women on unpaid work is high, and their contribution to the household's income and overall welfare remains unaccounted and unappreciated. The MGNREGS has helped women in converting some unpaid hours of work into paid hours of work with significant effects, especially for those women for whom MGNREGS is a primary work opportunity outside the home.

Income–consumption effects: By income–consumption effects, we mean an increase in the paid income of a woman worker and, consequently, her ability to choose her consumption baskets. Although income and consumption are related, yet we emphasise on consumption, as an increase in income sans the ability to consume or choose consumption baskets has little significance. For example, if a woman earns, but is unable to exercise any choice on how to spend those earnings and instead, say, surrenders her entire earnings to the head of the household, she does not influence the spending decision at all, and subsequently the element of empowerment is probably missing, in spite of the income effects. Paid work under the MGNREGS has helped rural women in realising income–consumption effects through: (*a*) monetised earnings and (*b*) better control over earnings because of monetised wages and account payment, leading to greater consumption effects.

Share in household income: A woman worker's earnings from the MGNREGS constituted 14 per cent (average of the four districts) of the total annual income of the household, 21 per cent in Dungarpur, 15 per cent in Kangra, 11 per cent in Ranchi, and 8 per cent in Gaya districts (Table 12.5). Her share might actually be more, as we have not accounted for her other contributions, in the form of either paid or unpaid work.

Underlining the significance of paid work and its effects on self-perception of women, one woman worker in a lighter vein told us that 'now she earns; her husband is ready even to prepare tea for her', something quite unlikely earlier. Some also shared that when they hand over either part or whole of their earnings to the head of their households or to any other male members, they feel a sense of worth and importance.

Table 12.5: Women's Contribution to Household's Income through MGNREGS (2008–09)

Districts	*Average Income of Households from MGNREGS (₹)*	*Women's Income from MGNREGS as Percentage of Total MGNREGS Income of Households*	*Share of Women's MGNREGS Income in the Total Annual Income of Households (%)*
Dungarpur	7,855	78.79	21.23
Gaya	2,755	61.47	7.90
Kangra	7,399	82.12	14.70
Ranchi	4,394	67.38	10.91
Total	**5,459**	**76.64**	**14.14**

Source: Survey.

Collecting and retaining wages: Earning is important, but equally important is retaining and exercising choice over the use of earnings. Sixty-eight per cent of the women workers (overall of the four districts) were collecting their wages themselves. This figure was higher in Dungarpur (98 per cent) followed by Kangra (60 per cent), and low in Ranchi (39 per cent) and Gaya (33 per cent). Similar results are found in another study (Khera and Nayak, 2009: 51).

Table 12.6: Who Collects Wages (per cent)

Districts	*Women Themselves*	*Male Members*	*Sometimes Male Members*
Dungarpur	97.5	2.5	0.0
Gaya	33.3	66.7	0.0
Kangra	60.0	9.1	30.9
Ranchi	38.6	61.4	0.0
Total	**68.2**	**23.2**	**8.6**

Source: Survey.

It appears that account payment leads to greater incidence of self-collection and control over wages. A high proportion of women in Dungarpur and Kangra, who collected their wages themselves was in fact coterminus with cent per cent account payment. On the other hand, in two-thirds cases in Gaya and slightly less in Ranchi, male members collected women's wages, as cash payment was still in practice and often payment was made to the male member on behalf of the household. The local social set-up accepts the practice of male members collecting wages of female family members, as often a household is identified by the name of the head of the household. Local officials and PRI representatives easily cooperate with male members to earn their local support and favour.

It was observed that sometimes women collect their wages, but hand it over either to the male heads of their households or to their husbands. Sometimes, they retain a portion and surrender the rest. Nevertheless, self-collection increases the chances of retaining control over wages.

Table 12.7: Retention of Earnings by Women

Proportion of MGNREGS Earnings Retained By Women Workers	*Percentage of Women Workers*				
	Dungarpur	*Gaya*	*Kangra*	*Ranchi*	*Total*
Up to 25%	50.5	69.1	50.0	52.3	**55.6**
25–50%	5.8	1.8	14.2	5.5	**6.8**
50–75%	4.9	0.0	3.8	0.9	**2.3**
75–100%	9.7	3.6	6.6	3.7	**5.8**
Nil	29.1	25.5	25.5	37.6	**29.4**
Total	**100.0**	**100.0**	**100.0**	**100.0**	**100.0**

Source: Survey.

Majority of women workers were found to be collecting and retaining their wages. Significantly, it was found that 55.6 per cent of sample women retained up to 25 per cent of their wages. The proportion of women who controlled up to 25 per cent of their MGNREGS wages for personal use/consumption was 50 per cent in Dungarpur, 69 per cent in Gaya, 50 per cent in Kangra and 52 per cent in Ranchi. Interestingly, 8.1 per cent women retained more than 50 per cent of their wage income. Still, 29 per cent women surrendered their entire earnings.

Retaining choice over the use of wages: A large number of women who retained either part or whole of their MGNREGS wages, also retained the choice over its use (Table 12.7). They used it for all kinds of purposes—on daily-consumption items, household durables, health and education of children, visiting relatives and social ceremonies, etc. They also used it to meet their personal needs. The most common items of personal needs women were spending on included clothes, cosmetics and bangles, personal health (medicines), visiting relatives and giving gifts at the time of marriage and festivals to near and dear ones.

The significance of this lies in reduced dependence on male and other family members. Before the MGNREGS, 44 per cent women said that they were able to meet their personal needs through their own earnings. Now, 71 per cent women were able to do so. The pre- and post-MGNREGS difference is quite significant in case of Kangra and Dungarpur, where the overall earning of women workers was relatively high because of the greater number of person-days worked by them. It seems that women are able to spare for personal needs only when they earn a minimum income, as other priorities of the household are equally pressing. This also registers the significance of realising a critical minimum number of person-days and wages for its better effects on women workers.

Interestingly, majority of women workers, even after getting own income through MGNREGS, continued to receive money from earlier sources to meet their personal needs, as per necessities and exigencies (Table 12.8). Of the total women workers, 78 per cent of them (85.3 per cent in Ranchi, 82.7 per cent in Gaya, 77.7 per cent in Dungarpur and 66 per cent in Kangra) continued to receive money from the earlier sources. This underlines the fact that cooperation and understanding continue to play a role in household affairs in rural India, notwithstanding the bargaining model of the household.

Table 12.8: Women's Own Income to Meet Personal Needs: Pre- and Post-MGNREGS

Districts	*Pre-MGNREGS Own Income to Meet Personal Needs*	*Post-MGNREGS Own Income to Meet Personal Needs*
Dungarpur	32	70.9
Gaya	59.1	74.5
Kangra	19.8	74.6
Ranchi	63.3	62.4
Total	**43.9**	**70.5**

Source: Survey.

Figure 12.1: Substitution Effect on Women's Earlier Sources of Income
Are earlier income sources to meet personal needs still available?

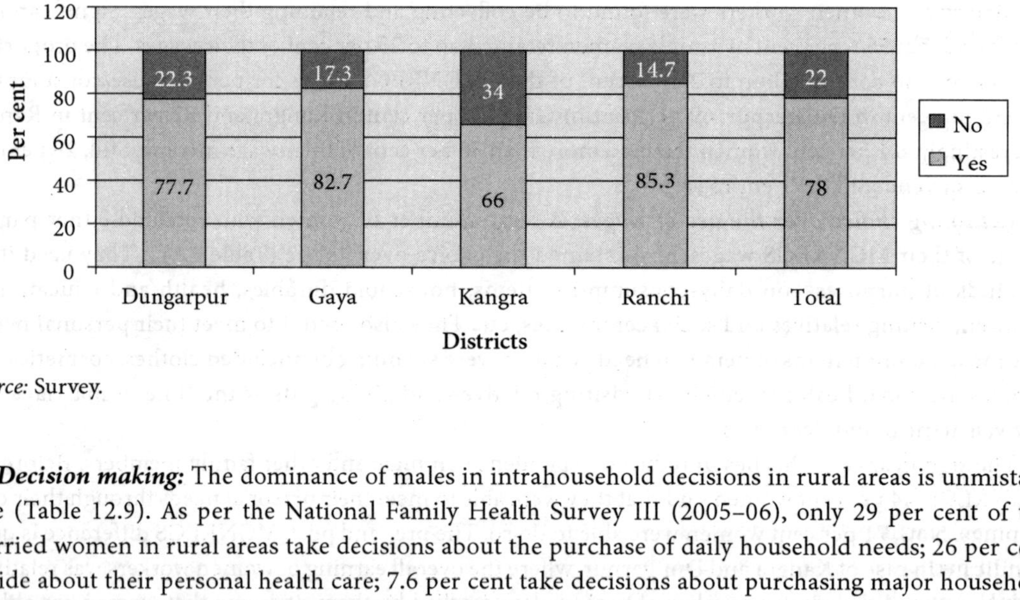

Source: Survey.

Decision making: The dominance of males in intrahousehold decisions in rural areas is unmistakable (Table 12.9). As per the National Family Health Survey III (2005–06), only 29 per cent of the married women in rural areas take decisions about the purchase of daily household needs; 26 per cent decide about their personal health care; 7.6 per cent take decisions about purchasing major household items and 10 per cent decide about visits to relatives (CSO, 2007:102).

If we compare this with observed changes in the case of MGNREGS women workers, the impact is remarkable. Now, 71 per cent of them retain certain portion of their income to spend it as per choice, related to purchase of household items, health care, visits of relatives, etc. Moreover, the domain of their decision making has also widened. One woman worker in Kangra used her MGNREGS income for the construction of a toilet inside her house, and interestingly, this was her own decision. Many of these women are now able to visit their relatives, mostly their maternal house (called *mayka* in north India), more frequently. Earlier, their visits were doubly controlled by both permission and the required money for the visit. Additionally, a number of women workers in Dungarpur had invested in fixed deposit for the sake of their children, earlier beyond the domain of their decision making.

Broadening of choice: The MGNREGS has broadened the choice for rural women in two ways. One, it has opened for them an entirely new avenue of paid employment opportunity. It has broadened their choice and capability because of the former. An important fact is that a large number of women decided on their own to work under the MGNREGS. Out of the four districts, 57.9 per cent joined MGNREGS works as their own decision, although 37.9 per cent were asked by the head of the household to work.

Table 12.9: Intrahousehold Decision to Participate in MGNREGS (in per cent)

Who decides	*Dungarpur*	*Gaya*	*Kangra*	*Ranchi*	*All*
Self (women workers)	75.7	37.3	78.3	42.2	**57.9**
Head of the household	20.4	59.1	20.8	49.5	**37.9**
Other family members	3.9	3.6	0.9	7.3	**4.0**
Others	0.0	0.0	0.0	0.9	**0.2**

Source: Survey.

Two, the MGNREGS has increased the choice of women by reducing economic dependence on other family members. In the case of dependence of a woman worker on the head of her household, the latter's discretion limits the choice or indulgence of the former by amount and timing. For example, if a woman wants to give 100 rupees as *kanyadan* on the occasion of the marriage ceremony of a girl, and the head of the household agrees to give only 50 rupees, then her choice is restricted by the amount. Similarly, if she wants to purchase a sari for herself at the time of the Holi festival and the head of the household agrees to provide money on the occasion of *Deepavali*, her choice is restricted by timing. The paid employment under the MGNREGS has enhanced both freedom and the choice to use earnings.

Community-level Effects

Participation in Social and Community Development Processes

Women's participation at the grass-roots community development process in general and decision making in particular remain weak in spite of their increased representation, following the 73rd Constitutional Amendment Act. Apart from low participation in the gram sabha and other decision-making fora, the problem of proxy (mostly male performing the role of women representatives) is frequently found to occur.

One of the latent objectives of the MGNREGS is to strengthen community development process through grass-roots institutions and to make the decision-making process at that level more inclusive and participatory. Women's participation in the procedural aspects under the MGNREGS, say, selection and implementation of works, social audit, asset management, etc., remains low, even though their participation as workers has surpassed the benchmark of 33 per cent at the all-India level in all the three years of implementation. The low procedural participation is a fact even in panchayats headed by women.

Procedural participation: The procedural participation is important for the realisation of entitlement. The first and foremost important issue is to know one's entitlements and process of realisation. Most of the women workers were aware of the basic provision of 100 days of guaranteed employment. But the level of awareness about the details of provisions including women-specific ones was low. This varied across districts.

Table 12.10: Level and Quality of Awareness about the MGNREGS (percentage of respondents)

Provisions	*Dungarpur*	*Gaya*	*Kangra*	*Ranchi*	*Total*
Up to 100 days of employment	99.0	60.0	98.1	78.0	**83.4**
Minimum wages	47.6	25.5	92.5	59.6	**56.1**
Equal wages	87.4	39.1	93.4	58.7	**69.2**
Wage payment within 15 days	49.5	21.8	75.5	27.5	**43.2**
Worksite facilities	94.2	21.8	74.5	40.4	**57.0**
Work within 5 km from residence	23.3	20.0	49.1	45.0	**34.3**
Unemployment allowance	7.8	11.8	37.7	10.1	**16.8**
One-third women workers	0.0	22.7	16.0	33.0	**18.2**

Source: Survey. Based on multiple answers.

Women workers were better informed of those provisions that had already been implemented, either partially or fully, and were least aware of those provisions that they were not availing of at all. Moreover, the level of awareness/information was generally higher in the better implemented places—Dungarpur and Kangra—and greater in case of provisions implemented effectively (Table 12.10). Literacy was another factor. Women in Kangra were more informed of most of the provisions, because of the relatively high literacy rate. Social mobilisation by civil society organisations is another factor that can overcome the handicap of low literacy rate.

Women's ability to search for the MGNREGS job themselves is another indicator of process participation. But only 5.4 per cent of women were found to have searched the MGNREGS job themselves, with GP head and panchayat secretary/rozgar sevak helping women in most of the cases. District-wise, the role of different agencies varied, and although the role of GP head/panchayat secretary/rozgar sevak was important in all the four districts, 'mates' especially played a critical role in Dungarpur.

Women's participation in the selection of MGNREG works and social monitoring including auditing was almost negligible. They were hardly involved in the management of assets created. This is important to derive lateral benefits of the assets. This happened even in the panchayats headed by woman *pradhans*.

A positive development is increased participation of women in gram sabha meetings. Forty-five per cent of them had attended gram sabha meetings held in connection with the MGNREGS. Women's participation in gram sabha was the highest in Kangra (89 per cent), followed by Dungarpur (55 per cent), Ranchi (26 per cent) and Gaya (14 per cent). The high participation in Kangra and Dungarpur was

Table 12.11: How did Women Search for the MGNREGS Job?

Who Helped Woman in Getting the Job?	*Percentage*				
	Dungarpur	*Gaya*	*Kangra*	*Ranchi*	*Total*
1. Searched herself	3.9	1.8	8.5	7.3	5.4
2. Family member	1.9	1.8	1.9	2.8	2.1
3. Fellow women worker	0.0	0.9	0.9	0.9	0.7
4. Mate	44.7	0.0	0.0	0.9	11.0
5. SHG/women group/association	0.0	2.7	0.0	0.9	0.9
6. GP head/ward member	46.6	70.0	75.5	38.5	57.7
7. Panchayat secretary/Rozgar sevak	2.9	12.7	13.2	14.7	11.0
8. Others	0.0	10.0	0.0	33.9	11.2

Source: Survey.

also because of better institutionalisation and functioning of PRIs in both the states, and greater social mobilisation in Rajasthan. It seems that women's participation in the gram sabha has been increasing. In another study of six north Indian states in 2008, only 33 per cent of male and female workers had attended the gram sabha meeting (Khera and Nayak, 2009: 56). It also seems that the holding of gram sabha meeting itself has become a more regular phenomenon post MGNREGS.

A large number of women also said that they spoke in the gram sabhas (Table 12.12). Seventy-three per cent of women who had attended the gram sabha, spoke in the meeting. The percentage of women who spoke in the meeting was once again the highest in Kangra (85 per cent), followed by Dungarpur (79 per cent), Ranchi (54 per cent) and Gaya (13 per cent). However, it was revealed that women speak mainly about the availability of job, wage payment and other related issues of personal interests, not of community interests like the selection of work, social monitoring, etc.

More women (MGNREGS workers) now also meet and interact with government officials and PRI representatives. Forty-six per cent of them had the chance to interact with government officials, with the percentage of women interacting with officials being the highest in Kangra (97 per cent), followed

Table 12.12: Women Workers' Participation in the Gram Sabha

Districts	*Percentage of Women Attending Gram Sabha*	*Percentage of Women Speaking in Gram Sabha*	*Percentage of Women Interacting with Officials*
Dungarpur	55.3	78.9	76.7
Gaya	13.6	13.3	5.5
Kangra	88.7	85.1	97.2
Ranchi	25.7	53.6	10.1
Total	**45.3**	**73.2**	**46.5**

Source: Survey.

by Dungarpur (77 per cent), Ranchi (10 per cent) and Gaya (5.5 per cent). This has larger effects in terms of increase in their confidence levels.

Before MGNREGS, only 16 per cent of women workers' households had an account in a bank or post office (Table 12.13). The figure was dismally low in Dungarpur (3.9 per cent) and no better in other places (Kangra, 19 per cent; Gaya, 17 per cent and Ranchi, 25 per cent). Now, 73 per cent of these households have access to bank or a post office account. The access had increased to 100 per cent in Dungarpur and Kangra. Moreover, pre-MGNREGS accounts were mostly in the name of male members. Now, 72 per cent of the women workers in Kangra, 33 per cent in Ranchi, 24 per cent in Dungarpur and 12.7 per cent even in Gaya have accounts in their own names. Since the government has instructed for account payment of MGNREGS wages, it is likely to be universalised in other places as well.

Table 12.13: Access to Bank/Post Office Account (Pre- and Post-MGNREGS in per cent)

Districts	*Pre-MGNREGS Household Access*	*Post-MGNREGS Household Access*	*Post-MGNREGS Individual Account of Women Workers*
Dungarpur	3.9	100.0	24.3
Gaya	17.4	41.8	12.7
Kangra	18.9	100.0	72.6
Ranchi	25.3	78.2	33.0
Total	**16.0**	**72.8**	**35.5**

Source: Survey.

Access to account payment of wages also creates some other effects. Apart from increasing the chance of greater control over earnings, it leads to development of the saving habit. Initially, most of these workers used to withdraw their entire wages at one go. Gradually, they have started withdrawing as per their needs. This has an added advantage as women are able to save money from wasteful expenditure, if husbands or other male members tend to spend on items like liquor. Women were also found investing in fixed deposit schemes in the same bank. Greater linkage of women with financial institutions may trigger many individual- and community-level social and economic effects (Kabeer, 2001b; Mayoux, 2001; Pit, Khandker and Cartwright, 2006; Mayoux and Hartl, 2009).

Male–female Wage Equality under MGNREGS: The practice of discriminatory wages in case of casual workers is found both in rural and urban areas. In 2004–05, the all-India average daily wage of a casual rural worker was 55.03 ₹ for male and 34.94 ₹ for female—a difference of about 20 ₹ (Karan and Selviraj, 2008: 43). In other words, the average daily wage of a female casual worker was only 63 per cent of that of a male worker. The difference was much higher in some states. There was a difference of 69.11 ₹ in Kerala, the highest among all the states.

Ensuring equal wages for male and female workers in the informal sector remains a major issue and challenge of gender equality. The MGNREGS has achieved it in some places and to some extent. In our survey, only in one out of 13 worksites, male and female workers were paid different wages. Group measurement system, social mobilisations including social audits, absence of contractors and the practice of daily wage system have helped in realising equal wages.

But payment of minimum wages through SOR still remains a challenge. Except HP, in all the three states, the actual wage of a woman worker was less than the prescribed minimum, even though it was quite high compared with the prevailing rural wage for female casual workers. The difference between prevailing market, actual and minimum wages under the MGNREGS are shown in Table 12.14.

Table 12.14: Difference between Market, Actual and MGNREGS Minimum Wages

Districts	*Average Earning of a Woman Worker (per day in ₹)*	*Minimum Wages Under MGNREGS (per day in ₹)#*	*District-wise Average Rural Wage of Casual Worker 2004–05 (per day in ₹)*
Dungarpur	81	100	52.06*
Gaya	65	89	36.17**
Kangra	100	100	
Ranchi	83	92	50.21***

Sources: * IHD and UNWFP (2010): 55.
** IHD and UNWFP (2009): 53.
*** IHD and UNWFP (2008): 45.
Note: # This was the prescribed minimum wage for unskilled workers at the time of the survey.

Realisation of equal wages under the MGNREGS has significant implications for the rural labour market.[13] If women are able to earn higher wages under the MGNREGS, there is a likelihood that in most cases, they would not be willing/available to work for less than what they are getting under the MGNREGS. The reduction in the supply of women labour force, because of their joining the MGNREGS, would create supply-side pressure on labour market that would push the wage floor. It was observed that many tea gardens in Kangra were finding it difficult to hire workers on the basis of their pre-MGNREGS wages. They had to increase the wages, and frequently this upward revision had to be done with consideration to MGNREGS wages. Some of these gardens were on the verge of closure, as they were finding it difficult to operate at profit with increased wage cost.

Changes in gender relations: Subtle changes in gender relations have been observed, but mostly at the household level. Increased say of women in decision making, greater recognition of their contribution to the household's income and reduced dependence on male members for meeting expenditure related to personal needs are some of those changes.

Because of weak participation in the process, larger community-level effects yet remain to be realised. Even in the case of the increased presence of women at the gram sabha, male members dominate the decision-making process. Entrenched gender relations are hard to fall: while we were interviewing women workers in Dungarpur, they refused to sit side by side on the cot in the presence of male members, as social norms prohibited them to do so.

Nevertheless, the worksite experiences were enriching. The introduction of the female mate system has allowed women to reverse the role of a male mate/supervisor. For male workers, working under a female mate is a new experience. This may not change the character of gender relations immediately, but will have a definite impact in the long run. Moreover, female mates were found to be more sensitive to the needs and requirements of women.

Working together gives women an opportunity to share grievances and personal problems and helps in the development of women's solidarity. Women were observed to be exchanging help, for example, borrowing money and bartering goods among themselves for which they were earlier dependent on other people. Some old and physically weak women were found to be working on the sites. In spite of group measurement system, nobody was complaining that these women were receiving the same wages, although their productivity was less. Rather, the group was considerate towards their old age and physical ability, and offered them easy and less strenuous tasks. In turn, some of the widows working at MGNREGS worksites said that coming out and working gave them a sense of purpose and belonging, rather than having to sit at home and getting bored.

Difficulties and Obstacles for Women Workers

However, MGNREGS benefits have not come easily—working hours for women have increased; their leisure time has vanished and they have to bear with physical and emotional strain. Women in Dungarpur told us that they get up quite early to fetch water, prepare food and make arrangements for the children before going to the worksite. Even during the official lunch break, some of them return home to take care of the children and other family members. Wage payment is linked to a task-based schedule of rate and since the SOR is prepared based on the average output of a healthy, invariably male worker, women have to work very hard to earn minimum wages. This is much more difficult for old, physically weak and lactating women. In the absence of (proper) crèche facilities, lactating women and women with young children leave their children at home while working at the worksite. Only 28 per cent of the women having children under the age of five brought them to the worksite; 62 per cent left their

Figure 12.2: The Status of Facilities at 13 Surveyed Worksites

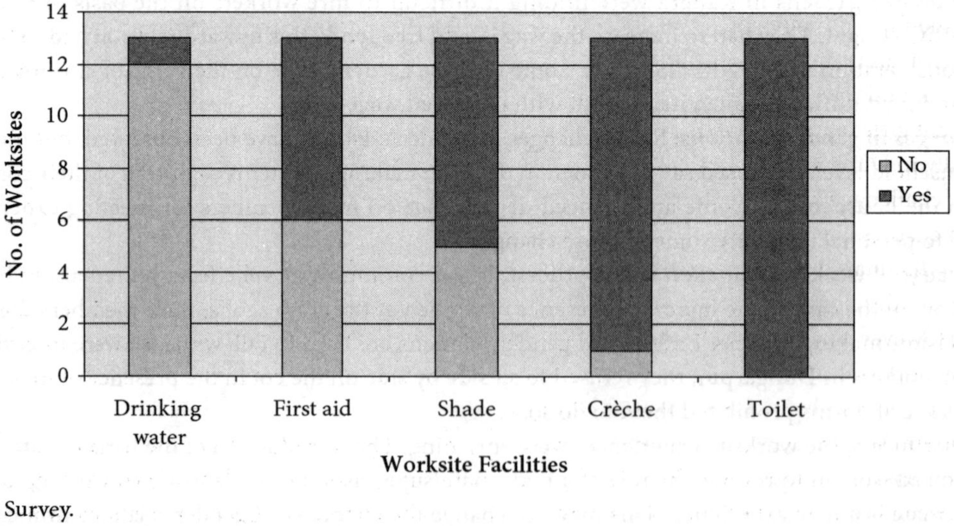

Source: Survey.
Note: The provision of attending toilets in privacy is not part of the official provision, although its necessity was emphasised by women workers.

children in the care of siblings/elders and another 10 per cent of women left their children without proper care. Since they have to remain away from home for a minimum of eight hours at the MGNREG worksite, they remain anxious about the well-being of their children. Eighty-one per cent confessed that they remain emotionally strained while they are working at the worksite and their children are left at home, either unattended or in another's care. There are also some reports of continued presence of contractors and harassment of women workers. Khera and Nayak in their 2008 study found that at worksites where contractors were present, 35 per cent of women reported various types of harassment. Also, worksite facilities were negligible on those worksites (Khera and Nayak, 2009: 54).

VI

Conclusion and Prospects

Empowerment of rural women has emerged as an unintended consequence of MGNREGS. Women have benefited more as workers than as a community. Women as individuals have gained because of their ability to earn independently, made possible due to the paid employment opportunity under the MGNREGS. Independent and monetised earning have increased consumption choices and reduced economic dependence. This has helped women in registering their tangible contribution to the household's income. The overall effects of the above have translated as increased say of women in household affairs (Figure 12.2).

Women as a community, however, have been slow in realising the potential benefits of the scheme. Nevertheless, their increased presence in the gram sabha; increasing number of women speaking out in the gram sabha; frequent interactions with the government officials and PRI representatives and access to bank and post offices are new developments. Additionally, the female mate system has reversed the traditional gender roles—of course, in a limited manner.

On the flip side, working hours for women have increased; the leisure time has vanished and there are physical and emotional strains related to such work. Lactating women and women with young children work under emotional strain, as they remain separated from their children for long hours. Some adolescent girls reported to have left their studies to avail of the job opportunity under the MGNREGS, especially in Dungarpur.

The challenges lie in horizontal and vertical expansion of benefits first. The high participation of women ensures horizontal spread of benefits, and realisation of greater number of person-days ensures better individual-level effects. Districts with high SC and ST population and states with high human and gender development indices and greater level of state and civil society mobilisation have benefited more. However, women, other than from the SCs, STs and OBCs, are not forthcoming in availing this paid job opportunity.

Apart from implementation issues, there are social and cultural contexts that restrict women's participation in some places. Persistent social and community mobilisation and proactive role of the state can compensate for some of these social and cultural deficits. This will also be helpful in bridging the gap between 'work participation' and 'process participation'.

Certain initiatives and changes can also prove helpful. Realisation of sufficient number of person-days to earn a critical minimum income that triggers household-level effects is the first condition.

Timely payment of wages through individual account of women workers encourages participation and greater control over earnings. Daily wage system instead of wages as per SOR has been helpful in realising minimum wages. The experience of HP is proof of this and the act does not prohibit it. Alternatively, gender-sensitive SOR, as has been introduced in Bihar,[14] can be experimented in other states as well. Working conditions need to be made more conducive by enforcing and strengthening of the existing provisions and adding new ones. For example, breastfeeding breaks for lactating women and flexibility in working hours may be considered. Crèche provision may be linked with the Anganwadi (ICDS) centres, panchayat bhavans, local school buildings, etc., to make it more practical for working purpose. Among others, maternity relief for women, along the lines of MEGS, makeshift toilets at the worksite and innovations in work instruments, so as to reduce work drudgery, may be adopted.

Increased participation in procedural aspects and greater control over the types and management of assets would increase larger social and community benefits. The Kerala model of linking MGNREGS with women's groups (Kudumbashree) may be useful for greater process participation. A minimum representation of women among the MGNREGS functionaries like programme officers, rozgar sevaks, ombudsmen, members of vigilance and monitoring committees, mates, etc., would be useful. Some of the assets created, if properly chosen, may reduce the load of unpaid work like fetching water, fodder, etc. Creation of skill-generating assets like horticulture or fisheries through ponds can also be further explored to ensure better lateral benefits from such assets.

Acknowledgements

This chapter was published in *Economic & Political Weekly*, July 24, 2010 XLV, No. 30. The authors thank *Economic and Political Weekly* for allowing them to include this chapter in this volume. This chapter is part of a two-phase study 'Women's Empowerment through Paid Employment', sponsored by the United Nations Development Fund for Women (UNIFEM now UNWomen).

Notes

1. There are three distinctively identified but overlapping perspectives of women's development. These are Women in Development–Women and Development–Gender and Development (WID–WAD–GAD). In fact, they have evolved in phases and in a chronological sequence. See, Boserup (1980), Rathgeber (1989), Moser (1993), Razavi and Miller (1995).
2. Because of little demand for wage employment in the developed states of Punjab and Haryana, their selection was ruled out ab initio. UP is a large state with at least four cultural–economic zones. One district sample is too small for a state such as UP and, hence, it was not included. However, in the second phase, the study included one district each from U.P., Karnataka, Andhra Pradesh and Maharashtra.
3. *Sarna* claim and insist on separate religious category and are offended when they are categorised as Hindus.
4. OBC can further be classified into OBC-I and OBC-II. OBC-I refers to lower OBC and OBC-II refers to upper OBC. This classification is applicable only in a few states. For example in Bihar, upper OBCs include Yadav, Koeri, Kurmi and others, and lower OBCs include Kevat, Mallah, Kahar, Mehtar, Nai and others.
5. Kudumbashree refers to a state poverty-eradication mission set up by the Kerala government. It is organised as neighbourhood groups of 15–40 households, and each household is represented by a woman member. In terms of organisation, it comprises (*a*) area development society (ADS) at the ward level and (*b*) community

development society (CDS) at the panchayat level. Synergisation of the MGNREGS implementation with Kudumbshree has increased women's participation in Kerala.

6. There is no conclusive evidence to show that the new gender differential SOR has improved women's participation in Bihar. Nevertheless, the share of women in total person-days has increased in the state.
7. Sainath illustrates the case of Ananthapura district of Andhra Pradesh where the work was allotted to groups of 2–3 families to get high output and productivity. This led to the exclusion of single, widowed and separated women. See, Sainath (2007). Bhatty finds exclusion of single women in Jhalawar district of Rajasthan. See, Bhatty (2008).
8. STs constitute only 1 per cent of the total state population after separation of Jharkhand.
9. Every alternative year is a drought year. While we were in the field, drought-relief works were in progress, and households that had already exhausted 100 days under the MGNREGS were given additional employment under relief work.
10. Because of the adoption of daily wage system in HP, everybody was getting minimum wages.
11. For their detailed socio-economic conditions, see the main study by Pankaj and Tankha (2009).
12. SNA activities refer to primary production activities such as crop farming, kitchen gardening, etc.; animal husbandry, fishing, forestry, horticulture, collection of fruit, water, plants, etc.; storing and hunting, processing and storage, mining, quarrying, digging, cutting, etc., and also secondary activities such as construction, manufacturing, trade, business and services. Extended SNA activities include household maintenance; management and shopping for own household; care for children, the sick, elderly and disabled for own household and community services and help to other households.
13. Ratna Sudarshan has examined rural labour market conditions in Palakkad district of Kerala and found that differential wages existed for men and women in non-formal agriculture and non-agriculture sectors. A women worker in Palakkad district earned about ₹70 upwards per day while a male worker earned about ₹150 upwards per day. In contrast to this, the MGNREGS provided equal wages for both male and female workers (₹125). See Sudarshan (2008).
14. For earning the same minimum wages in Bihar, a male worker has to work 80 cft in case of soft soil, 77 cft in case of semi-hard soil and 73 cft in case of hard soil. However, in order to earn the same minimum wages, women workers have to work 68 cft in case of soft soil, 63 cft in case of semi-hard soil and 60 cft in case of hard soil.

References

Acharya, Sarthi (1990) *The Maharashtra Employment Guarantee Scheme: A study of labour market intervention*. Working Paper, ILO, Asian Regional Team for Employment Promotion, Delhi.

Agarwal, Bina (1994) *A field of one's own: Gender and land rights in South* Asia. Cambridge: Cambridge University Press.

Becker, Gary S. (1981) *A treatise on the family*. Cambridge: Harvard University Press.

Bhatty, Kiran (2006) Employment guarantee and child rights. *Economic and Political Weekly* 41, No. 20: 1965–67.

——— (2008) Falling through the cracks. *The Hindu*, 16 March.

Boserup, Ester (1980) *Women's role in economic development*. New York: St. Martin's Press.

Central Statistical Organisation (2007) *Women and men in India 2007*, XI Issue, Central Statistical Organisation, Ministry of Statistics and Programme Implementation, Government of India.

Folbre, Nancy (1986) Hearts and spades: Paradigms of household economics. *World Development* 14, No. 2: 245–55.

——— (2009) How should we value unpaid work—theory, methodology and estimates, lecture delivered on 16 December, New Delhi, organised by the Institute of Economic Growth.

Ministry of Women and Child Development et al. (2009) Gendering Human Development Indices: Recasting the Gender Development Index and Gender Empowerment Measures for India. Delhi: Ministry of Women and Child Development, IIPA and UNDP.

Hirway, Indira and M. R. Saluja (2009) Engendering public works programme by addressing unpaid work of women in developing countries case study in India. Paper presentation at National Workshop on NREGA and Women's Empowerment, 31 August 2009, in New Delhi.

IHD and UN World Food Programme (2008) *Food security atlas of rural Jharkhand*. New Delhi: Institute for Human Development.

——— (2009) *Food security atlas of rural Bihar*. New Delhi: Institute for Human Development.

——— and UN World Food Programme (2010) *Food security atlas of rural Rajasthan*. Delhi: Institute for Human Development.

Kabeer, Naila (2001a) Reflections on the measurement of women's empowerment. In *Discussing women's empowerment—theory and practice*, SIDA Studies No.3, Swedish International Development Cooperation Agency.

——— (2001b): Conflict over credit: Re-evaluating the empowerment potential of loans to women in rural Bangladesh. *World Development* 29, No. 1: 63–84.

Karan, Anup K. and Sakthivel Selviraj (2008) *Trends in wages and earnings in India: Increasing wage differentials in a segmented labour market*, ILO Asia-Pacific Working Paper Series, ILO Subregional Office for South Asia, New Delhi.

Khera, Reetika (2008) Group measurement of NREGA work: The Jalore experiment. Paper presented at international conference on NREGS in India: Impacts and Implementation Experiences, 16–17 September, in New Delhi.

Khera, Reetika and Nandini Nayak (2009) Women workers and perceptions of the National Rural Employment Guarantee Act. *Economic and Political Weekly* 44, No. 43: 49–57.

Krishnaraj, Maithreyi, Divya Pandey and Aruna Kanchi (2004) Does EGS require restructuring for poverty alleviation and gender equality? II—Gender concerns and issues for restructuring. *Economic and Political Weekly* 39, No. 17: 1741–47.

Luttrell, Cecilia and Sitna Quiroz, with Claire Scrutton and Kate Bird (2009) Understanding and operationalising empowerment. Working Paper 308, Overseas Development Institute, London.

Mayoux, Linda (2001) Tackling the downside: Social capital, women's empowerment and micro-finance in Cameroon. *Development and Change* 32, No. 3: 435–65.

Mayoux, Linda and Maria Hartl (2009) *Gender and rural microfinance: Reaching and empowering women*. Rome: International Fund for Agricultural Development.

Mehrotra, Santosh (2008) NREG two years on: Where do we go from here? *Economic and Political Weekly* 43, No. 31: 27–35.

Ministry of Health and Family Welfare (2007) *National family health survey III (2005-06)*. Mumbai: International Institute for Population Sciences, Mumbai.

Molyneux, Maxine (1985) Mobilisation without emancipation: Women's interests, state and revolution in Nicaragua. *Feminist Studies* 2, No. 2: 227–54.

Moser, Caroline (1993) *Gender planning and development—theory, practice and training*. London: Routledge.

Narayanan, Sudha (2008) Employment guarantee, women's work and childcare. *Economic and Political Weekly* 43, No. 9: 10–13.

Pankaj, Ashok K. (2008a) *Processes, institutions and mechanisms of implementation of NREGA: Impact assessment of Bihar and Jharkhand*. Delhi: Institute for Human Development.

——— (2008b) Meeting social deficits through legislation: Bihar Panchayat Raj Act 2006. *Journal of Social Sciences* 10, No. 2: 273–84.

Pankaj, Ashok K. and M. P. Singh (2004) The changing socio-political profiles of local political elites (mukhias) of Bihar: A study of the 1978 and 2001 panchayat elections. *Contributions to Indian Sociology* 39, No. 3: 407–28.

Pankaj, Ashok K. and Rukmini Tankha (2009) *Women's empowerment through guaranteed employment*. Delhi: Institute for Human Development.

Pit Mark M., Shahidur R. Khandker, Jennifer Cartwright (2006) Empowering women with micro-finance: Evidence from Bangladesh. *Economic Development and Cultural Change* 54, No. 4: 791–831.

Raja, Annie (2007) Ensuring the right to work for women: A review of NREGA from the gender perspective. In *Gender and governance—reviewing the women's agenda in the National Common Minimum Programme*. Delhi: Wada Na Todo Abhiyan.

Rathgeber, Eva M. (1989) *WID, WAD, GAD: Trends in research and practice*. Ottawa: International Development Research Centre.

Razavi, Shahrashoub and Carol Miller (1995) *From WID to GAD: Conceptual shifts in the women and development discourse*. Geneva: United Nations Research Institute for Social Development.

Sainath, P. (2007) No place for single women. *The Hindu*, 28 May.

Sen, Amartya K. (1990) Gender and co-operative conflict. In *Persistent inequalities*, ed. Irene Tinker. Oxford: Oxford University Press.

——— (1996) Gender inequality and theories of justice. In *Women, culture, and development—a study of human capabilities*, ed. Martha C. Nussbaum and Jonathan Glover. New York: Oxford University Press.

Sudarshan, Ratna (2008) Impact of NREGA on rural labour market in Kerala: Preliminary findings on women's work. Presentation made at international conference on NREGS in India: Impacts and Implementation Experiences, 16–17 September, in New Delhi.

Talukdar, Ratna Bharali (2008) NREGA shines for Tripura women. *India Together*, 30 June. http://www.indiatogether.org/2008/jun/wom-nrega.htm.

Vijayakumar, B. and S. N Thomas (2008) Governance, institutions and National Rural Employment Guarantee Scheme. Paper presented at international conference on NREGS in India: Impacts and Implementation Experiences, 16–17 September, in New Delhi.

Zila Panchayat, Bastar. Chhattisgarh Rural Employment Guarantee Scheme—Land Development of BPL/SC/ST Households' Land by SHGs and Jatropha Plantation Handover to SHGs, http://nrega.nic.in/Attachments/Jagdalpur.pdf (accessed on 10 April 2010).

SECTION V

Prospects

13

Overcoming the Governance Challenges of Implementing MGNREGA?

Insight from Bihar Using Process-Influence-Mapping

Katharina Raabe, Regina Birner, Madhushree Sekher, K. G. Gayathridevi, Amrita Shilpi and Eva Schiffer

I

Introduction

In 2005, India's Parliament passed the MGNREGA, which is the central government's response to the constitutionally manifested right to work and a means to promote livelihood security in India's rural areas. To this end, the act guarantees 100 days of annual employment at statutory minimum wage rates to any rural household whose adult members are willing to do unskilled manual work. The manual work needs to create sustainable assets, which promote the economic and infrastructure development of villages.[1] Being implemented in three phases as of 2006, the act extended to all of rural India in April 2008. MGNREGA is an innovative answer to the long-standing problem of providing social safety nets in rural areas. Most important, it is a rights-based approach. In the words of social activist Aruna Roy (2009, quoted in UNDP, 2009), the MGNREGA exemplifies the features of a 'mature democracy', which provides 'the poor with the right to demand, the right to know and the right to dignity. Not the right to beg.'

There are two types of governance challenges that make the large-scale implementation of social safety nets in rural areas, such as those implemented under the MGNREGA, inherently difficult: (*a*) the challenge to avoid elite capture and to actually reach the poor and the disadvantaged, and (*b*) the challenge to manage the funds allocated to the programme effectively and to avoid leakages and corruption. As a public works programme, the MGNREGA uses a self-targeting mechanism to meet the first challenge. In fact, the programme has been remarkably successful in this regard. More than half of its beneficiaries belong to SC and ST, and more than half are women.[2]

The second challenge is more difficult to meet because the MGNREGA involves two features that have been highlighted in the literature as particularly challenging. First, the programme is 'transaction-intensive' in terms of time and space: It requires day-to-day action throughout a country that spans an entire subcontinent. Second, the programme requires discretion, since decision making on issues such as the type of infrastructure to be created under the programme cannot easily be standardised. As Pritchett and Woolcock (2004) have shown, there are no simple administrative solutions to the problem of managing programmes that are at the same time transaction intensive and discretionary.

Informed by India's far-ranging experience in managing rural welfare programmes, MGNREGA has already gone a long way in including innovative design features that aim at overcoming the well-known implementation challenges of such programmes. As further discussed below, MGNREGA is implemented in a decentralised manner and includes substantial checks and balances as well as oversight and complaint mechanisms. Yet, available evidence indicates that massive implementation problems remain (see section three). At the same time, there are constant efforts to adjust the implementation procedures to resolve these challenges. This contribution aims to support these efforts by analysing the administrative implementation procedures of the MGNREGA.

The chapter is based on the recognition that 'the devil is in the detail' when it comes to the implementation of programmes such as the MGNREGA. These details are often overlooked or treated as a 'black box' in the literature on programme implementation, yet their understanding is crucial to be able to find out how the governance challenges of programme implementation can be met. In particular, it is essential to identify how the actual process of programme implementation differs from what is foreseen in the implementation guidelines, and to identify where exactly the opportunities for leakage and mismanagement arise. Likewise, it is crucial to find out how much influence different actors have on the implementation process, and how local power structures and informal bureaucratic processes affect programme implementation.

This chapter uses a new research method, referred to as Process-Influence-Mapping, to throw light on these questions. The Process-Influence-Mapping is a participatory mapping technique, which is based on the Net-Map tool (Schiffer and Waale, 2008).[3] It combines elements of various tools that have been developed to analyse stakeholder interaction and political processes (World Bank, 2007). The technique can be used in interviews with individuals or groups and involves three main steps: (*a*) mapping all stakeholders or actors involved in a particular process, (*b*) drawing a flow chart of the different steps involved in the process and (*c*) ranking the influence of different actors on the process by using checkers game or carom board pieces for visualisation. The result is a three-dimensional map, which serves as a basis for further discussions with the interviewees. The maps can then also be used to identify problems in the implementation process, and to identify entry points for overcoming these problems.

This chapter presents the results from a case study, in which Process-Influence-Mapping was applied in two districts in Bihar to analyse the implementation of the MGNREGA. The case study was conducted jointly by researchers from the International Food Policy Research Institute, the Institute for Social and Economic Change, and the Tata Institute of Social Sciences. The study was carried out in the first district in April 2008 and the second district in January 2009. The time difference made it possible to gain some insights into the challenges in implementation of a change in the administrative structure of the MGNREGA project that involved the payment of wages through banks and post offices. The remainder of this chapter is structured as follows. Section two presents the guidelines for the administrative processes through which the MGNREGA is supposed to be implemented and section three reviews the existing literature about the MGNREGA implementation and its challenges. Section four describes the Process-Influence-Mapping tool in more detail, explains the selection of the case study location and reports the major insights regarding the governance challenges of MGNREGA implementation that have been derived from the Process-Influence-Mapping exercise. Section five uses the Process-Influence Maps to derive possible strategies for strengthening the effectiveness of the MGNREGA implementation process.

II

MGNREGA Implementation in Theory[4]

The implementation of the MGNREGA involves institutions at the centre and state level, and at all panchayat levels. The most important agency at the centre is the Ministry of Rural Development and the ministry-founded Central Employment Guarantee Council (CEGC). The ministry is responsible for ensuring the adequate and timely delivery of resources to the states and for reviewing, monitoring and evaluating the use of the resources, as well as the MGNREGA processes and outcomes. The CEGC advises the Central Government on MGNREGA-related matters and monitors and evaluates the implementation of the act. The council is mandated to prepare annual reports on the implementation of the MGNREGA and submits these to the parliament.

The pivotal institution at the state level is the state government which has to formulate a Rural Employment Guarantee Scheme (REGS) that conforms to the minimum features specified under the act. In addition, the state government has to constitute the State Employment Guarantee Council (SEGC), whose main responsibility is to advise the state government on MGNREGA-related matters and to monitor and evaluate the implementation of the act. Finally, the state government is responsible for ensuring the adequate and timely release of the state share of the REGS budget and facilitates the administrative, financial and technical support to all implementing bodies at the district, block and gram panchayat (GP) level (the three tiers of local government in India).

Since the MGNREGA foresees a decentralised implementation, the principal authorities for the implementation of the MGNREG schemes are the institutions at the district, block and GP levels. In order to provide employment in a timely and adequate manner, the panchayat institutions at all levels have to identify priority areas of employment-generating activities and propose, scrutinise and approve the respective REGS projects. At the district level, the identification of the REGS projects is guided by the five-year district perspective plan (DPP), which specifies the long-term employment generation and development perspectives of the district. In addition to the long-term plan, the panchayats at all levels also have to identify the activities to be taken up on priority in a year. At the GP level, these priority areas are decided during gram sabha and ward sabha meetings. Based on the recommendations formulated in the gram sabha and ward sabha, the GP prepares an annual plan and forwards it to the MGNREGA block programme officer (BPO) for technical sanction/approval.

The PO scrutinises the annual plans of the individual GPs for technical feasibility and submits a consolidated statement of approved proposals at the block level to the block (or intermediate) panchayat. The block panchayat discusses and approves the plan and forwards it to the district programme coordinator. The coordinator scrutinises the plan proposals of all block panchayats, and consolidates them into a district plan proposal with a block-wise shelf of projects (arranged by GP). For each project, the district plan indicates (*a*) the time frame, (*b*) the person-days of labour to be generated and (*c*) the full cost. This plan is discussed and approved by the district panchayat with the assistance of technical resource support groups. The latter group is asked to assess the technical feasibility and cost efficiency of works and to monitor and evaluate work implementation. Ultimately, the technical resource support groups help to define plans that can meet the demand for employment within 15 days of application. Following the approval of the development plans through the district panchayat, the GP has to execute at least 50 per cent of the works as well as monitor and audit the implementation of the REGS at the GP level. The responsibility for these activities at the GP rests with the Gram Rozgar Sevak, that is, the employment guarantee assistant. Considering the remaining 50 per cent of the development works, 30 per cent thereof can be executed by the block panchayat and 20 per cent can be realised through the zilla panchayat. Block- and district-level activities are expected to cover more than one GP and block panchayat, respectively. Examples are roads that connect several gram or block panchayats.

In addition to defining and implementing an annual work plan that identifies the activities to be taken up on priority in a year, the GPs are also responsible for verifying the households' registration for MGNREGA employment, for registering households for job cards, issuing and distributing job cards, allocating employment, initiating MGNREGA-related works, measuring and evaluating the completed work and remunerating the MGNREGA wage workers. The GPs are required to issue job cards free of cost within 14 days after the application for registration is filed in the presence of the local community (see GoI, 2008). Being valid for a period of five years, the job cards are required to carry the photograph of the adult members.

Following the issue of job cards, rural households have a right to seek employment from the GP or the MGNREGA PO after the state REGS is passed. Once the request for employment is submitted in writing to the GP or the PO, stating the registration number of the job card, the date from which employment is required, and the number of days of employment required, work is to be provided within a radius of 5 km of the village and within 15 days of the date of demand. If the state fails to provide work within the mandated period for whatever reason, the applicant is entitled to an unemployment allowance at prefixed rates, paid by the state government. If work cannot be provided within a radius of 5 km of the village, the rural workers are entitled to a markup which equals 10 per cent of their wages.

People who take up employment under the MGNREGA are entitled to receive wages between 7 to 15 days after the date on which the work was executed for a period of at least 14 days. The wage rate has to be at least as high as the minimum wage rate set by the centre or the state according to the Minimum Wages Act 1948 for agricultural labourers, and needs to be paid according to a piece rate or daily rate and disbursed on a weekly or fortnightly basis. The minimum wage should not be less than ₹60 per day and be the same for men and women (see GoI, 2008). Besides setting minimum wages, the MGNREGA also promotes livelihood security in rural areas by mandating a wage–material ratio of 60:40. To this end, the act bans the use of machinery as well as contractors. The latter are perceived to exploit unskilled worker and to use capital-intensive rather than labour-intensive production techniques.

In terms of funding, the MGNREGA activities are financed with funds from the central as well as the state government. The central government releases funds directly to the districts through the National Employment Guarantee Fund. The funds cover 75 per cent of the MGNREGA-related material and wage expenses of the semi-skilled and skilled workers. The central government is required to fund 100 per cent of the wage costs of the unskilled workers. The state government is mandated to provide the funds for the remaining 25 per cent expenses as well as the funds for the unemployment allowance payments and the administrative expenses of the State Employment Guarantee Council. To this end, the state government releases revolving funds under the REGS to the implementing agencies at the district, block and GP levels. At all levels, the implementation of the REGS is facilitated by line departments, NGOs, central and state government undertakings and SHGs.

III

MGNREGA in Reality—Insights from the Literature

As the MGNREGA was introduced in phases as of 2006, assessments regarding the procedural challenges of MGNREGS implementation predominantly prevail for the phase-one districts (2006–07). The present review mainly emphasises the performance assessment results of the 2008 comptroller and auditor general (CAG) social audit and the 2007 Poorest Area Civil Society (PACS) Programme-CSO survey (hereafter PACS-CSO).[5] The CAG evaluated the implementation of the National Rural Employment Act in 558 GPs and 141 blocks in 68 of those 200 districts that had been covered during the first phase of the MGNREGA programme (that is, February 2006 to March 2007). The 68 districts belong to 26 States. In comparison, the PACS-CSO survey emphasises the experience of six states which had been subject to interventions under both the MGNREGA and DFID's Poorest Area Civil Society Program. Accounting for differences in the socio-economic and geographic conditions, primary data were collected for 283 GPs and 600 villages from different socio-cultural backgrounds in 39 districts of the six PACS-intervened states.[6] In Bihar, the survey covered 8 districts, 50 GPs and 172 villages. The findings refer to the fiscal year 2006/2007.

Technical and Administrative Implementation

Under the MGNREGA, the maintenance and computerisation of records is an important approach for promoting accountability and transparency in the generation of guaranteed employment. Accountability and transparency are promoted through computerisation because records help to (*a*) authenticate the number of households that demanded and received employment, (*c*) substantiate the caste and gender distribution of MGNREGA employment, (*c*) identify the number of days of employment provided and (*d*) locate any discrepancies between the number of workdays demanded and provided.[7] In reality, the CAG audit report identifies pronounced deficiencies in the preparation and/or maintenance of all types of records at all panchayat levels. Major deficiencies concern the improper and untimely maintenance of the employment register, the application registration register, the job card register, the asset register, the muster roll receipt register or the complaint register.

For instance, the employment register in many GPs was not maintained or missed details on the type and duration of employment demanded, the employment allotted and the employment that was actually taken up. Muster rolls and the muster roll register did not carry the required unique identification numbers and did not furnish information on (*a*) the name of the person on work, (*b*) the respective job card number, (*c*) the work order number, (*d*) the number of days worked and (*e*) the wages paid. Due to these deficiencies, wages had been paid to unregistered and fictitious workers and to workers whose names had been recorded twice or thrice for the same time period, resulting in overpayment. In addition, the GPs did not keep photocopies of the muster rolls for public inspection and the BPO typically did not digitise the muster rolls (CAG, 2008: 51 and section 8.8.1).

One important reason for the absence of adequate registers is the absence of a sufficiently large number of trained support staff, especially at the level of the block and the GP. At the GP level, manpower constraints predominantly concern the absence of the gram rozgar sevak. As the gram rozgar sevak is instrumental for the maintenance of the MGNREGA-related records at the GP level, the absence of this agent limits access to basic information such as employment demand and employment allocation. This, in turn, causes employment generation under the MGNREGA to be a non-transparent and unaccountable process, which offers substantial scope for fraud and the misappropriation of funds. Unfortunately, the CAG and PACS-CSO reports do not assess or discuss the relative importance of the underlying incentive problems. Furthermore, potential beneficiaries of the REGSes do not have a contact at the local level who can easily be contacted for employment, let alone for local proximity.

At the block level, the CAG criticises the absence of a (full-time) BPO. In many instances, regional employment guarantee schemes are processed, approved, evaluated and monitored by the BDO. As the BDO is responsible for a large number of development programmes, he cannot pay adequate attention to the needs of the MGNREGA-related employment guarantee schemes. In addition, the block level suffers from chronic shortages of technical support staff and is, thus, short of people who assist in the planning, design and estimation of MGNREGA works and screen project proposals for their technical feasibility and cost-efficiency. In fact, most blocks implemented MGNREGA works through the same administrative and technical channels as other development programmes. With the same number of people implementing a larger number of programs, the BDO and the block-level staff lack the support infrastructure that would be needed for the adequate implementation of the provisions of the MGNREGA. This effect is further compounded by the absence of rules that specify the time for processing and approving proposals at different levels.

As regards the capacity of the administrative and technical staff, the PACS-CSO report emphasises the need for capacity-strengthening activities, especially at the panchayat level. Capacity strengthening should aim at improving the knowledge and skills of elected representatives to keep and maintain accounts and books, muster rolls; to measure the volume and quality of work and to conduct social audits (PACS-CSO, 2007: 46). The current level of capacity-strengthening support is considered to leave panchayat officials unable to deal with complex administrative and technical tasks. Outsourcing technical and administrative tasks to private resource persons in response to manpower constraints is unlikely to promote the effective implementation of MGNREGA activities unless they are qualified and accountable to the PRIs (see also Shah, 2008).

Plan Preparation and Work Execution

The CAG audit report notes that annual plans were not at all or inadequately prepared or checked at the district and GP levels. At the district level, the district programme coordinator often did not consolidate the plan proposals of the block panchayats into a district plan proposal with a block-wise shelf of projects. If a district plan existed, it frequently did not specify the time frame during which the projects should be carried out; did not indicate the *person-days* to be generated for each project or did not specify the full cost for each project. Furthermore, the district plans frequently promoted projects which were not evaluated in terms of their technical feasibility. Counter to the prediction of the act, the district plans also did not ensure that 50 per cent of the works were executed by the GPs (CAG: 17–18).

At the GP level, the CAG report and PACS-CSO report note that GPs frequently did not identify the low-wage areas of employment and the priority areas of GP work according to the principles of transparency and accountability. At the core of the problem are (*a*) elected GP representatives who are unaware of the steps that need to be taken for defining and executing the annual plans, (*b*) unannounced and unpublicised gram sabha meetings and (*c*) low gram sabha participation rates. According to the CAG report, the low gram sabha participation rates reflect the unawareness of the rural poor regarding the provisions of the MGNREGA. The level of unawareness is pronounced as the GPs do not (*a*) organise gram sabha meetings which explain the provisions of the act, (*b*) invite applications for registration and (*c*) verify applications so as to ensure that all those who are entitled to work under MGNREGA can demand and ultimately receive employment. In view of these constraints, the annual plans were frequently prepared by external agencies or by the block- or district-level officials without the participation and consultation of rural households and/or the gram sabha.

Another problem in the implementation of projects relates to the requirement to get all planned activities technically and administratively sanctioned. According to the PACS-CSO survey, 50 per cent of the sampled GPs from six states received the technical approval of the MGNREGA work within 7 to 15 days and the administrative approval and the respective funds for project implementation within another 7 to 15 days. That is, MGNREGA-related work could start after a total of 15 to 30 days in 2006–07. In Bihar, only 40 per cent of the sampled GPs received the technical approval within 7 to 15 days, while 29 per cent of the GPs had to wait for 31 to 60 days and 13 per cent had to wait for more than 60 days. For the same sample, 45 per cent received funds within 7 to 15 days after the technical sanction, while 23 per cent and 21 per cent were funded after, respectively, 31 to 60 days and more than 60 days.

The PACS-CSO report documents that the speed at which projects are technically sanctioned depends on the payment of commissions to the block-level functionaries. GPs that paid commissions got projects approved in a shorter period of time. Similarly, GPs with a sufficient number of well-trained personnel received the technical and administrative approvals faster. Still, the delay in the release of funds suggests that thorough planning on the part of GPs is required to ensure the timely access to employment under the MGNREGA whenever need for employment arises. Besides thorough planning, another determinant for the successful generation of employment under the MGNREGA is the willingness of the GP secretaries and executive officers to pursue and support MGNREGA-related activities. If these agents lack commitment, Ambasta, Shankar and Shah (2008: 44) argue that they may take active measures to discourage even committed panchayati raj leaders from implementing the act. One reason is the fear to be held (financially) responsible for any violations of MGNREGA provisions and guidelines and for any delays in the implementation of the MGNREGA.

Resource Utilisation

Under the MGNREGA, three-fourths of the funds are to be provided by the centre and one-fourth by the states, as indicated above. In order to measure the success of the states in implementing the act, the PACS-CSO study determines the degree of resource utilisation. The assumption is that states which utilise more resources implement a larger number of low-wage projects, generate more employment and labour income and create more infrastructure.

Using the official MGNREGA data from the Ministry of Panchayati Raj, the PACS-CSO report shows that the average state in India utilised 73 per cent of the MGNREGA-related funds in 2006/07. Bihar used only 60 per cent. Funds, thus, do not appear to be a binding constraint under the MGNREGA. The underutilisation of funds could reflect the non-compliance with explicit funding guidelines that prevail at the level of the state, district, block and GP. For instance, the state is required to release funds within 15 days of the release of the central funds. In order to transfer and use the funds and to ensure transparency and accountability, the state government is required to design a complete financial management system. Under this system, separate bank accounts for MGNREGA-related funds need to be opened at the level of the district, block and GP. At the same time, accounts need to be squared on a monthly basis in order to track the use of the funds and to ensure financial accountability. The CAG report documents examples of states, districts, blocks and GPs that did not follow these and other guidelines. For example, the Government of Bihar experienced a cut in central funds in 2006–07 because it did not inform the Government of India about the funds that had been spent by the District Rural Development Agency (DRDA) of two districts (CAG: section 8.9.2.212.2.1).

Turning to the wage–material ratio, Indian states complied on the average with the requirement of the act and maintain a wage–material ratio in excess of 60:40.[8] In fact, on the average, states spent 66.20 per cent of all funds on wages during the fiscal year 2006/07 (PACS-CSO, 2007: Table 2.4). Although resource utilisation was quite low, the wage–material ratio suggests that the pursued projects were labour-intensive. Bihar belongs to the states with a comparatively low wage–material ratio (58.73 per cent). The CAG report attributes the low wage–material ratio to the material-intensive construction of brick soling roads and to the failure of the GP to identify low-wage projects (CAG: 18). The PACS-CSO survey emphasises that care needs to be exercised when interpreting this data, as block, district and GP functionaries lack the capacity to fill up formats or to upload data on the indicator variables of MGNREGA performance. Given this, states like Bihar may actually comply with the required ratio of 60:40, but are said to spend too little on wages as records are not well maintained and stored.

Entitlement Realisation of Workers

Although funds are not fully utilised, the prevailing wage–material ratio suggests that the MGNREGA is an important instrument for providing income through employment-generating activities at least at the state level. In order to gain a better understanding about the extent to which the MGNREGA supports livelihood, this section summarises the existing evidence on the MGNREGA in terms of the number of job cards provided, the number of workdays received per household and the wage rate earned.

Ownership of a job card is the first step to demand employment, claim wages or unemployment allowance if a job is not provided within the time frame of 15 days. Using the official MGNREGA data, the PACS-CSO document shows that 37.85 million people have been issued job cards in 2006–07 all over India, which is equivalent to 70 per cent of the rural households. Bihar has issued fewer cards than is warranted by the 2001 census number of rural households, which could reflect the lack of awareness of people regarding the existence of a guaranteed employment scheme and the lack of publicly organised MGNREGA awareness-creation campaigns. In comparison to the results from the official MGNREGA data, the PACS-CSO survey suggests that 90 per cent of the households in the aggregate sample of the selected six states who registered for a job card had been issued a card. This value is influenced by the experience of Bihar, where only 74.3 per cent of the households who registered for a job card had been issued a card. The primary data of the PACS-CSO survey also suggests that only 42.9 per cent of the job cards were distributed to the households in the aggregate of the sampled states. This low number is again driven by Bihar, where only 21.3 per cent of the job cards were distributed.

The evidence from the PACS-CSO report (2007: 15–16) points to a substantial delay in the issuance and distribution of job cards, with households waiting up to eight months till they receive their card. In addition, distributed job cards were eventually taken back and kept with the gram sevak or with the GP president and GP secretaries. The latter were found to make wrong job card entries, such as over-reporting the number of workdays of MGNREGA employment provided. According to the PACS-CSO report, the GP officials inflate the actual number of workdays in order to accommodate the commissions for the block-level functionaries like the junior engineers and the BPOs.

Considering those households with a job card, they are entitled to receive employment within 15 days of employment registration. If the state fails to do so for whatever reason, the applicant is entitled to an unemployment allowance at prefixed rates, paid by the state government. Unemployment payments are typically not paid for a number of reasons. First, job cardholders demanding work typically do not obtain a receipt of the application and, thus, cannot prove the day of registration. As unemployment benefits need to be paid entirely by the state government, the government is reluctant to pay unemployment allowance and may, therefore, refuse to accept applications for work or actively discourage job cardholders from demanding work. Considering those workers who have received MGNREGA employment, they report a response time to call for employment of 15 to 30 days. That is, the time between submitting the application for work and getting work is less than one month in most states.

MGNREGA provides clear instructions on the manner and the time frame in which the workers can get their entitlements. One requirement mandates that at least 25 per cent of the wage payments involve cash, while 75 per cent can involve both cash and in-kind payments. The PACS-CSO survey documents that most workers in Bihar and in India receive cash payments (see Table 13.1). The MGNREGA also mandates that workers receive their wages at fixed rates between 7 to 15 days after the completion of the work. According to the PACS-CSO survey (section 3.5.5), the majority of workers received their wages within 30 days for the aggregate sample of Indian states and within 7 days for the sample of Bihar (Table 13.1). Delays in the payment of wages arise because wage payments are determined by looking at the amount of work completed on a day rather than by looking at the number of days worked. Numerous problems arise with measurement-based wage payments. First, assessments regarding the actual

Table 13.1: Wage Payment Characteristics (in per cent)

	Mode of Wage Payment		*Duration of Wage Payment after Work Completion*		
	Cash	*Cash and Kind*	*Less than 7 days*	*7 to 30 days*	*More than 30 days*
Bihar	84	16	58	35	7
Grand Total	92	8	33	55	13

Source: PACS-CSO (2007: section 3.5.4–3.5.6).
Note: The values are derived from graphical illustrations and are therefore approximations. Values may not sum to 100 due to rounding.

amount of work done are unclear and delayed, mainly because of an insufficient number of technical support staff (for example, civil engineers) that could measure the work output. Second, measurements regarding the amount of work completed are likely to be imprecise, with the worker getting less than what he would be entitled to. Third, the absence of properly maintained records (especially muster rolls and job cards) implies that neither the worker nor any vigilance committee can conclude whether full wages had been paid or not.[9]

One major provision of the MGNREGA is employment generation without gender discrimination. However, both the PACS-CSO report and Drèze and Oldiges (2007) point to the existence of gender discrimination in work creation. The gender bias is particularly strong in the northern states of India, especially in Bihar, UP, Jammu and Kashmir, West Bengal and Himachal Pradesh (HP), where less than one-fourth of all workdays are given to women. At the all-India level, women take up 40 per cent of the MGNREGA employment. Case study evidence compiled by PACS-CSO suggests that the low share of female workers, especially in the northern states, does not reflect a lack of demand, but the apprehension of panchayats to provide work opportunities to women, and the unwillingness of men to send their wives and daughters to work places in the public domain (PACS-CSO, 2007: 30). At the core of gender discrimination are traditional and cultural factors and beliefs, which typically also cumulate in wage discrimination against women. Wage discrimination arises from the vested belief that women are incapable of doing hard manual labour which, in turn, causes panchayats to pay lower wages to women than to men. In a study for Tamil Nadu, Narayanan (2008) suggests that women who bring their children to MGNREGA worksites in the absence of childcare facilities receive lower wages or are even turned away from worksites. The absence or lack of (sufficient) childcare facilities at MGNREGA worksites, thus, adversely affects female participation rates in MGNREGA implementation (see also Drèze and Oldiges, 2007).

Auditing, Monitoring and Grievance Redressal

In order to ensure the effective implementation of MGNREGA, the act includes provisions for social auditing, monitoring and grievance redressal. Social audits are required to verify 11 stages in the implementation of the MGNREGA, including the job card registration of households and the biannual mandatory social audit in the gram sabha (see the CAG report). Monitoring requires block-, district- and state-level officials to inspect 100 per cent, 10 per cent and 2 per cent of works every year, respectively. At the GP level, vigilance and monitoring committees have to monitor the progress and quality of work execution. In addition, the district authorities have to prepare financial audits. Finally, grievance redressal mechanisms and procedures at the block and district levels have to be devised by the state government. The mechanisms have to deal with any MGNREGA-related complaint by any person and need to specify the procedures that will be used to handle complaints.

The CAG report shows that the provisions for public auditing, monitoring and grievance redressal were not properly met under the MGNREGA at least during 2006/07. Although social audits are mandated to take place twice a year for all works taken up within the GP in the preceding year, the CAG report notes that the majority of sampled GPs did not implement any social audit. Ambasta, Shankar and Shah (2008) report narrative evidence according to which the social audits were not implemented due to the poor maintenance of records and the insufficient mobilisation of rural households to participate in gram sabha meetings.

Regarding monitoring, there is strong evidence that the state-, district- and block-level officials do not inspect the required number of works. At the GP level, monitoring is complicated by the non-existence of vigilance committees (see CAG). Ambasta, Shankar and Shah (2008) however note that even where vigilance committees exist, this might only be on paper. There are cases when GP secretaries selected proxy vigilance committee members without informing the respective persons about their membership or their duties and powers. Furthermore, the mandatory social audits were not properly conducted by the gram sabha even in the presence of vigilance committees, given the rural communities' unawareness regarding the audit objectives.

At all levels, monitoring was complicated by the absence of up-to-date information on key parameters of MGNREGA performance such as the number of registered workers, the registered demand for work, cost estimates, muster rolls, administrative decisions on the release and sanction of funds, the spending activities of the implementing agencies and works started and executed (see the CAG report). The inadequate flow of information reflects the absence of a well-functioning and integrated management information system (MIS) that contains timely and adequate data on the performance of the MGNREGA at all stages of implementation. According to Ambasta, Shankar and Shah (2008), the present MIS does not function effectively and comprehensively due to insufficient Internet connectivity and the lack of sufficiently trained personnel in data entry and posting. Instead, the implementation of MGNREGA presently relies on a non-transparent system of (incomplete and time-consuming) paper works. These factors combined preclude concurrent vigilance, public audit and transparency of MGNREGA-related activities. As a consequence, the MGNREG schemes are implemented in an environment conducive to malpractices, including corruption and the misappropriation of funds.

In order to create an effective, accountable, transparent and timely MIS that integrates all MGNREGA-related functions, functionaries and funds, and facilitates the timely transfer of data between all MGNREGA agents, Ambasta, Shankar and Shah (2008) emphasise the need for investments in Internet connectivity, especially in remote areas. At the same time, capacity training in data entry and posting is needed to promote the effective use of the MIS as well as the quality of the available information.

IV

Case Study

Case Selection and Research Methods

In order to gain deeper insights in the administrative procedures of MGNREGA implementation, a case study was conducted in two districts[10] in Bihar, as explained in the introduction.[11] The two districts were selected by using 2001 census information and the insights from a poverty and social assessment study of districts in Bihar, as prepared by the Asian Development Research Institute.[12] The latter clustered districts according to poverty, social vulnerability, livelihood potential and social capital criteria. Qualifying the data along a 1–5 scale, one district which performed better (referred to as District A) and one which performed worse (referred to as District B) than the average district in Bihar were purposely selected.

In each district, two blocks were purposely selected, one again being better developed than the other. The selection was guided by the 2001 census infrastructure data on the number of villages with drinking water, schooling, health, post office and public transportation facilities, among others. In addition, the selection was supported by insights from district officials. The better-off blocks in Districts A and B are referred to as Block A-A and B-A, respectively, while the less well-performing blocks are referred to as Block B-A and Block B-B. In District A, 19 villages were randomly selected in each selected block. With the assistance of block-level officials, one well-developed and one less well-developed village from the list of 10 villages were identified. In the selected case study sites, interviews were conducted with government officials at the district and block level and with MGNREGA beneficiaries in focus groups at the village level. As indicated in the introduction, the Process-Influence-Mapping tool was applied to gain an in-depth understanding of how the implementation of MGNREGA works in practice, which and how actors are involved and how much influence they have, in the perception of the respondents, on the ultimate outcome.

The remainder of this section describes the application of the Process-Influence-Mapping tool taking the interviews of focus groups as an example. Dependent on the interview, the focus groups included (*a*) both villagers and representatives of GPs such as the GP secretary or the gram rozgar sevak or (*b*) only the gram rozgar sevak or the MGNREGA Programme Officer at the block level. Regardless of the focus group composition, the interviewees were asked in three stages about the steps that are taken to provide MGNREGA employment and wage payments to the unskilled poor in rural areas. In step one, the interviewee identified the actors that are involved in providing MGNREGA employment and wage payments, which in turn are marked on a sheet of paper (Figure 13.1 Panel A). The second stage represents the different actors with little figures, and arrows are used to describe the actions that are needed for providing MGNREGA employment and MGNREGA wages (Figure 13.1 Panel B). In a third step, 'towers' of carom game pieces are built in order to visualise how much influence different actors have on providing MGNREGA employment and MGNREGA wage payments (Figure 13.1 Panel C). At that stage, it was emphasised that the level of influence was not about 'authority', but about the importance of actors for the implementation of MGNREGA as described in the Process-Influence-Mapping exercise.

Case Study Findings

The remainder of this section presents and discusses the results of the Process-Influence-Mapping tool from interviews with MGNREGA service providers (Block Programme Officer and gram rozgar sevak) and one village focus group. The interviewees identified the actors that are involved and the steps which are actually taken to provide MGNREGA wage employment and wage payments to the rural poor and unskilled.

In order to facilitate the comparison of the results across the different interviews, this section first summarises the administrative procedure as envisaged in the operational guidelines of the MGNREGA. The following sections report the evidence from Process-Influence-Mapping interviews with (*a*) one village focus group which implemented MGNREGA work at the block level in block A-A,[13] (*b*) one MGNREGA PO in block B-A and (*c*) one gram rozgar sevak in block B-A so as to identify the governance challenges in programme implementation. We supplement the results from the Process-Influence-Mapping with insights from interviews in which the Process-Influence-Mapping exercise could not be adequately applied. The respective evidence refers to interviews with one BDO in block A-B, one zilla parishad (the term used in Bihar for the district panchayat) president in district A and with MGNREGA beneficiaries in block B-A.

Figure 13.1: Process-Influence-Mapping

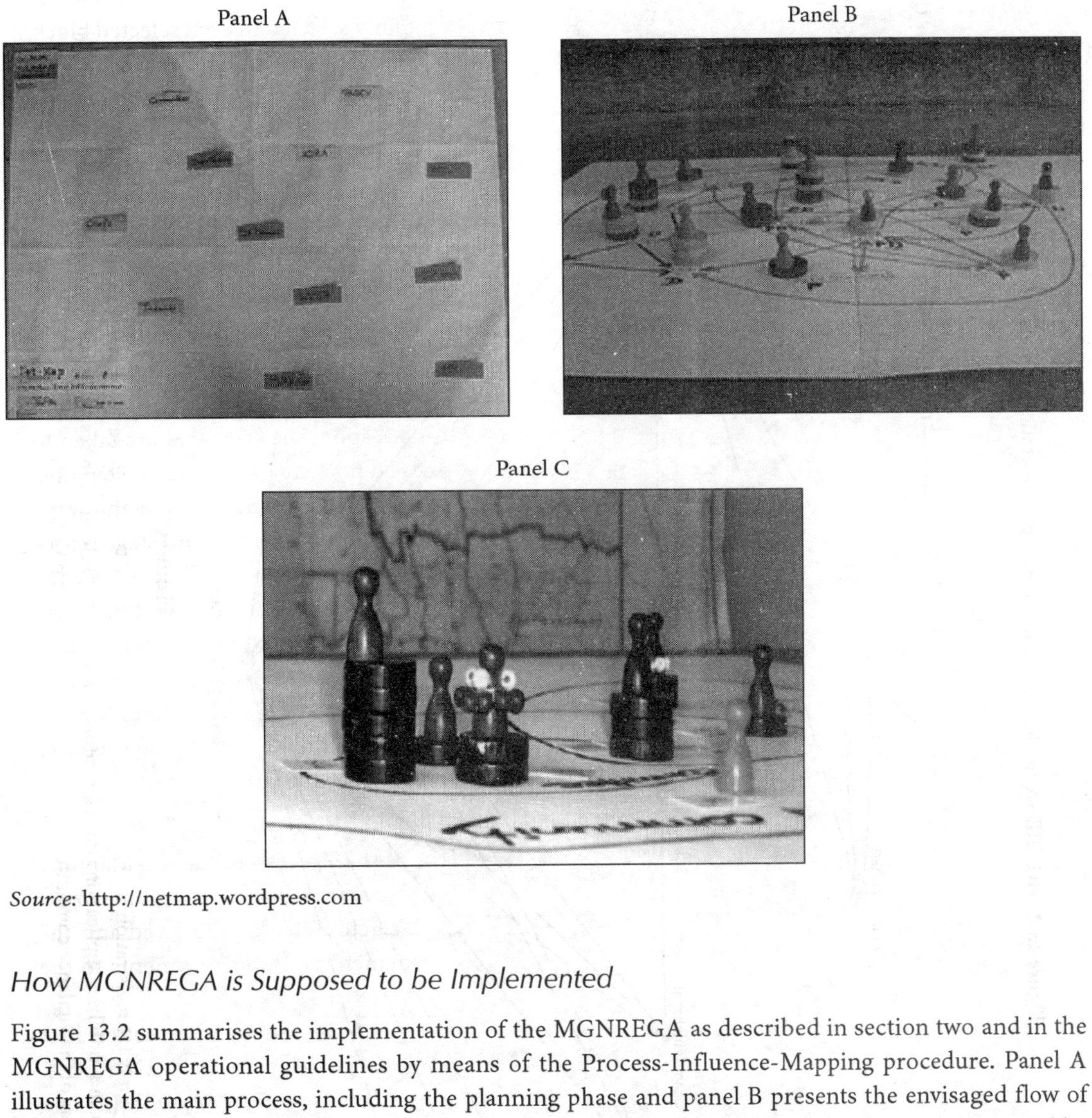

Source: http://netmap.wordpress.com

How MGNREGA is Supposed to be Implemented

Figure 13.2 summarises the implementation of the MGNREGA as described in section two and in the MGNREGA operational guidelines by means of the Process-Influence-Mapping procedure. Panel A illustrates the main process, including the planning phase and panel B presents the envisaged flow of funds and provides insights as to who controls whom in the implementation of the works executed by the gram, block or district panchayat. Figure 13.2 indicates that the implementation process mainly involves the MGNREGS workers and the BPO. The GP and the gram sabha are however important for the identification of the works that should be carried out under the MGNREGA.

MGNREGS workers are supposed to be proactive in the application for registration and employment as part of the demand- and rights-based employment programme. Figure 13.2 also suggests that the law seeks to provide a complex web of check and balance mechanisms that cover the flow of funds

Figure 13.2: MGNREGA Implementation According to Operational Guidelines

Panel A: Processes

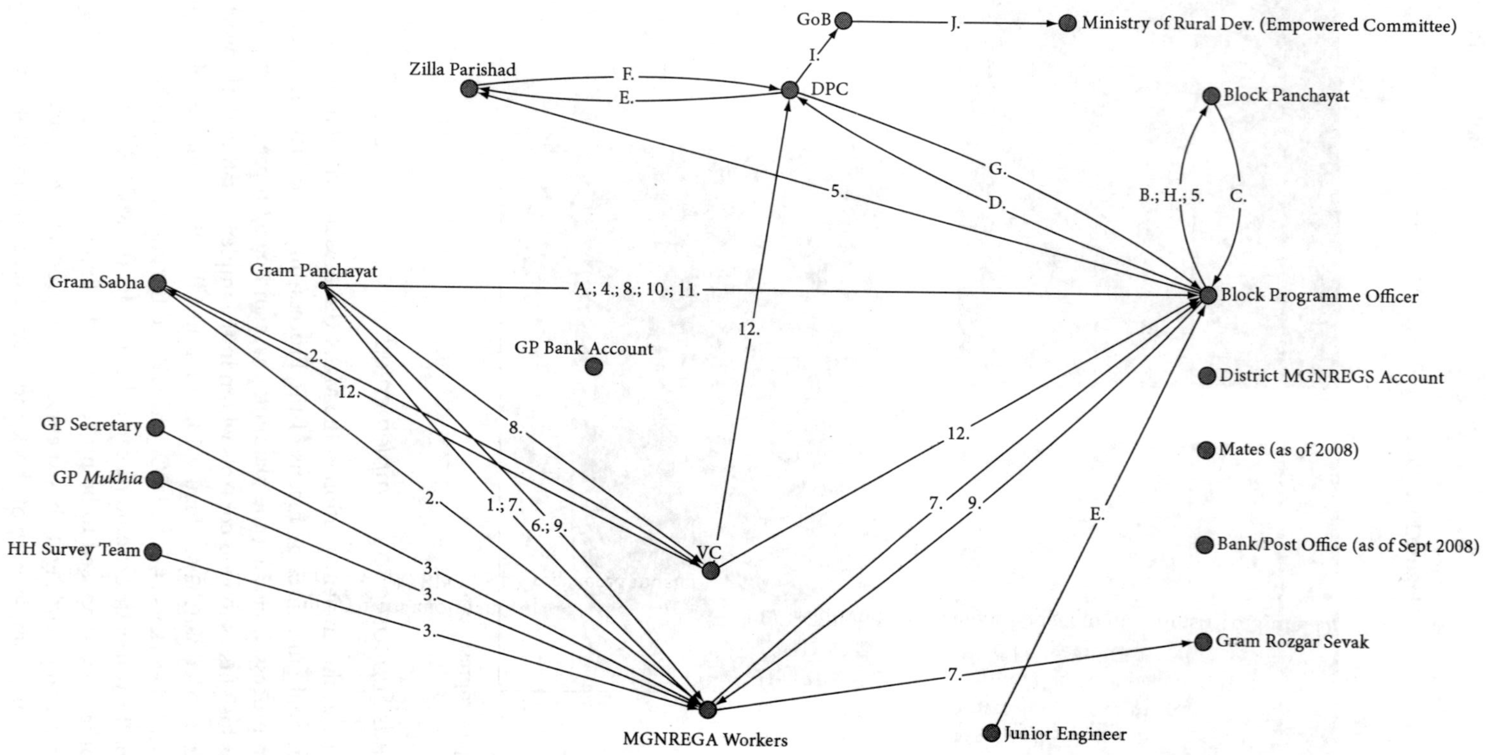

Process

1. Adult HH members apply for registration.
2. Gram sabha verifies and mobilises applications for registration. Gram sabha elects members of the vigilance committee.

Planning

A. GP forwards development plan and priorities to BPO.

B. BPO scrutinises, approves GP proposals. Sends consolidated GP proposals to BP.

3. HH survey for identification of households willing to register.
4. GP sends copy of registration to BPO.
5. BPO reports to BP and ZP.
6. GP issues employment cards to registered HHs.
7. Adult HH members apply for work at GP or present themselves to the gram RS. Gram RS records application in employment register. Application via BPO is a 'fallback' option only.
8. GP informs BPO about new work applications. GP informs VC of estimates regarding the work, time frame and quality parameters.
9. GP and BPO assign employment.
10. GP informs BPO about employment allotments made.
11. GP informs BPO about start of work. BPO issues registered muster rolls.
12. Upon completion of work, VC prepares report and submits that to the gram sabha, BPO, DPC.

C. BP sends approval.
D. BPO forwards shelf of GP proposals to DPC.
E. DPC consolidates block plans, prepares labour budget. Junior engineer assists BPO and develops and approves technical estimates. Sends them to ZP, which approves the block-wise shelf of projects and labour budget.
F. ZP reports approval to DPC.
G. DPC reports approved projects to BPO.
H. BPO forwards a copy of the block plan to GP.
I. DPC forwards labour budget to GoB.
J. GoB forwards labour budget to the Ministry of Rural Development.

(Figure 13.2 contd.)

(Figure 13.2 contd.)

Panel B: Flow of Funds and Control (Who Controls Whom?)

- Grey line = money flow
- Black line = Who controls whom/what?

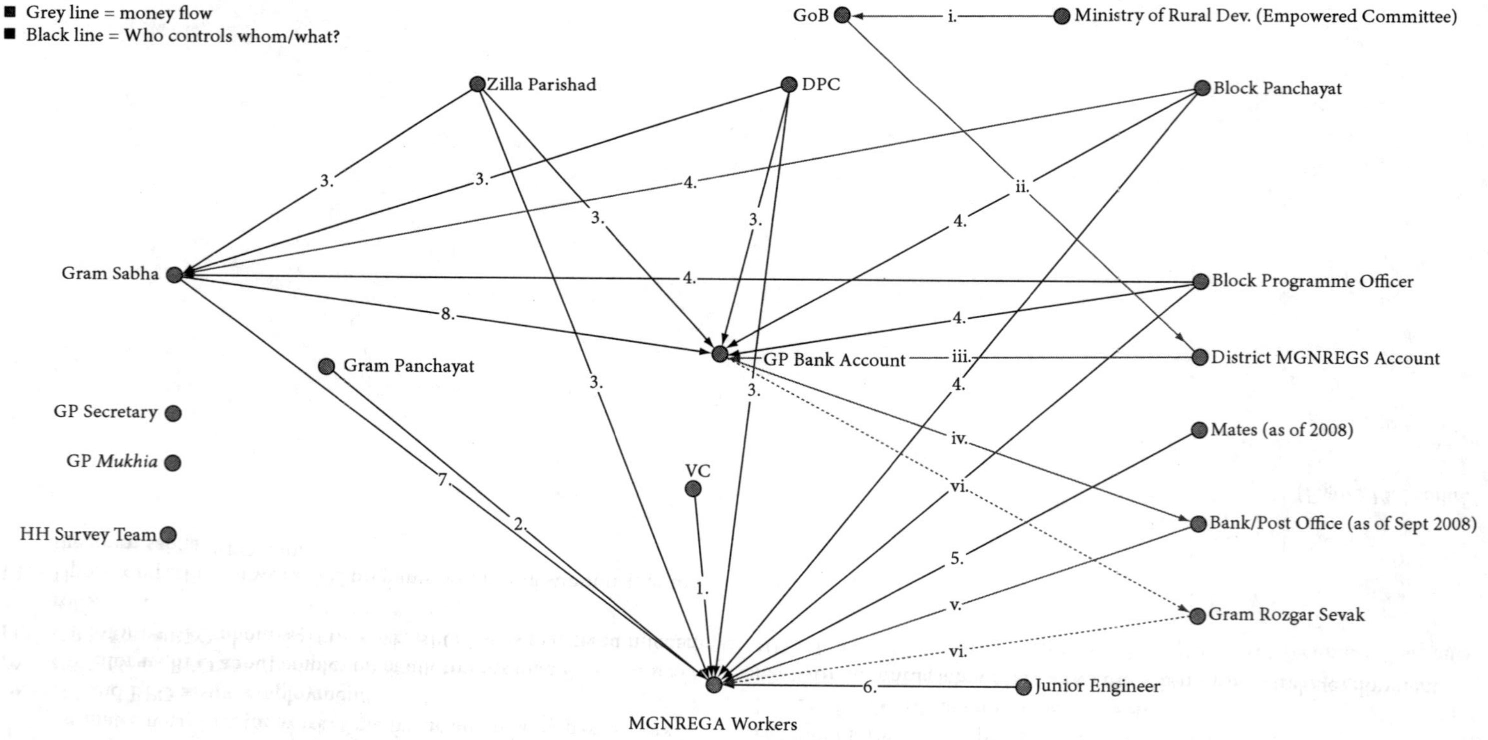

Who controls whom?

1. VC monitors work.
2. GP monitors work and related documents.
3. DPC and ZP monitor timely issue of job cards, provision of employment, social audits, flow of funds, progress and quality of works.

Flow of funds

i. Upon release of labour budget, flow of funds from the Ministry of Rural Development to GoB.
ii. Flow of fund from GoB to district MGNREGS account.
iii. Flow of funds from district MGNREGS account to GP MGNREGS account, which is jointly operated by GP *Mukhia* and GP secretary.

4. BP and the BPO monitor the registration of HHs, issue of job cards, employment demanded and provided, maintenance of muster rolls, unemployment allowances paid, social audits, flow of funds, timely and correct payment of wages and progress and quality of works.
5. Mate supervises work at project sites.
6. JE measures the work output.
7. Gram sabha monitors registration and issue of job cards, works at village level and employment provided.
8. Social audit of GP MGNREGS account through gram sabha.

iv. Upon completion of work, transfer of funds from GP to bank/post office account.
v. Upon completion of work, payment of workers through bank/post office account.
vi. Till September 2008, direct payment of MGNREGS worker through implementing agent.

Source: Constructed using information from Government of India (2005b).
Notes: BP=block panchayat/panchayat samiti; BPO=Block Programme Officer; DM=District Magistrate; DPC=District Programme Coordinator; GoB=Government of Bihar; GoI=Government of India; GP=Gram Panchayat; HH=Household; JE=Junior Engineer; PTA=Panchayat Technical Assistant; RS=Rozgar Sevak; VC=Vigilance Committee; ZP=Zilla Parishad.
The picture does not illustrate the interaction between parties in special cases like the unavailability of employment. See the Operational Guidelines for more details (GoI, 2008).
As regards wage payments, they are made through the implementing agent, which can be the GP, block and district panchayat, government line departments, among others. Figure 13.2 is constructed by assuming that the GP is the implementing agent.

and administrative procedures, and to create transparency and accountability, mainly through the creation of top-down state- and district-level control or accountability mechanisms and the social audit of MGNREGA-related works through villagers during gram sabha meetings and the gram sabha social audit forum. In addition, citizen information boards at worksites; vigilance monitoring committees and block-, district-, and state-level inspections are meant to foster transparency in the implementation of MGNREGA schemes.

Governance Challenges

This section emphasises the evidence from Process-Influence-Mapping interviews with one village focus group (Figure 13.3), one BPO (Figure 13.4) and one gram rozgar sevak (Figure 13.5) so as to identify the governance challenges in MGNREGA programme implementation. The village focus group describes the implementation of block panchayat–funded MGNREG schemes at the village level, while the gram rozgar sevak describes the implementation of GP-funded MGNREG schemes. The BPO provides a general description. We supplement the discussion from the Process-Influence-Mapping with insights from interviews of service providers and MGNREGS beneficiaries in which the net-mapping approach could not be adequately applied. In order to structure the analysis, the discussion identifies the governance challenges prevailing at different stages of MGNREGA implementation, that is, planning, issue of job cards and work execution.

A note of caution is required. The administrative procedures presented here reflect the implementation of MGNREGA as it is understood by different respondents. Actors or lines of administrative responsibility and fund flows may not coincide with the provisions of the operational guidelines as the interviewees are only aware of the procedures that they are directly exposed to.

Project Planning. The village focus group in block A-A (Figure 13.3) presents the administrative process involved in the implementation of a block panchayat–funded MGNREG scheme. The illustrations suggest that block panchayat–funded projects are implemented without the involvement of the GP. Instead, the implementation appears to depend on a farmers' committee, which identifies the MGNREGA-related activities. As the farmers' committee may promote activities that are of direct concern to the committee members, block panchayat–funded NREG schemes may face problems from local elite capture and targeting failures.

Additional support for this proposition is obtained from the fact that the block panchayat–funded MGNREG scheme was only implemented in the GP where the block panchayat member came from. This observation suggests that MGNREG schemes funded and implemented through block panchayats may not cover a wider set of GPs as envisaged in the block plan.

Considering the evidence from the interview with the BPO and the gram rozgar sevak in block B-A, the priority areas of work are identified during gram sabha meetings. Opposing the provisions of the act, the priority areas are not communicated to the GP and incorporated into the annual plan. Instead, they are directly communicated to the block panchayat. As there is evidence that gram sabha meetings are attended by villagers with vested interests (see Drèze, Khera and Siddharth, 2007), the set of priority areas may favour only few people and this, in turn, may reduce the commitment of villagers to programme implementation.

Maybe due to unawareness or irrelevance for their own tasks, the village focus group (Figure 13.3) and BPO (Figure 13.4) do not assign the BPO a role in the project planning procedure. According to the interviewees, the BPO does not receive the GP or block development plan for technical scrutiny and approval, while it may receive a final list of projects after the approval of the zilla parishad (Figure 13.3 and 13.5).

If the lack of involvement of the BPO is symptomatic for the implementation of MGNREGA, then development plans may (*a*) specify budget requirements that are too low to fund sufficient employment and (*b*) approve projects that are too small to generate sufficient employment for all concerned as the BPO is responsible for matching the demand for work at the block level with the employment opportunities. Given the interview responses of the BPO, the underestimation of funding requirements appears to be a binding constraint in the generation of MGNREGA employment. The constraint is such that households only receive MGNREGA employment for a period of 15 days.

In addition, if the BPO is not involved in the planning process, development plans might be passed which do not reflect local priorities and needs, but generate employment without increasing the local potential for productivity and income gains (in agriculture) or which fail to promote activities targeted towards weaker sections of the society (for example, land development works for small and marginal farmers).

Registration and Job Card Issue. According to the provisions of the MGNREGA, the GP is required to receive the application for registration, verify the registration applications, register households and issue employment cards. The village focus group interview suggests that employment cards are reviewed by the block panchayat and issued by the gram rozgar sevak. The information for the verification of the household's economic status is provided by the GP president, who in Bihar is referred to as *Mukhia*.

The Process-Influence maps suggest that the BPO does not receive information on the number of job card applicants. Again, we cannot conclude that this is a general property of MGNREGA implementation as it may reflect the unawareness of the interview respondents. However, if it holds true, then estimates of how many programs are needed in order to meet the prospective employment demand might be unreliable. In addition, according to the perceptions of the village focus group (Figure 13.3), employment demand is made to fit supply as employment cards are issued only once projects are identified and project funds are received. Although this finding casts doubt on the extent to which employment generation is rights-based and need-based, and inclusive, it should not be overemphasised as it reflects the perceptions of the interviewees, which could be imperfect mirror images of reality.

The case study evidence also points to financial irregularities in the job card issue procedure. In line with the CAG report finding, a group of MGNREGS workers in block B-A pointed out that the GP *Mukhia* required households applying for a job card to pay ₹10 per household applicant both at the time of submitting the job card application form and at the time of getting the job card issued. The cost for the photographs had to be borne by the job card applicants as well in spite of the clear operational guideline that the cost of the photographs and the job card are part of the programme cost. The focus group of MGNREGS workers also complained that the *Mukhia* only issued the job cards to those who voted for him during the GP election or those who were close to him. Closely related, the interview responses point to the existence of caste conflicts in the issue and distribution of job cards. For instance, the village focus group argued that the GP *Mukhia* preferably issued the job cards to members of his own caste within the SC group, while members of lower SC castes were less likely to receive it.

Figure 13.3: MGNREGA Implementation—Village Focus Group in Block A-A, April 2008

Panel A: Influence of Actors

- Level of influence on MGNREGA outcome from 0 to 10 (low to high in parentheses given).
- Grey line = money flow.

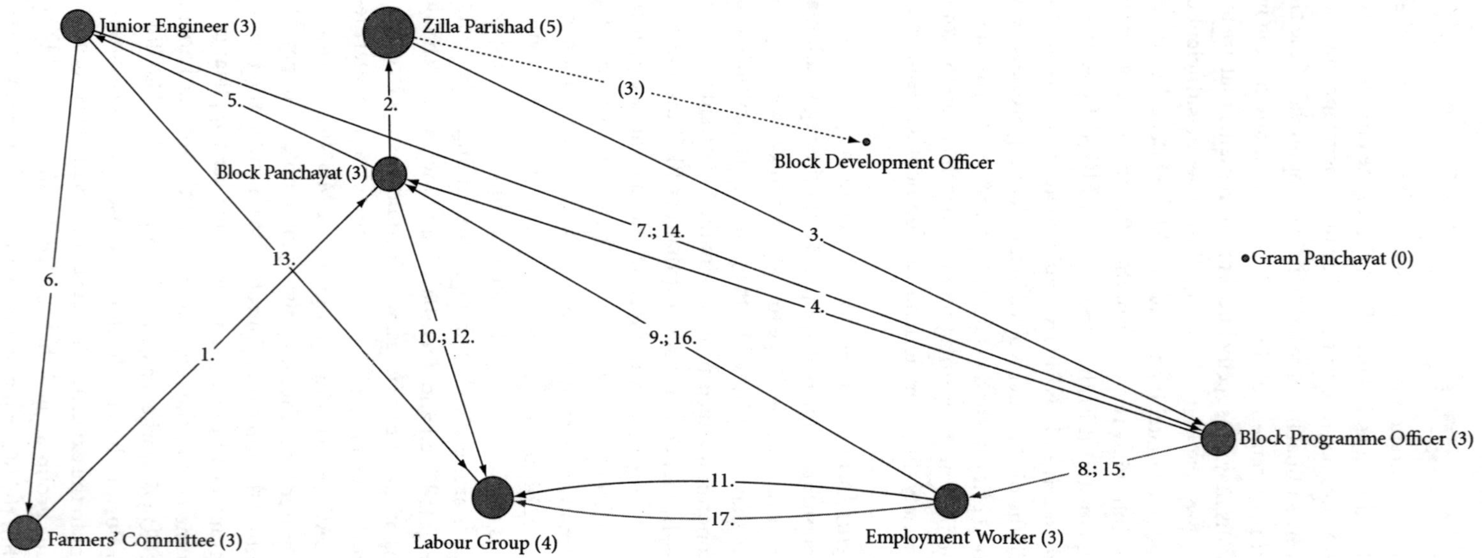

Panel B: Perceived Corruption of Actors

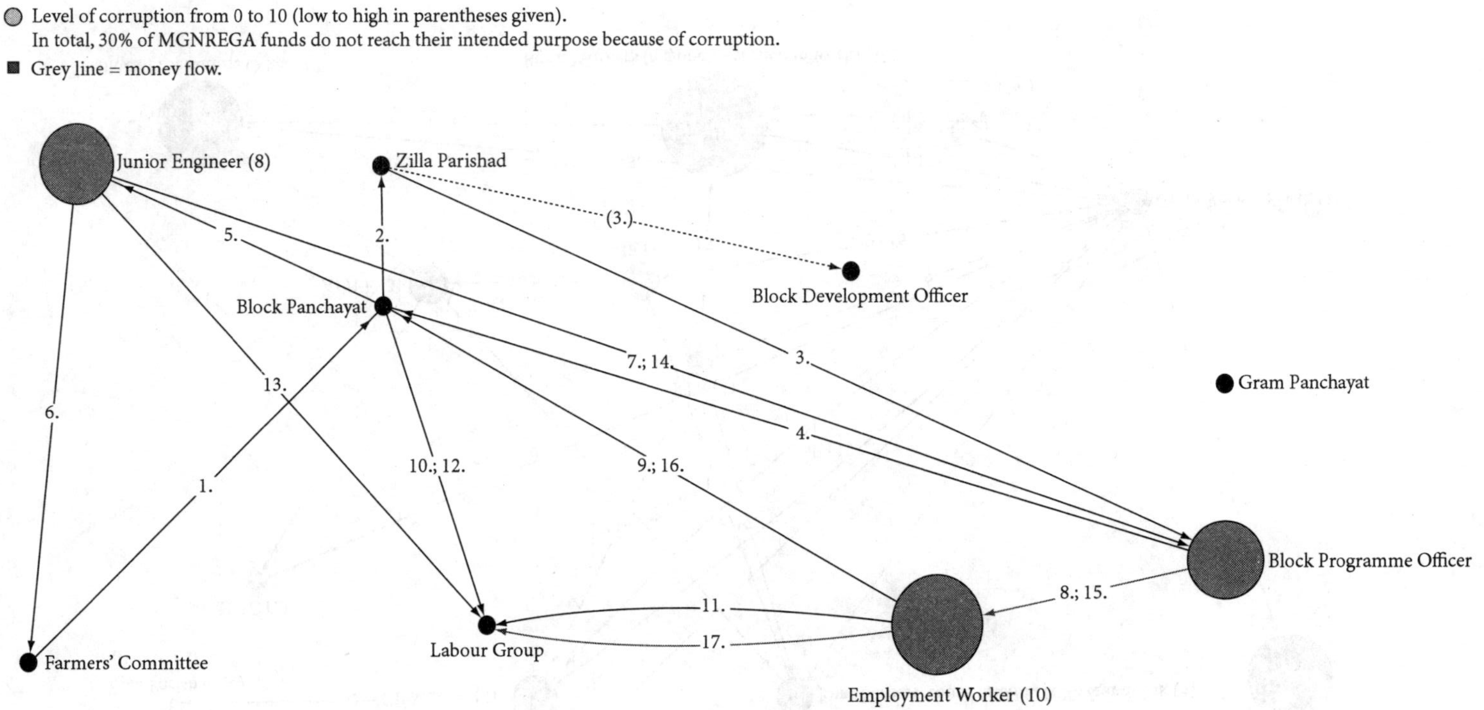

1. Decides about MGNREGA activities; informs.
2. Sends proposal for approval.
3. Informs about approval.
4. Informs about start of work.
5. Asks for estimate.
6. Goes to village, makes estimate.
7. Informs about estimate.
8. Calls, gives advance money.
9. Informs about advance money.
10. Informs to get people ready.
11. Issues employment cards and maintains attendance sheet.
12. Supervises the flow of money.
13. Measures the work and maintains books.
14. Informs about work done.
15. Provides money for work (signs checks).
16. Informs about money received.
17. Distributes money.

(3.) Till 2007, informs about approval.

Source: Authors.

Figure 13.4: MGNREGA Implementation—Block Programme Officer in Block B-A, January 2009

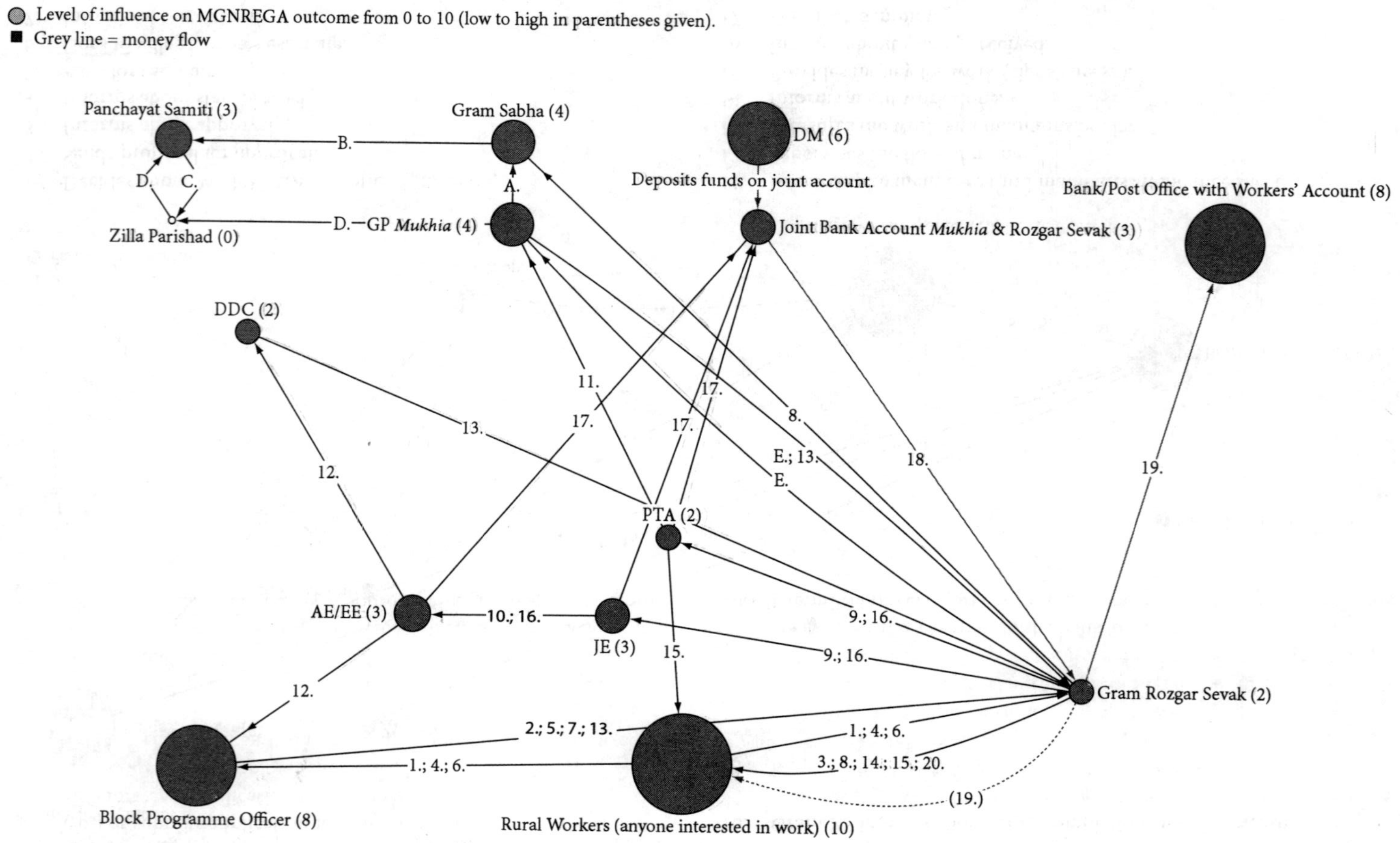

Process

1. Worker demands job card.
2. Channels job card application to gram RS.
3. Gram RS signs and issues the job card.
4. Worker submits application for employment.
5. BPO forwards application for employment to gram RS.
6. Worker demands employment from BPO and gram RS.
7. BPO informs about and transfers employment applications to the gram RS.
8. Gram RS informs people about shelf of projects among which they can choose the MGNREGS projects.
9. Gram RS informs about the selected MGNREGA work/scheme and asks for cost estimate/technical approval. Technical approval from (*a*) PTA for < ₹1 lakh schemes, (*b*) JE for > ₹1 lakh schemes.
10. JE seeks technical approval from (*a*) AE for ₹2–5 lakh schemes, (*b*) EE for > ₹5 lakh schemes.
11. GP *Mukhia* receives technical approval from (*a*) PTA for < ₹1 lakh scheme, (*b*) JE for ₹1–2 lakh scheme.
12. BPO is contacted for administrative approval of ₹2–5 lakh schemes. DDC is contacted for administrative approval of > ₹5 lakh schemes.
13. GP *Mukhia* grants administrative approval; asks gram RS to start < ₹1 lakh schemes. BPO grants administrative approval; asks gram RS to start ₹1–5 lakh schemes. DDC grants administrative approval; asks RS to start > ₹5 lakh schemes.
14. Gram RS informs rural workers about start of work within 15 days.
15. Monitoring of MGNREGA work/scheme implementation.
16. Gram RS informs about work completion, asks for measurement book (*a*) PTA for < ₹1 lakh schemes, (*b*) JE for > ₹1 lakh schemes. JE informs about work completion, asks for measurement book AE/EE for >₹2 lakh schemes.
17. Administrative release of funds.
18. Joint signature of GP *Mukhia* and gram RS releases funds to gram RS.
19. As of September 2008, RS sends consolidated statement of the workers' MGNREGS earnings to the bank/post office.
20. Gram RS informs workers about money transfer to bank/post office.

(19.) Till September 2008, RS paid workers directly in cash.

Planning Process

A. GP *Mukhia* calls gram sabha to decide the MGNREGS projects for the next year.
B. Projects selected in gram sabha are sent to panchayat samiti for approval.
C. Panchayat samiti informs about approval of projects.
D. ZP informs about approval of panchayat samiti or GP work/schemes.
E. GP *Mukhia* and gram RS jointly decide the work/scheme out of the set of schemes approved by ZP.

Source: Authors.

Notes: AE=Assistant Engineer; BP=Block Panchayat/Panchayat Samiti; BPO=Block Programme Officer; DM=District Magistrate; DDC=District Development Commissioner; DPC=District Programme Coordinator; EE=Executive Engineer; GoB=Government of Bihar; GoI=Government of India; GP=gram panchayat; HH=Household; JE=Junior Engineer; PTA=Panchayat Technical Assistant; RS=Rozgar Sevak; VC=Vigilance Committee; ZP=Zilla Parishad.

The Process-Influence map is characterised by a number of simultaneous rather than consecutive processes. Entries A to E denote the process of selecting NREGA schemes/works.

Figure 13.5: MGNREGA Implementation—Gram Rozgar Sevak in Block B-A, January 2009

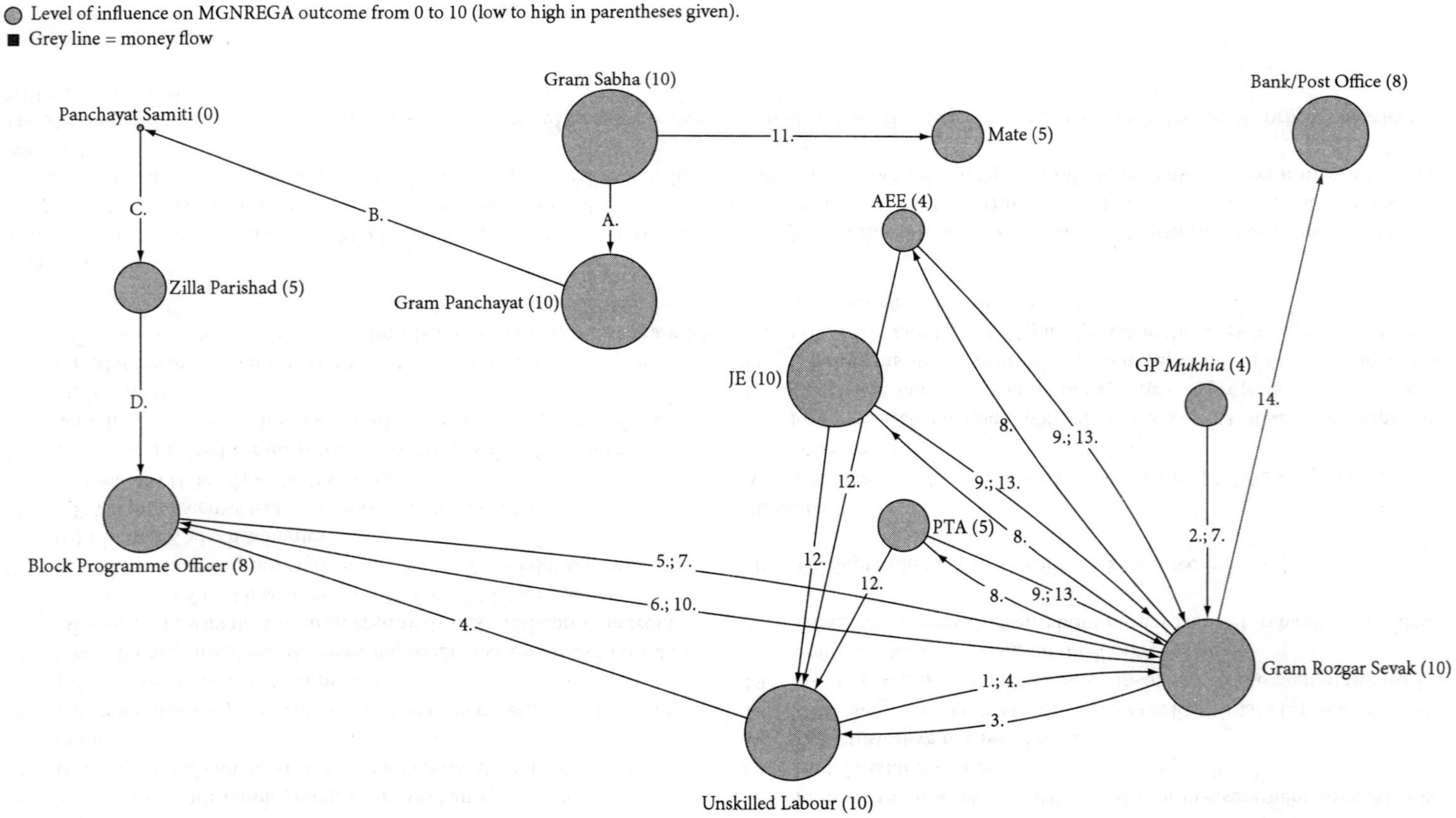

Process

1. Worker demands job card.
2. GP *Mukhia* provides background information on economic status of applicant.
3. Gram RS verifies application; issues job card.
4. Worker submits application for employment to gram RS or BPO (if gram RS is not present).
5. BPO forwards employment application to gram RS.
6. Gram RS informs BPO about the number of applications.
7. GP *Mukhia* grants administrative approval; asks gram RS to start < ₹1 lakh schemes. BPO grants administrative approval; asks gram RS to start ₹1–5 lakh schemes.
8. Gram RS asks for technical approval. Technical approval from (*a*) PTA for < ₹1 lakh schemes, (*b*) JE and AEE for > ₹1 lakh schemes.
9. PTA, JE, AEE send technical approval letter.
10. Gram RS informs BPO about formal start of work.
11. Gram sabha selects one labourer per worksite to be the mate. The mate maintains the attendance sheet.
12. Work supervision.
13. Preparation of measurement book and provision to gram RS.
14. Gram RS computes the consolidated amount of salaries and issues a check, which is jointly signed with GP *Mukhia* and sent to bank.

Planning Process

A. Gram sabha identifies MGNREGS projects for the next year.
B. GP sends projects for approval to panchayat samiti.
C. Panchayat samiti forwards list with schemes to ZP.
D. ZP approves schemes received from the panchayat samiti and sends final list of projects to BPO. BPO selects schemes that can employ the required number of people.

Source: Authors.
Note: See the notes to Figure 13.4. The process–influence map is characterised by a number of simultaneous rather than consecutive processes.

Allocation of Employment Opportunities, Work Execution and Wage Payments. The MGNREGA mandates the allocation of employment opportunities through the BPO and the GP. In order to coordinate works and employment at the block level, the GP is mandated to inform the BPO about the job allocation. However, the interviewees perceive that this is hardly done. According to the perceptions of the gram rozgar sevak in block B-A, he is the only one who communicates the start of the work to the BPO (Figure 13.5).

In addition, the act mandates the notification through a public notice at the offices of the GP and the BPO and through mail, but it is not evident whether this transparent process is actually followed. It could be due to the respondents' limited understanding of what is going on at the district level that none of them mentioned the district programme coordinator as authority that coordinates with the BPO and the GP (or other implementing agents) to ensure the generation of 100 days of MGNREGS employment per household per year. Unawareness may therefore also explain why the results of the Process-Influence map point to the complete detachment of MGNREGS work allocation and execution from the district programme coordinator.

It remained unclear as to what extent the findings from the Process-Influence-Mapping exercise are also the outcome of staff shortages. In particular, the implementation of NREG schemes is complicated by staff shortages at all government levels in Bihar. The shortages are due to substantial policy-driven restraints on the new hiring of district- and block-level staff and the consequent adverse development of the age composition of staff. As vacancies are not (permanently) filled, block- and district-level staff are frequently assigned several posts.[14] For instance, one BDO from block A-B made it clear in the interview with him that he was assigned the responsibility for six additional posts, the post of the BPO being just one of them. In another interview in District A, the district programme coordinator was found to be the district development commissioner. Obviously, the workload associated with every position implies that the respective interviewee cannot act as a full-time BPO or district programme coordinator and accordingly could not pay the required attention to or effectively monitor or administer the implementation of MGNREGA.[15]

Given the manpower problems (from unfilled vacancies) and the consequent lack of supervision, the 2008 MGNREGA operational guidelines specify the introduction of a mate who is supposed to be selected twice a month from the pool of MGNREGS workers 'through a fair, transparent and participatory process' (GoI, 2008: 30). After training, the selected MGNREGS workers are meant to become responsible for the local supervision and monitoring of worksites. As this includes the maintenance of muster rolls at the worksite and assessments regarding the quality of work, mates may not only reduce the workload of the gram rozgar sevak, but also increase the transparency and accountability of MGNREGS work implementation. Among the case studies, the gram rozgar sevak in block B-A referred to the mate as an actor who matters for the generation of MGNREGA-related wage employment by maintaining the attendance sheet. Per worksite, one mate was said to be selected from the pool of MGNREGS workers during gram sabha meetings.

In addition to the introduction of mates, the Government of Bihar incurred efforts to alleviate the manpower problems and the consequent high workload by hiring specific staff for the implementation of the NREG schemes outside the civil services and on a contract basis. For instance, the gram rozgar sevak in block B-A was hired on a contract basis to support the GP. Still, as it takes time for the measures to become effective, it could be in response to the shortage of manpower but also due to the traditional importance of contractors as employers of unskilled labour in Bihar that we find evidence for the implementation of MGNREGA projects through contractors despite the ban of private contractors under the MGNREGA. In district B, the MGNREGS workers in block A carried out work related to the renovation of traditional water bodies and the desilting of two tanks. In contrast to the provisions of the MGNREGA, the project was given to a contractor, who was associated with the political elite and deprived MGNREGS workers of approximately 40 per cent of the their wage entitlement. Instead of the agreed-upon wage of ₹82, the workers received only ₹50 per day.

The role of a contractor as implementing agent of MGNREGA-related works and the associated misappropriation of funds illustrates the imperfect functioning of public vigilance. The MGNREGA operational guidelines request the formation of one vigilance and monitoring committee for every work sanctioned to ensure transparency and accountability in MGNREGA programme implementation. We could not find support for the existence of vigilance and monitoring committees in the collected case studies. In addition, both the interviewed gram rozgar sevak in block B-A and the BPO in block B-A have not mentioned their mandated responsibility to ensure the implementation and organisation of social audits. This could be indicative of the absence of social audits (see Drèze, Khera and Siddharth, 2007, for comparable evidence from Orissa) and, thus, of the absence of a platform that could promote accountability and transparency in the planning, implementation, monitoring and evaluation of MGNREGS projects.

In addition to the contracting work, the evidence from the Process-Influence-Mapping tool suggests that corruption may also exist at the level of those authorities that assess the technical feasibility of project work and provide cost estimates of project implementation (that is, panchayat technical assistant, junior engineer, assistant engineer and executive engineer). In fact, the village focus group respondents in block A-A consider the Junior Engineer (overseer) to be one of the most corrupt agents in the implementation of MGNREGA (Figure 13.3 Panel B). The respective Process-Influence-Mapping method helps to identify the chain of mutually reinforcing actions through which junior engineers can misappropriate funds. To illustrate, the block panchayat asks the junior engineer to provide estimates of the costs associated with a particular MGNREG scheme (step 5).[16] As the junior engineer also measures the work and maintains related books (step 13) in the absence of effective supervision and accountability mechanisms, he can provide estimates (step 7) that exceed the true cost of work. Because the junior engineer also signs the document that authorises the release of funds, he may siphon off the difference between the true cost and the excess estimate, or share this difference with other actors involved.

The ability to control corruption at the technical level depends on the existence of well-functioning monitoring mechanisms (including the monitoring capacity of the BPO and the district magistrate) and enforcement mechanisms. Furthermore, incentive schemes for the technical staff are needed that increase the incentives for regular and reliable verifications and audits of the completed works. In addition to corruption at the technical level, the interviewed gram rozgar sevak (Figure 13.5) also complains about the corrupt behaviour of politically powerful villagers. The latter initiate disputes about the geographic area of MGNREGA worksites and pose financial requests for their permission to get MGNREGS work started in particular worksites.

Finally, the evidence from the Process-Influence-Mapping tool suggests that corruption may also exist at the level of the gram rozgar sevak and BPO, that is, those authorities that administer and handle the management of funds associated with the implementation of MGNREG schemes and the associated wage payments. The village focus group in block A-A assumed that approximately one-third of the MGNREGA funds were misused. Although the research team had no opportunity to cross-check this figure, the Process-Influence-Mapping tool can be used to assess the scope for corruption by identifying the channels through which funds can be misused.

The evidence from the village focus group interview (Figure 13.3) indicates that block panchayat–funded MGNREG schemes involve the flow of funds from the BPO (step 8 and 15) to the gram rozgar sevak and the subsequent distribution in form of wages to labour groups (step 17). In the absence of adequate supervision and monitoring mechanisms, the BPO and gram rozgar sevak might be corrupt along three related avenues. First, the BPO authorises the release of advanced and final payments to the gram rozgar sevak once he receives the work approval (step 3) and the information regarding work completion (step 14), respectively. The BPO can siphon off funds by turning a blind eye on junior engineers if they submit cost estimates and work output measures that are too high in comparison to conventional estimates (step 7 and 14). BPOs and junior engineers may share the differential between excess cost and true cost. Second, corrupt gram rozgar sevaks may deprive workers of their true wage entitlement (step 11 and 17) by imposing arbitrary upper bounds on the maximum daily output that qualifies for wage payments or by withholding the required minimum wage payment. Third, the gram rozgar sevak may demand money from job card applicants for issuing the employment card (step 11).

Due to the problem of misappropriation of funds through project implementing agencies, the 2008 operational guidelines introduced the payment of wages through the bank or post network so as to separate payment agencies from implementing agencies. The interview with the BPO and gram rozgar sevak in block B-A (Figures 13.4 and 13.5 respectively) suggests that this administrative change requires the gram rozgar sevak to submit a consolidated statement of workers' earnings to the bank/post office (see step 19, Figure 13.4; step 14, Figure 13.5). The operational guidelines argue that bank and post office accounts should be opened on behalf of the concerned MGNREGS workers by an appropriate authority (for example, bank or GP). Given the experience with the job card application procedure, concerns prevail regarding the extent to which intermediaries can facilitate the equitable access of all MGNREGS workers or households to bank accounts.

The experience with the job card application procedure suggests that intermediaries may impose a fee for the opening of a bank account. As this increases the opportunity costs of applying for employment under MGNREGA, it may deter potential MGNREGS workers from applying for MGNREGA work. Furthermore, there is evidence that banks refused to open bank accounts for MGNREGS workers as the consequent additional administrative burden results in additional costs. In addition, the BPO and gram rozgar sevak in block B-A (Figure 13.4 and 13.5 respectively) point to problems in the use of bank accounts and delays in the payment of wages when made through banks.

Among others, MGNREGS workers have to tell the bank in advance when they plan to withdraw the money as they cannot keep a large amount of funds after closure.[17] Drèze and Khera (2008) argue that the move towards bank payments is not a sufficient means for creating accountability in MGNREGA implementation as the banking system is prone to corruption as well. Another problem concerns the scattered location of bank and post office branches, which reduces the accounts' accessibility and increases the opportunity costs of MGNREGS workers to visit banks, let alone the high transaction costs and the time involved.

Influence of Actors on the Actual MGNREGA Implementation Outcomes. So far, the Process-Influence-Mapping tool was analysed with respect to the steps that are taken to provide MGNREGA employment and wage payments to the unskilled poor in rural areas. This section summarises the answers to the question: How much influence do the different actors have on the outcome of the MGNREG schemes? As can be inferred from the size of the nodes in Figure 13.3 to 13.5, the interviewees differ in their perceptions regarding the importance of actors. We represent differences in the importance of actors for the generation of MGNREGA wage employment by varying the size of nodes in the maps. The smaller the nodes are, the less important is a particular actor perceived to be in providing wage employment.

Given their view on the implementation of NREG schemes, the BPO (Figure 13.4) and gram rozgar sevak (Figure 13.5) consider the MGNREGA beneficiaries to be most important for providing MGNREGA wage employment as they are the ones who initiate the MGNREGA process by demanding employment. However, the respondents from the village focus group (Figure 13.3) do not share this perception, but consider the zilla parishad as the district authority that sanctions all projects to be most influential for the results of MGNREGA implementation. Except for the zilla parishad, the Process-Influence-Mapping exercise suggests that the dominant share of the interview respondents does not consider the district- or state-level functionaries to be influential to the generation of MGNREGA wage employment. Their role appears to be largely confined to the intermediation of funds. At least the gram rozgar sevak also assigns importance to the newly created function of the mate. However, as the mate does not appear to report to any other institution, the associated maintenance of attendance sheets may not strengthen supervision over work execution and the payment of workers.

Finally, the maps suggest that responsibilities in the administration of MGNREG schemes per se may provide an imperfect view on the perceived importance of actors for the implementation of projects. A case in point is the village focus group, which assigned the largest influence to the zilla parishad in spite of its proposed limited role in the implementation of MGNREG schemes.

V

Conclusion—What Can Be Done to Overcome the Governance Challenges?

Using the insights gained from Process-Influence-Mapping, this chapter has pointed to a number of governance challenges in the implementation of the MGNREGS, which limit the effectiveness of the programme. The findings are largely consistent with the literature reviewed in section three. The use of the mapping tool, however, made it possible to identify some challenges that have received less attention in the literature, and to provide more detailed insights regarding the specific features of the implementation process that create scope for the misappropriation of funds. We conclude this chapter with an overview of the five main MGNREGA implementation problems as revealed by the Process-Influence-Mapping tool, and discuss possible solutions.

Elite Capture in the Definition of Works

Consistent with the existing literature, this chapter shows that district and block officials play a limited role in defining the block and district plans for the generation of MGNREGA employment. However, while the existing literature (for example, the CAG audit report and PACS-CSO report) emphasised the lack of capacity of district and block officials to define the respective plans, the evidence from Process-Influence-Mapping also points to inadequate transparency and accountability mechanisms, which enable interest groups such as farmers' committees to exercise power in defining the priority areas of MGNREGA-related works. As a consequence, the projects may favour the interests of this particular group, whereas the GP, as a more inclusive body (with mandated reservation of seats for women and SC/ST members), might have chosen different projects. The case study also indicates that this problem can arise when block panchayat members implement works that do not cover several GPs (as foreseen under this mechanism), but rather cover only the location in which they reside. In such cases, it seems easy for block panchayat members to exclude the GP members from participating in the decision process, and instead involve interest groups that are close to them. This problem requires more attention in the future as it may indicate that the share of work to be implemented by the GPs, block panchayats and district panchayats should be changed in favour of the GPs.

Exclusion in Issuing Job Cards

It is well known from the literature and from the case studies that rural people face problems in getting the MGNREGA employment cards. It is also well known that many factors, especially corruption on the part of the card issuer, account for the failure of people to receive the employment card. The Process-Influence-Mapping exercise highlighted the role of local politics as an additional factor and showed that exclusion from getting employment cards can also arise due to caste conflicts *within* the SC group. At the core of the problem observed in the case study were electoral politics of the GP president and the lack of voice of the (SC) rural people to express their rights-based demand for MGNREGA employment. In order to improve the access of the rural population in general and of minorities in particular to MGNREGA-related services, it may be useful to concentrate more on awareness-creation campaigns that are targeted at disadvantaged (SC) citizens and inform them about their rights and duties, existing grievance mechanisms, the MGNREGA implementation process and the agents involved.

The need for capacity building among rural citizens seeking MGNREGA employment is not well recognised in the literature, which may be related to the challenge inherent in capacity building at that level. For instance, the PACS-CSO report (2007) mainly emphasises the need for strengthening the knowledge and skills of elected representatives. The Process-Influence-Mapping tool could be used to identify areas where the mobilisation of people, awareness-creation and capacity-strengthening activities could help to increase the effectiveness of the MGNREGA simply by removing structural and procedural misunderstandings regarding the implementation of the programme and the responsibilities of the different actors. In addition to the prevailing level of unawareness, one interviewee attributed the limited effectiveness of the MGNREGA to the value system of workers who are fast to assume that public programmes are 'gifts' provided by politicians to poor people. In order to strengthen the capacity of people to demand, monitor and evaluate MGNREGS-related services, a 'value for work' attitude needs to be developed that creates a sense of ownership over programme implementation. In addition, Process-Influence-Mapping can be used as a tool to identify possible changes in the administrative structure together with officials and stakeholders that could help to increase the transparency and accountability of MGNREGA programme implementation. Entry points for providing demand-based, inclusive and adequate MGNREGA employment could involve the mobilisation of local people through SHGs and other local groups and through media campaigns that are specifically designed to help rural citizens to claim their rights under the MGNREGA. Improvements in the availability of information related to, for example, tenders and contracts and progress reports will also help, even though a stronger sensitisation of the public may be required for an effective use of such documents for oversight purposes.[18]

Misappropriation of Funds

The problem related to the misappropriation of funds is widely documented in the literature, specifically in the audit reports discussed in section three, but Process-Influence-Mapping made it possible to specify more clearly where and how scope for misappropriation and corruption is created in the system. The Process-Influence-Mapping exercise suggests that the misappropriation is fostered by the complex structure of the administrative system and the programme design. Although resulting from the best of intentions to minimise corruption through the creation of an extensive check-and-balance system, the complex administrative system facilitates the misappropriation of funds as it adversely affects programme monitoring and evaluation. Although manpower shortages and capacity constraints explain insufficient programme monitoring and evaluation, additional hiring and training of staff may not necessarily reduce or even eliminate corruption as long as the scope for misappropriation is high. Hence, the case study shows that there are trade-offs in creating additional checks and balances and keeping the system simple, which need to be considered in further reforming the system. Moreover, in line with the existing literature, the study suggests that sustainable solutions to corruption require the mobilisation of rural people to become responsible for regular vigilance and monitoring as they are the ones who have the strongest stake in the ultimate outcome of the programme.

As the mobilisation of rural people involves a time-consuming process, the Government of India seeks to limit the misuse of funds and corruption by separating the payment agencies from the implementing agencies and by making different agents responsible for the maintenance of muster rolls and the payment of wages. To this end, the Government of India mandated the introduction of bank or post office accounts. The Process-Influence Map for block panchayat–funded MGNREG schemes (Figure 13.3) indicates that this approach may in fact increase the effectiveness of the MGNREG schemes as it eliminates those money flows that induce corruption among the gram rozgar sevak, the junior engineer and the BPO. As argued in the section 'Governance Challenges', the introduction of financial intermediaries is associated with new challenges, which include increased transaction costs (in terms of time required) for programme beneficiaries to access their payments. Still, the separation of payment and implementing agencies through the introduction of bank accounts appears to be a step in the right direction, provided it is associated with the effective operation of effective safeguard accountability and transparency mechanisms.

The use of technologies is another avenue to improve the vigilance over programme implementation. In fact, Internet and software tools are increasingly considered to be useful means for meeting the demand for data collection and reporting. For instance, the Government of Bihar recently decided to use the biometric devices for introducing the e–muster roll with the objective to improve the transparency of muster roll entries and to ensure timely and appropriate wage payments.[19] Being successfully pilot-tested in Andhra Pradesh, the biometric readers store the fingerprints and photographs of the MGNREGA programme beneficiaries and record the number of days worked and the date and time of wage payments. The information is ultimately stored in a central online database that traces all transactions and facilitates the timely availability of project implementation information. In addition to ensuring the unique identification of the MGNREGA beneficiaries, the biometric card is planned to eliminate all cash transactions once banks integrate it with their own technology. The main binding constraint in the operation of the biometric devices might not be electric power supply as the devices run on battery power, but the availability of a sufficient number of people who can properly use and maintain the devices. In addition, banks might be reluctant to incur the efforts of integrating another technology, a problem that might be particularly pronounced in remote rural areas where banks are sparsely located and poorly computerised. Nevertheless, the use of such technologies offers unique opportunities to meet some of the governance challenges inherent in implementing the MGNREGA.

Lack of Capacity Due To Staff Shortages and Lack of Training

The Process-Influence-Mapping exercise suggests that many challenges arise because the MGNREGA implementing agents and public officials are not sufficiently trained or related posts are vacant. These challenges are well known to the Government of India and—given the government's strong support of the programme—steps have been taken to address them by assigning responsibilities for programme implementation to contracted non-governmental agents and/or by modifying the administrative structure of MGNREGA implementation.

As regards training, the MGNREGA operational guidelines emphasise the importance of strengthening the capacity of all agents involved in MGNREGS planning, implementation, measurement, monitoring and evaluation to meet their respective responsibilities. Unfortunately, the guidelines are silent on who is responsible for the specification of the envisaged training calendar and training modules. In order to facilitate the access to training, information regarding the source of training and conditions for training eligibility should be easily accessible. In many instances, training needs to be given to agents who are employed for a limited period of time and/or on contract basis (gram rozgar sevak, BPO). The training of temporarily employed agents like the gram rozgar sevak is resource intensive and difficult to manage because of a high turnover rate and the sheer number of required employment workers. Proposed strategies like training of (master) trainers with the active participation of NGOs could increase the outreach of training, but also requires additional resources for the supervision of NGOs.

In order to effectively alleviate the constraints from unfilled vacancies, new functionaries are introduced, such as the mate. In addition, the Government of Bihar moves away from its stringent policy of no new hiring. The Process-Influence-Mapping instrument can be used to gain a better understanding as to the channels through which the introduction of additional (support) staff (for example, mate) affects the procedural and administrative implementation of NREG schemes, and thus, employment generation.

Overall, the case confirms that in programme implementation, the 'devil is in the detail' and catching this devil is important to identify reform options. Participatory techniques, such as Process-Influence-Mapping can help to better understand the intricacies of implementing complex large-scale programs such as the MGNREGA and to assess possible solutions. The authors hope that the insights from the case study will help the government and the stakeholders involved in their continued efforts to realise the vision of the MGNREGA as an innovative rights-based answer to the long-standing challenge of providing social safety to India's rural poor.

Notes

1. See Government of India (2005a) for additional information.
2. See figures on the official website of MGNREGA at http://nrega.nic.in/.
3. For details see http://netmap.wordpress.com.
4. This section builds on GoI (2005a, b) and the social audit implemented by the CAG in 2007.
5. This chapter does not review the socio-economic and infrastructural impact of NREG schemes. See Siddhartha and Vanaik (2008) and the PACS-CSO report for respective (tentative) evidence.
6. The States are UP, MP, Jharkhand, Chhattisgarh, Bihar, Maharashtra.
7. The most important records are the application registration register, the job card register, the employment register, the asset register, the muster rolls and muster roll issue and receipt register, and the complaint register. The majority of these registers need to be maintained by the panchayats.
8. The discussion on the wage share emphasises the amount of funds that is spent on the wage of unskilled workers. The amount of funds spent on semi-skilled or skilled workers is typically less than six per cent (PACS-CSO, Table 3.1 on p. 51 of the PACS-CSO report).
9. See the PACS-CSO report for more details on the approach used for determining the wage rate and the level of wages. As the present chapter is interested in the administrative process of providing wage employment, the wage rates are not further considered. Siddhartha and Vanaik (2008) and Drèze and Oldiges (2007) summarise the number of workdays that MGNREGA generates per household.
10. To ensure anonymity to the respondents, the names of the selected districts, blocks, GPs, villages and interviewees are not disclosed.
11. The study of MGNREGA was part of a more comprehensive case study that dealt with decentralised rural service provision. This study was sponsored by the International Food Policy Research Institute (IFPRI) and the World Bank through a Trust Fund Grant of the Bank-Netherlands Partnership Program (BNPP).
12. We thank Vera Vemuru—Senior Social Development Specialist at the World Bank—for pointing out this study.
13. As indicated in section two, MGNREGA work can be carried out at the district, block and GP level, with each level getting a certain percentage of funds for MGNREGA implementation (20, 30 and 50 per cent, respectively.)
14. In order to deal with manpower shortage in spite of government regulations against new hiring, some employment is done on a contract basis.
15. Also see Drèze, Khera and Siddharth (2007) for comparable evidence from Orissa.
16. Steps refer to the activities displayed in Figure 13.3 that lead to the provision of MGNREGA-related wage employment.
17. Drèze and Khera (2008) argue that the move towards bank payments is not a sufficient means for making the MGNREGA implementation process more accountable as the banking system is prone to corruption as well. Another problem concerns the scattered location of bank and post office branches, which reduces the accounts' accessibility and increases the opportunity and transaction costs of MGNREGS workers to visit banks. Furthermore, Drèze and Khera (2008) argue that the move to bank payments has reduced transparency in

MGNREGA wage payments as banks are not subject to the same transparency and publication rules of key MGNREGA documents (for example, muster rolls) as the MGNREGA implementing agents.

18. http://www.solutionexchange-un.net.in/emp/cr-public/cr-se-emp-decn-03040601-public.pdf.
19. See http://www.igovernment.in and http://www.civilsocietyonline.com/June07/india07ngrea.asp.

References

Ambasta, P., P. S Vijay Shankar, M. Shah (2008) Two years of NREGA: The road ahead. *Economic and Political Weekly* 43, No. 08: 41–50.

CAG (2008) *Performance audit of implementation of National Rural Employment Guarantee Act, 2005 (NREGA)*, Performance Audit Report No. 42, New Delhi.

Drèze, J. and C. Oldiges (2007) Commendable Act. *Frontline* 24, No. 14, 14–27 July.

Drèze, J. and R. Khera (2008). From accounts to accountability. *The Hindu*, 06 December 2008. http://www.sacw.net/article382.html (accessed 21 March 2009).

Drèze, J., R. Khera and Siddharth (2007). *NREGA in Orissa: Ten loopholes and the silver lining*, Interim Survey Report, 21 October 2007, Allahabad University. http://www.righttofoodindia.org/data/gbpant07orissa-social-audit-interim-report.pdf (accessed 21 March 2009).

Government of India (2005a) *National Rural Employment Guarantee Act 2005, No. 42 Of 2005*. http://www.commonlii.org/in/legis/num_act/nrega2005375 (accessed on 05 Sept 2008).

——— (2005b) *The National Rural Employment Guarantee Act 2005 (NREGA): Operational guidelines*. New Delhi: Ministry of Rural Development, Department of Rural Development.

——— (2008). *The National Rural Employment Guarantee Act 2005 (NREGA): Operational guidelines 2008*, 3rd edition. New Delhi: Ministry of Rural Development, Department of Rural Development. http://nrega.nic.in/NREGA_guidelinesEng.pdf (accessed on 16 March 2009).

Narayanan, S. (2008) Employment guarantee, women's work and childcare. *Economic and Political Weekly* 43, No. 9: 10–13.

PACS-CSO survey, Centre for Development Support (2007) *Status of NREGA implementation—Grassroots learning and ways forward*, 2nd monitoring report, 06 April to 07 March, Poorest Area Civil Society (PACS) Programme, Delhi.

Pritchett, L. and M. Woolcock (2004) Solutions when the solution is the problem: Arraying the disarray in development. World Development, 32, 191–212.

Schiffer, E. and D. Waale (2008) Tracing power and influence in networks: Net-map as a tool for research and strategic network planning. Discussion Paper No. 00772, Washington, D.C., International Food Policy Research Institute.

Shah, M. (2008) Governance reform key to NREGA success. *Hindu*, 14 March 2008.

Siddhartha and A. Vanaik (2008) CAG report on NREGA: Fact and fiction. *Economic and Political Weekly* 43, No. 25.

UNDP (2009) *Employment guarantee quickening India's march towards MDGs*. Report on an International seminar on rural poverty-key Initiatives in achieving Millennium Development Goals and the role of NREGA, 21–22 January 2009, National Agricultural Science Centre, New Delhi. United Nations Development Programme.

World Bank (2007) *Tools for Institutional, political and social analysis of policy reform—A sourcebook for development practitioners. Washington, D.C.: World Bank.*

14

MGNREGA and Rural Governance Reform

Growth with Inclusion through Panchayats

Pramathesh Ambasta

The Constitutional 73rd Amendment Act and the establishment of a local governance system in India through three-tier PRIs has marked a new chapter in the history of democratic decentralisation in India. The vision informing this decentralisation has been that these local government institutions will be the pivots fostering inclusion in an era of high economic growth. This chapter argues that the challenges of inclusion are formidable and the articulation of this vision has been hampered by an ineffective devolution of funds, functions and functionaries to the PRIs. In this context, it examines the experience of the MGNREGA to see how its outcomes have fallen short of its potential due to inadequate support structures at the grass roots. The chapter then attempts to spell out a blueprint of reforms that are needed for the MGNREGA to realise its true potential. Since funds to PRIs are not so much of an issue after MGNREGA, functionaries are the real bottleneck, which must be taken care of by a revisioning of the cutting edge of implementation of the MGNREGA. The chapter also examines in detail the information technology (IT) deployment for the MGNREGA and suggests how it can be strengthened. The chapter proposes that to ensure proper monitoring, evaluation, deployment of human resources and their development, IT innovations and for grievance redress, a national authority for the MGNREGA is needed to anchor and support MGNREGA implementation. The chapter further argues that while such support and resource deployment are necessary conditions, rural development and the empowerment of the poor cannot happen through techno-managerial provisioning alone, but needs grass-roots mobilisation. In the tasks of mobilisation and support to the gram sabhas and PRIs for making MGNREGA more effective, civil society has a role to play and this role needs to be mainstreamed. Such reforms in the MGNREGA can effectively transform governance at the grass roots and also empower rural communities. Over time, such reforms can become the way forward for all interventions targeting the rural poor.

I

The Context

The passage of the Constitutional 73rd Amendment Act by the Indian Parliament in 1992, followed by its extension to scheduled areas in 1996, has been heralded as the dawn of a new era in the history of India and also as the largest decentralisation project in the world (Widmalm, 2005). The vision informing this decentralisation project is that an elected three-tier local government structure, collectively known as PRIs, will take the lead in ensuring inclusion and empowerment in an era of high growth.[1] This systemic move towards decentralisation has paved the way for a host of people-centred legislations such as the MGNREGA, the Forest Rights Act and the upcoming National Food Security Act.

Yet the experience of the past decade and more has shown that the challenges of inclusion are formidable to say the least. In the era of market reforms, which were kicked off contemporaneously with decentralisation reforms, GDP growth has accelerated and the rate of GDP growth has consistently been above 5 per cent during the last two decades (Nagaraj, 2008). India is the 12th largest economy in the world in terms of GDP and is one of the fastest growing economies in the world today (World Bank, 2008). Yet this growth has remained confined to enclaves of prosperity surrounded by vast hinterlands of deprivation, home to 77 per cent of India's population or over 836 million people, with a per capita consumption expenditure of less than or equal to ₹20 per day (roughly $2 in Purchasing Power Parity [PPP] terms) (NCEUS, 2007; Sengupta, Kannan and Ravindran, 2008). The latest National Family Health Survey–3 of 2005–06 shows that the share of anaemic under-three children has risen to 79 per cent over the previous (NFHS-2) survey of 1998–99, when it was 74 per cent. Nearly half of India's under-three-year children continue to remain underweight. India has the highest percentage (87 per cent) of pregnant anaemic women in the world (World Bank, 2007). Moreover, as per the World Bank's World Development Indicators of 2005 and 2007, India's infant mortality and under-five mortality rates (63 per 1,000 and 87 per 1,000, respectively) are not only amongst the highest in the world, but are also substantially higher than that of Bangladesh (46 per 1,000 and 69 per 1,000, respectively), which has a substantially lower per capita gross national income.

Within an overall dismal national scenario, there is glaring evidence of inter-regional inequalities. Thus, for instance, states within India are in the same bracket as some of the poorer parts of the world in terms of infant mortality and under-5 mortality and malnourishment. There is also reason to believe that inequities in social sector provisioning such as health, both spatial and inter-group, have persisted, and have probably worsened (Shankar and Shah, 2009). It has further been shown that 'low-income and poorly-performing major states of UP, MP, Bihar, Orissa and Assam, have not only persisted with their low-growth syndrome but have also experienced further deceleration in growth rates in the 1990s' (EPWRF, 2003: 26). Deaton and Drèze (2002) find strong evidence that growth rates of per capita expenditure point to a significant increase in rural–urban inequalities at the all-India level, and also within most individual states, dampening the effects of growth on poverty reduction. This echoes the findings of Datt and Ravallion (2002) who find that 'the geographic and sectoral pattern of India's growth process has greatly attenuated its aggregate impact on poverty' (Datt and Ravallion, 2002: 1). Poverty and distress are increasingly concentrated in the dry lands of India and its hilly and tribal areas (Shah et al., 1998), which are also home to violent expressions of discontent. The Inter-ministry Task Group on Redressing Growing Regional Imbalances (Planning Commission, 2005) has developed a list of '170 most backward districts including 55 extremist affected districts'. One hundred and eighteen of these districts are located in five big states—Bihar, Jharkhand, Orissa, UP and MP (Shankar and Shah, 2009). At the other end of this spectrum are thousands of farmers continuing to commit suicide

(Ghosh, 2005). This is no ordinary crisis. It reflects the complete breakdown of governance in large parts of the country (Shah, 2007).

It is quite clear from the above that even if the mainstream economic development paradigm of market reforms has done nothing to worsen the poverty and inequity situation, it has done very little to improve it and, therefore, at the very best, is irrelevant to the process of inclusion. Given such a grave context, reforms of another kind for rural India are clearly an imperative. It is our view that the role of PRIs becomes critical in these alternative reforms and if PRIs are to play this role, the project of decentralisation has to deepen towards better governance at the grass roots.

In this chapter we look at how PRIs are poised to play this role and what needs to change to make them perform better. We place the discussion in the context of the MGNREGA. We briefly look at the experience of decentralisation and its problems. We then look at the potential of the MGNREGA to bring about inclusive growth, after which its performance on the ground is assessed. Problems in its implementation are discussed in order to draw out a blueprint for reforms in the MGNREGA implementation. The chapter argues that the outlined framework of necessary preparations required for making the MGNREGA successful are also what should inform all rural development interventions, though reforms of each intervention will necessarily be different and specific.

The Decentralisation Experience

While democratic decentralisation in India has made progress, there is still a long way to go. A major bottleneck in this regard has been insufficient progress in devolution of what is known as the three Fs—funds, functions and functionaries. Essentially, this means that while the legislation has been passed, the actual work of making PRIs in charge has proceeded very slowly and the progress has been uneven across states (Aiyar, 2005; Widmalm, 2005; ARC, 2007; MoPR, 2008). Thus, even if functions have been demarcated to be carried out by PRIs, the requisite funds have not been placed at their disposal but have been diverted by state governments, even if temporarily, to meet their own 'ways and means requirements' (Aiyar, 2005: 65), or the functionaries have not been made fully accountable to them, with line departments still maintaining their stranglehold (Social Watch India, 2009), or there has been a lack of clarity on demarcation of powers and functions to be performed between tiers of the PRI system. An index of devolution, based on scores for different parameters of devolution suggests that while there has been some progress in devolution, this progress has been uneven across states (NCAER, 2009). While devolution of funds between 1993–94 and 2002–03 grew, PRIs' own revenue per capita accounted for only 9 per cent of their expenditure per capita, indicating that fund control has not been effectively devolved (MoPR, 2008).

A serious consequence of such decentralisation without adequate preparation has been, on the one hand, a universalisation of basic social services without sufficient attention to quality (Shankar and Shah, 2009), and on the other, such 'subsidiarity without empowerment' has also the possible implication of effectively absolving the state of its responsibilities in the social sector (Shah, 2007).

Since 2004, however, one key element in this overall scenario has begun to change decisively—explosive rise in expenditure on rural development in particular, exemplified most of all by the MGNREGA.

II

MGNREGA: Potential, Performance and Problems

The Possibilities

The passage of the MGNREGA in 2005 marks a new chapter in Indian history as well as in the history of decentralisation in India. Through this Act, the state is committed to providing employment ('not less than one hundred days of such work in a financial year', NREGA, 2005: Ch. II) to every rural family which demands such work and whose adult members volunteer to do such work. Such work will be provided at the minimum wage rate and, as far as possible, within a five km radius of the village where the applicant resides. Failure to provide such wage employment within 15 days of the receipt of the application will entitle the applicant to receive a daily unemployment allowance. The act moves towards ensuring the right to work and lays the basis for development interventions which do not depend on the wilful benevolence of the state but legally bind the state to provide employment for any rural family that demands it. Since April 2008, the coverage of the act was expanded to all districts of India, making it the largest employment programme in the world.

The principal implementing agency under the act is the GP. The MGNREGA is also supported by unprecedented operational guidelines (GoI, 2005), which give central emphasis to community participation in quality planning, implementation, social audit and transparency. A remarkable feature of the MGNREGA through which it makes a decisive break with the past is that it places a complete ban on the use of contractors and also lays emphasis on labour-intensive work for water conservation, drought and flood proofing as priority works under the MGNREGA, underscoring water security as the prerequisite and foundation for rural transformation in India (NREGA, 2005, Schedule I).

The transformatory potential of the MGNREGA lies in creating sustainable livelihoods through well-targeted public investments in rural areas for creation of durable assets in priority works as listed above, thus easing the resource constraints faced by the poor, RLHs, a very high proportion of whom are actually owners of land (Labour Bureau, 2004).[2] This acquires particular significance in the light of growing realisation in economic thinking about the synergies between equity and growth (see Bourguignon, 2004; Shah, 2007, for a discussion of the issues involved). The reasons are one, in an unequal situation, the impact of growth on poverty would be muted (Datt and Ravallion, 2002; Deaton and Drèze, 2002). On the other hand, inverting the growth–poverty linkage argument, it can be understood that the poor remain poor because of lack of access to productive resources (say, for instance, due to imperfect credit markets or an unequal distribution of wealth (Bourguinon, 2004), which in turn inhibits their productive growth-oriented potential from being unlocked. Thus, the poor are not simply passive receptors of growth but, as producers, are contributors to it, representing both a 'slack' in the system and an opportunity which, with systematic and well-directed investments (such as the priority activities listed in Schedule I of the MGNREGA), could actually begin to contribute to the growth process itself. MGNREGA funds could be initially utilised to create the basic water infrastructure in villages through proper grassroots planning. Over time, this could serve as the basis for a range of income-generating livelihoods interventions. Together, these would ensure that the investments made are productive, put the economy on a sustainable growth path and further that the number of dependents on a state-sponsored guarantee would steadily decline. The recent amendment to allow MGNREGA work on lands of small and marginal farmers (MoRD, 2009), has further deepened the possibilities of working on such activities under the MGNREGA. However, for such possibilities to be fully articulated, the bottom-up architecture of the MGNREGA would have to become a reality, the key to which, in turn, is a deepening of democratic decentralisation. It is to an understanding of these issues that we now turn.

Performance and Achievements

Over the past four years or so, MGNREGA's performance according to key aggregate indicators has been quite impressive, particularly when compared with previous employment programmes. For one, budgetary allocation for the MGNREGA has expanded steadily from its base of about ₹11,300 crores in 2006–07 to ₹40,100 crores in 2009–10. As per data available from the MGNREGA website, the cumulative expenditure under MGNREGA works since 2006–07 has been ₹67,667.64 crores. The cumulative employment generated has been 578.65 crore person-days over the same period.

Since its launch, the benefits of MGNREGA has reached women, SC/ST families and the poor. Over the last four years, the share of SC/ST families in the work provided under MGNREGA has ranged between 51–56 per cent. 41 to 50 per cent of workers have been women. Nearly 8.50 lakh differently abled workers have so far been registered for work. With nearly eight crore bank/post office accounts opened for MGNREGA workers, and about 85 per cent of MGNREGA payments being made through them, MGNREGA has also moved financial inclusion of the poor several steps forward.

Major Issues in MGNREGA Implementation

Aggregate figures of achievement, however, hide several lacunae in the core MGNREGA objectives of people-centred planning, transparency and bottom-up architecture, even in states which are performing well on the employment-generation criterion (see Kumar, Rakesh Kumar and Seethalakshmi, 2008, for a discussion of such issues related to Andhra Pradesh). It has been observed that wage payments are delayed; works are of a poor quality; there is corruption; contractors tend to find ways to beat the system and planning and social audits do not involve people (see, for instance, Shah, 2009; Ambasta, 2009; Drèze, Bhatia and Khera, 2009).

A field assessment of the status of MGNREGA implementation in selected panchayats was undertaken by partner organisations of the National Consortium on MGNREGA (a loosely federated collective of CSOs committed to supporting and partnering PRIs to make MGNREGA implementation a success) in 15 districts of Gujarat, MP, Chhattisgarh and Orissa (Samaj Pragati Sahayog, 2008; see also Ambasta, Shah and Vijay Shankar, 2008 and National Consortium on MGNREGA, 2009 for detailed discussions). Table 14.1 summarises the main findings of the field assessment carried out.

Subsequent follow-ups by consortium partners do not find significant changes in the base situation. These field observations also find corroboration in the performance audit of MGNREGA carried out by the CAG (CAG, 2008),[3] which finds that plans were not prepared properly and with the involvement of the gram sabhas, several activities included under the plans were non-priority and there were delays in wage payments. In other words, MGNREGA seems to be heading towards becoming another instance of the 'universalization sans quality' syndrome.

Table 14.1: Field Assessment of MGNREGA Performance According to Major Indicators

Indicator	*Summary Observation*	*Remarks*
1. People-centred planning	Absent	1. Gram sabha's involvement in plan preparation minimal; its role often confined to a formality of approving what has already been done by the block 2. Choice of works not towards the priorities envisaged under the MGNREGA with a bias towards roads rural connectivity 3. The absence of plans meant that fund release not in tune with labour availability and work demand 4. In some instances, plans made were photocopies of plans prepared under NFFWP. List of such works put together has formed the MGNREGA plan 5. Lack of annual plans, with activities not well defined. 6. Lack of capacity in GP and shortage of technical staff with GPs for planning
2. Quality of works	Uniformly poor	1. Indifference of line departments to MGNREGA works 2. Poor planning results in poor results (plantations made, but no arrangement for watering meant plants died) 3. Several works left incomplete 4. Shortage of staff a serious issue in ensuring quality
3. Wages and wage payments	Delays and non-conformance with minimum wages observed	1. In some panchayats, delays cross two to three months 2. SOR militate against minimum wages 3. Long gaps between work and valuation also cause delays in wage payments 4. Shortage of funds at block level also reportedly a cause of delayed wage payments 5. Increases in task rates made at the state level do not translate into similar increases at the GP level because GP does not have the capacity to rework the estimates, and engineers who can do so are too few in number. 6. Banks do not have branches/staff, etc., to cater to MGNREGA wage payments
4. Use of machines and contractors	Prevalent	1. JCBs, machines used in MGNREGA work with muster rolls fudged to hide the fact 2. In some cases, functionaries appointed to work at GP level (Labour Leaders in Orissa) have become de facto contractors 3. Political patronage in line department works 4. Line department works need machinery and tractors 5. In some places (Raigarh and Jashpur, Chhattisgarh), following mobilisation of people, use of machines and contractors has come down
5. Transparency and social audit	Poor	1. No real social audit taking place in any location 2. Government reports and documents show that they are taking place 3. No active vigilance committees 4. Very often, panchayat secretaries simply write down the name of village people as vigilance committee members, without the people's knowledge

Indicator	Summary Observation	Remarks
		5. Where administration claims that social audit has been done, no records made available of the event 6. Disturbing trend of inviting tenders for social audit with assignment given to lowest bidder—far cry from the actual requirements of social audit
6. Work demand	Not correctly represented	1. Lack of awareness among people that MGNREGA guarantees work and that they have to demand it 2. Fear of legal action forces implementing agencies to suppress work demand 3. Bureaucratic machinery puts fear in PRI leadership of legal action in case of non-fulfilment of work demand so that real work demand does not get expressed

Source: Compiled from Samaj Pragati Sahayog (2008).

Funds, Functions and Functionaries

Funds and Functions

From a functions point of view, the main implementing agencies under the MGNREGA are PRIs. The central government assistance is routed directly to district-level panchayats from where it reaches the grass-roots implementing agency, namely, GPs. Regarding finances, since the MGNREGA is a legal right, the amount of funds made available to a GP is a function of the number of job cardholders in the GP and the number of days for which they demand work. If work demand under the MGNREGA is properly mobilised, given the constitutional commitment under the act, funds will have to be provided by the state.

An understanding of how the MGNREGA has made a difference to the financial situation of the GPs will necessitate a quantitative assessment of the funds available with GPs pre-MGNREGA. However, such data at the GP level is not available, caused largely due to variations in the methods adopted by different states with respect to devolution of funds. Hence, in what follows, we will attempt an estimation.

As per the Twelfth Finance Commission (2004), the total number of PRIs (across all tiers) was 237,824 in 2002–03. Their total revenues stood at ₹24,010 crores, or approximately ₹10 lakhs per PRI unit. Since this includes all tiers, it only gives us an approximate picture on the funds position of GPs, which is likely to be much less.[4] As per MoPR, 2008, the average expenditure per capita of PRIs across all three tiers for 15 major states (Andhra Pradesh, Assam, Bihar, Gujarat, Haryana, Karnataka, Kerala, MP, Maharashtra, Orissa, Punjab, Rajasthan, Tamil Nadu, UP and West Bengal) between 1998–2003 was ₹378 only.

Our projections for potential expenditures under MGNREGA in the same 15 states which formed part of the MoPR exercise are summarised in Table 14.2. They show that even under very modest assumptions,[5] the funds that can be potentially leveraged by these GPs for MGNREGA work alone is three times their pre-MGNREGA budget.

Thus, the MGNREGA has very clearly set the context for devolution of both finances and functions. Indeed, it would not be an exaggeration to say that compared to pre-MGNREGA base situations, there is an explosion of funds that can potentially be leveraged by GPs.

Table 14.2: Estimated Typical MGNREGA Budget for One Gram Panchayat

		All India	
		Unit	*Amount*
1.	Total no. of rural households (RHs) in 1999–2000 (Labour Bureau, 2004)	Crores	13.49
2.	Total no. of projected RHs in 2009–10 @1.93 % per annum rate of growth of population	Crores	16.02
3.	RLHs @40 % of RHs (0.40 × [2])	Crores	6.41
4.	No. of GPs	No	239,432
5.	RLH per GP [3/4]	No	268
6.	Persons offering themselves for MGNREGA work @1 adult in 90 % of RLH in GP) [0.90 × 5]	No	241
7.	Total job cards (=6)	No	241
8.	Person-days of employment if 100 days guarantee in one year (100 × [7])	No	24,091
9.	Wage bill @ ₹100 per person per day ([8] × 100)	₹	2,409,076
10.	Material cost assuming 60:40 wage to non-wage cost ([9] × 4/6)	₹	1,606,051
11.	**Total cost of guarantee (₹ Cr) for one GP [9] + [10]**	₹	**4,015,126**
		(₹ lakhs)	**40**
12.	Projected population of GPs (1.93 % per annum growth over 2000–01)	No	863,963,069
13.	**Potential GP MGNREGA budget per capita [13/12]**	₹	**1,202**

Source: Author.

Functionaries as a Major Bottleneck

A real bottleneck in MGNREGA implementation is a lack of functionaries at the cutting edge of implementation, with serious consequences for the bottom-up, people-centred architecture of MGNREGA. The shortage of staff has had a serious impact on key parameters like high-quality people-centred planning and implementation of works, availability of employment on time, timely measurements, and hence, timely payments, as shown above. It is clear that the sheer size of the guarantee makes it impossible to be carried out on an 'additional charge' syndrome. However, this is precisely what has been happening with MGNREGA.

CAG Report of 2008. The performance audit report of the CAG (CAG, 2008) found that 19 states had not appointed Programme Officers (POs) in 70 per cent of the blocks it surveyed. The report said that every state government was required to appoint, in each block, a full-time PO, exclusively dedicated to the implementation of the MGNREGA, with necessary support staff. The existing BDOs had been appointed POs and given 'additional charge' of the MGNREGA. An EGA was to be appointed in each GP, in view of the pivotal role of PRIs in the MGNREGA implementation. According to the CAG report, 52 per cent of the 513 GPs it surveyed had not appointed EGAs. The state governments were also required to constitute panels of accredited engineers at the district and block levels. Without timely and transparent costing of works and their measurement and valuation by such a panel, neither sanction of works nor payment to labour can happen on schedule. The CAG found the panel missing in as many as 20 of the states it studied. The state governments were also to appoint technical resource support groups at the state and district levels to assist in planning, design, monitoring, evaluation, quality audit, training and handholding. The CAG report finds that 23 states had not set up such groups at the state or district levels. According to the report,

> [N]on-appointment of a full-time dedicated PO, who is pivotal to the successful implementation of MGNREGA, and giving the additional charge of PO to BDOs, who were responsible for other developmental schemes at the block level, strikes at the root of effective implementation of MGNREGA. In the absence of dedicated technical resources, the administrative and technical scrutiny and approval of works was, thus, routed through the normal departmental channels burdened with existing responsibilities. This was further compounded by the failure to specify time-frames for processing and approval of proposals at different levels. This was reflected in the poor progress in taking up works. (CAG, 2008: 16–17)

Field Review by Consortium Partners. Field reviews carried out by partners of the National Consortium on MGNREGA (Samaj Pragati Sahayog, 2008), corroborate these observations of CAG as Table 14.3 shows.

Table 14.3: Field Assessment of Deployment of MGNREGA Functionaries: Selected Highlights

District/State in Which Consortium Partner Working	*Status of Appointment of:*		
	Programme Officers (POs)	*Technical Support Staff*	*Rozgar Sevaks, Mates*
Bolangir and Nuapada, Orissa	1. BDOs doubling up as MGNREGA Programme Officers.	1. Engineers of line departments given additional responsibility of MGNREGA. For a block of 140 villages, only 4–5 JENs available, two of whom are given additional responsibility for MGNREGA, while the others continue with their normal departmental work. 2. These two JENs, in charge of MGNREGA, also look after other schemes such as the BRGF, IAY, Revised Long Term Action Plan for KBK, Biju-KBK Scheme, Member of Parliament Local Area Development Scheme (MPLADS) and (Drought Prone Areas Programme) DPAP.	1. In Orissa, village labour leaders were appointed, who were organising village people for work and getting work done under the MGNREGA. These were found to be working as de facto contractors. 2. Move to appoint one male and one female *gram saathi* in each village to help with MGNREGA work. However, their selection procedure has been handed over to touts and their qualifications and fitness for the job are in doubt.

(Table 14.3 contd.)

(Table 14.3 contd.)

District/State in Which Consortium Partner Working	*Status of Appointment of:*		
	Programme Officers (POs)	*Technical Support Staff*	*Rozgar Sevaks, Mates*
		3. Sometimes an Assistant Engineer (AE) supervises the work in more than one block. 4. Thus, the whole process of planning and design of works, implementation, measurement and payment is marked with poor attention to quality and long delays.	
Dahod and Panchmahals, Gujarat	1. Officers being sent on deputation from other government departments, particularly the irrigation department, as POs 2. But such officers normally do not want to be posted in a remote tribal area. So they would like to be transferred out as soon as possible. 3. Also, having a full-time dedicated PO for the implementation of MGNREGA means that administrative costs go up. So the trend is being reversed and the BDOs are given additional charge.	1. Since 2007, there has been some move to induct technical personnel. 2. But actual appointments fall far short of what is required.	1. Independently of MGNREGA implementation, the state government has created the post of *gram mitras* (village friends) and made appointments to look after development works in the panchayats. 2. However, they are unable to exercise themselves in the interest of larger communities and are often under control of powerful PRI leaders and talati.
Shivpuri district, MP	1. Panchayat inspector was also PO MGNREGA (Pohari block) 2. Officers of other line departments have been appointed PO (Badarwas block)		

District/State in Which Consortium Partner Working	Status of Appointment of: Programme Officers (POs)	Technical Support Staff	Rozgar Sevaks, Mates
Tikamgarh District, MP	1. CEOs of block panchayats had been given additional charge of MGNREGA.	1. Rural Engineering Services (RES) and other line department engineers are also being given additional charge of MGNREGA. 2. Some appointment of engineers at the block or district level have been made but under contract for a limited tenure. 3. Delays of upto two months between submission of plan and sanction.	
Khandwa district, MP	1. CEOs of block panchayats had been given additional charge of MGNREGA	In Khandwa, there have been some contractual appointments but too few to make any difference.	
Raigarh District, Chhattisgarh	1. Government advertised for open market recruitment of POs. However, contract is for a limited period of a year. After this, the whole process is undertaken again. The present PO may be transferred to another block or may cease to be in service altogether. By the time the PO is in the saddle, it is time to make a move. 2. This uncertainty of tenure and resulting discontinuity has serious impacts on MGNREGA works. POs are demoralised and demotivated and feel that the work done by them has come to nothing.	1. In Raigarh and Jashpur districts, where JEs have been appointed, their tenure is for a period of one year, after which it has to be renewed. 2. Number of such JEs also falling far short of what is required.	1. Appointment of EGA is on a contractual basis for a tenure of a year. 2. Short tenure and the impending transfers affect the morale of these personnel adversely. 3. Also, in several panchayats, the post may be reserved for SC/ST or women candidates. This reservation is put up in the panchayat roster. This reservation category is also subject to change on an annual basis, forcing the panchayat to change the EGA. 4. If one year, an SC candidate is appointed EGA; next year, the GP may have to change the candidate to an ST person and so on.

(Table 14.3 contd.)

(Table 14.3 contd.)

District/State in Which Consortium Partner Working	Status of Appointment of: Programme Officers (POs)	Technical Support Staff	Rozgar Sevaks, Mates
			5. It may be several months before the next EGA is appointed. 6. An outmigration of skills from the GP since the EGA leaves and is posted to another GP or is out of the system altogether.
Sarguja district, Chhattisgarh	1. Similar contracts and tenures resulting in uncertainty and demoralisation of POs	1. In Wardrafnagar block of Sarguja district, for instance, four technical assistants have been appointed between 72 GPs. 2. No pool of engineers available at the district level either.	Same as above
Rajnandgaon district, Chhattisgarh	1. Similar contracts and tenures resulting in uncertainty and demoralisation of POs	1. Similar paucity of technical personnel reported	Same as above

Source: Compiled from Samaj Pragati Sahayog (2008).

III

Towards MGNREGA Reforms

In the light of the review above, we will now look at some of the ways in which MGNREGA implementation can be reformed to harness its true potential. It is our attempt to work out a minimum agenda for reform of MGNREGA implementation.

Decentralisation at the Cutting Edge of Implementation: Gram Vikas Sankul (Village Development Cluster)

It is obvious that the level of professional support to GPs has to be stepped up. Not only should there be dedicated staff for a programme with new, radical demands but also the number of such staff needs to increase to set up a proper implementation team. Such a larger team size naturally suggests that each block is broken down into implementation clusters to ensure proper division of responsibilities between different POs in the same block.

Such a cluster-based implementation unit would also become the cutting edge of implementation, instead of the block. This can be seen as an innovation in governance delivery in rural India, as decentralisation is deepened further beyond the current District → Block → GP model.

On an average, there are about 90 villages per block in India. We may divide the block into three parts, each to be called the village development cluster (gram vikas sankul, GVS) comprising 30 villages each or about 15 GPs.[6] This middle-tier GVS will be the cutting-edge level of MGNREGA implementation between the GP and the intermediate panchayat. Such a layer will be coterminus with optimum deployment of personnel, and will ensure:[7]

1. Proper planning
2. Greater cohesion and coordination between GPs and within project teams
3. Time-bound sanctions and releases, smoother functioning through a reduction in the critical distance between GP and MGNREGA implementation hub
4. Timely measurements and valuations of work
5. Powerful social mobilisation and social audit.

Apart from increasing human resource allocation at the cutting edge of implementation, the GVS also ensures a level of efficiency of use of such resources since they are collectively used by several GPs.

Dedicated Implementation Structure at Cluster Level

We further propose that along with this decentralisation of implementation, a fully dedicated professional support team for the MGNREGA is placed at the GVS. This team is recruited from the open market through a rigorous selection and screening process. The team members should be recruited on contract for a period not exceeding three years.

An Outline of the Professional Support Staff Required

The table below attempts to outline the staff requirements at the GVS level along with their proposed job description and the situation at present. This draws on the experiences of the partners of the National Consortium in supporting panchayats for better MGNREGA implementation.

To begin with, this placement of professional support can begin with 2,000 of the most backward blocks of the country where the MGNREGA is of the greatest importance. There is widespread evidence that within districts there are blocks that are much less developed than others and where demand for MGNREGA works is greater. Most tribal blocks would fall into this category. Extension of the act to the entire country became a case of spreading our resources too thin and achieving suboptimal outcomes across the board, rather than aiming for high-quality works where they are needed the most.

Costs of Professional Support

We present in Table 14.4 an indicative calculation of the costs involved in these reforms in the 2,000 most backward blocks of the country.[8] According to the 7th Rural Labour Enquiry Report (Labour Bureau, 2004), there were 13.71 crore rural households in the country in 1999–2000, of which 5.48 crore

Table 14.4: Professionals Required at Sankul Level with Work Description

Personnel	*Work Description*	*As Required Now (Though Not Always in Place)*	*Our Recommendations*
Programme officer (PO)	1. Overall responsibility for coordination of MGNREGA works undertaken by GPs and other implementing agencies 2. Leads team of social mobilisers and EGAs to take responsibility for social components of MGNREGA, such as: • raising awareness about provisions of MGNREGA • ensuring registration of workers and issue of job cards • mobilisation for raising work demand • conducting baseline socio-economic surveys • Participatory Rural Appraisals (PRAs), transect walks and rural appraisal exercises for planning • finalisation of action plan with village community • presentation and approval of action plan in gram sabha • formation of local vigilance committees • organising gram sabhas for continuous approval of work done • organisation of social audits and social audit forums • capacity building of EGAs, social mobilisers and PRI leadership • conflict resolution 3. Monitoring each stage of implementation 4. Redressing or taking responsibility for redressal of grievances 5. Reporting to block panchayats and DPC	1. One per block (invariably additional charge) 2. CAG report (2008) finds that 19 states had not appointed these officers in 70 per cent of the blocks they surveyed. The existing BDOs had been given 'additional charge' of MGNREGA.	1. One per GVS (two to three per block) 2. Full-time, professional PO, carefully selected from the open market, on contract; fully answerable to the block panchayat.
Civil engineer (AEN)	1. Overall technical head of GVS 2. Guide the process of technical planning, estimating, measuring and valuating works 3. Responsible of approval of plans and estimates at GVS level 4. Responsible for approval of measurements at GVS level 5. Building capacities of JENs, APOs and EGAs 6. Visits to work sites to provide handholding support to JENs and EGAs 7. Assist in monitoring of the programme	1. In some states, one AEN is in charge of more than 100 villages (invariably additional charge)	1. One per GVS (two to three per block), full time with experience of earthen works, carefully selected from the open market, on contract; reports to PO

Technical assistants (JEN)	1. Planning: • technical survey of possible work sites • preparation of technical drawings • preparation of cost estimates proper shelf of works 2. Execution: • layout at work site • supervision and monitoring of works • measurement of work done • preparation of musters • maintenance of site-specific records • preparation of work completion certificates • obtain technical approval from AEN • lead the grass-roots technical team of barefoot engineers	1. 1 per 20 GPs 2. Major lacuna in present set-up leading to enormous delays. According to the CAG report, JENs are not in place in 35 per cent of the blocks they surveyed. Official MGNREGA guidelines recommend 1 JEN for 10 GPs; CAG recommends 1 JEN for 5 GPs	1. We agree with the CAG that one full-time JEN is required for every five GPs or three per GVS full time (each in charge of 15 villages) with experience of earthen works, carefully selected from the open market, on contract; reports to civil engineer (AEN)
Social mobilisers	1. Work directly under guidance of PO and discharge social mobilisation functions such as: • awareness generation among village communities about the act and its entitlements • organise meetings/campaigns to raise level of work demand • ensure that work demand applications reach GPs and receipts are issued • assist in social aspects of micro-plan formulation • form and mobilise vigilance committees • carry out the fact-finding for social audits • assist in organising of social audits and other similar events • ensure that grievances reach POs and other redressal mechanism • assist in conflict resolution	None	1. One per two villages
EGA	1. Assists social mobilisers and barefoot engineers in all their tasks 2. Ensures maintenance of records at GP level 3. Ensures that job card and worker registration is maximised	1. Official guidelines suggest one EGA for every GP. According to the CAG report (2007), EGAs are not in place in over 50 per cent of the GPs they surveyed.	1. One per village
Data entry operator	1. Data entry at block level	1. Two DEOs per block already in place	1. One DEO per GVS (three per block)

Table 14.5: Estimated Costs of Extending Employment Guarantee across 2,000 Blocks

		Unit	*Amount*
1.	Total no. of RHs in 1999–2000 as per Labour Bureau (2004)	Crores	13.71
2.	Total no. of projected RHs in 2009–10 @1.93 % per annum rate of growth of population	Crores	16.6
3.	RLH] @40 % of RH (0.40 × [2])	Crores	6.64
4.	No. of blocks in India	No	6495
5.	No. of RLH in 2,000 most backward blocks	Crores	2.04
6.	Persons offering themselves for MGNREGA work @1 adult in 90 % of RLH in 2,000 most backward blocks (0.90 × [5])	Crores	1.84
7.	Total job cards (=6)	Crores	1.84
8.	Person-days of employment if 100 days guarantee in one year (100 × [7])	Crores	184.02
9.	Wage bill @ ₹100 per person per day ([8] × 100)	₹ Crores	18,401.85
10.	Material cost assuming 60:40 wage to non-wage cost ([9] × 4/6)	₹ Crores	12,267.9
11.	Total cost of guarantee (₹ Cr) for 2,000 most backward blocks ([9] + [10])	₹ Crores	30,669.75

Source: Author.

(40 per cent) were RLH. Projecting the number of RLH to grow at an annual compound rate of 1.93 per cent (the national rate of growth of population between 1991 and 2001), we get a figure of 6.64 crore RLH in 2009–10. Since there are 6,495 blocks in India, there would be around 2.04 crore RLH in the 2,000 most backward blocks. If we assume that 1 adult in 90 per cent of these RLH offer themselves for employment under the MGNREGA, the number of people for whom the 100-day job guarantee would have to be extended in the 2,000 most backward blocks comes to nearly 1.84 crores (Table 14.5).

Table 14.6 summarises the cost of professional deployment in the 6,000 GVSs in the 2,000 most backward blocks of India.

Table 14.6: Costs of Professional Support at Gram Vikas Sankul

			Salary Per Month (₹)	*Salary Bill Per Annum (₹ Cr)*
1.	Average no. of GVS per block	3	–	–
2.	Average no. of villages per GVS	30	–	–
3.	No. of GVS for 2,000 blocks ([1] × 2000)	6,000	–	–
4.	Project officers	6,000	20,000	144
5.	Civil engineers (=[2])	6,000	17,500	126
6.	Technical assistants (=[2] × 3)	18,000	12,000	259.2
7.	Social mobilisers (one per two villages)	90,000	2,500	270
8.	EGAs (one per village)	180,000	1,500	324
9.	Data entry operator (one per GVS)	6,000	5,000	36
	Total	–	–	**1,159.2**

Source: Author.

The above cost of professional support works out to a mere 3.78 per cent of total cost of extending the guarantee in the 2,000 most backward blocks. If the employment limit was relaxed beyond 100 days or extended to two adults per household, the above proportion would fall further. In addition, we also estimate that costs of administrative support to the cluster teams and their capacity building costs will not come to more than 1.35 per cent. Thus, the total cost of professional deployment will be a little over 5 per cent of total MGNREGA costs.

In order to attract the best professional talent for MGNREGA implementation, the recruitment of professionals also has to be done in a professional manner. This will need innovative criteria for selection of the right person for the right job and transparent and appropriate human resource policies which build in performance assessment and incentives for good performance.

Such recruitments could be outsourced to credible agencies, backed by administrative and political support. Such innovations in the contexts of specific projects have been tried by the state governments of Bihar, Rajasthan and Tamil Nadu with very good impacts.[9]

Information Technology for MGNREGA

In this section we have spelt out the kind of professional support that will have to be placed at the disposal of panchayats for them to be able to do justice to the demands of MGNREGA. In this endeavour, apart from professional assistance, IT will have a crucial role to play.

To ensure timely delivery of deliverables in any e-governance initiative, concurrent monitoring is a must. It is in this context that the IT for MGNREGA becomes crucial in ensuring best results. Already, the IT system for MGNREGA is a pioneer in terms of the huge amount of information that it has warehoused and made available. We look at how this good start could be made better.

The potential advantage of using IT systems for governance lies in:

1. the speed with which data can be processed and made available in meaningful forms;
2. the availability of data nearly concurrently with its online updation/entry through networks, so that information is available proactively and to a larger audience (in a paper system, this information would have to be dug out to become available);
3. the breaking of artificial barriers of geography, boundaries, etc., to allow flow of information (in paper systems, such boundaries do not automatically break. There is, therefore a systemic support for information suppression).

Of these, the last two are key to engendering transparency and, together, all three make for contributions in governance which only IT can make. Thus, IT systems can become tremendous potential allies in concurrent monitoring, enabling preventives to be placed in line before situations deteriorate. They can also directly enable attaining entitlements and finally, they can become potent tools for grievance redressal.

Usefulness of IT in the MGNREGA Context

We look at the present status of IT systems in the MGNREGA context and discuss how it can be improved. Table 14.7 illustrates the broad stages of MGNREGA workflow and the requirements of different stakeholders.

Table 14.7: MGNREGA Workflow and Stakeholder Expectations from IT

	Stakeholders and Objectives of IT Use		
	Wage seekers	*Implementers*	*Monitors/Grievance Redressers*
	Primary Objective: Getting Entitlement in the Act	*Primary Objective: Implementing and Planning Work to Fulfil Legal Mandate*	*Primary Objective:Monitor Programmes for Quality, Smooth Out Bottlenecks and Ensure that Entitlements Reach Wage Seekers on Time*
Stages of MGNREGA Workflow[10]	*What IT must Enable to Fulfil These Objectives*		
1. Worker registration and issue of job cards 2. Work demand applications 3. Planning and estimation[11] 4. Sanction of work 5. Estimating material requirements 6. Start of work 7. Daily attendance and preparation of muster rolls 8. Measurement and valuation at fixed intervals 9. Preparation of pay order 10. Payment to wage-seekers through bank accounts 11. Accounts/bookkeeping	1. Demand for work must be visible to the implementer 2. Work must be provided within the stipulated time 3. Wages for work done should be paid transparently, without any leakages and preferably at the doorstep 4. Work done must be visible to monitors to ensure that entitlements are fairly met 5. Non-fulfilment of demand or non-compliance with legal requirements of wage payments should become known to monitors for concurrent redressal	1. Information of work demand reaches them 2. Estimates and plans are drawn up in the shortest possible time to meet this demand 3. Estimates of cost are not bloated 4. The process of sanctions and releases is expedited 5. Work is started with minimum delay 6. Worker payments are made within a stipulated time 7. Wage payments reach workers and fraud and fudging is rooted out	1. Availability of updated information which is as close to reality as possible 2. Tracking of the implementation of the MGNREGA schemes as they go from stage to stage

However, for IT to be able to deliver along the above lines, a necessary condition is that it becomes central to the workflow and is tightly integrated end to end. In addition, for maximisation of benefits, it requires a system that is real time and online. The first is a case for better use of IT. The second requires better connectivity backbones and hardware and innovations to ensure that more and more such aspects of work are brought under the purview of IT, which are traditionally thought of as belonging to the domain of notesheets, files and red tape.

Lacunae in Current IT Set-up and How it can be Improved

Let us now examine the MGNREGA workflow and see how the situation on the ground looks for the MGNREGA. What is attempted in Table 14.8 is a stage-wise analysis of what is happening now and how IT can be made to deliver.

Table 14.8: MGNREGA Workflow, Stakeholders and How IT Can Be Used Effectively

Sl No.	*Stages*	*Current Status/Problems That can Occur*	*Stakeholders Impacted*	*How Can IT Effectively Be Used To Change the Situation*
1.	Worker registration and issue of job cards	Registration of bogus workers (dead men/ghosts)	**Monitors:** Information on wage-seekers is wrong, with possibilities of misappropriation	1. The Unique ID (UID) project through fresh surveys and tight screening can rule out such cases 2. The UID can function as a single window for all entitlements due from the government
2.	Work demand applications	1. Registered demand for work can invite penalties for implementers under the act if works are not opened within the stipulated time. So attempts are made to suppress or understate work demand. 2. A way to reconcile the work generated with work demanded is to show in the MIS all work generated as having been demanded[12]	**Wage seekers:** Their demand for work is suppressed, cannot find expression and, thus, their right is denied. **Monitors:** Since the system depends on paper at the local level, no one other than local functionaries need to know about the fact that applications are not being allowed to surface **Implementers:** Cannot properly reconcile work creation with work demand	1. UIDs, when issued, can be combined with biometrics and wireless networks with Portable Digital Assistants (PDAs), or even a cell phone–based system can be used to register work applications online. This makes actual work demand visible on the network for those monitoring the programme so that corrections can be put in place. 2. In case of complaints, a cell phone–based system like in UP can be used to make complaints **Expected Results:** Physical barriers to flow of information are broken and information is transparently available and status is visible
3.	Planning and estimation	Only in a few states like Andhra are computer-generated estimates and drawings actually used. In most states, this stage of work is not computerised, even though the MIS reportedly has the capability	**Implementers:** In the absence of sufficient personnel, time is lost preparing work estimates and shelf of works. Encourages improper planning methods (such as copying of earlier plans, etc.) Plans may be prepared which are non-priority, or with bloated estimates, or not according to standard acceptable norms **Monitoring:** Properly monitoring and tracking works available for sanction becomes impossible; affixing responsibility for non-preparation of plans becomes impossible, etc.[13]	Estimation must compulsorily be computerised as in Andhra Pradesh. This will help put in place a proper shelf of works and plan. **Results:** 1. Dependence on 'technical' personnel for this stage is reduced 2. By standardising norms for estimation, chances of bloated estimates is reduced 3. By making work estimates available on a network and visible, tracking of workflow becomes faster and simpler, so proper monitoring is aided 4. Computerised shelf of works makes possible quick comparisons and matching of demand for work with possible sources of supply so that appropriate action can be taken

(Table 14.8 contd.)

(Table 14.8 contd.)

Sl No.	*Stages*	*Current Status/Problems That can Occur*	*Stakeholders Impacted*	*How Can IT Effectively Be Used To Change the Situation*
4.	Sanction of plan	Two types of sanctions are required: technical and administrative. Neither is computerised so there is a reliance on paper sanctions	**Wage seekers**: Work will not open on site until sanction is accorded. So the entitlement of timely wage employment is denied, which is a violation of their right **Implementers**: Implementers are kept on hold because unless they receive sanctions, they cannot implement **Monitors:** Invisibility of proposal pending for sanction reduces chances of tracking delays between work planning and sanction, affixing responsibility and ensuring time-bound programme implementation.	1. Possible to have systems of computerised sanctions. Role-based privileged and differential access to the same data, coupled with digital signatures and encryption should make it possible to accord such sanctions online. In fact, the paper sanction should be a *report* emanating from online transactions, rather than the other way around **Result:** 1. Greater speed 2. Greater amenability to tracking 3. Control over bloating of estimates
5.	Material requirement/ estimation	1. Automated in Andhra Pradesh 2. Manual elsewhere, takes time, and is not available for peer review	**Implementers:** 1. Lack of automation may slow down procurement 2. Also may slow down payments to suppliers, accounts reconciliation, etc. **Monitors:** 1. May not be enough safeguards against choice of suppliers made by implementers 2. Difficult to track reasons for delays in material procurement if order placement itself is not online	Online database of suppliers (as in the case of the Andhra Pradesh Rural Employment Guarantee Scheme [APREGS]) limits scope for discretion and misuse in choice of suppliers. Better than post facto action and deterrents **Results:** 1. Material supply and accounts thereof can be seamlessly integrated and speeded up 2. Data on network makes tracking better
6.	Start of work	Currently no way of knowing when work *should* have started, since it is entered in MIS when it is started	**Monitors:** 1. Lack of online information on stages prior to start of work does not make for good monitoring and tracking	1. Tracking can be improved by making IT central to the workflow **Result:** Better and timely execution

7.	Daily attendance and muster rolls	1. Taken manually 2. Huge scope for fudging by contractors and others in the implementation interface 3. Most muster roll data is entered into MIS after a certain number of days of work have been completed	**Wage seekers:** 1. Do not know if information against their job card is entered correctly; are victims of corruption **Implementers:** 1. Can fudge, connive, etc., to make money 2. Seniors need not come to know if juniors are indulging in such malpractices **Monitors** 1. No means of verifying whether the muster roll details fed into the MIS are true or are fudged, so corruption cannot be tackled effectively 2. There is lack of updated information on labour employed	Use of UID biometric authentication, GPS-enabled handhelds along with 'MGNREGA correspondent model', wherein the correspondent or field worker is equipped with handheld devices which take the attendance 'digitally', can enable direct *real-time* updation of attendance and muster rolls. In such a system, muster rolls are *reports* generated out of the online system rather than data entry forms feeding data into the system. A pilot of this concept has been proposed by the MoRD for Andhra Pradesh, Orissa, Kerala, UP and Bihar (MoRD, Government of India). **Results:** 1. Greater transparency 2. Faster execution 3. Better monitoring
8.	Measurement and valuation	This is an activity which will have to be done on site. However, it is delayed and is sometimes subject to enormous delays for various reasons, because of which work completion, further instalments and wage payments are all delayed. 1. There is also need for verification of work done, which at present can only be done through periodic surveys/inspection of selected sights	**Wage seekers:** 1. Delays in measurements can often cause serious delays in wage disbursements in clear violation of the law 2. It can also put at risk further work prospects **Monitors:** 1. Lack of onsite verification can lead to corruption which can become very hard to establish post facto	1. If all previous stages are sufficiently 'IT-ised', then chances of tracking delays at this stage are maximised **Result:**Use of technologies such as those outlined in the row above can make possible real-time verification of sites
9.	Preparation of pay order	1. In Andhra, computerised wage lists, pay orders are sent to GP, post office or bank 2. Elsewhere this stage appears largely outside the purview of the MIS which is updated later	**Wage seekers:** No check on pay order generation and handing over could mean delays in wages **Monitors:** No real-time basis for knowing whether the pay order has been prepared or not; so if delays occur, they appear only after the event	Take a cue from Andhra and integrate this process it into the main MIS

(Table 14.8 contd.)

(Table 14.8 contd.)

Sl No.	Stages	Current Status/Problems That can Occur	Stakeholders Impacted	How Can IT Effectively Be Used To Change the Situation
10.	Wage payments to wage seekers through bank/ post offices	1. Bank-based/post office–based labour payments mandatory since 2008 to ensure transparency and separation of executing agency from paying agency 2. Not enough bank branches 3. Large number of small accounts are not seen as profitable by banks 4. At payment time, large number of wage-seekers come for cash withdrawal to be catered to by a small staff 5. Panchayats too do not have the human resources to help wage-seekers with all the paper formalities that banks require 6. Wage-seekers are often not aware of bank procedures 7. Bank branches are located at a distance from workers homes, so it is difficult for them to make frequent trips 8. Collusion mechanisms to beat the system and actually practise corruption have surfaced at different places	**Wage-seekers:** 1. Benefited to the extent that bank/ PO transfers check corruption 2. However, delays in wage payments take place frequently 3. Travelling to banks, negotiating with them for withdrawals, etc., may discourage wage-seekers 4. The poor can enter into arrangements with some people in the village for a 'consideration' to help them get cash withdrawals done **Monitors:** 1. No means of verification (except after the event type of social audits, etc.) whether the payment has actually reached the wage seeker or has been siphoned off 2. MIS does not reflect wage payment delays[14]	The bank correspondent model along with UID-based biometrics and handheld devices can ensure that payments reach the beneficiary at the doorstep **Results:** Problems with bank payments can be smoothened out Move towards greater transparency is strengthened

Taking a Cue from Andhra Pradesh

It is worthwhile to look at the APREGS software, developed by the Tata Consultancy Services which comes as close as possible under the current situation to being a good IT deployment (see Tata Consultancy Services, 2006).

All stages of MGNREGA work, from registration of workers to issue of job cards, preparation of estimates for works, muster rolls and transfer of payments to workers are effectively computerised, leading to reduction in time taken and administrative costs. Modules in the software related to estimation and planning make it possible for technical survey readings for a standard basket of activities, taken by a technical assistant or EGA, to be fed into the system and a work estimate generated on this basis. The estimate is given a unique ID, which is used to track the work, prepare muster rolls from the MIS system and also prepare orders for payments. The MIS has already ensured that most or all stages of MGNREGA implementation cannot bypass it. Thus, work estimates, pay orders, muster rolls, etc., must be generated from the system for work to continue.

The major contribution of this MIS is that it opens up MGNREGA for public scrutiny, engenders greater transparency and has become an invaluable tool for social audit. Timely wage payments have been made possible and any work registered in the system is alive, status-visible and amenable to tracking. Delays at any stage can thus be immediately identified and corrected (see Shah and Ambasta, 2008, for a discussion).

Biometrics and Banking Correspondents

Labour payments in MGNREGA through banks or post office accounts[15] have been made compulsory since 2008. With 80 million MGNREGA wage-seeker bank accounts opened and 80 per cent of MGNREGA wage payments already being made through this route, the MGNREGA has ushered in unprecedented financial inclusion. While this is a move to ensure transparency so that handling of cash for payments is ruled out, lack of sufficient preparation for this move has led to several problems (see Vanaik, Ashish and Siddhartha, 2008; Drèze and Khera, 2008) some of which have been outlined above. Despite its various problems, the basic premises of separating those in charge of work execution from those in charge of payments and doing away with the handling of cash is fundamentally sound.

Under the circumstances, it is desirable to think of ways in which the problems in the system are taken care of. Here IT has a big role to play. The potential of the use of IT to create transparent and empowering systems is best seen in the use of the banking correspondent model. The system is simple—the beneficiary may be given a smart card which is powered by Radio Frequency Identification Technology (RFID). Optionally a secure mobile coupled with biometric authentication may serve the same purpose. Instead of banks opening more and more branches to cater to the rural areas, they hire the services of a business development correspondent. This correspondent is equipped with a cell phone or a handheld device whose memory is buttressed by flash cards which also has records of beneficiary accounts. Beneficiaries swipe their cards (smart cards or otherwise) against the phone and use their thumbprint for biometric identification. The transaction is updated instantaneously (or optionally the data may be synchronised with back-end servers periodically) and the cash is delivered to the doorstep from the cash chest in the possession of the correspondent. A printer may give out details of the transaction as a paper record. The model has been piloted and tested with success.[16] Pushed by the Reserve Bank of India towards greater and greater inclusive banking, banks have started embracing this model of service delivery.

Real-time Online Systems and MGNREGA Correspondents

With the success of the above pilots in the banking sector, it is time to think of extending the use of such technologies to the core areas of MGNREGA implementation. In this regard, the placement of personnel and decentralisation of implementation must move pari passu with ensuring that the MIS is central to the MGNREGA workflow and further that real-time online technologies are at the cutting edge of the IT deployment. Such changes will ensure that transactions are captured as they happen (thus, real time rather than post facto or batch-mode, in that lags between an event occurring and the reporting of that event are made negligible, if not altogether eliminated), and made status visible across the network, further ensuring that data and system state at any given point of time are as fresh as they can be under any circumstances. This is a critical aid to concurrent monitoring and transparency as it liberates information from those who control it and the geographical boundaries where it is controlled.

Here, the recent Unique Identification project of the GoI can have a role to play in both engendering transparency and inclusion and in ensuring that crucial data are concurrently available for monitoring. The identity can function as a single window for the entitlements of the poor not only under the MGNREGA but all government schemes such as the proposed Food Security Act, health care, education and so on. The business of manual updation of job cards and the consequent bad practices of some people keeping workers cards will become redundant.

Real-time Online Muster Rolls and Work Attendance. A system can be visualised whereby handhelds are issued to field workers under the MGNREGA, and muster rolls are directly updated online to the state-level servers by biometric identification of the workers who are present on site. Such an immediate updation will go a long way in aiding concurrent monitoring. In fact, the paper muster roll can be a printout of the online muster. Fitted with GPS and webcam facilities, the system should further aid in verification of the work being done on the site at which it is reportedly being done (MoRD, n.d.). It seems that this has also already been piloted in different states by the MoRD. The results of this pilot should be made public and appropriate policies framed on the feedback.

Online Real-time Work Demand. Take also the question of work demand applications. It is possible to imagine a situation where the sarpanch is unwilling to accept the work demand application of a wage seeker. If MGNREGA correspondents with a handheld or a computer are available even within the perimeter of the GVS or the block, the application can be made online. For those monitoring the system, this is enough information to ask for explanations from the GP or others involved in the implementation, as to why the work application has not been made to the GP and why work has not been opened up. To counter for cases where even the PO is pressurised into not accepting the application, a cell phone–based online work demand application system can be worked out wherein a short message from a wage seeker's cell phone in a predefined format lodges itself on a server at the state or central level. The PO's office, which is also part of the network, takes cognisance of the application and ensures that employment is provided.

Online Real-time Grievance Redressal. A similar system can be visualised for complaints and their redressal. Either they are entered through handhelds or directly by the wage seeker through her cell phone and the complaint is lodged to a central server. A recent move in UP to enable a cell phone–based complaints and grievance redressal system is on similar lines (see Seth, 2010)

The major contribution of such IT reforms will be to ensure greater and tighter monitoring of MGNREGA work so that essential parameters of timely delivery are ensured. It will also support by making available current information for public scrutiny such as social audits. Together with decentralisation of implementation, this is the second step in ensuring that the core objectives of the MGNREGA are met.

A National Authority for MGNREGA

The previous two sections have discussed at length the kind of human and IT deployments that are needed in order that the MGNREGA delivers not only in physical terms but in the more crucial areas of transparency and governance reform. The MGNREGA has assigned several responsibilities of steering and guiding the programme to the central government and a comprehensive mandate to the CEGC (See NREGA, 2005: Section 11) to guide, monitor and evaluate the programme and introduce new changes. It is clear that an anchor role must be played at the central level (see also Drèze, Bhatia and Khera, 2009; Ambasta, 2009). We strongly believe that the largest employment programme in human history requires a separate authority to anchor it and to ensure that the legal entitlements are complied with. We propose the setting up of a National Authority for MGNREGA (NAM) as an autonomous body within the Ministry of Rural Development for discharging three of the most important functions to make MGNREGA effective:

1. Deploying IT and human resources to make MGNREGA implementation more effective
2. Social audit, monitoring and evaluation of MGNREGA implementation
3. Grievance redressal

Setting up of such an authority will help to separate the functions of executing the programme from those of monitoring, evaluation and grievance redressal, since as a matter of principle, the agency executing the programme should not be the one also assessing its own work.

In order to ensure maximum autonomy, the chairperson of NAM should be an individual of established integrity and eminence chosen from public life.

We propose that NAM has the following structure:

1. NAM is an autonomous body, registered under the Societies Registration Act, 1860.
2. The Central Employment Guarantee Council is the Governing Body of NAM with a chairperson.
3. NAM should also have a General Body comprising representatives from State Employment Guarantee Councils, state governments, elected representatives, domain experts, representatives of workers organisations, CSOs, etc.

4. NAM has an executive arm, which discharges on a day-to-day basis what the CEGC is mandated with, and reports periodically to the CEGC about its activities.
5. The executive arm is headed by a Director General (DG), who shall be an officer not below the rank of Secretary to the Government of India, and who should be selected from the open market after a careful search and screen process.[17] The process should identify potential candidates from within the government or outside. The DG of NAM will also be ex officio member secretary of the CEGC. She is the executive through whom the will of the CEGC is expressed in action. The DG will report to the chairperson, NAM and the CEGC.
6. The executive arm of the authority has the following departments:
   - *Monitoring, evaluation and social audit*: Headed by a Deputy Director General (DDG, whose recruitment is from the open market and who will report to the DG), responsible for concurrent monitoring of work under MGNREGA, mounting evaluations through a carefully selected panel of experts and consultants from across the country, ensuring that social audits are undertaken and monitoring the action taken on the findings of such social audits.
   - *Grievance redressal*: Headed by another DDG whose recruitment is from the open market and who will report to the DG, the department will be a window for immediate response to any complaint made by wage seekers, lay citizens, representatives of wage seekers, organisations working with wage seekers or any other agency or institution wishing to bring to the notice of the NAM and the CEGC any violation of the act or its operational guidelines in any part of the country. The department will appoint ombudsmen throughout the country who will work as the eyes, arms and legs of the NAM[18], looking into complaints and ensuring timely redressal through a tripartite process.
   - *IT department*: Also headed by a DDG, who will report to the DG, this department's role will be to assess ICT needs, in terms of both hardware and software, for providing a proper ICT backbone for MGNREGA implementation; to come up with a blueprint for effective ICT deployment for MGNREGA and to ensure that such deployments are made and complied with.
   - *Human resources department*: Also headed by a DDG, who will report to the DG, this department's primary responsibility will be:
     - to work out standards for human resources recruited for MGNREGA implementation;
     - to work out a system of certification for human resources, which all implementation structures have to comply with;
     - to identify and set standards for identifying training institutions across the country which can discharge the responsibilities of capacity building for the MGNREGA;
     - to work out syllabi for training courses that MGNREGA personnel should go through;
     - to arrange for trainings for these personnel.

The following diagram attempts to sum up the proposed structure of the NAM.

The Role of Civil Society

The reform steps outlined so far have been in the nature of necessary conditions. If we want MGNREGA to deliver on its core agenda of empowerment, these must be met. However, such techno-managerial inputs are not a magic bullet, the mere provisioning of which will by itself ensure that the complex task of

Figure 14.1: Possible Organisational Structure of NAM

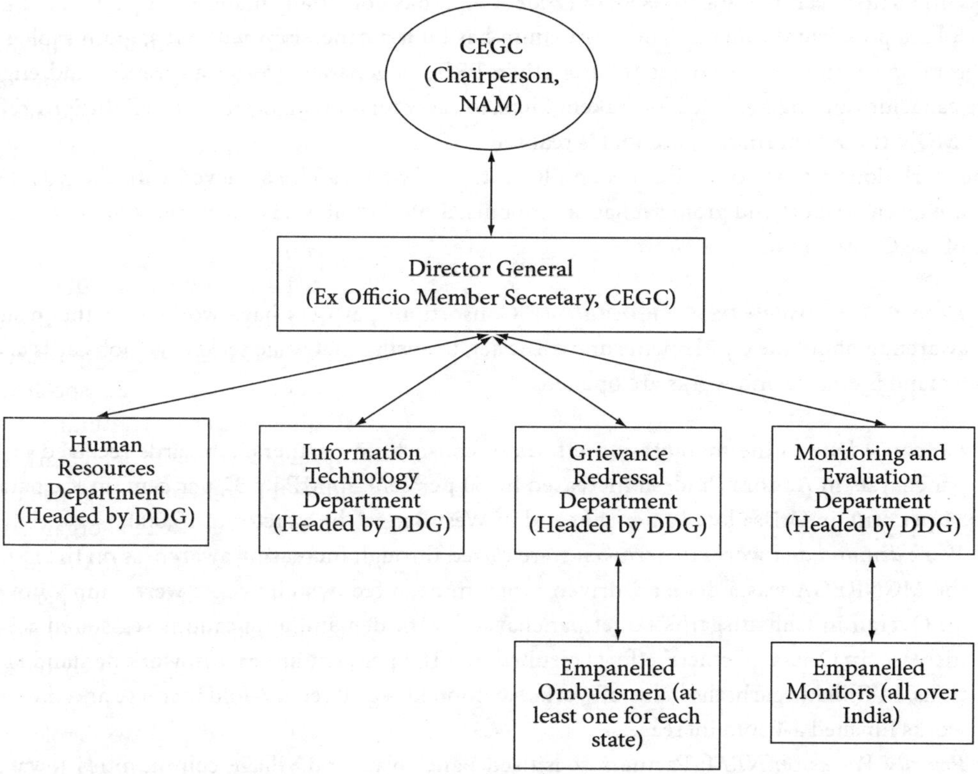

inclusive rural development is done. For it is worth reiterating that PRI elections and mere devolution of the three Fs does not by itself make PRIs pro-poor, pro-women, pro-marginalised, pro-Dalit, transparent and incorruptible. Indeed, not to recognise this and to see village communities as undifferentiated is not vindicated by reality.[19]

For this, what is needed is the mobilisation of the gram sabhas and their empowerment, so that they insist on their entitlements and to take the lead in the planning and implementation process. It is here that the civil society must play a leading role. Indeed, civil society initiatives can take the following forms:

1. Support to GPs in planning, implementation and social audit
2. Capacity building, mobilisation and monitoring
3. Social audit, vigilance and advocacy

Impact of Civil Society: National Consortium on NREGA

It is in recognition of the possibilities inherent in MGNREGA and the problems in the way of realisation of these possibilities that the National Consortium of Civil Society Organizations on NREGA was formed (Figure 14.1). The consortium has 51 CSO partners working across 59 blocks of 44 most backward districts in 11 states of India with a clear vision of working with GPs to make MGNREGA a success. In its first year of grass-roots work (2008–09), it has potentially made an impact on the lives of over 6.5 lakh poor, rural Indians. The consortium has built partnerships with GPs, gram sabhas, state and central governments. Its goal is to strengthen PRIs, to generate greater awareness and engender deeper capacities among MGNREGA stakeholders, to carry forward an agenda of MGNREGA reforms, so that MGNREGA's enormous potential is realised.

The work done by the consortium is an illustration of what can be achieved with the MGNREGA if GPs are given support and gram sabhas are mobilised. What follows is a summary of major achievements of the Consortium.

Mobilisation and Awareness Generation. Consortium partners have worked on the ground to create awareness about the entitlements under the act, to ensure that wage seekers get job cards and that work demand is created and works are opened.

1. *Job cards:* Due to the mobilisation efforts of consortium partners, job cards received in target panchayats in Andhra Pradesh increased by 60 per cent, in MP by 37 per cent, in Karnataka by 32 per cent, in Orissa by 210 per cent and in West Bengal, by a factor of 15,000.
2. *Work demand and works undertaken* were raised through increasing awareness on the issue that the MGNREGA was a demand-driven programme, a fact which people were simply not aware of. Overall in Chhattisgarh's target panchayats, work demand applications registered a 34-fold increase. In Orissa, partners' efforts resulted in a 182 per cent increase in work demand applications. In Chhattisgarh, the value of works sanctioned registered a 7-fold increase and the value of works finished a 4-fold increase.
3. *Priority Works on NRM:* Partners sensitised panchayats and village communities towards the need for giving priority to NRM-oriented works under the MGNREGA. In Karnataka, value of NRM works sanctioned rose from ₹28 lakhs to ₹3 crores. Share of NRM activities undertaken in panchayat plans increased from under 25 per cent to over 50 per cent. In Orissa, the same share increased from 24 per cent to 46 per cent.

Support to Gram Panchayats on Planning and Implementation. Partners in several locations have supported GPs to prepare detailed action plans with technical surveys, costing, drawings, etc. The value of these action plans is more than ₹125 crores in the first year alone and is rising as more plans are created. These plans are ratified by the GPs and put up to districts for approval. Wherever such plans have been implemented, the impact on incomes, indebtedness and migration are visible. In several instances, partners have built upon the water infrastructure created by the MGNREGA to dovetail livelihood interventions on agriculture and microcredit. There is need to create a network of CSOs with capability and credibility which can act as resource support centres for MGNREGA implementation.

Interface with Government MGNREGA Implementation Structure. Consortium partners have helped the interface of wage seekers with government in all locations. In Andhra Pradesh, for instance, through consistent dialogue, the state government has passed a series of orders for worksite facilities, tools and kits to be made available. State governments in UP and Andhra Pradesh have entered into

Memorandums of Understanding (MoUs) with consortium partners so that their inputs are assured in MGNREGA implementation. In Andhra Pradesh, a landmark MoU (see GoAP, 2010) was signed between the Government of Andhra Pradesh and CSOs, for the formation of an Andhra Pradesh NGO Alliance (APNA), which envisages coming on board of selected CSOs across the state to perform critical mobilisational and monitoring roles and build an interface between the government and wage seekers. Such roles can be envisaged for committed CSOs with a good track record, across the country.

Social Audits and Vigilance. Partners, depending on their base situations have pressed for social audits in their panchayats and activated vigilance committees. In Devgadh Baria block of Gujarat's Dahod district, social audit were completed on 446 worksites (from a base of none) as a result of the Rozi Roti Lok Jumbesh, spearheaded by consortium partner ANANDI. In Karnataka, Samuha has conducted 181 social audits in its target panchayats.

Training Material, Capacity Building and Support. Consortium partners have organised a wide variety of training, exposure and capacity building initiatives for PRI leaders, village community members, MGNREGA implementation staff and other stakeholders. Some partners of the consortium have also taken on the role of supporting other partners through capacity building, field support, production of training and resource material. Manuals (see Samaj Pragati Sahayog, 2006), films and communication material have been produced as a part of this effort. A website of the consortium also helps in bringing together resources on MGNREGA (see http://www.nregaconsortium.in).

Upscaling the Role of Civil Society

As the preceding discussion has shown, there is clearly room for civil society support to GPs. For this, to begin with, CSOs have to shed established mindsets of suspicion of GPs (for on several occasions, the work of CSOs and their support to the marginalised brings them in direct conflict with elements in the PRI structure which have been co-opted by the prevalent structures of power) and move forward with a new, positive vision of partnership.

It also entails a policy environment which explicitly welcomes such initiatives from the civil society. In this respect, some states have taken a lead. For example, MP has built watershed guidelines around the MGNREGA (see GoMP, 2007) in which CSOs are invited to participate as partners. In Andhra Pradesh, the constitution of APNA is another such example. In UP, the state government has identified selected CSOs to help the monitoring of MGNREGA works in different blocks. More such partnerships need to be forged and formalised.

In this move, institutions like the Council for Advancement of People's Action and Rural Technology (CAPART, GoI, an autonomous council for support to CSOs) must play a bigger role in bringing on board credible and committed CSOs. This will require a reorientation in their functions and vision. As a part of the process of bringing in reforms in CAPART, new schemes have already been proposed to cover flagship areas like the MGNREGA, Right to Food, Forest Rights Act and the RTI. It is further proposed that a fundamental building block of such partnerships should be a consortium-based approach in which CSOs are partners and work together on a thematic area. Such partnerships should have a clear mandate of working with PRIs for creation of models of excellence, which show the way forward on how implementation of such programmes must proceed. The MoRD has also recently proposed a lok sevak/lok karmi scheme for upscaling the involvement of CSOs. There is need to also bring on board established academic, research and training institutions, individual experts, CSOs, government and PRI resource agencies together and knit them into a national movement for capacity building, support and mobilisation for MGNREGA. Such efforts will help in pooling and mainstreaming the vast body of knowledge that has been generated in the course of civil society action in different areas, which can become a resource for the MGNREGA implementers throughout the country. They will also help in establishing resource support centres throughout the country which will help PRIs to make MGNREGA effective.

IV

Conclusion

In this chapter, we have tried to spell out a blueprint of reforms that are needed for MGNREGA to realise its true potential. This blueprint springs from a vision of deepening decentralisation and grass-roots democracy through devolution of funds, functions and functionaries to PRIs. Since funds are not so much of an issue after the MGNREGA, functionaries are the real bottleneck, which must be taken care of by a revisioning of the cutting edge of implementation of MGNREGA through the establishment of GVSes below the block level. We argue that such a reform is critically needed to deepen decentralisation and democracy at the grass roots, and while making MGNREGA more effective, it will also take forward the decentralisation project initiated through the Constitution 73rd Amendment. To further strengthen these MGNREGA reforms, the use of IT for monitoring and an agency like the proposed NAM have a crucial role to play. While such provisioning of the best talent and resources is commonplace for large infrastructure projects in the 'mainstream' of economic development, they are tragically not even thought of when rural development is envisioned. Bringing about these reforms, thus, will also play a big role in mainstreaming inclusion, rural development and decentralisation.

We further argue that while such support and resource deployment are necessary conditions, rural development and the empowerment of the poor cannot happen simply through such techno-managerial provisioning but needs grass-roots mobilisation. This, to begin with, entails an acceptance of the fact that rural communities are differentiated and there is no reason a priori to believe that mere creation of local government institutions will also make them pro-poor. In both tasks—of mobilisation and support to gram sabhas and PRIs for making MGNREGA more effective—civil society has a big role to play and its role needs to be mainstreamed.

Such an approach to the MGNREGA can effectively reform governance at the grass roots and also empower rural communities. Over time, this can become the way forward for all interventions targeting the rural poor.

Acknowledgement

This chapter is a revised version of the paper presented at an international conference on *Dynamics of Rural Transformation in Emerging Economies* held in April 2010 at Delhi. The invaluable inputs of Mihir Shah and P. S. Vijay Shankar to this chapter are gratefully acknowledged.

Notes

1. More than the aspects of decentralisation and devolution of political and administrative power (which are means to an end) it is this role of providing the 'missing link between accelerated growth and inclusive growth' (Ministry of Panchayati Raj (MoPR), Government of India, 2008), which needs to define PRIs. For, 'In the rapid changes that will take place in India, and indeed the world in the twenty first century, governance systems will have to be at the cutting edge of being the protectors of the poor, the oppressed, the vulnerable and the underprivileged' (MoPR, 2008) and the 'problematique' of 'globalisation, a political space characterised by a changing polity, and strong macroeconomic growth' has 'inclusion' at its very epicenter' (MoPR, 2008).
2. The share is around 50 per cent in Rajasthan and MP, 60 in Orissa and UP and over 70 in Chhattisgarh and Jharkhand. And if we focus on Adivasis, the proportion shoots up to as high as 76–87 per cent in Chhattisgarh, Jharkhand and Rajasthan (Shah, 2009).
3. The CAG report covers 513 GPs in 128 blocks of 68 districts in 26 states for the period February 2006 to March 2007.
4. Our field assessments of selected panchayats in Bagli Tehsil of Dewas district, MP, suggests that the average budget of a GP (excluding funds for the MGNREGA) is not more than ₹2.5 lakhs per annum in 2009–10. Only if MLA development funds are received by the GP or if it happens to be under the Tribal Sub Plan or a similar scheme does the budget rise to about ₹9 lakhs. If we include such allocations, the average budget of these selected panchayats rises to about ₹4 lakhs (about ₹272 per capita).
5. See Chandra (2010), who suggests on the basis of various surveys that the participation in MGNREGA is likely to be much higher with 75 per cent of all rural households wanting a full 100 days of work. In contrast, our calculations above assume that only 90 per cent of RLHs would demand 100 days of work
6. This is akin to the 'Mandal' of Andhra Pradesh introduced in the 1980s by the then Chief Minister of the state, N. T. Rama Rao. The Mandals of Andhra Pradesh comprise 20–25 GPs on an average. Despite its several challenges, some of the gains in APREGS in terms of social audit, planning and implementation are attributable to decentralisation below the block level.
7. To clarify, we are not proposing an elected panchayat layer for which separate elections have to be held. The GVS is a part of the block-level panchayat where it is located. However, it *is* the cutting-edge level of implementation as far as the MGNREGA is concerned. If this concept gains ground, the GVS could be the centre for implementation of all similar development schemes.
8. For an alternative estimate based on the assumption that MGNREGA will be extended at ₹100 per day to every adult individual (instead of household), as promised in the Congress Party manifesto of 2009, see National Consortium on NREGA, 2009. The experience of drought further places demands on MGNREGA to be expanded (see Sainath, 2009 and *Business Standard*, 2009), with concomitant increases in the size of the guarantee.
9. See Arya and Shubham (2009). The involvement of Self-reliant Initiatives through Joint Action (Srijan), an NGO, and SIDS, its consultancy arm, in the recruitment process for the Jeevika project of the Government of Bihar is an illustration of such outsourcing. The project is being executed by an autonomous agency, the Bihar Rural Livelihoods Promotion Society (BRLP) which also outsourced the recruitment process.
10. This does not attempt to capture all complexities involved in the workflow, but is offered more by way of illustration. A more detailed discussion on the workflow (as analysed for the APREGS) can be found in Tata Consultancy Services (TCS, 2006).

11. Although shown in a sequence, planning and estimation are not activities that need to wait for work demand. Nor should work demand be contingent upon work estimates prepared which seems to be the de facto situation today, because proper shelves of work rarely exist. So work demand on the MIS is always made equal to the work supplied by the simple method of normally entering work demand when a particular work has been estimated *and* sanctioned.
12. Drèze, Bhatia and Khera (2009) also point out that the MIS is entirely based on official data, and there is an issue with the credibility of the data, with a covering up of such information that may be seen to be violative of the act. Thus, the MGNREGA MIS routinely shows that the employment demanded is equal to that provided, whereas actually, the wage seekers may be routinely dissuaded from applying for work.
13. While it is possible to get all information without using IT, such information flows are prone to huge delays, as everyone knows, and lead to the question, 'why have an IT solution at all?'
14. Drèze et al. (2009) point out:

    Yet, delays in wage payments remain very common ... The casual treatment of this right is evident from the fact that in most states the Monitoring and Information System (MIS) does not include any tracking of the timeliness of wage payments: if payments are delayed, there is no trace of it in the MIS.
15. In this section, the term 'bank' is used to mean banks and post offices.
16. See Menon (2008), Leslie (2008), Dev (2006), NISG (2006), *Outlook* (2007) for some descriptions of the pilots and their success. See also, *Hindu Business Line* (2007).
17. The DG, DDGs and professionals can be appointed after the recommendations of a search committee consisting of the Cabinet Secretary as the chairperson, and two eminent professionals connected with MGNREGA implementation. Serving government officers can also apply for these posts.
18. This is akin to the system of Commissioners and Advisers set up by the Supreme Court in the Right to Food case.
19. See Shah et al., 1998, for an account of how PRIs can be captured by conventional axes of power to subvert the very purpose of such institutions. Indeed, if the state is an 'arena of conflict', then its decentralisation will decentralise the arena and not automagically 'wither away' the conflict. Strong people's institutions are needed to ensure that the gram sabhas are mobilised and that PRIs play the role they are mandated to.

References

Aiyar, Mani Shankar (2005) Panchayati raj: The way forward. In *Decentralisation and local governance*, ed. L. C. Jain. New Delhi: Orient Longman.

Ambasta, Pramathesh (2009) Programming NREGS to succeed. *Hindu*, 31 October, Chennai.

Ambasta, Pramathesh, Mihir Shah and P. S. Vijay Shankar (2008) Two years of NREGA: The road ahead. *Economic and Political Weekly* 43, No. 8: 41 to 50.

ARC (2007) *Local Governance: An Inspiring Journey into the Future*, Second Administrative Reforms Commission, 6th Report, Government of India, New Delhi.

Arya, Ved and Shubham (2009) *Recruitment and selection for development sector projects: Experience of Bihar rural livelihoods project (Jeevika)*, mimeo.

Bourguignon, Francois (2004) *The poverty-growth-inequality triangle*. Paper presented at Indian Council for International Economic Relations, ICRIER, 4 February, New Delhi.

Business Standard (2009) Job days under NREGA scheme could increase: Plan panel. *Business Standard*. http://www.business-standard.com/india/news/job-days-under-nrega-scheme-could-increase-plan-panel/69803/on.

CAG (2008). *Draft performance audit of implementation of NREGA*, Office of the Principal Director of Audit, Economic and Service Ministries, New Delhi, Comptroller and Auditor General.

Chandra, Nirmal Kumar (2010) *Inclusive Growth in Neoliberal India: A Facade? Economic and Political Weekly*, 45, No. 8: 43–56.

D'Monte, Leslie (2008) *Villagers across 12 states to benefit from mobile banking. Business Standard*, 20 February.

D'Monte, Leslie and Reetika Khera (2008) *From accounts to accountability. Hindu*, 6 December.

Datt, Gaurav and Martin Ravallion (2002) Is India's growth leaving the poor behind? *Journal of Economic Perspectives* 16, No. 3: 89–108.

Deaton, Angus and Jean Drèze (2002) Poverty and Inequality in India. *Economic and Political Weekly* 37, No. 36: 3729–48.

Dev, Kris (2006) *Biometrics, payment and rural communities*. http://tracnet.blogspot.com/

Drèze, Jean, Kartika Bhatia and Reetika Khera (2009) *Making NREGA work*, Unpublished report prepared for the NCEUS, National Commission for Enterprises in the Unorganized Sector.

EPWRF (2003) *Domestic product of states of India, 1960–61 to 2000–01*. Mumbai: Economic and Political Weekly Research Foundation.

Ghosh, Jayati (2005) *The political economy of farmers' suicides in India*. New Delhi: Centre for Environment and Food Security.

Government of Andhra Pradesh (2010) GOMS No. 80, on *Formation of Andhra Pradesh NGO alliance (APNA) for MGNREGA*, 19/2/2010. http://www.rd.ap.gov.in

Government of India (2005) *The National Rural Employment Guarantee Act 2005 operational guidelines*. New Delhi: Ministry of Rural Development, Government of India.

Government of Madhya Pradesh (2007). *Guidelines for watershed development*.

Hindu Business Line (2007) *Use biz correspondent model for effective financial inclusion*. Bureau Report, 11 August 2007. www.thehindubusinessline.com

Kumar, Ravi, D. Rakesh Kumar and S. Seethalakshmi (2008) *National Rural Employment Guarantee Act in Andhra Pradesh—Claims and questions in operationalisation (2007–08)*. http://www.nregaconsortium.in

Labour Bureau (2004) *7th Report of the rural labour enquiry (55*th *round of NSS) on employment and unemployment of rural households, 1999–2000*, Labour Bureau, Ministry of Labour and Employment, Government of India, Simla.

Menon, Amarnath K. (2008) Swiping reforms. *India Today*, 28 January, New Delhi.

Ministry of Panchayati Raj (2008a) Panchayat Directory, Ministry of Panchayat Raj, Government of India, New Delhi. http://www.panchayat.gov.in/directory (accessed 10 February).

——— (2008b) *State of panchayats report: An independent assessment*, Ministry of Panchayati Raj, Government of India.

Ministry of Rural Development (2009) *Order No. 11060/3/2009-NREGA, Amendment to Schedule I Para 1(iv) of NREG Act*, New Delhi, Ministry of Rural Development, Government of India, available at: http://nrega.nic.in

——— (n.d.) ICT pilot project: *Smartcard and Handheld Devices, A Concept Note*, New Delhi, Ministry of Rural Development, Government of India. http://nrega.nic.in

Nagaraj, R. (2008) *Development strategies and poverty reduction—Indian experience*. Paper for the UNRISD Project, Poverty Reduction and Policy Regimes (unpublished).

National Consortium on NREGA (2009) *NREGA reforms: Building rural India—First annual report of the National Consortium of Civil Society Organizations on NREGA*, Madhya Pradesh, National Consortium on NREGA, August. http://www.nregaconsortium.in

NCAER (2009) *An index of devolution for assessing environment for panchayati raj institutions in the states [final report]*, New Delhi, National Council for Applied Economic Research, March.

NCEUS (2007) *Report of the National Commission on Enterprises in Unorganised Sector*, Government of India, New Delhi.

NISG (2006) *ICT in NREGA implementation*, National Institute for Smart Government, www.nisg.org

NREGA (2005) Chapter II: *Guarantee of Employment in Rural India*, p. 3. http://rural.nic.in//rajaswa.pdf

——— (2005a) *The National Rural Employment Guarantee Act*, Gazette of India Extraordinary, 7th September 2005, Ministry of Law and Justice, Government of India.

Outlook (2007) *A New World Begins from Zero*, Report, 5 July.

Planning Commission (2005) *Report of the Inter-ministry Task Group on addressing regional imbalances*, Planning Commission, Government of India, New Delhi.

Sainath, P. (2009) Drought of justice, flood of funds. *Hindu*, 15 August.

Samaj Pragati Sahayog (2006) *National Rural Employment Guarantee Act: Watershed works manual*. Bagli: Samaj Pragati Sahayog.

——— (2008) *Status of NREGA implementation: Field reports of the National Consortium on NREGA Partners*, mimeo.

Sengupta, Arjun, K. P. Kannan and G. Ravindran (2008) India's common people: Who are they, how many are they and how do they live? *Economic and Political Weekly* 43, No. 11: 49–63.

Seth, Maulshree (2010) In Bundelkhand, Centre gets MNREGS Key. *Indian Express*, New Delhi, 24 February.
Shah, Mihir (2007) Employment guarantee, civil society and Indian democracy. *Economic and Political Weekly* 42, Nos. 45, 46: 43–51.
——— (2009) Multiplier accelerator synergy in NREGA, *Hindu*, 30 April, Chennai.
Shah, Mihir and Pramathesh Ambasta (2008): NREGA: Andhra shows the way, *The Hindu* (leader page), 8 September, Chennai.
Shah, Mihir, D. Banerji, P. S.Vijayshankar and Pramathesh Ambasta (1998) *India's drylands: Tribal societies and development through environmental regeneration*. New Delhi: Oxford University Press.
Shankar, P. S. Vijay and Mihir Shah (2009) *Rethinking reforms: A new vision for the social sector in India*, (unpublished), prepared for UNRISD project on Poverty Reduction and Policy Regimes.
Social Watch India (2009) *Citizen's report on governance and development 2008–09*, New Delhi, National Social Watch Coalition.
Tata Consultancy Services (2006) *APREGS application user manual*. Hyderabad: TCS. http://nrega.ap.gov.in/Nregs/GovtDocs/APEGS User Manual 22nd April 2006.doc
Twelfth Finance Commission (2004) *Report of twelfth finance commission*, chap. 8 and chap. 8 annexure. New Delhi: Government of India.
Vanaik, Ashish and Siddhartha (2008) *Bank payments: End of corruption in NREGA*. *Economic and Political Weekly* 43, No. 17: 33–39.
Widmalm, Sten (2005) *What are decentralization and panchayati raj reforms and who likes them?* In *Decentralisation and local governance*, ed. L. C. Jain. New Delhi: Orient Longman.
World Bank (2007) *World development indicators 2007*. New York: Oxford University Press.
——— (2008) *World development indicators 2008*. New York: Oxford University Press.

About the Editor and Contributors

Editor

Ashok K. Pankaj (Ph.D., LL.B.) is senior fellow at Institute for Human Development, Delhi. His area of interest and research is political economy of development in India and South Asia with a focus on public policies, institutions of governance and development, interface between development and democracy and society and polity. He has completed eight major projects on various issues of socio-economic development sponsored by UNDP, UNIFEM, UN Women, ICSSR, Ministry of Rural Development, Ministry of Panchayati Raj, Ministry of Minority Affairs (Government of India), Government of Bihar and World Bank, and is presently leading two major evaluation projects, sponsored by the Planning Commission of India. He has contributed about 60 articles including reviews and chapters in books. His articles and reviews have appeared in reputed professional journals like *South Asia Research* (SAGE, London), *Contribution to Indian Sociology* (SAGE, Delhi), *Journal of Asian and African Studies* (SAGE, Boston), *Economic and Political Weekly* (Mumbai), *International Studies* (SAGE, Delhi), *Journal of Commonwealth and Comparative Politics* (Routledge, Oxfordshire), *Social Scientist* (Delhi) *etc.*

Contributors

Diana Alarcón is Senior Economic Affairs Officer at UN Department for Economic and Social Affairs. She has done research and contributed to the development of programmes for employment creation, poverty reduction and social protection through her career at International Labor Office, Inter-American Development Bank, UNDP and DESA. Diana has taught in various universities in Mexico and the United States.

Pramathesh Ambasta is Co-Founder, Samaj Pragati Sahayog, a grass-roots voluntary organization headquartered in the tribal dry lands of Madhya Pradesh and National Coordinator, Civil Society Consortium on NREGA.

Regina Birner is Professor at University of Hohenheim, Germany, where she holds the Chair of 'Social and Institutional Change in Agricultural Development'. Her research interests include governance and public sector reforms in agriculture, the political economy of agricultural policymaking and the role of community-based organisations in agricultural and rural development. Prior to joining University of Hohenheim in 2010, she was Senior Research Fellow at International Food Policy Research Institute (IFPRI), where she led IFPRI's Research Program on 'Governance for Agricultural and Rural Development'. She also served as Assistant Professor at Institute of Rural Development at University of Göttingen, Germany, where her research focused on institutional and political questions of natural resource management. She holds a Ph.D. in Socioeconomics of Agricultural Development from University of Göttingen, and an M.Sc. in Agricultural Sciences from University of Munich-Weihenstephan, Germany.

Parvinder Kaur Dua is Lecturer in Economics, MBBGR Girls College, Mansowal, Hoshiarpur, Punjab. She is pursuing her Ph.D. degree on 'National Rural Employment Guarantee Act: A Case Study of Hoshiarpur District in Punjab' from Punjabi University, Patiala.

Shaik Galab, a development economist, is Professor at Centre for Economic and Social Studies. He was trained at Waltair School of Economics (M.A., 1978 and Ph.D., 1985) and Department of Statistics Andhra University, (M.Sc., 1980). His initial research interest at the university was Efficiency in Resource Utilisation in Agriculture. At Centre for Economic and Social Studies, he carried out research on Effectiveness of Public Policies related to poverty alleviation; Rehabilitation and Resettlement of Project Affected; Natural Resource Management; Handloom Sector; Solid Waste Management in Urban Areas; and Agrarian Distress. He has also conducted research on the welfare impact of Public Sector Reforms, apart from teaching and guiding M.Phil and Ph.D. students. His recent work focuses on social capital, land rights and land access to women, women's empowerment, child labour and livelihoods. He was a member of Farmers' Welfare Commission—a commission appointed by Government of Andhra Pradesh in response to the agrarian crisis in the state; permanent invitee on the expert group on agricultural indebtedness constituted by Government of India, and co-opted member on the subgroup to study on poverty constituted by Planning Commission, Government of India. He is one of the co-authors of the book *On Joint Forest Management in Andhra Pradesh*. His recent publications have appeared in journals such as *Development and Change* and *Economic and Political Weekly*. He is also leading the subgroup on agriculture for the 12th Five Year Plan in Andhra Pradesh. Presently he is leading Young Lives Project India on childhood poverty as Principal Investigator.

K. G. Gayathridevi (Ph.D.) is a senior faculty member at Institute for Social and Economic Change (ISEC), Bangalore, India. She is a sociologist by training and has been associated with ISEC for the last two decades. Her main areas of academic interest are empowerment of women, children and dalits; caste- and gender-based oppression; poverty and vulnerability; social issues in environmental protection; decentralization and development; and gender and governance. Before joining ISEC, she was a research consultant at Institute of Social Sciences, New Delhi in its Panchayati Raj project and also taught postgraduate and graduate students at Mysore and Bangalore universities for 8 years. She has worked on several research projects commissioned by IFPRI, The World Bank, Ford Foundation, ILO, SDC, Aghaz Foundation and ActionAid, India and has published three books with co-authors, a number of working papers and research articles. She was a research fellow at Department of Sociology, University of Glasgow, Scotland during July–September 1995, Visiting Fellow at University of Vienna in October 1995 and IFPRI, Washington D.C., in April 2009. Gayathridevi is on the board of studies of the departments of Sociology and Women's Study Centres of some universities in Karnataka. Currently, she is working on a project 'Engendering Governance in Karnataka' for the Agaz Foundation.

Ranjit Singh Ghuman is presently Chair Professor, Nehru SAIL Chair, Centre for Rural Research and Industrial Development (CRRID), Chandigarh. He was earlier Professor and Head, Department of

Economics; Coordinator, Centre for Advanced Study in Economics; Director, Centre for Research in Economic Change; and Coordinator South-West Asia Study Centre, Punjabi University, Patiala. He is Vice-president of Indian Society of Labour Economics and on the board of various academic and administrative bodies, such as Academic Council of Central University of Gujarat, ICSSR (North-West Regional Centre, Chandigarh) and State Advisory Committee of Punjab State Electricity Regulatory Commission. He has chaired Punjab Government Committee on Minimum Support Price and Price-Index. He has also been Visiting Scholar at Mainz University, Germany. He has published about 75 research papers and has authored and co-authored (edited) 9 books and completed 10 research projects.

T. Haque is currently Director, Council for Social Development, New Delhi. He has served as Chairman of Commission for Agricultural Costs and Price, Government of India for five years. He has also served as member of several professional groups, including Expert Group on MGNREGA under Ministry of Rural Development, Government of India. He has published about 75 research papers and 4 books.

Indira Hirway is Director and Professor of Economics at Centre for Development Alternatives (CFDA), Ahmedabad. She has been Visiting Faculty/Fellow at Erasmus University, Netherlands; University of Amsterdam, Netherlands; Queen Elizabeth House, University of Oxford; and University of Utah, USA. She is Associate at Levy Economics Institute, Bard College in New York State. She works in the area of development alternatives, employment and labour market structures, poverty and human development, environment and development, time use studies, gender and development, etc. She has written several books and published articles in reputed national and international journals. Her recent works include *Restructuring of Production and Labour under Globalization: Study of Textile and Garment Industries* (ILO, 2010), *Impact of the Global Financial Crisis on Workers and Small Producers in India: Emerging Issues and Implications* (2009), *Employment Guarantee Programme and Pro-poor Growth* (2010) and *Unpaid Work and the Economy: Gender, Time Use and Poverty* (edited with Rania Antonopoulos, 2009).

K. N. Joshi is Professor at Institute of Development Studies, Jaipur. His areas of specialization are remote sensing applications, desertification, land degradation, land use planning, watershed planning and development, and wasteland development. He has edited *Environmental Problems of Mining and their Management*, *Environmental Monitoring and Pollution Measures*, *Readings in Remote Sensing Applications* and *Studies in Arid Lands Management*. He has to his credit 25 research papers.

Varsha Joshi is Associate Professor at Institute of Development Studies, Jaipur. She is a cultural historian and is a Ph.D. from School of Oriental and African Studies, London. She has authored *Polygamy and Purdah: Women and Society amongst Rajputs* and co-edited *Multiple Histories: Culture and Society in the Study of Rajasthan*, *Institutions and Social Change*, *Culture, Polity and Economy* and edited *Culture, Community and Change*. She has published various papers in journals in Indian and abroad.

Katharina Raabe is a research fellow at Institute for Environmental Economics and World Trade at Leibniz University Hannover (Germany). Her research interests include governance and rural service provision for inclusive and sustainable agricultural and rural development and public sector implementation of development programmes. Her current research focuses on migration as rural livelihood support strategy in the light of environmental change and political, administrative and fiscal decentralisation. Prior to joining Leibniz University Hannover in 2009, she was a consultant and post-doctoral fellow in the Development Strategy and Governance Division at the International Food Policy Research Institute (IFPRI), living and working in India. Katharina is a German citizen and holds a Ph.D. and Masters degree in Economics with specialization in macro and monetary economics from Maastricht University, the Netherlands.

D. Narashimha Reddy was Professor of Economics at Hyderabad Central University and is currently Visiting Professor at Institute for Human Development, Delhi. His specialisation includes science policy studies, political economy of development and labour economics. He was a member of Farmers' Welfare Commission set up by Government of Andhra Pradesh to look into the issues of farmers' suicides and agriculture crisis. He has published more than 60 research articles in reputed professional journals and authored, co-authored and edited a number of books.

E. Revathi is currently Professor and Senior Fellow, ICSSR at Department of Economics, Kakatiya University, Warangal. She was Visiting Fellow at Centre for Economic and Social Studies (CESS), Hyderabad. She worked on 'Women Work and Technology in Agriculture' for her Ph.D., which has been published as a book. At CESS, she carried research on the issues of agrarian crisis in Andhra Pradesh, farmers and weavers suicides. She was involved in research projects on rural indebtedness and National Rural Employment Guarantee Programme in association with other scholars at CESS. She also worked in the area of regional inequalities. She contributed to the subgroup on Gender and Agriculture for the Eleventh Five Year Plan. She worked for a collaborative project with National Institute of Agricultural Extension Management sponsored by Ministry of Agriculture, New Delhi at CESS on 'State Policies, Women's Access to Land and Women Empowerment'. She is presently working on 'Land Access to Women and Women Empowerment—Under Different Situations in Andhra Pradesh' for Senior Fellowship. She teaches Macroeconomic Theory and Policy and Agricultural Economics.

Gerry Rodgers (M.A. [Cantab], D.Phil., University of Sussex) is currently Visiting Professor at Institute for Human Development, New Delhi. Formerly Director of the International Institute for Labour Studies, he held various other positions with the International Labour Office between 1972 and 2008. His work has mainly been concerned with poverty, inequality, labour and employment in low- and medium-income countries, especially in India and Latin America. Publications as author or co-author include *The ILO and the Quest for Social Justice, 1919–2009*; *The Institutional Approach to Labour and Development*; *Social Exclusion: Rhetoric, Reality, Response*; *Labour Institutions and Economic Development in India* and articles on Decent Work, globalization, labour market flexibility, development in rural Bihar and other topics.

Eva Schiffer (Ph.D.) is a social scientist and facilitator, working as independent consultant, helping groups and individuals to make most of their complex influence networks. She holds a Ph.D. in Human Geography from University of Bochum, Germany. Before starting her own business, she was a post-doctoral fellow for International Food Policy Research Institute living in Ghana, where she developed the participatory influence network mapping tool Net-Map. Since 2008, she has applied this method in various projects, collaborating, for example, with World Bank, United Nations University, USAID and The Gates Foundation. These projects focused on matters as diverse as avian influenza, innovation systems, public health and monitoring of development projects. For the development of Net-Map, she received 'CGIAR Promising Young Scientist of the Year Award' in 2008. Her main regional expertise lies in Africa, she comes from Germany and lives in Washington D.C.

Madhushree Sekher holds a Ph.D. in political science from Institute for Social and Economic Change (Bangalore University) in Bangalore, and is Associate Professor at TISS, Mumbai. She has completed her post-doctoral research under World Bank Robert McNamara Fellowship Program for young social scientists. She was a visiting fellow at University of Amsterdam, University of Alberta and Indiana University. Her research studies have mainly centred on the process of governing at the sub-state level (decentralised local governance), the State–society interrelationships and the nature of user/citizen involvement in the development process through participatory partnerships, and the institutional aspects involved. Her current research is on improving governance and gender equity in rural services, and the role of rural institutions in pro-poor agriculture-led development and food security concerns. She has authored a number of articles and research reports on related subjects, which have been published nationally and internationally.

Amita Shah (Ph.D.) is Professor of Economics and currently Director, Gujarat Institute of Development Research. She has been invited as a visiting scholar to academic institutions in the United Kingdom, China, France, the Netherlands and Canada. She has worked extensively in the field of development economics. Her major areas of research and interest include natural resource management, with special focus on dry land agriculture and forestry, environmental impact assessment, gender and environment, agriculture–industry interface, small scale and rural industries, employment–livelihood issues and chronic poverty. She has contributed about 50 research articles, 30 chapters in books and reports and more than 24 reports. Her books include *Dynamics of Development in Gujarat* (2002, co-edited), *Women in Agriculture* (2004, co-edited), *Water, Agriculture, and Sustainable Well-Being* (2009, co-edited), *Impact of Watershed Management on Women and Vulnerable Groups* (2010, co-edited).

Amrita Shilpi is assistant professor in the Department of Political Science, Kirorimal College, University of Delhi. She was previously research fellow in Indian Institute of Dalit Studies, New Delhi. She obtained her doctoral degree from Jawaharlal Nehru University. The focus of her research was on the patterns of participation of the scheduled castes, scheduled tribes and women in the rural local governance processes across the three states of Karnataka, Kerala and Bihar. This study of three government schemes in 36 village panchayats brings out interesting issues related to the participation and marginalization of the groups studied. Her research interests focus on issues of marginalization and governance processes.

Surjit Singh (Ph.D. in Economics) is Professor and Director, Institute of Development Studies, Jaipur. He served earlier as Chair Professor, Bank of India Chair on Rural Credit, Institute of Development

Studies, Jaipur during 1997 to 2000 and taught at Guru Nanak Dev University, Amritsar between 1984 and 1988. He has been Consultant, Bureau of Industrial Costs and Prices, Ministry of Industry, Government of India, New Delhi; Consultant, International Labour Organization, ILO-SAAT, New Delhi and Consultant, The World Bank, New Delhi. He has authored *Modelling Indian Economy* and *Urban Informal Sector*, co-authored *Agriculture Credit in India*, edited *Rural Credit: Issues for the Nineties* and co-edited *Political Economy of WTO Regime: Some Aspects of Globalisation and Governance, Sustainable Agriculture, Poverty and Food Security, Institutions and Social Change, Rajasthan: The Quest for Sustainable Development, Culture, Polity and Economy, Changing Contours of Asian Agriculture: Policies, Performance and Challenges, Rainfed Agriculture in India: Perspectives and Challenges, Globalization and Regional Economies: Economic and Social Perspectives and Climate Change: Asian Perspective.* He has written around 100 papers for national and international journals.

Rukmini Tankha was Research Associate at Institute for Human Development, Delhi, and is presently working as a consultant for Social and Human Sciences Sector, UNESCO, Delhi. She works on issues of public policy, social protection and gender development. She has worked mostly on MGNREGA and her papers have appeared in the *Economic and Political Weekly* and *IDS Bulletin*.

Eduardo Zepeda is Policy Adviser at Bureau for Development Policy of UN Development Programme. Prior to this, he was Senior Associate at Carnegie Endowment for International Peace and Senior Researcher at International Poverty Centre (Brasilia). He has done research and advised on employment and poverty issues and has taught at Mexican and US universities.

Index